BARRON'S FINANCIAL TABLES FOR BETTER MONEY MANAGEMENT

Savings and Loans

Stephen S. Solomon
M.S., Applied Mathematics

Clifford W. Marshall
Ph.D., Applied Mathematics
Professor of Mathematics
Polytechnic Institute of New York

Martin Pepper
Principal, Coopers & Lybrand
Fellow, Society of Actuaries

Barron's Educational Series, Inc.
New York • London • Toronto • Sydney

Great effort has been made to develop accurate tables; however, no warranty of absolute accuracy is given.

2745

All inquiries should be addressed to:
Barron's Educational Series, Inc.
250 Wireless Boulevard
Hauppauge, New York 11788

Library of Congress Catalog Card No. 83-15482

International Standard Book No. 0-8120-2745-0

Library of Congress Cataloging in Publication Data

Solomon, Stephen S.
  Barron's financial tables for better money management. Savings and loans.

  Includes index.
  1. Interest—Tables. 2. Investments—Tables.
I. Marshall, Clifford W., 1928-   . II. Pepper,
Martin. III. Title. IV. Title: Financial tables for
better money management. V. Title: Savings and loans.
HG1628.S75 1983   332.8'0212   83-15482
ISBN 0-8120-2745-0

PRINTED IN THE UNITED STATES OF AMERICA

89   900   9876

Contents

Introduction

The idea behind *Barron's Financial Tables for Better Money Management* is to provide assistance to anyone who invests, makes purchases, or borrows money. Since these guides require no financial or mathematical expertise, they can be used easily by the average investor or mortgage seeker. The tables are easy to read and are preceded by sample situations that show the nature and scope of the tables. Following each sample situation a short explanation tells how to use a particular table to find the desired answer and how to locate data on the table. After reading the situation and explanation you should be able to apply the same procedure to answer questions regarding your particular situation. If you spend time "walking through" all the situations given, you will better understand how to use the tables.

Because these tables are designed for the non-professional, no formulas or mathematical derivations are shown. Such derivations are not required for proper use of the tables.

Monthly Installment Loan Payments

Many times a person must borrow to pay for all or part of an item he or she wishes to purchase. Whether the borrowing is for an appliance, a home repair, travel, or an automobile, one of the most common sources of money is the installment loan. This involves installment payments, a series of equal periodic payments — usually due monthly — that are paid over a specified period of time to repay the loan.

The table that follows shows the monthly payments for such loans, based on interest rates of 8% to 24%, loan amounts of $100 to $70,000, and repayment periods of 6 months to 15 years. Here are some illustrative situations to help you understand and use the tables:

Situation 1

Mr. Hart wants to buy a new car that costs $12,000.00 and has a down payment of $2,000.00. He now seeks a loan for $10,000.00 that has a repayment period of 4 years. The stipulated interest rate at his neighborhood bank is 16%. To find the required monthly installment payment, Mr. Hart must (1) find the 16% pages of the table, (2) locate the column for 4 years, (3) look down the left side of the page to find the $10,000.00 line, and (4) read across to the 4-year column. The monthly payment amount is $283.40.

Situation 2

Mrs. Plum wishes to have two rooms of her house painted. The cost is $500.00 and she will borrow the money and pay it back through an installment loan for the full amount; the repayment period is 3 years and the interest rate is 14%. Mrs. Plum can determine what the monthly installment payment will be by (1) locating the 14% pages of the table, (2) finding the 3-year column heading, (3) looking down the left side of the page to the $500.00 line, and (4) scanning across to the 3-year column. There Mrs. Plum will find the amount of $17.09, which she will have to pay every month for 3 years.

8% Monthly Loan Payments

LOAN AMOUNT	½ YEAR	1 YEAR	1½ YEARS	2 YEARS	2½ YEARS	3 YEARS	3½ YEARS
100	17.06	8.70	5.91	4.52	3.69	3.13	2.7
200	34.12	17.40	11.83	9.05	7.38	6.27	5.4
300	51.17	26.10	17.74	13.57	11.07	9.40	8.2
400	68.23	34.80	23.66	18.09	14.76	12.53	10.9
500	85.29	43.49	29.57	22.61	18.44	15.67	13.6
600	102.35	52.19	35.48	27.14	22.13	18.80	16.4
700	119.40	60.89	41.40	31.66	25.82	21.94	19.1
800	136.46	69.59	47.31	36.18	29.51	25.07	21.9
900	153.52	78.29	53.23	40.70	33.20	28.20	24.6
1000	170.58	86.99	59.14	45.23	36.89	31.34	27.3
1500	255.87	130.48	88.71	67.84	55.33	47.00	41.0
2000	341.15	173.98	118.28	90.45	73.78	62.67	54.7
2500	426.44	217.47	147.85	113.07	92.22	78.34	68.4
3000	511.73	260.97	177.42	135.68	110.66	94.01	82.1
3500	597.02	304.46	206.99	158.30	129.11	109.68	95.8
4000	682.31	347.95	236.56	180.91	147.55	125.35	109.5
4500	767.60	391.45	266.13	203.52	166.00	141.01	123.2
5000	852.89	434.94	295.70	226.14	184.44	156.68	136.8
5500	938.17	478.44	325.27	248.75	202.89	172.35	150.5
6000	1023.46	521.93	354.84	271.36	221.33	188.02	164.2
6500	1108.75	565.42	384.41	293.98	239.77	203.69	177.9
7000	1194.04	608.92	413.98	316.59	258.22	219.35	191.6
7500	1279.33	652.41	443.55	339.20	276.66	235.02	205.3
8000	1364.62	695.91	473.12	361.82	295.11	250.69	219.0
8500	1449.91	739.40	502.69	384.43	313.55	266.36	232.7
9000	1535.19	782.90	532.26	407.05	331.99	282.03	246.3
9500	1620.48	826.39	561.83	429.66	350.44	297.70	260.0
10000	1705.77	869.88	591.40	452.27	368.88	313.36	273.7
11000	1876.35	956.87	650.54	497.50	405.77	344.70	301.1
12000	2046.93	1043.86	709.68	542.73	442.66	376.04	328.5
13000	2217.50	1130.85	768.82	587.95	479.55	407.37	355.9
14000	2388.08	1217.84	827.96	633.18	516.44	438.71	383.2
15000	2558.66	1304.83	887.10	678.41	553.32	470.05	410.6
16000	2729.23	1391.81	946.24	723.64	590.21	501.38	438.0
17000	2899.81	1478.80	1005.39	768.86	627.10	532.72	465.4
18000	3070.39	1565.79	1064.53	814.09	663.99	564.05	492.7
19000	3240.96	1652.78	1123.67	859.32	700.88	595.39	520.1
20000	3411.54	1739.77	1182.81	904.55	737.77	626.73	547.5
21000	3582.12	1826.76	1241.95	949.77	774.65	658.06	574.9
22000	3752.70	1913.75	1301.09	995.00	811.54	689.40	602.2
23000	3923.27	2000.73	1360.23	1040.23	848.43	720.74	629.6
24000	4093.85	2087.72	1419.37	1085.45	885.32	752.07	657.0
25000	4264.43	2174.71	1478.51	1130.68	922.21	783.41	684.4
26000	4435.00	2261.70	1537.65	1175.91	959.10	814.75	711.8
27000	4605.58	2348.69	1596.79	1221.14	995.98	846.08	739.1
28000	4776.16	2435.68	1655.93	1266.36	1032.87	877.42	766.5
29000	4946.74	2522.66	1715.07	1311.59	1069.76	908.75	793.9
30000	5117.31	2609.65	1774.21	1356.82	1106.65	940.09	821.3
31000	5287.89	2696.64	1833.35	1402.05	1143.54	971.43	848.6
32000	5458.47	2783.63	1892.49	1447.27	1180.43	1002.76	876.0
33000	5629.04	2870.62	1951.63	1492.50	1217.31	1034.10	903.4
34000	5799.62	2957.61	2010.77	1537.73	1254.20	1065.44	930.8
35000	5970.20	3044.60	2069.91	1582.96	1291.09	1096.77	958.1
40000	6823.08	3479.54	2365.61	1809.09	1475.53	1253.45	1095.0
45000	7675.97	3914.48	2661.31	2035.23	1659.97	1410.14	1231.9
50000	8528.85	4349.42	2957.01	2261.36	1844.42	1566.82	1368.8
55000	9381.74	4784.36	3252.72	2487.50	2028.86	1723.50	1505.7
60000	10234.63	5219.31	3548.42	2713.64	2213.30	1880.18	1642.6
65000	11087.51	5654.25	3844.12	2939.77	2397.74	2036.86	1779.5
70000	11940.40	6089.19	4139.82	3165.91	2582.18	2193.55	1916.3

Monthly Loan Payments 8%

LOAN AMOUNT	4 YEARS	4½ YEARS	5 YEARS	5½ YEARS	6 YEARS	6½ YEARS	7 YEARS
100	2.44	2.21	2.03	1.88	1.75	1.65	1.56
200	4.88	4.42	4.06	3.76	3.51	3.30	3.12
300	7.32	6.63	6.08	5.63	5.26	4.94	4.68
400	9.77	8.84	8.11	7.51	7.01	6.59	6.23
500	12.21	11.06	10.14	9.39	8.77	8.24	7.79
600	14.65	13.27	12.17	11.27	10.52	9.89	9.35
700	17.09	15.48	14.19	13.14	12.27	11.54	10.91
800	19.53	17.69	16.22	15.02	14.03	13.19	12.47
900	21.97	19.90	18.25	16.90	15.78	14.83	14.03
1000	24.41	22.11	20.28	18.78	17.53	16.48	15.59
1500	36.62	33.17	30.41	28.17	26.30	24.72	23.38
2000	48.83	44.22	40.55	37.56	35.07	32.97	31.17
2500	61.03	55.28	50.69	46.95	43.83	41.21	38.97
3000	73.24	66.34	60.83	56.33	52.60	49.45	46.76
3500	85.45	77.39	70.97	65.72	61.37	57.69	54.55
4000	97.65	88.45	81.11	75.11	70.13	65.93	62.34
4500	109.86	99.51	91.24	84.50	78.90	74.17	70.14
5000	122.06	110.56	101.38	93.89	87.67	82.42	77.93
5500	134.27	121.62	111.52	103.28	96.43	90.66	85.72
6000	146.48	132.67	121.66	112.67	105.20	98.90	93.52
6500	158.68	143.73	131.80	122.06	113.97	107.14	101.31
7000	170.89	154.79	141.93	131.45	122.73	115.38	109.10
7500	183.10	165.84	152.07	140.84	131.50	123.62	116.90
8000	195.30	176.90	162.21	150.23	140.27	131.87	124.69
8500	207.51	187.96	172.35	159.61	149.03	140.11	132.48
9000	219.72	199.01	182.49	169.00	157.80	148.35	140.28
9500	231.92	210.07	192.63	178.39	166.57	156.59	148.07
10000	244.13	221.12	202.76	187.78	175.33	164.83	155.86
11000	268.54	243.24	223.04	206.56	192.87	181.32	171.45
12000	292.96	265.35	243.32	225.34	210.40	197.80	187.03
13000	317.37	287.46	263.59	244.12	227.93	214.28	202.62
14000	341.78	309.57	283.87	262.89	245.47	230.76	218.21
15000	366.19	331.69	304.15	281.67	263.00	247.25	233.79
16000	390.61	353.80	324.42	300.45	280.53	263.73	249.38
17000	415.02	375.91	344.70	319.23	298.07	280.21	264.97
18000	439.43	398.02	364.98	338.01	315.60	296.70	280.55
19000	463.85	420.14	385.25	356.78	333.13	313.18	296.14
20000	488.26	442.25	405.53	375.56	350.66	329.66	311.72
21000	512.67	464.36	425.80	394.34	368.20	346.15	327.31
22000	537.08	486.47	446.08	413.12	385.73	362.63	342.90
23000	561.50	508.59	466.36	431.90	403.26	379.11	358.48
24000	585.91	530.70	486.63	450.68	420.80	395.60	374.07
25000	610.32	552.81	506.91	469.45	438.33	412.08	389.66
26000	634.74	574.92	527.19	488.23	455.86	428.56	405.24
27000	659.15	597.04	547.46	507.01	473.40	445.05	420.83
28000	683.56	619.15	567.74	525.79	490.93	461.53	436.41
29000	707.97	641.26	588.02	544.57	508.46	478.01	452.00
30000	732.39	663.37	608.29	563.34	526.00	494.50	467.59
31000	756.80	685.49	628.57	582.12	543.53	510.98	483.17
32000	781.21	707.60	648.84	600.90	561.06	527.46	498.76
33000	805.63	729.71	669.12	619.68	578.60	543.95	514.35
34000	830.04	751.82	689.40	638.46	596.13	560.43	529.93
35000	854.45	773.93	709.67	657.24	613.66	576.91	545.52
40000	976.52	884.50	811.06	751.13	701.33	659.33	623.45
45000	1098.58	995.06	912.44	845.02	789.00	741.74	701.38
50000	1220.65	1105.62	1013.82	938.91	876.66	824.16	779.31
55000	1342.71	1216.18	1115.20	1032.80	964.33	906.58	857.24
60000	1464.78	1326.75	1216.58	1126.69	1051.99	988.99	935.17
65000	1586.84	1437.31	1317.97	1220.58	1139.66	1071.41	1013.10
70000	1708.90	1547.87	1419.35	1314.47	1227.33	1153.82	1091.04

8%   Monthly Loan Payments

LOAN AMOUNT	7½ YEARS	8 YEARS	8½ YEARS	9 YEARS	9½ YEARS	10 YEARS	10½ YEARS
100	1.48	1.41	1.35	1.30	1.26	1.21	1.18
200	2.96	2.83	2.71	2.60	2.51	2.43	2.35
300	4.44	4.24	4.06	3.91	3.77	3.64	3.53
400	5.92	5.65	5.42	5.21	5.02	4.85	4.70
500	7.41	7.07	6.77	6.51	6.28	6.07	5.88
600	8.89	8.48	8.13	7.81	7.53	7.28	7.05
700	10.37	9.90	9.48	9.11	8.79	8.49	8.23
800	11.85	11.31	10.83	10.41	10.04	9.71	9.40
900	13.33	12.72	12.19	11.72	11.30	10.92	10.58
1000	14.81	14.14	13.54	13.02	12.55	12.13	11.76
1500	22.22	21.21	20.32	19.53	18.83	18.20	17.63
2000	29.62	28.27	27.09	26.04	25.10	24.27	23.51
2500	37.03	35.34	33.86	32.55	31.38	30.33	29.39
3000	44.44	42.41	40.63	39.06	37.65	36.40	35.27
3500	51.84	49.48	47.40	45.57	43.93	42.46	41.15
4000	59.25	56.55	54.17	52.07	50.21	48.53	47.02
4500	66.65	63.62	60.95	58.58	56.48	54.60	52.90
5000	74.06	70.68	67.72	65.09	62.76	60.66	58.78
5500	81.46	77.75	74.49	71.60	69.03	66.73	64.66
6000	88.87	84.82	81.26	78.11	75.31	72.80	70.54
6500	96.28	91.89	88.03	84.62	81.58	78.86	76.41
7000	103.68	98.96	94.80	91.13	87.86	84.93	82.29
7500	111.09	106.03	101.58	97.64	94.13	91.00	88.17
8000	118.49	113.09	108.35	104.15	100.41	97.06	94.05
8500	125.90	120.16	115.12	110.66	106.69	103.13	99.93
9000	133.31	127.23	121.89	117.17	112.96	109.19	105.80
9500	140.71	134.30	128.66	123.68	119.24	115.26	111.68
10000	148.12	141.37	135.44	130.19	125.51	121.33	117.56
11000	162.93	155.50	148.98	143.21	138.06	133.46	129.32
12000	177.74	169.64	162.52	156.22	150.62	145.59	141.07
13000	192.55	183.78	176.07	169.24	163.17	157.73	152.83
14000	207.36	197.91	189.61	182.26	175.72	169.86	164.58
15000	222.18	212.05	203.15	195.28	188.27	181.99	176.34
16000	236.99	226.19	216.70	208.30	200.82	194.12	188.10
17000	251.80	240.32	230.24	221.32	213.37	206.26	199.85
18000	266.61	254.46	243.78	234.34	225.92	218.39	211.61
19000	281.42	268.60	257.33	247.36	238.48	230.52	223.36
20000	296.23	282.73	270.87	260.37	251.03	242.66	235.12
21000	311.05	296.87	284.41	273.39	263.58	254.79	246.88
22000	325.86	311.01	297.96	286.41	276.13	266.92	258.63
23000	340.67	325.14	311.50	299.43	288.68	279.05	270.39
24000	355.48	339.28	325.05	312.45	301.23	291.19	282.14
25000	370.29	353.42	338.59	325.47	313.78	303.32	293.90
26000	385.10	367.55	352.13	338.49	326.33	315.45	305.66
27000	399.92	381.69	365.68	351.51	338.89	327.58	317.41
28000	414.73	395.83	379.22	364.52	351.44	339.72	329.17
29000	429.54	409.96	392.76	377.54	363.99	351.85	340.93
30000	444.35	424.10	406.31	390.56	376.54	363.98	352.68
31000	459.16	438.24	419.85	403.58	389.09	376.12	364.44
32000	473.97	452.37	433.39	416.60	401.64	388.25	376.19
33000	488.79	466.51	446.94	429.62	414.19	400.38	387.95
34000	503.60	480.65	460.48	442.64	426.74	412.51	399.71
35000	518.41	494.78	474.02	455.66	439.30	424.65	411.46
40000	592.47	565.47	541.74	520.75	502.05	485.31	470.24
45000	666.53	636.15	609.46	585.84	564.81	545.97	529.02
50000	740.59	706.83	677.18	650.94	627.57	606.64	587.80
55000	814.64	777.52	744.90	716.03	690.32	667.30	646.58
60000	888.70	848.20	812.61	781.12	753.08	727.97	705.36
65000	962.76	918.88	880.33	846.22	815.84	788.63	764.14
70000	1036.82	989.57	948.05	911.31	878.59	849.29	822.92

Monthly Loan Payments 8%

LOAN AMOUNT	11 YEARS	11½ YEARS	12 YEARS	12½ YEARS	13 YEARS	14 YEARS	15 YEARS
100	1.14	1.11	1.08	1.06	1.03	0.99	0.96
200	2.28	2.22	2.16	2.11	2.07	1.98	1.91
300	3.42	3.33	3.25	3.17	3.10	2.97	2.87
400	4.57	4.44	4.33	4.23	4.13	3.97	3.82
500	5.71	5.55	5.41	5.28	5.17	4.96	4.78
600	6.85	6.66	6.49	6.34	6.20	5.95	5.73
700	7.99	7.77	7.58	7.40	7.23	6.94	6.69
800	9.13	8.89	8.66	8.45	8.26	7.93	7.65
900	10.27	10.00	9.74	9.51	9.30	8.92	8.60
1000	11.42	11.11	10.82	10.57	10.33	9.91	9.56
1500	17.12	16.66	16.24	15.85	15.50	14.87	14.33
2000	22.83	22.21	21.65	21.13	20.66	19.83	19.11
2500	28.54	27.77	27.06	26.42	25.83	24.78	23.89
3000	34.25	33.32	32.47	31.70	30.99	29.74	28.67
3500	39.95	38.87	37.89	36.98	36.16	34.70	33.45
4000	45.66	44.43	43.30	42.27	41.32	39.65	38.23
4500	51.37	49.98	48.71	47.55	46.49	44.61	43.00
5000	57.08	55.53	54.12	52.83	51.65	49.57	47.78
5500	62.78	61.08	59.53	58.12	56.82	54.52	52.56
6000	68.49	66.64	64.95	63.40	61.98	59.48	57.34
6500	74.20	72.19	70.36	68.69	67.15	64.44	62.12
7000	79.91	77.74	75.77	73.97	72.32	69.39	66.90
7500	85.62	83.30	81.18	79.25	77.48	74.35	71.67
8000	91.32	88.85	86.60	84.54	82.65	79.31	76.45
8500	97.03	94.40	92.01	89.82	87.81	84.26	81.23
9000	102.74	99.96	97.42	95.10	92.98	89.22	86.01
9500	108.45	105.51	102.83	100.39	98.14	94.18	90.79
10000	114.15	111.06	108.25	105.67	103.31	99.13	95.57
11000	125.57	122.17	119.07	116.24	113.64	109.05	105.12
12000	136.99	133.28	129.89	126.80	123.97	118.96	114.68
13000	148.40	144.38	140.72	137.37	134.30	128.87	124.23
14000	159.82	155.49	151.54	147.94	144.63	138.78	133.79
15000	171.23	166.59	162.37	158.50	154.96	148.70	143.35
16000	182.65	177.70	173.19	169.07	165.29	158.61	152.90
17000	194.06	188.81	184.02	179.64	175.62	168.52	162.46
18000	205.48	199.91	194.84	190.21	185.95	178.44	172.02
19000	216.89	211.02	205.67	200.77	196.28	188.35	181.57
20000	228.31	222.13	216.49	211.34	206.61	198.26	191.13
21000	239.72	233.23	227.32	221.91	216.95	208.18	200.69
22000	251.14	244.34	238.14	232.47	227.28	218.09	210.24
23000	262.56	255.44	248.96	243.04	237.61	228.00	219.80
24000	273.97	266.55	259.79	253.61	247.94	237.92	229.36
25000	285.39	277.66	270.61	264.17	258.27	247.83	238.91
26000	296.80	288.76	281.44	274.74	268.60	257.74	248.47
27000	308.22	299.87	292.26	285.31	278.93	267.66	258.03
28000	319.63	310.98	303.09	295.87	289.26	277.57	267.58
29000	331.05	322.08	313.91	306.44	299.59	287.48	277.14
30000	342.46	333.19	324.74	317.01	309.92	297.40	286.70
31000	353.88	344.29	335.56	327.58	320.25	307.31	296.25
32000	365.29	355.40	346.38	338.14	330.58	317.22	305.81
33000	376.71	366.51	357.21	348.71	340.91	327.14	315.37
34000	388.13	377.61	368.03	359.28	351.25	337.05	324.92
35000	399.54	388.72	378.86	369.84	361.58	346.96	334.48
40000	456.62	444.25	432.98	422.68	413.23	396.53	382.26
45000	513.70	499.78	487.10	475.51	464.88	446.09	430.04
50000	570.77	555.31	541.23	528.35	516.54	495.66	477.83
55000	627.85	610.84	595.35	581.18	568.19	545.23	525.61
60000	684.93	666.38	649.47	634.02	619.84	594.79	573.39
65000	742.00	721.91	703.59	686.85	671.50	644.36	621.17
70000	799.08	777.44	757.72	739.69	723.15	693.92	668.96

8¼%   Monthly Loan Payments

LOAN AMOUNT	½ YEAR	1 YEAR	1½ YEARS	2 YEARS	2½ YEARS	3 YEARS	3½ YEARS
100	17.07	8.71	5.93	4.53	3.70	3.15	2.75
200	34.14	17.42	11.85	9.07	7.40	6.29	5.50
300	51.21	26.13	17.78	13.60	11.10	9.44	8.25
400	68.28	34.84	23.70	18.14	14.80	12.58	11.00
500	85.35	43.55	29.63	22.67	18.50	15.73	13.75
600	102.42	52.26	35.55	27.20	22.20	18.87	16.50
700	119.49	60.97	41.48	31.74	25.90	22.02	19.25
800	136.56	69.68	47.40	36.27	29.60	25.16	21.99
900	153.63	78.39	53.33	40.81	33.30	28.31	24.74
1000	170.70	87.10	59.25	45.34	37.00	31.45	27.49
1500	256.05	130.66	88.88	68.01	55.50	47.18	41.24
2000	341.40	174.21	118.51	90.68	74.01	62.90	54.99
2500	426.75	217.76	148.14	113.35	92.51	78.63	68.73
3000	512.10	261.31	177.76	136.02	111.01	94.36	82.48
3500	597.45	304.86	207.39	158.69	129.51	110.08	96.23
4000	682.80	348.42	237.02	181.37	148.01	125.81	109.97
4500	768.15	391.97	266.65	204.04	166.51	141.53	123.72
5000	853.50	435.52	296.27	226.71	185.01	157.26	137.47
5500	938.85	479.07	325.90	249.38	203.52	172.99	151.21
6000	1024.20	522.62	355.53	272.05	222.02	188.71	164.96
6500	1109.55	566.18	385.15	294.72	240.52	204.44	178.71
7000	1194.90	609.73	414.78	317.39	259.02	220.16	192.45
7500	1280.25	653.28	444.41	340.06	277.52	235.89	206.20
8000	1365.60	696.83	474.04	362.73	296.02	251.61	219.95
8500	1450.95	740.38	503.66	385.40	314.53	267.34	233.69
9000	1536.30	783.94	533.29	408.07	333.03	283.07	247.44
9500	1621.65	827.49	562.92	430.74	351.53	298.79	261.19
10000	1707.00	871.04	592.54	453.41	370.03	314.52	274.93
11000	1877.70	958.14	651.80	498.76	407.03	345.97	302.43
12000	2048.40	1045.25	711.05	544.10	444.04	377.42	329.92
13000	2219.10	1132.35	770.31	589.44	481.04	408.87	357.41
14000	2389.80	1219.46	829.56	634.78	518.04	440.33	384.91
15000	2560.50	1306.56	888.82	680.12	555.04	471.78	412.40
16000	2731.20	1393.67	948.07	725.46	592.05	503.23	439.89
17000	2901.90	1480.77	1007.33	770.80	629.05	534.68	467.39
18000	3072.60	1567.87	1066.58	816.15	666.05	566.13	494.88
19000	3243.30	1654.98	1125.83	861.49	703.06	597.58	522.37
20000	3414.00	1742.08	1185.09	906.83	740.06	629.04	549.87
21000	3584.70	1829.19	1244.34	952.17	777.06	660.49	577.36
22000	3755.40	1916.29	1303.60	997.51	814.07	691.94	604.86
23000	3926.10	2003.39	1362.85	1042.85	851.07	723.39	632.35
24000	4096.80	2090.50	1422.11	1088.19	888.07	754.84	659.84
25000	4267.50	2177.60	1481.36	1133.53	925.07	786.30	687.34
26000	4438.20	2264.71	1540.62	1178.88	962.08	817.75	714.83
27000	4608.90	2351.81	1599.87	1224.22	999.08	849.20	742.32
28000	4779.60	2438.91	1659.12	1269.56	1036.08	880.65	769.82
29000	4950.30	2526.02	1718.38	1314.90	1073.09	912.10	797.31
30000	5121.00	2613.12	1777.63	1360.24	1110.09	943.55	824.80
31000	5291.70	2700.23	1836.89	1405.58	1147.09	975.01	852.30
32000	5462.40	2787.33	1896.14	1450.92	1184.09	1006.46	879.79
33000	5633.10	2874.43	1955.40	1496.27	1221.10	1037.91	907.28
34000	5803.80	2961.54	2014.65	1541.61	1258.10	1069.36	934.78
35000	5974.50	3048.64	2073.91	1586.95	1295.10	1100.81	962.27
40000	6828.00	3484.16	2370.18	1813.66	1480.12	1258.07	1099.74
45000	7681.50	3919.68	2666.45	2040.36	1665.13	1415.33	1237.20
50000	8535.00	4355.20	2962.72	2267.07	1850.15	1572.59	1374.67
55000	9388.50	4790.72	3258.99	2493.78	2035.16	1729.85	1512.14
60000	10242.00	5226.24	3555.27	2720.48	2220.18	1887.11	1649.60
65000	11095.50	5661.76	3851.54	2947.19	2405.19	2044.37	1787.07
70000	11949.00	6097.28	4147.81	3173.90	2590.21	2201.63	1924.54

Monthly Loan Payments   8¼%

LOAN AMOUNT	4 YEARS	4½ YEARS	5 YEARS	5½ YEARS	6 YEARS	6½ YEARS	7 YEARS
100	2.45	2.22	2.04	1.89	1.77	1.66	1.57
200	4.91	4.45	4.08	3.78	3.53	3.32	3.14
300	7.36	6.67	6.12	5.67	5.30	4.98	4.71
400	9.81	8.89	8.16	7.56	7.06	6.64	6.28
500	12.27	11.12	10.20	9.45	8.83	8.30	7.86
600	14.72	13.34	12.24	11.34	10.59	9.96	9.43
700	17.17	15.56	14.28	13.23	12.36	11.62	11.00
800	19.62	17.78	16.32	15.12	14.12	13.29	12.57
900	22.08	20.01	18.36	17.01	15.89	14.95	14.14
1000	24.53	22.23	20.40	18.90	17.66	16.61	15.71
1500	36.80	33.35	30.59	28.35	26.48	24.91	23.57
2000	49.06	44.46	40.79	37.80	35.31	33.21	31.42
2500	61.33	55.58	50.99	47.25	44.14	41.52	39.28
3000	73.59	66.69	61.19	56.70	52.97	49.82	47.13
3500	85.86	77.81	71.39	66.15	61.79	58.12	54.99
4000	98.12	88.92	81.59	75.60	70.62	66.43	62.84
4500	110.39	100.04	91.78	85.05	79.45	74.73	70.70
5000	122.65	111.16	101.98	94.50	88.28	83.03	78.56
5500	134.92	122.27	112.18	103.95	97.11	91.34	86.41
6000	147.18	133.39	122.38	113.40	105.93	99.64	94.27
6500	159.45	144.50	132.58	122.85	114.76	107.94	102.12
7000	171.71	155.62	142.77	132.29	123.59	116.25	109.98
7500	183.98	166.73	152.97	141.74	132.42	124.55	117.83
8000	196.24	177.85	163.17	151.19	141.24	132.85	125.69
8500	208.51	188.96	173.37	160.64	150.07	141.16	133.54
9000	220.77	200.08	183.57	170.09	158.90	149.46	141.40
9500	233.04	211.20	193.76	179.54	167.73	157.76	149.26
10000	245.30	222.31	203.96	188.99	176.56	166.07	157.11
11000	269.83	244.54	224.36	207.89	194.21	182.67	172.82
12000	294.37	266.77	244.76	226.79	211.87	199.28	188.53
13000	318.90	289.00	265.15	245.69	229.52	215.89	204.24
14000	343.43	311.24	285.55	264.59	247.18	232.49	219.95
15000	367.96	333.47	305.94	283.49	264.83	249.10	235.67
16000	392.49	355.70	326.34	302.39	282.49	265.71	251.38
17000	417.02	377.93	346.74	321.29	300.14	282.31	267.09
18000	441.55	400.16	367.13	340.19	317.80	298.92	282.80
19000	466.08	422.39	387.53	359.09	335.46	315.53	298.51
20000	490.61	444.62	407.93	377.98	353.11	332.14	314.22
21000	515.14	466.85	428.32	396.88	370.77	348.74	329.93
22000	539.67	489.08	448.72	415.78	388.42	365.35	345.64
23000	564.20	511.32	469.11	434.68	406.08	381.96	361.35
24000	588.73	533.55	489.51	453.58	423.73	398.56	377.07
25000	613.26	555.78	509.91	472.48	441.39	415.17	392.78
26000	637.79	578.01	530.30	491.38	459.04	431.78	408.49
27000	662.32	600.24	550.70	510.28	476.70	448.38	424.20
28000	686.85	622.47	571.10	529.18	494.36	464.99	439.91
29000	711.38	644.70	591.49	548.08	512.01	481.60	455.62
30000	735.91	666.93	611.89	566.98	529.67	498.20	471.33
31000	760.44	689.16	632.28	585.88	547.32	514.81	487.04
32000	784.97	711.39	652.68	604.78	564.98	531.42	502.75
33000	809.50	733.63	673.08	623.67	582.63	548.02	518.46
34000	834.04	755.86	693.47	642.57	600.29	564.63	534.18
35000	858.57	778.09	713.87	661.47	617.94	581.24	549.89
40000	981.22	889.24	815.85	755.97	706.22	664.27	628.44
45000	1103.87	1000.40	917.83	850.47	794.50	747.30	707.00
50000	1226.52	1111.55	1019.81	944.96	882.78	830.34	785.55
55000	1349.17	1222.71	1121.79	1039.46	971.06	913.37	864.11
60000	1471.83	1333.87	1223.78	1133.95	1059.33	996.41	942.66
65000	1594.48	1445.02	1325.76	1228.45	1147.61	1079.44	1021.22
70000	1717.13	1556.18	1427.74	1322.95	1235.89	1162.47	1099.77

8¼%   Monthly Loan Payments

LOAN AMOUNT	7½ YEARS	8 YEARS	8½ YEARS	9 YEARS	9½ YEARS	10 YEARS	10½ YEARS
100	1.49	1.43	1.37	1.31	1.27	1.23	1.19
200	2.99	2.85	2.73	2.63	2.54	2.45	2.38
300	4.48	4.28	4.10	3.94	3.80	3.68	3.57
400	5.98	5.71	5.47	5.26	5.07	4.91	4.76
500	7.47	7.13	6.84	6.57	6.34	6.13	5.94
600	8.96	8.56	8.20	7.89	7.61	7.36	7.13
700	10.46	9.98	9.57	9.20	8.88	8.59	8.32
800	11.95	11.41	10.94	10.52	10.15	9.81	9.51
900	13.44	12.84	12.31	11.83	11.41	11.04	10.70
1000	14.94	14.26	13.67	13.15	12.68	12.27	11.89
1500	22.41	21.40	20.51	19.72	19.02	18.40	17.83
2000	29.88	28.53	27.34	26.30	25.37	24.53	23.78
2500	37.34	35.66	34.18	32.87	31.71	30.66	29.72
3000	44.81	42.79	41.02	39.45	38.05	36.80	35.67
3500	52.28	49.92	47.85	46.02	44.39	42.93	41.61
4000	59.75	57.06	54.69	52.59	50.73	49.06	47.56
4500	67.22	64.19	61.53	59.17	57.07	55.19	53.50
5000	74.69	71.32	68.36	65.74	63.41	61.33	59.45
5500	82.16	78.45	75.20	72.32	69.75	67.46	65.39
6000	89.63	85.58	82.03	78.89	76.10	73.59	71.34
6500	97.10	92.72	88.87	85.47	82.44	79.72	77.28
7000	104.56	99.85	95.71	92.04	88.78	85.86	83.23
7500	112.03	106.98	102.54	98.62	95.12	91.99	89.17
8000	119.50	114.11	109.38	105.19	101.46	98.12	95.12
8500	126.97	121.24	116.21	111.76	107.80	104.25	101.06
9000	134.44	128.38	123.05	118.34	114.14	110.39	107.01
9500	141.91	135.51	129.89	124.91	120.48	116.52	112.95
10000	149.38	142.64	136.72	131.49	126.83	122.65	118.90
11000	164.32	156.90	150.39	144.64	139.51	134.92	130.79
12000	179.25	171.17	164.07	157.78	152.19	147.18	142.68
13000	194.19	185.43	177.74	170.93	164.87	159.45	154.57
14000	209.13	199.70	191.41	184.08	177.56	171.71	166.46
15000	224.07	213.96	205.08	197.23	190.24	183.98	178.35
16000	239.01	228.23	218.76	210.38	202.92	196.24	190.24
17000	253.94	242.49	232.43	223.53	215.60	208.51	202.13
18000	268.88	256.75	246.10	236.68	228.29	220.77	214.02
19000	283.82	271.02	259.77	249.82	240.97	233.04	225.91
20000	298.76	285.28	273.44	262.97	253.65	245.31	237.80
21000	313.69	299.55	287.12	276.12	266.33	257.57	249.69
22000	328.63	313.81	300.79	289.27	279.02	269.84	261.58
23000	343.57	328.07	314.46	302.42	291.70	282.10	273.47
24000	358.51	342.34	328.13	315.57	304.38	294.37	285.36
25000	373.45	356.60	341.81	328.72	317.06	306.63	297.25
26000	388.38	370.87	355.48	341.87	329.75	318.90	309.14
27000	403.32	385.13	369.15	355.01	342.43	331.16	321.02
28000	418.26	399.39	382.82	368.16	355.11	343.43	332.91
29000	433.20	413.66	396.50	381.31	367.79	355.69	344.80
30000	448.13	427.92	410.17	394.46	380.48	367.96	356.69
31000	463.07	442.19	423.84	407.61	393.16	380.22	368.58
32000	478.01	456.45	437.51	420.76	405.84	392.49	380.47
33000	492.95	470.71	451.18	433.91	418.52	404.75	392.36
34000	507.89	484.98	464.86	447.05	431.21	417.02	404.25
35000	522.82	499.24	478.53	460.20	443.89	429.28	416.14
40000	597.51	570.56	546.89	525.95	507.30	490.61	475.59
45000	672.20	641.88	615.25	591.69	570.71	551.94	535.04
50000	746.89	713.20	683.61	657.43	634.13	613.26	594.49
55000	821.58	784.52	751.97	723.18	697.54	674.59	653.94
60000	896.27	855.84	820.33	788.92	760.95	735.92	713.39
65000	970.96	927.16	888.70	854.66	824.37	797.24	772.84
70000	1045.65	998.49	957.06	920.41	887.78	858.57	832.29

Monthly Loan Payments 8¼%

LOAN AMOUNT	11 YEARS	11½ YEARS	12 YEARS	12½ YEARS	13 YEARS	14 YEARS	15 YEARS
100	1.16	1.12	1.10	1.07	1.05	1.01	0.97
200	2.31	2.25	2.19	2.14	2.09	2.01	1.94
300	3.47	3.37	3.29	3.21	3.14	3.02	2.91
400	4.62	4.50	4.38	4.28	4.19	4.02	3.88
500	5.78	5.62	5.48	5.35	5.24	5.03	4.85
600	6.93	6.75	6.58	6.42	6.28	6.03	5.82
700	8.09	7.87	7.67	7.49	7.33	7.04	6.79
800	9.24	8.99	8.77	8.56	8.38	8.04	7.76
900	10.40	10.12	9.87	9.64	9.42	9.05	8.73
1000	11.55	11.24	10.96	10.71	10.47	10.06	9.70
1500	17.33	16.86	16.44	16.06	15.71	15.08	14.55
2000	23.10	22.49	21.92	21.41	20.94	20.11	19.40
2500	28.88	28.11	27.41	26.76	26.18	25.14	24.25
3000	34.65	33.73	32.89	32.12	31.41	30.17	29.10
3500	40.43	39.35	38.37	37.47	36.65	35.19	33.95
4000	46.20	44.97	43.85	42.82	41.88	40.22	38.81
4500	51.98	50.59	49.33	48.18	47.12	45.25	43.66
5000	57.75	56.21	54.81	53.53	52.35	50.28	48.51
5500	63.53	61.83	60.29	58.88	57.59	55.31	53.36
6000	69.30	67.46	65.77	64.23	62.82	60.33	58.21
6500	75.08	73.08	71.25	69.59	68.06	65.36	63.06
7000	80.85	78.70	76.73	74.94	73.30	70.39	67.91
7500	86.63	84.32	82.22	80.29	78.53	75.42	72.76
8000	92.40	89.94	87.70	85.65	83.77	80.45	77.61
8500	98.18	95.56	93.18	91.00	89.00	85.47	82.46
9000	103.95	101.18	98.66	96.35	94.24	90.50	87.31
9500	109.73	106.80	104.14	101.70	99.47	95.53	92.16
10000	115.50	112.43	109.62	107.06	104.71	100.56	97.01
11000	127.06	123.67	120.58	117.76	115.18	110.61	106.72
12000	138.61	134.91	131.54	128.47	125.65	120.67	116.42
13000	150.16	146.15	142.51	139.17	136.12	130.72	126.12
14000	161.71	157.40	153.47	149.88	146.59	140.78	135.82
15000	173.26	168.64	164.43	160.59	157.06	150.83	145.52
16000	184.81	179.88	175.39	171.29	167.53	160.89	155.22
17000	196.36	191.12	186.36	182.00	178.00	170.95	164.92
18000	207.91	202.37	197.32	192.70	188.47	181.00	174.63
19000	219.46	213.61	208.28	203.41	198.94	191.06	184.33
20000	231.01	224.85	219.24	214.11	209.42	201.11	194.03
21000	242.56	236.09	230.20	224.82	219.89	211.17	203.73
22000	254.11	247.34	241.17	235.53	230.36	221.22	213.43
23000	265.66	258.58	252.13	246.23	240.83	231.28	223.13
24000	277.21	269.82	263.09	256.94	251.30	241.34	232.83
25000	288.76	281.06	274.05	267.64	261.77	251.39	242.54
26000	300.31	292.31	285.01	278.35	272.24	261.45	252.24
27000	311.86	303.55	295.98	289.06	282.71	271.50	261.94
28000	323.41	314.79	306.94	299.76	293.18	281.56	271.64
29000	334.96	326.03	317.90	310.47	303.65	291.61	281.34
30000	346.51	337.28	328.86	321.17	314.12	301.67	291.04
31000	358.06	348.52	339.82	331.88	324.59	311.73	300.74
32000	369.62	359.76	350.79	342.58	335.06	321.78	310.44
33000	381.17	371.00	361.75	353.29	345.54	331.84	320.15
34000	392.72	382.25	372.71	364.00	356.01	341.89	329.85
35000	404.27	393.49	383.67	374.70	366.48	351.95	339.55
40000	462.02	449.70	438.48	428.23	418.83	402.23	388.06
45000	519.77	505.91	493.29	481.76	471.18	452.50	436.56
50000	577.52	562.13	548.10	535.29	523.54	502.78	485.07
55000	635.28	618.34	602.91	588.82	575.89	553.06	533.58
60000	693.03	674.55	657.72	642.34	628.25	603.34	582.08
65000	750.78	730.77	712.53	695.87	680.60	653.62	630.59
70000	808.53	786.98	767.35	749.40	732.95	703.90	679.10

8½%   Monthly Loan Payments

LOAN AMOUNT	½ YEAR	1 YEAR	1½ YEARS	2 YEARS	2½ YEARS	3 YEARS	3½ YEARS
100	17.08	8.72	5.94	4.55	3.71	3.16	2.76
200	34.16	17.44	11.87	9.09	7.42	6.31	5.52
300	51.25	26.17	17.81	13.64	11.14	9.47	8.28
400	68.33	34.89	23.75	18.18	14.85	12.63	11.04
500	85.41	43.61	29.68	22.73	18.56	15.78	13.81
600	102.49	52.33	35.62	27.27	22.27	18.94	16.57
700	119.58	61.05	41.56	31.82	25.98	22.10	19.33
800	136.66	69.78	47.49	36.36	29.69	25.25	22.09
900	153.74	78.50	53.43	40.91	33.41	28.41	24.85
1000	170.82	87.22	59.37	45.46	37.12	31.57	27.61
1500	256.23	130.83	89.05	68.18	55.68	47.35	41.42
2000	341.65	174.44	118.74	90.91	74.24	63.14	55.22
2500	427.06	218.05	148.42	113.64	92.79	78.92	69.03
3000	512.47	261.66	178.11	136.37	111.35	94.70	82.83
3500	597.88	305.27	207.79	159.09	129.91	110.49	96.64
4000	683.29	348.88	237.47	181.82	148.47	126.27	110.44
4500	768.70	392.49	267.16	204.55	167.03	142.05	124.25
5000	854.11	436.10	296.84	227.28	185.59	157.84	138.05
5500	939.53	479.71	326.53	250.01	204.15	173.62	151.86
6000	1024.94	523.32	356.21	272.73	222.71	189.41	165.66
6500	1110.35	566.93	385.90	295.46	241.27	205.19	179.47
7000	1195.76	610.54	415.58	318.19	259.82	220.97	193.27
7500	1281.17	654.15	445.27	340.92	278.38	236.76	207.08
8000	1366.58	697.76	474.95	363.65	296.94	252.54	220.88
8500	1451.99	741.37	504.63	386.37	315.50	268.32	234.69
9000	1537.41	784.98	534.32	409.10	334.06	284.11	248.49
9500	1622.82	828.59	564.00	431.83	352.62	299.89	262.30
10000	1708.23	872.20	593.69	454.56	371.18	315.68	276.10
11000	1879.05	959.42	653.06	500.01	408.30	347.24	303.71
12000	2049.87	1046.64	712.42	545.47	445.41	378.81	331.32
13000	2220.70	1133.86	771.79	590.92	482.53	410.38	358.93
14000	2391.52	1221.08	831.16	636.38	519.65	441.95	386.54
15000	2562.34	1308.30	890.53	681.84	556.77	473.51	414.15
16000	2733.17	1395.52	949.90	727.29	593.89	505.08	441.76
17000	2903.99	1482.74	1009.27	772.75	631.00	536.65	469.37
18000	3074.81	1569.96	1068.64	818.20	668.12	568.22	496.98
19000	3245.64	1657.18	1128.01	863.66	705.24	599.78	524.59
20000	3416.46	1744.40	1187.37	909.11	742.36	631.35	552.20
21000	3587.28	1831.62	1246.74	954.57	779.47	662.92	579.81
22000	3758.10	1918.84	1306.11	1000.02	816.59	694.49	607.42
23000	3928.93	2006.05	1365.48	1045.48	853.71	726.05	635.03
24000	4099.75	2093.27	1424.85	1090.94	890.83	757.62	662.64
25000	4270.57	2180.49	1484.22	1136.39	927.95	789.19	690.25
26000	4441.40	2267.71	1543.59	1181.85	965.06	820.76	717.86
27000	4612.22	2354.93	1602.96	1227.30	1002.18	852.32	745.47
28000	4783.04	2442.15	1662.32	1272.76	1039.30	883.89	773.08
29000	4953.86	2529.37	1721.69	1318.21	1076.42	915.46	800.69
30000	5124.69	2616.59	1781.06	1363.67	1113.53	947.03	828.30
31000	5295.51	2703.81	1840.43	1409.13	1150.65	978.59	855.91
32000	5466.33	2791.03	1899.80	1454.58	1187.77	1010.16	883.52
33000	5637.16	2878.25	1959.17	1500.04	1224.89	1041.73	911.13
34000	5807.98	2965.47	2018.54	1545.49	1262.01	1073.30	938.75
35000	5978.80	3052.69	2077.91	1590.95	1299.12	1104.86	966.36
40000	6832.92	3488.79	2374.75	1818.23	1484.71	1262.70	1104.41
45000	7687.03	3924.89	2671.59	2045.51	1670.30	1420.54	1242.46
50000	8541.15	4360.99	2968.44	2272.78	1855.89	1578.38	1380.51
55000	9395.26	4797.09	3265.28	2500.06	2041.48	1736.21	1518.56
60000	10249.37	5233.19	3562.12	2727.34	2227.07	1894.05	1656.61
65000	11103.49	5669.29	3858.97	2954.62	2412.66	2051.89	1794.66
70000	11957.60	6105.38	4155.81	3181.90	2598.25	2209.73	1932.71

Monthly Loan Payments 8½%

LOAN AMOUNT	4 YEARS	4½ YEARS	5 YEARS	5½ YEARS	6 YEARS	6½ YEARS	7 YEARS
100	2.46	2.24	2.05	1.90	1.78	1.67	1.58
200	4.93	4.47	4.10	3.80	3.56	3.35	3.17
300	7.39	6.71	6.15	5.71	5.33	5.02	4.75
400	9.86	8.94	8.21	7.61	7.11	6.69	6.33
500	12.32	11.18	10.26	9.51	8.89	8.37	7.92
600	14.79	13.41	12.31	11.41	10.67	10.04	9.50
700	17.25	15.65	14.36	13.31	12.44	11.71	11.09
800	19.72	17.88	16.41	15.22	14.22	13.38	12.67
900	22.18	20.12	18.46	17.12	16.00	15.06	14.25
1000	24.65	22.35	20.52	19.02	17.78	16.73	15.84
1500	36.97	33.53	30.77	28.53	26.67	25.10	23.75
2000	49.30	44.70	41.03	38.04	35.56	33.46	31.67
2500	61.62	55.88	51.29	47.55	44.45	41.83	39.59
3000	73.94	67.05	61.55	57.06	53.34	50.19	47.51
3500	86.27	78.23	71.81	66.57	62.22	58.56	55.43
4000	98.59	89.40	82.07	76.08	71.11	66.92	63.35
4500	110.92	100.58	92.32	85.59	80.00	75.29	71.26
5000	123.24	111.75	102.58	95.10	88.89	83.65	79.18
5500	135.57	122.93	112.84	104.61	97.78	92.02	87.10
6000	147.89	134.10	123.10	114.12	106.67	100.39	95.02
6500	160.21	145.28	133.36	123.64	115.56	108.75	102.94
7000	172.54	156.45	143.62	133.15	124.45	117.12	110.86
7500	184.86	167.63	153.87	142.66	133.34	125.48	118.77
8000	197.19	178.80	164.13	152.17	142.23	133.85	126.69
8500	209.51	189.98	174.39	161.68	151.12	142.21	134.61
9000	221.83	201.15	184.65	171.19	160.01	150.58	142.53
9500	234.16	212.33	194.91	180.70	168.89	158.94	150.45
10000	246.48	223.50	205.17	190.21	177.78	167.31	158.36
11000	271.13	245.85	225.68	209.23	195.56	184.04	174.20
12000	295.78	268.20	246.20	228.25	213.34	200.77	190.04
13000	320.43	290.55	266.71	247.27	231.12	217.50	205.87
14000	345.08	312.90	287.23	266.29	248.90	234.23	221.71
15000	369.72	335.25	307.75	285.31	266.68	250.96	237.55
16000	394.37	357.60	328.26	304.33	284.45	267.69	253.38
17000	419.02	379.95	348.78	323.35	302.23	284.42	269.22
18000	443.67	402.30	369.30	342.37	320.01	301.16	285.06
19000	468.32	424.65	389.81	361.39	337.79	317.89	300.89
20000	492.97	447.00	410.33	380.42	355.57	334.62	316.73
21000	517.61	469.35	430.85	399.44	373.35	351.35	332.57
22000	542.26	491.70	451.36	418.46	391.12	368.08	348.40
23000	566.91	514.05	471.88	437.48	408.90	384.81	364.24
24000	591.56	536.40	492.40	456.50	426.68	401.54	380.08
25000	616.21	558.75	512.91	475.52	444.46	418.27	395.91
26000	640.86	581.10	533.43	494.54	462.24	435.00	411.75
27000	665.50	603.45	553.95	513.56	480.02	451.73	427.59
28000	690.15	625.80	574.46	532.58	497.79	468.46	443.42
29000	714.80	648.15	594.98	551.60	515.57	485.20	459.26
30000	739.45	670.50	615.50	570.62	533.35	501.93	475.09
31000	764.10	692.85	636.01	589.64	551.13	518.66	490.93
32000	788.75	715.20	656.53	608.66	568.91	535.39	506.77
33000	813.39	737.55	677.05	627.69	586.69	552.12	522.60
34000	838.04	759.90	697.56	646.71	604.47	568.85	538.44
35000	862.69	782.25	718.08	665.73	622.24	585.58	554.28
40000	985.93	894.01	820.66	760.83	711.14	669.24	633.46
45000	1109.17	1005.76	923.24	855.93	800.03	752.89	712.64
50000	1232.42	1117.51	1025.83	951.04	888.92	836.54	791.82
55000	1355.66	1229.26	1128.41	1046.14	977.81	920.20	871.01
60000	1478.90	1341.01	1230.99	1141.25	1066.70	1003.85	950.19
65000	1602.14	1452.76	1333.57	1236.35	1155.59	1087.51	1029.37
70000	1725.38	1564.51	1436.16	1331.45	1244.49	1171.16	1108.55

8½% Monthly Loan Payments

LOAN AMOUNT	7½ YEARS	8 YEARS	8½ YEARS	9 YEARS	9½ YEARS	10 YEARS	10½ YEARS
100	1.51	1.44	1.38	1.33	1.28	1.24	1.20
200	3.01	2.88	2.76	2.66	2.56	2.48	2.40
300	4.52	4.32	4.14	3.98	3.84	3.72	3.61
400	6.03	5.76	5.52	5.31	5.13	4.96	4.81
500	7.53	7.20	6.90	6.64	6.41	6.20	6.01
600	9.04	8.64	8.28	7.97	7.69	7.44	7.21
700	10.55	10.07	9.66	9.30	8.97	8.68	8.42
800	12.05	11.51	11.04	10.62	10.25	9.92	9.62
900	13.56	12.95	12.42	11.95	11.53	11.16	10.82
1000	15.06	14.39	13.80	13.28	12.81	12.40	12.02
1500	22.60	21.59	20.70	19.92	19.22	18.60	18.04
2000	30.13	28.78	27.60	26.56	25.63	24.80	24.05
2500	37.66	35.98	34.50	33.20	32.04	31.00	30.06
3000	45.19	43.18	41.40	39.84	38.44	37.20	36.07
3500	52.73	50.37	48.31	46.48	44.85	43.39	42.09
4000	60.26	57.57	55.21	53.12	51.26	49.59	48.10
4500	67.79	64.76	62.11	59.76	57.67	55.79	54.11
5000	75.32	71.96	69.01	66.40	64.07	61.99	60.12
5500	82.86	79.16	75.91	73.04	70.48	68.19	66.13
6000	90.39	86.35	82.81	79.68	76.89	74.39	72.15
6500	97.92	93.55	89.71	86.32	83.29	80.59	78.16
7000	105.45	100.74	96.61	92.96	89.70	86.79	84.17
7500	112.98	107.94	103.51	99.60	96.11	92.99	90.18
8000	120.52	115.14	110.41	106.23	102.52	99.19	96.20
8500	128.05	122.33	117.31	112.87	108.92	105.39	102.21
9000	135.58	129.53	124.21	119.51	115.33	111.59	108.22
9500	143.11	136.73	131.12	126.15	121.74	117.79	114.23
10000	150.65	143.92	138.02	132.79	128.15	123.99	120.24
11000	165.71	158.31	151.82	146.07	140.96	136.38	132.27
12000	180.77	172.71	165.62	159.35	153.77	148.78	144.29
13000	195.84	187.10	179.42	172.63	166.59	161.18	156.32
14000	210.90	201.49	193.22	185.91	179.40	173.58	168.34
15000	225.97	215.88	207.02	199.19	192.22	185.98	180.37
16000	241.03	230.27	220.83	212.47	205.03	198.38	192.39
17000	256.10	244.67	234.63	225.75	217.85	210.78	204.42
18000	271.16	259.06	248.43	239.03	230.66	223.17	216.44
19000	286.23	273.45	262.23	252.31	243.48	235.57	228.46
20000	301.29	287.84	276.03	265.59	256.29	247.97	240.49
21000	316.36	302.23	289.83	278.87	269.11	260.37	252.51
22000	331.42	316.63	303.64	292.15	281.92	272.77	264.54
23000	346.48	331.02	317.44	305.43	294.73	285.17	276.56
24000	361.55	345.41	331.24	318.70	307.55	297.57	288.59
25000	376.61	359.80	345.04	331.98	320.36	309.96	300.61
26000	391.68	374.20	358.84	345.26	333.18	322.36	312.64
27000	406.74	388.59	372.64	358.54	345.99	334.76	324.66
28000	421.81	402.98	386.45	371.82	358.81	347.16	336.68
29000	436.87	417.37	400.25	385.10	371.62	359.56	348.71
30000	451.94	431.76	414.05	398.38	384.44	371.96	360.73
31000	467.00	446.16	427.85	411.66	397.25	384.36	372.76
32000	482.07	460.55	441.65	424.94	410.07	396.75	384.78
33000	497.13	474.94	455.45	438.22	422.88	409.15	396.81
34000	512.20	489.33	469.25	451.50	435.69	421.55	408.83
35000	527.26	503.72	483.06	464.78	448.51	433.95	420.85
40000	602.58	575.69	552.06	531.17	512.58	495.94	480.98
45000	677.91	647.65	621.07	597.57	576.65	557.94	541.10
50000	753.23	719.61	690.08	663.97	640.73	619.93	601.22
55000	828.55	791.57	759.09	730.36	704.80	681.92	661.34
60000	903.87	863.53	828.10	796.76	768.87	743.91	721.47
65000	979.20	935.49	897.11	863.16	832.95	805.91	781.59
70000	1054.52	1007.45	966.11	929.55	897.02	867.90	841.71

Monthly Loan Payments 8½%

LOAN AMOUNT	11 YEARS	11½ YEARS	12 YEARS	12½ YEARS	13 YEARS	14 YEARS	15 YEARS
100	1.17	1.14	1.11	1.08	1.06	1.02	0.98
200	2.34	2.28	2.22	2.17	2.12	2.04	1.97
300	3.51	3.41	3.33	3.25	3.18	3.06	2.95
400	4.67	4.55	4.44	4.34	4.24	4.08	3.94
500	5.84	5.69	5.55	5.42	5.31	5.10	4.92
600	7.01	6.83	6.66	6.51	6.37	6.12	5.91
700	8.18	7.97	7.77	7.59	7.43	7.14	6.89
800	9.35	9.10	8.88	8.68	8.49	8.16	7.88
900	10.52	10.24	9.99	9.76	9.55	9.18	8.86
1000	11.69	11.38	11.10	10.85	10.61	10.20	9.85
1500	17.53	17.07	16.65	16.27	15.92	15.30	14.77
2000	23.37	22.76	22.20	21.69	21.22	20.40	19.69
2500	29.22	28.45	27.75	27.11	26.53	25.50	24.62
3000	35.06	34.14	33.30	32.54	31.84	30.60	29.54
3500	40.90	39.83	38.85	37.96	37.14	35.70	34.47
4000	46.75	45.52	44.40	43.38	42.45	40.80	39.39
4500	52.59	51.21	49.95	48.80	47.75	45.90	44.31
5000	58.43	56.90	55.50	54.23	53.06	51.00	49.24
5500	64.28	62.59	61.05	59.65	58.36	56.10	54.16
6000	70.12	68.28	66.60	65.07	63.67	61.20	59.08
6500	75.96	73.97	72.15	70.50	68.98	66.29	64.01
7000	81.80	79.66	77.70	75.92	74.28	71.39	68.93
7500	87.65	85.35	83.25	81.34	79.59	76.49	73.86
8000	93.49	91.04	88.80	86.76	84.89	81.59	78.78
8500	99.33	96.73	94.35	92.19	90.20	86.69	83.70
9000	105.18	102.42	99.91	97.61	95.51	91.79	88.63
9500	111.02	108.11	105.46	103.03	100.81	96.89	93.55
10000	116.86	113.80	111.01	108.46	106.12	101.99	98.47
11000	128.55	125.18	122.11	119.30	116.73	112.19	108.32
12000	140.24	136.56	133.21	130.15	127.34	122.39	118.17
13000	151.92	147.94	144.31	140.99	137.95	132.59	128.02
14000	163.61	159.32	155.41	151.84	148.57	142.79	137.86
15000	175.30	170.70	166.51	162.68	159.18	152.99	147.71
16000	186.98	182.08	177.61	173.53	169.79	163.19	157.56
17000	198.67	193.46	188.71	184.37	180.40	173.39	167.41
18000	210.36	204.84	199.81	195.22	191.01	183.59	177.25
19000	222.04	216.22	210.91	206.06	201.62	193.78	187.10
20000	233.73	227.59	222.01	216.91	212.24	203.98	196.95
21000	245.41	238.97	233.11	227.76	222.85	214.18	206.80
22000	257.10	250.35	244.21	238.60	233.46	224.38	216.64
23000	268.79	261.73	255.31	249.45	244.07	234.58	226.49
24000	280.47	273.11	266.41	260.29	254.68	244.78	236.34
25000	292.16	284.49	277.51	271.14	265.29	254.98	246.18
26000	303.85	295.87	288.61	281.98	275.91	265.18	256.03
27000	315.53	307.25	299.72	292.83	286.52	275.38	265.88
28000	327.22	318.63	310.82	303.67	297.13	285.58	275.73
29000	338.91	330.01	321.92	314.52	307.74	295.78	285.57
30000	350.59	341.39	333.02	325.37	318.35	305.98	295.42
31000	362.28	352.77	344.12	336.21	328.97	316.17	305.27
32000	373.96	364.15	355.22	347.06	339.58	326.37	315.12
33000	385.65	375.53	366.32	357.90	350.19	336.57	324.96
34000	397.34	386.91	377.42	368.75	360.80	346.77	334.81
35000	409.02	398.29	388.52	379.59	371.41	356.97	344.66
40000	467.46	455.19	444.02	433.82	424.47	407.97	393.90
45000	525.89	512.09	499.53	488.05	477.53	458.96	443.13
50000	584.32	568.99	555.03	542.28	530.59	509.96	492.37
55000	642.75	625.89	610.53	596.50	583.65	560.96	541.61
60000	701.18	682.78	666.03	650.73	636.71	611.95	590.84
65000	759.62	739.68	721.54	704.96	689.77	662.95	640.08
70000	818.05	796.58	777.04	759.19	742.83	713.94	689.32

8¾%   Monthly Loan Payments

LOAN AMOUNT	½ YEAR	1 YEAR	1½ YEARS	2 YEARS	2½ YEARS	3 YEARS	3½ YEARS
100	17.09	8.73	5.95	4.56	3.72	3.17	2.77
200	34.19	17.47	11.90	9.11	7.45	6.34	5.55
300	51.28	26.20	17.84	13.67	11.17	9.51	8.32
400	68.38	34.93	23.79	18.23	14.89	12.67	11.09
500	85.47	43.67	29.74	22.79	18.62	15.84	13.86
600	102.57	52.40	35.69	27.34	22.34	19.01	16.64
700	119.66	61.13	41.64	31.90	26.06	22.18	19.41
800	136.76	69.87	47.59	36.46	29.79	25.35	22.18
900	153.85	78.60	53.53	41.01	33.51	28.52	24.95
1000	170.95	87.34	59.48	45.57	37.23	31.68	27.73
1500	256.42	131.00	89.22	68.36	55.85	47.53	41.59
2000	341.89	174.67	118.97	91.14	74.47	63.37	55.45
2500	427.36	218.34	148.71	113.93	93.08	79.21	69.32
3000	512.84	262.01	178.45	136.71	111.70	95.05	83.18
3500	598.31	305.67	208.19	159.50	130.32	110.89	97.05
4000	683.78	349.34	237.93	182.28	148.93	126.73	110.91
4500	769.26	393.01	267.67	205.07	167.55	142.58	124.77
5000	854.73	436.68	297.42	227.85	186.16	158.42	138.64
5500	940.20	480.35	327.16	250.64	204.78	174.26	152.50
6000	1025.68	524.01	356.90	273.42	223.40	190.10	166.36
6500	1111.15	567.68	386.64	296.21	242.01	205.94	180.23
7000	1196.62	611.35	416.38	318.99	260.63	221.78	194.09
7500	1282.09	655.02	446.12	341.78	279.25	237.63	207.95
8000	1367.57	698.68	475.87	364.56	297.86	253.47	221.82
8500	1453.04	742.35	505.61	387.35	316.48	269.31	235.68
9000	1538.51	786.02	535.35	410.13	335.10	285.15	249.54
9500	1623.99	829.69	565.09	432.92	353.71	300.99	263.41
10000	1709.46	873.36	594.83	455.70	372.33	316.84	277.27
11000	1880.40	960.69	654.31	501.27	409.56	348.52	305.00
12000	2051.35	1048.03	713.80	546.84	446.79	380.20	332.73
13000	2222.30	1135.36	773.28	592.41	484.03	411.89	360.45
14000	2393.24	1222.70	832.76	637.98	521.26	443.57	388.18
15000	2564.19	1310.03	892.25	683.55	558.49	475.25	415.91
16000	2735.13	1397.37	951.73	729.12	595.73	506.94	443.63
17000	2906.08	1484.70	1011.21	774.69	632.96	538.62	471.36
18000	3077.03	1572.04	1070.70	820.26	670.19	570.30	499.09
19000	3247.97	1659.38	1130.18	865.83	707.42	601.99	526.82
20000	3418.92	1746.71	1189.66	911.40	744.66	633.67	554.54
21000	3589.86	1834.05	1249.15	956.97	781.89	665.35	582.27
22000	3760.81	1921.38	1308.63	1002.54	819.12	697.04	610.00
23000	3931.76	2008.72	1368.11	1048.11	856.36	728.72	637.73
24000	4102.70	2096.05	1427.60	1093.68	893.59	760.40	665.45
25000	4273.65	2183.39	1487.08	1139.25	930.82	792.09	693.18
26000	4444.59	2270.73	1546.56	1184.82	968.05	823.77	720.91
27000	4615.54	2358.06	1606.04	1230.39	1005.29	855.45	748.63
28000	4786.48	2445.40	1665.53	1275.96	1042.52	887.14	776.36
29000	4957.43	2532.73	1725.01	1321.53	1079.75	918.82	804.09
30000	5128.38	2620.07	1784.49	1367.10	1116.99	950.51	831.82
31000	5299.32	2707.40	1843.98	1412.67	1154.22	982.19	859.54
32000	5470.27	2794.74	1903.46	1458.24	1191.45	1013.87	887.27
33000	5641.21	2882.07	1962.94	1503.81	1228.69	1045.56	915.00
34000	5812.16	2969.41	2022.43	1549.38	1265.92	1077.24	942.72
35000	5983.11	3056.75	2081.91	1594.95	1303.15	1108.92	970.45
40000	6837.84	3493.42	2379.33	1822.80	1489.32	1267.34	1109.09
45000	7692.57	3930.10	2676.74	2050.66	1675.48	1425.76	1247.72
50000	8547.29	4366.78	2974.16	2278.51	1861.64	1584.18	1386.36
55000	9402.02	4803.46	3271.57	2506.36	2047.81	1742.59	1525.00
60000	10256.75	5240.14	3568.99	2734.21	2233.97	1901.01	1663.63
65000	11111.48	5676.81	3866.40	2962.06	2420.14	2059.43	1802.27
70000	11966.21	6113.49	4163.82	3189.91	2606.30	2217.85	1940.90

16

Monthly Loan Payments 8¾%

LOAN AMOUNT	4 YEARS	4½ YEARS	5 YEARS	5½ YEARS	6 YEARS	6½ YEARS	7 YEARS
100	2.48	2.25	2.06	1.91	1.79	1.69	1.60
200	4.95	4.49	4.13	3.83	3.58	3.37	3.19
300	7.43	6.74	6.19	5.74	5.37	5.06	4.79
400	9.91	8.99	8.25	7.66	7.16	6.74	6.38
500	12.38	11.23	10.32	9.57	8.95	8.43	7.98
600	14.86	13.48	12.38	11.49	10.74	10.11	9.58
700	17.34	15.73	14.45	13.40	12.53	11.80	11.17
800	19.81	17.98	16.51	15.31	14.32	13.48	12.77
900	22.29	20.22	18.57	17.23	16.11	15.17	14.37
1000	24.77	22.47	20.64	19.14	17.90	16.86	15.96
1500	37.15	33.70	30.96	28.71	26.85	25.28	23.94
2000	49.53	44.94	41.27	38.29	35.80	33.71	31.92
2500	61.92	56.17	51.59	47.86	44.75	42.14	39.91
3000	74.30	67.41	61.91	57.43	53.71	50.57	47.89
3500	86.68	78.64	72.23	67.00	62.66	58.99	55.87
4000	99.07	89.88	82.55	76.57	71.61	67.42	63.85
4500	111.45	101.11	92.87	86.14	80.56	75.85	71.83
5000	123.83	112.35	103.19	95.71	89.51	84.28	79.81
5500	136.22	123.58	113.50	105.29	98.46	92.71	87.79
6000	148.60	134.82	123.82	114.86	107.41	101.13	95.77
6500	160.98	146.05	134.14	124.43	116.36	109.56	103.76
7000	173.37	157.29	144.46	134.00	125.31	117.99	111.74
7500	185.75	168.52	154.78	143.57	134.26	126.42	119.72
8000	198.13	179.76	165.10	153.14	143.21	134.84	127.70
8500	210.52	190.99	175.42	162.71	152.16	143.27	135.68
9000	222.90	202.23	185.74	172.28	161.12	151.70	143.66
9500	235.28	213.46	196.05	181.86	170.07	160.13	151.64
10000	247.67	224.70	206.37	191.43	179.02	168.56	159.62
11000	272.43	247.17	227.01	210.57	196.92	185.41	175.59
12000	297.20	269.63	247.65	229.71	214.82	202.27	191.55
13000	321.96	292.10	268.28	248.86	232.72	219.12	207.51
14000	346.73	314.57	288.92	268.00	250.62	235.98	223.47
15000	371.50	337.04	309.56	287.14	268.53	252.83	239.44
16000	396.26	359.51	330.20	306.28	286.43	269.69	255.40
17000	421.03	381.98	350.83	325.43	304.33	286.54	271.36
18000	445.80	404.45	371.47	344.57	322.23	303.40	287.32
19000	470.56	426.92	392.11	363.71	340.13	320.26	303.29
20000	495.33	449.39	412.74	382.86	358.03	337.11	319.25
21000	520.10	471.86	433.38	402.00	375.94	353.97	335.21
22000	544.86	494.33	454.02	421.14	393.84	370.82	351.17
23000	569.63	516.80	474.66	440.28	411.74	387.68	367.14
24000	594.40	539.27	495.29	459.43	429.64	404.53	383.10
25000	619.16	561.74	515.93	478.57	447.54	421.39	399.06
26000	643.93	584.21	536.57	497.71	465.44	438.24	415.02
27000	668.70	606.68	557.21	516.85	483.35	455.10	430.99
28000	693.46	629.15	577.84	536.00	501.25	471.96	446.95
29000	718.23	651.62	598.48	555.14	519.15	488.81	462.91
30000	743.00	674.09	619.12	574.28	537.05	505.67	478.87
31000	767.76	696.56	639.75	593.43	554.95	522.52	494.84
32000	792.53	719.03	660.39	612.57	572.85	539.38	510.80
33000	817.29	741.50	681.03	631.71	590.76	556.23	526.76
34000	842.06	763.97	701.67	650.85	608.66	573.09	542.72
35000	866.83	786.43	722.30	670.00	626.56	589.94	558.69
40000	990.66	898.78	825.49	765.71	716.07	674.22	638.50
45000	1114.49	1011.13	928.68	861.42	805.58	758.50	718.31
50000	1238.33	1123.48	1031.86	957.14	895.09	842.78	798.12
55000	1362.16	1235.83	1135.05	1052.85	984.59	927.05	877.94
60000	1485.99	1348.17	1238.23	1148.57	1074.10	1011.33	957.75
65000	1609.82	1460.52	1341.42	1244.28	1163.61	1095.61	1037.56
70000	1733.66	1572.87	1444.61	1339.99	1253.12	1179.89	1117.37

8¾% Monthly Loan Payments

LOAN AMOUNT	7½ YEARS	8 YEARS	8½ YEARS	9 YEARS	9½ YEARS	10 YEARS	10½ YEARS
100	1.52	1.45	1.39	1.34	1.29	1.25	1.22
200	3.04	2.90	2.79	2.68	2.59	2.51	2.43
300	4.56	4.36	4.18	4.02	3.88	3.76	3.65
400	6.08	5.81	5.57	5.36	5.18	5.01	4.86
500	7.60	7.26	6.97	6.71	6.47	6.27	6.08
600	9.12	8.71	8.36	8.05	7.77	7.52	7.30
700	10.63	10.16	9.75	9.39	9.06	8.77	8.51
800	12.15	11.62	11.15	10.73	10.36	10.03	9.73
900	13.67	13.07	12.54	12.07	11.65	11.28	10.94
1000	15.19	14.52	13.93	13.41	12.95	12.53	12.16
1500	22.79	21.78	20.90	20.12	19.42	18.80	18.24
2000	30.38	29.04	27.86	26.82	25.89	25.07	24.32
2500	37.98	36.30	34.83	33.53	32.37	31.33	30.40
3000	45.58	43.56	41.80	40.23	38.84	37.60	36.48
3500	53.17	50.82	48.76	46.94	45.32	43.86	42.56
4000	60.77	58.08	55.73	53.64	51.79	50.13	48.64
4500	68.36	65.34	62.69	60.35	58.26	56.40	54.72
5000	75.96	72.60	69.66	67.05	64.74	62.66	60.80
5500	83.56	79.86	76.62	73.76	71.21	68.93	66.88
6000	91.15	87.13	83.59	80.46	77.68	75.20	72.96
6500	98.75	94.39	90.56	87.17	84.16	81.46	79.04
7000	106.34	101.65	97.52	93.88	90.63	87.73	85.12
7500	113.94	108.91	104.49	100.58	97.10	94.00	91.20
8000	121.54	116.17	111.45	107.29	103.58	100.26	97.28
8500	129.13	123.43	118.42	113.99	110.05	106.53	103.36
9000	136.73	130.69	125.39	120.70	116.53	112.79	109.44
9500	144.32	137.95	132.35	127.40	123.00	119.06	115.52
10000	151.92	145.21	139.32	134.11	129.47	125.33	121.60
11000	167.11	159.73	153.25	147.52	142.42	137.86	133.76
12000	182.30	174.25	167.18	160.93	155.37	150.39	145.92
13000	197.49	188.77	181.11	174.34	168.32	162.92	158.08
14000	212.69	203.29	195.04	187.75	181.26	175.46	170.24
15000	227.88	217.81	208.98	201.16	194.21	187.99	182.40
16000	243.07	232.33	222.91	214.57	207.16	200.52	194.56
17000	258.26	246.85	236.84	227.98	220.10	213.06	206.72
18000	273.45	261.38	250.77	241.39	233.05	225.59	218.88
19000	288.65	275.90	264.70	254.80	246.00	238.12	231.04
20000	303.84	290.42	278.63	268.22	258.95	250.65	243.20
21000	319.03	304.94	292.57	281.63	271.89	263.19	255.36
22000	334.22	319.46	306.50	295.04	284.84	275.72	267.52
23000	349.41	333.98	320.43	308.45	297.79	288.25	279.68
24000	364.61	348.50	334.36	321.86	310.74	300.78	291.84
25000	379.80	363.02	348.29	335.27	323.68	313.32	304.00
26000	394.99	377.54	362.22	348.68	336.63	325.85	316.16
27000	410.18	392.06	376.16	362.09	349.58	338.38	328.32
28000	425.37	406.58	390.09	375.50	362.52	350.91	340.48
29000	440.57	421.10	404.02	388.91	375.47	363.45	352.64
30000	455.76	435.63	417.95	402.32	388.42	375.98	364.80
31000	470.95	450.15	431.88	415.73	401.37	388.51	376.96
32000	486.14	464.67	445.81	429.14	414.31	401.05	389.12
33000	501.33	479.19	459.75	442.56	427.26	413.58	401.28
34000	516.53	493.71	473.68	455.97	440.21	426.11	413.44
35000	531.72	508.23	487.61	469.38	453.16	438.64	425.60
40000	607.68	580.83	557.27	536.43	517.89	501.31	486.39
45000	683.64	653.44	626.93	603.48	582.63	563.97	547.19
50000	759.60	726.04	696.58	670.54	647.37	626.63	607.99
55000	835.56	798.65	766.24	737.59	712.10	689.30	668.79
60000	911.52	871.25	835.90	804.65	776.84	751.96	729.59
65000	987.47	943.85	905.56	871.70	841.58	814.62	790.39
70000	1063.43	1016.46	975.22	938.75	906.31	877.29	851.19

Monthly Loan Payments 8¾%

LOAN AMOUNT	11 YEARS	11½ YEARS	12 YEARS	12½ YEARS	13 YEARS	14 YEARS	15 YEARS
100	1.18	1.15	1.12	1.10	1.08	1.03	1.00
200	2.36	2.30	2.25	2.20	2.15	2.07	2.00
300	3.55	3.46	3.37	3.30	3.23	3.10	3.00
400	4.73	4.61	4.50	4.39	4.30	4.14	4.00
500	5.91	5.76	5.62	5.49	5.38	5.17	5.00
600	7.09	6.91	6.74	6.59	6.45	6.21	6.00
700	8.28	8.06	7.87	7.69	7.53	7.24	7.00
800	9.46	9.21	8.99	8.79	8.60	8.28	8.00
900	10.64	10.37	10.12	9.89	9.68	9.31	9.00
1000	11.82	11.52	11.24	10.99	10.75	10.34	9.99
1500	17.73	17.28	16.86	16.48	16.13	15.52	14.99
2000	23.65	23.04	22.48	21.97	21.51	20.69	19.99
2500	29.56	28.79	28.10	27.47	26.88	25.86	24.99
3000	35.47	34.55	33.72	32.96	32.26	31.03	29.98
3500	41.38	40.31	39.34	38.45	37.64	36.20	34.98
4000	47.29	46.07	44.96	43.94	43.02	41.38	39.98
4500	53.20	51.83	50.58	49.44	48.39	46.55	44.98
5000	59.12	57.59	56.20	54.93	53.77	51.72	49.97
5500	65.03	63.35	61.82	60.42	59.15	56.89	54.97
6000	70.94	69.11	67.44	65.92	64.52	62.06	59.97
6500	76.85	74.87	73.06	71.41	69.90	67.23	64.96
7000	82.76	80.62	78.68	76.90	75.28	72.41	69.96
7500	88.67	86.38	84.30	82.40	80.65	77.58	74.96
8000	94.59	92.14	89.92	87.89	86.03	82.75	79.96
8500	100.50	97.90	95.54	93.38	91.41	87.92	84.95
9000	106.41	103.66	101.16	98.88	96.78	93.09	89.95
9500	112.32	109.42	106.78	104.37	102.16	98.27	94.95
10000	118.23	115.18	112.40	109.86	107.54	103.44	99.94
11000	130.05	126.70	123.64	120.85	118.29	113.78	109.94
12000	141.88	138.21	134.88	131.83	129.05	124.13	119.93
13000	153.70	149.73	146.12	142.82	139.80	134.47	129.93
14000	165.52	161.25	157.36	153.81	150.55	144.81	139.92
15000	177.35	172.77	168.60	164.79	161.31	155.16	149.92
16000	189.17	184.29	179.84	175.78	172.06	165.50	159.91
17000	200.99	195.80	191.08	186.77	182.81	175.84	169.91
18000	212.82	207.32	202.32	197.75	193.57	186.19	179.90
19000	224.64	218.84	213.56	208.74	204.32	196.53	189.90
20000	236.46	230.36	224.80	219.72	215.08	206.88	199.89
21000	248.29	241.87	236.04	230.71	225.83	217.22	209.88
22000	260.11	253.39	247.28	241.70	236.58	227.56	219.88
23000	271.93	264.43	258.52	252.68	247.34	237.91	229.87
24000	283.76	276.43	269.76	263.67	258.09	248.25	239.87
25000	295.58	287.95	281.00	274.66	268.85	258.59	249.86
26000	307.40	299.46	292.24	285.64	279.60	268.94	259.86
27000	319.23	310.98	303.48	296.63	290.35	279.28	269.85
28000	331.05	322.50	314.72	307.61	301.11	289.63	279.85
29000	342.87	334.02	325.96	318.60	311.86	299.97	289.84
30000	354.70	345.54	337.20	329.59	322.61	310.31	299.83
31000	366.52	357.05	348.44	340.57	333.37	320.66	309.83
32000	378.34	368.57	359.68	351.56	344.12	331.00	319.82
33000	390.16	380.09	370.92	362.55	354.88	341.34	329.82
34000	401.99	391.61	382.16	373.53	365.63	351.69	339.81
35000	413.81	403.12	393.40	384.52	376.38	362.03	349.81
40000	472.93	460.71	449.60	439.45	430.15	413.75	399.78
45000	532.04	518.30	505.80	494.38	483.92	465.47	449.75
50000	591.16	575.89	562.00	549.31	537.69	517.19	499.72
55000	650.27	633.48	618.20	604.24	591.46	568.91	549.70
60000	709.39	691.07	674.40	659.17	645.23	620.63	599.67
65000	768.51	748.66	730.60	714.10	699.00	672.34	649.64
70000	827.62	806.25	786.80	769.04	752.77	724.06	699.61

19

9% Monthly Loan Payments

LOAN AMOUNT	½ YEAR	1 YEAR	1½ YEARS	2 YEARS	2½ YEARS	3 YEARS	3½ YEARS
100	17.11	8.75	5.96	4.57	3.73	3.18	2.78
200	34.21	17.49	11.92	9.14	7.47	6.36	5.57
300	51.32	26.24	17.88	13.71	11.20	9.54	8.35
400	68.43	34.98	23.84	18.27	14.94	12.72	11.14
500	85.53	43.73	29.80	22.84	18.67	15.90	13.92
600	102.64	52.47	35.76	27.41	22.41	19.08	16.71
700	119.75	61.22	41.72	31.98	26.14	22.26	19.49
800	136.86	69.96	47.68	36.55	29.88	25.44	22.28
900	153.96	78.71	53.64	41.12	33.61	28.62	25.06
1000	171.07	87.45	59.60	45.68	37.35	31.80	27.84
1500	256.60	131.18	89.40	68.53	56.02	47.70	41.77
2000	342.14	174.90	119.20	91.37	74.70	63.60	55.69
2500	427.67	218.63	148.99	114.21	93.37	79.50	69.61
3000	513.21	262.35	178.79	137.05	112.04	95.40	83.53
3500	598.74	306.08	208.59	159.90	130.72	111.30	97.46
4000	684.28	349.81	238.39	182.74	149.39	127.20	111.38
4500	769.81	393.53	268.19	205.58	168.07	143.10	125.30
5000	855.34	437.26	297.99	228.42	186.74	159.00	139.22
5500	940.88	480.98	327.79	251.27	205.41	174.90	153.14
6000	1026.41	524.71	357.59	274.11	224.09	190.80	167.07
6500	1111.95	568.43	387.38	296.95	242.76	206.70	180.99
7000	1197.48	612.16	417.18	319.79	261.44	222.60	194.91
7500	1283.02	655.89	446.98	342.64	280.11	238.50	208.83
8000	1368.55	699.61	476.78	365.48	298.79	254.40	222.76
8500	1454.09	743.34	506.58	388.32	317.46	270.30	236.68
9000	1539.62	787.06	536.38	411.16	336.13	286.20	250.60
9500	1625.15	830.79	566.18	434.01	354.81	302.10	264.52
10000	1710.69	874.51	595.98	456.85	373.48	318.00	278.45
11000	1881.76	961.97	655.57	502.53	410.83	349.80	306.29
12000	2052.83	1049.42	715.17	548.22	448.18	381.60	334.13
13000	2223.90	1136.87	774.77	593.90	485.53	413.40	361.98
14000	2394.96	1224.32	834.37	639.59	522.87	445.20	389.82
15000	2566.03	1311.77	893.96	685.27	560.22	477.00	417.67
16000	2737.10	1399.22	953.56	730.96	597.57	508.80	445.51
17000	2908.17	1486.68	1013.16	776.64	634.92	540.60	473.36
18000	3079.24	1574.13	1072.76	822.33	672.27	572.40	501.20
19000	3250.31	1661.58	1132.36	868.01	709.62	604.19	529.05
20000	3421.38	1749.03	1191.95	913.69	746.96	635.99	556.89
21000	3592.45	1836.48	1251.55	959.38	784.31	667.79	584.73
22000	3763.52	1923.93	1311.15	1005.06	821.66	699.59	612.58
23000	3934.58	2011.38	1370.75	1050.75	859.01	731.39	640.42
24000	4105.65	2098.84	1430.34	1096.43	896.36	763.19	668.27
25000	4276.72	2186.29	1489.94	1142.12	933.70	794.99	696.11
26000	4447.79	2273.74	1549.54	1187.80	971.05	826.79	723.96
27000	4618.86	2361.19	1609.14	1233.49	1008.40	858.59	751.80
28000	4789.93	2448.64	1668.73	1279.17	1045.75	890.39	779.65
29000	4961.00	2536.09	1728.33	1324.86	1083.10	922.19	807.49
30000	5132.07	2623.54	1787.93	1370.54	1120.44	953.99	835.34
31000	5303.14	2711.00	1847.53	1416.23	1157.79	985.79	863.18
32000	5474.21	2798.45	1907.13	1461.91	1195.14	1017.59	891.02
33000	5645.27	2885.90	1966.72	1507.60	1232.49	1049.39	918.87
34000	5816.34	2973.35	2026.32	1553.28	1269.84	1081.19	946.71
35000	5987.41	3060.80	2085.92	1598.97	1307.19	1112.99	974.56
40000	6842.76	3498.06	2383.91	1827.39	1493.93	1271.99	1113.78
45000	7698.10	3935.32	2681.89	2055.81	1680.67	1430.99	1253.00
50000	8553.45	4372.57	2979.88	2284.24	1867.41	1589.99	1392.23
55000	9408.79	4809.83	3277.87	2512.66	2054.15	1748.99	1531.45
60000	10264.13	5247.09	3575.86	2741.08	2240.89	1907.98	1670.67
65000	11119.48	5684.35	3873.85	2969.51	2427.63	2066.98	1809.89
70000	11974.82	6121.60	4171.84	3197.93	2614.37	2225.98	1949.12

Monthly Loan Payments 9%

LOAN AMOUNT	4 YEARS	4½ YEARS	5 YEARS	5½ YEARS	6 YEARS	6½ YEARS	7 YEARS
100	2.49	2.26	2.08	1.93	1.80	1.70	1.61
200	4.98	4.52	4.15	3.85	3.61	3.40	3.22
300	7.47	6.78	6.23	5.78	5.41	5.09	4.83
400	9.95	9.04	8.30	7.71	7.21	6.79	6.44
500	12.44	11.29	10.38	9.63	9.01	8.49	8.04
600	14.93	13.55	12.46	11.56	10.82	10.19	9.65
700	17.42	15.81	14.53	13.49	12.62	11.89	11.26
800	19.91	18.07	16.61	15.41	14.42	13.58	12.87
900	22.40	20.33	18.68	17.34	16.22	15.28	14.48
1000	24.89	22.59	20.76	19.27	18.03	16.98	16.09
1500	37.33	33.88	31.14	28.90	27.04	25.47	24.13
2000	49.77	45.18	41.52	38.53	36.05	33.96	32.18
2500	62.21	56.47	51.90	48.16	45.06	42.45	40.22
3000	74.66	67.77	62.28	57.80	54.08	50.94	48.27
3500	87.10	79.06	72.65	67.43	63.09	59.43	56.31
4000	99.54	90.36	83.03	77.06	72.10	67.92	64.36
4500	111.98	101.65	93.41	86.69	81.11	76.41	72.40
5000	124.43	112.95	103.79	96.33	90.13	84.90	80.45
5500	136.87	124.24	114.17	105.96	99.14	93.39	88.49
6000	149.31	135.54	124.55	115.59	108.15	101.88	96.53
6500	161.75	146.83	134.93	125.22	117.17	110.37	104.58
7000	174.20	158.13	145.31	134.86	126.18	118.87	112.62
7500	186.64	169.42	155.69	144.49	135.19	127.36	120.67
8000	199.08	180.72	166.07	154.12	144.20	135.85	128.71
8500	211.52	192.01	176.45	163.75	153.22	144.34	136.76
9000	223.97	203.30	186.83	173.39	162.23	152.83	144.80
9500	236.41	214.60	197.20	183.02	171.24	161.32	152.85
10000	248.85	225.89	207.58	192.65	180.26	169.81	160.89
11000	273.74	248.48	228.34	211.92	198.28	186.79	176.98
12000	298.62	271.07	249.10	231.18	216.31	203.77	193.07
13000	323.51	293.66	269.86	250.45	234.33	220.75	209.16
14000	348.39	316.25	290.62	269.71	252.36	237.73	225.25
15000	373.28	338.84	311.38	288.98	270.38	254.71	241.34
16000	398.16	361.43	332.13	308.24	288.41	271.69	257.43
17000	423.05	384.02	352.89	327.51	306.43	288.67	273.51
18000	447.93	406.61	373.65	346.77	324.46	305.65	289.60
19000	472.82	429.20	394.41	366.04	342.49	322.63	305.69
20000	497.70	451.79	415.17	385.30	360.51	339.61	321.78
21000	522.59	474.38	435.93	404.57	378.54	356.60	337.87
22000	547.47	496.97	456.68	423.84	396.56	373.58	353.96
23000	572.36	519.56	477.44	443.10	414.59	390.56	370.05
24000	597.24	542.15	498.20	462.37	432.61	407.54	386.14
25000	622.13	564.73	518.96	481.63	450.64	424.52	402.23
26000	647.01	587.32	539.72	500.90	468.66	441.50	418.32
27000	671.90	609.91	560.48	520.16	486.69	458.48	434.41
28000	696.78	632.50	581.23	539.43	504.72	475.46	450.49
29000	721.67	655.09	601.99	558.69	522.74	492.44	466.58
30000	746.55	677.68	622.75	577.96	540.77	509.42	482.67
31000	771.44	700.27	643.51	597.22	558.79	526.40	498.76
32000	796.32	722.86	664.27	616.49	576.82	543.38	514.85
33000	821.21	745.45	685.03	635.75	594.84	560.36	530.94
34000	846.09	768.04	705.78	655.02	612.87	577.35	547.03
35000	870.98	790.63	726.54	674.28	630.89	594.33	563.12
40000	995.40	903.58	830.33	770.61	721.02	679.23	643.56
45000	1119.83	1016.52	934.13	866.94	811.15	764.13	724.01
50000	1244.25	1129.47	1037.92	963.26	901.28	849.04	804.45
55000	1368.68	1242.42	1141.71	1059.59	991.40	933.94	884.90
60000	1493.10	1355.36	1245.50	1155.91	1081.53	1018.84	965.34
65000	1617.53	1468.31	1349.29	1252.24	1171.66	1103.75	1045.79
70000	1741.95	1581.26	1453.08	1348.57	1261.79	1188.65	1126.24

9%   Monthly Loan Payments

LOAN AMOUNT	7½ YEARS	8 YEARS	8½ YEARS	9 YEARS	9½ YEARS	10 YEARS	10½ YEARS
100	1.53	1.47	1.41	1.35	1.31	1.27	1.23
200	3.06	2.93	2.81	2.71	2.62	2.53	2.46
300	4.60	4.40	4.22	4.06	3.92	3.80	3.69
400	6.13	5.86	5.62	5.42	5.23	5.07	4.92
500	7.66	7.33	7.03	6.77	6.54	6.33	6.15
600	9.19	8.79	8.44	8.13	7.85	7.60	7.38
700	10.72	10.26	9.84	9.48	9.16	8.87	8.61
800	12.26	11.72	11.25	10.83	10.46	10.13	9.84
900	13.79	13.19	12.66	12.19	11.77	11.40	11.07
1000	15.32	14.65	14.06	13.54	13.08	12.67	12.30
1500	22.98	21.98	21.09	20.31	19.62	19.00	18.44
2000	30.64	29.30	28.12	27.09	26.16	25.34	24.59
2500	38.30	36.63	35.16	33.86	32.70	31.67	30.74
3000	45.96	43.95	42.19	40.63	39.24	38.00	36.89
3500	53.62	51.28	49.22	47.40	45.78	44.34	43.04
4000	61.28	58.60	56.25	54.17	52.32	50.67	49.18
4500	68.94	65.93	63.28	60.94	58.86	57.00	55.33
5000	76.60	73.25	70.31	67.71	65.40	63.34	61.48
5500	84.26	80.58	77.34	74.49	71.94	69.67	67.63
6000	91.92	87.90	84.37	81.26	78.49	76.01	73.78
6500	99.58	95.23	91.41	88.03	85.03	82.34	79.92
7000	107.24	102.55	98.44	94.80	91.57	88.67	86.07
7500	114.90	109.88	105.47	101.57	98.11	95.01	92.22
8000	122.56	117.20	112.50	108.34	104.65	101.34	98.37
8500	130.22	124.53	119.53	115.11	111.19	107.67	104.52
9000	137.88	131.85	126.56	121.89	117.73	114.01	110.67
9500	145.54	139.18	133.59	128.66	124.27	120.34	116.81
10000	153.20	146.50	140.62	135.43	130.81	126.68	122.96
11000	168.52	161.15	154.69	148.97	143.89	139.34	135.26
12000	183.84	175.80	168.75	162.51	156.97	152.01	147.55
13000	199.16	190.45	182.81	176.06	170.05	164.68	159.85
14000	214.48	205.10	196.87	189.60	183.13	177.35	172.15
15000	229.80	219.75	210.94	203.14	196.21	190.01	184.44
16000	245.12	234.40	225.00	216.69	209.29	202.68	196.74
17000	260.44	249.05	239.06	230.23	222.37	215.35	209.03
18000	275.76	263.70	253.12	243.77	235.46	228.02	221.33
19000	291.08	278.35	267.19	257.32	248.54	240.68	233.63
20000	306.40	293.00	281.25	270.86	261.62	253.35	245.92
21000	321.72	307.65	295.31	284.40	274.70	266.02	258.22
22000	337.04	322.30	309.37	297.94	287.78	278.69	270.52
23000	352.36	336.95	323.44	311.49	300.86	291.35	282.81
24000	367.68	351.60	337.50	325.03	313.94	304.02	295.11
25000	383.00	366.26	351.56	338.57	327.02	316.69	307.40
26000	398.32	380.91	365.62	352.12	340.10	329.36	319.70
27000	413.64	395.56	379.69	365.66	353.18	342.02	332.00
28000	428.96	410.21	393.75	379.20	366.26	354.69	344.29
29000	444.28	424.86	407.81	392.74	379.34	367.36	356.59
30000	459.60	439.51	421.87	406.29	392.43	380.03	368.88
31000	474.92	454.16	435.94	419.83	405.51	392.69	381.18
32000	490.24	468.81	450.00	433.37	418.59	405.36	393.48
33000	505.56	483.46	464.06	446.92	431.67	418.03	405.77
34000	520.88	498.11	478.12	460.46	444.75	430.70	418.07
35000	536.20	512.76	492.19	474.00	457.83	443.37	430.36
40000	612.80	586.01	562.50	541.72	523.23	506.70	491.85
45000	689.40	659.26	632.81	609.43	588.64	570.04	553.33
50000	765.99	732.51	703.12	677.15	654.04	633.38	614.81
55000	842.59	805.76	773.43	744.86	719.45	696.72	676.29
60000	919.19	879.01	843.75	812.57	784.85	760.05	737.77
65000	995.79	952.26	914.06	880.29	850.25	823.39	799.25
70000	1072.39	1025.51	984.37	948.00	915.66	886.73	860.73

Monthly Loan Payments 9%

LOAN AMOUNT	11 YEARS	11½ YEARS	12 YEARS	12½ YEARS	13 YEARS	14 YEARS	15 YEARS
100	1.20	1.17	1.14	1.11	1.09	1.05	1.01
200	2.39	2.33	2.28	2.23	2.18	2.10	2.03
300	3.59	3.50	3.41	3.34	3.27	3.15	3.04
400	4.78	4.66	4.55	4.45	4.36	4.20	4.06
500	5.98	5.83	5.69	5.56	5.45	5.24	5.07
600	7.18	6.99	6.83	6.68	6.54	6.29	6.09
700	8.37	8.16	7.97	7.79	7.63	7.34	7.10
800	9.57	9.33	9.10	8.90	8.72	8.39	8.11
900	10.76	10.49	10.24	10.02	9.81	9.44	9.13
1000	11.96	11.66	11.38	11.13	10.90	10.49	10.14
1500	17.94	17.49	17.07	16.69	16.35	15.73	15.21
2000	23.92	23.31	22.76	22.26	21.79	20.98	20.29
2500	29.90	29.14	28.45	27.82	27.24	26.22	25.36
3000	35.88	34.97	34.14	33.38	32.69	31.47	30.43
3500	41.86	40.80	39.83	38.95	38.14	36.71	35.50
4000	47.84	46.63	45.52	44.51	43.59	41.96	40.57
4500	53.82	52.46	51.21	50.08	49.04	47.20	45.64
5000	59.80	58.28	56.90	55.64	54.48	52.45	50.71
5500	65.78	64.11	62.59	61.20	59.93	57.69	55.78
6000	71.76	69.94	68.28	66.77	65.38	62.94	60.86
6500	77.75	75.77	73.97	72.33	70.83	68.18	65.93
7000	83.73	81.60	79.66	77.90	76.28	73.43	71.00
7500	89.71	87.43	85.35	83.46	81.73	78.67	76.07
8000	95.69	93.25	91.04	89.02	87.17	83.92	81.14
8500	101.67	99.08	96.73	94.59	92.62	89.16	86.21
9000	107.65	104.91	102.42	100.15	98.07	94.40	91.28
9500	113.63	110.74	108.11	105.72	103.52	99.65	96.36
10000	119.61	116.57	113.80	111.28	108.97	104.89	101.43
11000	131.57	128.23	125.18	122.41	119.86	115.38	111.57
12000	143.53	139.88	136.56	133.53	130.76	125.87	121.71
13000	155.49	151.54	147.94	144.66	141.66	136.36	131.85
14000	167.45	163.20	159.32	155.79	152.56	146.85	142.00
15000	179.41	174.85	170.70	166.92	163.45	157.34	152.14
16000	191.37	186.51	182.08	178.05	174.35	167.83	162.28
17000	203.33	198.17	193.47	189.17	185.25	178.32	172.43
18000	215.29	209.82	204.85	200.30	196.14	188.81	182.57
19000	227.26	221.48	216.23	211.43	207.04	199.30	192.71
20000	239.22	233.14	227.61	222.56	217.94	209.79	202.85
21000	251.18	244.79	238.99	233.69	228.83	220.28	213.00
22000	263.14	256.45	250.37	244.81	239.73	230.77	223.14
23000	275.10	268.11	261.75	255.94	250.63	241.26	233.28
24000	287.06	279.76	273.13	267.07	261.52	251.75	243.42
25000	299.02	291.42	284.51	278.20	272.42	262.23	253.57
26000	310.98	303.08	295.89	289.33	283.32	272.72	263.71
27000	322.94	314.73	307.27	300.45	294.21	283.21	273.85
28000	334.90	326.39	318.65	311.58	305.11	293.70	283.99
29000	346.86	338.05	330.03	322.71	316.01	304.19	294.14
30000	358.82	349.71	341.41	333.84	326.90	314.68	304.28
31000	370.78	361.36	352.79	344.96	337.80	325.17	314.42
32000	382.75	373.02	364.17	356.09	348.70	335.66	324.57
33000	394.71	384.68	375.55	367.22	359.59	346.15	334.71
34000	406.67	396.33	386.93	378.35	370.49	356.64	344.85
35000	418.63	407.99	398.31	389.48	381.39	367.13	354.99
40000	478.43	466.27	455.21	445.12	435.87	419.58	405.71
45000	538.24	524.56	512.11	500.76	490.36	472.02	456.42
50000	598.04	582.84	569.02	556.39	544.84	524.47	507.13
55000	657.84	641.13	625.92	612.03	599.32	576.92	557.85
60000	717.65	699.41	682.82	667.67	653.81	629.36	608.56
65000	777.45	757.69	739.72	723.31	708.29	681.81	659.27
70000	837.26	815.98	796.62	778.95	762.78	734.26	709.99

23

9¼% Monthly Loan Payments

LOAN AMOUNT	½ YEAR	1 YEAR	1½ YEARS	2 YEARS	2½ YEARS	3 YEARS	3½ YEAR
100	17.12	8.76	5.97	4.58	3.75	3.19	2.8
200	34.24	17.51	11.94	9.16	7.49	6.38	5.8
300	51.36	26.27	17.91	13.74	11.24	9.57	8.3
400	68.48	35.03	23.88	18.32	14.99	12.77	11.1
500	85.60	43.78	29.86	22.90	18.73	15.96	13.9
600	102.72	52.54	35.83	27.48	22.48	19.15	16.7
700	119.83	61.30	41.80	32.06	26.22	22.34	19.5
800	136.95	70.05	47.77	36.64	29.97	25.53	22.3
900	154.07	78.81	53.74	41.22	33.72	28.72	25.1
1000	171.19	87.57	59.71	45.80	37.46	31.92	27.9
1500	256.79	131.35	89.57	68.70	56.20	47.87	41.9
2000	342.38	175.13	119.42	91.60	74.93	63.83	55.9
2500	427.98	218.92	149.28	114.50	93.66	79.79	69.9
3000	513.58	262.70	179.14	137.40	112.39	95.75	83.8
3500	599.17	306.49	208.99	160.30	131.12	111.71	97.8
4000	684.77	350.27	238.85	183.20	149.85	127.66	111.8
4500	770.36	394.05	268.71	206.10	168.59	143.62	125.8
5000	855.96	437.84	298.56	229.00	187.32	159.58	139.8
5500	941.56	481.62	328.42	251.90	206.05	175.54	153.7
6000	1027.15	525.40	358.27	274.80	224.78	191.50	167.7
6500	1112.75	569.19	388.13	297.70	243.51	207.46	181.7
7000	1198.34	612.97	417.99	320.60	262.25	223.41	195.7
7500	1283.94	656.76	447.84	343.50	280.98	239.37	209.7
8000	1369.54	700.54	477.70	366.40	299.71	255.33	223.7
8500	1455.13	744.32	507.55	389.30	318.44	271.29	237.6
9000	1540.73	788.11	537.41	412.20	337.17	287.25	251.6
9500	1626.32	831.89	567.27	435.10	355.90	303.20	265.6
10000	1711.92	875.67	597.12	458.00	374.64	319.16	279.6
11000	1883.11	963.24	656.84	503.79	412.10	351.08	307.5
12000	2054.30	1050.81	716.55	549.59	449.56	382.99	335.5
13000	2225.50	1138.38	776.26	595.39	487.03	414.91	363.5
14000	2396.69	1225.94	835.97	641.19	524.49	446.83	391.4
15000	2567.88	1313.51	895.68	686.99	561.95	478.74	419.4
16000	2739.07	1401.08	955.40	732.79	599.42	510.66	447.3
17000	2910.26	1488.65	1015.11	778.59	636.88	542.58	475.
18000	3081.46	1576.21	1074.82	824.39	674.35	574.49	503.3
19000	3252.65	1663.78	1134.53	870.19	711.81	606.41	531.2
20000	3423.84	1751.35	1194.25	915.99	749.27	638.32	559.2
21000	3595.03	1838.92	1253.96	961.79	786.74	670.24	587.2
22000	3766.22	1926.48	1313.67	1007.59	824.20	702.16	615.
23000	3937.42	2014.05	1373.38	1053.39	861.66	734.07	643.
24000	4108.61	2101.62	1433.10	1099.19	899.13	765.99	671.0
25000	4279.80	2189.19	1492.81	1144.99	936.59	797.91	699.0
26000	4450.99	2276.75	1552.52	1190.79	974.05	829.82	727.0
27000	4622.18	2364.32	1612.23	1236.59	1011.52	861.74	754.0
28000	4793.38	2451.89	1671.95	1282.39	1048.98	893.65	782.9
29000	4964.57	2539.46	1731.66	1328.19	1086.45	925.57	810.9
30000	5135.76	2627.02	1791.37	1373.99	1123.91	957.49	838.8
31000	5306.95	2714.59	1851.08	1419.79	1161.37	989.40	866.8
32000	5478.14	2802.16	1910.79	1465.59	1198.84	1021.32	894.
33000	5649.33	2889.73	1970.51	1511.38	1236.30	1053.24	922.
34000	5820.53	2977.29	2030.22	1557.18	1273.76	1085.15	950.
35000	5991.72	3064.86	2089.93	1602.98	1311.23	1117.07	978.
40000	6847.68	3502.70	2388.49	1831.98	1498.55	1276.65	1118.
45000	7703.64	3940.54	2687.05	2060.98	1685.86	1436.23	1258.
50000	8559.60	4378.37	2985.62	2289.98	1873.18	1595.81	1398.
55000	9415.56	4816.21	3284.18	2518.97	2060.50	1755.39	1537.9
60000	10271.52	5254.05	3582.74	2747.97	2247.82	1914.97	1677.
65000	11127.48	5691.88	3881.30	2976.97	2435.14	2074.55	1817.9
70000	11983.44	6129.72	4179.86	3205.97	2622.46	2234.13	1957.

Monthly Loan Payments 9¼%

LOAN AMOUNT	4 YEARS	4½ YEARS	5 YEARS	5½ YEARS	6 YEARS	6½ YEARS	7 YEARS
100	2.50	2.27	2.09	1.94	1.81	1.71	1.62
200	5.00	4.54	4.18	3.88	3.63	3.42	3.24
300	7.50	6.81	6.26	5.82	5.44	5.13	4.86
400	10.00	9.08	8.35	7.76	7.26	6.84	6.49
500	12.50	11.35	10.44	9.69	9.07	8.55	8.11
600	15.00	13.63	12.53	11.63	10.89	10.26	9.73
700	17.50	15.90	14.62	13.57	12.70	11.97	11.35
800	20.00	18.17	16.70	15.51	14.52	13.69	12.97
900	22.50	20.44	18.79	17.45	16.33	15.40	14.59
1000	25.00	22.71	20.88	19.39	18.15	17.11	16.22
1500	37.51	34.06	31.32	29.08	27.22	25.66	24.32
2000	50.01	45.42	41.76	38.78	36.30	34.21	32.43
2500	62.51	56.77	52.20	48.47	45.37	42.77	40.54
3000	75.01	68.13	62.64	58.16	54.45	51.32	48.65
3500	87.51	79.48	73.08	67.86	63.52	59.87	56.76
4000	100.02	90.84	83.52	77.55	72.60	68.43	64.86
4500	112.52	102.19	93.96	87.25	81.67	76.98	72.97
5000	125.02	113.55	104.40	96.94	90.75	85.53	81.08
5500	137.52	124.90	114.84	106.63	99.82	94.09	89.19
6000	150.02	136.26	125.28	116.33	108.90	102.64	97.30
6500	162.53	147.61	135.72	126.02	117.97	111.19	105.41
7000	175.03	158.97	146.16	135.72	127.05	119.75	113.51
7500	187.53	170.32	156.60	145.41	136.12	128.30	121.62
8000	200.03	181.68	167.04	155.11	145.20	136.85	129.73
8500	212.53	193.03	177.48	164.80	154.27	145.41	137.84
9000	225.04	204.39	187.92	174.49	163.35	153.96	145.95
9500	237.54	215.74	198.36	184.19	172.42	162.51	154.05
10000	250.04	227.10	208.80	193.88	181.50	171.06	162.16
11000	275.04	249.81	229.68	213.27	199.65	188.17	178.38
12000	300.05	272.51	250.56	232.66	217.80	205.28	194.59
13000	325.05	295.22	271.44	252.05	235.95	222.38	210.81
14000	350.05	317.93	292.32	271.43	254.10	239.49	227.03
15000	375.06	340.64	313.20	290.82	272.25	256.60	243.24
16000	400.06	363.35	334.08	310.21	290.40	273.70	259.46
17000	425.07	386.06	354.96	329.60	308.55	290.81	275.68
18000	450.07	408.77	375.84	348.99	326.70	307.92	291.89
19000	475.07	431.48	396.72	368.38	344.85	325.02	308.11
20000	500.08	454.19	417.60	387.76	363.00	342.13	324.32
21000	525.08	476.90	438.48	407.15	381.15	359.24	340.54
22000	550.09	499.61	459.36	426.54	399.30	376.34	356.76
23000	575.09	522.32	480.24	445.93	417.45	393.45	372.97
24000	600.09	545.03	501.12	465.32	435.60	410.56	389.19
25000	625.10	567.74	522.00	484.70	453.75	427.66	405.41
26000	650.10	590.45	542.88	504.09	471.90	444.77	421.62
27000	675.11	613.16	563.76	523.48	490.05	461.88	437.84
28000	700.11	635.87	584.64	542.87	508.20	478.98	454.06
29000	725.12	658.58	605.52	562.26	526.35	496.09	470.27
30000	750.12	681.29	626.40	581.64	544.50	513.19	486.49
31000	775.12	704.00	647.28	601.03	562.65	530.30	502.70
32000	800.13	726.71	668.16	620.42	580.80	547.41	518.92
33000	825.13	749.42	689.00	639.81	598.95	564.51	535.14
34000	850.14	772.13	709.92	659.20	617.10	581.62	551.35
35000	875.14	794.83	730.80	678.59	635.25	598.73	567.57
40000	1000.16	908.38	835.20	775.53	725.99	684.26	648.65
45000	1125.18	1021.93	939.60	872.47	816.74	769.79	729.73
50000	1250.20	1135.48	1043.99	969.41	907.49	855.32	810.81
55000	1375.22	1249.03	1148.39	1066.35	998.24	940.86	891.89
60000	1500.24	1362.57	1252.79	1163.29	1088.99	1026.39	972.97
65000	1625.25	1476.12	1357.19	1260.23	1179.74	1111.92	1054.06
70000	1750.27	1589.67	1461.59	1357.17	1270.49	1197.45	1135.14

9¼%   Monthly Loan Payments

LOAN AMOUNT	7½ YEARS	8 YEARS	8½ YEARS	9 YEARS	9½ YEARS	10 YEARS	10½ YEARS
100	1.54	1.48	1.42	1.37	1.32	1.28	1.24
200	3.09	2.96	2.84	2.74	2.64	2.56	2.49
300	4.63	4.43	4.26	4.10	3.96	3.84	3.73
400	6.18	5.91	5.68	5.47	5.29	5.12	4.97
500	7.72	7.39	7.10	6.84	6.61	6.40	6.22
600	9.27	8.87	8.52	8.21	7.93	7.68	7.46
700	10.81	10.35	9.94	9.57	9.25	8.96	8.70
800	12.36	11.82	11.36	10.94	10.57	10.24	9.95
900	13.90	13.30	12.77	12.31	11.89	11.52	11.19
1000	15.45	14.78	14.19	13.68	13.22	12.80	12.43
1500	23.17	22.17	21.29	20.51	19.82	19.20	18.65
2000	30.90	29.56	28.39	27.35	26.43	25.61	24.87
2500	38.62	36.95	35.48	34.19	33.04	32.01	31.08
3000	46.35	44.34	42.58	41.03	39.65	38.41	37.30
3500	54.07	51.73	49.68	47.87	46.25	44.81	43.52
4000	61.79	59.12	56.78	54.70	52.86	51.21	49.73
4500	69.52	66.51	63.87	61.54	59.47	57.61	55.95
5000	77.24	73.90	70.97	68.38	66.08	64.02	62.17
5500	84.97	81.29	78.07	75.22	72.68	70.42	68.38
6000	92.69	88.68	85.16	82.05	79.29	76.82	74.60
6500	100.42	96.07	92.26	88.89	85.90	83.22	80.82
7000	108.14	103.46	99.36	95.73	92.51	89.62	87.03
7500	115.86	110.85	106.45	102.57	99.11	96.02	93.25
8000	123.59	118.24	113.55	109.41	105.72	102.43	99.47
8500	131.31	125.63	120.65	116.24	112.33	108.83	105.68
9000	139.04	133.02	127.74	123.08	118.94	115.23	111.90
9500	146.76	140.41	134.84	129.92	125.54	121.63	118.12
10000	154.48	147.80	141.94	136.76	132.15	128.03	124.33
11000	169.93	162.58	156.13	150.43	145.37	140.84	136.77
12000	185.38	177.36	170.33	164.11	158.58	153.64	149.20
13000	200.83	192.14	184.52	177.79	171.80	166.44	161.63
14000	216.28	206.92	198.71	191.46	185.01	179.25	174.07
15000	231.73	221.70	212.91	205.14	198.23	192.05	186.50
16000	247.18	236.48	227.10	218.81	211.44	204.85	198.93
17000	262.62	251.26	241.30	232.49	224.66	217.66	211.37
18000	278.07	266.04	255.49	246.16	237.87	230.46	223.80
19000	293.52	280.82	269.68	259.84	251.09	243.26	236.23
20000	308.97	295.60	283.88	273.52	264.30	256.07	248.66
21000	324.42	310.38	298.07	287.19	277.52	268.87	261.10
22000	339.87	325.16	312.27	300.87	290.73	281.67	273.53
23000	355.32	339.95	326.46	314.54	303.95	294.48	285.96
24000	370.76	354.73	340.65	328.22	317.16	307.28	298.40
25000	386.21	369.51	354.85	341.89	330.38	320.08	310.83
26000	401.66	384.29	369.04	355.57	343.59	332.89	323.26
27000	417.11	399.07	383.23	369.25	356.81	345.69	335.70
28000	432.56	413.85	397.43	382.92	370.02	358.49	348.13
29000	448.01	428.63	411.62	396.60	383.24	371.29	360.56
30000	463.45	443.41	425.82	410.27	396.45	384.10	373.00
31000	478.90	458.19	440.01	423.95	409.67	396.90	385.43
32000	494.35	472.97	454.20	437.62	422.88	409.70	397.86
33000	509.80	487.75	468.40	451.30	436.10	422.51	410.30
34000	525.25	502.53	482.59	464.98	449.31	435.31	422.73
35000	540.70	517.31	496.79	478.65	462.53	448.11	435.16
40000	617.94	591.21	567.76	547.03	528.60	512.13	497.33
45000	695.18	665.11	638.72	615.41	594.68	576.15	559.50
50000	772.42	739.01	709.69	683.79	660.76	640.16	621.66
55000	849.67	812.91	780.66	752.17	726.83	704.18	683.83
60000	926.91	886.81	851.63	820.55	792.91	768.20	745.99
65000	1004.15	960.71	922.60	888.93	858.98	832.21	808.16
70000	1081.39	1034.62	993.57	957.30	925.06	896.23	870.33

Monthly Loan Payments 9¼%

LOAN AMOUNT	11 YEARS	11½ YEARS	12 YEARS	12½ YEARS	13 YEARS	14 YEARS	15 YEARS
100	1.21	1.18	1.15	1.13	1.10	1.06	1.03
200	2.42	2.36	2.30	2.25	2.21	2.13	2.06
300	3.63	3.54	3.46	3.38	3.31	3.19	3.09
400	4.84	4.72	4.61	4.51	4.42	4.25	4.12
500	6.05	5.90	5.76	5.64	5.52	5.32	5.15
600	7.26	7.08	6.91	6.76	6.62	6.38	6.18
700	8.47	8.26	8.07	7.89	7.73	7.45	7.20
800	9.68	9.44	9.22	9.02	8.83	8.51	8.23
900	10.89	10.62	10.37	10.14	9.94	9.57	9.26
1000	12.10	11.80	11.52	11.27	11.04	10.64	10.29
1500	18.15	17.70	17.28	16.91	16.56	15.95	15.44
2000	24.20	23.59	23.04	22.54	22.08	21.27	20.58
2500	30.25	29.49	28.80	28.18	27.60	26.59	25.73
3000	36.30	35.39	34.56	33.81	33.12	31.91	30.88
3500	42.35	41.29	40.33	39.45	38.64	37.23	36.02
4000	48.40	47.19	46.09	45.08	44.16	42.54	41.17
4500	54.45	53.09	51.85	50.72	49.68	47.86	46.31
5000	60.50	58.98	57.61	56.35	55.20	53.18	51.46
5500	66.55	64.88	63.37	61.99	60.72	58.50	56.61
6000	72.60	70.78	69.13	67.62	66.24	63.82	61.75
6500	78.65	76.68	74.89	73.26	71.77	69.13	66.90
7000	84.70	82.58	80.65	78.89	77.29	74.45	72.04
7500	90.74	88.48	86.41	84.53	82.81	79.77	77.19
8000	96.79	94.37	92.17	90.16	88.33	85.09	82.34
8500	102.84	100.27	97.93	95.80	93.85	90.41	87.48
9000	108.89	106.17	103.69	101.43	99.37	95.72	92.63
9500	114.94	112.07	109.45	107.07	104.89	101.04	97.77
10000	120.99	117.97	115.22	112.71	110.41	106.36	102.92
11000	133.09	129.76	126.74	123.98	121.45	117.00	113.21
12000	145.19	141.56	138.26	135.25	132.49	127.63	123.50
13000	157.29	153.36	149.78	146.52	143.53	138.27	133.79
14000	169.39	165.15	161.30	157.79	154.57	148.90	144.09
15000	181.49	176.95	172.82	169.06	165.61	159.54	154.38
16000	193.59	188.75	184.35	180.33	176.65	170.18	164.67
17000	205.69	200.54	195.87	191.60	187.69	180.81	174.96
18000	217.79	212.34	207.39	202.87	198.73	191.45	185.25
19000	229.89	224.14	218.91	214.14	209.77	202.08	195.55
20000	241.99	235.93	230.43	225.41	220.82	212.72	205.84
21000	254.09	247.73	241.95	236.68	231.86	223.36	216.13
22000	266.18	259.53	253.47	247.95	242.90	233.99	226.42
23000	278.28	271.32	265.00	259.22	253.94	244.63	236.71
24000	290.38	283.12	276.52	270.49	264.98	255.26	247.01
25000	302.48	294.92	288.04	281.76	276.02	265.90	257.30
26000	314.58	306.71	299.56	293.03	287.06	276.54	267.59
27000	326.68	318.51	311.08	304.30	298.10	287.17	277.88
28000	338.78	330.31	322.60	315.57	309.14	297.81	288.17
29000	350.88	342.10	334.13	326.85	320.18	308.44	298.47
30000	362.98	353.90	345.65	338.12	331.22	319.08	308.76
31000	375.08	365.70	357.17	349.39	342.26	329.72	319.05
32000	387.18	377.50	368.69	360.66	353.30	340.35	329.34
33000	399.28	389.29	380.21	371.93	364.35	350.99	339.63
34000	411.38	401.09	391.73	383.20	375.39	361.62	349.93
35000	423.48	412.89	403.25	394.47	386.43	372.26	360.22
40000	483.97	471.87	460.86	450.82	441.63	425.44	411.68
45000	544.47	530.85	518.47	507.17	496.84	478.62	463.14
50000	604.96	589.84	576.08	563.53	552.04	531.80	514.60
55000	665.46	648.82	633.69	619.88	607.24	584.98	566.06
60000	725.96	707.80	691.29	676.23	662.45	638.16	617.52
65000	786.45	766.79	748.90	732.58	717.65	691.34	668.97
70000	846.95	825.77	806.51	788.94	772.85	744.52	720.43

9½% Monthly Loan Payments

LOAN AMOUNT	½ YEAR	1 YEAR	1½ YEARS	2 YEARS	2½ YEARS	3 YEARS	3½ YEARS
100	17.13	8.77	5.98	4.59	3.76	3.20	2.81
200	34.26	17.54	11.97	9.18	7.52	6.41	5.62
300	51.39	26.31	17.95	13.77	11.27	9.61	8.42
400	68.53	35.07	23.93	18.37	15.03	12.81	11.23
500	85.66	43.84	29.91	22.96	18.79	16.02	14.04
600	102.79	52.61	35.90	27.55	22.55	19.22	16.85
700	119.92	61.38	41.88	32.14	26.31	22.42	19.66
800	137.05	70.15	47.86	36.73	30.06	25.63	22.46
900	154.18	78.92	53.84	41.32	33.82	28.83	25.27
1000	171.32	87.68	59.83	45.91	37.58	32.03	28.08
1500	256.97	131.53	89.74	68.87	56.37	48.05	42.12
2000	342.63	175.37	119.65	91.83	75.16	64.07	56.16
2500	428.29	219.21	149.57	114.79	93.95	80.08	70.20
3000	513.95	263.05	179.48	137.74	112.74	96.10	84.24
3500	599.60	306.89	209.39	160.70	131.53	112.12	98.28
4000	685.26	350.73	239.31	183.66	150.32	128.13	112.32
4500	770.92	394.58	269.22	206.62	169.11	144.15	126.36
5000	856.58	438.42	299.14	229.57	187.90	160.16	140.40
5500	942.23	482.26	329.05	252.53	206.69	176.18	154.44
6000	1027.89	526.10	358.96	275.49	225.48	192.20	168.48
6500	1113.55	569.94	388.88	298.44	244.27	208.21	182.52
7000	1199.21	613.78	418.79	321.40	263.06	224.23	196.56
7500	1284.86	657.63	448.70	344.36	281.85	240.25	210.60
8000	1370.52	701.47	478.62	367.32	300.63	256.26	224.64
8500	1456.18	745.31	508.53	390.27	319.42	272.28	238.68
9000	1541.84	789.15	538.44	413.23	338.21	288.30	252.72
9500	1627.49	832.99	568.36	436.19	357.00	304.31	266.76
10000	1713.15	876.84	598.27	459.14	375.79	320.33	280.80
11000	1884.47	964.52	658.10	505.06	413.37	352.36	308.88
12000	2055.78	1052.20	717.93	550.97	450.95	384.40	336.96
13000	2227.10	1139.89	777.75	596.89	488.53	416.43	365.04
14000	2398.41	1227.57	837.58	642.80	526.11	448.46	393.1
15000	2569.73	1315.25	897.41	688.72	563.69	480.49	421.2
16000	2741.04	1402.94	957.23	734.63	601.27	512.53	449.2
17000	2912.36	1490.62	1017.06	780.55	638.85	544.56	477.3
18000	3083.67	1578.30	1076.89	826.46	676.43	576.59	505.4
19000	3254.99	1665.99	1136.72	872.38	714.01	608.63	533.5
20000	3426.30	1753.67	1196.54	918.29	751.59	640.66	561.6
21000	3597.62	1841.35	1256.37	964.20	789.17	672.69	589.6
22000	3768.93	1929.04	1316.20	1010.12	826.75	704.72	617.7
23000	3940.25	2016.72	1376.02	1056.03	864.33	736.76	645.8
24000	4111.56	2104.40	1435.85	1101.95	901.90	768.79	673.9
25000	4282.88	2192.09	1495.68	1147.86	939.48	800.82	702.0
26000	4454.19	2279.77	1555.51	1193.78	977.06	832.86	730.0
27000	4625.51	2367.45	1615.33	1239.69	1014.64	864.89	758.1
28000	4796.82	2455.14	1675.16	1285.61	1052.22	896.92	786.2
29000	4968.14	2542.82	1734.99	1331.52	1089.80	928.96	814.3
30000	5139.45	2630.51	1794.81	1377.43	1127.38	960.99	842.4
31000	5310.77	2718.19	1854.64	1423.35	1164.96	993.02	870.4
32000	5482.08	2805.87	1914.47	1469.26	1202.54	1025.05	898.5
33000	5653.40	2893.56	1974.29	1515.18	1240.12	1057.09	926.6
34000	5824.71	2981.24	2034.12	1561.09	1277.70	1089.12	954.7
35000	5996.03	3068.92	2093.95	1607.01	1315.28	1121.15	982.8
40000	6852.60	3507.34	2393.08	1836.58	1503.17	1281.32	1123.2
45000	7709.18	3945.76	2692.22	2066.15	1691.07	1441.48	1263.6
50000	8565.75	4384.18	2991.36	2295.72	1878.97	1601.65	1404.0
55000	9422.33	4822.59	3290.49	2525.30	2066.86	1761.81	1544.4
60000	10278.90	5261.01	3589.63	2754.87	2254.76	1921.98	1684.8
65000	11135.48	5699.43	3888.76	2984.44	2442.66	2082.14	1825.2
70000	11992.05	6137.85	4187.90	3214.01	2630.56	2242.31	1965.6

Monthly Loan Payments 9½%

LOAN AMOUNT	4 YEARS	4½ YEARS	5 YEARS	5½ YEARS	6 YEARS	6½ YEARS	7 YEARS
100	2.51	2.28	2.10	1.95	1.83	1.72	1.63
200	5.02	4.57	4.20	3.90	3.65	3.45	3.27
300	7.54	6.85	6.30	5.85	5.48	5.17	4.90
400	10.05	9.13	8.40	7.80	7.31	6.89	6.54
500	12.56	11.42	10.50	9.76	9.14	8.62	8.17
600	15.07	13.70	12.60	11.71	10.96	10.34	9.81
700	17.59	15.98	14.70	13.66	12.79	12.06	11.44
800	20.10	18.26	16.80	15.61	14.62	13.79	13.08
900	22.61	20.55	18.90	17.56	16.45	15.51	14.71
1000	25.12	22.83	21.00	19.51	18.27	17.23	16.34
1500	37.68	34.25	31.50	29.27	27.41	25.85	24.52
2000	50.25	45.66	42.00	39.02	36.55	34.47	32.69
2500	62.81	57.08	52.50	48.78	45.69	43.08	40.86
3000	75.37	68.49	63.01	58.53	54.82	51.70	49.03
3500	87.93	79.91	73.51	68.29	63.96	60.31	57.20
4000	100.49	91.32	84.01	78.05	73.10	68.93	65.38
4500	113.05	102.74	94.51	87.80	82.24	77.55	73.55
5000	125.62	114.15	105.01	97.56	91.37	86.16	81.72
5500	138.18	125.57	115.51	107.31	100.51	94.78	89.89
6000	150.74	136.98	126.01	117.07	109.65	103.40	98.06
6500	163.30	148.40	136.51	126.83	118.79	112.01	106.24
7000	175.86	159.81	147.01	136.58	127.92	120.63	114.41
7500	188.42	171.23	157.51	146.34	137.06	129.25	122.58
8000	200.99	182.64	168.01	156.09	146.20	137.86	130.75
8500	213.55	194.06	178.52	165.85	155.33	146.48	138.92
9000	226.11	205.47	189.02	175.60	164.47	155.09	147.10
9500	238.67	216.89	199.52	185.36	173.61	163.71	155.27
10000	251.23	228.30	210.02	195.12	182.75	172.33	163.44
11000	276.35	251.13	231.02	214.63	201.02	189.56	179.78
12000	301.48	273.96	252.02	234.14	219.30	206.79	196.13
13000	326.60	296.79	273.02	253.65	237.57	224.03	212.47
14000	351.72	319.62	294.03	273.16	255.85	241.26	228.82
15000	376.85	342.45	315.03	292.67	274.12	258.49	245.16
16000	401.97	365.28	336.03	312.18	292.40	275.72	261.50
17000	427.09	388.11	357.03	331.70	310.67	292.96	277.85
18000	452.22	410.94	378.03	351.21	328.94	310.19	294.19
19000	477.34	433.77	399.04	370.72	347.22	327.42	310.54
20000	502.46	456.60	420.04	390.23	365.49	344.66	326.88
21000	527.59	479.43	441.04	409.74	383.77	361.89	343.22
22000	552.71	502.26	462.04	429.25	402.04	379.12	359.57
23000	577.83	525.09	483.04	448.77	420.32	396.35	375.91
24000	602.96	547.92	504.04	468.28	438.59	413.59	392.26
25000	628.08	570.75	525.05	487.79	456.87	430.82	408.60
26000	653.20	593.58	546.05	507.30	475.14	448.05	424.94
27000	678.32	616.41	567.05	526.81	493.42	465.28	441.29
28000	703.45	639.24	588.05	546.32	511.69	482.52	457.63
29000	728.57	662.07	609.05	565.84	529.97	499.75	473.98
30000	753.69	684.90	630.06	585.35	548.24	516.98	490.32
31000	778.82	707.73	651.06	604.86	566.52	534.22	506.66
32000	803.94	730.56	672.06	624.37	584.79	551.45	523.01
33000	829.06	753.39	693.06	643.88	603.06	568.68	539.35
34000	854.19	776.22	714.06	663.39	621.34	585.91	555.70
35000	879.31	799.05	735.07	682.90	639.61	603.15	572.04
40000	1004.93	913.21	840.07	780.46	730.99	689.31	653.76
45000	1130.54	1027.36	945.08	878.02	822.36	775.47	735.48
50000	1256.16	1141.51	1050.09	975.58	913.73	861.64	817.20
55000	1381.77	1255.66	1155.10	1073.14	1005.11	947.80	898.92
60000	1507.39	1369.81	1260.11	1170.69	1096.48	1033.97	980.64
65000	1633.00	1483.96	1365.12	1268.25	1187.85	1120.13	1062.36
70000	1758.62	1598.11	1470.13	1365.81	1279.23	1206.29	1144.08

9½%   Monthly Loan Payments

LOAN AMOUNT	7½ YEARS	8 YEARS	8½ YEARS	9 YEARS	9½ YEARS	10 YEARS	10½ YEARS
100	1.56	1.49	1.43	1.38	1.34	1.29	1.26
200	3.12	2.98	2.87	2.76	2.67	2.59	2.51
300	4.67	4.47	4.30	4.14	4.01	3.88	3.77
400	6.23	5.96	5.73	5.52	5.34	5.18	5.03
500	7.79	7.46	7.16	6.90	6.68	6.47	6.29
600	9.35	8.95	8.60	8.29	8.01	7.76	7.54
700	10.90	10.44	10.03	9.67	9.35	9.06	8.80
800	12.46	11.93	11.46	11.05	10.68	10.35	10.06
900	14.02	13.42	12.89	12.43	12.02	11.65	11.31
1000	15.58	14.91	14.33	13.81	13.35	12.94	12.57
1500	23.37	22.37	21.49	20.71	20.03	19.41	18.86
2000	31.16	29.82	28.65	27.62	26.70	25.88	25.14
2500	38.94	37.28	35.82	34.52	33.38	32.35	31.43
3000	46.73	44.73	42.98	41.43	40.05	38.82	37.71
3500	54.52	52.19	50.14	48.33	46.73	45.29	44.00
4000	62.31	59.64	57.30	55.24	53.40	51.76	50.28
4500	70.10	67.10	64.47	62.14	60.08	58.23	56.57
5000	77.89	74.55	71.63	69.05	66.75	64.70	62.86
5500	85.68	82.01	78.79	75.95	73.43	71.17	69.14
6000	93.47	89.47	85.96	82.86	80.10	77.64	75.43
6500	101.25	96.92	93.12	89.76	86.78	84.11	81.71
7000	109.04	104.38	100.28	96.67	93.45	90.58	88.00
7500	116.83	111.83	107.45	103.57	100.13	97.05	94.28
8000	124.62	119.29	114.61	110.47	106.80	103.52	100.57
8500	132.41	126.74	121.77	117.38	113.48	109.99	106.85
9000	140.20	134.20	128.93	124.28	120.15	116.46	113.14
9500	147.99	141.65	136.10	131.19	126.83	122.93	119.43
10000	155.78	149.11	143.26	138.09	133.50	129.40	125.71
11000	171.35	164.02	157.59	151.90	146.85	142.34	138.28
12000	186.93	178.93	171.91	165.71	160.20	155.28	150.85
13000	202.51	193.84	186.24	179.52	173.55	168.22	163.43
14000	218.09	208.75	200.56	193.33	186.90	181.16	176.00
15000	233.67	223.66	214.89	207.14	200.25	194.10	188.57
16000	249.24	238.57	229.22	220.95	213.60	207.04	201.14
17000	264.82	253.49	243.54	234.76	226.95	219.98	213.71
18000	280.40	268.40	257.87	248.57	240.30	232.92	226.28
19000	295.98	283.31	272.19	262.38	253.65	245.86	238.85
20000	311.55	298.22	286.52	276.19	267.00	258.80	251.42
21000	327.13	313.13	300.85	290.00	280.35	271.73	263.99
22000	342.71	328.04	315.17	303.81	293.70	284.67	276.57
23000	358.29	342.95	329.50	317.62	307.05	297.61	289.14
24000	373.86	357.86	343.82	331.42	320.40	310.55	301.71
25000	389.44	372.77	358.15	345.23	333.75	323.49	314.28
26000	405.02	387.68	372.48	359.04	347.10	336.43	326.85
27000	420.60	402.59	386.80	372.85	360.45	349.37	339.42
28000	436.18	417.50	401.13	386.66	373.80	362.31	351.99
29000	451.75	432.42	415.45	400.47	387.15	375.25	364.56
30000	467.33	447.33	429.78	414.28	400.50	388.19	377.13
31000	482.91	462.24	444.11	428.09	413.85	401.13	389.71
32000	498.49	477.15	458.43	441.90	427.21	414.07	402.28
33000	514.06	492.06	472.76	455.71	440.56	427.01	414.85
34000	529.64	506.97	487.08	469.52	453.91	439.95	427.42
35000	545.22	521.88	501.41	483.33	467.26	452.89	439.99
40000	623.11	596.44	573.04	552.37	534.01	517.59	502.85
45000	701.00	670.99	644.67	621.42	600.76	582.29	565.70
50000	778.88	745.54	716.30	690.47	667.51	646.99	628.56
55000	856.77	820.10	787.93	759.51	734.26	711.69	691.41
60000	934.66	894.65	859.56	828.56	801.01	776.39	754.27
65000	1012.55	969.21	931.19	897.61	867.76	841.08	817.13
70000	1090.44	1043.76	1002.82	966.66	934.51	905.78	879.98

Monthly Loan Payments 9½%

LOAN AMOUNT	11 YEARS	11½ YEARS	12 YEARS	12½ YEARS	13 YEARS	14 YEARS	15 YEARS
100	1.22	1.19	1.17	1.14	1.12	1.08	1.04
200	2.45	2.39	2.33	2.28	2.24	2.16	2.09
300	3.67	3.58	3.50	3.42	3.36	3.24	3.13
400	4.90	4.77	4.67	4.57	4.47	4.31	4.18
500	6.12	5.97	5.83	5.71	5.59	5.39	5.22
600	7.34	7.16	7.00	6.85	6.71	6.47	6.27
700	8.57	8.36	8.16	7.99	7.83	7.55	7.31
800	9.79	9.55	9.33	9.13	8.95	8.63	8.35
900	11.01	10.74	10.50	10.27	10.07	9.71	9.40
1000	12.24	11.94	11.66	11.41	11.19	10.78	10.44
1500	18.36	17.91	17.50	17.12	16.78	16.18	15.66
2000	24.48	23.87	23.33	22.83	22.37	21.57	20.88
2500	30.60	29.84	29.16	28.54	27.96	26.96	26.11
3000	36.72	35.81	34.99	34.24	33.56	32.35	31.33
3500	42.84	41.78	40.82	39.95	39.15	37.74	36.55
4000	48.95	47.75	46.65	45.66	44.74	43.13	41.77
4500	55.07	53.72	52.49	51.36	50.34	48.53	46.99
5000	61.19	59.69	58.32	57.07	55.93	53.92	52.21
5500	67.31	65.66	64.15	62.78	61.52	59.31	57.43
6000	73.43	71.62	69.98	68.48	67.11	64.70	62.65
6500	79.55	77.59	75.81	74.19	72.71	70.09	67.87
7000	85.67	83.56	81.65	79.90	78.30	75.49	73.10
7500	91.79	89.53	87.48	85.61	83.89	80.88	78.32
8000	97.91	95.50	93.31	91.31	89.49	86.27	83.54
8500	104.03	101.47	99.14	97.02	95.08	91.66	88.76
9000	110.15	107.44	104.97	102.73	100.67	97.05	93.98
9500	116.27	113.41	110.81	108.43	106.26	102.44	99.20
10000	122.39	119.37	116.64	114.14	111.86	107.84	104.42
11000	134.63	131.31	128.30	125.55	123.04	118.62	114.86
12000	146.86	143.25	139.96	136.97	134.23	129.40	125.31
13000	159.10	155.19	151.63	148.38	145.41	140.19	135.75
14000	171.34	167.12	163.29	159.80	156.60	150.97	146.19
15000	183.58	179.06	174.96	171.21	167.79	161.76	156.63
16000	195.82	191.00	186.62	182.63	178.97	172.54	167.08
17000	208.06	202.94	198.28	194.04	190.16	183.32	177.52
18000	220.30	214.87	209.95	205.45	201.34	194.11	187.96
19000	232.53	226.81	221.61	216.87	212.53	204.89	198.40
20000	244.77	238.75	233.27	228.28	223.71	215.67	208.84
21000	257.01	250.69	244.94	239.70	234.90	226.46	219.29
22000	269.25	262.62	256.60	251.11	246.09	237.24	229.73
23000	281.49	274.56	268.27	262.52	257.27	248.02	240.17
24000	293.73	286.50	279.93	273.94	268.46	258.81	250.61
25000	305.97	298.44	291.59	285.35	279.64	269.59	261.06
26000	318.20	310.37	303.26	296.77	290.83	280.38	271.50
27000	330.44	322.31	314.92	308.18	302.01	291.16	281.94
28000	342.68	334.25	326.58	319.59	313.20	301.94	292.38
29000	354.92	346.19	338.25	331.01	324.39	312.73	302.83
30000	367.16	358.12	349.91	342.42	335.57	323.51	313.27
31000	379.40	370.06	361.58	353.84	346.76	334.29	323.71
32000	391.64	382.00	373.24	365.25	357.94	345.08	334.15
33000	403.88	393.94	384.90	376.66	369.13	355.86	344.59
34000	416.11	405.87	396.57	388.08	380.31	366.65	355.04
35000	428.35	417.81	408.23	399.49	391.50	377.43	365.48
40000	489.55	477.50	466.55	456.56	447.43	431.35	417.69
45000	550.74	537.19	524.87	513.63	503.36	485.27	469.90
50000	611.93	596.87	583.19	570.70	559.29	539.18	522.11
55000	673.13	656.56	641.51	627.77	615.21	593.10	574.32
60000	734.32	716.25	699.82	684.84	671.14	647.02	626.53
65000	795.51	775.94	758.14	741.92	727.07	700.94	678.75
70000	856.71	835.62	816.46	798.99	783.00	754.86	730.96

31

9¾% Monthly Loan Payments

LOAN AMOUNT	½ YEAR	1 YEAR	1½ YEARS	2 YEARS	2½ YEARS	3 YEARS	3½ YEARS
100	17.14	8.78	5.99	4.60	3.77	3.21	2.82
200	34.29	17.56	11.99	9.21	7.54	6.43	5.64
300	51.43	26.34	17.98	13.81	11.31	9.64	8.46
400	68.58	35.12	23.98	18.41	15.08	12.86	11.28
500	85.72	43.90	29.97	23.01	18.85	16.07	14.10
600	102.86	52.68	35.97	27.62	22.62	19.29	16.92
700	120.01	61.46	41.96	32.22	26.39	22.50	19.74
800	137.15	70.24	47.95	36.82	30.16	25.72	22.56
900	154.29	79.02	53.95	41.43	33.93	28.93	25.38
1000	171.44	87.80	59.94	46.03	37.70	32.15	28.20
1500	257.16	131.70	89.91	69.04	56.54	48.22	42.30
2000	342.88	175.60	119.88	92.06	75.39	64.30	56.40
2500	428.60	219.50	149.86	115.07	94.24	80.37	70.50
3000	514.31	263.40	179.83	138.09	113.09	96.45	84.59
3500	600.03	307.30	209.80	161.10	131.93	112.52	98.69
4000	685.75	351.20	239.77	184.12	150.78	128.60	112.79
4500	771.47	395.10	269.74	207.13	169.63	144.67	126.89
5000	857.19	439.00	299.71	230.15	188.48	160.75	140.99
5500	942.91	482.90	329.68	253.16	207.32	176.82	155.09
6000	1028.63	526.80	359.65	276.18	226.17	192.90	169.19
6500	1114.35	570.70	389.62	299.19	245.02	208.97	183.29
7000	1200.07	614.60	419.59	322.21	263.87	225.05	197.39
7500	1285.79	658.50	449.57	345.22	282.71	241.12	211.49
8000	1371.51	702.40	479.54	368.24	301.56	257.20	225.59
8500	1457.22	746.30	509.51	391.25	320.41	273.27	239.69
9000	1542.94	790.20	539.48	414.27	339.26	289.35	253.78
9500	1628.66	834.10	569.45	437.28	358.11	305.42	267.88
10000	1714.38	878.00	599.42	460.30	376.95	321.50	281.98
11000	1885.82	965.80	659.36	506.33	414.65	353.65	310.18
12000	2057.26	1053.60	719.30	552.36	452.34	385.80	338.38
13000	2228.70	1141.40	779.25	598.39	490.04	417.95	366.58
14000	2400.13	1229.20	839.19	644.41	527.73	450.10	394.78
15000	2571.57	1316.99	899.13	690.44	565.43	482.25	422.97
16000	2743.01	1404.79	959.07	736.47	603.12	514.40	451.17
17000	2914.45	1492.59	1019.01	782.50	640.82	546.55	479.37
18000	3085.89	1580.39	1078.96	828.53	678.52	578.70	507.57
19000	3257.33	1668.19	1138.90	874.56	716.21	610.85	535.77
20000	3428.76	1755.99	1198.84	920.59	753.91	643.00	563.97
21000	3600.20	1843.79	1258.78	966.62	791.60	675.15	592.16
22000	3771.64	1931.59	1318.72	1012.65	829.30	707.30	620.36
23000	3943.08	2019.39	1378.67	1058.68	866.99	739.45	648.56
24000	4114.52	2107.19	1438.61	1104.71	904.69	771.60	676.76
25000	4285.96	2194.99	1498.55	1150.74	942.38	803.75	704.96
26000	4457.39	2282.79	1558.49	1196.77	980.08	835.90	733.16
27000	4628.83	2370.59	1618.43	1242.80	1017.77	868.05	761.35
28000	4800.27	2458.39	1678.38	1288.83	1055.47	900.20	789.55
29000	4971.71	2546.19	1738.32	1334.86	1093.16	932.35	817.75
30000	5143.15	2633.99	1798.26	1380.89	1130.86	964.50	845.95
31000	5314.58	2721.79	1858.20	1426.92	1168.55	996.65	874.15
32000	5486.02	2809.59	1918.15	1472.95	1206.25	1028.80	902.35
33000	5657.46	2897.39	1978.09	1518.98	1243.94	1060.95	930.54
34000	5828.90	2985.19	2038.03	1565.01	1281.64	1093.10	958.74
35000	6000.34	3072.99	2097.97	1611.04	1319.33	1125.25	986.94
40000	6857.53	3511.99	2397.68	1841.18	1507.81	1286.00	1127.93
45000	7714.72	3950.98	2697.39	2071.33	1696.29	1446.75	1268.92
50000	8571.91	4389.98	2997.10	2301.48	1884.76	1607.50	1409.91
55000	9429.10	4828.98	3296.81	2531.63	2073.24	1768.25	1550.91
60000	10286.29	5267.98	3596.52	2761.78	2261.72	1929.00	1691.90
65000	11143.48	5706.98	3896.23	2991.93	2450.19	2089.75	1832.89
70000	12000.67	6145.98	4195.94	3222.07	2638.67	2250.50	1973.88

Monthly Loan Payments 9¾%

LOAN AMOUNT	4 YEARS	4½ YEARS	5 YEARS	5½ YEARS	6 YEARS	6½ YEARS	7 YEARS
100	2.52	2.30	2.11	1.96	1.84	1.74	1.65
200	5.05	4.59	4.22	3.93	3.68	3.47	3.29
300	7.57	6.89	6.34	5.89	5.52	5.21	4.94
400	10.10	9.18	8.45	7.85	7.36	6.94	6.59
500	12.62	11.48	10.56	9.82	9.20	8.68	8.24
600	15.15	13.77	12.67	11.78	11.04	10.42	9.88
700	17.67	16.07	14.79	13.74	12.88	12.15	11.53
800	20.19	18.36	16.90	15.71	14.72	13.89	13.18
900	22.72	20.66	19.01	17.67	16.56	15.62	14.83
1000	25.24	22.95	21.12	19.64	18.40	17.36	16.47
1500	37.86	34.43	31.69	29.45	27.60	26.04	24.71
2000	50.49	45.90	42.25	39.27	36.80	34.72	32.94
2500	63.11	57.38	52.81	49.09	46.00	43.40	41.18
3000	75.73	68.85	63.37	58.91	55.20	52.08	49.42
3500	88.35	80.33	73.93	68.72	64.40	60.76	57.65
4000	100.97	91.80	84.50	78.54	73.60	69.44	65.89
4500	113.59	103.28	95.06	88.36	82.80	78.12	74.13
5000	126.21	114.76	105.62	98.18	92.00	86.80	82.36
5500	138.83	126.23	116.18	107.99	101.20	95.48	90.60
6000	151.46	137.71	126.75	117.81	110.40	104.16	98.83
6500	164.08	149.18	137.31	127.63	119.60	112.84	107.07
7000	176.70	160.66	147.87	137.45	128.80	121.52	115.31
7500	189.32	172.13	158.43	147.27	138.00	130.20	123.54
8000	201.94	183.61	168.99	157.08	147.20	138.88	131.78
8500	214.56	195.08	179.56	166.90	156.40	147.56	140.01
9000	227.18	206.56	190.12	176.72	165.60	156.24	148.25
9500	239.81	218.04	200.68	186.54	174.80	164.92	156.49
10000	252.43	229.51	211.24	196.35	184.00	173.60	164.72
11000	277.67	252.46	232.37	215.99	202.40	190.96	181.20
12000	302.91	275.41	253.49	235.62	220.80	208.31	197.67
13000	328.15	298.36	274.62	255.26	239.20	225.67	214.14
14000	353.40	321.32	295.74	274.90	257.60	243.03	230.61
15000	378.64	344.27	316.86	294.53	276.00	260.39	247.08
16000	403.88	367.22	337.99	314.17	294.40	277.75	263.56
17000	429.13	390.17	359.11	333.80	312.80	295.11	280.03
18000	454.37	413.12	380.24	353.44	331.20	312.47	296.50
19000	479.61	436.07	401.36	373.07	349.60	329.83	312.97
20000	504.85	459.02	422.48	392.71	368.00	347.19	329.45
21000	530.10	481.97	443.61	412.34	386.40	364.55	345.92
22000	555.34	504.92	464.73	431.98	404.80	381.91	362.39
23000	580.58	527.87	485.86	451.61	423.20	399.27	378.86
24000	605.82	550.83	506.98	471.25	441.60	416.63	395.34
25000	631.07	573.78	528.11	490.88	460.00	433.99	411.81
26000	656.31	596.73	549.23	510.52	478.40	451.35	428.28
27000	681.55	619.68	570.35	530.16	496.80	468.71	444.75
28000	706.80	642.63	591.48	549.79	515.20	486.07	461.22
29000	732.04	665.58	612.60	569.43	533.60	503.43	477.70
30000	757.28	688.53	633.73	589.06	552.00	520.79	494.17
31000	782.52	711.48	654.85	608.70	570.40	538.15	510.64
32000	807.77	734.43	675.98	628.33	588.80	555.51	527.11
33000	833.01	757.39	697.10	647.97	607.20	572.87	543.59
34000	858.25	780.34	718.22	667.60	625.60	590.23	560.06
35000	883.49	803.29	739.35	687.24	644.00	607.59	576.53
40000	1009.71	918.04	844.97	785.42	736.00	694.38	658.89
45000	1135.92	1032.80	950.59	883.59	828.00	781.18	741.25
50000	1262.13	1147.55	1056.21	981.77	920.00	867.98	823.61
55000	1388.35	1262.31	1161.83	1079.95	1012.00	954.78	905.98
60000	1514.56	1377.06	1267.45	1178.12	1104.00	1041.57	988.34
65000	1640.77	1491.82	1373.08	1276.30	1196.00	1128.37	1070.70
70000	1766.99	1606.58	1478.70	1374.48	1288.00	1215.17	1153.06

9¾%   Monthly Loan Payments

LOAN AMOUNT	7½ YEARS	8 YEARS	8½ YEARS	9 YEARS	9½ YEARS	10 YEARS	10½ YEARS
100	1.57	1.50	1.45	1.39	1.35	1.31	1.27
200	3.14	3.01	2.89	2.79	2.70	2.62	2.54
300	4.71	4.51	4.34	4.18	4.05	3.92	3.81
400	6.28	6.02	5.78	5.58	5.39	5.23	5.08
500	7.85	7.52	7.23	6.97	6.74	6.54	6.35
600	9.42	9.03	8.68	8.37	8.09	7.85	7.63
700	11.00	10.53	10.12	9.76	9.44	9.15	8.90
800	12.57	12.03	11.57	11.15	10.79	10.46	10.17
900	14.14	13.54	13.01	12.55	12.14	11.77	11.44
1000	15.71	15.04	14.46	13.94	13.49	13.08	12.71
1500	23.56	22.56	21.69	20.92	20.23	19.62	19.06
2000	31.42	30.08	28.92	27.89	26.97	26.15	25.42
2500	39.27	37.61	36.15	34.86	33.71	32.69	31.77
3000	47.12	45.13	43.38	41.83	40.46	39.23	38.13
3500	54.98	52.65	50.61	48.80	47.20	45.77	44.48
4000	62.83	60.17	57.84	55.77	53.94	52.31	50.84
4500	70.68	67.69	65.06	62.75	60.69	58.85	57.19
5000	78.54	75.21	72.29	69.72	67.43	65.39	63.55
5500	86.39	82.73	79.52	76.69	74.17	71.92	69.90
6000	94.25	90.25	86.75	83.66	80.92	78.46	76.26
6500	102.10	97.77	93.98	90.63	87.66	85.00	82.61
7000	109.95	105.30	101.21	97.61	94.40	91.54	88.97
7500	117.81	112.82	108.44	104.58	101.14	98.08	95.32
8000	125.66	120.34	115.67	111.55	107.89	104.62	101.68
8500	133.51	127.86	122.90	118.52	114.63	111.15	108.03
9000	141.37	135.38	130.13	125.49	121.37	117.69	114.39
9500	149.22	142.90	137.36	132.46	128.12	124.23	120.74
10000	157.08	150.42	144.59	139.44	134.86	130.77	127.10
11000	172.78	165.46	159.05	153.38	148.35	143.85	139.81
12000	188.49	180.51	173.51	167.32	161.83	156.92	152.52
13000	204.20	195.55	187.96	181.27	175.32	170.00	165.23
14000	219.91	210.59	202.42	195.21	188.80	183.08	177.94
15000	235.61	225.63	216.88	209.15	202.29	196.16	190.65
16000	251.32	240.68	231.34	223.10	215.78	209.23	203.36
17000	267.03	255.72	245.80	237.04	229.26	222.31	216.07
18000	282.74	270.76	260.26	250.99	242.75	235.39	228.78
19000	298.44	285.80	274.72	264.93	256.23	248.46	241.49
20000	314.15	300.84	289.18	278.87	269.72	261.54	254.20
21000	329.86	315.89	303.64	292.82	283.20	274.62	266.91
22000	345.57	330.93	318.09	306.76	296.69	287.69	279.62
23000	361.27	345.97	332.55	320.70	310.18	300.77	292.33
24000	376.98	361.01	347.01	334.65	323.66	313.85	305.04
25000	392.69	376.06	361.47	348.59	337.15	326.93	317.75
26000	408.40	391.10	375.93	362.54	350.63	340.00	330.46
27000	424.10	406.14	390.39	376.48	364.12	353.08	343.17
28000	439.81	421.18	404.85	390.42	377.61	366.16	355.88
29000	455.52	436.22	419.31	404.37	391.09	379.23	368.59
30000	471.23	451.27	433.76	418.31	404.58	392.31	381.30
31000	486.93	466.31	448.22	432.25	418.06	405.39	394.01
32000	502.64	481.35	462.68	446.20	431.55	418.46	406.72
33000	518.35	496.39	477.14	460.14	445.04	431.54	419.43
34000	534.06	511.43	491.60	474.08	458.52	444.62	432.14
35000	549.76	526.48	506.06	488.03	472.01	457.70	444.85
40000	628.30	601.69	578.35	557.75	539.44	523.08	508.40
45000	706.84	676.90	650.65	627.46	606.87	588.47	571.95
50000	785.38	752.11	722.94	697.18	674.30	653.85	635.49
55000	863.91	827.32	795.23	766.90	741.73	719.24	699.04
60000	942.45	902.53	867.53	836.62	809.16	784.62	762.59
65000	1020.99	977.74	939.82	906.34	876.59	850.01	826.14
70000	1099.53	1052.95	1012.12	976.06	944.02	915.39	889.69

Monthly Loan Payments 9¾%

LOAN AMOUNT	11 YEARS	11½ YEARS	12 YEARS	12½ YEARS	13 YEARS	14 YEARS	15 YEARS
100	1.24	1.21	1.18	1.16	1.13	1.09	1.06
200	2.48	2.42	2.36	2.31	2.27	2.19	2.12
300	3.71	3.62	3.54	3.47	3.40	3.28	3.18
400	4.95	4.83	4.72	4.62	4.53	4.37	4.24
500	6.19	6.04	5.90	5.78	5.67	5.47	5.30
600	7.43	7.25	7.08	6.94	6.80	6.56	6.36
700	8.67	8.46	8.26	8.09	7.93	7.65	7.42
800	9.90	9.66	9.45	9.25	9.07	8.75	8.47
900	11.14	10.87	10.63	10.40	10.20	9.84	9.53
1000	12.38	12.08	11.81	11.56	11.33	10.93	10.59
1500	18.57	18.12	17.71	17.34	17.00	16.40	15.89
2000	24.76	24.16	23.61	23.12	22.66	21.86	21.19
2500	30.95	30.20	29.52	28.90	28.33	27.33	26.48
3000	37.14	36.24	35.42	34.68	33.99	32.80	31.78
3500	43.33	42.28	41.32	40.46	39.66	38.26	37.08
4000	49.52	48.32	47.23	46.23	45.33	43.73	42.37
4500	55.70	54.36	53.13	52.01	50.99	49.20	47.67
5000	61.89	60.40	59.03	57.79	56.66	54.66	52.97
5500	68.08	66.44	64.94	63.57	62.32	60.13	58.26
6000	74.27	72.47	70.84	69.35	67.99	65.59	63.56
6500	80.46	78.51	76.74	75.13	73.66	71.06	68.86
7000	86.65	84.55	82.65	80.91	79.32	76.53	74.16
7500	92.84	90.59	88.55	86.69	84.99	81.99	79.45
8000	99.03	96.63	94.45	92.47	90.65	87.46	84.75
8500	105.22	102.67	100.36	98.25	96.32	92.92	90.05
9000	111.41	108.71	106.26	104.03	101.98	98.39	95.34
9500	117.60	114.75	112.16	109.81	107.65	103.86	100.64
10000	123.79	120.79	118.07	115.59	113.32	109.32	105.94
11000	136.17	132.87	129.87	127.14	124.65	120.26	116.53
12000	148.55	144.95	141.68	138.70	135.98	131.19	127.12
13000	160.92	157.03	153.49	150.26	147.31	142.12	137.72
14000	173.30	169.11	165.30	161.82	158.64	153.05	148.31
15000	185.68	181.19	177.10	173.38	169.97	163.99	158.90
16000	198.06	193.27	188.91	184.94	181.31	174.92	169.50
17000	210.44	205.35	200.72	196.50	192.64	185.85	180.09
18000	222.82	217.42	212.52	208.05	203.97	196.78	190.69
19000	235.20	229.50	224.33	219.61	215.30	207.71	201.28
20000	247.58	241.58	236.14	231.17	226.63	218.65	211.87
21000	259.96	253.66	247.94	242.73	237.96	229.58	222.47
22000	272.33	265.74	259.75	254.29	249.30	240.51	233.06
23000	284.71	277.82	271.56	265.85	260.63	251.44	243.65
24000	297.09	289.90	283.36	277.41	271.96	262.38	254.25
25000	309.47	301.98	295.17	288.96	283.29	273.31	264.84
26000	321.85	314.06	306.98	300.52	294.62	284.24	275.43
27000	334.23	326.14	318.78	312.08	305.95	295.17	286.03
28000	346.61	338.22	330.59	323.64	317.29	306.11	296.62
29000	358.99	350.29	342.40	335.20	328.62	317.04	307.22
30000	371.37	362.37	354.20	346.76	339.95	327.97	317.81
31000	383.74	374.45	366.01	358.32	351.28	338.90	328.40
32000	396.12	386.53	377.82	369.87	362.61	349.84	339.00
33000	408.50	398.61	389.62	381.43	373.94	360.77	349.59
34000	420.88	410.69	401.43	392.99	385.28	371.70	360.18
35000	433.26	422.77	413.24	404.55	396.61	382.63	370.78
40000	495.15	483.16	472.27	462.34	453.27	437.29	423.75
45000	557.05	543.56	531.31	520.14	509.92	491.96	476.71
50000	618.94	603.96	590.34	577.93	566.58	546.62	529.68
55000	680.84	664.35	649.37	635.72	623.24	601.28	582.65
60000	742.73	724.75	708.41	693.51	679.90	655.94	635.62
65000	804.62	785.14	767.44	751.31	736.56	710.60	688.59
70000	866.52	845.54	826.48	809.10	793.21	765.26	741.55

10% Monthly Loan Payments

LOAN AMOUNT	½ YEAR	1 YEAR	1½ YEARS	2 YEARS	2½ YEARS	3 YEARS	3½ YEARS
100	17.16	8.79	6.01	4.61	3.78	3.23	2.83
200	34.31	17.58	12.01	9.23	7.56	6.45	5.66
300	51.47	26.37	18.02	13.84	11.34	9.68	8.50
400	68.62	35.17	24.02	18.46	15.12	12.91	11.33
500	85.78	43.96	30.03	23.07	18.91	16.13	14.16
600	102.94	52.75	36.03	27.69	22.69	19.36	16.99
700	120.09	61.54	42.04	32.30	26.47	22.59	19.82
800	137.25	70.33	48.05	36.92	30.25	25.81	22.65
900	154.41	79.12	54.05	41.53	34.03	29.04	25.49
1000	171.56	87.92	60.06	46.14	37.81	32.27	28.32
1500	257.34	131.87	90.09	69.22	56.72	48.40	42.48
2000	343.12	175.83	120.11	92.29	75.62	64.53	56.63
2500	428.90	219.79	150.14	115.36	94.53	80.67	70.79
3000	514.68	263.75	180.17	138.43	113.43	96.80	84.95
3500	600.46	307.71	210.20	161.51	132.34	112.94	99.11
4000	686.25	351.66	240.23	184.58	151.25	129.07	113.27
4500	772.03	395.62	270.26	207.65	170.15	145.20	127.43
5000	857.81	439.58	300.29	230.72	189.06	161.34	141.58
5500	943.59	483.54	330.31	253.80	207.96	177.47	155.74
6000	1029.37	527.50	360.34	276.87	226.87	193.60	169.90
6500	1115.15	571.45	390.37	299.94	245.77	209.74	184.06
7000	1200.93	615.41	420.40	323.01	264.68	225.87	198.22
7500	1286.71	659.37	450.43	346.09	283.59	242.00	212.38
8000	1372.49	703.33	480.46	369.16	302.49	258.14	226.53
8500	1458.27	747.29	510.49	392.23	321.40	274.27	240.69
9000	1544.05	791.24	540.51	415.30	340.30	290.40	254.85
9500	1629.83	835.20	570.54	438.38	359.21	306.54	269.01
10000	1715.61	879.16	600.57	461.45	378.11	322.67	283.17
11000	1887.18	967.07	660.63	507.59	415.93	354.94	311.49
12000	2058.74	1054.99	720.68	553.74	453.74	387.21	339.80
13000	2230.30	1142.91	780.74	599.88	491.55	419.47	368.12
14000	2401.86	1230.82	840.80	646.03	529.36	451.74	396.44
15000	2573.42	1318.74	900.86	692.17	567.17	484.01	424.75
16000	2744.98	1406.65	960.91	738.32	604.98	516.27	453.07
17000	2916.54	1494.57	1020.97	784.46	642.79	548.54	481.39
18000	3088.11	1582.49	1081.03	830.61	680.61	580.81	509.70
19000	3259.67	1670.40	1141.08	876.75	718.42	613.08	538.02
20000	3431.23	1758.32	1201.14	922.90	756.23	645.34	566.34
21000	3602.79	1846.23	1261.20	969.04	794.04	677.61	594.65
22000	3774.35	1934.15	1321.26	1015.19	831.85	709.88	622.97
23000	3945.91	2022.07	1381.31	1061.33	869.66	742.15	651.29
24000	4117.47	2109.98	1441.37	1107.48	907.47	774.41	679.60
25000	4289.03	2197.90	1501.43	1153.62	945.29	806.68	707.92
26000	4460.60	2285.81	1561.48	1199.77	983.10	838.95	736.24
27000	4632.16	2373.73	1621.54	1245.91	1020.91	871.21	764.55
28000	4803.72	2461.64	1681.60	1292.06	1058.72	903.48	792.87
29000	4975.28	2549.56	1741.66	1338.20	1096.53	935.75	821.19
30000	5146.84	2637.48	1801.71	1384.35	1134.34	968.02	849.50
31000	5318.40	2725.39	1861.77	1430.49	1172.15	1000.28	877.82
32000	5489.96	2813.31	1921.83	1476.64	1209.97	1032.55	906.14
33000	5661.53	2901.22	1981.88	1522.78	1247.78	1064.82	934.46
34000	5833.09	2989.14	2041.94	1568.93	1285.59	1097.08	962.77
35000	6004.65	3077.06	2102.00	1615.07	1323.40	1129.35	991.09
40000	6862.46	3516.64	2402.28	1845.80	1512.46	1290.69	1132.67
45000	7720.26	3956.21	2702.57	2076.52	1701.51	1452.02	1274.26
50000	8578.07	4395.79	3002.85	2307.25	1890.57	1613.36	1415.84
55000	9435.88	4835.37	3303.14	2537.97	2079.63	1774.70	1557.43
60000	10293.68	5274.95	3603.42	2768.70	2268.68	1936.03	1699.01
65000	11151.49	5714.53	3903.71	2999.42	2457.74	2097.37	1840.59
70000	12009.30	6154.11	4204.00	3230.14	2646.80	2258.70	1982.18

Monthly Loan Payments 10%

LOAN AMOUNT	4 YEARS	4½ YEARS	5 YEARS	5½ YEARS	6 YEARS	6½ YEARS	7 YEARS
100	2.54	2.31	2.12	1.98	1.85	1.75	1.66
200	5.07	4.61	4.25	3.95	3.71	3.50	3.32
300	7.61	6.92	6.37	5.93	5.56	5.25	4.98
400	10.15	9.23	8.50	7.90	7.41	6.99	6.64
500	12.68	11.54	10.62	9.88	9.26	8.74	8.30
600	15.22	13.84	12.75	11.86	11.12	10.49	9.96
700	17.75	16.15	14.87	13.83	12.97	12.24	11.62
800	20.29	18.46	17.00	15.81	14.82	13.99	13.28
900	22.83	20.77	19.12	17.78	16.67	15.74	14.94
1000	25.36	23.07	21.25	19.76	18.53	17.49	16.60
1500	38.04	34.61	31.87	29.64	27.79	26.23	24.90
2000	50.73	46.14	42.49	39.52	37.05	34.97	33.20
2500	63.41	57.68	53.12	49.40	46.31	43.72	41.50
3000	76.09	69.22	63.74	59.28	55.58	52.46	49.80
3500	88.77	80.75	74.36	69.16	64.84	61.20	58.10
4000	101.45	92.29	84.99	79.04	74.10	69.95	66.40
4500	114.13	103.83	95.61	88.92	83.37	78.69	74.71
5000	126.81	115.36	106.24	98.80	92.63	87.43	83.01
5500	139.49	126.90	116.86	108.68	101.89	96.18	91.31
6000	152.18	138.43	127.48	118.56	111.16	104.92	99.61
6500	164.86	149.97	138.11	128.44	120.42	113.67	107.91
7000	177.54	161.51	148.73	138.32	129.68	122.41	116.21
7500	190.22	173.04	159.35	148.20	138.94	131.15	124.51
8000	202.90	184.58	169.98	158.08	148.21	139.90	132.81
8500	215.58	196.12	180.60	167.96	157.47	148.64	141.11
9000	228.26	207.65	191.22	177.84	166.73	157.38	149.41
9500	240.94	219.19	201.85	187.72	176.00	166.13	157.71
10000	253.63	230.72	212.47	197.60	185.26	174.87	166.01
11000	278.99	253.80	233.72	217.36	203.78	192.36	182.61
12000	304.35	276.87	254.96	237.12	222.31	209.84	199.21
13000	329.71	299.94	276.21	256.88	240.84	227.33	215.82
14000	355.08	323.01	297.46	276.64	259.36	244.82	232.42
15000	380.44	346.09	318.71	296.40	277.89	262.30	249.02
16000	405.80	369.16	339.95	316.16	296.41	279.79	265.62
17000	431.16	392.23	361.20	335.91	314.94	297.28	282.22
18000	456.53	415.30	382.45	355.67	333.47	314.76	298.82
19000	481.89	438.38	403.69	375.43	351.99	332.25	315.42
20000	507.25	461.45	424.94	395.19	370.52	349.74	332.02
21000	532.61	484.52	446.19	414.95	389.04	367.23	348.62
22000	557.98	507.59	467.43	434.71	407.57	384.71	365.23
23000	583.34	530.67	488.68	454.47	426.09	402.20	381.83
24000	608.70	553.74	509.93	474.23	444.62	419.69	398.43
25000	634.06	576.81	531.18	493.99	463.15	437.17	415.03
26000	659.43	599.88	552.42	513.75	481.67	454.66	431.63
27000	684.79	622.95	573.67	533.51	500.20	472.15	448.23
28000	710.15	646.03	594.92	553.27	518.72	489.63	464.83
29000	735.51	669.10	616.16	573.03	537.25	507.12	481.43
30000	760.88	692.17	637.41	592.79	555.78	524.61	498.04
31000	786.24	715.24	658.66	612.55	574.30	542.09	514.64
32000	811.60	738.32	679.91	632.31	592.83	559.58	531.24
33000	836.97	761.39	701.15	652.07	611.35	577.07	547.84
34000	862.33	784.46	722.40	671.83	629.88	594.56	564.44
35000	887.69	807.53	743.65	691.59	648.40	612.04	581.04
40000	1014.50	922.90	849.88	790.39	741.03	699.48	664.05
45000	1141.32	1038.26	956.12	889.19	833.66	786.91	747.05
50000	1268.13	1153.62	1062.35	987.98	926.29	874.35	830.06
55000	1394.94	1268.98	1168.59	1086.78	1018.92	961.78	913.07
60000	1521.76	1384.34	1274.82	1185.58	1111.55	1049.22	996.07
65000	1648.57	1499.71	1381.06	1284.38	1204.18	1136.65	1079.08
70000	1775.38	1615.07	1487.29	1383.18	1296.81	1224.09	1162.08

10% Monthly Loan Payments

LOAN AMOUNT	7½ YEARS	8 YEARS	8½ YEARS	9 YEARS	9½ YEARS	10 YEARS	10½ YEARS
100	1.58	1.52	1.46	1.41	1.36	1.32	1.28
200	3.17	3.03	2.92	2.82	2.72	2.64	2.57
300	4.75	4.55	4.38	4.22	4.09	3.96	3.85
400	6.34	6.07	5.84	5.63	5.45	5.29	5.14
500	7.92	7.59	7.30	7.04	6.81	6.61	6.42
600	9.50	9.10	8.76	8.45	8.17	7.93	7.71
700	11.09	10.62	10.21	9.86	9.54	9.25	8.99
800	12.67	12.14	11.67	11.26	10.90	10.57	10.28
900	14.25	13.66	13.13	12.67	12.26	11.89	11.56
1000	15.84	15.17	14.59	14.08	13.62	13.22	12.85
1500	23.76	22.76	21.89	21.12	20.43	19.82	19.27
2000	31.68	30.35	29.18	28.16	27.24	26.43	25.70
2500	39.59	37.94	36.48	35.20	34.06	33.04	32.12
3000	47.51	45.52	43.78	42.24	40.87	39.65	38.55
3500	55.43	53.11	51.07	49.28	47.68	46.25	44.97
4000	63.35	60.70	58.37	56.31	54.49	52.86	51.40
4500	71.27	68.28	65.67	63.35	61.30	59.47	57.82
5000	79.19	75.87	72.96	70.39	68.11	66.08	64.25
5500	87.11	83.46	80.26	77.43	74.92	72.68	70.67
6000	95.03	91.04	87.55	84.47	81.73	79.29	77.10
6500	102.95	98.63	94.85	91.51	88.55	85.90	83.52
7000	110.87	106.22	102.15	98.55	95.36	92.51	89.95
7500	118.78	113.81	109.44	105.59	102.17	99.11	96.37
8000	126.70	121.39	116.74	112.63	108.98	105.72	102.80
8500	134.62	128.98	124.03	119.67	115.79	112.33	109.22
9000	142.54	136.57	131.33	126.71	122.60	118.94	115.65
9500	150.46	144.15	138.63	133.75	129.41	125.54	122.07
10000	158.38	151.74	145.92	140.79	136.22	132.15	128.49
11000	174.22	166.92	160.52	154.87	149.85	145.37	141.34
12000	190.06	182.09	175.11	168.94	163.47	158.58	154.19
13000	205.89	197.26	189.70	183.02	177.09	171.80	167.04
14000	221.73	212.44	204.29	197.10	190.71	185.01	179.89
15000	237.57	227.61	218.88	211.18	204.34	198.23	192.74
16000	253.41	242.79	233.48	225.26	217.96	211.44	205.59
17000	269.24	257.96	248.07	239.34	231.58	224.66	218.44
18000	285.08	273.13	262.66	253.42	245.20	237.87	231.29
19000	300.92	288.31	277.25	267.50	258.83	251.09	244.14
20000	316.76	303.48	291.85	281.57	272.45	264.30	256.99
21000	332.60	318.66	306.44	295.65	286.07	277.52	269.84
22000	348.43	333.83	321.03	309.73	299.69	290.73	282.69
23000	364.27	349.01	335.62	323.81	313.32	303.95	295.54
24000	380.11	364.18	350.22	337.89	326.94	317.16	308.39
25000	395.95	379.35	364.81	351.97	340.56	330.38	321.24
26000	411.79	394.53	379.40	366.05	354.18	343.59	334.09
27000	427.62	409.70	393.99	380.12	367.81	356.81	346.94
28000	443.46	424.88	408.58	394.20	381.43	370.02	359.78
29000	459.30	440.05	423.18	408.28	395.05	383.24	372.63
30000	475.14	455.22	437.77	422.36	408.67	396.45	385.48
31000	490.98	470.40	452.36	436.44	422.30	409.67	398.33
32000	506.81	485.57	466.95	450.52	435.92	422.88	411.18
33000	522.65	500.75	481.55	464.60	449.54	436.10	424.03
34000	538.49	515.92	496.14	478.68	463.16	449.31	436.88
35000	554.33	531.10	510.73	492.75	476.79	462.53	449.73
40000	633.52	606.97	583.69	563.15	544.90	528.60	513.98
45000	712.71	682.84	656.65	633.54	613.01	594.68	578.23
50000	791.90	758.71	729.62	703.93	681.12	660.75	642.47
55000	871.09	834.58	802.58	774.33	749.24	726.83	706.72
60000	950.28	910.45	875.54	844.72	817.35	792.90	770.97
65000	1029.47	986.32	948.50	915.11	885.46	858.98	835.21
70000	1108.65	1062.19	1021.46	985.51	953.57	925.06	899.46

Monthly Loan Payments 10%

LOAN AMOUNT	11 YEARS	11½ YEARS	12 YEARS	12½ YEARS	13 YEARS	14 YEARS	15 YEARS
100	1.25	1.22	1.20	1.17	1.15	1.11	1.07
200	2.50	2.44	2.39	2.34	2.30	2.22	2.15
300	3.76	3.67	3.59	3.51	3.44	3.32	3.22
400	5.01	4.89	4.78	4.68	4.59	4.43	4.30
500	6.26	6.11	5.98	5.85	5.74	5.54	5.37
600	7.51	7.33	7.17	7.02	6.89	6.65	6.45
700	8.76	8.56	8.37	8.19	8.03	7.76	7.52
800	10.02	9.78	9.56	9.36	9.18	8.87	8.60
900	11.27	11.00	10.76	10.53	10.33	9.97	9.67
1000	12.52	12.22	11.95	11.70	11.48	11.08	10.75
1500	18.78	18.33	17.93	17.56	17.22	16.62	16.12
2000	25.04	24.44	23.90	23.41	22.96	22.16	21.49
2500	31.30	30.55	29.88	29.26	28.70	27.71	26.87
3000	37.56	36.66	35.85	35.11	34.44	33.25	32.24
3500	43.82	42.78	41.83	40.96	40.17	38.79	37.61
4000	50.08	48.89	47.80	46.82	45.91	44.33	42.98
4500	56.34	55.00	53.78	52.67	51.65	49.87	48.36
5000	62.60	61.11	59.75	58.52	57.39	55.41	53.73
5500	68.86	67.22	65.73	64.37	63.13	60.95	59.10
6000	75.12	73.33	71.70	70.22	68.87	66.49	64.48
6500	81.38	79.44	77.68	76.08	74.61	72.03	69.85
7000	87.64	85.55	83.66	81.93	80.35	77.57	75.22
7500	93.90	91.66	89.63	87.78	86.09	83.12	80.60
8000	100.16	97.77	95.61	93.63	91.83	88.66	85.97
8500	106.42	103.88	101.58	99.48	97.57	94.20	91.34
9000	112.68	109.99	107.56	105.34	103.31	99.74	96.71
9500	118.94	116.11	113.53	111.19	109.05	105.28	102.09
10000	125.20	122.22	119.51	117.04	114.78	110.82	107.46
11000	137.72	134.44	131.46	128.74	126.26	121.90	118.21
12000	150.24	146.66	143.41	140.45	137.74	132.98	128.95
13000	162.76	158.88	155.36	152.15	149.22	144.07	139.70
14000	175.28	171.10	167.31	163.86	160.70	155.15	150.44
15000	187.80	183.32	179.26	175.56	172.18	166.23	161.19
16000	200.32	195.55	191.21	187.26	183.66	177.31	171.94
17000	212.84	207.77	203.16	198.97	195.13	188.39	182.68
18000	225.36	219.99	215.11	210.67	206.61	199.48	193.43
19000	237.88	232.21	227.06	222.38	218.09	210.56	204.17
20000	250.40	244.43	239.02	234.08	229.57	221.64	214.92
21000	262.92	256.65	250.97	245.78	241.05	232.72	225.67
22000	275.44	268.88	262.92	257.49	252.53	243.80	236.41
23000	287.96	281.10	274.87	269.19	264.01	254.89	247.16
24000	300.48	293.32	286.82	280.90	275.48	265.97	257.91
25000	313.00	305.54	298.77	292.60	286.96	277.05	268.65
26000	325.52	317.76	310.72	304.30	298.44	288.13	279.40
27000	338.04	329.98	322.67	316.01	309.92	299.21	290.14
28000	350.56	342.21	334.62	327.71	321.40	310.30	300.89
29000	363.08	354.43	346.57	339.42	332.88	321.38	311.64
30000	375.60	366.65	358.52	351.12	344.35	332.46	322.38
31000	388.12	378.87	370.47	362.82	355.83	343.54	333.13
32000	400.64	391.09	382.43	374.53	367.31	354.62	343.87
33000	413.16	403.31	394.38	386.23	378.79	365.71	354.62
34000	425.68	415.54	406.33	397.94	390.27	376.79	365.37
35000	438.20	427.76	418.28	409.64	401.75	387.87	376.11
40000	500.80	488.87	478.03	468.16	459.14	443.28	429.84
45000	563.39	549.97	537.79	526.68	516.53	498.69	483.57
50000	625.99	611.08	597.54	585.20	573.92	554.10	537.30
55000	688.59	672.19	657.29	643.72	631.32	609.51	591.03
60000	751.19	733.30	717.05	702.24	688.71	664.92	644.76
65000	813.79	794.41	776.80	760.76	746.10	720.33	698.49
70000	876.39	855.51	836.55	819.28	803.49	775.74	752.22

10¼% Monthly Loan Payments

LOAN AMOUNT	½ YEAR	1 YEAR	1½ YEARS	2 YEARS	2½ YEARS	3 YEARS	3½ YEARS
100	17.17	8.80	6.02	4.63	3.79	3.24	2.84
200	34.34	17.61	12.03	9.25	7.59	6.48	5.69
300	51.51	26.41	18.05	13.88	11.38	9.72	8.53
400	68.67	35.21	24.07	18.50	15.17	12.95	11.37
500	85.84	44.02	30.09	23.13	18.96	16.19	14.22
600	103.01	52.82	36.10	27.76	22.76	19.43	17.06
700	120.18	61.62	42.12	32.38	26.55	22.67	19.90
800	137.35	70.43	48.14	37.01	30.34	25.91	22.75
900	154.52	79.23	54.16	41.63	34.13	29.15	25.59
1000	171.68	88.03	60.17	46.26	37.93	32.38	28.44
1500	257.53	132.05	90.26	69.39	56.89	48.58	42.65
2000	343.37	176.06	120.34	92.52	75.86	64.77	56.87
2500	429.21	220.08	150.43	115.65	94.82	80.96	71.09
3000	515.05	264.10	180.52	138.78	113.78	97.15	85.31
3500	600.90	308.11	210.60	161.91	132.75	113.35	99.52
4000	686.74	352.13	240.69	185.04	151.71	129.54	113.74
4500	772.58	396.14	270.78	208.17	170.67	145.73	127.96
5000	858.42	440.16	300.86	231.30	189.64	161.92	142.18
5500	944.27	484.18	330.95	254.43	208.60	178.12	156.40
6000	1030.11	528.19	361.03	277.56	227.57	194.31	170.61
6500	1115.95	572.21	391.12	300.69	246.53	210.50	184.83
7000	1201.79	616.23	421.21	323.82	265.49	226.69	199.05
7500	1287.63	660.24	451.29	346.95	284.46	242.89	213.27
8000	1373.48	704.26	481.38	370.08	303.42	259.08	227.49
8500	1459.32	748.27	511.46	393.21	322.39	275.27	241.70
9000	1545.16	792.29	541.55	416.34	341.35	291.46	255.92
9500	1631.00	836.31	571.64	439.47	360.31	307.65	270.14
10000	1716.85	880.32	601.72	462.60	379.28	323.85	284.36
11000	1888.53	968.35	661.89	508.86	417.21	356.23	312.79
12000	2060.22	1056.39	722.07	555.12	455.13	388.62	341.23
13000	2231.90	1144.42	782.24	601.39	493.06	421.00	369.66
14000	2403.58	1232.45	842.41	647.65	530.99	453.39	398.10
15000	2575.27	1320.48	902.58	693.91	568.92	485.77	426.53
16000	2746.95	1408.52	962.76	740.17	606.84	518.16	454.97
17000	2918.64	1496.55	1022.93	786.43	644.77	550.54	483.41
18000	3090.32	1584.58	1083.10	832.69	682.70	582.92	511.84
19000	3262.01	1672.61	1143.27	878.95	720.63	615.31	540.28
20000	3433.69	1760.64	1203.45	925.21	758.56	647.69	568.71
21000	3605.38	1848.68	1263.62	971.47	796.48	680.08	597.15
22000	3777.06	1936.71	1323.79	1017.73	834.41	712.46	625.58
23000	3948.75	2024.74	1383.96	1063.99	872.34	744.85	654.02
24000	4120.43	2112.77	1444.13	1110.25	910.27	777.23	682.46
25000	4292.12	2200.81	1504.31	1156.51	948.19	809.62	710.89
26000	4463.80	2288.84	1564.48	1202.77	986.12	842.00	739.33
27000	4635.48	2376.87	1624.65	1249.03	1024.05	874.39	767.76
28000	4807.17	2464.90	1684.82	1295.29	1061.98	906.77	796.20
29000	4978.85	2552.93	1745.00	1341.55	1099.90	939.16	824.63
30000	5150.54	2640.97	1805.17	1387.81	1137.83	971.54	853.07
31000	5322.22	2729.00	1865.34	1434.07	1175.76	1003.93	881.50
32000	5493.91	2817.03	1925.51	1480.33	1213.69	1036.31	909.94
33000	5665.59	2905.06	1985.68	1526.59	1251.62	1068.69	938.38
34000	5837.28	2993.09	2045.86	1572.85	1289.54	1101.08	966.81
35000	6008.96	3081.13	2106.03	1619.11	1327.47	1133.46	995.25
40000	6867.38	3521.29	2406.89	1850.42	1517.11	1295.39	1137.43
45000	7725.81	3961.45	2707.75	2081.72	1706.75	1457.31	1279.60
50000	8584.23	4401.61	3008.61	2313.02	1896.39	1619.23	1421.78
55000	9442.65	4841.77	3309.47	2544.32	2086.03	1781.16	1563.96
60000	10301.08	5281.93	3610.34	2775.62	2275.67	1943.08	1706.14
65000	11159.50	5722.09	3911.20	3006.93	2465.30	2105.00	1848.32
70000	12017.92	6162.25	4212.06	3238.23	2654.94	2266.93	1990.49

Monthly Loan Payments 10¼%

LOAN AMOUNT	4 YEARS	4½ YEARS	5 YEARS	5½ YEARS	6 YEARS	6½ YEARS	7 YEARS
100	2.55	2.32	2.14	1.99	1.87	1.76	1.67
200	5.10	4.64	4.27	3.98	3.73	3.52	3.35
300	7.64	6.96	6.41	5.97	5.60	5.28	5.02
400	10.19	9.28	8.55	7.95	7.46	7.05	6.69
500	12.74	11.60	10.69	9.94	9.33	8.81	8.37
600	15.29	13.92	12.82	11.93	11.19	10.57	10.04
700	17.84	16.24	14.96	13.92	13.06	12.33	11.71
800	20.39	18.56	17.10	15.91	14.92	14.09	13.38
900	22.93	20.87	19.23	17.90	16.79	15.85	15.06
1000	25.48	23.19	21.37	19.88	18.65	17.61	16.73
1500	38.22	34.79	32.06	29.83	27.98	26.42	25.10
2000	50.97	46.39	42.74	39.77	37.30	35.23	33.46
2500	63.71	57.99	53.43	49.71	46.63	44.04	41.83
3000	76.45	69.58	64.11	59.65	55.96	52.84	50.19
3500	89.19	81.18	74.80	69.60	65.28	61.65	58.56
4000	101.93	92.78	85.48	79.54	74.61	70.46	66.92
4500	114.67	104.37	96.17	89.48	83.93	79.27	75.29
5000	127.41	115.97	106.85	99.42	93.26	88.07	83.65
5500	140.16	127.57	117.54	109.36	102.59	96.88	92.02
6000	152.90	139.16	128.22	119.31	111.91	105.69	100.38
6500	165.64	150.76	138.91	129.25	121.24	114.50	108.75
7000	178.38	162.36	149.59	139.19	130.57	123.30	117.11
7500	191.12	173.96	160.28	149.13	139.89	132.11	125.48
8000	203.86	185.55	170.96	159.08	149.22	140.92	133.85
8500	216.60	197.15	181.65	169.02	158.54	149.73	142.21
9000	229.35	208.75	192.33	178.96	167.87	158.53	150.58
9500	242.09	220.34	203.02	188.90	177.20	167.34	158.94
10000	254.83	231.94	213.70	198.84	186.52	176.15	167.31
11000	280.31	255.14	235.07	218.73	205.17	193.76	184.04
12000	305.79	278.33	256.44	238.61	223.83	211.38	200.77
13000	331.28	301.52	277.81	258.50	242.48	228.99	217.50
14000	356.76	324.72	299.18	278.38	261.13	246.61	234.23
15000	382.24	347.91	320.55	298.27	279.78	264.22	250.96
16000	407.73	371.11	341.92	318.15	298.43	281.84	267.69
17000	433.21	394.30	363.29	338.04	317.09	299.45	284.42
18000	458.69	417.49	384.66	357.92	335.74	317.07	301.15
19000	484.17	440.69	406.04	377.80	354.39	334.68	317.88
20000	509.66	463.88	427.41	397.69	373.04	352.30	334.61
21000	535.14	487.08	448.78	417.57	391.70	369.91	351.34
22000	560.62	510.27	470.15	437.46	410.35	387.53	368.07
23000	586.10	533.46	491.52	457.34	429.00	405.14	384.80
24000	611.59	556.66	512.89	477.23	447.65	422.76	401.54
25000	637.07	579.85	534.26	497.11	466.30	440.37	418.27
26000	662.55	603.05	555.63	517.00	484.96	457.99	435.00
27000	688.04	626.24	577.00	536.88	503.61	475.60	451.73
28000	713.52	649.44	598.37	556.76	522.26	493.21	468.46
29000	739.00	672.63	619.74	576.65	540.91	510.83	485.19
30000	764.48	695.82	641.11	596.53	559.56	528.44	501.92
31000	789.97	719.02	662.48	616.42	578.22	546.06	518.65
32000	815.45	742.21	683.85	636.30	596.87	563.67	535.38
33000	840.93	765.41	705.22	656.19	615.52	581.29	552.11
34000	866.42	788.60	726.59	676.07	634.17	598.90	568.84
35000	891.90	811.79	747.96	695.96	652.83	616.52	585.57
40000	1019.31	927.76	854.81	795.38	746.09	704.59	669.23
45000	1146.73	1043.74	961.66	894.80	839.35	792.67	752.88
50000	1274.14	1159.71	1068.51	994.22	932.61	880.74	836.53
55000	1401.55	1275.68	1175.36	1093.65	1025.87	968.82	920.19
60000	1528.97	1391.65	1282.22	1193.07	1119.13	1056.89	1003.84
65000	1656.38	1507.62	1389.07	1292.49	1212.39	1144.96	1087.49
70000	1783.80	1623.59	1495.92	1391.91	1305.65	1233.04	1171.15

10¼%   Monthly Loan Payments

LOAN AMOUNT	7½ YEARS	8 YEARS	8½ YEARS	9 YEARS	9½ YEARS	10 YEARS	10½ YEARS
100	1.60	1.53	1.47	1.42	1.38	1.34	1.30
200	3.19	3.06	2.95	2.84	2.75	2.67	2.60
300	4.79	4.59	4.42	4.26	4.13	4.01	3.90
400	6.39	6.12	5.89	5.69	5.50	5.34	5.20
500	7.98	7.65	7.36	7.11	6.88	6.68	6.49
600	9.58	9.18	8.84	8.53	8.26	8.01	7.79
700	11.18	10.71	10.31	9.95	9.63	9.35	9.09
800	12.78	12.25	11.78	11.37	11.01	10.68	10.39
900	14.37	13.78	13.25	12.79	12.38	12.02	11.69
1000	15.97	15.31	14.73	14.21	13.76	13.35	12.99
1500	23.95	22.96	22.09	21.32	20.64	20.03	19.48
2000	31.94	30.61	29.45	28.43	27.52	26.71	25.98
2500	39.92	38.27	36.82	35.54	34.40	33.38	32.47
3000	47.91	45.92	44.18	42.64	41.28	40.06	38.97
3500	55.89	53.57	51.54	49.75	48.16	46.74	45.46
4000	63.88	61.23	58.91	56.86	55.04	53.42	51.96
4500	71.86	68.88	66.27	63.96	61.92	60.09	58.45
5000	79.84	76.53	73.63	71.07	68.80	66.77	64.95
5500	87.83	84.19	81.00	78.18	75.68	73.45	71.44
6000	95.81	91.84	88.36	85.29	82.56	80.12	77.94
6500	103.80	99.49	95.72	92.39	89.44	86.80	84.43
7000	111.78	107.15	103.09	99.50	96.32	93.48	90.93
7500	119.77	114.80	110.45	106.61	103.20	100.15	97.42
8000	127.75	122.45	117.81	113.72	110.08	106.83	103.92
8500	135.74	130.11	125.18	120.82	116.96	113.51	110.41
9000	143.72	137.76	132.54	127.93	123.84	120.19	116.91
9500	151.71	145.41	139.90	135.04	130.72	126.86	123.40
10000	159.69	153.07	147.26	142.14	137.60	133.54	129.90
11000	175.66	168.37	161.99	156.36	151.36	146.89	142.89
12000	191.63	183.68	176.72	170.57	165.12	160.25	155.88
13000	207.60	198.99	191.44	184.79	178.88	173.60	168.87
14000	223.57	214.29	206.17	199.00	192.64	186.95	181.86
15000	239.53	229.60	220.90	213.22	206.40	200.31	194.85
16000	255.50	244.91	235.62	227.43	220.16	213.66	207.84
17000	271.47	260.22	250.35	241.65	233.92	227.02	220.83
18000	287.44	275.52	265.08	255.86	247.68	240.37	233.82
19000	303.41	290.83	279.80	270.07	261.44	253.72	246.81
20000	319.38	306.14	294.53	284.29	275.20	267.08	259.80
21000	335.35	321.44	309.26	298.50	288.96	280.43	272.79
22000	351.32	336.75	323.98	312.72	302.72	293.79	285.78
23000	367.29	352.06	338.71	326.93	316.47	307.14	298.77
24000	383.26	367.36	353.44	341.15	330.23	320.49	311.76
25000	399.22	382.67	368.16	355.36	343.99	333.85	324.75
26000	415.19	397.98	382.89	369.57	357.75	347.20	337.73
27000	431.16	413.28	397.62	383.79	371.51	360.56	350.72
28000	447.13	428.59	412.34	398.00	385.27	373.91	363.71
29000	463.10	443.90	427.07	412.22	399.03	387.26	376.70
30000	479.07	459.20	441.79	426.43	412.79	400.62	389.69
31000	495.04	474.51	456.52	440.65	426.55	413.97	402.68
32000	511.01	489.82	471.25	454.86	440.31	427.32	415.67
33000	526.98	505.12	485.97	469.08	454.07	440.68	428.66
34000	542.94	520.43	500.70	483.29	467.83	454.03	441.65
35000	558.91	535.74	515.43	497.50	481.59	467.39	454.64
40000	638.76	612.27	589.06	568.58	550.39	534.16	519.59
45000	718.60	688.80	662.69	639.65	619.19	600.93	584.54
50000	798.45	765.34	736.32	710.72	687.99	667.70	649.49
55000	878.29	841.87	809.96	781.79	756.79	734.46	714.44
60000	958.14	918.41	883.59	852.87	825.59	801.23	779.39
65000	1037.98	994.94	957.22	923.94	894.39	868.00	844.34
70000	1117.83	1071.47	1030.85	995.01	963.18	934.77	909.29

Monthly Loan Payments 10¼%

LOAN AMOUNT	11 YEARS	11½ YEARS	12 YEARS	12½ YEARS	13 YEARS	14 YEARS	15 YEARS
100	1.27	1.24	1.21	1.19	1.16	1.12	1.09
200	2.53	2.47	2.42	2.37	2.33	2.25	2.18
300	3.80	3.71	3.63	3.56	3.49	3.37	3.27
400	5.06	4.95	4.84	4.74	4.65	4.49	4.36
500	6.33	6.18	6.05	5.93	5.81	5.62	5.45
600	7.60	7.42	7.26	7.11	6.98	6.74	6.54
700	8.86	8.66	8.47	8.30	8.14	7.86	7.63
800	10.13	9.89	9.68	9.48	9.30	8.99	8.72
900	11.40	11.13	10.89	10.67	10.46	10.11	9.81
1000	12.66	12.37	12.10	11.85	11.63	11.23	10.90
1500	18.99	18.55	18.14	17.78	17.44	16.85	16.35
2000	25.32	24.73	24.19	23.70	23.25	22.47	21.80
2500	31.65	30.91	30.24	29.63	29.07	28.08	27.25
3000	37.99	37.10	36.29	35.55	34.88	33.70	32.70
3500	44.32	43.28	42.33	41.48	40.69	39.31	38.15
4000	50.65	49.46	48.38	47.40	46.51	44.93	43.60
4500	56.98	55.64	54.43	53.33	52.32	50.55	49.05
5000	63.31	61.83	60.48	59.25	58.13	56.16	54.50
5500	69.64	68.01	66.53	65.18	63.94	61.78	59.95
6000	75.97	74.19	72.57	71.10	69.76	67.40	65.40
6500	82.30	80.37	78.62	77.03	75.57	73.01	70.85
7000	88.63	86.56	84.67	82.95	81.38	78.63	76.30
7500	94.96	92.74	90.72	88.88	87.20	84.25	81.75
8000	101.29	98.92	96.77	94.80	93.01	89.86	87.20
8500	107.62	105.10	102.81	100.73	98.82	95.48	92.65
9000	113.96	111.29	108.86	106.65	104.64	101.09	98.10
9500	120.29	117.47	114.91	112.58	110.45	106.71	103.55
10000	126.62	123.65	120.96	118.50	116.26	112.33	109.00
11000	139.28	136.02	133.05	130.35	127.89	123.56	119.89
12000	151.94	148.38	145.15	142.20	139.52	134.79	130.79
13000	164.60	160.75	157.24	154.05	151.14	146.03	141.69
14000	177.26	173.11	169.34	165.90	162.77	157.26	152.59
15000	189.93	185.48	181.43	177.76	174.39	168.49	163.49
16000	202.59	197.84	193.53	189.61	186.02	179.72	174.39
17000	215.25	210.21	205.63	201.46	197.65	190.96	185.29
18000	227.91	222.57	217.72	213.31	209.27	202.19	196.19
19000	240.57	234.94	229.82	225.16	220.90	213.42	207.09
20000	253.24	247.30	241.91	237.01	232.53	224.65	217.99
21000	265.90	259.67	254.01	248.86	244.15	235.89	228.89
22000	278.56	272.03	266.10	260.71	255.78	247.12	239.79
23000	291.22	284.40	278.20	272.56	267.40	258.35	250.69
24000	303.88	296.76	290.30	284.41	279.03	269.58	261.59
25000	316.54	309.13	302.39	296.26	290.66	280.82	272.49
26000	329.21	321.49	314.49	308.11	302.28	292.05	283.39
27000	341.87	333.86	326.58	319.96	313.91	303.28	294.29
28000	354.53	346.22	338.68	331.81	325.54	314.52	305.19
29000	367.19	358.59	350.77	343.66	337.16	325.75	316.09
30000	379.85	370.95	362.87	355.51	348.79	336.98	326.99
31000	392.51	383.32	374.97	367.36	360.41	348.21	337.88
32000	405.18	395.68	387.06	379.21	372.04	359.45	348.78
33000	417.84	408.05	399.16	391.06	383.67	370.68	359.68
34000	430.50	420.41	411.25	402.91	395.29	381.91	370.58
35000	443.16	432.78	423.35	414.76	406.92	393.14	381.48
40000	506.47	494.60	483.83	474.01	465.05	449.31	435.98
45000	569.78	556.43	544.30	533.27	523.18	505.47	490.48
50000	633.09	618.25	604.78	592.52	581.31	561.63	544.98
55000	696.40	680.08	665.26	651.77	639.45	617.80	599.47
60000	759.71	741.90	725.74	711.02	697.58	673.96	653.97
65000	823.01	803.73	786.22	770.27	755.71	730.13	708.47
70000	886.32	865.55	846.70	829.52	813.84	786.29	762.97

10½%   Monthly Loan Payments

LOAN AMOUNT	½ YEAR	1 YEAR	1½ YEARS	2 YEARS	2½ YEARS	3 YEARS	3½ YEARS
100	17.18	8.81	6.03	4.64	3.80	3.25	2.86
200	34.36	17.63	12.06	9.28	7.61	6.50	5.71
300	51.54	26.44	18.09	13.91	11.41	9.75	8.57
400	68.72	35.26	24.12	18.55	15.22	13.00	11.42
500	85.90	44.07	30.14	23.19	19.02	16.25	14.28
600	103.08	52.89	36.17	27.83	22.83	19.50	17.13
700	120.27	61.70	42.20	32.46	26.63	22.75	19.99
800	137.45	70.52	48.23	37.10	30.44	26.00	22.84
900	154.63	79.33	54.26	41.74	34.24	29.25	25.70
1000	171.81	88.15	60.29	46.38	38.04	32.50	28.55
1500	257.71	132.22	90.43	69.56	57.07	48.75	42.83
2000	343.62	176.30	120.58	92.75	76.09	65.00	57.11
2500	429.52	220.37	150.72	115.94	95.11	81.26	71.39
3000	515.42	264.45	180.86	139.13	114.13	97.51	85.66
3500	601.33	308.52	211.01	162.32	133.16	113.76	99.94
4000	687.23	352.59	241.15	185.50	152.18	130.01	114.22
4500	773.14	396.67	271.29	208.69	171.20	146.26	128.50
5000	859.04	440.74	301.44	231.88	190.22	162.51	142.77
5500	944.94	484.82	331.58	255.07	209.24	178.76	157.05
6000	1030.85	528.89	361.73	278.26	228.27	195.01	171.33
6500	1116.75	572.97	391.87	301.44	247.29	211.27	185.61
7000	1202.66	617.04	422.01	324.63	266.31	227.52	199.88
7500	1288.56	661.11	452.16	347.82	285.33	243.77	214.16
8000	1374.46	705.19	482.30	371.01	304.35	260.02	228.44
8500	1460.37	749.26	512.44	394.20	323.38	276.27	242.72
9000	1546.27	793.34	542.59	417.38	342.40	292.52	256.99
9500	1632.17	837.41	572.73	440.57	361.42	308.77	271.27
10000	1718.08	881.49	602.88	463.76	380.44	325.02	285.55
11000	1889.89	969.63	663.16	510.14	418.49	357.53	314.10
12000	2061.69	1057.78	723.45	556.51	456.53	390.03	342.66
13000	2233.50	1145.93	783.74	602.89	494.58	422.53	371.21
14000	2405.31	1234.08	844.03	649.26	532.62	455.03	399.77
15000	2577.12	1322.23	904.31	695.64	570.66	487.54	428.32
16000	2748.93	1410.38	964.60	742.02	608.71	520.04	456.88
17000	2920.73	1498.53	1024.89	788.39	646.75	552.54	485.43
18000	3092.54	1586.67	1085.18	834.77	684.80	585.04	513.99
19000	3264.35	1674.82	1145.46	881.14	722.84	617.55	542.54
20000	3436.16	1762.97	1205.75	927.52	760.89	650.05	571.09
21000	3607.97	1851.12	1266.04	973.90	798.93	682.55	599.65
22000	3779.77	1939.27	1326.33	1020.27	836.97	715.05	628.20
23000	3951.58	2027.42	1386.61	1066.65	875.02	747.56	656.76
24000	4123.39	2115.57	1446.90	1113.02	913.06	780.06	685.31
25000	4295.20	2203.72	1507.19	1159.40	951.11	812.56	713.87
26000	4467.01	2291.86	1567.48	1205.78	989.15	845.06	742.42
27000	4638.81	2380.01	1627.76	1252.15	1027.20	877.57	770.98
28000	4810.62	2468.16	1688.05	1298.53	1065.24	910.07	799.53
29000	4982.43	2556.31	1748.34	1344.91	1103.29	942.57	828.09
30000	5154.24	2644.46	1808.63	1391.28	1141.33	975.07	856.64
31000	5326.04	2732.61	1868.91	1437.66	1179.37	1007.58	885.20
32000	5497.85	2820.76	1929.20	1484.03	1217.42	1040.08	913.75
33000	5669.66	2908.90	1989.49	1530.41	1255.46	1072.58	942.31
34000	5841.47	2997.05	2049.78	1576.79	1293.51	1105.08	970.86
35000	6013.28	3085.20	2110.06	1623.16	1331.55	1137.59	999.42
40000	6872.32	3525.94	2411.50	1855.04	1521.77	1300.10	1142.19
45000	7731.35	3966.69	2712.94	2086.92	1711.99	1462.61	1284.96
50000	8590.39	4407.43	3014.38	2318.80	1902.22	1625.12	1427.74
55000	9449.43	4848.17	3315.82	2550.68	2092.44	1787.63	1570.51
60000	10308.47	5288.92	3617.25	2782.56	2282.66	1950.15	1713.28
65000	11167.51	5729.66	3918.69	3014.44	2472.88	2112.66	1856.06
70000	12026.55	6170.40	4220.13	3246.32	2663.10	2275.17	1998.83

Monthly Loan Payments 10½%

LOAN AMOUNT	4 YEARS	4½ YEARS	5 YEARS	5½ YEARS	6 YEARS	6½ YEARS	7 YEARS
100	2.56	2.33	2.15	2.00	1.88	1.77	1.69
200	5.12	4.66	4.30	4.00	3.76	3.55	3.37
300	7.68	6.99	6.45	6.00	5.63	5.32	5.06
400	10.24	9.33	8.60	8.00	7.51	7.10	6.74
500	12.80	11.66	10.75	10.00	9.39	8.87	8.43
600	15.36	13.99	12.90	12.01	11.27	10.65	10.12
700	17.92	16.32	15.05	14.01	13.15	12.42	11.80
800	20.48	18.65	17.20	16.01	15.02	14.19	13.49
900	23.04	20.98	19.34	18.01	16.90	15.97	15.17
1000	25.60	23.32	21.49	20.01	18.78	17.74	16.86
1500	38.41	34.97	32.24	30.01	28.17	26.61	25.29
2000	51.21	46.63	42.99	40.02	37.56	35.49	33.72
2500	64.01	58.29	53.73	50.02	46.95	44.36	42.15
3000	76.81	69.95	64.48	60.03	56.34	53.23	50.58
3500	89.61	81.61	75.23	70.03	65.73	62.10	59.01
4000	102.41	93.26	85.98	80.04	75.12	70.97	67.44
4500	115.22	104.92	96.72	90.04	84.51	79.84	75.87
5000	128.02	116.58	107.47	100.05	93.89	88.72	84.30
5500	140.82	128.24	118.22	110.05	103.28	97.59	92.73
6000	153.62	139.90	128.96	120.06	112.67	106.46	101.16
6500	166.42	151.56	139.71	130.06	122.06	115.33	109.59
7000	179.22	163.21	150.46	140.07	131.45	124.20	118.02
7500	192.03	174.87	161.20	150.07	140.84	133.07	126.46
8000	204.83	186.53	171.95	160.08	150.23	141.95	134.89
8500	217.63	198.19	182.70	170.08	159.62	150.82	143.32
9000	230.43	209.85	193.45	180.09	169.01	159.69	151.75
9500	243.23	221.50	204.19	190.09	178.40	168.56	160.18
10000	256.03	233.16	214.94	200.10	187.79	177.43	168.61
11000	281.64	256.48	236.43	220.11	206.57	195.18	185.47
12000	307.24	279.79	257.93	240.12	225.35	212.92	202.33
13000	332.84	303.11	279.42	260.13	244.13	230.66	219.19
14000	358.45	326.43	300.91	280.14	262.91	248.41	236.05
15000	384.05	349.74	322.41	300.15	281.68	266.15	252.91
16000	409.65	373.06	343.90	320.15	300.46	283.89	269.77
17000	435.26	396.38	365.40	340.16	319.24	301.64	286.63
18000	460.86	419.69	386.89	360.17	338.02	319.38	303.49
19000	486.46	443.01	408.38	380.18	356.80	337.12	320.35
20000	512.07	466.32	429.88	400.19	375.58	354.86	337.21
21000	537.67	489.64	451.37	420.20	394.36	372.61	354.07
22000	563.27	512.96	472.87	440.21	413.14	390.35	370.93
23000	588.88	536.27	494.36	460.22	431.92	408.09	387.80
24000	614.48	559.59	515.85	480.23	450.70	425.84	404.66
25000	640.08	582.90	537.35	500.24	469.47	443.58	421.52
26000	665.69	606.22	558.84	520.25	488.25	461.32	438.38
27000	691.29	629.54	580.34	540.26	507.03	479.07	455.24
28000	716.89	652.85	601.83	560.27	525.81	496.81	472.10
29000	742.50	676.17	623.32	580.28	544.59	514.55	488.96
30000	768.10	699.49	644.82	600.29	563.37	532.30	505.82
31000	793.70	722.80	666.31	620.30	582.15	550.04	522.68
32000	819.31	746.12	687.80	640.31	600.93	567.78	539.54
33000	844.91	769.43	709.30	660.32	619.71	585.53	556.40
34000	870.51	792.75	730.79	680.33	638.48	603.27	573.26
35000	896.12	816.07	752.29	700.34	657.26	621.01	590.12
40000	1024.14	932.65	859.76	800.39	751.16	709.73	674.43
45000	1152.15	1049.23	967.23	900.44	845.05	798.45	758.73
50000	1280.17	1165.81	1074.70	1000.48	938.95	887.16	843.03
55000	1408.19	1282.39	1182.16	1100.53	1032.84	975.88	927.34
60000	1536.20	1398.97	1289.63	1200.58	1126.74	1064.59	1011.64
65000	1664.22	1515.55	1397.10	1300.63	1220.63	1153.31	1095.94
70000	1792.24	1632.13	1504.57	1400.68	1314.53	1242.03	1180.25

10½% Monthly Loan Payments

LOAN AMOUNT	7½ YEARS	8 YEARS	8½ YEARS	9 YEARS	9½ YEARS	10 YEARS	10½ YEARS
100	1.61	1.54	1.49	1.44	1.39	1.35	1.31
200	3.22	3.09	2.97	2.87	2.78	2.70	2.63
300	4.83	4.63	4.46	4.31	4.17	4.05	3.94
400	6.44	6.18	5.94	5.74	5.56	5.40	5.25
500	8.05	7.72	7.43	7.18	6.95	6.75	6.57
600	9.66	9.26	8.92	8.61	8.34	8.10	7.88
700	11.27	10.81	10.40	10.05	9.73	9.45	9.19
800	12.88	12.35	11.89	11.48	11.12	10.79	10.50
900	14.49	13.90	13.38	12.92	12.51	12.14	11.82
1000	16.10	15.44	14.86	14.35	13.90	13.49	13.13
1500	24.15	23.16	22.29	21.53	20.85	20.24	19.70
2000	32.20	30.88	29.72	28.70	27.80	26.99	26.26
2500	40.25	38.60	37.15	35.88	34.74	33.73	32.83
3000	48.30	46.32	44.58	43.05	41.69	40.48	39.39
3500	56.35	54.04	52.01	50.23	48.64	47.23	45.96
4000	64.40	61.76	59.45	57.40	55.59	53.97	52.52
4500	72.45	69.48	66.88	64.58	62.54	60.72	59.09
5000	80.50	77.20	74.31	71.75	69.49	67.47	65.65
5500	88.55	84.92	81.74	78.93	76.44	74.21	72.22
6000	96.60	92.64	89.17	86.11	83.39	80.96	78.79
6500	104.65	100.36	96.60	93.28	90.34	87.71	85.35
7000	112.70	108.08	104.03	100.46	97.28	94.45	91.92
7500	120.75	115.80	111.46	107.63	104.23	101.20	98.48
8000	128.80	123.52	118.89	114.81	111.18	107.95	105.05
8500	136.86	131.24	126.32	121.98	118.13	114.69	111.61
9000	144.91	138.96	133.75	129.16	125.08	121.44	118.18
9500	152.96	146.68	141.18	136.33	132.03	128.19	124.74
10000	161.01	154.40	148.61	143.51	138.98	134.93	131.31
11000	177.11	169.84	163.47	157.86	152.88	148.43	144.44
12000	193.21	185.28	178.34	172.21	166.77	161.92	157.57
13000	209.31	200.72	193.20	186.56	180.67	175.42	170.70
14000	225.41	216.16	208.06	200.91	194.57	188.91	183.83
15000	241.51	231.60	222.92	215.26	208.47	202.40	196.96
16000	257.61	247.04	237.78	229.61	222.36	215.90	210.10
17000	273.71	262.48	252.64	243.96	236.26	229.39	223.23
18000	289.81	277.92	267.50	258.32	250.16	242.88	236.36
19000	305.91	293.36	282.37	272.67	264.06	256.38	249.49
20000	322.01	308.80	297.23	287.02	277.96	269.87	262.62
21000	338.11	324.24	312.09	301.37	291.85	283.36	275.75
22000	354.21	339.68	326.95	315.72	305.75	296.86	288.88
23000	370.31	355.12	341.81	330.07	319.65	310.35	302.01
24000	386.41	370.56	356.67	344.42	333.55	323.84	315.14
25000	402.51	386.00	371.53	358.77	347.44	337.34	328.27
26000	418.62	401.44	386.39	373.12	361.34	350.83	341.41
27000	434.72	416.88	401.26	387.47	375.24	364.32	354.54
28000	450.82	432.32	416.12	401.82	389.14	377.82	367.67
29000	466.92	447.76	430.98	416.17	403.04	391.31	380.80
30000	483.02	463.20	445.84	430.53	416.93	404.80	393.93
31000	499.12	478.64	460.70	444.88	430.83	418.30	407.06
32000	515.22	494.08	475.56	459.23	444.73	431.79	420.19
33000	531.32	509.52	490.42	473.58	458.63	445.29	433.32
34000	547.42	524.96	505.29	487.93	472.53	458.78	446.45
35000	563.52	540.40	520.15	502.28	486.42	472.27	459.58
40000	644.02	617.60	594.45	574.03	555.91	539.74	525.24
45000	724.53	694.80	668.76	645.79	625.40	607.21	590.89
50000	805.03	772.00	743.07	717.54	694.89	674.67	656.55
55000	885.53	849.20	817.37	789.30	764.38	742.14	722.20
60000	966.04	926.40	891.68	861.05	833.87	809.61	787.86
65000	1046.54	1003.60	965.99	932.81	903.36	877.08	853.51
70000	1127.04	1080.80	1040.29	1004.56	972.85	944.54	919.17

Monthly Loan Payments 10½%

LOAN AMOUNT	11 YEARS	11½ YEARS	12 YEARS	12½ YEARS	13 YEARS	14 YEARS	15 YEARS
100	1.28	1.25	1.22	1.20	1.18	1.14	1.11
200	2.56	2.50	2.45	2.40	2.36	2.28	2.21
300	3.84	3.75	3.67	3.60	3.53	3.42	3.32
400	5.12	5.00	4.90	4.80	4.71	4.55	4.42
500	6.40	6.25	6.12	6.00	5.89	5.69	5.53
600	7.68	7.51	7.34	7.20	7.07	6.83	6.63
700	8.96	8.76	8.57	8.40	8.24	7.97	7.74
800	10.24	10.01	9.79	9.60	9.42	9.11	8.84
900	11.52	11.26	11.02	10.80	10.60	10.25	9.95
1000	12.80	12.51	12.24	12.00	11.78	11.38	11.05
1500	19.21	18.76	18.36	18.00	17.66	17.08	16.58
2000	25.61	25.02	24.48	24.00	23.55	22.77	22.11
2500	32.01	31.27	30.60	29.99	29.44	28.46	27.63
3000	38.41	37.53	36.72	35.99	35.33	34.15	33.16
3500	44.82	43.78	42.84	41.99	41.21	39.85	38.69
4000	51.22	50.04	48.97	47.99	47.10	45.54	44.22
4500	57.62	56.29	55.09	53.99	52.99	51.23	49.74
5000	64.02	62.55	61.21	59.99	58.88	56.92	55.27
5500	70.42	68.80	67.33	65.99	64.76	62.61	60.80
6000	76.83	75.06	73.45	71.99	70.65	68.31	66.32
6500	83.23	81.31	79.57	77.98	76.54	74.00	71.85
7000	89.63	87.56	85.69	83.98	82.43	79.69	77.38
7500	96.03	93.82	91.81	89.98	88.31	85.38	82.90
8000	102.44	100.07	97.93	95.98	94.20	91.07	88.43
8500	108.84	106.33	104.05	101.98	100.09	96.77	93.96
9000	115.24	112.58	110.17	107.98	105.98	102.46	99.49
9500	121.64	118.84	116.29	113.98	111.86	108.15	105.01
10000	128.04	125.09	122.41	119.98	117.75	113.84	110.54
11000	140.85	137.60	134.66	131.97	129.53	125.23	121.59
12000	153.65	150.11	146.90	143.97	141.30	136.61	132.65
13000	166.46	162.62	159.14	155.97	153.08	148.00	143.70
14000	179.26	175.13	171.38	167.97	164.85	159.38	154.76
15000	192.07	187.64	183.62	179.96	176.63	170.77	165.81
16000	204.87	200.15	195.86	191.96	188.40	182.15	176.86
17000	217.68	212.66	208.10	203.96	200.18	193.53	187.92
18000	230.48	225.17	220.35	215.96	211.95	204.92	198.97
19000	243.28	237.68	232.59	227.95	223.73	216.30	210.03
20000	256.09	250.19	244.83	239.95	235.50	227.69	221.08
21000	268.89	262.69	257.07	251.95	247.28	239.07	232.13
22000	281.70	275.20	269.31	263.95	259.05	250.46	243.19
23000	294.50	287.71	281.55	275.94	270.83	261.84	254.24
24000	307.31	300.22	293.79	287.94	282.60	273.22	265.30
25000	320.11	312.73	306.04	299.94	294.38	284.61	276.35
26000	332.92	325.24	318.28	311.94	306.15	295.99	287.40
27000	345.72	337.75	330.52	323.94	317.93	307.38	298.46
28000	358.52	350.26	342.76	335.93	329.70	318.76	309.51
29000	371.33	362.77	355.00	347.93	341.48	330.15	320.57
30000	384.13	375.28	367.24	359.93	353.25	341.53	331.62
31000	396.94	387.79	379.48	371.93	365.03	352.91	342.67
32000	409.74	400.30	391.73	383.92	376.80	364.30	353.73
33000	422.55	412.81	403.97	395.92	388.58	375.68	364.78
34000	435.35	425.31	416.21	407.92	400.35	387.07	375.84
35000	448.16	437.82	428.45	419.92	412.13	398.45	386.89
40000	512.18	500.37	489.66	479.90	471.00	455.37	442.16
45000	576.20	562.92	550.86	539.89	529.88	512.30	497.43
50000	640.22	625.46	612.07	599.88	588.75	569.22	552.70
55000	704.25	688.01	673.28	659.87	647.63	626.14	607.97
60000	768.27	750.56	734.48	719.86	706.50	683.06	663.24
65000	832.29	813.10	795.69	779.84	765.38	739.98	718.51
70000	896.31	875.65	856.90	839.83	824.25	796.90	773.78

47

10¾% Monthly Loan Payments

LOAN AMOUNT	½ YEAR	1 YEAR	1½ YEARS	2 YEARS	2½ YEARS	3 YEARS	3½ YEARS
100	17.19	8.83	6.04	4.65	3.82	3.26	2.8
200	34.39	17.65	12.08	9.30	7.63	6.52	5.7
300	51.58	26.48	18.12	13.95	11.45	9.79	8.6
400	68.77	35.31	24.16	18.60	15.26	13.05	11.4
500	85.97	44.13	30.20	23.25	19.08	16.31	14.3
600	103.16	52.96	36.24	27.90	22.90	19.57	17.2
700	120.35	61.79	42.28	32.54	26.71	22.83	20.0
800	137.54	70.61	48.32	37.19	30.53	26.10	22.9
900	154.74	79.44	54.36	41.84	34.34	29.36	25.8
1000	171.93	88.27	60.40	46.49	38.16	32.62	28.6
1500	257.90	132.40	90.60	69.74	57.24	48.93	43.0
2000	343.86	176.53	120.81	92.98	76.32	65.24	57.3
2500	429.83	220.66	151.01	116.23	95.40	81.55	71.6
3000	515.79	264.80	181.21	139.48	114.48	97.86	86.0
3500	601.76	308.93	211.41	162.72	133.56	114.17	100.3
4000	687.72	353.06	241.61	185.97	152.64	130.48	114.7
4500	773.69	397.19	271.81	209.21	171.72	146.79	129.0
5000	859.66	441.33	302.01	232.46	190.81	163.10	143.3
5500	945.62	485.46	332.22	255.71	209.89	179.41	157.7
6000	1031.59	529.59	362.42	278.95	228.97	195.72	172.0
6500	1117.55	573.72	392.62	302.20	248.05	212.03	186.3
7000	1203.52	617.86	422.82	325.44	267.13	228.34	200.7
7500	1289.48	661.99	453.02	348.69	286.21	244.65	215.0
8000	1375.45	706.12	483.22	371.93	305.29	260.96	229.3
8500	1461.42	750.25	513.43	395.18	324.37	277.27	243.7
9000	1547.38	794.39	543.63	418.43	343.45	293.58	258.0
9500	1633.35	838.52	573.83	441.67	362.53	309.89	272.4
10000	1719.31	882.65	604.03	464.92	381.61	326.20	286.7
11000	1891.24	970.92	664.43	511.41	419.77	358.82	315.4
12000	2063.17	1059.18	724.84	557.90	457.93	391.45	344.0
13000	2235.11	1147.45	785.24	604.39	496.09	424.07	372.7
14000	2407.04	1235.71	845.64	650.89	534.26	456.69	401.4
15000	2578.97	1323.98	906.04	697.38	572.42	489.31	430.1
16000	2750.90	1412.24	966.45	743.87	610.58	521.93	458.7
17000	2922.83	1500.51	1026.85	790.36	648.74	554.55	487.4
18000	3094.76	1588.77	1087.25	836.85	686.90	587.17	516.1
19000	3266.69	1677.04	1147.66	883.35	725.06	619.79	544.8
20000	3438.62	1765.30	1208.06	929.84	763.22	652.41	573.4
21000	3610.56	1853.57	1268.46	976.33	801.38	685.03	602.1
22000	3782.49	1941.83	1328.87	1022.82	839.54	717.65	630.8
23000	3954.42	2030.10	1389.27	1069.31	877.70	750.27	659.5
24000	4126.35	2118.36	1449.67	1115.80	915.87	782.89	688.1
25000	4298.28	2206.63	1510.07	1162.30	954.03	815.51	716.8
26000	4470.21	2294.89	1570.48	1208.79	992.19	848.13	745.5
27000	4642.14	2383.16	1630.88	1255.28	1030.35	880.75	774.2
28000	4814.07	2471.42	1691.28	1301.77	1068.51	913.37	802.8
29000	4986.00	2559.69	1751.69	1348.26	1106.67	945.99	831.5
30000	5157.94	2647.95	1812.09	1394.76	1144.83	978.61	860.2
31000	5329.87	2736.22	1872.49	1441.25	1182.99	1011.23	888.9
32000	5501.80	2824.48	1932.90	1487.74	1221.15	1043.85	917.5
33000	5673.73	2912.75	1993.30	1534.23	1259.32	1076.47	946.2
34000	5845.66	3001.01	2053.70	1580.72	1297.48	1109.10	974.9
35000	6017.59	3089.28	2114.10	1627.21	1335.64	1141.72	1003.6
40000	6877.25	3530.60	2416.12	1859.67	1526.44	1304.82	1146.9
45000	7736.90	3971.93	2718.13	2092.13	1717.25	1467.92	1290.3
50000	8596.56	4413.25	3020.15	2324.59	1908.05	1631.02	1433.7
55000	9456.22	4854.58	3322.16	2557.05	2098.86	1794.12	1577.0
60000	10315.87	5295.91	3624.18	2789.51	2289.66	1957.23	1720.4
65000	11175.53	5737.23	3926.19	3021.97	2480.47	2120.33	1863.8
70000	12035.18	6178.56	4228.21	3254.43	2671.28	2283.43	2007.1

Monthly Loan Payments 10¾%

LOAN AMOUNT	4 YEARS	4½ YEARS	5 YEARS	5½ YEARS	6 YEARS	6½ YEARS	7 YEARS
100	2.57	2.34	2.16	2.01	1.89	1.79	1.70
200	5.14	4.69	4.32	4.03	3.78	3.57	3.40
300	7.72	7.03	6.49	6.04	5.67	5.36	5.10
400	10.29	9.38	8.65	8.05	7.56	7.15	6.80
500	12.86	11.72	10.81	10.07	9.45	8.94	8.50
600	15.43	14.06	12.97	12.08	11.34	10.72	10.19
700	18.01	16.41	15.13	14.09	13.23	12.51	11.89
800	20.58	18.75	17.29	16.11	15.13	14.30	13.59
900	23.15	21.09	19.46	18.12	17.02	16.08	15.29
1000	25.72	23.44	21.62	20.14	18.91	17.87	16.99
1500	38.59	35.16	32.43	30.20	28.36	26.81	25.49
2000	51.45	46.88	43.24	40.27	37.81	35.74	33.98
2500	64.31	58.60	54.04	50.34	47.27	44.68	42.48
3000	77.17	70.32	64.85	60.41	56.72	53.62	50.97
3500	90.03	82.04	75.66	70.47	66.17	62.55	59.47
4000	102.90	93.75	86.47	80.54	75.63	71.49	67.97
4500	115.76	105.47	97.28	90.61	85.08	80.42	76.46
5000	128.62	117.19	108.09	100.68	94.53	89.36	84.96
5500	141.48	128.91	118.90	110.74	103.98	98.30	93.45
6000	154.35	140.63	129.71	120.81	113.44	107.23	101.95
6500	167.21	152.35	140.52	130.88	122.89	116.17	110.44
7000	180.07	164.07	151.33	140.95	132.34	125.11	118.94
7500	192.93	175.79	162.13	151.02	141.80	134.04	127.43
8000	205.79	187.51	172.94	161.08	151.25	142.98	135.93
8500	218.66	199.23	183.75	171.15	160.70	151.91	144.43
9000	231.52	210.95	194.56	181.22	170.16	160.85	152.92
9500	244.38	222.67	205.37	191.29	179.61	169.79	161.42
10000	257.24	234.39	216.18	201.35	189.06	178.72	169.91
11000	282.97	257.83	237.80	221.49	207.97	196.59	186.90
12000	308.69	281.26	259.42	241.62	226.88	214.47	203.90
13000	334.42	304.70	281.03	261.76	245.78	232.34	220.89
14000	360.14	328.14	302.65	281.89	264.69	250.21	237.88
15000	385.86	351.58	324.27	302.03	283.59	268.08	254.87
16000	411.59	375.02	345.89	322.17	302.50	285.96	271.86
17000	437.31	398.46	367.51	342.30	321.41	303.83	288.85
18000	463.04	421.90	389.12	362.44	340.31	321.70	305.84
19000	488.76	445.33	410.74	382.57	359.22	339.57	322.83
20000	514.49	468.77	432.36	402.71	378.13	357.44	339.83
21000	540.21	492.21	453.98	422.84	397.03	375.32	356.82
22000	565.93	515.65	475.59	442.98	415.94	393.19	373.81
23000	591.66	539.09	497.21	463.11	434.84	411.06	390.80
24000	617.38	562.53	518.83	483.25	453.75	428.93	407.79
25000	643.11	585.97	540.45	503.38	472.66	446.80	424.78
26000	668.83	609.40	562.07	523.52	491.56	464.68	441.77
27000	694.56	632.84	583.68	543.65	510.47	482.55	458.76
28000	720.28	656.28	605.30	563.79	529.38	500.42	475.76
29000	746.00	679.72	626.92	583.93	548.28	518.29	492.75
30000	771.73	703.16	648.54	604.06	567.19	536.17	509.74
31000	797.45	726.60	670.16	624.20	586.09	554.04	526.73
32000	823.18	750.04	691.77	644.33	605.00	571.91	543.72
33000	848.90	773.48	713.39	664.47	623.91	589.78	560.71
34000	874.63	796.91	735.01	684.60	642.81	607.65	577.70
35000	900.35	820.35	756.63	704.74	661.72	625.53	594.69
40000	1028.97	937.55	864.72	805.41	756.25	714.89	679.65
45000	1157.59	1054.74	972.81	906.09	850.78	804.25	764.61
50000	1286.21	1171.93	1080.90	1006.77	945.31	893.61	849.56
55000	1414.84	1289.13	1188.99	1107.44	1039.85	982.97	934.52
60000	1543.46	1406.32	1297.08	1208.12	1134.38	1072.33	1019.48
65000	1672.08	1523.51	1405.17	1308.80	1228.91	1161.69	1104.43
70000	1800.70	1640.71	1513.26	1409.47	1323.44	1251.05	1189.39

10¾%   Monthly Loan Payments

LOAN AMOUNT	7½ YEARS	8 YEARS	8½ YEARS	9 YEARS	9½ YEARS	10 YEARS	10½ YEARS
100	1.62	1.56	1.50	1.45	1.40	1.36	1.33
200	3.25	3.11	3.00	2.90	2.81	2.73	2.65
300	4.87	4.67	4.50	4.35	4.21	4.09	3.98
400	6.49	6.23	6.00	5.80	5.61	5.45	5.31
500	8.12	7.79	7.50	7.24	7.02	6.82	6.64
600	9.74	9.34	9.00	8.69	8.42	8.18	7.96
700	11.36	10.90	10.50	10.14	9.83	9.54	9.29
800	12.99	12.46	12.00	11.59	11.23	10.91	10.62
900	14.61	14.02	13.50	13.04	12.63	12.27	11.95
1000	16.23	15.57	14.99	14.49	14.04	13.63	13.27
1500	24.35	23.36	22.50	21.73	21.05	20.45	19.91
2000	32.47	31.15	29.99	28.98	28.07	27.27	26.55
2500	40.58	38.93	37.49	36.22	35.09	34.08	33.18
3000	48.70	46.72	44.99	43.46	42.11	40.90	39.82
3500	56.81	54.51	52.49	50.71	49.13	47.72	46.46
4000	64.93	62.30	59.99	57.95	56.15	54.54	53.09
4500	73.05	70.08	67.49	65.20	63.16	61.35	59.73
5000	81.16	77.87	74.98	72.44	70.18	68.17	66.36
5500	89.28	85.66	82.48	79.68	77.20	74.99	73.00
6000	97.40	93.44	89.98	86.93	84.22	81.80	79.64
6500	105.51	101.23	97.48	94.17	91.24	88.62	86.27
7000	113.63	109.02	104.98	101.42	98.26	95.44	92.91
7500	121.75	116.80	112.48	108.66	105.27	102.25	99.55
8000	129.86	124.59	119.97	115.90	112.29	109.07	106.18
8500	137.98	132.38	127.47	123.15	119.31	115.89	112.82
9000	146.10	140.17	134.97	130.39	126.33	122.70	119.46
9500	154.21	147.95	142.47	137.64	133.35	129.52	126.09
10000	162.33	155.74	149.97	144.88	140.37	136.34	132.73
11000	178.56	171.31	164.97	159.37	154.40	149.97	146.00
12000	194.79	186.89	179.96	173.86	168.44	163.61	159.28
13000	211.03	202.46	194.96	188.34	182.48	177.24	172.55
14000	227.26	218.03	209.96	202.83	196.51	190.87	185.82
15000	243.49	233.61	224.95	217.32	210.55	204.51	199.09
16000	259.73	249.18	239.95	231.81	224.59	218.14	212.37
17000	275.96	264.76	254.95	246.30	238.62	231.78	225.64
18000	292.19	280.33	269.94	260.78	252.66	245.41	238.91
19000	308.42	295.90	284.94	275.27	266.69	259.04	252.19
20000	324.66	311.48	299.94	289.76	280.73	272.68	265.46
21000	340.89	327.05	314.93	304.25	294.77	286.31	278.73
22000	357.12	342.63	329.93	318.74	308.80	299.95	292.00
23000	373.36	358.20	344.93	333.22	322.84	313.58	305.28
24000	389.59	373.77	359.92	347.71	336.88	327.21	318.55
25000	405.82	389.35	374.92	362.20	350.91	340.85	331.82
26000	422.05	404.92	389.92	376.69	364.95	354.48	345.10
27000	438.29	420.50	404.92	391.18	378.99	368.11	358.37
28000	454.52	436.07	419.91	405.66	393.02	381.75	371.64
29000	470.75	451.64	434.91	420.15	407.06	395.38	384.91
30000	486.99	467.22	449.91	434.64	421.10	409.02	398.19
31000	503.22	482.79	464.90	449.13	435.13	422.65	411.46
32000	519.45	498.36	479.90	463.62	449.17	436.28	424.73
33000	535.68	513.94	494.90	478.10	463.21	449.92	438.01
34000	551.92	529.51	509.89	492.59	477.24	463.55	451.28
35000	568.15	545.09	524.89	507.08	491.28	477.19	464.55
40000	649.31	622.96	599.87	579.52	561.46	545.35	530.92
45000	730.48	700.83	674.86	651.96	631.65	613.52	597.28
50000	811.64	778.70	749.84	724.40	701.83	681.69	663.65
55000	892.81	856.56	824.83	796.84	772.01	749.86	730.01
60000	973.97	934.43	899.81	869.28	842.19	818.03	796.38
65000	1055.13	1012.30	974.80	941.72	912.38	886.20	862.74
70000	1136.30	1090.17	1049.78	1014.16	982.56	954.37	929.10

50

Monthly Loan Payments   10¾%

LOAN AMOUNT	11 YEARS	11½ YEARS	12 YEARS	12½ YEARS	13 YEARS	14 YEARS	15 YEARS
100	1.29	1.27	1.24	1.21	1.19	1.15	1.12
200	2.59	2.53	2.48	2.43	2.38	2.31	2.24
300	3.88	3.80	3.72	3.64	3.58	3.46	3.36
400	5.18	5.06	4.96	4.86	4.77	4.61	4.48
500	6.47	6.33	6.19	6.07	5.96	5.77	5.60
600	7.77	7.59	7.43	7.29	7.15	6.92	6.73
700	9.06	8.86	8.67	8.50	8.35	8.08	7.85
800	10.36	10.12	9.91	9.72	9.54	9.23	8.97
900	11.65	11.39	11.15	10.93	10.73	10.38	10.09
1000	12.95	12.65	12.39	12.15	11.92	11.54	11.21
1500	19.42	18.98	18.58	18.22	17.89	17.31	16.81
2000	25.90	25.31	24.78	24.29	23.85	23.07	22.42
2500	32.37	31.64	30.97	30.36	29.81	28.84	28.02
3000	38.84	37.96	37.16	36.44	35.77	34.61	33.63
3500	45.32	44.29	43.36	42.51	41.74	40.38	39.23
4000	51.79	50.62	49.55	48.58	47.70	46.15	44.84
4500	58.27	56.94	55.75	54.66	53.66	51.92	50.44
5000	64.74	63.27	61.94	60.73	59.62	57.68	56.05
5500	71.21	69.60	68.13	66.80	65.59	63.45	61.65
6000	77.69	75.93	74.33	72.87	71.55	69.22	67.26
6500	84.16	82.25	80.52	78.95	77.51	74.99	72.86
7000	90.64	88.58	86.72	85.02	83.47	80.76	78.47
7500	97.11	94.91	92.91	91.09	89.44	86.53	84.07
8000	103.58	101.23	99.10	97.17	95.40	92.30	89.68
8500	110.06	107.56	105.30	103.24	101.36	98.06	95.28
9000	116.53	113.89	111.49	109.31	107.32	103.83	100.89
9500	123.01	120.22	117.69	115.38	113.28	109.60	106.49
10000	129.48	126.54	123.88	121.46	119.25	115.37	112.09
11000	142.43	139.20	136.27	133.60	131.17	126.91	123.30
12000	155.38	151.85	148.66	145.75	143.10	138.44	134.51
13000	168.32	164.51	161.04	157.89	155.02	149.98	145.72
14000	181.27	177.16	173.43	170.04	166.95	161.52	156.93
15000	194.22	189.82	185.82	182.19	178.87	173.05	168.14
16000	207.17	202.47	198.21	194.33	190.79	184.59	179.35
17000	220.12	215.12	210.60	206.48	202.72	196.13	190.56
18000	233.06	227.78	222.98	218.62	214.64	207.67	201.77
19000	246.01	240.43	235.37	230.77	226.57	219.20	212.98
20000	258.96	253.09	247.76	242.92	238.49	230.74	224.19
21000	271.91	265.74	260.15	255.06	250.42	242.28	235.40
22000	284.86	278.40	272.54	267.21	262.34	253.81	246.61
23000	297.80	291.05	284.92	279.35	274.27	265.35	257.82
24000	310.75	303.70	297.31	291.50	286.19	276.89	269.03
25000	323.70	316.36	309.70	303.64	298.12	288.42	280.24
26000	336.65	329.01	322.09	315.79	310.04	299.96	291.45
27000	349.60	341.67	334.48	327.94	321.97	311.50	302.66
28000	362.54	354.32	346.87	340.08	333.89	323.03	313.87
29000	375.49	366.98	359.25	352.23	345.82	334.57	325.07
30000	388.44	379.63	371.64	364.37	357.74	346.11	336.28
31000	401.39	392.28	384.03	376.52	369.67	357.65	347.49
32000	414.34	404.94	396.42	388.66	381.59	369.18	358.70
33000	427.28	417.59	408.81	400.81	393.51	380.72	369.91
34000	440.23	430.25	421.19	412.96	405.44	392.26	381.12
35000	453.18	442.90	433.58	425.10	417.36	403.79	392.33
40000	517.92	506.17	495.52	485.83	476.99	461.48	448.38
45000	582.66	569.45	557.46	546.56	536.61	519.16	504.43
50000	647.40	632.72	619.40	607.29	596.23	576.85	560.47
55000	712.14	695.99	681.34	668.02	655.86	634.53	616.52
60000	776.88	759.26	743.28	728.75	715.48	692.22	672.57
65000	841.62	822.53	805.22	789.47	775.10	749.90	728.62
70000	906.36	885.80	867.16	850.20	834.73	807.59	784.66

11% Monthly Loan Payments

LOAN AMOUNT	½ YEAR	1 YEAR	1½ YEARS	2 YEARS	2½ YEARS	3 YEARS	3½ YEARS
100	17.21	8.84	6.05	4.66	3.83	3.27	2.8
200	34.41	17.68	12.10	9.32	7.66	6.55	5.7
300	51.62	26.51	18.16	13.98	11.48	9.82	8.6
400	68.82	35.35	24.21	18.64	15.31	13.10	11.5
500	86.03	44.19	30.26	23.30	19.14	16.37	14.4
600	103.23	53.03	36.31	27.96	22.97	19.64	17.2
700	120.44	61.87	42.36	32.63	26.79	22.92	20.1
800	137.64	70.71	48.41	37.29	30.62	26.19	23.0
900	154.85	79.54	54.47	41.95	34.45	29.46	25.9
1000	172.05	88.38	60.52	46.61	38.28	32.74	28.7
1500	258.08	132.57	90.78	69.91	57.42	49.11	43.1
2000	344.11	176.76	121.04	93.22	76.56	65.48	57.5
2500	430.14	220.95	151.30	116.52	95.70	81.85	71.9
3000	516.16	265.14	181.56	139.82	114.83	98.22	86.3
3500	602.19	309.34	211.81	163.13	133.97	114.59	100.7
4000	688.22	353.53	242.07	186.43	153.11	130.95	115.1
4500	774.25	397.72	272.33	209.74	172.25	147.32	129.5
5000	860.27	441.91	302.59	233.04	191.39	163.69	143.9
5500	946.30	486.10	332.85	256.34	210.53	180.06	158.3
6000	1032.33	530.29	363.11	279.65	229.67	196.43	172.7
6500	1118.35	574.48	393.37	302.95	248.81	212.80	187.1
7000	1204.38	618.67	423.63	326.25	267.95	229.17	201.5
7500	1290.41	662.86	453.89	349.56	287.09	245.54	215.9
8000	1376.44	707.05	484.15	372.86	306.22	261.91	230.3
8500	1462.46	751.24	514.41	396.17	325.36	278.28	244.7
9000	1548.49	795.43	544.67	419.47	344.50	294.65	259.1
9500	1634.52	839.63	574.93	442.77	363.64	311.02	273.5
10000	1720.55	883.82	605.19	466.08	382.78	327.39	287.9
11000	1892.60	972.20	665.70	512.69	421.06	360.13	316.7
12000	2064.65	1060.58	726.22	559.29	459.34	392.86	345.5
13000	2236.71	1148.96	786.74	605.90	497.61	425.60	374.3
14000	2408.76	1237.34	847.26	652.51	535.89	458.34	403.1
15000	2580.82	1325.72	907.78	699.12	574.17	491.08	431.9
16000	2752.87	1414.11	968.30	745.73	612.45	523.82	460.7
17000	2924.93	1502.49	1028.82	792.33	650.73	556.56	489.5
18000	3096.98	1590.87	1089.33	838.94	689.01	589.30	518.2
19000	3269.04	1679.25	1149.85	885.55	727.28	622.04	547.0
20000	3441.09	1767.63	1210.37	932.16	765.56	654.77	575.8
21000	3613.15	1856.01	1270.89	978.76	803.84	687.51	604.6
22000	3785.20	1944.40	1331.41	1025.37	842.12	720.25	633.4
23000	3957.25	2032.78	1391.93	1071.98	880.40	752.99	662.2
24000	4129.31	2121.16	1452.45	1118.59	918.67	785.73	691.0
25000	4301.36	2209.54	1512.96	1165.20	956.95	818.47	719.8
26000	4473.42	2297.92	1573.48	1211.80	995.23	851.21	748.6
27000	4645.47	2386.30	1634.00	1258.41	1033.51	883.95	777.4
28000	4817.53	2474.69	1694.52	1305.02	1071.79	916.68	806.2
29000	4989.58	2563.07	1755.04	1351.63	1110.06	949.42	835.0
30000	5161.64	2651.45	1815.56	1398.24	1148.34	982.16	863.8
31000	5333.69	2739.83	1876.07	1444.84	1186.62	1014.90	892.6
32000	5505.75	2828.21	1936.59	1491.45	1224.90	1047.64	921.4
33000	5677.80	2916.59	1997.11	1538.06	1263.18	1080.38	950.2
34000	5849.85	3004.98	2057.63	1584.67	1301.45	1113.12	978.9
35000	6021.91	3093.36	2118.15	1631.27	1339.73	1145.86	1007.7
40000	6882.18	3535.27	2420.74	1864.31	1531.12	1309.55	1151.7
45000	7742.45	3977.17	2723.33	2097.35	1722.51	1473.24	1295.7
50000	8602.73	4419.08	3025.93	2330.39	1913.90	1636.94	1439.6
55000	9463.00	4860.99	3328.52	2563.43	2105.29	1800.63	1583.6
60000	10323.27	5302.90	3631.11	2796.42	2296.68	1964.32	1727.6
65000	11183.55	5744.81	3933.71	3029.51	2488.07	2128.02	1871.6
70000	12043.82	6186.72	4236.30	3262.55	2679.46	2291.71	2015.5

Monthly Loan Payments   11%

LOAN AMOUNT	4 YEARS	4½ YEARS	5 YEARS	5½ YEARS	6 YEARS	6½ YEARS	7 YEARS
100	2.58	2.36	2.17	2.03	1.90	1.80	1.71
200	5.17	4.71	4.35	4.05	3.81	3.60	3.42
300	7.75	7.07	6.52	6.08	5.71	5.40	5.14
400	10.34	9.42	8.70	8.10	7.61	7.20	6.85
500	12.92	11.78	10.87	10.13	9.52	9.00	8.56
600	15.51	14.14	13.05	12.16	11.42	10.80	10.27
700	18.09	16.49	15.22	14.18	13.32	12.60	11.99
800	20.68	18.85	17.39	16.21	15.23	14.40	13.70
900	23.26	21.21	19.57	18.24	17.13	16.20	15.41
1000	25.85	23.56	21.74	20.26	19.03	18.00	17.12
1500	38.77	35.34	32.61	30.39	28.55	27.00	25.68
2000	51.69	47.12	43.48	40.52	38.07	36.00	34.24
2500	64.61	58.90	54.36	50.65	47.59	45.00	42.81
3000	77.54	70.68	65.23	60.78	57.10	54.01	51.37
3500	90.46	82.47	76.10	70.92	66.62	63.01	59.93
4000	103.38	94.25	86.97	81.05	76.14	72.01	68.49
4500	116.30	106.03	97.84	91.18	85.65	81.01	77.05
5000	129.23	117.81	108.71	101.31	95.17	90.01	85.61
5500	142.15	129.59	119.58	111.44	104.69	99.01	94.17
6000	155.07	141.37	130.45	121.57	114.20	108.01	102.73
6500	168.00	153.15	141.33	131.70	123.72	117.01	111.30
7000	180.92	164.93	152.20	141.83	133.24	126.01	119.86
7500	193.84	176.71	163.07	151.96	142.76	135.01	128.42
8000	206.76	188.49	173.94	162.09	152.27	144.01	136.98
8500	219.69	200.27	184.81	172.22	161.79	153.01	145.54
9000	232.61	212.05	195.68	182.35	171.31	162.02	154.10
9500	245.53	223.83	206.55	192.48	180.82	171.02	162.66
10000	258.46	235.61	217.42	202.61	190.34	180.02	171.22
11000	284.30	259.18	239.17	222.88	209.37	198.02	188.35
12000	310.15	282.74	260.91	243.14	228.41	216.02	205.47
13000	335.99	306.30	282.65	263.40	247.44	234.02	222.59
14000	361.84	329.86	304.39	283.66	266.48	252.02	239.71
15000	387.68	353.42	326.14	303.92	285.51	270.03	256.84
16000	413.53	376.98	347.88	324.18	304.55	288.03	273.96
17000	439.37	400.55	369.62	344.45	323.58	306.03	291.08
18000	465.22	424.11	391.36	364.71	342.61	324.03	308.20
19000	491.06	447.67	413.11	384.97	361.65	342.03	325.33
20000	516.91	471.23	434.85	405.23	380.68	360.03	342.45
21000	542.76	494.79	456.59	425.49	399.72	378.04	359.57
22000	568.60	518.35	478.33	445.75	418.75	396.04	376.69
23000	594.45	541.91	500.08	466.01	437.78	414.04	393.82
24000	620.29	565.48	521.82	486.28	456.82	432.04	410.94
25000	646.14	589.04	543.56	506.54	475.85	450.04	428.06
26000	671.98	612.60	565.30	526.80	494.89	468.04	445.18
27000	697.83	636.16	587.05	547.06	513.92	486.05	462.31
28000	723.67	659.72	608.79	567.32	532.95	504.05	479.43
29000	749.52	683.28	630.53	587.58	551.99	522.05	496.55
30000	775.37	706.84	652.27	607.84	571.02	540.05	513.67
31000	801.21	730.41	674.02	628.11	590.06	558.05	530.80
32000	827.06	753.97	695.76	648.37	609.09	576.05	547.92
33000	852.90	777.53	717.50	668.63	628.12	594.06	565.04
34000	878.75	801.09	739.24	688.89	647.16	612.06	582.16
35000	904.59	824.65	760.98	709.15	666.19	630.06	599.29
40000	1033.82	942.46	869.70	810.46	761.36	720.07	684.90
45000	1163.05	1060.27	978.41	911.77	856.53	810.08	770.51
50000	1292.28	1178.07	1087.12	1013.07	951.70	900.08	856.12
55000	1421.50	1295.88	1195.83	1114.38	1046.87	990.09	941.73
60000	1550.73	1413.69	1304.55	1215.69	1142.04	1080.10	1027.35
65000	1679.96	1531.50	1413.26	1317.00	1237.22	1170.11	1112.96
70000	1809.19	1649.30	1521.97	1418.30	1332.39	1260.12	1198.57

11%   Monthly Loan Payments

LOAN AMOUNT	7½ YEARS	8 YEARS	8½ YEARS	9 YEARS	9½ YEARS	10 YEARS	10½ YEARS
100	1.64	1.57	1.51	1.46	1.42	1.38	1.34
200	3.27	3.14	3.03	2.93	2.84	2.76	2.68
300	4.91	4.71	4.54	4.39	4.25	4.13	4.02
400	6.55	6.28	6.05	5.85	5.67	5.51	5.37
500	8.18	7.85	7.57	7.31	7.09	6.89	6.71
600	9.82	9.43	9.08	8.78	8.51	8.27	8.05
700	11.46	11.00	10.59	10.24	9.92	9.64	9.39
800	13.09	12.57	12.11	11.70	11.34	11.02	10.73
900	14.73	14.14	13.62	13.16	12.76	12.40	12.07
1000	16.37	15.71	15.13	14.63	14.18	13.78	13.42
1500	24.55	23.56	22.70	21.94	21.26	20.66	20.12
2000	32.73	31.42	30.27	29.25	28.35	27.55	26.83
2500	40.91	39.27	37.83	36.56	35.44	34.44	33.54
3000	49.10	47.13	45.40	43.88	42.53	41.33	40.25
3500	57.28	54.98	52.97	51.19	49.62	48.21	46.95
4000	65.46	62.83	60.53	58.50	56.70	55.10	53.66
4500	73.65	70.69	68.10	65.82	63.79	61.99	60.37
5000	81.83	78.54	75.67	73.13	70.88	68.88	67.08
5500	90.01	86.40	83.23	80.44	77.97	75.76	73.79
6000	98.19	94.25	90.80	87.76	85.06	82.65	80.49
6500	106.38	102.10	98.36	95.07	92.14	89.54	87.20
7000	114.56	109.96	105.93	102.38	99.23	96.43	93.91
7500	122.74	117.81	113.50	109.69	106.32	103.31	100.62
8000	130.93	125.67	121.06	117.01	113.41	110.20	107.33
8500	139.11	133.52	128.63	124.32	120.50	117.09	114.03
9000	147.29	141.38	136.20	131.63	127.58	123.98	120.74
9500	155.47	149.23	143.76	138.95	134.67	130.86	127.45
10000	163.66	157.08	151.33	146.26	141.76	137.75	134.16
11000	180.02	172.79	166.46	160.88	155.94	151.53	147.57
12000	196.39	188.50	181.60	175.51	170.11	165.30	160.99
13000	212.75	204.21	196.73	190.14	184.29	179.08	174.40
14000	229.12	219.92	211.86	204.76	198.46	192.85	187.82
15000	245.49	235.63	227.00	219.39	212.64	206.63	201.24
16000	261.85	251.33	242.13	234.01	226.82	220.40	214.65
17000	278.22	267.04	257.26	248.64	240.99	234.18	228.07
18000	294.58	282.75	272.39	263.27	255.17	247.95	241.48
19000	310.95	298.46	287.53	277.89	269.35	261.73	254.90
20000	327.31	314.17	302.66	292.52	283.52	275.50	268.31
21000	343.68	329.88	317.79	307.14	297.70	289.28	281.73
22000	360.05	345.59	332.93	321.77	311.87	303.05	295.14
23000	376.41	361.29	348.06	336.39	326.05	316.83	308.56
24000	392.78	377.00	363.19	351.02	340.23	330.60	321.98
25000	409.14	392.71	378.33	365.65	354.40	344.38	335.39
26000	425.51	408.42	393.46	380.27	368.58	358.15	348.81
27000	441.87	424.13	408.59	394.90	382.75	371.93	362.22
28000	458.24	439.84	423.73	409.52	396.93	385.70	375.64
29000	474.61	455.54	438.86	424.15	411.11	399.48	389.05
30000	490.97	471.25	453.99	438.78	425.28	413.25	402.47
31000	507.34	486.96	469.12	453.40	439.46	427.03	415.89
32000	523.70	502.67	484.26	468.03	453.63	440.80	429.30
33000	540.07	518.38	499.39	482.65	467.81	454.58	442.72
34000	556.43	534.09	514.52	497.28	481.99	468.35	456.13
35000	572.80	549.79	529.66	511.91	496.16	482.13	469.55
40000	654.63	628.34	605.32	585.03	567.04	551.00	536.63
45000	736.46	706.88	680.99	658.16	637.92	619.88	603.71
50000	818.28	785.42	756.65	731.29	708.80	688.75	670.78
55000	900.11	863.96	832.32	804.42	779.68	757.63	737.86
60000	981.94	942.51	907.98	877.55	850.56	826.50	804.94
65000	1063.77	1021.05	983.65	950.68	921.44	895.38	872.02
70000	1145.60	1099.59	1059.31	1023.81	992.32	964.25	939.10

Monthly Loan Payments 11%

LOAN AMOUNT	11 YEARS	11½ YEARS	12 YEARS	12½ YEARS	13 YEARS	14 YEARS	15 YEARS
100	1.31	1.28	1.25	1.23	1.21	1.17	1.14
200	2.62	2.56	2.51	2.46	2.42	2.34	2.27
300	3.93	3.84	3.76	3.69	3.62	3.51	3.41
400	5.24	5.12	5.01	4.92	4.83	4.68	4.55
500	6.55	6.40	6.27	6.15	6.04	5.85	5.68
600	7.86	7.68	7.52	7.38	7.25	7.01	6.82
700	9.16	8.96	8.77	8.61	8.45	8.18	7.96
800	10.47	10.24	10.03	9.84	9.66	9.35	9.09
900	11.78	11.52	11.28	11.07	10.87	10.52	10.23
1000	13.09	12.80	12.54	12.29	12.08	11.69	11.37
1500	19.64	19.20	18.80	18.44	18.11	17.54	17.05
2000	26.18	25.60	25.07	24.59	24.15	23.38	22.73
2500	32.73	32.00	31.34	30.74	30.19	29.23	28.41
3000	39.28	38.40	37.61	36.88	36.23	35.07	34.10
3500	45.82	44.80	43.87	43.03	42.26	40.92	39.78
4000	52.37	51.20	50.14	49.18	48.30	46.76	45.46
4500	58.92	57.60	56.41	55.33	54.34	52.61	51.15
5000	65.46	64.00	62.68	61.47	60.38	58.45	56.83
5500	72.01	70.40	68.95	67.62	66.41	64.30	62.51
6000	78.55	76.80	75.21	73.77	72.45	70.14	68.20
6500	85.10	83.20	81.48	79.92	78.49	75.99	73.88
7000	91.65	89.60	87.75	86.06	84.53	81.83	79.56
7500	98.19	96.00	94.02	92.21	90.56	87.68	85.24
8000	104.74	102.40	100.28	98.36	96.60	93.52	90.93
8500	111.28	108.80	106.55	104.51	102.64	99.37	96.61
9000	117.83	115.20	112.82	110.65	108.68	105.21	102.29
9500	124.38	121.60	119.09	116.80	114.72	111.06	107.98
10000	130.92	128.00	125.36	122.95	120.75	116.91	113.66
11000	144.02	140.80	137.89	135.24	132.83	128.60	125.03
12000	157.11	153.60	150.43	147.54	144.90	140.29	136.39
13000	170.20	166.40	162.96	159.83	156.98	151.98	147.76
14000	183.29	179.20	175.50	172.13	169.05	163.67	159.12
15000	196.39	192.00	188.03	184.42	181.13	175.36	170.49
16000	209.48	204.80	200.57	196.72	193.20	187.05	181.86
17000	222.57	217.60	213.10	209.01	205.28	198.74	193.22
18000	235.66	230.41	225.64	221.31	217.35	210.43	204.59
19000	248.75	243.21	238.18	233.60	229.43	222.12	215.95
20000	261.85	256.01	250.71	245.90	241.51	233.81	227.32
21000	274.94	268.81	263.25	258.19	253.58	245.50	238.69
22000	288.03	281.61	275.78	270.49	265.66	257.19	250.05
23000	301.12	294.41	288.32	282.78	277.73	268.88	261.42
24000	314.22	307.21	300.85	295.08	289.81	280.57	272.78
25000	327.31	320.01	313.39	307.37	301.88	292.26	284.15
26000	340.40	332.81	325.92	319.67	313.96	303.95	295.52
27000	353.49	345.61	338.46	331.96	326.03	315.64	306.88
28000	366.59	358.41	351.00	344.25	338.11	327.34	318.25
29000	379.68	371.21	363.53	356.55	350.18	339.03	329.61
30000	392.77	384.01	376.07	368.84	362.26	350.72	340.98
31000	405.86	396.81	388.60	381.14	374.33	362.41	352.35
32000	418.96	409.61	401.14	393.43	386.41	374.10	363.71
33000	432.05	422.41	413.67	405.73	398.48	385.79	375.08
34000	445.14	435.21	426.21	418.02	410.56	397.48	386.44
35000	458.23	448.01	438.74	430.32	422.63	409.17	397.81
40000	523.69	512.01	501.42	491.79	483.01	467.62	454.64
45000	589.16	576.01	564.10	553.27	543.39	526.07	511.47
50000	654.62	640.01	626.78	614.74	603.76	584.53	568.30
55000	720.08	704.02	689.46	676.21	664.14	642.98	625.13
60000	785.54	768.02	752.13	737.69	724.52	701.43	681.96
65000	851.00	832.02	814.81	799.16	784.89	759.89	738.79
70000	916.46	896.02	877.49	860.64	845.27	818.34	795.62

11¼% Monthly Loan Payments

LOAN AMOUNT	½ YEAR	1 YEAR	1½ YEARS	2 YEARS	2½ YEARS	3 YEARS	3½ YEARS
100	17.22	8.85	6.06	4.67	3.84	3.29	2.89
200	34.44	17.70	12.13	9.34	7.68	6.57	5.78
300	51.65	26.55	18.19	14.02	11.52	9.86	8.67
400	68.87	35.40	24.25	18.69	15.36	13.14	11.57
500	86.09	44.25	30.32	23.36	19.20	16.43	14.46
600	103.31	53.10	36.38	28.03	23.04	19.71	17.35
700	120.52	61.95	42.44	32.71	26.88	23.00	20.24
800	137.74	70.80	48.51	37.38	30.72	26.29	23.13
900	154.96	79.65	54.57	42.05	34.56	29.57	26.02
1000	172.18	88.50	60.63	46.72	38.40	32.86	28.91
1500	258.27	132.75	90.95	70.09	57.59	49.29	43.37
2000	344.36	177.00	121.27	93.45	76.79	65.71	57.83
2500	430.44	221.25	151.59	116.81	95.99	82.14	72.28
3000	516.53	265.49	181.90	140.17	115.19	98.57	86.74
3500	602.62	309.74	212.22	163.53	134.38	115.00	101.20
4000	688.71	353.99	242.54	186.90	153.58	131.43	115.66
4500	774.80	398.24	272.85	210.26	172.78	147.86	130.11
5000	860.89	442.49	303.17	233.62	191.98	164.29	144.57
5500	946.98	486.74	333.49	256.98	211.17	180.71	159.03
6000	1033.07	530.99	363.81	280.34	230.37	197.14	173.48
6500	1119.16	575.24	394.12	303.71	249.57	213.57	187.94
7000	1205.25	619.49	424.44	327.07	268.77	230.00	202.40
7500	1291.33	663.74	454.76	350.43	287.96	246.43	216.85
8000	1377.42	707.99	485.07	373.79	307.16	262.86	231.31
8500	1463.51	752.24	515.39	397.15	326.36	279.29	245.77
9000	1549.60	796.48	545.71	420.52	345.56	295.72	260.22
9500	1635.69	840.73	576.03	443.88	364.75	312.14	274.68
10000	1721.78	884.98	606.34	467.24	383.95	328.57	289.14
11000	1893.96	973.48	666.98	513.96	422.35	361.43	318.05
12000	2066.14	1061.98	727.61	560.69	460.74	394.29	346.97
13000	2238.31	1150.48	788.24	607.41	499.14	427.14	375.88
14000	2410.49	1238.98	848.88	654.14	537.53	460.00	404.79
15000	2582.67	1327.47	909.51	700.86	575.93	492.86	433.71
16000	2754.85	1415.97	970.15	747.58	614.32	525.72	462.62
17000	2927.02	1504.47	1030.78	794.31	652.72	558.57	491.54
18000	3099.20	1592.97	1091.42	841.03	691.11	591.43	520.45
19000	3271.38	1681.47	1152.05	887.76	729.51	624.29	549.36
20000	3443.56	1769.97	1212.68	934.48	767.91	657.14	578.28
21000	3615.74	1858.46	1273.32	981.20	806.30	690.00	607.19
22000	3787.91	1946.96	1333.95	1027.93	844.70	722.86	636.10
23000	3960.09	2035.46	1394.59	1074.65	883.09	755.72	665.02
24000	4132.27	2123.96	1455.22	1121.38	921.49	788.57	693.93
25000	4304.45	2212.46	1515.86	1168.10	959.88	821.43	722.85
26000	4476.63	2300.96	1576.49	1214.82	998.28	854.29	751.76
27000	4648.80	2389.45	1637.12	1261.55	1036.67	887.15	780.67
28000	4820.98	2477.95	1697.76	1308.27	1075.07	920.00	809.59
29000	4993.16	2566.45	1758.39	1355.00	1113.46	952.86	838.50
30000	5165.34	2654.95	1819.03	1401.72	1151.86	985.72	867.42
31000	5337.52	2743.45	1879.66	1448.44	1190.25	1018.57	896.33
32000	5509.69	2831.95	1940.30	1495.17	1228.65	1051.43	925.24
33000	5681.87	2920.44	2000.93	1541.89	1267.04	1084.29	954.16
34000	5854.05	3008.94	2061.56	1588.62	1305.44	1117.15	983.07
35000	6026.23	3097.44	2122.20	1635.34	1343.83	1150.00	1011.99
40000	6887.12	3539.93	2425.37	1868.46	1535.81	1314.29	1156.55
45000	7748.01	3982.42	2728.54	2102.58	1727.79	1478.58	1301.12
50000	8608.90	4424.92	3031.71	2336.20	1919.76	1642.86	1445.69
55000	9469.79	4867.41	3334.88	2569.82	2111.74	1807.15	1590.26
60000	10330.68	5309.90	3638.05	2803.44	2303.72	1971.43	1734.83
65000	11191.57	5752.39	3941.22	3037.06	2495.69	2135.72	1879.40
70000	12052.46	6194.88	4244.40	3270.68	2687.67	2300.01	2023.97

Monthly Loan Payments 11¼%

LOAN AMOUNT	4 YEARS	4½ YEARS	5 YEARS	5½ YEARS	6 YEARS	6½ YEARS	7 YEARS
100	2.60	2.37	2.19	2.04	1.92	1.81	1.73
200	5.19	4.74	4.37	4.08	3.83	3.63	3.45
300	7.79	7.11	6.56	6.12	5.75	5.44	5.18
400	10.39	9.47	8.75	8.16	7.66	7.25	6.90
500	12.98	11.84	10.93	10.19	9.58	9.07	8.63
600	15.58	14.21	13.12	12.23	11.50	10.88	10.35
700	18.18	16.58	15.31	14.27	13.41	12.69	12.08
800	20.77	18.95	17.49	16.31	15.33	14.51	13.80
900	23.37	21.32	19.68	18.35	17.25	16.32	15.53
1000	25.97	23.68	21.87	20.39	19.16	18.13	17.25
1500	38.95	35.53	32.80	30.58	28.74	27.20	25.88
2000	51.93	47.37	43.73	40.78	38.32	36.26	34.51
2500	64.92	59.21	54.67	50.97	47.91	45.33	43.14
3000	77.90	71.05	65.60	61.16	57.49	54.40	51.76
3500	90.88	82.90	76.54	71.36	67.07	63.46	60.39
4000	103.87	94.74	87.47	81.55	76.65	72.53	69.02
4500	116.85	106.58	98.40	91.75	86.23	81.59	77.64
5000	129.84	118.42	109.34	101.94	95.81	90.66	86.27
5500	142.82	130.27	120.27	112.13	105.39	99.72	94.90
6000	155.80	142.11	131.20	122.33	114.97	108.79	103.53
6500	168.79	153.95	142.14	132.52	124.56	117.86	112.15
7000	181.77	165.79	153.07	142.72	134.14	126.92	120.78
7500	194.75	177.64	164.00	152.91	143.72	135.99	129.41
8000	207.74	189.48	174.94	163.10	153.30	145.05	138.03
8500	220.72	201.32	185.87	173.30	162.88	154.12	146.66
9000	233.70	213.16	196.81	183.49	172.46	163.19	155.29
9500	246.69	225.00	207.74	193.69	182.04	172.25	163.91
10000	259.67	236.85	218.67	203.88	191.62	181.32	172.54
11000	285.64	260.53	240.54	224.27	210.79	199.45	189.80
12000	311.61	284.22	262.41	244.66	229.95	217.58	207.05
13000	337.57	307.90	284.28	265.04	249.11	235.71	224.30
14000	363.54	331.59	306.14	285.43	268.27	253.84	241.56
15000	389.51	355.27	328.01	305.82	287.44	271.98	258.81
16000	415.47	378.96	349.88	326.21	306.60	290.11	276.07
17000	441.44	402.64	371.74	346.60	325.76	308.24	293.32
18000	467.41	426.32	393.61	366.99	344.92	326.37	310.58
19000	493.37	450.01	415.48	387.37	364.09	344.50	327.83
20000	519.34	473.69	437.35	407.76	383.25	362.63	345.08
21000	545.31	497.38	459.21	428.15	402.41	380.77	362.34
22000	571.28	521.06	481.08	448.54	421.57	398.90	379.59
23000	597.24	544.75	502.95	468.93	440.73	417.03	396.85
24000	623.21	568.43	524.82	489.31	459.90	435.16	414.10
25000	649.18	592.12	546.68	509.70	479.06	453.29	431.35
26000	675.14	615.80	568.55	530.09	498.22	471.42	448.61
27000	701.11	639.49	590.42	550.48	517.38	489.56	465.86
28000	727.08	663.17	612.28	570.87	536.55	507.69	483.12
29000	753.05	686.86	634.15	591.25	555.71	525.82	500.37
30000	779.01	710.54	656.02	611.64	574.87	543.95	517.63
31000	804.98	734.23	677.89	632.03	594.03	562.08	534.88
32000	830.95	757.91	699.75	652.42	613.20	580.21	552.13
33000	856.91	781.60	721.62	672.81	632.36	598.35	569.39
34000	882.88	805.28	743.49	693.19	651.52	616.48	586.64
35000	908.85	828.96	765.36	713.58	670.68	634.61	603.90
40000	1038.68	947.39	874.69	815.52	766.49	725.27	690.17
45000	1168.52	1065.81	984.03	917.46	862.31	815.93	776.44
50000	1298.35	1184.23	1093.37	1019.40	958.12	906.58	862.71
55000	1428.19	1302.66	1202.70	1121.34	1053.93	997.24	948.98
60000	1558.03	1421.08	1312.04	1223.28	1149.74	1087.90	1035.25
65000	1687.86	1539.51	1421.38	1325.22	1245.55	1178.56	1121.52
70000	1817.70	1657.93	1530.71	1427.16	1341.37	1269.22	1207.79

11¼% Monthly Loan Payments

LOAN AMOUNT	7½ YEARS	8 YEARS	8½ YEARS	9 YEARS	9½ YEARS	10 YEARS	10½ YEARS
100	1.65	1.58	1.53	1.48	1.43	1.39	1.36
200	3.30	3.17	3.05	2.95	2.86	2.78	2.71
300	4.95	4.75	4.58	4.43	4.29	4.18	4.07
400	6.60	6.34	6.11	5.91	5.73	5.57	5.42
500	8.25	7.92	7.63	7.38	7.16	6.96	6.78
600	9.90	9.51	9.16	8.86	8.59	8.35	8.14
700	11.55	11.09	10.69	10.34	10.02	9.74	9.49
800	13.20	12.67	12.22	11.81	11.45	11.13	10.85
900	14.85	14.26	13.74	13.29	12.88	12.53	12.20
1000	16.50	15.84	15.27	14.76	14.32	13.92	13.56
1500	24.75	23.77	22.90	22.15	21.47	20.88	20.34
2000	33.00	31.69	30.54	29.53	28.63	27.83	27.12
2500	41.25	39.61	38.17	36.91	35.79	34.79	33.90
3000	49.50	47.53	45.81	44.29	42.95	41.75	40.68
3500	57.75	55.45	53.44	51.68	50.11	48.71	47.46
4000	66.00	63.37	61.08	59.06	57.27	55.67	54.24
4500	74.25	71.30	68.71	66.44	64.42	62.63	61.02
5000	82.50	79.22	76.35	73.82	71.58	69.58	67.80
5500	90.75	87.14	83.98	81.20	78.74	76.54	74.58
6000	98.99	95.06	91.62	88.59	85.90	83.50	81.36
6500	107.24	102.98	99.25	95.97	93.06	90.46	88.13
7000	115.49	110.91	106.89	103.35	100.21	97.42	94.91
7500	123.74	118.83	114.52	110.73	107.37	104.38	101.69
8000	131.99	126.75	122.16	118.12	114.53	111.34	108.47
8500	140.24	134.67	129.79	125.50	121.69	118.29	115.25
9000	148.49	142.59	137.43	132.88	128.85	125.25	122.03
9500	156.74	150.51	145.06	140.26	136.00	132.21	128.81
10000	164.99	158.44	152.70	147.64	143.16	139.17	135.59
11000	181.49	174.28	167.97	162.41	157.48	153.09	149.15
12000	197.99	190.12	183.24	177.17	171.80	167.00	162.71
13000	214.49	205.97	198.51	191.94	186.11	180.92	176.27
14000	230.99	221.81	213.78	206.70	200.43	194.84	189.83
15000	247.49	237.65	229.05	221.47	214.74	208.75	203.39
16000	263.99	253.50	244.32	236.23	229.06	222.67	216.95
17000	280.49	269.34	259.59	251.00	243.38	236.59	230.51
18000	296.98	285.18	274.86	265.76	257.69	250.50	244.07
19000	313.48	301.03	290.13	280.52	272.01	264.42	257.63
20000	329.98	316.87	305.40	295.29	286.33	278.34	271.18
21000	346.48	332.72	320.67	310.05	300.64	292.25	284.74
22000	362.98	348.56	335.94	324.82	314.96	306.17	298.30
23000	379.48	364.40	351.21	339.58	329.27	320.09	311.86
24000	395.98	380.25	366.48	354.35	343.59	334.01	325.42
25000	412.48	396.09	381.75	369.11	357.91	347.92	338.98
26000	428.98	411.93	397.02	383.87	372.22	361.84	352.54
27000	445.48	427.78	412.29	398.64	386.54	375.76	366.10
28000	461.98	443.62	427.56	413.40	400.86	389.67	379.66
29000	478.47	459.46	442.83	428.17	415.17	403.59	393.22
30000	494.97	475.31	458.10	442.93	429.49	417.51	406.78
31000	511.47	491.15	473.37	457.70	443.81	431.42	420.34
32000	527.97	506.99	488.64	472.46	458.12	445.34	433.89
33000	544.47	522.84	503.91	487.23	472.44	459.26	447.45
34000	560.97	538.68	519.18	501.99	486.75	473.17	461.01
35000	577.47	554.53	534.45	516.75	501.07	487.09	474.57
40000	659.97	633.74	610.80	590.58	572.65	556.68	542.37
45000	742.46	712.96	687.15	664.40	644.23	626.26	610.16
50000	824.96	792.18	763.50	738.22	715.81	695.84	677.96
55000	907.45	871.40	839.84	812.04	787.40	765.43	745.76
60000	989.95	950.62	916.19	885.86	858.98	835.01	813.55
65000	1072.44	1029.83	992.54	959.69	930.56	904.60	881.35
70000	1154.94	1109.05	1068.89	1033.51	1002.14	974.18	949.15

Monthly Loan Payments 11¼%

LOAN AMOUNT	11 YEARS	11½ YEARS	12 YEARS	12½ YEARS	13 YEARS	14 YEARS	15 YEARS
100	1.32	1.29	1.27	1.24	1.22	1.18	1.15
200	2.65	2.59	2.54	2.49	2.45	2.37	2.30
300	3.97	3.88	3.81	3.73	3.67	3.55	3.46
400	5.30	5.18	5.07	4.98	4.89	4.74	4.61
500	6.62	6.47	6.34	6.22	6.11	5.92	5.76
600	7.94	7.77	7.61	7.47	7.34	7.11	6.91
700	9.27	9.06	8.88	8.71	8.56	8.29	8.07
800	10.59	10.36	10.15	9.96	9.78	9.48	9.22
900	11.91	11.65	11.42	11.20	11.00	10.66	10.37
1000	13.24	12.95	12.68	12.44	12.23	11.85	11.52
1500	19.86	19.42	19.03	18.67	18.34	17.77	17.29
2000	26.48	25.89	25.37	24.89	24.45	23.69	23.05
2500	33.09	32.37	31.71	31.11	30.57	29.61	28.81
3000	39.71	38.84	38.05	37.33	36.68	35.54	34.57
3500	46.33	45.31	44.39	43.56	42.79	41.46	40.33
4000	52.95	51.79	50.74	49.78	48.91	47.38	46.09
4500	59.57	58.26	57.08	56.00	55.02	53.30	51.86
5000	66.19	64.74	63.42	62.22	61.13	59.23	57.62
5500	72.81	71.21	69.76	68.45	67.25	65.15	63.38
6000	79.43	77.68	76.10	74.67	73.36	71.07	69.14
6500	86.04	84.16	82.45	80.89	79.47	76.99	74.90
7000	92.66	90.63	88.79	87.11	85.59	82.92	80.66
7500	99.28	97.10	95.13	93.34	91.70	88.84	86.43
8000	105.90	103.58	101.47	99.56	97.81	94.76	92.19
8500	112.52	110.05	107.81	105.78	103.93	100.68	97.95
9000	119.14	116.52	114.16	112.00	110.04	106.61	103.71
9500	125.76	123.00	120.50	118.23	116.15	112.53	109.47
10000	132.38	129.47	126.84	124.45	122.27	118.45	115.23
11000	145.61	142.42	139.52	136.89	134.49	130.30	126.76
12000	158.85	155.36	152.21	149.34	146.72	142.14	138.28
13000	172.09	168.31	164.89	161.78	158.95	153.99	149.80
14000	185.33	181.26	177.58	174.23	171.17	165.83	161.33
15000	198.56	194.21	190.26	186.67	183.40	177.68	172.85
16000	211.80	207.15	202.94	199.12	195.63	189.52	184.38
17000	225.04	220.10	215.63	211.56	207.86	201.37	195.90
18000	238.28	233.05	228.31	224.01	220.08	213.21	207.42
19000	251.51	245.99	240.99	236.45	232.31	225.06	218.95
20000	264.75	258.94	253.68	248.90	244.54	236.90	230.47
21000	277.99	271.89	266.36	261.34	256.76	248.75	241.99
22000	291.23	284.84	279.05	273.78	268.99	260.59	253.52
23000	304.46	297.78	291.73	286.23	281.22	272.44	265.04
24000	317.70	310.73	304.41	298.67	293.44	284.28	276.56
25000	330.94	323.68	317.10	311.12	305.67	296.13	288.09
26000	344.18	336.62	329.78	323.56	317.90	307.97	299.61
27000	357.41	349.57	342.47	336.01	330.12	319.82	311.13
28000	370.65	362.52	355.15	348.45	342.35	331.66	322.66
29000	383.89	375.47	367.83	360.90	354.58	343.51	334.18
30000	397.13	388.41	380.52	373.34	366.80	355.35	345.70
31000	410.36	401.36	393.20	385.79	379.03	367.20	357.23
32000	423.60	414.31	405.89	398.23	391.26	379.04	368.75
33000	436.84	427.25	418.57	410.68	403.48	390.89	380.27
34000	450.08	440.20	431.25	423.12	415.71	402.73	391.80
35000	463.31	453.15	443.94	435.57	427.94	414.58	403.32
40000	529.50	517.88	507.36	497.79	489.07	473.80	460.94
45000	595.69	582.62	570.78	560.01	550.20	533.03	518.56
50000	661.88	647.35	634.20	622.24	611.34	592.25	576.17
55000	728.06	712.09	697.62	684.46	672.47	651.48	633.79
60000	794.25	776.82	761.04	746.69	733.61	710.70	691.41
65000	860.44	841.56	824.46	808.91	794.74	769.93	749.02
70000	926.63	906.30	887.88	871.13	855.87	829.16	806.64

11½%   Monthly Loan Payments

LOAN AMOUNT	½ YEAR	1 YEAR	1½ YEARS	2 YEARS	2½ YEARS	3 YEARS	3½ YEARS
100	17.23	8.86	6.08	4.68	3.85	3.30	2.90
200	34.46	17.72	12.15	9.37	7.70	6.60	5.81
300	51.69	26.58	18.23	14.05	11.55	9.89	8.71
400	68.92	35.45	24.30	18.74	15.41	13.19	11.61
500	86.15	44.31	30.38	23.42	19.26	16.49	14.52
600	103.38	53.17	36.45	28.10	23.11	19.79	17.42
700	120.61	62.03	42.53	32.79	26.96	23.08	20.32
800	137.84	70.89	48.60	37.47	30.81	26.38	23.23
900	155.07	79.75	54.68	42.16	34.66	29.68	26.13
1000	172.30	88.62	60.75	46.84	38.51	32.98	29.03
1500	258.45	132.92	91.13	70.26	57.77	49.46	43.55
2000	344.60	177.23	121.50	93.68	77.03	65.95	58.07
2500	430.75	221.54	151.88	117.10	96.28	82.44	72.59
3000	516.90	265.85	182.25	140.52	115.54	98.93	87.10
3500	603.05	310.15	212.63	163.94	134.79	115.42	101.62
4000	689.21	354.46	243.00	187.36	154.05	131.90	116.14
4500	775.36	398.77	273.38	210.78	173.31	148.39	130.65
5000	861.51	443.08	303.75	234.20	192.56	164.88	145.17
5500	947.66	487.38	334.13	257.62	211.82	181.37	159.69
6000	1033.81	531.69	364.50	281.04	231.08	197.86	174.20
6500	1119.96	576.00	394.88	304.46	250.33	214.34	188.72
7000	1206.11	620.31	425.25	327.88	269.59	230.83	203.24
7500	1292.26	664.61	455.63	351.30	288.84	247.32	217.76
8000	1378.41	708.92	486.00	374.72	308.10	263.81	232.27
8500	1464.56	753.23	516.38	398.14	327.36	280.30	246.79
9000	1550.71	797.54	546.75	421.56	346.61	296.78	261.31
9500	1636.86	841.84	577.13	444.98	365.87	313.27	275.82
10000	1723.01	886.15	607.50	468.40	385.13	329.76	290.34
11000	1895.32	974.77	668.25	515.24	423.64	362.74	319.38
12000	2067.62	1063.38	729.00	562.08	462.15	395.71	348.41
13000	2239.92	1152.00	789.75	608.92	500.66	428.69	377.44
14000	2412.22	1240.61	850.50	655.76	539.18	461.66	406.48
15000	2584.52	1329.23	911.25	702.60	577.69	494.64	435.51
16000	2756.82	1417.84	972.00	749.45	616.20	527.62	464.55
17000	2929.12	1506.46	1032.75	796.29	654.72	560.59	493.58
18000	3101.42	1595.07	1093.50	843.13	693.23	593.57	522.61
19000	3273.73	1683.69	1154.25	889.97	731.74	626.54	551.65
20000	3446.03	1772.30	1215.00	936.81	770.25	659.52	580.68
21000	3618.33	1860.92	1275.75	983.65	808.77	692.50	609.72
22000	3790.63	1949.53	1336.50	1030.49	847.28	725.47	638.75
23000	3962.93	2038.15	1397.25	1077.33	885.79	758.45	667.79
24000	4135.23	2126.76	1458.00	1124.17	924.30	791.42	696.82
25000	4307.53	2215.38	1518.75	1171.01	962.82	824.40	725.85
26000	4479.84	2303.99	1579.50	1217.85	1001.33	857.38	754.89
27000	4652.14	2392.61	1640.25	1264.69	1039.84	890.35	783.92
28000	4824.44	2481.22	1701.00	1311.53	1078.35	923.33	812.96
29000	4996.74	2569.84	1761.75	1358.37	1116.87	956.30	841.99
30000	5169.04	2658.45	1822.50	1405.21	1155.38	989.28	871.02
31000	5341.34	2747.07	1883.25	1452.05	1193.89	1022.26	900.06
32000	5513.64	2835.68	1944.00	1498.89	1232.41	1055.23	929.09
33000	5685.95	2924.30	2004.75	1545.73	1270.92	1088.21	958.13
34000	5858.25	3012.91	2065.50	1592.57	1309.43	1121.18	987.16
35000	6030.55	3101.53	2126.25	1639.41	1347.94	1154.16	1016.20
40000	6892.05	3544.60	2430.00	1873.61	1540.51	1319.04	1161.37
45000	7753.56	3987.68	2733.75	2107.81	1733.07	1483.92	1306.54
50000	8615.07	4430.75	3037.50	2342.02	1925.63	1648.80	1451.71
55000	9476.58	4873.83	3341.25	2576.22	2118.20	1813.68	1596.88
60000	10338.08	5316.90	3645.00	2810.42	2310.76	1978.56	1742.05
65000	11199.59	5759.98	3948.75	3044.62	2503.32	2143.44	1887.22
70000	12061.10	6203.05	4252.50	3278.82	2695.89	2308.32	2032.39

Monthly Loan Payments 11½%

LOAN AMOUNT	4 YEARS	4½ YEARS	5 YEARS	5½ YEARS	6 YEARS	6½ YEARS	7 YEARS
100	2.61	2.38	2.20	2.05	1.93	1.83	1.74
200	5.22	4.76	4.40	4.10	3.86	3.65	3.48
300	7.83	7.14	6.60	6.15	5.79	5.48	5.22
400	10.44	9.52	8.80	8.21	7.72	7.30	6.95
500	13.04	11.90	11.00	10.26	9.65	9.13	8.69
600	15.65	14.28	13.20	12.31	11.57	10.96	10.43
700	18.26	16.67	15.39	14.36	13.50	12.78	12.17
800	20.87	19.05	17.59	16.41	15.43	14.61	13.91
900	23.48	21.43	19.79	18.46	17.36	16.44	15.65
1000	26.09	23.81	21.99	20.52	19.29	18.26	17.39
1500	39.13	35.71	32.99	30.77	28.94	27.39	26.08
2000	52.18	47.62	43.99	41.03	38.58	36.52	34.77
2500	65.22	59.52	54.98	51.29	48.23	45.66	43.47
3000	78.27	71.42	65.98	61.55	57.87	54.79	52.16
3500	91.31	83.33	76.97	71.80	67.52	63.92	60.85
4000	104.36	95.23	87.97	82.06	77.16	73.05	69.55
4500	117.40	107.14	98.97	92.32	86.81	82.18	78.24
5000	130.45	119.04	109.96	102.58	96.46	91.31	86.93
5500	143.49	130.95	120.96	112.83	106.10	100.44	95.63
6000	156.53	142.85	131.96	123.09	115.75	109.57	104.32
6500	169.58	154.75	142.95	133.35	125.39	118.70	113.01
7000	182.62	166.66	153.95	143.61	135.04	127.84	121.71
7500	195.67	178.56	164.94	153.86	144.68	136.97	130.40
8000	208.71	190.47	175.94	164.12	154.33	146.10	139.09
8500	221.76	202.37	186.94	174.38	163.97	155.23	147.78
9000	234.80	214.27	197.93	184.64	173.62	164.36	156.48
9500	247.85	226.18	208.93	194.89	183.27	173.49	165.17
10000	260.89	238.08	219.93	205.15	192.91	182.62	173.86
11000	286.98	261.89	241.92	225.67	212.20	200.88	191.25
12000	313.07	285.70	263.91	246.18	231.49	219.15	208.64
13000	339.16	309.51	285.90	266.70	250.79	237.41	226.02
14000	365.25	333.32	307.90	287.21	270.08	255.67	243.41
15000	391.34	357.12	329.89	307.73	289.37	273.93	260.80
16000	417.42	380.93	351.88	328.24	308.66	292.20	278.18
17000	443.51	404.74	373.87	348.76	327.95	310.46	295.57
18000	469.60	428.55	395.87	369.27	347.25	328.72	312.96
19000	495.69	452.36	417.86	389.79	366.53	346.98	330.34
20000	521.78	476.17	439.85	410.30	385.82	365.24	347.73
21000	547.87	499.97	461.84	430.82	405.11	383.51	365.12
22000	573.96	523.78	483.84	451.33	424.41	401.77	382.50
23000	600.05	547.59	505.83	471.85	443.70	420.03	399.89
24000	626.14	571.40	527.82	492.36	462.99	438.29	417.28
25000	652.23	595.21	549.82	512.88	482.28	456.56	434.66
26000	678.31	619.02	571.81	533.39	501.57	474.82	452.05
27000	704.40	642.82	593.80	553.91	520.86	493.08	469.43
28000	730.49	666.63	615.79	574.42	540.15	511.34	486.82
29000	756.58	690.44	637.79	594.94	559.44	529.60	504.21
30000	782.67	714.25	659.78	615.45	578.73	547.87	521.59
31000	808.76	738.06	681.77	635.97	598.03	566.13	538.98
32000	834.85	761.87	703.76	656.48	617.32	584.39	556.37
33000	860.94	785.67	725.76	677.00	636.61	602.65	573.75
34000	887.03	809.48	747.75	697.51	655.90	620.92	591.14
35000	913.12	833.29	769.74	718.03	675.19	639.18	608.53
40000	1043.56	952.33	879.70	820.60	771.65	730.49	695.46
45000	1174.01	1071.37	989.67	923.18	868.10	821.80	782.39
50000	1304.45	1190.41	1099.63	1025.75	964.56	913.11	869.32
55000	1434.90	1309.46	1209.59	1128.33	1061.01	1004.42	956.26
60000	1565.34	1428.50	1319.56	1230.91	1157.47	1095.73	1043.19
65000	1695.79	1547.54	1429.52	1333.48	1253.93	1187.04	1130.12
70000	1826.23	1666.58	1539.48	1436.06	1350.38	1278.36	1217.05

11½% Monthly Loan Payments

LOAN AMOUNT	7½ YEARS	8 YEARS	8½ YEARS	9 YEARS	9½ YEARS	10 YEARS	10½ YEARS
100	1.66	1.60	1.54	1.49	1.45	1.41	1.37
200	3.33	3.20	3.08	2.98	2.89	2.81	2.74
300	4.99	4.79	4.62	4.47	4.34	4.22	4.11
400	6.65	6.39	6.16	5.96	5.78	5.62	5.48
500	8.32	7.99	7.70	7.45	7.23	7.03	6.85
600	9.98	9.59	9.24	8.94	8.67	8.44	8.22
700	11.64	11.19	10.79	10.43	10.12	9.84	9.59
800	13.31	12.78	12.33	11.92	11.57	11.25	10.96
900	14.97	14.38	13.87	13.41	13.01	12.65	12.33
1000	16.63	15.98	15.41	14.90	14.46	14.06	13.70
1500	24.95	23.97	23.11	22.36	21.69	21.09	20.56
2000	33.27	31.96	30.81	29.81	28.91	28.12	27.41
2500	41.58	39.95	38.52	37.26	36.14	35.15	34.26
3000	49.90	47.94	46.22	44.71	43.37	42.18	41.11
3500	58.22	55.93	53.93	52.16	50.60	49.21	47.96
4000	66.53	63.92	61.63	59.61	57.83	56.24	54.81
4500	74.85	71.91	69.33	67.07	65.06	63.27	61.67
5000	83.17	79.90	77.04	74.52	72.29	70.30	68.52
5500	91.48	87.89	84.74	81.97	79.51	77.33	75.37
6000	99.80	95.88	92.44	89.42	86.74	84.36	82.22
6500	108.12	103.87	100.15	96.87	93.97	91.39	89.07
7000	116.43	111.86	107.85	104.33	101.20	98.42	95.92
7500	124.75	119.85	115.56	111.78	108.43	105.45	102.78
8000	133.07	127.83	123.26	119.23	115.66	112.48	109.63
8500	141.38	135.82	130.96	126.68	122.89	119.51	116.48
9000	149.70	143.81	138.67	134.13	130.12	126.54	123.33
9500	158.02	151.80	146.37	141.58	137.34	133.57	130.18
10000	166.33	159.79	154.07	149.04	144.57	140.60	137.04
11000	182.97	175.77	169.48	163.94	159.03	154.65	150.74
12000	199.60	191.75	184.89	178.84	173.49	168.71	164.44
13000	216.23	207.73	200.30	193.75	187.94	182.77	178.15
14000	232.86	223.71	215.70	208.65	202.40	196.83	191.85
15000	249.50	239.69	231.11	223.55	216.86	210.89	205.55
16000	266.13	255.67	246.52	238.46	231.32	224.95	219.26
17000	282.76	271.65	261.93	253.36	245.77	239.01	232.96
18000	299.40	287.63	277.33	268.27	260.23	253.07	246.66
19000	316.03	303.61	292.74	283.17	274.69	267.13	260.37
20000	332.66	319.59	308.15	298.07	289.14	281.19	274.07
21000	349.30	335.57	323.56	312.98	303.60	295.25	287.77
22000	365.93	351.55	338.96	327.88	318.06	309.31	301.48
23000	382.56	367.53	354.37	342.78	332.52	323.37	315.18
24000	399.20	383.50	369.78	357.69	346.97	337.43	328.88
25000	415.83	399.48	385.19	372.59	361.43	351.49	342.59
26000	432.46	415.46	400.59	387.50	375.89	365.55	356.29
27000	449.10	431.44	416.00	402.40	390.35	379.61	370.00
28000	465.73	447.42	431.41	417.30	404.80	393.67	383.70
29000	482.36	463.40	446.82	432.21	419.26	407.73	397.40
30000	499.00	479.38	462.22	447.11	433.72	421.79	411.11
31000	515.63	495.36	477.63	462.01	448.17	435.85	424.81
32000	532.26	511.34	493.04	476.92	462.63	449.91	438.51
33000	548.90	527.32	508.45	491.82	477.09	463.96	452.22
34000	565.53	543.30	523.85	506.72	491.55	478.02	465.92
35000	582.16	559.28	539.26	521.63	506.00	492.08	479.62
40000	665.33	639.17	616.30	596.15	578.29	562.38	548.14
45000	748.49	719.07	693.33	670.66	650.58	632.68	616.66
50000	831.66	798.97	770.37	745.18	722.86	702.98	685.18
55000	914.83	878.87	847.41	819.70	795.15	773.27	753.69
60000	997.99	958.76	924.45	894.22	867.43	843.57	822.21
65000	1081.16	1038.66	1001.48	968.74	939.72	913.87	890.73
70000	1164.32	1118.56	1078.52	1043.26	1012.01	984.17	959.25

Monthly Loan Payments 11½%

LOAN AMOUNT	11 YEARS	11½ YEARS	12 YEARS	12½ YEARS	13 YEARS	14 YEARS	15 YEARS
100	1.34	1.31	1.28	1.26	1.24	1.20	1.17
200	2.68	2.62	2.57	2.52	2.48	2.40	2.34
300	4.02	3.93	3.85	3.78	3.71	3.60	3.50
400	5.35	5.24	5.13	5.04	4.95	4.80	4.67
500	6.69	6.55	6.42	6.30	6.19	6.00	5.84
600	8.03	7.86	7.70	7.56	7.43	7.20	7.01
700	9.37	9.17	8.98	8.82	8.67	8.40	8.18
800	10.71	10.48	10.27	10.08	9.90	9.60	9.35
900	12.05	11.79	11.55	11.34	11.14	10.80	10.51
1000	13.38	13.09	12.83	12.60	12.38	12.00	11.68
1500	20.08	19.64	19.25	18.89	18.57	18.00	17.52
2000	26.77	26.19	25.67	25.19	24.76	24.00	23.36
2500	33.46	32.74	32.08	31.49	30.95	30.00	29.20
3000	40.15	39.28	38.50	37.79	37.14	36.00	35.05
3500	46.84	45.83	44.92	44.08	43.33	42.00	40.89
4000	53.53	52.38	51.33	50.38	49.52	48.00	46.73
4500	60.23	58.93	57.75	56.68	55.71	54.00	52.57
5000	66.92	65.47	64.17	62.98	61.90	60.00	58.41
5500	73.61	72.02	70.58	69.28	68.09	66.00	64.25
6000	80.30	78.57	77.00	75.57	74.28	72.00	70.09
6500	86.99	85.12	83.42	81.87	80.46	78.00	75.93
7000	93.68	91.66	89.83	88.17	86.65	84.00	81.77
7500	100.38	98.21	96.25	94.47	92.84	90.00	87.61
8000	107.07	104.76	102.67	100.76	99.03	96.00	93.46
8500	113.76	111.30	109.08	107.06	105.22	102.00	99.30
9000	120.45	117.85	115.50	113.36	111.41	108.00	105.14
9500	127.14	124.40	121.92	119.66	117.60	114.01	110.98
10000	133.84	130.95	128.33	125.96	123.79	120.01	116.82
11000	147.22	144.04	141.16	138.55	136.17	132.01	128.50
12000	160.60	157.14	154.00	151.15	148.55	144.01	140.18
13000	173.99	170.23	166.83	163.74	160.93	156.01	151.86
14000	187.37	183.33	179.66	176.34	173.31	168.01	163.55
15000	200.75	196.42	192.50	188.93	185.69	180.01	175.23
16000	214.14	209.52	205.33	201.53	198.07	192.01	186.91
17000	227.52	222.61	218.16	214.13	210.45	204.01	198.59
18000	240.90	235.70	231.00	226.72	222.83	216.01	210.27
19000	254.29	248.80	243.83	239.32	235.20	228.01	221.96
20000	267.67	261.89	256.66	251.91	247.58	240.01	233.64
21000	281.05	274.99	269.50	264.51	259.96	252.01	245.32
22000	294.44	288.08	282.33	277.10	272.34	264.01	257.00
23000	307.82	301.18	295.16	289.70	284.72	276.01	268.68
24000	321.20	314.27	308.00	302.29	297.10	288.01	280.37
25000	334.59	327.37	320.83	314.89	309.48	300.01	292.05
26000	347.97	340.46	333.66	327.49	321.86	312.01	303.73
27000	361.35	353.56	346.50	340.08	334.24	324.01	315.41
28000	374.74	366.65	359.33	352.68	346.62	336.02	327.09
29000	388.12	379.75	372.16	365.27	359.00	348.02	338.78
30000	401.51	392.84	384.99	377.87	371.38	360.02	350.46
31000	414.89	405.94	397.83	390.46	383.75	372.02	362.14
32000	428.27	419.03	410.66	403.06	396.13	384.02	373.82
33000	441.66	432.12	423.49	415.65	408.51	396.02	385.50
34000	455.04	445.22	436.33	428.25	420.89	408.02	397.18
35000	468.42	458.31	449.16	440.85	433.27	420.02	408.87
40000	535.34	523.79	513.33	503.82	495.17	480.02	467.28
45000	602.26	589.26	577.49	566.80	557.06	540.02	525.69
50000	669.18	654.73	641.66	629.78	618.96	600.03	584.09
55000	736.09	720.21	705.82	692.76	680.85	660.03	642.50
60000	803.01	785.68	769.99	755.74	742.75	720.03	700.91
65000	869.93	851.16	834.16	818.71	804.65	780.04	759.32
70000	936.85	916.63	898.32	881.69	866.54	840.04	817.73

11¾%   Monthly Loan Payments

LOAN AMOUNT	½ YEAR	1 YEAR	1½ YEARS	2 YEARS	2½ YEARS	3 YEARS	3½ YEARS
100	17.24	8.87	6.09	4.70	3.86	3.31	2.92
200	34.48	17.75	12.17	9.39	7.73	6.62	5.83
300	51.73	26.62	18.26	14.09	11.59	9.93	8.75
400	68.97	35.49	24.35	18.78	15.45	13.24	11.66
500	86.21	44.37	30.43	23.48	19.32	16.55	14.58
600	103.45	53.24	36.52	28.17	23.18	19.86	17.49
700	120.70	62.11	42.61	32.87	27.04	23.17	20.41
800	137.94	70.99	48.69	37.57	30.90	26.48	23.32
900	155.18	79.86	54.78	42.26	34.77	29.79	26.24
1000	172.42	88.73	60.87	46.96	38.63	33.10	29.15
1500	258.64	133.10	91.30	70.44	57.95	49.64	43.73
2000	344.85	177.46	121.73	93.91	77.26	66.19	58.31
2500	431.06	221.83	152.16	117.39	96.58	82.74	72.89
3000	517.27	266.20	182.60	140.87	115.89	99.29	87.46
3500	603.49	310.56	213.03	164.35	135.21	115.83	102.04
4000	689.70	354.93	243.46	187.83	154.52	132.38	116.62
4500	775.91	399.29	273.90	211.31	173.84	148.93	131.20
5000	862.12	443.66	304.33	234.78	193.15	165.48	145.77
5500	948.34	488.03	334.76	258.26	212.47	182.02	160.35
6000	1034.55	532.39	365.20	281.74	231.78	198.57	174.93
6500	1120.76	576.76	395.63	305.22	251.10	215.12	189.51
7000	1206.97	621.12	426.06	328.70	270.41	231.67	204.08
7500	1293.19	665.49	456.49	352.18	289.73	248.21	218.66
8000	1379.40	709.86	486.93	375.65	309.04	264.76	233.24
8500	1465.61	754.22	517.36	399.13	328.36	281.31	247.82
9000	1551.82	798.59	547.79	422.61	347.67	297.86	262.39
9500	1638.04	842.95	578.23	446.09	366.99	314.40	276.97
10000	1724.25	887.32	608.66	469.57	386.30	330.95	291.55
11000	1896.67	976.05	669.53	516.52	424.93	364.05	320.70
12000	2069.10	1064.78	730.39	563.48	463.56	397.14	349.86
13000	2241.52	1153.51	791.26	610.44	502.19	430.24	379.01
14000	2413.95	1242.25	852.12	657.40	540.82	463.33	408.17
15000	2586.37	1330.98	912.99	704.35	579.45	496.43	437.32
16000	2758.80	1419.71	973.86	751.31	618.08	529.52	466.48
17000	2931.22	1508.44	1034.72	798.27	656.71	562.62	495.63
18000	3103.65	1597.17	1095.59	845.22	695.35	595.71	524.79
19000	3276.07	1685.91	1156.45	892.18	733.98	628.81	553.94
20000	3448.50	1774.64	1217.32	939.14	772.61	661.90	583.09
21000	3620.92	1863.37	1278.19	986.09	811.24	695.00	612.25
22000	3793.35	1952.10	1339.05	1033.05	849.87	728.09	641.40
23000	3965.77	2040.83	1399.92	1080.01	888.50	761.19	670.56
24000	4138.20	2129.57	1460.78	1126.96	927.13	794.28	699.71
25000	4310.62	2218.30	1521.65	1173.92	965.76	827.38	728.87
26000	4483.05	2307.03	1582.52	1220.88	1004.39	860.47	758.02
27000	4655.47	2395.76	1643.38	1267.83	1043.02	893.57	787.18
28000	4827.90	2484.49	1704.25	1314.79	1081.65	926.66	816.33
29000	5000.32	2573.22	1765.11	1361.75	1120.28	959.76	845.49
30000	5172.75	2661.96	1825.98	1408.70	1158.91	992.85	874.64
31000	5345.17	2750.69	1886.85	1455.66	1197.54	1025.95	903.80
32000	5517.60	2839.42	1947.71	1502.62	1236.17	1059.04	932.95
33000	5690.02	2928.15	2008.58	1549.57	1274.80	1092.14	962.11
34000	5862.44	3016.88	2069.44	1596.53	1313.43	1125.23	991.26
35000	6034.87	3105.62	2130.31	1643.49	1352.06	1158.33	1020.42
40000	6896.99	3549.28	2434.64	1878.27	1545.21	1323.80	1166.19
45000	7759.12	3992.93	2738.97	2113.06	1738.36	1489.28	1311.96
50000	8621.24	4436.59	3043.30	2347.84	1931.51	1654.75	1457.74
55000	9483.37	4880.25	3347.63	2582.62	2124.67	1820.23	1603.51
60000	10345.49	5323.91	3651.96	2817.41	2317.82	1985.70	1749.28
65000	11207.62	5767.57	3956.29	3052.19	2510.97	2151.18	1895.06
70000	12069.74	6211.23	4260.62	3286.98	2704.12	2316.65	2040.83

Monthly Loan Payments 11¾%

LOAN AMOUNT	4 YEARS	4½ YEARS	5 YEARS	5½ YEARS	6 YEARS	6½ YEARS	7 YEARS
100	2.62	2.39	2.21	2.06	1.94	1.84	1.75
200	5.24	4.79	4.42	4.13	3.88	3.68	3.50
300	7.86	7.18	6.64	6.19	5.83	5.52	5.26
400	10.48	9.57	8.85	8.26	7.77	7.36	7.01
500	13.11	11.97	11.06	10.32	9.71	9.20	8.76
600	15.73	14.36	13.27	12.39	11.65	11.04	10.51
700	18.35	16.75	15.48	14.45	13.59	12.88	12.26
800	20.97	19.15	17.69	16.51	15.54	14.71	14.02
900	23.59	21.54	19.91	18.58	17.48	16.55	15.77
1000	26.21	23.93	22.12	20.64	19.42	18.39	17.52
1500	39.32	35.90	33.18	30.96	29.13	27.59	26.28
2000	52.42	47.86	44.24	41.29	38.84	36.79	35.04
2500	65.53	59.83	55.30	51.61	48.55	45.98	43.80
3000	78.63	71.80	66.35	61.93	58.26	55.18	52.56
3500	91.74	83.76	77.41	72.25	67.97	64.38	61.32
4000	104.85	95.73	88.47	82.57	77.68	73.57	70.08
4500	117.95	107.70	99.53	92.89	87.39	82.77	78.84
5000	131.06	119.66	110.59	103.21	97.10	91.97	87.60
5500	144.16	131.63	121.65	113.53	106.81	101.16	96.36
6000	157.27	143.59	132.71	123.86	116.52	110.36	105.12
6500	170.37	155.56	143.77	134.18	126.23	119.56	113.88
7000	183.48	167.53	154.83	144.50	135.94	128.75	122.64
7500	196.58	179.49	165.89	154.82	145.65	137.95	131.39
8000	209.69	191.46	176.95	165.14	155.36	147.15	140.15
8500	222.80	203.42	188.01	175.46	165.07	156.34	148.91
9000	235.90	215.39	199.06	185.78	174.78	165.54	157.67
9500	249.01	227.36	210.12	196.10	184.49	174.74	166.43
10000	262.11	239.32	221.18	206.43	194.20	183.93	175.19
11000	288.32	263.25	243.30	227.07	213.62	202.33	192.71
12000	314.54	287.19	265.42	247.71	233.05	220.72	210.23
13000	340.75	311.12	287.54	268.35	252.47	239.11	227.75
14000	366.96	335.05	309.66	289.00	271.89	257.51	245.27
15000	393.17	358.98	331.77	309.64	291.31	275.90	262.79
16000	419.38	382.92	353.89	330.28	310.73	294.29	280.31
17000	445.59	406.85	376.01	350.92	330.15	312.69	297.83
18000	471.80	430.78	398.13	371.57	349.57	331.08	315.35
19000	498.01	454.71	420.25	392.21	368.99	349.47	332.87
20000	524.23	478.64	442.37	412.85	388.41	367.87	350.39
21000	550.44	502.58	464.48	433.49	407.83	386.26	367.91
22000	576.65	526.51	486.60	454.14	427.25	404.65	385.42
23000	602.86	550.44	508.72	474.78	446.67	423.05	402.94
24000	629.07	574.37	530.84	495.42	466.09	441.44	420.46
25000	655.28	598.31	552.96	516.06	485.51	459.83	437.98
26000	681.49	622.24	575.08	536.71	504.93	478.23	455.50
27000	707.70	646.17	597.19	557.35	524.35	496.62	473.02
28000	733.92	670.10	619.31	577.99	543.77	515.01	490.54
29000	760.13	694.04	641.43	598.63	563.19	533.41	508.06
30000	786.34	717.97	663.55	619.28	582.61	551.80	525.58
31000	812.55	741.90	685.67	639.92	602.03	570.19	543.10
32000	838.76	765.83	707.79	660.56	621.45	588.59	560.62
33000	864.97	789.76	729.90	681.21	640.87	606.98	578.14
34000	891.18	813.70	752.02	701.85	660.29	625.37	595.66
35000	917.39	837.63	774.14	722.49	679.72	643.77	613.18
40000	1048.45	957.29	884.73	825.70	776.82	735.73	700.77
45000	1179.51	1076.95	995.32	928.92	873.92	827.70	788.37
50000	1310.56	1196.61	1105.92	1032.13	971.02	919.66	875.97
55000	1441.62	1316.27	1216.51	1135.34	1068.12	1011.63	963.56
60000	1572.68	1435.93	1327.10	1238.55	1165.23	1103.60	1051.16
65000	1703.73	1555.60	1437.69	1341.77	1262.33	1195.56	1138.76
70000	1834.79	1675.26	1548.28	1444.98	1359.43	1287.53	1226.35

11¾% Monthly Loan Payments

LOAN AMOUNT	7½ YEARS	8 YEARS	8½ YEARS	9 YEARS	9½ YEARS	10 YEARS	10½ YEARS
100	1.68	1.61	1.55	1.50	1.46	1.42	1.38
200	3.35	3.22	3.11	3.01	2.92	2.84	2.77
300	5.03	4.83	4.66	4.51	4.38	4.26	4.15
400	6.71	6.45	6.22	6.02	5.84	5.68	5.54
500	8.38	8.06	7.77	7.52	7.30	7.10	6.92
600	10.06	9.67	9.33	9.03	8.76	8.52	8.31
700	11.74	11.28	10.88	10.53	10.22	9.94	9.69
800	13.41	12.89	12.44	12.03	11.68	11.36	11.08
900	15.09	14.50	13.99	13.54	13.14	12.78	12.46
1000	16.77	16.12	15.55	15.04	14.60	14.20	13.85
1500	25.15	24.17	23.32	22.57	21.90	21.30	20.77
2000	33.54	32.23	31.09	30.09	29.20	28.41	27.70
2500	41.92	40.29	38.86	37.61	36.50	35.51	34.62
3000	50.30	48.35	46.64	45.13	43.80	42.61	41.55
3500	58.69	56.41	54.41	52.65	51.10	49.71	48.47
4000	67.07	64.46	62.18	60.17	58.40	56.81	55.39
4500	75.46	72.52	69.96	67.70	65.70	63.91	62.32
5000	83.84	80.58	77.73	75.22	72.99	71.01	69.24
5500	92.22	88.64	85.50	82.74	80.29	78.12	76.17
6000	100.61	96.69	93.27	90.26	87.59	85.22	83.09
6500	108.99	104.75	101.05	97.78	94.89	92.32	90.02
7000	117.37	112.81	108.82	105.31	102.19	99.42	96.94
7500	125.76	120.87	116.59	112.83	109.49	106.52	103.86
8000	134.14	128.93	124.36	120.35	116.79	113.62	110.79
8500	142.53	136.98	132.14	127.87	124.09	120.73	117.71
9000	150.91	145.04	139.91	135.39	131.39	127.83	124.64
9500	159.29	153.10	147.68	142.91	138.69	134.93	131.56
10000	167.68	161.16	155.46	150.44	145.99	142.03	138.49
11000	184.45	177.27	171.00	165.48	160.59	156.23	152.34
12000	201.21	193.39	186.55	180.52	175.19	170.44	166.18
13000	217.98	209.51	202.09	195.57	189.79	184.64	180.03
14000	234.75	225.62	217.64	210.61	204.39	198.84	193.88
15000	251.52	241.74	233.18	225.65	218.98	213.04	207.73
16000	268.29	257.85	248.73	240.70	233.58	227.25	221.58
17000	285.05	273.97	264.28	255.74	248.18	241.45	235.43
18000	301.82	290.08	279.82	270.78	262.78	255.65	249.28
19000	318.59	306.20	295.37	285.83	277.38	269.86	263.12
20000	335.36	322.32	310.91	300.87	291.98	284.06	276.97
21000	352.12	338.43	326.46	315.92	306.58	298.26	290.82
22000	368.89	354.55	342.00	330.96	321.18	312.46	304.67
23000	385.66	370.66	357.55	346.00	335.78	326.67	318.52
24000	402.43	386.78	373.09	361.05	350.37	340.87	332.37
25000	419.20	402.89	388.64	376.09	364.97	355.07	346.22
26000	435.96	419.01	404.19	391.13	379.57	369.28	360.06
27000	452.73	435.13	419.73	406.18	394.17	383.48	373.91
28000	469.50	451.24	435.28	421.22	408.77	397.68	387.76
29000	486.27	467.36	450.82	436.26	423.37	411.89	401.61
30000	503.03	483.47	466.37	451.31	437.97	426.09	415.46
31000	519.80	499.59	481.91	466.35	452.57	440.29	429.31
32000	536.57	515.71	497.46	481.40	467.17	454.49	443.16
33000	553.34	531.82	513.01	496.44	481.76	468.70	457.01
34000	570.11	547.94	528.55	511.48	496.36	482.90	470.85
35000	586.87	564.05	544.10	526.53	510.96	497.10	484.70
40000	670.71	644.63	621.82	601.74	583.96	568.12	553.95
45000	754.55	725.21	699.55	676.96	656.95	639.13	623.19
50000	838.39	805.79	777.28	752.18	729.95	710.15	692.43
55000	922.23	886.37	855.01	827.40	802.94	781.16	761.68
60000	1006.07	966.95	932.74	902.62	875.94	852.18	830.92
65000	1089.91	1047.53	1010.47	977.83	948.93	923.19	900.16
70000	1173.75	1128.11	1088.19	1053.05	1021.93	994.21	969.41

Monthly Loan Payments 11¾%

LOAN AMOUNT	11 YEARS	11½ YEARS	12 YEARS	12½ YEARS	13 YEARS	14 YEARS	15 YEARS
100	1.35	1.32	1.30	1.27	1.25	1.22	1.18
200	2.71	2.65	2.60	2.55	2.51	2.43	2.37
300	4.06	3.97	3.89	3.82	3.76	3.65	3.55
400	5.41	5.30	5.19	5.10	5.01	4.86	4.74
500	6.77	6.62	6.49	6.37	6.27	6.08	5.92
600	8.12	7.95	7.79	7.65	7.52	7.29	7.10
700	9.47	9.27	9.09	8.92	8.77	8.51	8.29
800	10.82	10.59	10.39	10.20	10.03	9.73	9.47
900	12.18	11.92	11.68	11.47	11.28	10.94	10.66
1000	13.53	13.24	12.98	12.75	12.53	12.16	11.84
1500	20.30	19.86	19.47	19.12	18.80	18.24	17.76
2000	27.06	26.49	25.97	25.49	25.06	24.31	23.68
2500	33.83	33.11	32.46	31.87	31.33	30.39	29.60
3000	40.59	39.73	38.95	38.24	37.60	36.47	35.52
3500	47.36	46.35	45.44	44.62	43.86	42.55	41.44
4000	54.12	52.97	51.93	50.99	50.13	48.63	47.37
4500	60.89	59.59	58.42	57.36	56.40	54.71	53.29
5000	67.65	66.22	64.92	63.74	62.66	60.78	59.21
5500	74.42	72.84	71.41	70.11	68.93	66.86	65.13
6000	81.18	79.46	77.90	76.48	75.19	72.94	71.05
6500	87.95	86.08	84.39	82.86	81.46	79.02	76.97
7000	94.71	92.70	90.88	89.23	87.73	85.10	82.89
7500	101.48	99.32	97.37	95.60	93.99	91.18	88.81
8000	108.24	105.95	103.87	101.98	100.26	97.26	94.73
8500	115.01	112.57	110.36	108.35	106.53	103.33	100.65
9000	121.77	119.19	116.85	114.73	112.79	109.41	106.57
9500	128.54	125.81	123.34	121.10	119.06	115.49	112.49
10000	135.30	132.43	129.83	127.47	125.32	121.57	118.41
11000	148.83	145.67	142.82	140.22	137.86	133.73	130.25
12000	162.36	158.92	155.80	152.97	150.39	145.88	142.10
13000	175.89	172.16	168.78	165.71	162.92	158.04	153.94
14000	189.42	185.40	181.77	178.46	175.45	170.20	165.78
15000	202.95	198.65	194.75	191.21	187.99	182.35	177.62
16000	216.48	211.89	207.73	203.96	200.52	194.51	189.46
17000	230.01	225.13	220.72	216.70	213.05	206.67	201.30
18000	243.55	238.38	233.70	229.45	225.58	218.83	213.14
19000	257.08	251.62	246.68	242.20	238.12	230.98	224.98
20000	270.61	264.86	259.67	254.95	250.65	243.14	236.83
21000	284.14	278.11	272.65	267.69	263.18	255.30	248.67
22000	297.67	291.35	285.63	280.44	275.71	267.45	260.51
23000	311.20	304.59	298.61	293.19	288.25	279.61	272.35
24000	324.73	317.84	311.60	305.94	300.78	291.77	284.19
25000	338.26	331.08	324.58	318.68	313.31	303.92	296.03
26000	351.79	344.32	337.56	331.43	325.84	316.08	307.87
27000	365.32	357.56	350.55	344.18	338.38	328.24	319.72
28000	378.85	370.81	363.53	356.92	350.91	340.39	331.56
29000	392.38	384.05	376.51	369.67	363.44	352.55	343.40
30000	405.91	397.29	389.50	382.42	375.97	364.71	355.24
31000	419.44	410.54	402.48	395.17	388.51	376.87	367.08
32000	432.97	423.78	415.46	407.91	401.04	389.02	378.92
33000	446.50	437.02	428.45	420.66	413.57	401.18	390.76
34000	460.03	450.27	441.43	433.41	426.10	413.34	402.60
35000	473.56	463.51	454.41	446.16	438.64	425.49	414.45
40000	541.21	529.73	519.33	509.89	501.30	486.28	473.65
45000	608.86	595.94	584.25	573.63	563.96	547.06	532.86
50000	676.51	662.16	649.16	637.37	626.62	607.85	592.07
55000	744.17	728.37	714.08	701.10	689.29	668.63	651.27
60000	811.82	794.59	779.00	764.84	751.95	729.42	710.48
65000	879.47	860.80	843.91	828.57	814.61	790.20	769.69
70000	947.12	927.02	908.83	892.31	877.27	850.99	828.89

12%　　Monthly Loan Payments

LOAN AMOUNT	½ YEAR	1 YEAR	1½ YEARS	2 YEARS	2½ YEARS	3 YEARS	3½ YEARS
100	17.25	8.88	6.10	4.71	3.87	3.32	2.93
200	34.51	17.77	12.20	9.41	7.75	6.64	5.86
300	51.76	26.65	18.29	14.12	11.62	9.96	8.78
400	69.02	35.54	24.39	18.83	15.50	13.29	11.71
500	86.27	44.42	30.49	23.54	19.37	16.61	14.64
600	103.53	53.31	36.59	28.24	23.25	19.93	17.57
700	120.78	62.19	42.69	32.95	27.12	23.25	20.49
800	138.04	71.08	48.79	37.66	31.00	26.57	23.42
900	155.29	79.96	54.88	42.37	34.87	29.89	26.35
1000	172.55	88.85	60.98	47.07	38.75	33.21	29.28
1500	258.82	133.27	91.47	70.61	58.12	49.82	43.91
2000	345.10	177.70	121.96	94.15	77.50	66.43	58.55
2500	431.37	222.12	152.46	117.68	96.87	83.04	73.19
3000	517.65	266.55	182.95	141.22	116.24	99.64	87.83
3500	603.92	310.97	213.44	164.76	135.62	116.25	102.46
4000	690.19	355.40	243.93	188.29	154.99	132.86	117.10
4500	776.47	399.82	274.42	211.83	174.37	149.46	131.74
5000	862.74	444.24	304.91	235.37	193.74	166.07	146.38
5500	949.02	488.67	335.40	258.90	213.11	182.68	161.02
6000	1035.29	533.09	365.89	282.44	232.49	199.29	175.65
6500	1121.56	577.52	396.38	305.98	251.86	215.89	190.29
7000	1207.84	621.94	426.87	329.51	271.24	232.50	204.93
7500	1294.11	666.37	457.37	353.05	290.61	249.11	219.57
8000	1380.39	710.79	487.86	376.59	309.98	265.71	234.21
8500	1466.66	755.21	518.35	400.12	329.36	282.32	248.84
9000	1552.94	799.64	548.84	423.66	348.73	298.93	263.48
9500	1639.21	844.06	579.33	447.20	368.11	315.54	278.12
10000	1725.48	888.49	609.82	470.73	387.48	332.14	292.76
11000	1898.03	977.34	670.80	517.81	426.23	365.36	322.03
12000	2070.58	1066.19	731.78	564.88	464.98	398.57	351.31
13000	2243.13	1155.03	792.77	611.96	503.73	431.79	380.58
14000	2415.68	1243.88	853.75	659.03	542.47	465.00	409.86
15000	2588.23	1332.73	914.73	706.10	581.22	498.21	439.13
16000	2760.77	1421.58	975.71	753.18	619.97	531.43	468.41
17000	2933.32	1510.43	1036.69	800.25	658.72	564.64	497.69
18000	3105.87	1599.28	1097.68	847.32	697.47	597.86	526.96
19000	3278.42	1688.13	1158.66	894.40	736.21	631.07	556.24
20000	3450.97	1776.98	1219.64	941.47	774.96	664.29	585.51
21000	3623.52	1865.82	1280.62	988.54	813.71	697.50	614.79
22000	3796.06	1954.67	1341.61	1035.62	852.46	730.71	644.06
23000	3968.61	2043.52	1402.59	1082.69	891.21	763.93	673.34
24000	4141.16	2132.37	1463.57	1129.76	929.95	797.14	702.62
25000	4313.71	2221.22	1524.55	1176.84	968.70	830.36	731.89
26000	4486.26	2310.07	1585.53	1223.91	1007.45	863.57	761.17
27000	4658.81	2398.92	1646.52	1270.98	1046.20	896.79	790.44
28000	4831.35	2487.77	1707.50	1318.06	1084.95	930.00	819.72
29000	5003.90	2576.61	1768.48	1365.13	1123.70	963.21	848.99
30000	5176.45	2665.46	1829.46	1412.20	1162.44	996.43	878.27
31000	5349.00	2754.31	1890.44	1459.28	1201.19	1029.64	907.54
32000	5521.55	2843.16	1951.43	1506.35	1239.94	1062.86	936.82
33000	5694.10	2932.01	2012.41	1553.42	1278.69	1096.07	966.10
34000	5866.64	3020.86	2073.39	1600.50	1317.44	1129.29	995.37
35000	6039.19	3109.71	2134.37	1647.57	1356.18	1162.50	1024.65
40000	6901.93	3553.95	2439.28	1882.94	1549.92	1328.57	1171.03
45000	7764.68	3998.20	2744.19	2118.31	1743.67	1494.64	1317.40
50000	8627.42	4442.44	3049.10	2353.67	1937.41	1660.72	1463.78
55000	9490.16	4886.68	3354.01	2589.04	2131.15	1826.79	1610.16
60000	10352.90	5330.93	3658.92	2824.41	2324.89	1992.86	1756.54
65000	11215.64	5775.17	3963.83	3059.78	2518.63	2158.93	1902.92
70000	12078.39	6219.42	4268.74	3295.14	2712.37	2325.00	2049.29

Monthly Loan Payments 12%

LOAN AMOUNT	4 YEARS	4½ YEARS	5 YEARS	5½ YEARS	6 YEARS	6½ YEARS	7 YEARS
100	2.63	2.41	2.22	2.08	1.96	1.85	1.77
200	5.27	4.81	4.45	4.15	3.91	3.70	3.53
300	7.90	7.22	6.67	6.23	5.87	5.56	5.30
400	10.53	9.62	8.90	8.31	7.82	7.41	7.06
500	13.17	12.03	11.12	10.39	9.78	9.26	8.83
600	15.80	14.43	13.35	12.46	11.73	11.11	10.59
700	18.43	16.84	15.57	14.54	13.69	12.97	12.36
800	21.07	19.25	17.80	16.62	15.64	14.82	14.12
900	23.70	21.65	20.02	18.69	17.60	16.67	15.89
1000	26.33	24.06	22.24	20.77	19.55	18.52	17.65
1500	39.50	36.08	33.37	31.16	29.33	27.79	26.48
2000	52.67	48.11	44.49	41.54	39.10	37.05	35.31
2500	65.83	60.14	55.61	51.93	48.88	46.31	44.13
3000	79.00	72.17	66.73	62.31	58.65	55.57	52.96
3500	92.17	84.20	77.86	72.70	68.43	64.84	61.78
4000	105.34	96.23	88.98	83.08	78.20	74.10	70.61
4500	118.50	108.25	100.10	93.47	87.98	83.36	79.44
5000	131.67	120.28	111.22	103.85	97.75	92.62	88.26
5500	144.84	132.31	122.34	114.24	107.53	101.89	97.09
6000	158.00	144.34	133.47	124.62	117.30	111.15	105.92
6500	171.17	156.37	144.59	135.01	127.08	120.41	114.74
7000	184.34	168.40	155.71	145.39	136.85	129.67	123.57
7500	197.50	180.42	166.83	155.78	146.63	138.94	132.40
8000	210.67	192.45	177.96	166.16	156.40	148.20	141.22
8500	223.84	204.48	189.08	176.55	166.18	157.46	150.05
9000	237.00	216.51	200.20	186.93	175.95	166.72	158.87
9500	250.17	228.54	211.32	197.32	185.73	175.99	167.70
10000	263.34	240.57	222.44	207.71	195.50	185.25	176.53
11000	289.67	264.62	244.69	228.48	215.05	203.77	194.18
12000	316.01	288.68	266.93	249.25	234.60	222.30	211.83
13000	342.34	312.74	289.18	270.02	254.15	240.82	229.49
14000	368.67	336.79	311.42	290.79	273.70	259.35	247.14
15000	395.01	360.85	333.67	311.56	293.25	277.87	264.79
16000	421.34	384.91	355.91	332.33	312.80	296.40	282.44
17000	447.68	408.96	378.16	353.10	332.35	314.92	300.10
18000	474.01	433.02	400.40	373.87	351.90	333.45	317.75
19000	500.34	457.08	422.64	394.64	371.45	351.97	335.40
20000	526.68	481.13	444.89	415.41	391.00	370.50	353.05
21000	553.01	505.19	467.13	436.18	410.55	389.02	370.71
22000	579.34	529.24	489.38	456.95	430.10	407.55	388.36
23000	605.68	553.30	511.62	477.72	449.65	426.07	406.01
24000	632.01	577.36	533.87	498.49	469.20	444.60	423.67
25000	658.35	601.41	556.11	519.26	488.75	463.12	441.32
26000	684.68	625.47	578.36	540.03	508.31	481.65	458.97
27000	711.01	649.53	600.60	560.80	527.86	500.17	476.62
28000	737.35	673.58	622.84	581.57	547.41	518.70	494.28
29000	763.68	697.64	645.09	602.35	566.96	537.22	511.93
30000	790.02	721.70	667.33	623.12	586.51	555.75	529.58
31000	816.35	745.75	689.58	643.89	606.06	574.27	547.23
32000	842.68	769.81	711.82	664.66	625.61	592.80	564.89
33000	869.02	793.87	734.07	685.43	645.16	611.32	582.54
34000	895.35	817.92	756.31	706.20	664.71	629.85	600.19
35000	921.68	841.98	778.56	726.97	684.26	648.37	617.85
40000	1053.35	962.26	889.78	830.82	782.01	741.00	706.11
45000	1185.02	1082.55	1001.00	934.67	879.76	833.62	794.37
50000	1316.69	1202.83	1112.22	1038.53	977.51	926.24	882.64
55000	1448.36	1323.11	1223.44	1142.38	1075.26	1018.87	970.90
60000	1580.03	1443.39	1334.67	1246.23	1173.01	1111.49	1059.16
65000	1711.70	1563.68	1445.89	1350.08	1270.76	1204.12	1147.43
70000	1843.37	1683.96	1557.11	1453.94	1368.51	1296.74	1235.69

12% Monthly Loan Payments

LOAN AMOUNT	7½ YEARS	8 YEARS	8½ YEARS	9 YEARS	9½ YEARS	10 YEARS	10½ YEARS
100	1.63	1.63	1.57	1.52	1.47	1.43	1.40
200	3.38	3.25	3.14	3.04	2.95	2.87	2.80
300	5.07	4.88	4.71	4.56	4.42	4.30	4.20
400	6.76	6.50	6.27	6.07	5.90	5.74	5.60
500	8.45	8.13	7.84	7.59	7.37	7.17	7.00
600	10.14	9.75	9.41	9.11	8.84	8.61	8.40
700	11.83	11.38	10.98	10.63	10.32	10.04	9.80
800	13.52	13.00	12.55	12.15	11.79	11.48	11.20
900	15.21	14.63	14.12	13.67	13.27	12.91	12.60
1000	16.90	16.25	15.68	15.18	14.74	14.35	13.99
1500	25.35	24.38	23.53	22.78	22.11	21.52	20.99
2000	33.81	32.51	31.37	30.37	29.48	28.69	27.99
2500	42.26	40.63	39.21	37.96	36.85	35.87	34.99
3000	50.71	48.76	47.05	45.55	44.22	43.04	41.98
3500	59.16	56.88	54.90	53.14	51.59	50.21	48.98
4000	67.61	65.01	62.74	60.74	58.97	57.39	55.98
4500	76.06	73.14	70.58	68.33	66.34	64.56	62.98
5000	84.52	81.26	78.42	75.92	73.71	71.74	69.97
5500	92.97	89.39	86.26	83.51	81.08	78.91	76.97
6000	101.42	97.52	94.11	91.11	88.45	86.08	83.97
6500	109.87	105.64	101.95	98.70	95.82	93.26	90.96
7000	118.32	113.77	109.79	106.29	103.19	100.43	97.96
7500	126.77	121.90	117.63	113.88	110.56	107.60	104.96
8000	135.22	130.02	125.48	121.47	117.93	114.78	111.96
8500	143.68	138.15	133.32	129.07	125.30	121.95	118.95
9000	152.13	146.28	141.16	136.66	132.67	129.12	125.95
9500	160.58	154.40	149.00	144.25	140.04	136.30	132.95
10000	169.03	162.53	156.84	151.84	147.41	143.47	139.95
11000	185.93	178.78	172.53	167.03	162.15	157.82	153.94
12000	202.84	195.03	188.21	182.21	176.90	172.17	167.93
13000	219.74	211.29	203.90	197.40	191.64	186.51	181.93
14000	236.64	227.54	219.58	212.58	206.38	200.86	195.92
15000	253.55	243.79	235.27	227.76	221.12	215.21	209.92
16000	270.45	260.05	250.95	242.95	235.86	229.55	223.91
17000	287.35	276.30	266.64	258.13	250.60	243.90	237.91
18000	304.26	292.55	282.32	273.32	265.34	258.25	251.90
19000	321.16	308.80	298.00	288.50	280.09	272.59	265.90
20000	338.06	325.06	313.69	303.68	294.83	286.94	279.89
21000	354.96	341.31	329.37	318.87	309.57	301.29	293.89
22000	371.87	357.56	345.06	334.05	324.31	315.64	307.88
23000	388.77	373.82	360.74	349.24	339.05	329.98	321.87
24000	405.67	390.07	376.43	364.42	353.79	344.33	335.87
25000	422.58	406.32	392.11	379.61	368.53	358.68	349.86
26000	439.48	422.57	407.80	394.79	383.27	373.02	363.86
27000	456.38	438.83	423.48	409.97	398.02	387.37	377.85
28000	473.29	455.08	439.17	425.16	412.76	401.72	391.85
29000	490.19	471.33	454.85	440.34	427.50	416.07	405.84
30000	507.09	487.59	470.53	455.53	442.24	430.41	419.84
31000	523.99	503.84	486.22	470.71	456.98	444.76	433.83
32000	540.90	520.09	501.90	485.90	471.72	459.11	447.82
33000	557.80	536.34	517.59	501.08	486.46	473.45	461.82
34000	574.70	552.60	533.27	516.26	501.21	487.80	475.81
35000	591.61	568.85	548.96	531.45	515.95	502.15	489.81
40000	676.12	650.11	627.38	607.37	589.65	573.88	559.78
45000	760.64	731.38	705.80	683.29	663.36	645.62	629.75
50000	845.15	812.64	784.22	759.21	737.07	717.35	699.73
55000	929.67	893.91	862.65	835.13	810.77	789.09	769.70
60000	1014.18	975.17	941.07	911.05	884.48	860.83	839.67
65000	1098.70	1056.43	1019.49	986.98	958.19	932.56	909.64
70000	1183.21	1137.70	1097.91	1062.90	1031.89	1004.30	979.62

Monthly Loan Payments 12%

LOAN AMOUNT	11 YEARS	11½ YEARS	12 YEARS	12½ YEARS	13 YEARS	14 YEARS	15 YEARS
100	1.37	1.34	1.31	1.29	1.27	1.23	1.20
200	2.74	2.68	2.63	2.58	2.54	2.46	2.40
300	4.10	4.02	3.94	3.87	3.81	3.69	3.60
400	5.47	5.36	5.25	5.16	5.07	4.93	4.80
500	6.84	6.70	6.57	6.45	6.34	6.16	6.00
600	8.21	8.04	7.88	7.74	7.61	7.39	7.20
700	9.57	9.37	9.19	9.03	8.88	8.62	8.40
800	10.94	10.71	10.51	10.32	10.15	9.85	9.60
900	12.31	12.05	11.82	11.61	11.42	11.08	10.80
1000	13.68	13.39	13.13	12.90	12.69	12.31	12.00
1500	20.52	20.09	19.70	19.35	19.03	18.47	18.00
2000	27.36	26.78	26.27	25.80	25.37	24.63	24.00
2500	34.19	33.48	32.84	32.25	31.72	30.79	30.00
3000	41.03	40.18	39.40	38.70	38.06	36.94	36.01
3500	47.87	46.87	45.97	45.15	44.40	43.10	42.01
4000	54.71	53.57	52.54	51.60	50.75	49.26	48.01
4500	61.55	60.27	59.10	58.05	57.09	55.41	54.01
5000	68.39	66.96	65.67	64.50	63.43	61.57	60.01
5500	75.23	73.66	72.24	70.95	69.78	67.73	66.01
6000	82.07	80.35	78.81	77.40	76.12	73.89	72.01
6500	88.91	87.05	85.37	83.85	82.46	80.04	78.01
7000	95.75	93.75	91.94	90.30	88.81	86.20	84.01
7500	102.58	100.44	98.51	96.75	95.15	92.36	90.01
8000	109.42	107.14	105.07	103.20	101.49	98.51	96.01
8500	116.26	113.84	111.64	109.65	107.84	104.67	102.01
9000	123.10	120.53	118.21	116.10	114.18	110.83	108.02
9500	129.94	127.23	124.77	122.55	120.52	116.99	114.02
10000	136.78	133.92	131.34	129.00	126.87	123.14	120.02
11000	150.46	147.32	144.48	141.90	139.55	135.46	132.02
12000	164.13	160.71	157.61	154.80	152.24	147.77	144.02
13000	177.81	174.10	170.74	167.70	164.93	160.09	156.02
14000	191.49	187.49	183.88	180.60	177.61	172.40	168.02
15000	205.17	200.89	197.01	193.50	190.30	184.71	180.03
16000	218.85	214.28	210.15	206.40	202.99	197.03	192.03
17000	232.52	227.67	223.28	219.30	215.67	209.34	204.03
18000	246.20	241.06	236.42	232.20	228.36	221.66	216.03
19000	259.88	254.46	249.55	245.10	241.05	233.97	228.03
20000	273.56	267.85	262.68	258.00	253.73	246.29	240.03
21000	287.24	281.24	275.82	270.90	266.42	258.60	252.04
22000	300.91	294.63	288.95	283.80	279.11	270.91	264.04
23000	314.59	308.03	302.09	296.70	291.79	283.23	276.04
24000	328.27	321.42	315.22	309.60	304.48	295.54	288.04
25000	341.95	334.81	328.35	322.50	317.17	307.86	300.04
26000	355.62	348.20	341.49	335.40	329.85	320.17	312.04
27000	369.30	361.60	354.62	348.30	342.54	332.49	324.05
28000	382.98	374.99	367.76	361.20	355.23	344.80	336.05
29000	396.66	388.38	380.89	374.10	367.91	357.11	348.05
30000	410.34	401.77	394.03	387.00	380.60	369.43	360.05
31000	424.01	415.16	407.16	399.90	393.29	381.74	372.05
32000	437.69	428.56	420.29	412.80	405.97	394.06	384.05
33000	451.37	441.95	433.43	425.70	418.66	406.37	396.06
34000	465.05	455.34	446.56	438.60	431.35	418.69	408.06
35000	478.73	468.73	459.70	451.50	444.03	431.00	420.06
40000	547.12	535.70	525.37	516.00	507.47	492.57	480.07
45000	615.50	602.66	591.04	580.49	570.90	554.14	540.08
50000	683.89	669.62	656.71	644.99	634.33	615.71	600.08
55000	752.28	736.58	722.38	709.49	697.77	677.29	660.09
60000	820.67	803.55	788.05	773.99	761.20	738.86	720.10
65000	889.06	870.51	853.72	838.49	824.63	800.43	780.11
70000	957.45	937.47	919.39	902.99	888.07	862.00	840.12

12¼%   Monthly Loan Payments

LOAN AMOUNT	½ YEAR	1 YEAR	1½ YEARS	2 YEARS	2½ YEARS	3 YEARS	3½ YEAR
100	17.27	8.90	6.11	4.72	3.89	3.33	2.
200	34.53	17.79	12.22	9.44	7.77	6.67	5.
300	51.80	26.69	18.33	14.16	11.66	10.00	8.
400	69.07	35.59	24.44	18.88	15.55	13.33	11.
500	86.34	44.48	30.55	23.60	19.43	16.67	14.
600	103.60	53.38	36.66	28.31	23.32	20.00	17.
700	120.87	62.28	42.77	33.03	27.21	23.33	20.
800	138.14	71.17	48.88	37.75	31.09	26.67	23.
900	155.40	80.07	54.99	42.47	34.98	30.00	26.
1000	172.67	88.97	61.10	47.19	38.87	33.33	29.
1500	259.01	133.45	91.65	70.79	58.30	50.00	44.
2000	345.34	177.93	122.20	94.38	77.73	66.67	58.
2500	431.68	222.41	152.75	117.98	97.17	83.33	73.
3000	518.02	266.90	183.29	141.57	116.60	100.00	88.
3500	604.35	311.38	213.84	165.17	136.03	116.67	102.
4000	690.69	355.86	244.39	188.76	155.46	133.34	117.
4500	777.02	400.35	274.94	212.36	174.90	150.00	132.
5000	863.36	444.83	305.49	235.95	194.33	166.67	146.
5500	949.70	489.31	336.04	259.55	213.76	183.34	161.
6000	1036.03	533.79	366.59	283.14	233.20	200.00	176.
6500	1122.37	578.28	397.14	306.74	252.63	216.67	191.
7000	1208.70	622.76	427.69	330.33	272.06	233.34	205.
7500	1295.04	667.24	458.24	353.93	291.50	250.00	220.
8000	1381.38	711.73	488.79	377.52	310.93	266.67	235.
8500	1467.71	756.21	519.34	401.12	330.36	283.34	249.
9000	1554.05	800.69	549.88	424.71	349.80	300.00	264.
9500	1640.38	845.17	580.43	448.31	369.23	316.67	279.
10000	1726.72	889.66	610.98	471.90	388.66	333.34	293.
11000	1899.39	978.62	672.08	519.09	427.53	366.67	323.
12000	2072.06	1067.59	733.18	566.28	466.39	400.01	352.
13000	2244.74	1156.56	794.28	613.47	505.26	433.34	382.
14000	2417.41	1245.52	855.38	660.66	544.13	466.67	411.
15000	2590.08	1334.49	916.47	707.85	582.99	500.01	440.
16000	2762.75	1423.45	977.57	755.04	621.86	533.34	470.
17000	2935.42	1512.42	1038.67	802.24	660.72	566.68	499.
18000	3108.09	1601.38	1099.77	849.43	699.59	600.01	529.
19000	3280.77	1690.35	1160.87	896.62	738.46	633.34	558.
20000	3453.44	1779.32	1221.96	943.81	777.32	666.68	587.
21000	3626.11	1868.28	1283.06	991.00	816.19	700.01	617.
22000	3798.78	1957.25	1344.16	1038.19	855.06	733.34	646.
23000	3971.45	2046.21	1405.26	1085.38	893.92	766.68	676.
24000	4144.13	2135.18	1466.36	1132.57	932.79	800.01	705.
25000	4316.80	2224.14	1527.46	1179.76	971.65	833.35	734.
26000	4489.47	2313.11	1588.55	1226.95	1010.52	866.68	764.
27000	4662.14	2402.08	1649.65	1274.14	1049.39	900.01	793.
28000	4834.81	2491.04	1710.75	1321.33	1088.25	933.35	823.
29000	5007.49	2580.01	1771.85	1368.52	1127.12	966.68	852.
30000	5180.16	2668.97	1832.95	1415.71	1165.98	1000.02	881.
31000	5352.83	2757.94	1894.05	1462.90	1204.85	1033.35	911.
32000	5525.50	2846.91	1955.14	1510.00	1243.72	1066.68	940.
33000	5698.17	2935.87	2016.24	1557.28	1282.58	1100.02	970.
34000	5870.85	3024.84	2077.34	1604.47	1321.45	1133.35	999.
35000	6043.52	3113.80	2138.44	1651.66	1360.32	1166.68	1028.
40000	6906.88	3558.63	2443.90	1887.61	1554.65	1333.35	1175.
45000	7770.24	4003.46	2749.42	2123.56	1748.98	1500.02	1322.
50000	8633.60	4448.29	3054.91	2359.52	1943.31	1666.69	1469.
55000	9496.96	4893.12	3360.40	2595.47	2137.64	1833.36	1616.
60000	10360.32	5337.95	3665.89	2831.42	2331.97	2000.03	1763.
65000	11223.68	5782.78	3971.39	3067.37	2526.30	2166.70	1910.
70000	12087.03	6227.60	4276.88	3303.32	2720.63	2333.37	2057.

72

Monthly Loan Payments 12¼%

LOAN AMOUNT	4 YEARS	4½ YEARS	5 YEARS	5½ YEARS	6 YEARS	6½ YEARS	7 YEARS
100	2.65	2.42	2.24	2.09	1.97	1.87	1.78
200	5.29	4.84	4.47	4.18	3.94	3.73	3.56
300	7.94	7.25	6.71	6.27	5.90	5.60	5.34
400	10.58	9.67	8.95	8.36	7.87	7.46	7.11
500	13.23	12.09	11.19	10.45	9.84	9.33	8.89
600	15.87	14.51	13.42	12.54	11.81	11.19	10.67
700	18.52	16.93	15.66	14.63	13.78	13.06	12.45
800	21.17	19.35	17.90	16.72	15.74	14.93	14.23
900	23.81	21.76	20.13	18.81	17.71	16.79	16.01
1000	26.46	24.18	22.37	20.90	19.68	18.66	17.79
1500	39.69	36.27	33.56	31.35	29.52	27.99	26.68
2000	52.91	48.36	44.74	41.80	39.36	37.31	35.57
2500	66.14	60.45	55.93	52.25	49.20	46.64	44.47
3000	79.37	72.54	67.11	62.70	59.04	55.97	53.36
3500	92.60	84.63	78.30	73.15	68.88	65.30	62.25
4000	105.83	96.73	89.48	83.60	78.72	74.63	71.15
4500	119.06	108.82	100.67	94.05	88.56	83.96	80.04
5000	132.28	120.91	111.85	104.49	98.40	93.28	88.93
5500	145.51	133.00	123.04	114.94	108.24	102.61	97.83
6000	158.74	145.09	134.23	125.39	118.08	111.94	106.72
6500	171.97	157.18	145.41	135.84	127.92	121.27	115.61
7000	185.20	169.27	156.60	146.29	137.76	130.60	124.51
7500	198.43	181.36	167.78	156.74	147.60	139.93	133.40
8000	211.65	193.45	178.97	167.19	157.44	149.26	142.29
8500	224.88	205.54	190.15	177.64	167.28	158.58	151.19
9000	238.11	217.63	201.34	188.09	177.12	167.91	160.08
9500	251.34	229.72	212.52	198.54	186.96	177.24	168.97
10000	264.57	241.81	223.71	208.99	196.80	186.57	177.87
11000	291.02	265.99	246.08	229.89	216.48	205.23	195.65
12000	317.48	290.18	268.45	250.79	236.17	223.88	213.44
13000	343.94	314.36	290.82	271.69	255.85	242.54	231.23
14000	370.39	338.54	313.19	292.58	275.53	261.20	249.01
15000	396.85	362.72	335.56	313.48	295.21	279.85	266.80
16000	423.31	386.90	357.94	334.38	314.89	298.51	284.59
17000	449.76	411.08	380.31	355.28	334.57	317.17	302.37
18000	476.22	435.26	402.68	376.18	354.25	335.83	320.16
19000	502.68	459.44	425.05	397.08	373.93	354.48	337.95
20000	529.14	483.63	447.42	417.98	393.61	373.14	355.73
21000	555.59	507.81	469.79	438.88	413.29	391.80	373.52
22000	582.05	531.99	492.16	459.78	432.97	410.45	391.31
23000	608.51	556.17	514.53	480.67	452.65	429.11	409.09
24000	634.96	580.35	536.90	501.57	472.33	447.77	426.88
25000	661.42	604.53	559.27	522.47	492.01	466.42	444.67
26000	687.88	628.71	581.65	543.37	511.69	485.08	462.45
27000	714.33	652.89	604.02	564.27	531.37	503.74	480.24
28000	740.79	677.08	626.39	585.17	551.05	522.40	498.03
29000	767.25	701.26	648.76	606.07	570.73	541.05	515.81
30000	793.70	725.44	671.13	626.97	590.41	559.71	533.60
31000	820.16	749.62	693.50	647.87	610.09	578.37	551.39
32000	846.62	773.80	715.87	668.77	629.77	597.02	569.17
33000	873.07	797.98	738.24	689.66	649.45	615.68	586.96
34000	899.53	822.16	760.61	710.56	669.14	634.34	604.75
35000	925.99	846.35	782.98	731.46	688.82	652.99	622.53
40000	1058.27	967.25	894.84	835.96	787.22	746.28	711.47
45000	1190.55	1088.16	1006.69	940.45	885.62	839.56	800.40
50000	1322.84	1209.06	1118.45	1044.95	984.02	932.85	889.34
55000	1455.12	1329.97	1230.40	1149.44	1082.42	1026.13	978.27
60000	1587.41	1450.88	1342.26	1253.93	1180.83	1119.42	1067.20
65000	1719.69	1571.78	1454.11	1358.43	1279.23	1212.70	1156.14
70000	1851.97	1692.69	1565.97	1462.92	1377.63	1305.99	1245.07

12¼%   Monthly Loan Payments

LOAN AMOUNT	7½ YEARS	8 YEARS	8½ YEARS	9 YEARS	9½ YEARS	10 YEARS	10½ YEARS
100	1.70	1.64	1.58	1.53	1.49	1.45	1.41
200	3.41	3.28	3.16	3.07	2.98	2.90	2.83
300	5.11	4.92	4.75	4.60	4.47	4.35	4.24
400	6.82	6.56	6.33	6.13	5.95	5.80	5.66
500	8.52	8.20	7.91	7.66	7.44	7.25	7.07
600	10.22	9.83	9.49	9.20	8.93	8.70	8.48
700	11.93	11.47	11.08	10.73	10.42	10.14	9.90
800	13.63	13.11	12.66	12.26	11.91	11.59	11.31
900	15.34	14.75	14.24	13.79	13.40	13.04	12.73
1000	17.04	16.39	15.82	15.33	14.88	14.49	14.14
1500	25.56	24.59	23.74	22.99	22.33	21.74	21.21
2000	34.08	32.78	31.65	30.65	29.77	28.98	28.28
2500	42.60	40.98	39.56	38.31	37.21	36.23	35.35
3000	51.12	49.17	47.47	45.98	44.65	43.48	42.42
3500	59.64	57.37	55.38	53.64	52.10	50.72	49.49
4000	68.16	65.56	63.30	61.30	59.54	57.97	56.56
4500	76.68	73.76	71.21	68.96	66.98	65.21	63.64
5000	85.19	81.95	79.12	76.63	74.42	72.46	70.71
5500	93.71	90.15	87.03	84.29	81.86	79.71	77.78
6000	102.23	98.34	94.94	91.95	89.31	86.95	84.85
6500	110.75	106.54	102.86	99.62	96.75	94.20	91.92
7000	119.27	114.73	110.77	107.28	104.19	101.44	98.99
7500	127.79	122.93	118.68	114.94	111.63	108.69	106.06
8000	136.31	131.12	126.59	122.60	119.08	115.94	113.13
8500	144.83	139.32	134.50	130.27	126.52	123.18	120.20
9000	153.35	147.51	142.42	137.93	133.96	130.43	127.27
9500	161.87	155.71	150.33	145.59	141.40	137.67	134.34
10000	170.39	163.91	158.24	153.26	148.84	144.92	141.41
11000	187.43	180.30	174.06	168.58	163.73	159.41	155.55
12000	204.47	196.69	189.89	183.91	178.61	173.90	169.69
13000	221.51	213.08	205.71	199.23	193.50	188.40	183.84
14000	238.54	229.47	221.54	214.56	208.38	202.89	197.98
15000	255.58	245.86	237.36	229.88	223.27	217.38	212.12
16000	272.62	262.25	253.18	245.21	238.15	231.87	226.26
17000	289.66	278.64	269.01	260.53	253.04	246.36	240.40
18000	306.70	295.03	284.83	275.86	267.92	260.86	254.54
19000	323.74	311.42	300.66	291.19	282.80	275.35	268.68
20000	340.78	327.81	316.48	306.51	297.69	289.84	282.82
21000	357.82	344.20	332.30	321.84	312.57	304.33	296.96
22000	374.86	360.59	348.13	337.16	327.46	318.82	311.11
23000	391.89	376.98	363.95	352.49	342.34	333.32	325.25
24000	408.93	393.37	379.78	367.81	357.23	347.81	339.39
25000	425.97	409.76	395.60	383.14	372.11	362.30	353.53
26000	443.01	426.15	411.42	398.46	387.00	376.79	367.67
27000	460.05	442.54	427.25	413.79	401.88	391.28	381.81
28000	477.09	458.93	443.07	429.12	416.76	405.78	395.95
29000	494.13	475.32	458.90	444.44	431.65	420.27	410.09
30000	511.17	491.72	474.72	459.77	446.53	434.76	424.24
31000	528.21	508.11	490.54	475.09	461.42	449.25	438.38
32000	545.24	524.50	506.37	490.42	476.30	463.74	452.52
33000	562.28	540.89	522.19	505.74	491.19	478.24	466.66
34000	579.32	557.28	538.01	521.07	506.07	492.73	480.80
35000	596.36	573.67	553.84	536.39	520.96	507.22	494.94
40000	681.56	655.62	632.96	613.02	595.38	579.68	565.65
45000	766.75	737.57	712.08	689.65	669.80	652.14	636.35
50000	851.94	819.53	791.20	766.28	744.22	724.60	707.06
55000	937.14	901.48	870.32	842.91	818.64	797.06	777.76
60000	1022.33	983.43	949.44	919.53	893.07	869.52	848.47
65000	1107.53	1065.38	1028.56	996.16	967.49	941.98	919.18
70000	1192.72	1147.34	1107.68	1072.79	1041.91	1014.44	989.88

Monthly Loan Payments 12¼%

LOAN AMOUNT	11 YEARS	11½ YEARS	12 YEARS	12½ YEARS	13 YEARS	14 YEARS	15 YEARS
100	1.38	1.35	1.33	1.31	1.28	1.25	1.22
200	2.77	2.71	2.66	2.61	2.57	2.49	2.43
300	4.15	4.06	3.99	3.92	3.85	3.74	3.65
400	5.53	5.42	5.31	5.22	5.14	4.99	4.87
500	6.91	6.77	6.64	6.53	6.42	6.24	6.08
600	8.30	8.13	7.97	7.83	7.71	7.48	7.30
700	9.68	9.48	9.30	9.14	8.99	8.73	8.51
800	11.06	10.83	10.63	10.44	10.27	9.98	9.73
900	12.44	12.19	11.96	11.75	11.56	11.23	10.95
1000	13.83	13.54	13.29	13.05	12.84	12.47	12.16
1500	20.74	20.31	19.93	19.58	19.26	18.71	18.24
2000	27.65	27.09	26.57	26.11	25.68	24.95	24.33
2500	34.57	33.86	33.21	32.63	32.10	31.18	30.41
3000	41.48	40.63	39.86	39.16	38.53	37.42	36.49
3500	48.39	47.40	46.50	45.69	44.95	43.65	42.57
4000	55.31	54.17	53.14	52.21	51.37	49.89	48.65
4500	62.22	60.94	59.79	58.74	57.79	56.13	54.73
5000	69.13	67.71	66.43	65.27	64.21	62.36	60.81
5500	76.04	74.48	73.07	71.79	70.63	68.60	66.90
6000	82.96	81.26	79.72	78.32	77.05	74.84	72.98
6500	89.87	88.03	86.36	84.85	83.47	81.07	79.06
7000	96.78	94.80	93.00	91.37	89.89	87.31	85.14
7500	103.70	101.57	99.64	97.90	96.31	93.54	91.22
8000	110.61	108.34	106.29	104.43	102.73	99.78	97.30
8500	117.52	115.11	112.93	110.95	109.15	106.02	103.39
9000	124.44	121.88	119.57	117.48	115.58	112.25	109.47
9500	131.35	128.65	126.22	124.01	122.00	118.49	115.55
10000	138.26	135.43	132.86	130.53	128.42	124.73	121.63
11000	152.09	148.97	146.15	143.59	141.26	137.20	133.79
12000	165.92	162.51	159.43	156.64	154.10	149.67	145.96
13000	179.74	176.05	172.72	169.69	166.94	162.14	158.12
14000	193.57	189.60	186.00	182.75	179.78	174.62	170.28
15000	207.39	203.14	199.29	195.80	192.63	187.09	182.44
16000	221.22	216.68	212.58	208.85	205.47	199.56	194.61
17000	235.05	230.22	225.86	221.91	218.31	212.03	206.77
18000	248.87	243.77	239.15	234.96	231.15	224.51	218.93
19000	262.70	257.31	252.43	248.01	243.99	236.98	231.10
20000	276.53	270.85	265.72	261.07	256.83	249.45	243.26
21000	290.35	284.39	279.01	274.12	269.68	261.92	255.42
22000	304.18	297.94	292.29	287.17	282.52	274.40	267.59
23000	318.00	311.48	305.58	300.23	295.36	286.87	279.75
24000	331.83	325.02	318.86	313.28	308.20	299.34	291.91
25000	345.66	338.56	332.15	326.33	321.04	311.81	304.07
26000	359.48	352.11	345.44	339.39	333.88	324.29	316.24
27000	373.31	365.65	358.72	352.44	346.73	336.76	328.40
28000	387.14	379.19	372.01	365.49	359.57	349.23	340.56
29000	400.96	392.73	385.29	378.55	372.41	361.70	352.73
30000	414.79	406.28	398.58	391.60	385.25	374.18	364.89
31000	428.61	419.82	411.86	404.65	398.09	386.65	377.05
32000	442.44	433.36	425.15	417.71	410.94	399.12	389.22
33000	456.27	446.90	438.44	430.76	423.78	411.59	401.38
34000	470.09	460.45	451.72	443.81	436.62	424.07	413.54
35000	483.92	473.99	465.01	456.87	449.46	436.54	425.70
40000	553.05	541.70	531.44	522.13	513.67	498.90	486.52
45000	622.18	609.41	597.87	587.40	577.88	561.26	547.33
50000	691.31	677.13	664.30	652.67	642.09	623.63	608.15
55000	760.44	744.84	730.73	717.93	706.29	685.99	668.96
60000	829.58	812.55	797.16	783.20	770.50	748.35	729.78
65000	898.71	880.26	863.59	848.47	834.71	810.72	790.59
70000	967.84	947.98	930.02	913.73	898.92	873.08	851.41

12½% Monthly Loan Payments

LOAN AMOUNT	½ YEAR	1 YEAR	1½ YEARS	2 YEARS	2½ YEARS	3 YEARS	3½ YEARS
100	17.28	8.91	6.12	4.73	3.90	3.35	2.9
200	34.56	17.82	12.24	9.46	7.80	6.69	5.9
300	51.84	26.72	18.36	14.19	11.70	10.04	8.8
400	69.12	35.63	24.49	18.92	15.59	13.38	11.8
500	86.40	44.54	30.61	23.65	19.49	16.73	14.7
600	103.68	53.45	36.73	28.38	23.39	20.07	17.7
700	120.96	62.36	42.85	33.12	27.29	23.42	20.6
800	138.24	71.27	48.97	37.85	31.19	26.76	23.6
900	155.52	80.17	55.09	42.58	35.09	30.11	26.5
1000	172.80	89.08	61.21	47.31	38.98	33.45	29.5
1500	259.19	133.62	91.82	70.96	58.48	50.18	44.2
2000	345.59	178.17	122.43	94.61	77.97	66.91	59.0
2500	431.99	222.71	153.04	118.27	97.46	83.63	73.8
3000	518.39	267.25	183.64	141.92	116.95	100.36	88.5
3500	604.78	311.79	214.25	165.58	136.45	117.09	103.3
4000	691.18	356.33	244.86	189.23	155.94	133.81	118.0
4500	777.58	400.87	275.47	212.88	175.43	150.54	132.8
5000	863.98	445.41	306.07	236.54	194.92	167.27	147.5
5500	950.38	489.96	336.68	260.19	214.41	183.99	162.3
6000	1036.77	534.50	367.29	283.84	233.91	200.72	177.1
6500	1123.17	579.04	397.89	307.50	253.40	217.45	191.8
7000	1209.57	623.58	428.50	331.15	272.89	234.18	206.6
7500	1295.97	668.12	459.11	354.80	292.38	250.90	221.3
8000	1382.36	712.66	489.72	378.46	311.88	267.63	236.1
8500	1468.76	757.20	520.32	402.11	331.37	284.36	250.9
9000	1555.16	801.75	550.93	425.77	350.86	301.08	265.6
9500	1641.56	846.29	581.54	449.42	370.35	317.81	280.4
10000	1727.96	890.83	612.15	473.07	389.84	334.54	295.1
11000	1900.75	979.91	673.36	520.38	428.83	367.99	324.7
12000	2073.55	1068.99	734.57	567.69	467.81	401.44	354.2
13000	2246.34	1158.08	795.78	615.00	506.80	434.90	383.7
14000	2419.14	1247.16	857.00	662.30	545.78	468.35	413.2
15000	2591.93	1336.24	918.22	709.61	584.77	501.80	442.7
16000	2764.73	1425.33	979.43	756.92	623.75	535.26	472.2
17000	2937.52	1514.41	1040.65	804.22	662.73	568.71	501.8
18000	3110.32	1603.49	1101.86	851.53	701.72	602.17	531.3
19000	3283.11	1692.57	1163.08	898.84	740.70	635.62	560.8
20000	3455.91	1781.66	1224.29	946.15	779.69	669.07	590.3
21000	3628.71	1870.74	1285.51	993.45	818.67	702.53	619.8
22000	3801.50	1959.82	1346.72	1040.76	857.66	735.98	649.4
23000	3974.30	2048.91	1407.94	1088.07	896.64	769.43	678.9
24000	4147.09	2137.99	1469.15	1135.38	935.63	802.89	708.4
25000	4319.89	2227.07	1530.36	1182.68	974.61	836.34	737.9
26000	4492.68	2316.15	1591.58	1229.99	1013.59	869.79	767.4
27000	4665.48	2405.24	1652.79	1277.30	1052.58	903.25	796.9
28000	4838.27	2494.32	1714.01	1324.60	1091.56	936.70	826.5
29000	5011.07	2583.40	1775.22	1371.91	1130.55	970.16	856.0
30000	5183.87	2672.49	1836.44	1419.22	1169.53	1003.61	885.5
31000	5356.66	2761.57	1897.65	1466.53	1208.52	1037.06	915.0
32000	5529.46	2850.65	1958.87	1513.83	1247.50	1070.52	944.5
33000	5702.25	2939.73	2020.08	1561.14	1286.49	1103.97	974.1
34000	5875.05	3028.82	2081.30	1608.45	1325.47	1137.42	1003.6
35000	6047.84	3117.90	2142.51	1655.76	1364.45	1170.88	1033.1
40000	6911.82	3563.31	2448.58	1892.29	1559.38	1338.15	1180.7
45000	7775.80	4008.73	2754.66	2128.83	1754.30	1505.41	1328.3
50000	8639.78	4454.14	3060.73	2365.37	1949.22	1672.68	1475.9
55000	9503.75	4899.56	3366.80	2601.90	2144.14	1839.95	1623.5
60000	10367.73	5344.97	3672.87	2838.44	2339.06	2007.42	1771.1
65000	11231.71	5790.39	3978.95	3074.98	2533.99	2174.49	1918.6
70000	12095.69	6235.80	4285.02	3311.51	2728.91	2341.75	2066.2

Monthly Loan Payments 12½%

LOAN AMOUNT	4 YEARS	4½ YEARS	5 YEARS	5½ YEARS	6 YEARS	6½ YEARS	7 YEARS
100	2.66	2.43	2.25	2.10	1.98	1.88	1.79
200	5.32	4.86	4.50	4.21	3.96	3.76	3.58
300	7.97	7.29	6.75	6.31	5.94	5.64	5.38
400	10.63	9.72	9.00	8.41	7.92	7.52	7.17
500	13.29	12.15	11.25	10.51	9.91	9.39	8.96
600	15.95	14.58	13.50	12.62	11.89	11.27	10.75
700	18.61	17.01	15.75	14.72	13.87	13.15	12.54
800	21.26	19.45	18.00	16.82	15.85	15.03	14.34
900	23.92	21.88	20.25	18.92	17.83	16.91	16.13
1000	26.58	24.31	22.50	21.03	19.81	18.79	17.92
1500	39.87	36.46	33.75	31.54	29.72	28.18	26.88
2000	53.16	48.61	45.00	42.06	39.62	37.58	35.84
2500	66.45	60.77	56.24	52.57	49.53	46.97	44.80
3000	79.74	72.92	67.49	63.08	59.43	56.37	53.76
3500	93.03	85.07	78.74	73.60	69.34	65.76	62.72
4000	106.32	97.23	89.99	84.11	79.24	75.16	71.68
4500	119.61	109.38	101.24	94.62	89.15	84.55	80.65
5000	132.90	121.53	112.49	105.14	99.06	93.95	89.61
5500	146.19	133.69	123.74	115.65	108.96	103.34	98.57
6000	159.48	145.84	134.99	126.17	118.87	112.74	107.53
6500	172.77	157.99	146.24	136.68	128.77	122.13	116.49
7000	186.06	170.14	157.49	147.19	138.68	131.53	125.45
7500	199.35	182.30	168.73	157.71	148.58	140.92	134.41
8000	212.64	194.45	179.98	168.22	158.49	150.32	143.37
8500	225.93	206.60	191.23	178.74	168.40	159.71	152.33
9000	239.22	218.76	202.48	189.25	178.30	169.11	161.29
9500	252.51	230.91	213.73	199.76	188.21	178.50	170.25
10000	265.80	243.06	224.98	210.28	198.11	187.90	179.21
11000	292.38	267.37	247.48	231.31	217.92	206.69	197.13
12000	318.96	291.68	269.98	252.33	237.73	225.48	215.05
13000	345.54	315.98	292.47	273.36	257.55	244.27	232.98
14000	372.12	340.29	314.97	294.39	277.36	263.05	250.90
15000	398.70	364.60	337.47	315.42	297.17	281.84	268.82
16000	425.28	388.90	359.97	336.44	316.98	300.63	286.74
17000	451.86	413.21	382.46	357.47	336.79	319.42	304.66
18000	478.44	437.51	404.96	378.50	356.60	338.21	322.58
19000	505.02	461.82	427.46	399.53	376.41	357.00	340.50
20000	531.60	486.13	449.96	420.55	396.22	375.79	358.42
21000	558.18	510.43	472.46	441.58	416.03	394.58	376.35
22000	584.76	534.74	494.95	462.61	435.85	413.37	394.27
23000	611.34	559.05	517.45	483.64	455.66	432.16	412.19
24000	637.92	583.35	539.95	504.67	475.47	450.95	430.11
25000	664.50	607.66	562.45	525.69	495.28	469.74	448.03
26000	691.08	631.97	584.95	546.72	515.09	488.53	465.95
27000	717.66	656.27	607.44	567.75	534.90	507.32	483.87
28000	744.24	680.58	629.94	588.78	554.71	526.11	501.79
29000	770.82	704.88	652.44	609.80	574.52	544.90	519.72
30000	797.40	729.19	674.94	630.83	594.34	563.69	537.64
31000	823.98	753.50	697.44	651.86	614.15	582.48	555.56
32000	850.56	777.80	719.93	672.89	633.96	601.27	573.48
33000	877.14	802.11	742.43	693.92	653.77	620.06	591.40
34000	903.72	826.42	764.93	714.94	673.58	638.85	609.32
35000	930.30	850.72	787.43	735.97	693.39	657.64	627.24
40000	1063.20	972.26	899.92	841.11	792.45	751.59	716.85
45000	1196.10	1093.79	1012.41	946.25	891.50	845.53	806.46
50000	1329.00	1215.32	1124.90	1051.39	990.56	939.48	896.06
55000	1461.90	1336.85	1237.39	1156.53	1089.61	1033.43	985.67
60000	1594.80	1458.38	1349.88	1261.66	1188.67	1127.38	1075.27
65000	1727.70	1579.91	1462.37	1366.80	1287.73	1221.33	1164.88
70000	1860.60	1701.45	1574.86	1471.94	1386.78	1315.27	1254.49

12½%   Monthly Loan Payments

LOAN AMOUNT	7½ YEARS	8 YEARS	8½ YEARS	9 YEARS	9½ YEARS	10 YEARS	10½ YEARS
100	1.72	1.65	1.60	1.55	1.50	1.46	1.43
200	3.44	3.31	3.19	3.09	3.01	2.93	2.86
300	5.15	4.96	4.79	4.64	4.51	4.39	4.29
400	6.87	6.61	6.39	6.19	6.01	5.86	5.72
500	8.59	8.26	7.98	7.73	7.51	7.32	7.14
600	10.31	9.92	9.58	9.28	9.02	8.78	8.57
700	12.02	11.57	11.17	10.83	10.52	10.25	10.00
800	13.74	13.22	12.77	12.37	12.02	11.71	11.43
900	15.46	14.88	14.37	13.92	13.53	13.17	12.86
1000	17.18	16.53	15.96	15.47	15.03	14.64	14.29
1500	25.76	24.79	23.95	23.20	22.54	21.96	21.43
2000	34.35	33.06	31.93	30.94	30.06	29.28	28.58
2500	42.94	41.32	39.91	38.67	37.57	36.59	35.72
3000	51.53	49.59	47.89	46.40	45.08	43.91	42.87
3500	60.11	57.85	55.87	54.14	52.60	51.23	50.01
4000	68.70	66.12	63.86	61.87	60.11	58.55	57.15
4500	77.29	74.38	71.84	69.60	67.63	65.87	64.30
5000	85.88	82.64	79.82	77.34	75.14	73.19	71.44
5500	94.46	90.91	87.80	85.07	82.66	80.51	78.59
6000	103.05	99.17	95.78	92.81	90.17	87.83	85.73
6500	111.64	107.44	103.77	100.54	97.68	95.14	92.88
7000	120.23	115.70	111.75	108.27	105.20	102.46	100.02
7500	128.81	123.97	119.73	116.01	112.71	109.78	107.16
8000	137.40	132.23	127.71	123.74	120.23	117.10	114.31
8500	145.99	140.49	135.70	131.47	127.74	124.42	121.45
9000	154.58	148.76	143.68	139.21	135.25	131.74	128.60
9500	163.17	157.02	151.66	146.94	142.77	139.06	135.74
10000	171.75	165.29	159.64	154.68	150.28	146.38	142.89
11000	188.93	181.82	175.61	170.14	165.31	161.01	157.17
12000	206.10	198.35	191.57	185.61	180.34	175.65	171.46
13000	223.28	214.87	207.53	201.08	195.37	190.29	185.75
14000	240.45	231.40	223.50	216.55	210.40	204.93	200.04
15000	257.63	247.93	239.46	232.01	225.42	219.56	214.33
16000	274.80	264.46	255.43	247.48	240.45	234.20	228.62
17000	291.98	280.99	271.39	262.95	255.48	248.84	242.91
18000	309.16	297.52	287.35	278.42	270.51	263.48	257.19
19000	326.33	314.05	303.32	293.88	285.54	278.11	271.48
20000	343.51	330.58	319.28	309.35	300.57	292.75	285.77
21000	360.68	347.10	335.25	324.82	315.59	307.39	300.06
22000	377.86	363.63	351.21	340.29	330.62	322.03	314.35
23000	395.03	380.16	367.17	355.75	345.65	336.67	328.64
24000	412.21	396.69	383.14	371.22	360.68	351.30	342.93
25000	429.38	413.22	399.10	386.69	375.71	365.94	357.21
26000	446.56	429.75	415.07	402.16	390.73	380.58	371.50
27000	463.73	446.28	431.03	417.62	405.76	395.22	385.79
28000	480.91	462.81	447.00	433.09	420.79	409.85	400.08
29000	498.08	479.34	462.96	448.56	435.82	424.49	414.37
30000	515.26	495.86	478.92	464.03	450.85	439.13	428.66
31000	532.43	512.39	494.89	479.49	465.88	453.77	442.95
32000	549.61	528.92	510.85	494.96	480.90	468.40	457.23
33000	566.79	545.45	526.82	510.43	495.93	483.04	471.52
34000	583.96	561.98	542.78	525.90	510.96	497.68	485.81
35000	601.14	578.51	558.74	541.36	525.99	512.32	500.10
40000	687.01	661.15	638.56	618.70	601.13	585.50	571.54
45000	772.89	743.80	718.39	696.04	676.27	658.69	642.99
50000	858.77	826.44	798.21	773.38	751.41	731.88	714.43
55000	944.64	909.08	878.03	850.72	826.55	805.07	785.87
60000	1030.52	991.73	957.85	928.05	901.70	878.26	857.32
65000	1116.40	1074.37	1037.67	1005.39	976.84	951.45	928.76
70000	1202.27	1157.02	1117.49	1082.73	1051.98	1024.63	1000.20

Monthly Loan Payments 12½%

LOAN AMOUNT	11 YEARS	11½ YEARS	12 YEARS	12½ YEARS	13 YEARS	14 YEARS	15 YEARS
100	1.40	1.37	1.34	1.32	1.30	1.26	1.23
200	2.80	2.74	2.69	2.64	2.60	2.53	2.47
300	4.19	4.11	4.03	3.96	3.90	3.79	3.70
400	5.59	5.48	5.38	5.28	5.20	5.05	4.93
500	6.99	6.85	6.72	6.60	6.50	6.32	6.16
600	8.39	8.22	8.06	7.92	7.80	7.58	7.40
700	9.78	9.59	9.41	9.25	9.10	8.84	8.63
800	11.18	10.95	10.75	10.57	10.40	10.11	9.86
900	12.58	12.32	12.09	11.89	11.70	11.37	11.09
1000	13.98	13.69	13.44	13.21	13.00	12.63	12.33
1500	20.96	20.54	20.16	19.81	19.50	18.95	18.49
2000	27.95	27.39	26.88	26.42	26.00	25.26	24.65
2500	34.94	34.23	33.60	33.02	32.49	31.58	30.81
3000	41.93	41.08	40.32	39.62	38.99	37.90	36.98
3500	48.91	47.93	47.04	46.23	45.49	44.21	43.14
4000	55.90	54.77	53.75	52.83	51.99	50.53	49.30
4500	62.89	61.62	60.47	59.43	58.49	56.84	55.46
5000	69.88	68.47	67.19	66.04	64.99	63.16	61.63
5500	76.86	75.31	73.91	72.64	71.49	69.47	67.79
6000	83.85	82.16	80.63	79.25	77.99	75.79	73.95
6500	90.84	89.01	87.35	85.85	84.48	82.11	80.11
7000	97.83	95.85	94.07	92.45	90.98	88.42	86.28
7500	104.82	102.70	100.79	99.06	97.48	94.74	92.44
8000	111.80	109.55	107.51	105.66	103.98	101.05	98.60
8500	118.79	116.39	114.23	112.26	110.48	107.37	104.76
9000	125.78	123.24	120.95	118.87	116.98	113.69	110.93
9500	132.77	130.09	127.67	125.47	123.48	120.00	117.09
10000	139.75	136.93	134.39	132.08	129.98	126.32	123.25
11000	153.73	150.63	147.82	145.28	142.97	138.95	135.58
12000	167.71	164.32	161.26	158.49	155.97	151.58	147.90
13000	181.68	178.01	174.70	171.70	168.97	164.21	160.23
14000	195.66	191.71	188.14	184.91	181.97	176.84	172.55
15000	209.63	205.40	201.58	198.11	194.96	189.48	184.88
16000	223.61	219.09	215.02	211.32	207.96	202.11	197.20
17000	237.58	232.79	228.46	224.53	220.96	214.74	209.53
18000	251.56	246.48	241.89	237.74	233.96	227.37	221.85
19000	265.53	260.17	255.33	250.94	246.96	240.00	234.18
20000	279.51	273.87	268.77	264.15	259.95	252.63	246.50
21000	293.48	287.56	282.21	277.36	272.95	265.27	258.83
22000	307.46	301.26	295.65	290.57	285.95	277.90	271.15
23000	321.43	314.95	309.09	303.77	298.95	290.53	283.48
24000	335.41	328.64	322.53	316.98	311.94	303.16	295.80
25000	349.39	342.34	335.96	330.19	324.94	315.79	308.13
26000	363.36	356.03	349.40	343.40	337.94	328.42	320.46
27000	377.34	369.72	362.84	356.61	350.94	341.06	332.78
28000	391.31	383.42	376.28	369.81	363.93	353.69	345.11
29000	405.29	397.11	389.72	383.02	376.93	366.32	357.43
30000	419.26	410.80	403.16	396.23	389.93	378.95	369.76
31000	433.24	424.50	416.60	409.44	402.93	391.58	382.08
32000	447.21	438.19	430.03	422.64	415.93	404.21	394.41
33000	461.19	451.88	443.47	435.85	428.92	416.85	406.73
34000	475.16	465.58	456.91	449.06	441.92	429.48	419.06
35000	489.14	479.27	470.35	462.27	454.92	442.11	431.38
40000	559.02	547.74	537.54	528.30	519.91	505.27	493.01
45000	628.89	616.20	604.74	594.34	584.89	568.43	554.63
50000	698.77	684.67	671.93	660.38	649.88	631.58	616.26
55000	768.65	753.14	739.12	726.42	714.87	694.74	677.89
60000	838.53	821.60	806.31	792.46	779.86	757.90	739.51
65000	908.40	890.07	873.51	858.49	844.85	821.06	801.14
70000	978.28	958.54	940.70	924.53	909.84	884.22	862.77

12¾%   Monthly Loan Payments

LOAN AMOUNT	½ YEAR	1 YEAR	1½ YEARS	2 YEARS	2½ YEARS	3 YEARS	3½ YEARS
100	17.29	8.92	6.13	4.74	3.91	3.36	2.9
200	34.58	17.84	12.27	9.48	7.82	6.71	5.9
300	51.88	26.76	18.40	14.23	11.73	10.07	8.89
400	69.17	35.68	24.53	18.97	15.64	13.43	11.86
500	86.46	44.60	30.67	23.71	19.55	16.79	14.82
600	103.75	53.52	36.80	28.45	23.46	20.14	17.78
700	121.04	62.44	42.93	33.20	27.37	23.50	20.75
800	138.34	71.36	49.06	37.94	31.28	26.86	23.7
900	155.63	80.28	55.20	42.68	35.19	30.22	26.6
1000	172.92	89.20	61.33	47.42	39.10	33.57	29.6
1500	259.38	133.80	92.00	71.14	58.65	50.36	44.4
2000	345.84	178.40	122.66	94.85	78.21	67.15	59.2
2500	432.30	223.00	153.33	118.56	97.76	83.93	74.1
3000	518.76	267.60	183.99	142.27	117.31	100.72	88.9
3500	605.22	312.20	214.66	165.99	136.86	117.51	103.7
4000	691.68	356.80	245.32	189.70	156.41	134.29	118.5
4500	778.14	401.40	275.99	213.41	175.96	151.08	133.3
5000	864.60	446.00	306.66	237.12	195.51	167.87	148.2
5500	951.06	490.60	337.32	260.83	215.07	184.66	163.0
6000	1037.52	535.20	367.99	284.55	234.62	201.44	177.8
6500	1123.97	579.80	398.65	308.26	254.17	218.23	192.6
7000	1210.43	624.40	429.32	331.97	273.72	235.02	207.4
7500	1296.89	669.00	459.98	355.68	293.27	251.80	222.3
8000	1383.35	713.60	490.65	379.40	312.82	268.59	237.1
8500	1469.81	758.20	521.31	403.11	332.37	285.38	251.9
9000	1556.27	802.80	551.98	426.82	351.93	302.16	266.7
9500	1642.73	847.40	582.64	450.53	371.48	318.95	281.5
10000	1729.19	892.00	613.31	474.24	391.03	335.74	296.4
11000	1902.11	981.20	674.64	521.67	430.13	369.31	326.0
12000	2075.03	1070.40	735.97	569.09	469.23	402.88	355.6
13000	2247.95	1159.60	797.30	616.52	508.34	436.46	385.3
14000	2420.87	1248.80	858.63	663.94	547.44	470.03	414.9
15000	2593.79	1338.00	919.97	711.37	586.54	503.60	444.6
16000	2766.71	1427.20	981.30	758.79	625.65	537.18	474.2
17000	2939.63	1516.40	1042.63	806.22	664.75	570.75	503.8
18000	3112.55	1605.60	1103.96	853.64	703.85	604.33	533.5
19000	3285.46	1694.80	1165.29	901.07	742.95	637.90	563.1
20000	3458.38	1784.00	1226.62	948.49	782.06	671.47	592.8
21000	3631.30	1873.20	1287.95	995.91	821.16	705.05	622.4
22000	3804.22	1962.40	1349.28	1043.34	860.26	738.62	652.0
23000	3977.14	2051.60	1410.61	1090.76	899.37	772.19	681.7
24000	4150.06	2140.80	1471.94	1138.19	938.47	805.77	711.3
25000	4322.98	2230.00	1533.28	1185.61	977.57	839.34	741.0
26000	4495.90	2319.20	1594.61	1233.04	1016.67	872.92	770.6
27000	4668.82	2408.40	1655.94	1280.46	1055.78	906.49	800.2
28000	4841.74	2497.60	1717.27	1327.89	1094.88	940.06	829.9
29000	5014.66	2586.80	1778.60	1375.31	1133.98	973.64	859.5
30000	5187.58	2676.00	1839.93	1422.73	1173.09	1007.21	889.2
31000	5360.49	2765.20	1901.26	1470.16	1212.19	1040.78	918.8
32000	5533.41	2854.40	1962.59	1517.58	1251.29	1074.36	948.4
33000	5706.33	2943.60	2023.92	1565.01	1290.39	1107.93	978.1
34000	5879.25	3032.80	2085.25	1612.43	1329.50	1141.50	1007.7
35000	6052.17	3122.00	2146.59	1659.86	1368.60	1175.08	1037.4
40000	6916.77	3568.00	2453.24	1896.98	1564.11	1342.95	1185.6
45000	7781.36	4014.00	2759.90	2134.10	1759.63	1510.81	1333.8
50000	8645.96	4460.00	3066.55	2371.22	1955.14	1678.68	1482.0
55000	9510.55	4906.00	3373.21	2608.35	2150.66	1846.55	1630.2
60000	10375.15	5352.00	3679.86	2845.47	2346.17	2014.42	1778.4
65000	11239.75	5798.00	3986.52	3082.59	2541.69	2182.29	1926.6
70000	12104.34	6244.00	4293.17	3319.71	2737.20	2350.16	2074.8

Monthly Loan Payments 12¾%

LOAN AMOUNT	4 YEARS	4½ YEARS	5 YEARS	5½ YEARS	6 YEARS	6½ YEARS	7 YEARS
100	2.67	2.44	2.26	2.12	1.99	1.89	1.81
200	5.34	4.89	4.53	4.23	3.99	3.78	3.61
300	8.01	7.33	6.79	6.35	5.98	5.68	5.42
400	10.68	9.77	9.05	8.46	7.98	7.57	7.22
500	13.35	12.22	11.31	10.58	9.97	9.46	9.03
600	16.02	14.66	13.58	12.69	11.97	11.35	10.83
700	18.69	17.10	15.84	14.81	13.96	13.25	12.64
800	21.36	19.55	18.10	16.93	15.95	15.14	14.45
900	24.03	21.99	20.36	19.04	17.95	17.03	16.25
1000	26.70	24.43	22.63	21.16	19.94	18.92	18.06
1500	40.06	36.65	33.94	31.74	29.91	28.38	27.08
2000	53.41	48.86	45.25	42.31	39.88	37.85	36.11
2500	66.76	61.08	56.56	52.89	49.86	47.31	45.14
3000	80.11	73.30	67.88	63.47	59.83	56.77	54.17
3500	93.46	85.51	79.19	74.05	69.80	66.23	63.20
4000	106.81	97.73	90.50	84.63	79.77	75.69	72.23
4500	120.17	109.94	101.81	95.21	89.74	85.15	81.25
5000	133.52	122.16	113.13	105.79	99.71	94.61	90.28
5500	146.87	134.38	124.44	116.36	109.68	104.08	99.31
6000	160.22	146.59	135.75	126.94	119.65	113.54	108.34
6500	173.57	158.81	147.06	137.52	129.63	123.00	117.37
7000	186.93	171.02	158.38	148.10	139.60	132.46	126.39
7500	200.28	183.24	169.69	158.68	149.57	141.92	135.42
8000	213.63	195.45	181.00	169.26	159.54	151.38	144.45
8500	226.98	207.67	192.32	179.83	169.51	160.84	153.48
9000	240.33	219.89	203.63	190.41	179.48	170.31	162.51
9500	253.68	232.10	214.94	200.99	189.45	179.77	171.54
10000	267.04	244.32	226.25	211.57	199.42	189.23	180.56
11000	293.74	268.75	248.88	232.73	219.37	208.15	198.62
12000	320.44	293.18	271.50	253.88	239.31	227.07	216.68
13000	347.15	317.61	294.13	275.04	259.25	246.00	234.73
14000	373.85	342.05	316.75	296.20	279.19	264.92	252.79
15000	400.55	366.48	339.38	317.36	299.14	283.84	270.84
16000	427.26	390.91	362.00	338.51	319.08	302.76	288.90
17000	453.96	415.34	384.63	359.67	339.02	321.69	306.96
18000	480.66	439.77	407.26	380.83	358.96	340.61	325.01
19000	507.37	464.20	429.88	401.98	378.91	359.53	343.07
20000	534.07	488.64	452.51	423.14	398.85	378.46	361.13
21000	560.78	513.07	475.13	444.30	418.79	397.38	379.18
22000	587.48	537.50	497.76	465.45	438.73	416.30	397.24
23000	614.18	561.93	520.38	486.61	458.68	435.22	415.30
24000	640.89	586.36	543.01	507.77	478.62	454.15	433.35
25000	667.59	610.80	565.63	528.93	498.56	473.07	451.41
26000	694.29	635.23	588.26	550.08	518.50	491.99	469.46
27000	721.00	659.66	610.88	571.24	538.44	510.92	487.52
28000	747.70	684.09	633.51	592.40	558.39	529.84	505.58
29000	774.40	708.52	656.13	613.55	578.33	548.76	523.63
30000	801.11	732.95	678.76	634.71	598.27	567.68	541.69
31000	827.81	757.39	701.38	655.87	618.21	586.61	559.75
32000	854.51	781.82	724.01	677.03	638.16	605.53	577.80
33000	881.22	806.25	746.63	698.18	658.10	624.45	595.86
34000	907.92	830.68	769.26	719.34	678.04	643.37	613.92
35000	934.63	855.11	791.89	740.50	697.98	662.30	631.97
40000	1068.14	977.27	905.01	846.28	797.70	756.91	722.25
45000	1201.66	1099.43	1018.14	952.07	897.41	851.53	812.53
50000	1335.18	1221.59	1131.27	1057.85	997.12	946.14	902.82
55000	1468.70	1343.75	1244.39	1163.64	1096.83	1040.75	993.10
60000	1602.21	1465.91	1357.52	1269.42	1196.54	1135.37	1083.38
65000	1735.73	1588.07	1470.64	1375.21	1296.26	1229.98	1173.66
70000	1869.25	1710.23	1583.77	1480.99	1395.97	1324.59	1263.94

12¾%   Monthly Loan Payments

LOAN AMOUNT	7½ YEARS	8 YEARS	8½ YEARS	9 YEARS	9½ YEARS	10 YEARS	10½ YEARS
100	1.73	1.67	1.61	1.56	1.52	1.48	1.44
200	3.46	3.33	3.22	3.12	3.03	2.96	2.89
300	5.19	5.00	4.83	4.68	4.55	4.44	4.33
400	6.92	6.67	6.44	6.24	6.07	5.91	5.77
500	8.66	8.33	8.05	7.81	7.59	7.39	7.22
600	10.39	10.00	9.66	9.37	9.10	8.87	8.66
700	12.12	11.67	11.27	10.93	10.62	10.35	10.11
800	13.85	13.33	12.88	12.49	12.14	11.83	11.55
900	15.58	15.00	14.49	14.05	13.66	13.31	12.99
1000	17.31	16.67	16.10	15.61	15.17	14.78	14.44
1500	25.97	25.00	24.16	23.42	22.76	22.18	21.66
2000	34.62	33.34	32.21	31.22	30.35	29.57	28.87
2500	43.28	41.67	40.26	39.03	37.93	36.96	36.09
3000	51.94	50.00	48.31	46.83	45.52	44.35	43.31
3500	60.59	58.34	56.37	54.64	53.10	51.74	50.53
4000	69.25	66.67	64.42	62.44	60.69	59.14	57.75
4500	77.91	75.00	72.47	70.25	68.28	66.53	64.97
5000	86.56	83.34	80.52	78.05	75.86	73.92	72.18
5500	95.22	91.67	88.58	85.86	83.45	81.31	79.40
6000	103.87	100.01	96.63	93.66	91.04	88.70	86.62
6500	112.53	108.34	104.68	101.47	98.62	96.10	93.84
7000	121.19	116.67	112.73	109.27	106.21	103.49	101.06
7500	129.84	125.01	120.79	117.08	113.80	110.88	108.28
8000	138.50	133.34	128.84	124.88	121.38	118.27	115.49
8500	147.15	141.68	136.89	132.69	128.97	125.66	122.71
9000	155.81	150.01	144.94	140.49	136.56	133.06	129.93
9500	164.47	158.34	153.00	148.30	144.14	140.45	137.15
10000	173.12	166.68	161.05	156.10	151.73	147.84	144.37
11000	190.44	183.34	177.15	171.71	166.90	162.62	158.80
12000	207.75	200.01	193.26	187.32	182.07	177.41	173.24
13000	225.06	216.68	209.36	202.93	197.25	192.19	187.68
14000	242.37	233.35	225.47	218.54	212.42	206.98	202.11
15000	259.68	250.02	241.57	234.15	227.59	221.76	216.55
16000	277.00	266.68	257.68	249.76	242.76	236.54	230.99
17000	294.31	283.35	273.78	265.37	257.94	251.33	245.42
18000	311.62	300.02	289.89	280.98	273.11	266.11	259.86
19000	328.93	316.69	305.99	296.59	288.28	280.90	274.30
20000	346.25	333.35	322.10	312.20	303.46	295.68	288.74
21000	363.56	350.02	338.20	327.81	318.63	310.46	303.17
22000	380.87	366.69	354.31	343.43	333.80	325.25	317.61
23000	398.18	383.36	370.41	359.04	348.97	340.03	332.05
24000	415.50	400.03	386.52	374.65	364.15	354.82	346.48
25000	432.81	416.69	402.62	390.26	379.32	369.60	360.92
26000	450.12	433.36	418.73	405.87	394.49	384.38	375.36
27000	467.43	450.03	434.83	421.48	409.67	399.17	389.79
28000	484.74	466.70	450.94	437.09	424.84	413.95	404.23
29000	502.06	483.36	467.04	452.70	440.01	428.74	418.67
30000	519.37	500.03	483.15	468.31	455.18	443.52	433.10
31000	536.68	516.70	499.25	483.92	470.36	458.30	447.54
32000	553.99	533.37	515.36	499.53	485.53	473.09	461.98
33000	571.31	550.03	531.46	515.14	500.70	487.87	476.41
34000	588.62	566.70	547.57	530.75	515.88	502.66	490.85
35000	605.93	583.37	563.67	546.36	531.05	517.44	505.29
40000	692.49	666.71	644.20	624.41	606.91	591.36	577.47
45000	779.05	750.05	724.72	702.46	682.78	665.28	649.65
50000	865.62	833.39	805.25	780.51	758.64	739.20	721.84
55000	952.18	916.72	885.77	858.56	834.50	813.12	794.02
60000	1038.74	1000.06	966.30	936.61	910.37	887.04	866.21
65000	1125.30	1083.40	1046.82	1014.67	986.23	960.96	938.39
70000	1211.86	1166.74	1127.35	1092.72	1062.10	1034.88	1010.57

Monthly Loan Payments 12¾%

LOAN AMOUNT	11 YEARS	11½ YEARS	12 YEARS	12½ YEARS	13 YEARS	14 YEARS	15 YEARS
100	1.41	1.38	1.36	1.34	1.32	1.28	1.25
200	2.83	2.77	2.72	2.67	2.63	2.56	2.50
300	4.24	4.15	4.08	4.01	3.95	3.84	3.75
400	5.65	5.54	5.44	5.35	5.26	5.12	5.00
500	7.06	6.92	6.80	6.68	6.58	6.40	6.24
600	8.48	8.31	8.16	8.02	7.89	7.68	7.49
700	9.89	9.69	9.51	9.35	9.21	8.95	8.74
800	11.30	11.08	10.87	10.69	10.52	10.23	9.99
900	12.71	12.46	12.23	12.03	11.84	11.51	11.24
1000	14.13	13.85	13.59	13.36	13.15	12.79	12.49
1500	21.19	20.77	20.39	20.04	19.73	19.19	18.73
2000	28.25	27.69	27.18	26.73	26.31	25.58	24.98
2500	35.31	34.61	33.98	33.41	32.89	31.98	31.22
3000	42.38	41.54	40.78	40.09	39.46	38.38	37.47
3500	49.44	48.46	47.57	46.77	46.04	44.77	43.71
4000	56.50	55.38	54.37	53.45	52.62	51.17	49.95
4500	63.56	62.30	61.16	60.13	59.20	57.56	56.20
5000	70.63	69.23	67.96	66.81	65.77	63.96	62.44
5500	77.69	76.15	74.76	73.49	72.35	70.35	68.69
6000	84.75	83.07	81.55	80.18	78.93	76.75	74.93
6500	91.81	89.99	88.35	86.86	85.50	83.15	81.17
7000	98.88	96.92	95.14	93.54	92.08	89.54	87.42
7500	105.94	103.84	101.94	100.22	98.66	95.94	93.66
8000	113.00	110.76	108.74	106.90	105.24	102.33	99.91
8500	120.07	117.68	115.53	113.59	111.81	108.73	106.15
9000	127.13	124.61	122.33	120.26	118.39	115.13	112.40
9500	134.19	131.53	129.12	126.94	124.97	121.52	118.64
10000	141.25	138.45	135.92	133.63	131.54	127.92	124.88
11000	155.38	152.30	149.51	146.99	144.70	140.71	137.37
12000	169.50	166.14	163.10	160.35	157.85	153.50	149.86
13000	183.63	179.99	176.70	173.72	171.01	166.29	162.35
14000	197.76	193.83	190.29	187.08	184.16	179.08	174.84
15000	211.88	207.68	203.88	200.44	197.32	191.88	187.33
16000	226.01	221.52	217.47	213.80	210.47	204.67	199.81
17000	240.13	235.37	231.08	227.17	223.63	217.46	212.30
18000	254.26	249.21	244.66	240.53	236.78	230.25	224.79
19000	268.38	263.06	258.25	253.89	249.93	243.04	237.28
20000	282.51	276.90	271.84	267.25	263.09	255.83	249.77
21000	296.63	290.75	285.43	280.62	276.24	268.63	262.26
22000	310.76	304.59	299.02	293.98	289.40	281.42	274.74
23000	324.88	318.44	312.62	307.34	302.55	294.21	287.23
24000	339.01	332.28	326.21	320.71	315.71	307.00	299.72
25000	353.13	346.13	339.80	334.07	328.86	319.79	312.21
26000	367.26	359.97	353.39	347.43	342.02	332.58	324.70
27000	381.39	373.82	366.98	360.79	355.17	345.38	337.19
28000	395.51	387.66	380.58	374.16	368.32	358.17	349.67
29000	409.64	401.51	394.17	387.52	381.48	370.96	362.16
30000	423.76	415.35	407.76	400.88	394.63	383.75	374.65
31000	437.89	429.20	421.35	414.24	407.79	396.54	387.14
32000	452.01	443.04	434.94	427.61	420.94	409.34	399.63
33000	466.14	456.89	448.54	440.97	434.10	422.13	412.12
34000	480.26	470.73	462.13	454.33	447.25	434.92	424.60
35000	494.39	484.58	475.72	467.70	460.41	447.71	437.09
40000	565.02	553.80	543.68	534.51	526.18	511.67	499.53
45000	635.64	623.03	611.64	601.32	591.95	575.63	561.98
50000	706.27	692.26	679.60	668.14	657.72	639.59	624.42
55000	776.90	761.48	747.56	734.95	723.50	703.54	686.86
60000	847.52	830.71	815.52	801.76	789.27	767.50	749.30
65000	918.15	899.93	883.48	868.58	855.04	831.46	811.74
70000	988.78	969.16	951.44	935.39	920.81	895.42	874.19

LOAN AMOUNT	½ YEAR	1 YEAR	1½ YEARS	2 YEARS	2½ YEARS	3 YEARS	3½ YEARS
100	17.30	8.93	6.14	4.75	3.92	3.37	2.9
200	34.61	17.86	12.29	9.51	7.84	6.74	5.9
300	51.91	26.80	18.43	14.26	11.77	10.11	8.9
400	69.22	35.73	24.58	19.02	15.69	13.48	11.9
500	86.52	44.66	30.72	23.77	19.61	16.85	14.8
600	103.83	53.59	36.87	28.53	23.53	20.22	17.8
700	121.13	62.52	43.01	33.28	27.46	23.59	20.8
800	138.43	71.45	49.16	38.03	31.38	26.96	23.8
900	155.74	80.39	55.30	42.79	35.30	30.32	26.7
1000	173.04	89.32	61.45	47.54	39.22	33.69	29.7
1500	259.56	133.98	92.17	71.31	58.83	50.54	44.6
2000	346.09	178.63	122.90	95.08	78.44	67.39	59.5
2500	432.61	223.29	153.62	118.85	98.05	84.23	74.4
3000	519.13	267.95	184.34	142.63	117.66	101.08	89.2
3500	605.65	312.61	215.07	166.40	137.28	117.93	104.1
4000	692.17	357.27	245.79	190.17	156.89	134.78	119.0
4500	778.69	401.93	276.51	213.94	176.50	151.62	133.9
5000	865.21	446.59	307.24	237.71	196.11	168.47	148.8
5500	951.74	491.25	337.96	261.48	215.72	185.32	163.6
6000	1038.26	535.90	368.69	285.25	235.33	202.16	178.5
6500	1124.78	580.56	399.41	309.02	254.94	219.01	193.4
7000	1211.30	625.22	430.13	332.79	274.55	235.86	208.3
7500	1297.82	669.88	460.86	356.56	294.16	252.70	223.2
8000	1384.34	714.54	491.58	380.33	313.77	269.55	238.1
8500	1470.86	759.20	522.30	404.11	333.38	286.40	252.9
9000	1557.39	803.86	553.03	427.88	352.99	303.25	267.8
9500	1643.91	848.51	583.75	451.65	372.60	320.09	282.7
10000	1730.43	893.17	614.48	475.42	392.22	336.94	297.6
11000	1903.47	982.49	675.92	522.96	431.44	370.63	327.3
12000	2076.51	1071.81	737.37	570.50	470.66	404.33	357.1
13000	2249.56	1161.12	798.82	618.04	509.88	438.02	386.9
14000	2422.60	1250.44	860.27	665.59	549.10	471.72	416.6
15000	2595.64	1339.76	921.71	713.13	588.32	505.41	446.4
16000	2768.69	1429.08	983.16	760.67	627.54	539.10	476.1
17000	2941.73	1518.39	1044.61	808.21	666.77	572.80	505.9
18000	3114.77	1607.71	1106.06	855.75	705.99	606.49	535.7
19000	3287.81	1697.03	1167.50	903.29	745.21	640.19	565.4
20000	3460.86	1786.35	1228.95	950.84	784.43	673.88	595.2
21000	3633.90	1875.66	1290.40	998.38	823.65	707.57	625.0
22000	3806.94	1964.98	1351.85	1045.92	862.87	741.27	654.7
23000	3979.99	2054.30	1413.29	1093.46	902.10	774.96	684.5
24000	4153.03	2143.61	1474.74	1141.00	941.32	808.65	714.2
25000	4326.07	2232.93	1536.19	1188.55	980.54	842.35	744.0
26000	4499.11	2322.25	1597.64	1236.09	1019.76	876.04	773.8
27000	4672.16	2411.57	1659.09	1283.63	1058.98	909.74	803.5
28000	4845.20	2500.88	1720.53	1331.17	1098.20	943.43	833.3
29000	5018.24	2590.20	1781.98	1378.71	1137.42	977.12	863.1
30000	5191.29	2679.52	1843.43	1426.25	1176.65	1010.82	892.8
31000	5364.33	2768.84	1904.88	1473.80	1215.87	1044.51	922.6
32000	5537.37	2858.15	1966.32	1521.34	1255.09	1078.21	952.3
33000	5710.41	2947.47	2027.77	1568.88	1294.31	1111.90	982.1
34000	5883.46	3036.79	2089.22	1616.42	1333.53	1145.59	1011.9
35000	6056.50	3126.10	2150.67	1663.96	1372.75	1179.29	1041.6
40000	6921.71	3572.69	2457.90	1901.67	1568.86	1347.76	1190.4
45000	7786.93	4019.28	2765.14	2139.38	1764.97	1516.23	1339.2
50000	8652.14	4465.86	3072.38	2377.09	1961.08	1684.70	1488.10
55000	9517.36	4912.45	3379.62	2614.80	2157.19	1853.17	1636.9
60000	10382.57	5359.04	3686.86	2852.51	2353.29	2021.64	1785.7
65000	11247.79	5805.62	3994.09	3090.22	2549.40	2190.11	1934.5
70000	12113.00	6252.21	4301.33	3327.93	2745.51	2358.58	2083.3

Monthly Loan Payments 13%

LOAN AMOUNT	4 YEARS	4½ YEARS	5 YEARS	5½ YEARS	6 YEARS	6½ YEARS	7 YEARS
100	2.68	2.46	2.28	2.13	2.01	1.91	1.82
200	5.37	4.91	4.55	4.26	4.01	3.81	3.64
300	8.05	7.37	6.83	6.39	6.02	5.72	5.46
400	10.73	9.82	9.10	8.51	8.03	7.62	7.28
500	13.41	12.28	11.38	10.64	10.04	9.53	9.10
600	16.10	14.73	13.65	12.77	12.04	11.43	10.92
700	18.78	17.19	15.93	14.90	14.05	13.34	12.73
800	21.46	19.65	18.20	17.03	16.06	15.25	14.55
900	24.14	22.10	20.48	19.16	18.07	17.15	16.37
1000	26.83	24.56	22.75	21.29	20.07	19.06	18.19
1500	40.24	36.84	34.13	31.93	30.11	28.58	27.29
2000	53.65	49.12	45.51	42.57	40.15	38.11	36.38
2500	67.07	61.39	56.88	53.22	50.19	47.64	45.48
3000	80.48	73.67	68.26	63.86	60.22	57.17	54.58
3500	93.90	85.95	79.64	74.50	70.26	66.70	63.67
4000	107.31	98.23	91.01	85.15	80.30	76.23	72.77
4500	120.72	110.51	102.39	95.79	90.33	85.75	81.86
5000	134.14	122.79	113.77	106.43	100.37	95.28	90.96
5500	147.55	135.07	125.14	117.08	110.41	104.81	100.06
6000	160.96	147.35	136.52	127.72	120.44	114.34	109.15
6500	174.38	159.62	147.89	138.36	130.48	123.87	118.25
7000	187.79	171.90	159.27	149.01	140.52	133.40	127.34
7500	201.21	184.18	170.65	159.65	150.56	142.92	136.44
8000	214.62	196.46	182.02	170.29	160.59	152.45	145.54
8500	228.03	208.74	193.40	180.94	170.63	161.98	154.63
9000	241.45	221.02	204.78	191.58	180.67	171.51	163.73
9500	254.86	233.30	216.15	202.22	190.70	181.04	172.82
10000	268.27	245.58	227.53	212.87	200.74	190.56	181.92
11000	295.10	270.13	250.28	234.15	220.82	209.62	200.11
12000	321.93	294.69	273.04	255.44	240.89	228.68	218.30
13000	348.76	319.25	295.79	276.73	260.96	247.73	236.50
14000	375.58	343.81	318.54	298.01	281.04	266.79	254.69
15000	402.41	368.36	341.30	319.30	301.11	285.85	272.88
16000	429.24	392.92	364.05	340.59	321.19	304.90	291.07
17000	456.07	417.48	386.80	361.88	341.26	323.96	309.26
18000	482.89	442.04	409.56	383.16	361.33	343.02	327.46
19000	509.72	466.60	432.31	404.45	381.41	362.07	345.65
20000	536.55	491.15	455.06	425.74	401.48	381.13	363.84
21000	563.38	515.71	477.81	447.02	421.56	400.19	382.03
22000	590.20	540.27	500.57	468.31	441.63	419.24	400.22
23000	617.03	564.83	523.32	489.60	461.70	438.30	418.42
24000	643.86	589.38	546.07	510.88	481.78	457.36	436.61
25000	670.69	613.94	568.83	532.17	501.85	476.41	454.80
26000	697.51	638.50	591.58	553.46	521.93	495.47	472.99
27000	724.34	663.06	614.33	574.74	542.00	514.52	491.18
28000	751.17	687.61	637.09	596.03	562.07	533.58	509.37
29000	778.00	712.17	659.84	617.32	582.15	552.64	527.57
30000	804.82	736.73	682.59	638.60	602.22	571.69	545.76
31000	831.65	761.29	705.35	659.89	622.30	590.75	563.95
32000	858.48	785.85	728.10	681.18	642.37	609.81	582.14
33000	885.31	810.40	750.85	702.46	662.45	628.86	600.33
34000	912.13	834.96	773.60	723.75	682.52	647.92	618.53
35000	938.96	859.52	796.36	745.04	702.59	666.98	636.72
40000	1073.10	982.31	910.12	851.47	802.96	762.26	727.68
45000	1207.24	1105.09	1023.89	957.90	903.33	857.54	818.64
50000	1341.37	1227.88	1137.65	1064.34	1003.71	952.82	909.60
55000	1475.51	1350.67	1251.42	1170.77	1104.08	1048.11	1000.56
60000	1609.65	1473.46	1365.18	1277.21	1204.45	1143.39	1091.52
65000	1743.79	1596.25	1478.95	1383.64	1304.82	1238.67	1182.48
70000	1877.92	1719.04	1592.72	1490.07	1405.19	1333.95	1273.44

13% Monthly Loan Payments

LOAN AMOUNT	7½ YEARS	8 YEARS	8½ YEARS	9 YEARS	9½ YEARS	10 YEARS	10½ YEARS
100	1.74	1.68	1.62	1.58	1.53	1.49	1.46
200	3.49	3.36	3.25	3.15	3.06	2.99	2.92
300	5.23	5.04	4.87	4.73	4.60	4.48	4.38
400	6.98	6.72	6.50	6.30	6.13	5.97	5.83
500	8.72	8.40	8.12	7.88	7.66	7.47	7.29
600	10.47	10.08	9.75	9.45	9.19	8.96	8.75
700	12.21	11.77	11.37	11.03	10.72	10.45	10.21
800	13.96	13.45	13.00	12.60	12.25	11.94	11.67
900	15.70	15.13	14.62	14.18	13.79	13.44	13.13
1000	17.45	16.81	16.25	15.75	15.32	14.93	14.59
1500	26.17	25.21	24.37	23.63	22.98	22.40	21.88
2000	34.90	33.61	32.49	31.51	30.64	29.86	29.17
2500	43.62	42.02	40.62	39.38	38.30	37.33	36.46
3000	52.35	50.42	48.74	47.26	45.95	44.79	43.76
3500	61.07	58.83	56.86	55.14	53.61	52.26	51.05
4000	69.80	67.23	64.99	63.01	61.27	59.72	58.34
4500	78.52	75.63	73.11	70.89	68.93	67.19	65.64
5000	87.25	84.04	81.23	78.77	76.59	74.66	72.93
5500	95.97	92.44	89.36	86.64	84.25	82.12	80.22
6000	104.70	100.84	97.48	94.52	91.91	89.59	87.51
6500	113.42	109.25	105.60	102.40	99.57	97.05	94.81
7000	122.15	117.65	113.72	110.28	107.23	104.52	102.10
7500	130.87	126.05	121.85	118.15	114.89	111.98	109.39
8000	139.60	134.46	129.97	126.03	122.54	119.45	116.69
8500	148.32	142.86	138.09	133.91	130.20	126.91	123.98
9000	157.05	151.27	146.22	141.78	137.86	134.38	131.27
9500	165.77	159.67	154.34	149.66	145.52	141.85	138.56
10000	174.50	168.07	162.46	157.54	153.18	149.31	145.86
11000	191.95	184.88	178.71	173.29	168.50	164.24	160.44
12000	209.40	201.69	194.96	189.04	183.82	179.17	175.03
13000	226.85	218.49	211.20	204.80	199.13	194.10	189.61
14000	244.30	235.30	227.45	220.55	214.45	209.04	204.20
15000	261.75	252.11	243.70	236.30	229.77	223.97	218.79
16000	279.20	268.92	259.94	252.06	245.09	238.90	233.37
17000	296.65	285.72	276.19	267.81	260.41	253.83	247.96
18000	314.10	302.53	292.43	283.56	275.72	268.76	262.54
19000	331.55	319.34	308.68	299.32	291.04	283.69	277.13
20000	349.00	336.15	324.93	315.07	306.36	298.62	291.71
21000	366.45	352.95	341.17	330.83	321.68	313.55	306.30
22000	383.90	369.76	357.42	346.58	337.00	328.48	320.88
23000	401.35	386.57	373.67	362.33	352.31	343.41	335.47
24000	418.80	403.37	389.91	378.09	367.63	358.35	350.06
25000	436.25	420.18	406.16	393.84	382.95	373.28	364.64
26000	453.70	436.99	422.41	409.59	398.27	388.21	379.23
27000	471.15	453.80	438.65	425.35	413.59	403.14	393.81
28000	488.60	470.60	454.90	441.10	428.91	418.07	408.40
29000	506.05	487.41	471.15	456.85	444.22	433.00	422.98
30000	523.50	504.22	487.39	472.61	459.54	447.93	437.57
31000	540.95	521.02	503.64	488.36	474.86	462.86	452.16
32000	558.40	537.83	519.88	504.11	490.18	477.79	466.74
33000	575.85	554.64	536.13	519.87	505.50	492.73	481.33
34000	593.30	571.45	552.38	535.62	520.81	507.66	495.91
35000	610.75	588.25	568.62	551.38	536.13	522.59	510.50
40000	698.00	672.29	649.86	630.14	612.72	597.24	583.43
45000	785.25	756.33	731.09	708.91	689.31	671.90	656.36
50000	872.50	840.36	812.32	787.68	765.90	746.55	729.28
55000	959.74	924.40	893.55	866.45	842.49	821.21	802.21
60000	1046.99	1008.44	974.78	945.22	919.08	895.86	875.14
65000	1134.24	1092.47	1056.01	1023.98	995.67	970.52	948.07
70000	1221.49	1176.51	1137.25	1102.75	1072.26	1045.18	1021.00

Monthly Loan Payments 13%

LOAN AMOUNT	11 YEARS	11½ YEARS	12 YEARS	12½ YEARS	13 YEARS	14 YEARS	15 YEARS
100	1.43	1.40	1.37	1.35	1.33	1.30	1.27
200	2.86	2.80	2.75	2.70	2.66	2.59	2.53
300	4.28	4.20	4.12	4.06	3.99	3.89	3.80
400	5.71	5.60	5.50	5.41	5.32	5.18	5.06
500	7.14	7.00	6.87	6.76	6.66	6.48	6.33
600	8.57	8.40	8.25	8.11	7.99	7.77	7.59
700	9.99	9.80	9.62	9.46	9.32	9.07	8.86
800	11.42	11.20	11.00	10.81	10.65	10.36	10.12
900	12.85	12.60	12.37	12.17	11.98	11.66	11.39
1000	14.28	14.00	13.75	13.52	13.31	12.95	12.65
1500	21.41	21.00	20.62	20.28	19.97	19.43	18.98
2000	28.55	28.00	27.49	27.04	26.62	25.91	25.30
2500	35.69	34.99	34.37	33.80	33.28	32.38	31.63
3000	42.83	41.99	41.24	40.56	39.94	38.86	37.96
3500	49.97	48.99	48.11	47.32	46.59	45.33	44.28
4000	57.10	55.99	54.99	54.07	53.25	51.81	50.61
4500	64.24	62.99	61.86	60.83	59.90	58.29	56.94
5000	71.38	69.99	68.73	67.59	66.56	64.76	63.26
5500	78.52	76.99	75.60	74.35	73.22	71.24	69.59
6000	85.66	83.99	82.48	81.11	79.87	77.72	75.91
6500	92.79	90.98	89.35	87.87	86.53	84.19	82.24
7000	99.93	97.98	96.22	94.63	93.18	90.67	88.57
7500	107.07	104.98	103.10	101.39	99.84	97.14	94.89
8000	114.21	111.98	109.97	108.15	106.50	103.62	101.22
8500	121.35	118.98	116.84	114.91	113.15	110.10	107.55
9000	128.48	125.98	123.72	121.67	119.81	116.57	113.87
9500	135.62	132.98	130.59	128.43	126.46	123.05	120.20
10000	142.76	139.98	137.46	135.19	133.12	129.53	126.52
11000	157.04	153.97	151.21	148.71	146.43	142.48	139.18
12000	171.31	167.97	164.96	162.22	159.75	155.43	151.83
13000	185.59	181.97	178.70	175.74	173.06	168.38	164.48
14000	199.87	195.97	192.45	189.26	186.37	181.34	177.13
15000	214.14	209.96	206.19	202.78	199.68	194.29	189.79
16000	228.42	223.96	219.94	216.30	212.99	207.24	202.44
17000	242.69	237.96	233.69	229.82	226.31	220.19	215.09
18000	256.97	251.96	247.43	243.34	239.62	233.15	227.74
19000	271.25	265.95	261.18	256.86	252.93	246.10	240.40
20000	285.52	279.95	274.93	270.37	266.24	259.05	253.05
21000	299.80	293.95	288.67	283.89	279.55	272.01	265.70
22000	314.07	307.95	302.42	297.41	292.87	284.96	278.35
23000	328.35	321.95	316.16	310.93	306.18	297.91	291.01
24000	342.63	335.94	329.91	324.45	319.49	310.86	303.66
25000	356.90	349.94	343.66	337.97	332.80	323.82	316.31
26000	371.18	363.94	357.40	351.49	346.11	336.77	328.96
27000	385.45	377.94	371.15	365.00	359.43	349.72	341.62
28000	399.73	391.93	384.90	378.52	372.74	362.67	354.27
29000	414.01	405.93	398.64	392.04	386.05	375.63	366.92
30000	428.28	419.93	412.39	405.56	399.36	388.58	379.57
31000	442.56	433.93	426.13	419.08	412.68	401.53	392.23
32000	456.84	447.92	439.88	432.60	425.99	414.48	404.88
33000	471.11	461.92	453.63	446.12	439.30	427.44	417.53
34000	485.39	475.92	467.37	459.64	452.61	440.39	430.18
35000	499.66	489.92	481.12	473.15	465.92	453.34	442.83
40000	571.04	559.90	549.85	540.75	532.48	518.11	506.10
45000	642.42	629.89	618.58	608.34	599.04	582.87	569.36
50000	713.81	699.88	687.31	675.93	665.61	647.63	632.62
55000	785.19	769.87	756.04	743.53	732.17	712.39	695.88
60000	856.57	839.86	824.78	811.12	798.73	777.16	759.15
65000	927.95	909.85	893.51	878.71	865.29	841.92	822.41
70000	999.33	979.83	962.24	946.31	931.85	906.68	885.67

13¼%   Monthly Loan Payments

LOAN AMOUNT	½ YEAR	1 YEAR	1½ YEARS	2 YEARS	2½ YEARS	3 YEARS	3½ YEARS
100	17.32	8.94	6.16	4.77	3.93	3.38	2.99
200	34.63	17.89	12.31	9.53	7.87	6.76	5.98
300	51.95	26.83	18.47	14.30	11.80	10.14	8.97
400	69.27	35.77	24.63	19.06	15.74	13.53	11.95
500	86.58	44.72	30.78	23.83	19.67	16.91	14.94
600	103.90	53.66	36.94	28.60	23.60	20.29	17.93
700	121.22	62.60	43.10	33.36	27.54	23.67	20.92
800	138.53	71.55	49.25	38.13	31.47	27.05	23.91
900	155.85	80.49	55.41	42.89	35.41	30.43	26.90
1000	173.17	89.43	61.56	47.66	39.34	33.81	29.88
1500	259.75	134.15	92.35	71.49	59.01	50.72	44.83
2000	346.33	178.87	123.13	95.32	78.68	67.63	59.77
2500	432.92	223.59	153.91	119.15	98.35	84.54	74.71
3000	519.50	268.30	184.69	142.98	118.02	101.44	89.65
3500	606.08	313.02	215.48	166.81	137.69	118.35	104.60
4000	692.67	357.74	246.26	190.64	157.36	135.26	119.54
4500	779.25	402.46	277.04	214.47	177.03	152.17	134.48
5000	865.83	447.17	307.82	238.30	196.70	169.07	149.42
5500	952.42	491.89	338.60	262.13	216.37	185.98	164.36
6000	1039.00	536.61	369.39	285.96	236.04	202.89	179.31
6500	1125.59	581.32	400.17	309.79	255.71	219.79	194.25
7000	1212.17	626.04	430.95	333.62	275.38	236.70	209.19
7500	1298.75	670.76	461.73	357.45	295.05	253.61	224.13
8000	1385.33	715.48	492.51	381.27	314.72	270.52	239.08
8500	1471.92	760.19	523.30	405.10	334.39	287.42	254.02
9000	1558.50	804.91	554.08	428.93	354.06	304.33	268.96
9500	1645.08	849.63	584.86	452.76	373.73	321.24	283.90
10000	1731.67	894.35	615.64	476.59	393.40	338.14	298.84
11000	1904.83	983.78	677.21	524.25	432.74	371.96	328.73
12000	2078.00	1073.22	738.77	571.91	472.09	405.77	358.61
13000	2251.17	1162.65	800.34	619.57	511.43	439.59	388.50
14000	2424.33	1252.08	861.90	667.23	550.77	473.40	418.38
15000	2597.50	1341.52	923.46	714.89	590.11	507.22	448.27
16000	2770.67	1430.95	985.03	762.55	629.45	541.03	478.15
17000	2943.83	1520.39	1046.59	810.21	668.79	574.85	508.04
18000	3117.00	1609.82	1108.16	857.87	708.13	608.66	537.92
19000	3290.16	1699.26	1169.72	905.53	747.47	642.48	567.80
20000	3463.33	1788.69	1231.29	953.19	786.81	676.29	597.69
21000	3636.50	1878.13	1292.85	1000.85	826.15	710.10	627.57
22000	3809.66	1967.56	1354.41	1048.51	865.49	743.92	657.46
23000	3982.83	2057.00	1415.98	1096.16	904.83	777.73	687.34
24000	4156.00	2146.43	1477.54	1143.82	944.17	811.55	717.23
25000	4329.16	2235.87	1539.11	1191.48	983.51	845.36	747.11
26000	4502.33	2325.30	1600.67	1239.14	1022.85	879.18	777.00
27000	4675.50	2414.73	1662.24	1286.80	1062.19	912.99	806.88
28000	4848.66	2504.17	1723.80	1334.46	1101.53	946.81	836.76
29000	5021.83	2593.60	1785.36	1382.12	1140.87	980.62	866.65
30000	5195.00	2683.04	1846.93	1429.78	1180.21	1014.43	896.53
31000	5368.16	2772.47	1908.49	1477.44	1219.55	1048.25	926.42
32000	5541.33	2861.91	1970.06	1525.10	1258.89	1082.06	956.30
33000	5714.50	2951.34	2031.62	1572.76	1298.23	1115.88	986.19
34000	5887.66	3040.78	2093.19	1620.42	1337.57	1149.69	1016.07
35000	6060.83	3130.21	2154.75	1668.08	1376.92	1183.51	1045.96
40000	6926.66	3577.38	2462.57	1906.37	1573.62	1352.58	1195.38
45000	7792.50	4024.56	2770.39	2144.67	1770.32	1521.65	1344.80
50000	8658.33	4471.73	3078.21	2382.97	1967.02	1690.72	1494.22
55000	9524.16	4918.90	3386.04	2621.26	2163.72	1859.80	1643.64
60000	10389.99	5366.08	3693.86	2859.56	2360.43	2028.87	1793.07
65000	11255.83	5813.25	4001.68	3097.86	2557.13	2197.94	1942.49
70000	12121.66	6260.42	4309.50	3336.15	2753.83	2367.01	2091.91

Monthly Loan Payments 13¼%

LOAN AMOUNT	4 YEARS	4½ YEARS	5 YEARS	5½ YEARS	6 YEARS	6½ YEARS	7 YEARS
100	2.70	2.47	2.29	2.14	2.02	1.92	1.83
200	5.39	4.94	4.58	4.28	4.04	3.84	3.67
300	8.09	7.41	6.86	6.43	6.06	5.76	5.50
400	10.78	9.87	9.15	8.57	8.08	7.68	7.33
500	13.48	12.34	11.44	10.71	10.10	9.60	9.16
600	16.17	14.81	13.73	12.85	12.12	11.51	11.00
700	18.87	17.28	16.02	14.99	14.14	13.43	12.83
800	21.56	19.75	18.31	17.13	16.17	15.35	14.66
900	24.26	22.22	20.59	19.28	18.19	17.27	16.50
1000	26.95	24.68	22.88	21.42	20.21	19.19	18.33
1500	40.43	37.03	34.32	32.13	30.31	28.79	27.49
2000	53.90	49.37	45.76	42.83	40.41	38.38	36.66
2500	67.38	61.71	57.20	53.54	50.52	47.98	45.82
3000	80.86	74.05	68.64	64.25	60.62	57.57	54.98
3500	94.33	86.39	80.08	74.96	70.72	67.17	64.15
4000	107.81	98.74	91.53	85.67	80.83	76.76	73.31
4500	121.28	111.08	102.97	96.38	90.93	86.36	82.48
5000	134.76	123.42	114.41	107.08	101.03	95.95	91.64
5500	148.23	135.76	125.85	117.79	111.13	105.55	100.80
6000	161.71	148.10	137.29	128.50	121.24	115.14	109.97
6500	175.19	160.45	148.73	139.21	131.34	124.74	119.13
7000	188.66	172.79	160.17	149.92	141.44	134.33	128.30
7500	202.14	185.13	171.61	160.63	151.55	143.93	137.46
8000	215.61	197.47	183.05	171.34	161.65	153.53	146.63
8500	229.09	209.81	194.49	182.04	171.75	163.12	155.79
9000	242.57	222.15	205.93	192.75	181.86	172.72	164.95
9500	256.04	234.50	217.37	203.46	191.96	182.31	174.12
10000	269.52	246.84	228.81	214.17	202.06	191.91	183.28
11000	296.47	271.52	251.69	235.59	222.27	211.10	201.61
12000	323.42	296.21	274.58	257.00	242.48	230.29	219.94
13000	350.37	320.89	297.46	278.42	262.68	249.48	238.27
14000	377.32	345.57	320.34	299.84	282.89	268.67	256.59
15000	404.28	370.26	343.22	321.25	303.09	287.86	274.92
16000	431.23	394.94	366.10	342.67	323.30	307.05	293.25
17000	458.18	419.63	388.98	364.09	343.51	326.24	311.58
18000	485.13	444.31	411.86	385.51	363.71	345.43	329.91
19000	512.08	468.99	434.74	406.92	383.92	364.62	348.23
20000	539.03	493.68	457.63	428.34	404.13	383.81	366.56
21000	565.99	518.36	480.51	449.76	424.33	403.00	384.89
22000	592.94	543.04	503.39	471.17	444.54	422.19	403.22
23000	619.89	567.73	526.27	492.59	464.74	441.38	421.55
24000	646.84	592.41	549.15	514.01	484.95	460.58	439.88
25000	673.79	617.10	572.03	535.42	505.16	479.77	458.20
26000	700.75	641.78	594.91	556.84	525.36	498.96	476.53
27000	727.70	666.46	617.79	578.26	545.57	518.15	494.86
28000	754.65	691.15	640.68	599.67	565.77	537.34	513.19
29000	781.60	715.83	663.56	621.09	585.98	556.53	531.52
30000	808.55	740.52	686.44	642.51	606.19	575.72	549.84
31000	835.50	765.20	709.32	663.93	626.40	594.91	568.17
32000	862.46	789.88	732.20	685.34	646.60	614.10	586.50
33000	889.41	814.57	755.08	706.76	666.81	633.29	604.83
34000	916.36	839.25	777.96	728.18	687.01	652.48	623.16
35000	943.31	863.94	800.84	749.59	707.22	671.67	641.49
40000	1078.07	987.35	915.25	856.68	808.25	767.63	733.13
45000	1212.83	1110.77	1029.66	963.76	909.28	863.58	824.77
50000	1347.59	1234.19	1144.06	1070.85	1010.31	959.53	916.41
55000	1482.35	1357.61	1258.47	1177.93	1111.35	1055.49	1008.05
60000	1617.10	1481.03	1372.88	1285.02	1212.38	1151.44	1099.69
65000	1751.86	1604.45	1487.28	1392.10	1313.41	1247.39	1191.33
70000	1886.62	1727.87	1601.69	1499.19	1414.44	1343.35	1282.97

13¼%   Monthly Loan Payments

LOAN AMOUNT	7½ YEARS	8 YEARS	8½ YEARS	9 YEARS	9½ YEARS	10 YEARS	10½ YEARS
100	1.76	1.69	1.64	1.59	1.55	1.51	1.47
200	3.52	3.39	3.28	3.18	3.09	3.02	2.95
300	5.28	5.08	4.92	4.77	4.64	4.52	4.42
400	7.04	6.78	6.56	6.36	6.19	6.03	5.89
500	8.79	8.47	8.19	7.95	7.73	7.54	7.37
600	10.55	10.17	9.83	9.54	9.28	9.05	8.84
700	12.31	11.86	11.47	11.13	10.82	10.56	10.31
800	14.07	13.56	13.11	12.72	12.37	12.06	11.79
900	15.83	15.25	14.75	14.31	13.92	13.57	13.26
1000	17.59	16.95	16.39	15.90	15.46	15.08	14.74
1500	26.38	25.42	24.58	23.85	23.20	22.62	22.10
2000	35.18	33.89	32.78	31.80	30.93	30.16	29.47
2500	43.97	42.37	40.97	39.74	38.66	37.70	36.84
3000	52.76	50.84	49.17	47.69	46.39	45.24	44.21
3500	61.56	59.32	57.36	55.64	54.12	52.78	51.57
4000	70.35	67.79	65.55	63.59	61.86	60.32	58.94
4500	79.15	76.26	73.75	71.54	69.59	67.86	66.31
5000	87.94	84.74	81.94	79.49	77.32	75.39	73.68
5500	96.73	93.21	90.14	87.44	85.05	82.93	81.04
6000	105.53	101.68	98.33	95.39	92.78	90.47	88.41
6500	114.32	110.16	106.53	103.33	100.52	98.01	95.78
7000	123.12	118.63	114.72	111.28	108.25	105.55	103.15
7500	131.91	127.11	122.91	119.23	115.98	113.09	110.52
8000	140.70	135.58	131.11	127.18	123.71	120.63	117.88
8500	149.50	144.05	139.30	135.13	131.44	128.17	125.25
9000	158.29	152.53	147.50	143.08	139.18	135.71	132.62
9500	167.09	161.00	155.69	151.03	146.91	143.25	139.99
10000	175.88	169.47	163.88	158.98	154.64	150.79	147.35
11000	193.47	186.42	180.27	174.87	170.10	165.87	162.09
12000	211.06	203.37	196.66	190.77	185.57	180.95	176.82
13000	228.65	220.32	213.05	206.67	201.03	196.03	191.56
14000	246.23	237.26	229.44	222.57	216.50	211.10	206.29
15000	263.82	254.21	245.83	238.46	231.96	226.18	221.03
16000	281.41	271.16	262.22	254.36	247.42	241.26	235.77
17000	299.00	288.11	278.60	270.26	262.89	256.34	250.50
18000	316.59	305.05	294.99	286.16	278.35	271.42	265.24
19000	334.17	322.00	311.38	302.05	293.82	286.50	279.97
20000	351.76	338.95	327.77	317.95	309.28	301.58	294.71
21000	369.35	355.90	344.16	333.85	324.74	316.66	309.44
22000	386.94	372.84	360.55	349.75	340.21	331.74	324.18
23000	404.53	389.79	376.94	365.65	355.67	346.81	338.91
24000	422.11	406.74	393.32	381.54	371.14	361.89	353.65
25000	439.70	423.69	409.71	397.44	386.60	376.97	368.38
26000	457.29	440.63	426.10	413.34	402.06	392.05	383.12
27000	474.88	457.58	442.49	429.24	417.53	407.13	397.85
28000	492.47	474.53	458.88	445.13	432.99	422.21	412.59
29000	510.05	491.47	475.27	461.03	448.46	437.29	427.33
30000	527.64	508.42	491.65	476.93	463.92	452.37	442.06
31000	545.23	525.37	508.04	492.83	479.38	467.45	456.80
32000	562.82	542.32	524.43	508.72	494.85	482.52	471.53
33000	580.41	559.26	540.82	524.62	510.31	497.60	486.27
34000	597.99	576.21	557.21	540.52	525.78	512.68	501.00
35000	615.58	593.16	573.60	556.42	541.24	527.76	515.74
40000	703.52	677.90	655.54	635.90	618.56	603.16	589.41
45000	791.46	762.63	737.48	715.39	695.88	678.55	663.09
50000	879.40	847.37	819.42	794.88	773.20	753.94	736.77
55000	967.34	932.11	901.37	874.37	850.52	829.34	810.44
60000	1055.29	1016.84	983.31	953.86	927.84	904.73	884.12
65000	1143.23	1101.58	1065.25	1033.35	1005.16	980.13	957.80
70000	1231.17	1186.32	1147.19	1112.83	1082.48	1055.52	1031.47

Monthly Loan Payments 13¼%

LOAN AMOUNT	11 YEARS	11½ YEARS	12 YEARS	12½ YEARS	13 YEARS	14 YEARS	15 YEARS
100	1.44	1.42	1.39	1.37	1.35	1.31	1.28
200	2.89	2.83	2.78	2.74	2.69	2.62	2.56
300	4.33	4.25	4.17	4.10	4.04	3.93	3.85
400	5.77	5.66	5.56	5.47	5.39	5.25	5.13
500	7.21	7.08	6.95	6.84	6.74	6.56	6.41
600	8.66	8.49	8.34	8.21	8.08	7.87	7.69
700	10.10	9.91	9.73	9.57	9.43	9.18	8.97
800	11.54	11.32	11.12	10.94	10.78	10.49	10.25
900	12.98	12.74	12.51	12.31	12.12	11.80	11.54
1000	14.43	14.15	13.90	13.68	13.47	13.11	12.82
1500	21.64	21.23	20.85	20.51	20.21	19.67	19.23
2000	28.86	28.30	27.80	27.35	26.94	26.23	25.63
2500	36.07	35.38	34.75	34.19	33.68	32.79	32.04
3000	43.28	42.45	41.70	41.03	40.41	39.34	38.45
3500	50.50	49.53	48.65	47.86	47.15	45.90	44.86
4000	57.71	56.60	55.61	54.70	53.88	52.46	51.27
4500	64.92	63.68	62.56	61.54	60.62	59.01	57.68
5000	72.14	70.75	69.51	68.38	67.35	65.57	64.09
5500	79.35	77.83	76.46	75.22	74.09	72.13	70.50
6000	86.57	84.91	83.41	82.05	80.82	78.69	76.90
6500	93.78	91.98	90.36	88.89	87.56	85.24	83.31
7000	100.99	99.06	97.31	95.73	94.29	91.80	89.72
7500	108.21	106.13	104.26	102.57	101.03	98.36	96.13
8000	115.42	113.21	111.21	109.40	107.76	104.92	102.54
8500	122.63	120.28	118.16	116.24	114.50	111.47	108.95
9000	129.85	127.36	125.11	123.08	121.24	118.03	115.36
9500	137.06	134.43	132.06	129.92	127.97	124.59	121.76
10000	144.28	141.51	139.01	136.75	134.71	131.14	128.17
11000	158.70	155.66	152.91	150.43	148.18	144.26	140.99
12000	173.13	169.81	166.82	164.11	161.65	157.37	153.81
13000	187.56	183.96	180.72	177.78	175.12	170.49	166.63
14000	201.99	198.11	194.62	191.46	188.59	183.60	179.44
15000	216.41	212.26	208.52	205.13	202.06	196.72	192.26
16000	230.84	226.41	222.42	218.81	215.53	209.83	205.08
17000	245.27	240.57	236.32	232.48	229.00	222.95	217.90
18000	259.70	254.72	250.22	246.16	242.47	236.06	230.71
19000	274.12	268.87	264.12	259.83	255.94	249.17	243.53
20000	288.55	283.02	278.03	273.51	269.41	262.29	256.35
21000	302.98	297.17	291.93	287.19	282.88	275.40	269.16
22000	317.41	311.32	305.83	300.86	296.35	288.52	281.98
23000	331.83	325.47	319.73	314.54	309.82	301.63	294.80
24000	346.26	339.62	333.63	328.21	323.29	314.75	307.62
25000	360.69	353.77	347.53	341.89	336.76	327.86	320.43
26000	375.12	367.92	361.43	355.56	350.24	340.97	333.25
27000	389.55	382.07	375.34	369.24	363.71	354.09	346.07
28000	403.97	396.23	389.24	382.91	377.18	367.20	358.89
29000	418.40	410.38	403.14	396.59	390.65	380.32	371.70
30000	432.83	424.53	417.04	410.26	404.12	393.43	384.52
31000	447.26	438.68	430.94	423.94	417.59	406.55	397.34
32000	461.68	452.83	444.84	437.62	431.06	419.66	410.16
33000	476.11	466.98	458.74	451.29	444.53	432.78	422.97
34000	490.54	481.13	472.64	464.97	458.00	445.89	435.79
35000	504.97	495.28	486.55	478.64	471.47	459.00	448.61
40000	577.10	566.04	556.05	547.02	538.82	524.58	512.69
45000	649.24	636.79	625.56	615.40	606.18	590.15	576.78
50000	721.38	707.55	695.07	683.77	673.53	655.72	640.87
55000	793.52	778.30	764.57	752.15	740.88	721.29	704.96
60000	865.66	849.05	834.08	820.53	808.24	786.87	769.04
65000	937.79	919.81	903.59	888.91	875.59	852.44	833.13
70000	1009.93	990.56	973.09	957.28	942.94	918.01	897.22

13½% Monthly Loan Payments

LOAN AMOUNT	½ YEAR	1 YEAR	1½ YEARS	2 YEARS	2½ YEARS	3 YEARS	3½ YEARS
100	17.33	8.96	6.17	4.78	3.95	3.39	3.0
200	34.66	17.91	12.34	9.56	7.89	6.79	6.00
300	51.99	26.87	18.50	14.33	11.84	10.18	9.00
400	69.32	35.82	24.67	19.11	15.78	13.57	12.00
500	86.65	44.78	30.84	23.89	19.73	16.97	15.00
600	103.97	53.73	37.01	28.67	23.68	20.36	18.00
700	121.30	62.69	43.18	33.44	27.62	23.75	21.00
800	138.63	71.64	49.34	38.22	31.57	27.15	24.01
900	155.96	80.60	55.51	43.00	35.51	30.54	27.0
1000	173.29	89.55	61.68	47.78	39.46	33.94	30.0
1500	259.94	134.33	92.52	71.67	59.19	50.90	45.0
2000	346.58	179.10	123.36	95.55	78.92	67.87	60.0
2500	433.23	223.88	154.20	119.44	98.65	84.84	75.0
3000	519.87	268.66	185.04	143.33	118.38	101.81	90.0
3500	606.52	313.43	215.88	167.22	138.11	118.77	105.0
4000	693.16	358.21	246.72	191.11	157.84	135.74	120.0
4500	779.81	402.98	277.57	215.00	177.57	152.71	135.0
5000	866.45	447.76	308.41	238.89	197.30	169.68	150.0
5500	953.10	492.54	339.25	262.77	217.03	186.64	165.0
6000	1039.74	537.31	370.09	286.66	236.76	203.61	180.0
6500	1126.39	582.09	400.93	310.55	256.49	220.58	195.0
7000	1213.03	626.86	431.77	334.44	276.22	237.55	210.0
7500	1299.68	671.64	462.61	358.33	295.95	254.51	225.0
8000	1386.32	716.42	493.45	382.22	315.68	271.48	240.0
8500	1472.97	761.19	524.29	406.10	335.41	288.45	255.0
9000	1559.61	805.97	555.13	429.99	355.14	305.42	270.0
9500	1646.26	850.74	585.97	453.88	374.87	322.39	285.0
10000	1732.90	895.52	616.81	477.77	394.60	339.35	300.0
11000	1906.19	985.07	678.49	525.55	434.05	373.29	330.0
12000	2079.48	1074.62	740.17	573.32	473.51	407.22	360.0
13000	2252.77	1164.16	801.85	621.10	512.97	441.16	390.09
14000	2426.06	1253.73	863.54	668.88	552.43	475.09	420.1
15000	2599.36	1343.28	925.22	716.66	591.89	509.03	450.1
16000	2772.65	1432.83	986.90	764.43	631.35	542.96	480.1
17000	2945.94	1522.38	1048.58	812.21	670.81	576.90	510.1
18000	3119.23	1611.94	1110.26	859.99	710.27	610.84	540.1
19000	3292.52	1701.49	1171.94	907.76	749.73	644.77	570.1
20000	3465.81	1791.04	1233.62	955.54	789.19	678.71	600.1
21000	3639.10	1880.59	1295.30	1003.32	828.65	712.64	630.1
22000	3812.39	1970.14	1356.98	1051.09	868.11	746.58	660.1
23000	3985.68	2059.70	1418.67	1098.87	907.57	780.51	690.1
24000	4158.97	2149.25	1480.35	1146.65	947.03	814.45	720.1
25000	4332.26	2238.80	1542.03	1194.43	986.49	848.38	750.1
26000	4505.55	2328.35	1603.71	1242.20	1025.95	882.32	780.1
27000	4678.84	2417.90	1665.39	1289.98	1065.41	916.25	810.1
28000	4852.13	2507.46	1727.07	1337.76	1104.87	950.19	840.2
29000	5025.42	2597.01	1788.75	1385.53	1144.33	984.12	870.2
30000	5198.71	2686.56	1850.43	1433.31	1183.79	1018.06	900.2
31000	5372.00	2776.11	1912.12	1481.09	1223.25	1051.99	930.2
32000	5545.29	2865.66	1973.80	1528.86	1262.71	1085.93	960.2
33000	5718.58	2955.22	2035.48	1576.64	1302.16	1119.86	990.2
34000	5891.87	3044.77	2097.16	1624.42	1341.62	1153.80	1020.2
35000	6065.16	3134.32	2158.84	1672.20	1381.08	1187.74	1050.2
40000	6931.61	3582.08	2467.25	1911.08	1578.38	1357.41	1200.2
45000	7798.07	4029.84	2775.65	2149.97	1775.68	1527.09	1350.3
50000	8664.52	4477.60	3084.06	2388.85	1972.98	1696.76	1500.3
55000	9530.97	4925.36	3392.46	2627.74	2170.27	1866.44	1650.3
60000	10397.42	5373.12	3700.87	2866.62	2367.57	2036.12	1800.4
65000	11263.87	5820.88	4009.27	3105.51	2564.87	2205.79	1950.4
70000	12130.32	6268.64	4317.68	3344.39	2762.17	2375.47	2100.5

Monthly Loan Payments 13½%

LOAN AMOUNT	4 YEARS	4½ YEARS	5 YEARS	5½ YEARS	6 YEARS	6½ YEARS	7 YEARS
100	2.71	2.48	2.30	2.15	2.03	1.93	1.85
200	5.42	4.96	4.60	4.31	4.07	3.87	3.69
300	8.12	7.44	6.90	6.46	6.10	5.80	5.54
400	10.83	9.92	9.20	8.62	8.14	7.73	7.39
500	13.54	12.41	11.50	10.77	10.17	9.66	9.23
600	16.25	14.89	13.81	12.93	12.20	11.60	11.08
700	18.95	17.37	16.11	15.08	14.24	13.53	12.93
800	21.66	19.85	18.41	17.24	16.27	15.46	14.77
900	24.37	22.33	20.71	19.39	18.31	17.39	16.62
1000	27.08	24.81	23.01	21.55	20.34	19.33	18.46
1500	40.61	37.22	34.51	32.32	30.51	28.99	27.70
2000	54.15	49.62	46.02	43.10	40.68	38.65	36.93
2500	67.69	62.03	57.52	53.87	50.85	48.31	46.16
3000	81.23	74.43	69.03	64.64	61.02	57.98	55.39
3500	94.77	86.84	80.53	75.42	71.19	67.64	64.63
4000	108.31	99.24	92.04	86.19	81.36	77.30	73.86
4500	121.84	111.65	103.54	96.96	91.53	86.96	83.09
5000	135.38	124.05	115.05	107.74	101.69	96.63	92.32
5500	148.92	136.46	126.55	118.51	111.86	106.29	101.56
6000	162.46	148.86	138.06	129.29	122.03	115.95	110.79
6500	176.00	161.27	149.56	140.06	132.20	125.61	120.02
7000	189.53	173.67	161.07	150.83	142.37	135.28	129.25
7500	203.07	186.08	172.57	161.61	152.54	144.94	138.49
8000	216.61	198.48	184.08	172.38	162.71	154.60	147.72
8500	230.15	210.89	195.58	183.15	172.88	164.27	156.95
9000	243.69	223.29	207.09	193.93	183.05	173.93	166.18
9500	257.23	235.70	218.59	204.70	193.22	183.59	175.42
10000	270.76	248.10	230.10	215.48	203.39	193.25	184.65
11000	297.84	272.91	253.11	237.02	223.73	212.58	203.11
12000	324.92	297.73	276.12	258.57	244.07	231.90	221.58
13000	351.99	322.54	299.13	280.12	264.41	251.23	240.04
14000	379.07	347.35	322.14	301.67	284.75	270.56	258.51
15000	406.14	372.16	345.15	323.21	305.08	289.88	276.97
16000	433.22	396.97	368.16	344.76	325.42	309.21	295.44
17000	460.30	421.78	391.17	366.31	345.76	328.53	313.90
18000	487.37	446.59	414.18	387.86	366.10	347.86	332.37
19000	514.45	471.40	437.19	409.40	386.44	367.18	350.83
20000	541.53	496.21	460.20	430.95	406.78	386.51	369.30
21000	568.60	521.02	483.21	452.50	427.12	405.83	387.76
22000	595.68	545.83	506.22	474.05	447.46	425.16	406.23
23000	622.76	570.64	529.23	495.59	467.80	444.48	424.69
24000	649.83	595.45	552.24	517.14	488.14	463.81	443.16
25000	676.91	620.26	575.25	538.69	508.47	483.13	461.62
26000	703.98	645.07	598.26	560.24	528.81	502.46	480.09
27000	731.06	669.88	621.27	581.78	549.15	521.78	498.55
28000	758.14	694.69	644.28	603.33	569.49	541.11	517.02
29000	785.21	719.50	667.29	624.88	589.83	560.44	535.48
30000	812.29	744.31	690.30	646.43	610.17	579.76	553.95
31000	839.37	769.12	713.31	667.98	630.51	599.09	572.41
32000	866.44	793.93	736.32	689.52	650.85	618.41	590.88
33000	893.52	818.74	759.32	711.07	671.19	637.74	609.34
34000	920.59	843.55	782.33	732.62	691.52	657.06	627.81
35000	947.67	868.36	805.34	754.17	711.86	676.39	646.27
40000	1083.05	992.42	920.39	861.90	813.56	773.01	738.60
45000	1218.43	1116.47	1035.44	969.64	915.25	869.64	830.92
50000	1353.82	1240.52	1150.49	1077.38	1016.95	966.27	923.24
55000	1489.20	1364.57	1265.54	1185.12	1118.64	1062.89	1015.57
60000	1624.58	1488.63	1380.59	1292.85	1220.34	1159.52	1107.89
65000	1759.96	1612.68	1495.64	1400.59	1322.03	1256.15	1200.22
70000	1895.34	1736.73	1610.69	1508.33	1423.73	1352.78	1292.54

13½% Monthly Loan Payments

LOAN AMOUNT	7½ YEARS	8 YEARS	8½ YEARS	9 YEARS	9½ YEARS	10 YEARS	10½ YEARS
100	1.77	1.71	1.65	1.60	1.56	1.52	1.49
200	3.55	3.42	3.31	3.21	3.12	3.05	2.98
300	5.32	5.13	4.96	4.81	4.68	4.57	4.47
400	7.09	6.84	6.61	6.42	6.24	6.09	5.95
500	8.86	8.54	8.27	8.02	7.81	7.61	7.44
600	10.64	10.25	9.92	9.63	9.37	9.14	8.93
700	12.41	11.96	11.57	11.23	10.93	10.66	10.42
800	14.18	13.67	13.22	12.83	12.49	12.18	11.91
900	15.95	15.38	14.88	14.44	14.05	13.70	13.40
1000	17.73	17.09	16.53	16.04	15.61	15.23	14.89
1500	26.59	25.63	24.80	24.06	23.42	22.84	22.33
2000	35.45	34.18	33.06	32.08	31.22	30.45	29.77
2500	44.32	42.72	41.33	40.11	39.03	38.07	37.21
3000	53.18	51.26	49.59	48.13	46.83	45.68	44.66
3500	62.04	59.81	57.86	56.15	54.64	53.30	52.10
4000	70.91	68.35	66.12	64.17	62.44	60.91	59.54
4500	79.77	76.90	74.39	72.19	70.25	68.52	66.99
5000	88.63	85.44	82.66	80.21	78.05	76.14	74.43
5500	97.50	93.98	90.92	88.23	85.86	83.75	81.87
6000	106.36	102.53	99.19	96.25	93.66	91.36	89.31
6500	115.22	111.07	107.45	104.28	101.47	98.98	96.76
7000	124.09	119.62	115.72	112.30	109.27	106.59	104.20
7500	132.95	128.16	123.98	120.32	117.08	114.21	111.64
8000	141.81	136.71	132.25	128.34	124.88	121.82	119.09
8500	150.68	145.25	140.52	136.36	132.69	129.43	126.53
9000	159.54	153.79	148.78	144.38	140.50	137.05	133.97
9500	168.40	162.34	157.05	152.40	148.30	144.66	141.41
10000	177.27	170.88	165.31	160.42	156.11	152.27	148.86
11000	195.00	187.97	181.84	176.47	171.72	167.50	163.74
12000	212.72	205.06	198.37	192.51	187.33	182.73	178.63
13000	230.45	222.15	214.91	208.55	202.94	197.96	193.51
14000	248.18	239.23	231.44	224.59	218.55	213.18	208.40
15000	265.90	256.32	247.97	240.63	234.16	228.41	223.29
16000	283.63	273.41	264.50	256.68	249.77	243.64	238.17
17000	301.36	290.50	281.03	272.72	265.38	258.87	253.06
18000	319.08	307.59	297.56	288.76	280.99	274.09	267.94
19000	336.81	324.68	314.09	304.80	296.60	289.32	282.83
20000	354.54	341.76	330.62	320.85	312.21	304.55	297.72
21000	372.26	358.85	347.16	336.89	327.82	319.78	312.60
22000	389.99	375.94	363.69	352.93	343.43	335.00	327.49
23000	407.72	393.03	380.22	368.97	359.04	350.23	342.37
24000	425.44	410.12	396.75	385.02	374.65	365.46	357.26
25000	443.17	427.20	413.28	401.06	390.27	380.69	372.14
26000	460.90	444.29	429.81	417.10	405.88	395.91	387.03
27000	478.62	461.38	446.34	433.14	421.49	411.14	401.92
28000	496.35	478.47	462.87	449.18	437.10	426.37	416.80
29000	514.08	495.56	479.41	465.23	452.71	441.60	431.69
30000	531.81	512.64	495.94	481.27	468.32	456.82	446.57
31000	549.53	529.73	512.47	497.31	483.93	472.05	461.46
32000	567.26	546.82	529.00	513.35	499.54	487.28	476.34
33000	584.99	563.91	545.53	529.40	515.15	502.51	491.23
34000	602.71	581.00	562.06	545.44	530.76	517.73	506.12
35000	620.44	598.09	578.59	561.48	546.37	532.96	521.00
40000	709.07	683.53	661.25	641.69	624.42	609.10	595.43
45000	797.71	768.97	743.90	721.90	702.48	685.23	669.86
50000	886.34	854.41	826.56	802.12	780.53	761.37	744.29
55000	974.98	939.85	909.22	882.33	858.58	837.51	818.72
60000	1063.61	1025.29	991.87	962.54	936.64	913.65	893.15
65000	1152.24	1110.73	1074.53	1042.75	1014.69	989.78	967.57
70000	1240.88	1196.17	1157.19	1122.96	1092.74	1065.92	1042.00

Monthly Loan Payments 13½%

LOAN AMOUNT	11 YEARS	11½ YEARS	12 YEARS	12½ YEARS	13 YEARS	14 YEARS	15 YEARS
100	1.46	1.43	1.41	1.38	1.36	1.33	1.30
200	2.92	2.86	2.81	2.77	2.73	2.66	2.60
300	4.37	4.29	4.22	4.15	4.09	3.98	3.89
400	5.83	5.72	5.62	5.53	5.45	5.31	5.19
500	7.29	7.15	7.03	6.92	6.81	6.64	6.49
600	8.75	8.58	8.43	8.30	8.18	7.97	7.79
700	10.21	10.01	9.84	9.68	9.54	9.29	9.09
800	11.66	11.44	11.25	11.07	10.90	10.62	10.39
900	13.12	12.87	12.65	12.45	12.27	11.95	11.68
1000	14.58	14.30	14.06	13.83	13.63	13.28	12.98
1500	21.87	21.46	21.09	20.75	20.44	19.92	19.47
2000	29.16	28.61	28.11	27.67	27.26	26.55	25.97
2500	36.45	35.76	35.14	34.58	34.07	33.19	32.46
3000	43.74	42.91	42.17	41.50	40.89	39.83	38.95
3500	51.03	50.07	49.20	48.42	47.70	46.47	45.44
4000	58.32	57.22	56.23	55.33	54.52	53.11	51.93
4500	65.61	64.37	63.26	62.25	61.33	59.75	58.42
5000	72.90	71.52	70.29	69.17	68.15	66.39	64.92
5500	80.19	78.68	77.31	76.08	74.96	73.02	71.41
6000	87.48	85.83	84.34	83.00	81.78	79.66	77.90
6500	94.77	92.98	91.37	89.92	88.59	86.30	84.39
7000	102.06	100.13	98.40	96.83	95.41	92.94	90.88
7500	109.35	107.29	105.43	103.75	102.22	99.58	97.37
8000	116.64	114.44	112.46	110.66	109.04	106.22	103.87
8500	123.93	121.59	119.49	117.58	115.85	112.86	110.36
9000	131.22	128.74	126.51	124.50	122.67	119.49	116.85
9500	138.51	135.90	133.54	131.41	129.48	126.13	123.34
10000	145.80	143.05	140.57	138.33	136.30	132.77	129.83
11000	160.38	157.35	154.63	152.16	149.93	146.05	142.82
12000	174.96	171.66	168.69	166.00	163.56	159.32	155.80
13000	189.54	185.96	182.74	179.83	177.19	172.60	168.78
14000	204.12	200.27	196.80	193.66	190.82	185.88	181.76
15000	218.70	214.57	210.86	207.50	204.45	199.16	194.75
16000	233.28	228.88	224.91	221.33	218.08	212.43	207.73
17000	247.86	243.18	238.97	235.16	231.71	225.71	220.71
18000	262.44	257.49	253.03	249.00	245.34	238.99	233.70
19000	277.02	271.79	267.09	262.83	258.97	252.26	246.68
20000	291.60	286.10	281.14	276.66	272.60	265.54	259.66
21000	306.18	300.40	295.20	290.49	286.23	278.82	272.65
22000	320.76	314.71	309.26	304.33	299.86	292.10	285.63
23000	335.34	329.01	323.31	318.16	313.49	305.37	298.61
24000	349.92	343.32	337.37	331.99	327.12	318.65	311.60
25000	364.50	357.62	351.43	345.83	340.75	331.93	324.58
26000	379.08	371.93	365.49	359.66	354.38	345.20	337.56
27000	393.66	386.23	379.54	373.49	368.01	358.48	350.55
28000	408.24	400.54	393.60	387.33	381.64	371.76	363.53
29000	422.82	414.84	407.66	401.16	395.27	385.03	376.51
30000	437.40	429.15	421.72	414.99	408.90	398.31	389.50
31000	451.98	443.45	435.77	428.83	422.53	411.59	402.48
32000	466.56	457.76	449.83	442.66	436.16	424.87	415.46
33000	481.14	472.06	463.89	456.49	449.79	438.14	428.45
34000	495.72	486.37	477.94	470.32	463.42	451.42	441.43
35000	510.30	500.67	492.00	484.16	477.05	464.70	454.41
40000	583.19	572.20	562.29	553.32	545.20	531.08	519.33
45000	656.09	643.72	632.57	622.49	613.35	597.47	584.24
50000	728.99	715.25	702.86	691.65	681.50	663.85	649.16
55000	801.89	786.77	773.14	760.82	749.65	730.24	714.08
60000	874.79	858.30	843.43	829.98	817.80	796.62	778.99
65000	947.69	929.82	913.72	899.15	885.94	863.01	843.91
70000	1020.59	1001.35	984.00	968.32	954.09	929.39	908.82

13¾%   Monthly Loan Payments

LOAN AMOUNT	½ YEAR	1 YEAR	1½ YEARS	2 YEARS	2½ YEARS	3 YEARS	3½ YEARS
100	17.34	8.97	6.18	4.79	3.96	3.41	3.0
200	34.68	17.93	12.36	9.58	7.92	6.81	6.0
300	52.02	26.90	18.54	14.37	11.87	10.22	9.0
400	69.37	35.87	24.72	19.16	15.83	13.62	12.0
500	86.71	44.83	30.90	23.95	19.79	17.03	15.0
600	104.05	53.80	37.08	28.74	23.75	20.43	18.0
700	121.39	62.77	43.26	33.53	27.71	23.84	21.0
800	138.73	71.74	49.44	38.32	31.66	27.25	24.1
900	156.07	80.70	55.62	43.11	35.62	30.65	27.1
1000	173.41	89.67	61.80	47.89	39.58	34.06	30.1
1500	260.12	134.50	92.70	71.84	59.37	51.08	45.2
2000	346.83	179.34	123.60	95.79	79.16	68.11	60.2
2500	433.54	224.17	154.50	119.74	98.95	85.14	75.3
3000	520.24	269.01	185.39	143.68	118.74	102.17	90.3
3500	606.95	313.84	216.29	167.63	138.53	119.20	105.4
4000	693.66	358.68	247.19	191.58	158.32	136.23	120.5
4500	780.36	403.51	278.09	215.53	178.10	153.25	135.5
5000	867.07	448.35	308.99	239.47	197.89	170.28	150.6
5500	953.78	493.18	339.89	263.42	217.68	187.31	165.7
6000	1040.48	538.02	370.79	287.37	237.47	204.34	180.7
6500	1127.19	582.85	401.69	311.32	257.26	221.37	195.8
7000	1213.90	627.69	432.59	335.26	277.05	238.39	210.9
7500	1300.61	672.52	463.49	359.21	296.84	255.42	225.9
8000	1387.31	717.36	494.38	383.16	316.63	272.45	241.0
8500	1474.02	762.19	525.28	407.11	336.42	289.48	256.1
9000	1560.73	807.03	556.18	431.05	356.21	306.51	271.1
9500	1647.43	851.86	587.08	455.00	376.00	323.54	286.2
10000	1734.14	896.70	617.98	478.95	395.79	340.56	301.3
11000	1907.56	986.36	679.78	526.84	435.37	374.62	331.4
12000	2080.97	1076.03	741.58	574.74	474.95	408.68	361.5
13000	2254.38	1165.70	803.38	622.63	514.52	442.73	391.6
14000	2427.80	1255.37	865.17	670.53	554.10	476.79	421.8
15000	2601.21	1345.04	926.97	718.42	593.68	510.84	451.9
16000	2774.63	1434.71	988.77	766.32	633.26	544.90	482.0
17000	2948.04	1524.38	1050.57	814.21	672.84	578.96	512.2
18000	3121.45	1614.05	1112.37	862.11	712.42	613.01	542.3
19000	3294.87	1703.72	1174.16	910.00	752.00	647.07	572.4
20000	3468.28	1793.39	1235.96	957.90	791.58	681.13	602.6
21000	3641.70	1883.06	1297.76	1005.79	831.16	715.18	632.7
22000	3815.11	1972.73	1359.56	1053.69	870.73	749.24	662.8
23000	3988.53	2062.40	1421.36	1101.58	910.31	783.30	692.9
24000	4161.94	2152.07	1483.15	1149.48	949.89	817.35	723.1
25000	4335.35	2241.74	1544.95	1197.37	989.47	851.41	753.2
26000	4508.77	2331.41	1606.75	1245.27	1029.05	885.46	783.3
27000	4682.18	2421.08	1668.55	1293.16	1068.63	919.52	813.5
28000	4855.60	2510.75	1730.35	1341.06	1108.21	953.58	843.6
29000	5029.01	2600.42	1792.14	1388.95	1147.79	987.63	873.7
30000	5202.42	2690.09	1853.94	1436.85	1187.37	1021.69	903.9
31000	5375.84	2779.76	1915.74	1484.74	1226.94	1055.75	934.0
32000	5549.25	2869.42	1977.54	1532.64	1266.52	1089.80	964.1
33000	5722.67	2959.09	2039.44	1580.53	1306.10	1123.86	994.2
34000	5896.08	3048.76	2101.13	1628.43	1345.68	1157.92	1024.4
35000	6069.50	3138.43	2162.93	1676.32	1385.26	1191.97	1054.5
40000	6936.57	3586.78	2471.92	1915.79	1583.15	1362.25	1205.2
45000	7803.64	4035.13	2780.91	2155.27	1781.05	1532.53	1355.8
50000	8670.71	4483.48	3089.90	2394.74	1978.94	1702.82	1506.5
55000	9537.78	4931.82	3398.89	2634.22	2176.84	1873.10	1657.1
60000	10404.85	5380.17	3707.69	2873.69	2374.73	2043.38	1807.8
65000	11271.92	5828.52	4016.88	3113.17	2572.62	2213.66	1958.4
70000	12138.99	6276.87	4325.87	3352.64	2770.52	2383.94	2109.1

Monthly Loan Payments 13¾%

LOAN AMOUNT	4 YEARS	4½ YEARS	5 YEARS	5½ YEARS	6 YEARS	6½ YEARS	7 YEARS
100	2.72	2.49	2.31	2.17	2.05	1.95	1.86
200	5.44	4.99	4.63	4.34	4.09	3.89	3.72
300	8.16	7.48	6.94	6.50	6.14	5.84	5.58
400	10.88	9.97	9.26	8.67	8.19	7.78	7.44
500	13.60	12.47	11.57	10.84	10.24	9.73	9.30
600	16.32	14.96	13.88	13.01	12.28	11.68	11.16
700	19.04	17.46	16.20	15.18	14.33	13.62	13.02
800	21.76	19.95	18.51	17.34	16.38	15.57	14.88
900	24.48	22.44	20.82	19.51	18.42	17.51	16.74
1000	27.20	24.94	23.14	21.68	20.47	19.46	18.60
1500	40.80	37.41	34.71	32.52	30.71	29.19	27.90
2000	54.40	49.87	46.28	43.36	40.94	38.92	37.20
2500	68.00	62.34	57.85	54.20	51.18	48.65	46.51
3000	81.60	74.81	69.42	65.04	61.42	58.38	55.81
3500	95.20	87.28	80.99	75.88	71.65	68.11	65.11
4000	108.80	99.75	92.56	86.71	81.89	77.84	74.41
4500	122.41	112.22	104.12	97.55	92.12	87.57	83.71
5000	136.01	124.69	115.69	108.39	102.36	97.30	93.01
5500	149.61	137.16	127.26	119.23	112.60	107.03	102.31
6000	163.21	149.62	138.83	130.07	122.83	116.76	111.61
6500	176.81	162.09	150.40	140.91	133.07	126.49	120.91
7000	190.41	174.56	161.97	151.75	143.30	136.22	130.22
7500	204.01	187.03	173.54	162.59	153.54	145.95	139.52
8000	217.61	199.50	185.11	173.43	163.78	155.68	148.82
8500	231.21	211.97	196.68	184.27	174.01	165.41	158.12
9000	244.81	224.44	208.25	195.11	184.25	175.15	167.42
9500	258.41	236.90	219.82	205.95	194.49	184.88	176.72
10000	272.01	249.37	231.39	216.79	204.72	194.61	186.02
11000	299.21	274.31	254.53	238.47	225.19	214.07	204.62
12000	326.41	299.25	277.67	260.14	245.67	233.53	223.23
13000	353.62	324.19	300.80	281.82	266.14	252.99	241.83
14000	380.82	349.12	323.94	303.50	286.61	272.45	260.43
15000	408.02	374.06	347.08	325.18	307.08	291.91	279.03
16000	435.22	399.00	370.22	346.86	327.55	311.37	297.63
17000	462.42	423.94	393.36	368.54	348.03	330.83	316.24
18000	489.62	448.87	416.50	390.22	368.50	350.29	334.84
19000	516.82	473.81	439.64	411.89	388.97	369.75	353.44
20000	544.02	498.75	462.78	433.57	409.44	389.21	372.04
21000	571.23	523.68	485.92	455.25	429.91	408.67	390.65
22000	598.43	548.62	509.05	476.93	450.39	428.13	409.25
23000	625.63	573.56	532.19	498.61	470.86	447.59	427.85
24000	652.83	598.50	555.33	520.29	491.33	467.05	446.45
25000	680.03	623.43	578.47	541.97	511.80	486.51	465.05
26000	707.23	648.37	601.61	563.65	532.27	505.98	483.66
27000	734.43	673.31	624.75	585.32	552.75	525.44	502.26
28000	761.63	698.25	647.89	607.00	573.22	544.90	520.86
29000	788.84	723.18	671.03	628.68	593.69	564.36	539.46
30000	816.04	748.12	694.17	650.36	614.16	583.82	558.07
31000	843.24	773.06	717.30	672.04	634.64	603.28	576.67
32000	870.44	798.00	740.44	693.72	655.11	622.74	595.27
33000	897.64	822.93	763.58	715.40	675.58	642.20	613.87
34000	924.84	847.87	786.72	737.07	696.05	661.66	632.47
35000	952.04	872.81	809.86	758.75	716.52	681.12	651.08
40000	1088.05	997.49	925.55	867.15	818.88	778.42	744.09
45000	1224.06	1122.18	1041.25	975.54	921.25	875.73	837.10
50000	1360.06	1246.87	1156.94	1083.93	1023.61	973.03	930.11
55000	1496.07	1371.56	1272.64	1192.33	1125.97	1070.33	1023.12
60000	1632.07	1496.24	1388.33	1300.72	1228.33	1167.63	1116.13
65000	1768.08	1620.93	1504.02	1409.11	1330.69	1264.94	1209.14
70000	1904.09	1745.62	1619.72	1517.51	1433.05	1362.24	1302.15

13¾%   Monthly Loan Payments

LOAN AMOUNT	7½ YEARS	8 YEARS	8½ YEARS	9 YEARS	9½ YEARS	10 YEARS	10½ YEARS
100	1.79	1.72	1.67	1.62	1.58	1.54	1.50
200	3.57	3.45	3.33	3.24	3.15	3.08	3.01
300	5.36	5.17	5.00	4.86	4.73	4.61	4.51
400	7.15	6.89	6.67	6.48	6.30	6.15	6.01
500	8.93	8.61	8.34	8.09	7.88	7.69	7.52
600	10.72	10.34	10.00	9.71	9.45	9.23	9.02
700	12.51	12.06	11.67	11.33	11.03	10.76	10.53
800	14.29	13.78	13.34	12.95	12.61	12.30	12.03
900	16.08	15.51	15.01	14.57	14.18	13.84	13.53
1000	17.87	17.23	16.67	16.19	15.76	15.38	15.04
1500	26.80	25.84	25.01	24.28	23.64	23.07	22.56
2000	35.73	34.46	33.35	32.38	31.52	30.75	30.07
2500	44.67	43.07	41.69	40.47	39.39	38.44	37.59
3000	53.60	51.69	50.02	48.56	47.27	46.13	45.11
3500	62.53	60.30	58.36	56.66	55.15	53.82	52.63
4000	71.46	68.92	66.70	64.75	63.03	61.51	60.15
4500	80.40	77.53	75.04	72.84	70.91	69.20	67.67
5000	89.33	86.15	83.37	80.94	78.79	76.88	75.18
5500	98.26	94.76	91.71	89.03	86.67	84.57	82.70
6000	107.20	103.38	100.05	97.13	94.55	92.26	90.22
6500	116.13	111.99	108.38	105.22	102.43	99.95	97.74
7000	125.06	120.61	116.72	113.31	110.31	107.64	105.26
7500	134.00	129.22	125.06	121.41	118.18	115.33	112.78
8000	142.93	137.84	133.40	129.50	126.06	123.01	120.30
8500	151.86	146.45	141.73	137.60	133.94	130.70	127.81
9000	160.80	155.07	150.07	145.69	141.82	138.39	135.33
9500	169.73	163.68	158.41	153.78	149.70	146.08	142.85
10000	178.66	172.30	166.75	161.88	157.58	153.77	150.37
11000	196.53	189.52	183.42	178.06	173.34	169.14	165.41
12000	214.39	206.75	200.10	194.25	189.10	184.52	180.44
13000	232.26	223.98	216.77	210.44	204.85	199.90	195.48
14000	250.13	241.21	233.44	226.63	220.61	215.27	210.52
15000	267.99	258.44	250.12	242.82	236.37	230.65	225.55
16000	285.86	275.67	266.79	259.00	252.13	246.03	240.59
17000	303.73	292.90	283.47	275.19	267.88	261.40	255.63
18000	321.59	310.13	300.14	291.38	283.64	276.78	270.66
19000	339.46	327.36	316.82	307.57	299.40	292.16	285.70
20000	357.32	344.59	333.49	323.75	315.16	307.53	300.74
21000	375.19	361.82	350.17	339.94	330.92	322.91	315.78
22000	393.06	379.05	366.84	356.13	346.67	338.29	330.81
23000	410.92	396.28	383.52	372.32	362.43	353.66	345.85
24000	428.79	413.51	400.19	388.50	378.19	369.04	360.89
25000	446.65	430.74	416.86	404.69	393.95	384.42	375.92
26000	464.52	447.97	433.54	420.88	409.71	399.79	390.96
27000	482.39	465.20	450.21	437.07	425.46	415.17	406.00
28000	500.25	482.43	466.89	453.25	441.22	430.54	421.03
29000	518.12	499.66	483.56	469.44	456.98	445.92	436.07
30000	535.99	516.89	500.24	485.63	472.74	461.30	451.11
31000	553.85	534.12	516.91	501.82	488.50	476.68	466.14
32000	571.72	551.34	533.59	518.00	504.25	492.05	481.18
33000	589.58	568.57	550.26	534.19	520.01	507.43	496.22
34000	607.45	585.80	566.94	550.38	535.77	522.81	511.26
35000	625.32	603.03	583.61	566.57	551.53	538.18	526.29
40000	714.65	689.18	666.98	647.51	630.32	615.07	601.48
45000	803.98	775.33	750.36	728.45	709.11	691.95	676.66
50000	893.31	861.48	833.73	809.38	787.90	768.83	751.85
55000	982.64	947.62	917.10	890.32	866.69	845.72	827.03
60000	1071.97	1033.77	1000.48	971.26	945.48	922.60	902.22
65000	1161.30	1119.92	1083.85	1052.20	1024.27	999.48	977.40
70000	1250.63	1206.07	1167.22	1133.14	1103.05	1076.37	1052.58

Monthly Loan Payments 13¾%

LOAN AMOUNT	11 YEARS	11½ YEARS	12 YEARS	12½ YEARS	13 YEARS	14 YEARS	15 YEARS
100	1.47	1.45	1.42	1.40	1.38	1.34	1.31
200	2.95	2.89	2.84	2.80	2.76	2.69	2.63
300	4.42	4.34	4.26	4.20	4.14	4.03	3.94
400	5.89	5.78	5.69	5.60	5.52	5.38	5.26
500	7.37	7.23	7.11	7.00	6.90	6.72	6.57
600	8.84	8.68	8.53	8.39	8.27	8.06	7.89
700	10.31	10.12	9.95	9.79	9.65	9.41	9.20
800	11.79	11.57	11.37	11.19	11.03	10.75	10.52
900	13.26	13.01	12.79	12.59	12.41	12.10	11.83
1000	14.73	14.46	14.21	13.99	13.79	13.44	13.15
1500	22.10	21.69	21.32	20.99	20.69	20.16	19.72
2000	29.47	28.92	28.43	27.98	27.58	26.88	26.30
2500	36.83	36.15	35.53	34.98	34.48	33.60	32.87
3000	44.20	43.38	42.64	41.97	41.37	40.32	39.45
3500	51.57	50.61	49.75	48.97	48.27	47.04	46.02
4000	58.93	57.84	56.86	55.97	55.16	53.76	52.60
4500	66.30	65.07	63.96	62.96	62.06	60.48	59.17
5000	73.66	72.30	71.07	69.96	68.95	67.20	65.75
5500	81.03	79.53	78.18	76.95	75.85	73.92	72.32
6000	88.40	86.76	85.28	83.95	82.74	80.64	78.90
6500	95.76	93.99	92.39	90.94	89.64	87.36	85.47
7000	103.13	101.22	99.50	97.94	96.53	94.08	92.05
7500	110.50	108.45	106.60	104.94	103.43	100.80	98.62
8000	117.86	115.68	113.71	111.93	110.32	107.52	105.20
8500	125.23	122.91	120.82	118.93	117.22	114.24	111.77
9000	132.60	130.14	127.92	125.92	124.11	120.97	118.35
9500	139.96	137.37	135.03	132.92	131.01	127.69	124.92
10000	147.33	144.60	142.14	139.92	137.90	134.41	131.50
11000	162.06	159.06	156.35	153.91	151.69	147.85	144.65
12000	176.79	173.52	170.57	167.90	165.48	161.29	157.80
13000	191.53	187.98	184.78	181.89	179.27	174.73	170.95
14000	206.26	202.44	198.99	195.88	193.06	188.17	184.10
15000	220.99	216.90	213.21	209.87	206.85	201.61	197.25
16000	235.73	231.36	227.42	223.86	220.64	215.05	210.40
17000	250.46	245.82	241.64	237.86	234.43	228.49	223.55
18000	265.19	260.28	255.85	251.85	248.22	241.93	236.70
19000	279.92	274.74	270.06	265.84	262.01	255.37	249.85
20000	294.66	289.20	284.28	279.83	275.80	268.81	263.00
21000	309.39	303.66	298.49	293.82	289.59	282.25	276.15
22000	324.12	318.12	312.70	307.81	303.38	295.69	289.30
23000	338.86	332.58	326.92	321.80	317.17	309.13	302.45
24000	353.59	347.04	341.13	335.80	330.96	322.57	315.60
25000	368.32	361.50	355.35	349.79	344.75	336.01	328.75
26000	383.05	375.96	369.56	363.78	358.54	349.45	341.90
27000	397.79	390.42	383.77	377.77	372.33	362.90	355.05
28000	412.52	404.88	397.99	391.76	386.12	376.34	368.20
29000	427.25	419.34	412.20	405.75	399.91	389.78	381.35
30000	441.99	433.80	426.41	419.75	413.70	403.22	394.50
31000	456.72	448.26	440.63	433.74	427.49	416.66	407.65
32000	471.45	462.72	454.84	447.73	441.28	430.10	420.80
33000	486.19	477.17	469.06	461.72	455.07	443.54	433.95
34000	500.92	491.63	483.27	475.71	468.86	456.98	447.10
35000	515.65	506.09	497.48	489.70	482.65	470.42	460.25
40000	589.32	578.39	568.55	559.66	551.60	537.62	525.99
45000	662.98	650.69	639.62	629.62	620.55	604.83	591.74
50000	736.64	722.99	710.69	699.58	689.50	672.03	657.49
55000	810.31	795.29	781.76	769.53	758.45	739.23	723.24
60000	883.97	867.59	852.83	839.49	827.40	806.43	788.99
65000	957.64	939.89	923.90	909.45	896.35	873.64	854.74
70000	1031.30	1012.19	994.97	979.41	965.30	940.84	920.49

14% Monthly Loan Payments

LOAN AMOUNT	½ YEAR	1 YEAR	1½ YEARS	2 YEARS	2½ YEARS	3 YEARS	3½ YEARS
100	17.35	8.98	6.19	4.80	3.97	3.42	3.0?
200	34.71	17.96	12.38	9.60	7.94	6.84	6.0?
300	52.06	26.94	18.57	14.40	11.91	10.25	9.0?
400	69.42	35.91	24.77	19.21	15.88	13.67	12.1?
500	86.77	44.89	30.96	24.01	19.85	17.09	15.1?
600	104.12	53.87	37.15	28.81	23.82	20.51	18.1?
700	121.48	62.85	43.34	33.61	27.79	23.92	21.1?
800	138.83	71.83	49.53	38.41	31.76	27.34	24.2?
900	156.18	80.81	55.72	43.21	35.73	30.76	27.2?
1000	173.54	89.79	61.92	48.01	39.70	34.18	30.2?
1500	260.31	134.68	92.87	72.02	59.55	51.27	45.3?
2000	347.08	179.57	123.83	96.03	79.40	68.36	60.5?
2500	433.84	224.47	154.79	120.03	99.25	85.44	75.6?
3000	520.61	269.36	185.75	144.04	119.10	102.53	90.7?
3500	607.38	314.25	216.70	168.05	138.94	119.62	105.8?
4000	694.15	359.15	247.66	192.05	158.79	136.71	121.0?
4500	780.92	404.04	278.62	216.06	178.64	153.80	136.1?
5000	867.69	448.94	309.58	240.06	198.49	170.89	151.2?
5500	954.46	493.83	340.53	264.07	218.34	187.98	166.3?
6000	1041.23	538.72	371.49	288.08	238.19	205.07	181.5?
6500	1128.00	583.62	402.45	312.08	258.04	222.15	196.6?
7000	1214.77	628.51	433.41	336.09	277.89	239.24	211.7?
7500	1301.53	673.40	464.36	360.10	297.74	256.33	226.9?
8000	1388.30	718.30	495.32	384.10	317.59	273.42	242.0?
8500	1475.07	763.19	526.28	408.11	337.44	290.51	257.1?
9000	1561.84	808.08	557.24	432.12	357.29	307.60	272.2?
9500	1648.61	852.98	588.19	456.12	377.13	324.69	287.4?
10000	1735.38	897.87	619.15	480.13	396.98	341.78	302.5?
11000	1908.92	987.66	681.07	528.14	436.68	375.95	332.7?
12000	2082.46	1077.45	742.98	576.15	476.38	410.13	363.0?
13000	2255.99	1167.23	804.90	624.17	516.08	444.31	393.2?
14000	2429.53	1257.02	866.81	672.18	555.78	478.49	423.5?
15000	2603.07	1346.81	928.73	720.19	595.48	512.66	453.8?
16000	2776.61	1436.59	990.64	768.21	635.17	546.84	484.0?
17000	2950.15	1526.38	1052.56	816.22	674.87	581.02	514.3?
18000	3123.68	1616.17	1114.47	864.23	714.57	615.20	544.5?
19000	3297.22	1705.96	1176.39	912.24	754.27	649.37	574.8?
20000	3470.76	1795.74	1238.30	960.26	793.97	683.55	605.0?
21000	3644.30	1885.53	1300.22	1008.27	833.67	717.73	635.3?
22000	3817.84	1975.32	1362.13	1056.28	873.36	751.91	665.5?
23000	3991.37	2065.11	1424.05	1104.30	913.06	786.09	695.8?
24000	4164.91	2154.89	1485.96	1152.31	952.76	820.26	726.0?
25000	4338.45	2244.68	1547.88	1200.32	992.46	854.44	756.3?
26000	4511.99	2334.47	1609.79	1248.33	1032.16	888.62	786.5?
27000	4685.53	2424.25	1671.71	1296.35	1071.86	922.80	816.8?
28000	4859.06	2514.04	1733.62	1344.36	1111.55	956.97	847.0?
29000	5032.60	2603.83	1795.54	1392.37	1151.25	991.15	877.3?
30000	5206.14	2693.61	1857.46	1440.39	1190.95	1025.33	907.6?
31000	5379.68	2783.40	1919.37	1488.40	1230.65	1059.51	937.8?
32000	5553.22	2873.19	1981.29	1536.41	1270.35	1093.68	968.1?
33000	5726.75	2962.97	2043.20	1584.43	1310.05	1127.86	998.3?
34000	5900.29	3052.76	2105.12	1632.44	1349.74	1162.04	1028.6?
35000	6073.83	3142.55	2167.03	1680.45	1389.44	1196.22	1058.8?
40000	6941.52	3591.48	2476.61	1920.52	1587.93	1367.11	1210.1?
45000	7809.21	4040.42	2786.18	2160.58	1786.43	1537.99	1361.4?
50000	8676.90	4489.36	3095.76	2400.64	1984.92	1708.88	1512.6?
55000	9544.59	4938.29	3405.33	2640.71	2183.41	1879.77	1663.9?
60000	10412.28	5387.23	3714.91	2880.77	2381.90	2050.66	1815.1?
65000	11279.97	5836.16	4024.49	3120.84	2580.39	2221.55	1966.4?
70000	12147.66	6285.10	4334.06	3360.90	2778.89	2392.43	2117.7?

Monthly Loan Payments 14%

LOAN AMOUNT	4 YEARS	4½ YEARS	5 YEARS	5½ YEARS	6 YEARS	6½ YEARS	7 YEARS
100	2.73	2.51	2.33	2.18	2.06	1.96	1.87
200	5.47	5.01	4.65	4.36	4.12	3.92	3.75
300	8.20	7.52	6.98	6.54	6.18	5.88	5.62
400	10.93	10.03	9.31	8.72	8.24	7.84	7.50
500	13.66	12.53	11.63	10.91	10.30	9.80	9.37
600	16.40	15.04	13.96	13.09	12.36	11.76	11.24
700	19.13	17.55	16.29	15.27	14.42	13.72	13.12
800	21.86	20.05	18.61	17.45	16.48	15.68	14.99
900	24.59	22.56	20.94	19.63	18.55	17.64	16.87
1000	27.33	25.06	23.27	21.81	20.61	19.60	18.74
1500	40.99	37.60	34.90	32.72	30.91	29.39	28.11
2000	54.65	50.13	46.54	43.62	41.21	39.19	37.48
2500	68.32	62.66	58.17	54.53	51.51	48.99	46.85
3000	81.98	75.19	69.80	65.43	61.82	58.79	56.22
3500	95.64	87.73	81.44	76.34	72.12	68.59	65.59
4000	109.31	100.26	93.07	87.24	82.42	78.39	74.96
4500	122.97	112.79	104.71	98.15	92.73	88.18	84.33
5000	136.63	125.32	116.34	109.05	103.03	97.98	93.70
5500	150.30	137.86	127.98	119.96	113.33	107.78	103.07
6000	163.96	150.39	139.61	130.86	123.63	117.58	112.44
6500	177.62	162.92	151.24	141.77	133.94	127.38	121.81
7000	191.29	175.45	162.88	152.67	144.24	137.17	131.18
7500	204.95	187.99	174.51	163.58	154.54	146.97	140.55
8000	218.61	200.52	186.15	174.48	164.85	156.77	149.92
8500	232.28	213.05	197.78	185.39	175.15	166.57	159.29
9000	245.94	225.58	209.41	196.29	185.45	176.37	168.66
9500	259.60	238.11	221.05	207.20	195.75	186.17	178.03
10000	273.26	250.65	232.68	218.10	206.06	195.96	187.40
11000	300.59	275.71	255.95	239.91	226.66	215.56	206.14
12000	327.92	300.78	279.22	261.72	247.27	235.16	224.88
13000	355.24	325.84	302.49	283.53	267.87	254.75	243.62
14000	382.57	350.91	325.76	305.34	288.48	274.35	262.36
15000	409.90	375.97	349.02	327.15	309.09	293.94	281.10
16000	437.22	401.03	372.29	348.96	329.69	313.54	299.84
17000	464.55	426.10	395.56	370.77	350.30	333.14	318.58
18000	491.88	451.16	418.83	392.58	370.90	352.73	337.32
19000	519.20	476.23	442.10	414.39	391.51	372.33	356.06
20000	546.53	501.29	465.37	436.20	412.11	391.93	374.80
21000	573.86	526.36	488.63	458.01	432.72	411.52	393.54
22000	601.18	551.42	511.90	479.82	453.33	431.12	412.28
23000	628.51	576.49	535.17	501.63	473.93	450.72	431.02
24000	655.84	601.55	558.44	523.44	494.54	470.31	449.76
25000	683.16	626.62	581.71	545.25	515.14	489.91	468.50
26000	710.49	651.68	604.97	567.06	535.75	509.50	487.24
27000	737.81	676.75	628.24	588.87	556.35	529.10	505.98
28000	765.14	701.81	651.51	610.68	576.96	548.70	524.72
29000	792.47	726.88	674.78	632.49	597.57	568.29	543.46
30000	819.79	751.94	698.05	654.31	618.17	587.89	562.20
31000	847.12	777.01	721.32	676.12	638.78	607.49	580.94
32000	874.45	802.07	744.58	697.93	659.38	627.08	599.68
33000	901.77	827.13	767.85	719.74	679.99	646.68	618.42
34000	929.10	852.20	791.12	741.55	700.60	666.27	637.16
35000	956.43	877.26	814.39	763.36	721.20	685.87	655.90
40000	1093.06	1002.59	930.73	872.41	824.23	783.85	749.60
45000	1229.69	1127.91	1047.07	981.46	927.26	881.83	843.30
50000	1366.32	1253.23	1163.40	1090.51	1030.29	979.82	937.00
55000	1502.96	1378.58	1279.75	1199.56	1133.32	1077.80	1030.70
60000	1639.59	1503.88	1396.10	1308.61	1236.34	1175.78	1124.40
65000	1776.22	1629.20	1512.44	1417.66	1339.37	1273.76	1218.10
70000	1912.85	1754.53	1628.78	1526.71	1442.40	1371.74	1311.80

14%   Monthly Loan Payments

LOAN AMOUNT	7½ YEARS	8 YEARS	8½ YEARS	9 YEARS	9½ YEARS	10 YEARS	10½ YEARS
100	1.80	1.74	1.68	1.63	1.59	1.55	1.52
200	3.60	3.47	3.36	3.27	3.18	3.11	3.04
300	5.40	5.21	5.05	4.90	4.77	4.66	4.56
400	7.20	6.95	6.73	6.53	6.36	6.21	6.08
500	9.00	8.69	8.41	8.17	7.95	7.76	7.59
600	10.80	10.42	10.09	9.80	9.54	9.32	9.11
700	12.60	12.16	11.77	11.43	11.13	10.87	10.63
800	14.40	13.90	13.45	13.07	12.72	12.42	12.15
900	16.21	15.63	15.14	14.70	14.32	13.97	13.67
1000	18.01	17.37	16.82	16.33	15.91	15.53	15.19
1500	27.01	26.06	25.23	24.50	23.86	23.29	22.78
2000	36.01	34.74	33.64	32.67	31.81	31.05	30.38
2500	45.02	43.43	42.05	40.83	39.76	38.82	37.97
3000	54.02	52.11	50.46	49.00	47.72	46.58	45.57
3500	63.02	60.80	58.87	57.17	55.67	54.34	53.16
4000	72.02	69.49	67.27	65.33	63.62	62.11	60.76
4500	81.03	78.17	75.68	73.50	71.58	69.87	68.35
5000	90.03	86.86	84.09	81.67	79.53	77.63	75.94
5500	99.03	95.54	92.50	89.84	87.48	85.40	83.54
6000	108.04	104.23	100.91	98.00	95.44	93.16	91.13
6500	117.04	112.91	109.32	106.17	103.39	100.92	98.73
7000	126.04	121.60	117.73	114.34	111.34	108.69	106.32
7500	135.05	130.29	126.14	122.50	119.29	116.45	113.92
8000	144.05	138.97	134.55	130.67	127.25	124.21	121.51
8500	153.05	147.66	142.96	138.84	135.20	131.98	129.10
9000	162.05	156.34	151.37	147.00	143.15	139.74	136.70
9500	171.06	165.03	159.78	155.17	151.11	147.50	144.29
10000	180.06	173.72	168.19	163.34	159.06	155.27	151.89
11000	198.07	191.09	185.00	179.67	174.97	170.79	167.08
12000	216.08	208.46	201.82	196.00	190.87	186.32	182.27
13000	234.08	225.83	218.64	212.34	206.78	201.85	197.45
14000	252.09	243.20	235.46	228.67	222.68	217.37	212.64
15000	270.10	260.57	252.28	245.01	238.59	232.90	227.83
16000	288.10	277.94	269.10	261.34	254.49	248.43	243.02
17000	306.10	295.32	285.92	277.67	270.40	263.95	258.21
18000	324.11	312.69	302.74	294.01	286.31	279.48	273.40
19000	342.12	330.06	319.55	310.34	302.21	295.01	288.59
20000	360.12	347.43	336.37	326.67	318.12	310.53	303.78
21000	378.13	364.80	353.19	343.01	334.02	326.06	318.96
22000	396.13	382.17	370.01	359.34	349.93	341.59	334.15
23000	414.14	399.54	386.83	375.68	365.84	357.11	349.34
24000	432.15	416.92	403.65	392.01	381.74	372.64	364.53
25000	450.15	434.29	420.47	408.34	397.65	388.17	379.72
26000	468.16	451.66	437.28	424.68	413.55	403.69	394.91
27000	486.16	469.03	454.10	441.01	429.46	419.22	410.10
28000	504.17	486.40	470.92	457.34	445.37	434.75	425.29
29000	522.18	503.77	487.74	473.68	461.27	450.27	440.48
30000	540.18	521.15	504.56	490.01	477.18	465.80	455.66
31000	558.19	538.52	521.38	506.34	493.08	481.33	470.85
32000	576.19	555.89	538.20	522.68	508.99	496.85	486.04
33000	594.20	573.26	555.01	539.01	524.90	512.38	501.23
34000	612.21	590.63	571.83	555.35	540.80	527.91	516.42
35000	630.21	608.00	588.65	571.68	556.71	543.43	531.61
40000	720.24	694.86	672.74	653.35	636.24	621.07	607.55
45000	810.27	781.72	756.84	735.02	715.77	698.70	683.50
50000	900.30	868.58	840.93	816.69	795.30	776.33	759.44
55000	990.33	955.43	925.02	898.35	874.83	853.97	835.38
60000	1080.37	1042.29	1009.12	980.02	954.36	931.60	911.33
65000	1170.40	1129.15	1093.21	1061.69	1033.89	1009.23	987.27
70000	1260.43	1216.01	1177.30	1143.36	1113.42	1086.87	1063.22

Monthly Loan Payments 14%

LOAN AMOUNT	11 YEARS	11½ YEARS	12 YEARS	12½ YEARS	13 YEARS	14 YEARS	15 YEARS
100	1.49	1.46	1.44	1.42	1.40	1.36	1.33
200	2.98	2.92	2.87	2.83	2.79	2.72	2.66
300	4.47	4.38	4.31	4.25	4.19	4.08	4.00
400	5.95	5.85	5.75	5.66	5.58	5.44	5.33
500	7.44	7.31	7.19	7.08	6.98	6.80	6.66
600	8.93	8.77	8.62	8.49	8.37	8.16	7.99
700	10.42	10.23	10.06	9.91	9.77	9.52	9.32
800	11.91	11.69	11.50	11.32	11.16	10.88	10.65
900	13.40	13.15	12.93	12.74	12.56	12.24	11.99
1000	14.89	14.62	14.37	14.15	13.95	13.60	13.32
1500	22.33	21.92	21.56	21.23	20.93	20.41	19.98
2000	29.77	29.23	28.74	28.30	27.90	27.21	26.63
2500	37.22	36.54	35.93	35.38	34.88	34.01	33.29
3000	44.66	43.85	43.11	42.45	41.85	40.81	39.95
3500	52.10	51.15	50.30	49.53	48.83	47.62	46.61
4000	59.55	58.46	57.49	56.60	55.80	54.42	53.27
4500	66.99	65.77	64.67	63.68	62.78	61.22	59.93
5000	74.43	73.08	71.86	70.75	69.76	68.02	66.59
5500	81.88	80.39	79.04	77.83	76.73	74.83	73.25
6000	89.32	87.69	86.23	84.90	83.71	81.63	79.90
6500	96.76	95.00	93.41	91.98	90.68	88.43	86.56
7000	104.21	102.31	100.60	99.06	97.66	95.23	93.22
7500	111.65	109.62	107.78	106.13	104.63	102.04	99.88
8000	119.09	116.92	114.97	113.21	111.61	108.84	106.54
8500	126.54	124.23	122.16	120.28	118.58	115.64	113.20
9000	133.98	131.54	129.34	127.36	125.56	122.44	119.86
9500	141.42	138.85	136.53	134.43	132.53	129.25	126.52
10000	148.87	146.15	143.71	141.51	139.51	136.05	133.17
11000	163.75	160.77	158.08	155.66	153.46	149.65	146.49
12000	178.64	175.39	172.46	169.81	167.41	163.26	159.81
13000	193.53	190.00	186.83	183.96	181.36	176.86	173.13
14000	208.41	204.62	201.20	198.11	195.31	190.47	186.44
15000	223.30	219.23	215.57	212.26	209.27	204.07	199.76
16000	238.19	233.85	229.94	226.41	223.22	217.68	213.08
17000	253.07	248.46	244.31	240.56	237.17	231.28	226.40
18000	267.96	263.08	258.68	254.71	251.12	244.89	239.71
19000	282.85	277.69	273.05	268.86	265.07	258.49	253.03
20000	297.73	292.31	287.43	283.01	279.02	272.10	266.35
21000	312.62	306.92	301.80	297.17	292.97	285.70	279.67
22000	327.51	321.54	316.17	311.32	306.92	299.31	292.98
23000	342.39	336.16	330.54	325.47	320.87	312.91	306.30
24000	357.28	350.77	344.91	339.62	334.82	326.52	319.62
25000	372.17	365.39	359.28	353.77	348.78	340.12	332.94
26000	387.05	380.00	373.65	367.92	362.73	353.73	346.25
27000	401.94	394.62	388.02	382.07	376.68	367.33	359.57
28000	416.83	409.23	402.40	396.22	390.63	380.94	372.89
29000	431.71	423.85	416.77	410.37	404.58	394.54	386.21
30000	446.60	438.46	431.14	424.52	418.53	408.15	399.52
31000	461.49	453.08	445.51	438.67	432.48	421.75	412.84
32000	476.37	467.70	459.88	452.82	446.43	435.36	426.16
33000	491.26	482.31	474.25	466.97	460.38	448.96	439.47
34000	506.15	496.93	488.62	481.12	474.34	462.57	452.79
35000	521.03	511.54	502.99	495.28	488.29	476.17	466.11
40000	595.47	584.62	574.85	566.03	558.04	544.20	532.70
45000	669.90	657.70	646.71	636.78	627.80	612.22	599.28
50000	744.33	730.77	718.56	707.54	697.55	680.24	665.87
55000	818.77	803.85	790.42	778.29	767.31	748.27	732.46
60000	893.20	876.93	862.28	849.04	837.06	816.29	799.04
65000	967.63	950.01	934.13	919.80	906.82	884.32	865.63
70000	1042.07	1023.08	1005.99	990.55	976.57	952.34	932.22

14¼% Monthly Loan Payments

LOAN AMOUNT	½ YEAR	1 YEAR	1½ YEARS	2 YEARS	2½ YEARS	3 YEARS	3½ YEARS
100	17.37	8.99	6.20	4.81	3.98	3.13	3.04
200	34.73	17.98	12.41	9.63	7.96	6.86	6.08
300	52.10	26.97	18.61	14.44	11.95	10.29	9.11
400	69.46	35.96	24.81	19.25	15.93	13.72	12.15
500	86.83	44.95	31.02	24.07	19.91	17.15	15.19
600	104.20	53.94	37.22	28.88	23.89	20.58	18.23
700	121.56	62.93	43.42	33.69	27.87	24.01	21.26
800	138.93	71.92	49.63	38.50	31.85	27.44	24.30
900	156.30	80.91	55.83	43.32	35.84	30.87	27.34
1000	173.66	89.90	62.03	48.13	39.82	34.30	30.38
1500	260.49	134.86	93.05	72.20	59.73	51.45	45.57
2000	347.32	179.81	124.06	96.26	79.64	68.60	60.75
2500	434.15	224.76	155.08	120.33	99.55	85.75	75.94
3000	520.99	269.71	186.10	144.39	119.45	102.90	91.13
3500	607.82	314.67	217.11	168.46	139.36	120.05	106.32
4000	694.65	359.62	248.13	192.52	159.27	137.20	121.51
4500	781.48	404.57	279.15	216.59	179.18	154.35	136.70
5000	868.31	449.52	310.16	240.66	199.09	171.50	151.88
5500	955.14	494.48	341.18	264.72	219.00	188.65	167.07
6000	1041.97	539.43	372.19	288.79	238.91	205.80	182.26
6500	1128.80	584.38	403.21	312.85	258.82	222.94	197.45
7000	1215.63	629.33	434.23	336.92	278.73	240.09	212.64
7500	1302.46	674.29	465.24	360.98	298.64	257.24	227.83
8000	1389.30	719.24	496.26	385.05	318.54	274.39	243.01
8500	1476.13	764.19	527.28	409.11	338.45	291.54	258.20
9000	1562.96	809.14	558.29	433.18	358.36	308.69	273.39
9500	1649.79	854.10	589.31	457.25	378.27	325.84	288.58
10000	1736.62	899.05	620.32	481.31	398.18	342.99	303.77
11000	1910.28	988.95	682.36	529.44	438.00	377.29	334.14
12000	2083.94	1078.86	744.39	577.57	477.82	411.59	364.52
13000	2257.60	1168.76	806.42	625.70	517.64	445.89	394.90
14000	2431.27	1258.67	868.45	673.83	557.45	480.19	425.27
15000	2604.93	1348.57	930.49	721.97	597.27	514.49	455.65
16000	2778.59	1438.48	992.52	770.10	637.09	548.79	486.03
17000	2952.25	1528.38	1054.55	818.23	676.91	583.09	516.40
18000	3125.91	1618.29	1116.58	866.36	716.73	617.39	546.78
19000	3299.58	1708.19	1178.62	914.49	756.54	651.68	577.16
20000	3473.24	1798.10	1240.65	962.62	796.36	685.98	607.54
21000	3646.90	1888.00	1302.68	1010.75	836.18	720.28	637.91
22000	3820.56	1977.91	1364.71	1058.88	876.00	754.58	668.29
23000	3994.22	2067.81	1426.74	1107.01	915.82	788.88	698.67
24000	4167.89	2157.71	1488.78	1155.15	955.63	823.18	729.04
25000	4341.55	2247.62	1550.81	1203.28	995.45	857.48	759.42
26000	4515.21	2337.52	1612.84	1251.41	1035.27	891.78	789.80
27000	4688.87	2427.43	1674.87	1299.54	1075.09	926.08	820.17
28000	4862.53	2517.33	1736.91	1347.67	1114.91	960.38	850.55
29000	5036.19	2607.24	1798.94	1395.80	1154.72	994.68	880.93
30000	5209.86	2697.14	1860.97	1443.93	1194.54	1028.98	911.30
31000	5383.52	2787.05	1923.00	1492.06	1234.36	1063.27	941.68
32000	5557.18	2876.95	1985.04	1540.19	1274.18	1097.57	972.06
33000	5730.84	2966.86	2047.07	1588.33	1314.00	1131.87	1002.43
34000	5904.50	3056.76	2109.10	1636.46	1353.82	1166.17	1032.81
35000	6078.17	3146.67	2171.13	1684.59	1393.63	1200.47	1063.19
40000	6946.48	3596.19	2481.30	1925.24	1592.72	1371.97	1215.07
45000	7814.79	4045.72	2791.46	2165.90	1791.81	1543.46	1366.95
50000	8683.09	4495.24	3101.62	2406.55	1990.90	1714.96	1518.84
55000	9551.40	4944.76	3411.78	2647.21	2190.00	1886.45	1670.72
60000	10419.71	5394.29	3721.94	2887.86	2389.09	2057.95	1822.61
65000	11288.02	5843.81	4032.11	3128.52	2588.18	2229.45	1974.49
70000	12156.33	6293.34	4342.27	3369.17	2787.27	2400.94	2126.37

Monthly Loan Payments 14¼%

LOAN AMOUNT	4 YEARS	4½ YEARS	5 YEARS	5½ YEARS	6 YEARS	6½ YEARS	7 YEARS
100	2.75	2.52	2.34	2.19	2.07	1.97	1.89
200	5.49	5.04	4.68	4.39	4.15	3.95	3.78
300	8.24	7.56	7.02	6.58	6.22	5.92	5.66
400	10.98	10.08	9.36	8.78	8.30	7.89	7.55
500	13.73	12.60	11.70	10.97	10.37	9.87	9.44
600	16.47	15.12	14.04	13.17	12.44	11.84	11.33
700	19.22	17.63	16.38	15.36	14.52	13.81	13.21
800	21.96	20.15	18.72	17.55	16.59	15.79	15.10
900	24.71	22.67	21.06	19.75	18.67	17.76	16.99
1000	27.45	25.19	23.40	21.94	20.74	19.73	18.88
1500	41.18	37.79	35.10	32.91	31.11	29.60	28.32
2000	54.90	50.38	46.80	43.88	41.48	39.47	37.76
2500	68.63	62.98	58.50	54.86	51.85	49.33	47.20
3000	82.36	75.58	70.19	65.83	62.22	59.20	56.64
3500	96.08	88.17	81.89	76.80	72.59	69.06	66.07
4000	109.81	100.77	93.59	87.77	82.96	78.93	75.51
4500	123.53	113.37	105.29	98.74	93.33	88.80	84.95
5000	137.26	125.96	116.99	109.71	103.70	98.66	94.39
5500	150.99	138.56	128.69	120.68	114.07	108.53	103.83
6000	164.71	151.15	140.39	131.65	124.44	118.40	113.27
6500	178.44	163.75	152.09	142.62	134.81	128.26	122.71
7000	192.16	176.35	163.79	153.59	145.18	138.13	132.15
7500	205.89	188.94	175.49	164.57	155.55	147.99	141.59
8000	219.62	201.54	187.18	175.54	165.92	157.86	151.03
8500	233.34	214.14	198.88	186.51	176.29	167.73	160.47
9000	247.07	226.73	210.58	197.48	186.66	177.59	169.91
9500	260.79	239.33	222.28	208.45	197.03	187.46	179.34
10000	274.52	251.92	233.98	219.42	207.40	197.33	188.78
11000	301.97	277.12	257.38	241.36	228.14	217.06	207.66
12000	329.42	302.31	280.78	263.31	248.88	236.79	226.54
13000	356.88	327.50	304.17	285.25	269.62	256.52	245.42
14000	384.33	352.69	327.57	307.19	290.36	276.26	264.30
15000	411.78	377.89	350.97	329.13	311.10	295.99	283.18
16000	439.23	403.08	374.37	351.07	331.84	315.72	302.05
17000	466.68	428.27	397.77	373.02	352.58	335.45	320.93
18000	494.14	453.46	421.17	394.96	373.32	355.19	339.81
19000	521.59	478.65	444.56	416.90	394.06	374.92	358.69
20000	549.04	503.85	467.96	438.84	414.80	394.65	377.57
21000	576.49	529.04	491.36	460.78	435.54	414.38	396.45
22000	603.95	554.23	514.76	482.73	456.28	434.12	415.32
23000	631.40	579.42	538.16	504.67	477.02	453.85	434.20
24000	658.85	604.62	561.55	526.61	497.76	473.58	453.08
25000	686.30	629.81	584.95	548.55	518.50	493.31	471.96
26000	713.75	655.00	608.35	570.50	539.24	513.05	490.84
27000	741.21	680.19	631.75	592.44	559.98	532.78	509.72
28000	768.66	705.39	655.15	614.38	580.72	552.51	528.59
29000	796.11	730.58	678.54	636.32	601.46	572.24	547.47
30000	823.56	755.77	701.94	658.26	622.20	591.98	566.35
31000	851.01	780.96	725.34	680.21	642.94	611.71	585.23
32000	878.47	806.16	748.74	702.15	663.68	631.44	604.11
33000	905.92	831.35	772.14	724.09	684.41	651.17	622.99
34000	933.37	856.54	795.53	746.03	705.15	670.91	641.87
35000	960.82	881.73	818.93	767.97	725.89	690.64	660.74
40000	1098.08	1007.69	935.92	877.69	829.59	789.30	755.14
45000	1235.34	1133.66	1052.91	987.40	933.29	887.97	849.53
50000	1372.60	1259.62	1169.90	1097.11	1036.99	986.63	943.92
55000	1509.86	1385.58	1286.89	1206.82	1140.69	1085.29	1038.31
60000	1647.12	1511.54	1403.88	1316.53	1244.39	1183.95	1132.70
65000	1784.38	1637.50	1520.87	1426.24	1348.09	1282.62	1227.10
70000	1921.64	1763.46	1637.86	1535.95	1451.79	1381.28	1321.49

14¼%   Monthly Loan Payments

LOAN AMOUNT	7½ YEARS	8 YEARS	8½ YEARS	9 YEARS	9½ YEARS	10 YEARS	10½ YEARS
100	1.81	1.75	1.70	1.65	1.61	1.57	1.53
200	3.63	3.50	3.39	3.30	3.21	3.14	3.07
300	5.44	5.25	5.09	4.94	4.82	4.70	4.60
400	7.26	7.01	6.79	6.59	6.42	6.27	6.14
500	9.07	8.76	8.48	8.24	8.03	7.84	7.67
600	10.89	10.51	10.18	9.89	9.63	9.41	9.20
700	12.70	12.26	11.87	11.54	11.24	10.97	10.74
800	14.52	14.01	13.57	13.18	12.84	12.54	12.27
900	16.33	15.76	15.27	14.83	14.45	14.11	13.81
1000	18.15	17.51	16.96	16.48	16.05	15.68	15.34
1500	27.22	26.27	25.44	24.72	24.08	23.52	23.01
2000	36.29	35.03	33.93	32.96	32.11	31.35	30.68
2500	45.37	43.79	42.41	41.20	40.14	39.19	38.35
3000	54.44	52.54	50.89	49.44	48.16	47.03	46.02
3500	63.51	61.30	59.37	57.68	56.19	54.87	53.69
4000	72.59	70.06	67.85	65.92	64.22	62.71	61.37
4500	81.66	78.81	76.33	74.16	72.25	70.55	69.04
5000	90.73	87.57	84.82	82.40	80.27	78.39	76.71
5500	99.81	96.33	93.30	90.64	88.30	86.23	84.38
6000	108.88	105.08	101.78	98.88	96.33	94.06	92.05
6500	117.95	113.84	110.26	107.12	104.36	101.90	99.72
7000	127.03	122.60	118.74	115.36	112.38	109.74	107.39
7500	136.10	131.36	127.22	123.60	120.41	117.58	115.06
8000	145.17	140.11	135.71	131.84	128.44	125.42	122.73
8500	154.25	148.87	144.19	140.08	136.46	133.26	130.40
9000	163.32	157.63	152.67	148.32	144.49	141.10	138.07
9500	172.39	166.38	161.15	156.56	152.52	148.93	145.74
10000	181.47	175.14	169.63	164.80	160.55	156.77	153.41
11000	199.61	192.65	186.60	181.28	176.60	172.45	168.76
12000	217.76	210.17	203.56	197.76	192.66	188.13	184.10
13000	235.91	227.68	220.52	214.24	208.71	203.81	199.44
14000	254.05	245.20	237.49	230.73	224.76	219.48	214.78
15000	272.20	262.71	254.45	247.21	240.82	235.16	230.12
16000	290.35	280.23	271.41	263.69	256.87	250.84	245.46
17000	308.49	297.74	288.38	280.17	272.93	266.51	260.80
18000	326.64	315.25	305.34	296.65	288.98	282.19	276.15
19000	344.78	332.77	322.30	313.13	305.04	297.87	291.49
20000	362.93	350.28	339.27	329.61	321.09	313.55	306.83
21000	381.08	367.80	356.23	346.09	337.15	329.22	322.17
22000	399.22	385.31	373.19	362.57	353.20	344.90	337.51
23000	417.37	402.82	390.15	379.05	369.26	360.58	352.85
24000	435.52	420.34	407.12	395.53	385.31	376.26	368.19
25000	453.66	437.85	424.08	412.01	401.37	391.93	383.54
26000	471.81	455.37	441.04	428.49	417.42	407.61	398.88
27000	489.96	472.88	458.01	444.97	433.47	423.29	414.22
28000	508.10	490.39	474.97	461.45	449.53	438.96	429.56
29000	526.25	507.91	491.93	477.93	465.58	454.64	444.90
30000	544.40	525.42	508.90	494.41	481.64	470.32	460.24
31000	562.54	542.94	525.86	510.89	497.69	486.00	475.58
32000	580.69	560.45	542.82	527.37	513.75	501.67	490.93
33000	598.84	577.96	559.79	543.85	529.80	517.35	506.27
34000	616.98	595.48	576.75	560.33	545.86	533.03	521.61
35000	635.13	612.99	593.71	576.81	561.91	548.71	536.95
40000	725.86	700.56	678.53	659.22	642.19	627.09	613.66
45000	816.60	788.13	763.35	741.62	722.46	705.48	690.36
50000	907.33	875.70	848.16	824.02	802.73	783.87	767.07
55000	998.06	963.27	932.98	906.42	883.00	862.25	843.78
60000	1088.79	1050.84	1017.80	988.82	963.28	940.64	920.48
65000	1179.53	1138.42	1102.61	1071.22	1043.55	1019.03	997.19
70000	1270.26	1225.99	1187.43	1153.63	1123.82	1097.41	1073.90

Monthly Loan Payments 14¼%

LOAN AMOUNT	11 YEARS	11½ YEARS	12 YEARS	12½ YEARS	13 YEARS	14 YEARS	15 YEARS
100	1.50	1.48	1.45	1.43	1.41	1.38	1.35
200	3.01	2.95	2.91	2.86	2.82	2.75	2.70
300	4.51	4.43	4.36	4.29	4.23	4.13	4.05
400	6.02	5.91	5.81	5.72	5.65	5.51	5.39
500	7.52	7.39	7.26	7.16	7.06	6.89	6.74
600	9.02	8.86	8.72	8.59	8.47	8.26	8.09
700	10.53	10.34	10.17	10.02	9.88	9.64	9.44
800	12.03	11.82	11.62	11.45	11.29	11.02	10.79
900	13.54	13.29	13.08	12.88	12.70	12.39	12.14
1000	15.04	14.77	14.53	14.31	14.11	13.77	13.49
1500	22.56	22.16	21.79	21.47	21.17	20.66	20.23
2000	30.08	29.54	29.06	28.62	28.23	27.54	26.97
2500	37.60	36.93	36.32	35.78	35.28	34.43	33.71
3000	45.12	44.32	43.59	42.93	42.34	41.31	40.46
3500	52.64	51.70	50.85	50.09	49.39	48.20	47.20
4000	60.16	59.09	58.12	57.24	56.45	55.08	53.94
4500	67.69	66.47	65.38	64.40	63.51	61.97	60.69
5000	75.21	73.86	72.65	71.55	70.56	68.85	67.43
5500	82.73	81.25	79.91	78.71	77.62	75.74	74.17
6000	90.25	88.63	87.18	85.86	84.68	82.62	80.91
6500	97.77	96.02	94.44	93.02	91.73	89.51	87.66
7000	105.29	103.40	101.71	100.18	98.79	96.39	94.40
7500	112.81	110.79	108.97	107.33	105.85	103.28	101.14
8000	120.33	118.17	116.24	114.49	112.90	110.16	107.89
8500	127.85	125.56	123.50	121.64	119.96	117.05	114.63
9000	135.37	132.95	130.77	128.80	127.02	123.93	121.37
9500	142.89	140.33	138.03	135.95	134.07	130.82	128.12
10000	150.41	147.72	145.29	143.11	141.13	137.70	134.86
11000	165.45	162.49	159.82	157.42	155.24	151.47	148.34
12000	180.49	177.26	174.35	171.73	169.35	165.24	161.83
13000	195.54	192.03	188.88	186.04	183.47	179.01	175.32
14000	210.58	206.81	203.41	200.35	197.58	192.78	188.80
15000	225.62	221.58	217.94	214.66	211.69	206.55	202.29
16000	240.66	236.35	232.47	228.97	225.80	220.32	215.77
17000	255.70	251.12	247.00	243.28	239.92	234.09	229.26
18000	270.74	265.89	261.53	257.59	254.03	247.86	242.74
19000	285.78	280.67	276.06	271.90	268.14	261.63	256.23
20000	300.82	295.44	290.59	286.21	282.26	275.40	269.72
21000	315.86	310.21	305.12	300.53	296.37	289.17	283.20
22000	330.91	324.98	319.65	314.84	310.48	302.94	296.69
23000	345.95	339.75	334.18	329.15	324.59	316.71	310.17
24000	360.99	354.52	348.71	343.46	338.71	330.48	323.66
25000	376.03	369.30	363.24	357.77	352.82	344.25	337.14
26000	391.07	384.07	377.77	372.08	366.93	358.02	350.63
27000	406.11	398.84	392.30	386.39	381.05	371.79	364.12
28000	421.15	413.61	406.83	400.70	395.16	385.56	377.60
29000	436.19	428.38	421.36	415.01	409.27	399.33	391.09
30000	451.24	443.16	435.88	429.32	423.38	413.10	404.57
31000	466.28	457.93	450.41	443.63	437.50	426.87	418.06
32000	481.32	472.70	464.94	457.94	451.61	440.64	431.55
33000	496.36	487.47	479.47	472.25	465.72	454.41	445.03
34000	511.40	502.24	494.00	486.57	479.84	468.18	458.52
35000	526.44	517.02	508.53	500.88	493.95	481.95	472.00
40000	601.65	590.87	581.18	572.43	564.51	550.80	539.43
45000	676.85	664.73	653.83	643.98	635.08	619.65	606.86
50000	752.06	738.59	726.47	715.54	705.64	688.50	674.29
55000	827.26	812.45	799.12	787.09	776.20	757.35	741.72
60000	902.47	886.31	871.77	858.64	846.77	826.20	809.15
65000	977.68	960.17	944.42	930.20	917.33	895.05	876.58
70000	1052.88	1034.03	1017.06	1001.75	987.90	963.90	944.01

14½%   Monthly Loan Payments

LOAN AMOUNT	½ YEAR	1 YEAR	1½ YEARS	2 YEARS	2½ YEARS	3 YEARS	3½ YEARS
100	17.38	9.00	6.21	4.82	3.99	3.44	3.05
200	34.76	18.00	12.43	9.65	7.99	6.88	6.10
300	52.14	27.01	18.64	14.47	11.98	10.33	9.15
400	69.51	36.01	24.86	19.30	15.98	13.77	12.20
500	86.89	45.01	31.07	24.12	19.97	17.21	15.25
600	104.27	54.01	37.29	28.95	23.96	20.65	18.30
700	121.65	63.02	43.50	33.77	27.96	24.09	21.35
800	139.03	72.02	49.72	38.60	31.95	27.54	24.40
900	156.41	81.02	55.93	43.42	35.94	30.98	27.45
1000	173.79	90.02	62.15	48.25	39.94	34.42	30.50
1500	260.68	135.03	93.22	72.37	59.91	51.63	45.75
2000	347.57	180.05	124.30	96.50	79.88	68.84	61.00
2500	434.46	225.06	155.37	120.62	99.85	86.05	76.25
3000	521.36	270.07	186.45	144.75	119.81	103.26	91.50
3500	608.25	315.08	217.52	168.87	139.78	120.47	106.75
4000	695.14	360.09	248.60	193.00	159.75	137.68	122.00
4500	782.04	405.10	279.67	217.12	179.72	154.89	137.25
5000	868.93	450.11	310.75	241.25	199.69	172.10	152.50
5500	955.82	495.12	341.82	265.37	219.66	189.32	167.75
6000	1042.71	540.14	372.90	289.50	239.63	206.53	183.00
6500	1129.61	585.15	403.97	313.62	259.60	223.74	198.25
7000	1216.50	630.16	435.05	337.75	279.57	240.95	213.50
7500	1303.39	675.17	466.12	361.87	299.54	258.16	228.75
8000	1390.29	720.18	497.20	386.00	319.50	275.37	244.00
8500	1477.18	765.19	528.27	410.12	339.47	292.58	259.25
9000	1564.07	810.20	559.35	434.24	359.44	309.79	274.51
9500	1650.97	855.21	590.42	458.37	379.41	327.00	289.76
10000	1737.86	900.23	621.50	482.49	399.38	344.21	305.01
11000	1911.64	990.25	683.65	530.74	439.32	378.63	335.51
12000	2085.43	1080.27	745.80	578.99	479.26	413.05	366.01
13000	2259.22	1170.29	807.95	627.24	519.19	447.47	396.51
14000	2433.00	1260.32	870.10	675.49	559.13	481.89	427.01
15000	2606.79	1350.34	932.25	723.74	599.07	516.31	457.51
16000	2780.57	1440.36	994.40	771.99	639.01	550.74	488.01
17000	2954.36	1530.38	1056.55	820.24	678.95	585.16	518.51
18000	3128.14	1620.41	1118.70	868.49	718.88	619.58	549.01
19000	3301.93	1710.43	1180.84	916.74	758.82	654.00	579.51
20000	3475.72	1800.45	1242.99	964.99	798.76	688.42	610.01
21000	3649.50	1890.47	1305.14	1013.24	838.70	722.84	640.51
22000	3823.29	1980.50	1367.29	1061.49	878.64	757.26	671.01
23000	3997.07	2070.52	1429.44	1109.74	918.57	791.68	701.51
24000	4170.86	2160.54	1491.59	1157.99	958.51	826.10	732.01
25000	4344.65	2250.56	1553.74	1206.24	998.45	860.52	762.51
26000	4518.43	2340.59	1615.89	1254.49	1038.39	894.95	793.01
27000	4692.22	2430.61	1678.04	1302.73	1078.33	929.37	823.52
28000	4866.00	2520.63	1740.19	1350.98	1118.26	963.79	854.02
29000	5039.79	2610.65	1802.34	1399.23	1158.20	998.21	884.52
30000	5213.57	2700.68	1864.49	1447.48	1198.14	1032.63	915.02
31000	5387.36	2790.70	1926.64	1495.73	1238.08	1067.05	945.52
32000	5561.15	2880.72	1988.79	1543.98	1278.02	1101.47	976.02
33000	5734.93	2970.74	2050.94	1592.23	1317.96	1135.89	1006.52
34000	5908.72	3060.77	2113.09	1640.48	1357.89	1170.31	1037.02
35000	6082.50	3150.79	2175.24	1688.73	1397.83	1204.73	1067.52
40000	6951.43	3600.90	2485.99	1929.98	1597.52	1376.84	1220.02
45000	7820.36	4051.01	2796.74	2171.22	1797.21	1548.94	1372.53
50000	8689.29	4501.13	3107.49	2412.47	1996.90	1721.05	1525.03
55000	9558.22	4951.24	3418.23	2653.72	2196.59	1893.15	1677.53
60000	10427.15	5401.35	3728.98	2894.97	2396.28	2065.26	1830.03
65000	11296.08	5851.47	4039.73	3136.21	2595.97	2237.36	1982.54
70000	12165.01	6301.58	4350.48	3377.46	2795.66	2409.47	2135.04

Monthly Loan Payments 14½%

LOAN AMOUNT	4 YEARS	4½ YEARS	5 YEARS	5½ YEARS	6 YEARS	6½ YEARS	7 YEARS
100	2.76	2.53	2.35	2.21	2.09	1.99	1.90
200	5.52	5.06	4.71	4.41	4.17	3.97	3.80
300	8.27	7.60	7.06	6.62	6.26	5.96	5.71
400	11.03	10.13	9.41	8.83	8.35	7.95	7.61
500	13.79	12.66	11.76	11.04	10.44	9.93	9.51
600	16.55	15.19	14.12	13.24	12.52	11.92	11.41
700	19.30	17.72	16.47	15.45	14.61	13.91	13.31
800	22.06	20.26	18.82	17.66	16.70	15.90	15.21
900	24.82	22.79	21.18	19.87	18.79	17.88	17.12
1000	27.58	25.32	23.53	22.07	20.87	19.87	19.02
1500	41.37	37.98	35.29	33.11	31.31	29.80	28.53
2000	55.16	50.64	47.06	44.15	41.75	39.74	38.03
2500	68.94	63.30	58.82	55.19	52.19	49.67	47.54
3000	82.73	75.96	70.58	66.22	62.62	59.61	57.05
3500	96.52	88.62	82.35	77.26	73.06	69.54	66.56
4000	110.31	101.28	94.11	88.30	83.50	79.48	76.07
4500	124.10	113.94	105.88	99.34	93.93	89.41	85.58
5000	137.89	126.60	117.64	110.37	104.37	99.35	95.09
5500	151.68	139.26	129.41	121.41	114.81	109.28	104.60
6000	165.47	151.92	141.17	132.45	125.25	119.22	114.10
6500	179.26	164.58	152.93	143.48	135.68	129.15	123.61
7000	193.05	177.24	164.70	154.52	146.12	139.09	133.12
7500	206.83	189.90	176.46	165.56	156.56	149.02	142.63
8000	220.62	202.56	188.23	176.60	167.00	158.95	152.14
8500	234.41	215.22	199.99	187.63	177.43	168.89	161.65
9000	248.20	227.88	211.75	198.67	187.87	178.82	171.16
9500	261.99	240.54	223.52	209.71	198.31	188.76	180.66
10000	275.78	253.20	235.28	220.75	208.74	198.69	190.17
11000	303.36	278.52	258.81	242.82	229.62	218.56	209.19
12000	330.94	303.84	282.34	264.89	250.49	238.43	228.21
13000	358.51	329.17	305.87	286.97	271.37	258.30	247.22
14000	386.09	354.49	329.40	309.04	292.24	278.17	266.24
15000	413.67	379.81	352.92	331.12	313.12	298.04	285.26
16000	441.25	405.13	376.45	353.19	333.99	317.91	304.28
17000	468.83	430.45	399.98	375.27	354.87	337.78	323.29
18000	496.40	455.77	423.51	397.34	375.74	357.65	342.31
19000	523.98	481.09	447.04	419.42	396.61	377.52	361.33
20000	551.56	506.41	470.57	441.49	417.49	397.39	380.35
21000	579.14	531.73	494.09	463.57	438.36	417.26	399.36
22000	606.71	557.05	517.62	485.64	459.24	437.13	418.38
23000	634.29	582.37	541.15	507.71	480.11	456.99	437.40
24000	661.87	607.69	564.68	529.79	500.99	476.86	456.42
25000	689.45	633.01	588.21	551.86	521.86	496.73	475.43
26000	717.03	658.33	611.74	573.94	542.74	516.60	494.45
27000	744.60	683.65	635.26	596.01	563.61	536.47	513.47
28000	772.18	708.97	658.79	618.09	584.48	556.34	532.48
29000	799.76	734.29	682.32	640.16	605.36	576.21	551.50
30000	827.34	759.61	705.85	662.24	626.23	596.08	570.52
31000	854.92	784.93	729.38	684.31	647.11	615.95	589.54
32000	882.49	810.25	752.90	706.38	667.98	635.82	608.55
33000	910.07	835.57	776.43	728.46	688.86	655.69	627.57
34000	937.65	860.89	799.96	750.53	709.73	675.56	646.59
35000	965.23	886.21	823.49	772.61	730.60	695.43	665.61
40000	1103.12	1012.82	941.13	882.98	834.98	794.77	760.69
45000	1241.01	1139.42	1058.77	993.35	939.35	894.12	855.78
50000	1378.90	1266.02	1176.41	1103.73	1043.72	993.47	950.87
55000	1516.79	1392.62	1294.06	1214.10	1148.09	1092.81	1045.95
60000	1654.68	1519.22	1411.70	1324.47	1252.47	1192.16	1141.04
65000	1792.57	1645.83	1529.34	1434.84	1356.84	1291.51	1236.12
70000	1930.46	1772.43	1646.98	1545.22	1461.21	1390.85	1331.21

14½%　　Monthly Loan Payments

LOAN AMOUNT	7½ YEARS	8 YEARS	8½ YEARS	9 YEARS	9½ YEARS	10 YEARS	10½ YEARS
100	1.83	1.77	1.71	1.66	1.62	1.58	1.55
200	3.66	3.53	3.42	3.33	3.24	3.17	3.10
300	5.49	5.30	5.13	4.99	4.86	4.75	4.65
400	7.32	7.06	6.84	6.65	6.48	6.33	6.20
500	9.14	8.83	8.55	8.31	8.10	7.91	7.75
600	10.97	10.59	10.27	9.98	9.72	9.50	9.30
700	12.80	12.36	11.98	11.64	11.34	11.08	10.85
800	14.63	14.13	13.69	13.30	12.96	12.66	12.40
900	16.46	15.89	15.40	14.96	14.58	14.25	13.95
1000	18.29	17.66	17.11	16.63	16.20	15.83	15.49
1500	27.43	26.49	25.66	24.94	24.31	23.74	23.24
2000	36.58	35.31	34.22	33.26	32.41	31.66	30.99
2500	45.72	44.14	42.77	41.57	40.51	39.57	38.74
3000	54.86	52.97	51.33	49.88	48.61	47.49	46.48
3500	64.01	61.80	59.88	58.20	56.71	55.40	54.23
4000	73.15	70.63	68.43	66.51	64.82	63.31	61.98
4500	82.29	79.46	76.99	74.82	72.92	71.23	69.73
5000	91.44	88.29	85.54	83.14	81.02	79.14	77.47
5500	100.58	97.11	94.10	91.45	89.12	87.06	85.22
6000	109.73	105.94	102.65	99.77	97.22	94.97	92.97
6500	118.87	114.77	111.21	108.08	105.33	102.89	100.72
7000	128.01	123.60	119.76	116.39	113.43	110.80	108.46
7500	137.16	132.43	128.31	124.71	121.53	118.72	116.21
8000	146.30	141.26	136.87	133.02	129.63	126.63	123.96
8500	155.44	150.09	145.42	141.34	137.73	134.54	131.71
9000	164.59	158.92	153.98	149.65	145.84	142.46	139.45
9500	173.73	167.74	162.53	157.96	153.94	150.37	147.20
10000	182.88	176.57	171.09	166.28	162.04	158.29	154.95
11000	201.16	194.23	188.19	182.90	178.24	174.12	170.44
12000	219.45	211.89	205.30	199.53	194.45	189.94	185.94
13000	237.74	229.54	222.41	216.16	210.65	205.77	201.43
14000	256.03	247.20	239.52	232.79	226.86	221.60	216.93
15000	274.31	264.86	256.63	249.42	243.06	237.43	232.42
16000	292.60	282.52	273.74	266.04	259.26	253.26	247.92
17000	310.89	300.17	290.84	282.67	275.47	269.09	263.41
18000	329.18	317.83	307.95	299.30	291.67	284.92	278.91
19000	347.47	335.49	325.06	315.93	307.88	300.74	294.40
20000	365.75	353.15	342.17	332.55	324.08	316.57	309.89
21000	384.04	370.80	359.28	349.18	340.28	332.40	325.39
22000	402.33	388.46	376.39	365.81	356.49	348.23	340.88
23000	420.62	406.12	393.50	382.44	372.69	364.06	356.38
24000	438.90	423.77	410.60	399.07	388.90	379.89	371.87
25000	457.19	441.43	427.71	415.69	405.10	395.72	387.37
26000	475.48	459.09	444.82	432.32	421.30	411.55	402.86
27000	493.77	476.75	461.93	448.95	437.51	427.37	418.36
28000	512.05	494.40	479.04	465.58	453.71	443.20	433.85
29000	530.34	512.06	496.15	482.20	469.92	459.03	449.35
30000	548.63	529.72	513.26	498.83	486.12	474.86	464.84
31000	566.92	547.37	530.36	515.46	502.32	490.69	480.34
32000	585.20	565.03	547.47	532.09	518.53	506.52	495.83
33000	603.49	582.69	564.58	548.71	534.73	522.35	511.33
34000	621.78	600.35	581.69	565.34	550.94	538.18	526.82
35000	640.07	618.00	598.80	581.97	567.14	554.00	542.32
40000	731.51	706.29	684.34	665.11	648.16	633.15	619.79
45000	822.94	794.58	769.88	748.25	729.18	712.29	697.26
50000	914.38	882.86	855.43	831.39	810.20	791.43	774.74
55000	1005.82	971.15	940.97	914.52	891.22	870.58	852.21
60000	1097.26	1059.44	1026.51	997.66	972.24	949.72	929.68
65000	1188.70	1147.72	1112.05	1080.80	1053.26	1028.86	1007.16
70000	1280.13	1236.01	1197.60	1163.94	1134.28	1108.01	1084.63

Monthly Loan Payments 14½%

LOAN AMOUNT	11 YEARS	11½ YEARS	12 YEARS	12½ YEARS	13 YEARS	14 YEARS	15 YEARS
100	1.52	1.49	1.47	1.45	1.43	1.39	1.37
200	3.04	2.99	2.94	2.89	2.86	2.79	2.73
300	4.56	4.48	4.41	4.34	4.28	4.18	4.10
400	6.08	5.97	5.88	5.79	5.71	5.57	5.46
500	7.60	7.46	7.34	7.24	7.14	6.97	6.83
600	9.12	8.96	8.81	8.68	8.57	8.36	8.19
700	10.64	10.45	10.28	10.13	9.99	9.76	9.56
800	12.16	11.94	11.75	11.58	11.42	11.15	10.92
900	13.68	13.44	13.22	13.02	12.85	12.54	12.29
1000	15.20	14.93	14.69	14.47	14.28	13.94	13.66
1500	22.79	22.39	22.03	21.71	21.41	20.90	20.48
2000	30.39	29.86	29.38	28.94	28.55	27.87	27.31
2500	37.99	37.32	36.72	36.18	35.69	34.84	34.14
3000	45.59	44.79	44.07	43.41	42.83	41.81	40.97
3500	53.19	52.25	51.41	50.65	49.96	48.78	47.79
4000	60.79	59.72	58.75	57.89	57.10	55.74	54.62
4500	68.38	67.18	66.10	65.12	64.24	62.71	61.45
5000	75.98	74.65	73.44	72.36	71.38	69.68	68.28
5500	83.58	82.11	80.79	79.59	78.51	76.65	75.10
6000	91.18	89.57	88.13	86.83	85.65	83.62	81.93
6500	98.78	97.04	95.48	94.07	92.79	90.58	88.76
7000	106.38	104.50	102.82	101.30	99.93	97.55	95.59
7500	113.97	111.97	110.16	108.54	107.07	104.52	102.41
8000	121.57	119.43	117.51	115.77	114.20	111.49	109.24
8500	129.17	126.90	124.85	123.01	121.34	118.46	116.07
9000	136.77	134.36	132.20	130.24	128.48	125.42	122.90
9500	144.37	141.83	139.54	137.48	135.62	132.39	129.72
10000	151.96	149.29	146.88	144.72	142.75	139.36	136.55
11000	167.16	164.22	161.57	159.19	157.03	153.30	150.21
12000	182.36	179.15	176.26	173.66	171.30	167.23	163.86
13000	197.55	194.08	190.95	188.13	185.58	181.17	177.52
14000	212.75	209.01	205.64	202.60	199.86	195.10	191.17
15000	227.95	223.94	220.33	217.07	214.13	209.04	204.83
16000	243.14	238.86	235.02	231.54	228.41	222.98	218.48
17000	258.34	253.79	249.70	246.02	242.68	236.91	232.14
18000	273.54	268.72	264.39	260.49	256.96	250.85	245.79
19000	288.73	283.65	279.08	274.96	271.23	264.78	259.45
20000	303.93	298.58	293.77	289.43	285.51	278.72	273.10
21000	319.13	313.51	308.46	303.90	299.78	292.66	286.76
22000	334.32	328.44	323.15	318.37	314.06	306.59	300.41
23000	349.52	343.37	337.84	332.85	328.33	320.53	314.07
24000	364.71	358.30	352.52	347.32	342.61	334.46	327.72
25000	379.91	373.23	367.21	361.79	356.88	348.40	341.38
26000	395.11	388.15	381.90	376.26	371.16	362.34	355.03
27000	410.30	403.08	396.59	390.73	385.44	376.27	368.69
28000	425.50	418.01	411.28	405.20	399.71	390.21	382.34
29000	440.70	432.94	425.97	419.68	413.99	404.14	396.00
30000	455.89	447.87	440.65	434.15	428.26	418.08	409.65
31000	471.09	462.80	455.34	448.62	442.54	432.02	423.31
32000	486.29	477.73	470.03	463.09	456.81	445.95	436.96
33000	501.48	492.66	484.72	477.56	471.09	459.89	450.62
34000	516.68	507.59	499.41	492.03	485.36	473.83	464.27
35000	531.88	522.52	514.10	506.50	499.64	487.76	477.93
40000	607.86	597.16	587.54	578.86	571.02	557.44	546.20
45000	683.84	671.81	660.98	651.22	642.39	627.12	614.48
50000	759.82	746.45	734.42	723.58	713.77	696.80	682.75
55000	835.80	821.10	807.87	795.94	785.15	766.48	751.03
60000	911.79	895.74	881.31	868.29	856.52	836.16	819.30
65000	987.77	970.39	954.75	940.65	927.90	905.84	887.58
70000	1063.75	1045.03	1028.19	1013.01	999.28	975.52	955.85

14¾%   Monthly Loan Payments

LOAN AMOUNT	½ YEAR	1 YEAR	1½ YEARS	2 YEARS	2½ YEARS	3 YEARS	3½ YEARS
100	17.39	9.01	6.23	4.84	4.01	3.45	3.06
200	34.78	18.03	12.45	9.67	8.01	6.91	6.12
300	52.17	27.04	18.68	14.51	12.02	10.36	9.19
400	69.56	36.06	24.91	19.35	16.02	13.82	12.25
500	86.95	45.07	31.13	24.18	20.03	17.27	15.31
600	104.35	54.08	37.36	29.02	24.03	20.73	18.37
700	121.74	63.10	43.59	33.86	28.04	24.18	21.44
800	139.13	72.11	49.81	38.69	32.05	27.63	24.50
900	156.52	81.13	56.04	43.53	36.05	31.09	27.56
1000	173.91	90.14	62.27	48.37	40.06	34.54	30.62
1500	260.86	135.21	93.40	72.55	60.09	51.81	45.94
2000	347.82	180.28	124.53	96.74	80.12	69.09	61.25
2500	434.77	225.35	155.67	120.92	100.15	86.36	76.56
3000	521.73	270.42	186.80	145.10	120.17	103.63	91.87
3500	608.68	315.49	217.94	169.29	140.20	120.90	107.19
4000	695.64	360.56	249.07	193.47	160.23	138.17	122.50
4500	782.59	405.63	280.20	217.66	180.26	155.44	137.81
5000	869.65	450.70	311.34	241.84	200.29	172.72	153.12
5500	956.50	495.77	342.47	266.02	220.32	189.99	168.44
6000	1043.46	540.84	373.60	290.21	240.35	207.26	183.75
6500	1130.41	585.91	404.74	314.39	260.38	224.53	199.06
7000	1217.37	630.98	435.87	338.58	280.41	241.80	214.37
7500	1304.32	676.05	467.00	362.76	300.44	259.07	229.69
8000	1391.28	721.12	498.14	386.94	320.47	276.34	245.00
8500	1478.23	766.19	529.27	411.13	340.49	293.62	260.31
9000	1565.19	811.26	560.40	435.31	360.52	310.89	275.62
9500	1652.14	856.33	591.54	459.50	380.55	328.16	290.93
10000	1739.10	901.40	622.67	483.68	400.58	345.43	306.25
11000	1913.01	991.54	684.94	532.05	440.64	379.97	336.87
12000	2086.92	1081.68	747.21	580.42	480.70	414.52	367.50
13000	2260.83	1171.83	809.47	628.78	520.76	449.06	398.12
14000	2434.74	1261.97	871.74	677.15	560.81	483.60	428.75
15000	2608.65	1352.11	934.01	725.52	600.87	518.15	459.37
16000	2782.56	1442.25	996.28	773.89	640.93	552.69	489.99
17000	2956.47	1532.39	1058.54	822.26	680.99	587.23	520.62
18000	3130.38	1622.53	1120.81	870.62	721.05	621.77	551.24
19000	3304.29	1712.67	1183.08	918.99	761.11	656.32	581.87
20000	3478.20	1802.81	1245.34	967.36	801.16	690.86	612.49
21000	3652.11	1892.95	1307.61	1015.73	841.22	725.40	643.12
22000	3826.02	1983.09	1369.88	1064.09	881.28	759.95	673.74
23000	3999.93	2073.23	1432.15	1112.46	921.34	794.49	704.37
24000	4173.84	2163.37	1494.41	1160.83	961.40	829.03	734.99
25000	4347.74	2253.51	1556.68	1209.20	1001.45	863.58	765.62
26000	4521.65	2343.65	1618.95	1257.57	1041.51	898.12	796.24
27000	4695.56	2433.79	1681.21	1305.93	1081.57	932.66	826.87
28000	4869.47	2523.93	1743.48	1354.30	1121.63	967.20	857.49
29000	5043.38	2614.07	1805.75	1402.67	1161.69	1001.75	888.12
30000	5217.29	2704.21	1868.02	1451.04	1201.75	1036.29	918.74
31000	5391.20	2794.35	1930.28	1499.41	1241.80	1070.83	949.36
32000	5565.11	2884.49	1992.55	1547.77	1281.86	1105.38	979.99
33000	5739.02	2974.63	2054.82	1596.14	1321.92	1139.92	1010.61
34000	5912.93	3064.77	2117.08	1644.51	1361.98	1174.46	1041.24
35000	6086.84	3154.91	2179.35	1692.88	1402.04	1209.01	1071.86
40000	6956.39	3605.62	2490.69	1934.72	1602.33	1381.72	1224.99
45000	7825.94	4056.32	2802.02	2176.56	1802.62	1554.44	1378.11
50000	8695.49	4507.02	3113.36	2418.40	2002.91	1727.15	1531.23
55000	9565.04	4957.72	3424.70	2660.24	2203.20	1899.87	1684.36
60000	10434.59	5408.42	3736.03	2902.08	2403.49	2072.58	1837.48
65000	11304.14	5859.13	4047.37	3143.92	2603.78	2245.30	1990.60
70000	12173.69	6309.83	4358.70	3385.76	2804.07	2418.01	2143.73

Monthly Loan Payments 14¾%

LOAN AMOUNT	4 YEARS	4½ YEARS	5 YEARS	5½ YEARS	6 YEARS	6½ YEARS	7 YEARS
100	2.77	2.54	2.37	2.22	2.10	2.00	1.92
200	5.54	5.09	4.73	4.44	4.20	4.00	3.83
300	8.31	7.63	7.10	6.66	6.30	6.00	5.75
400	11.08	10.18	9.46	8.88	8.40	8.00	7.66
500	13.85	12.72	11.83	11.10	10.50	10.00	9.58
600	16.62	15.27	14.20	13.32	12.61	12.00	11.49
700	19.39	17.81	16.56	15.55	14.71	14.00	13.41
800	22.16	20.36	18.93	17.77	16.81	16.01	15.33
900	24.93	22.90	21.29	19.99	18.91	18.01	17.24
1000	27.70	25.45	23.66	22.21	21.01	20.01	19.16
1500	41.56	38.17	35.49	33.31	31.51	30.01	28.74
2000	55.41	50.90	47.32	44.41	42.02	40.01	38.31
2500	69.26	63.62	59.15	55.52	52.52	50.02	47.89
3000	83.11	76.35	70.98	66.62	63.03	60.02	57.47
3500	96.96	89.07	82.81	77.73	73.53	70.02	67.05
4000	110.82	101.80	94.64	88.83	84.04	80.03	76.63
4500	124.67	114.52	106.47	99.93	94.54	90.03	86.21
5000	138.52	127.24	118.29	111.04	105.05	100.03	95.78
5500	152.37	139.97	130.12	122.14	115.55	110.04	105.36
6000	166.23	152.69	141.95	133.24	126.06	120.04	114.94
6500	180.08	165.42	153.78	144.35	136.56	130.04	124.52
7000	193.93	178.14	165.61	155.45	147.07	140.05	134.10
7500	207.78	190.87	177.44	166.56	157.57	150.05	143.68
8000	221.63	203.59	189.27	177.66	168.08	160.05	153.25
8500	235.49	216.31	201.10	188.76	178.58	170.06	162.83
9000	249.34	229.04	212.93	199.87	189.09	180.06	172.41
9500	263.19	241.76	224.76	210.97	199.59	190.06	181.99
10000	277.04	254.49	236.59	222.07	210.09	200.07	191.57
11000	304.75	279.94	260.25	244.28	231.10	220.07	210.72
12000	332.45	305.39	283.91	266.49	252.11	240.08	229.88
13000	360.15	330.83	307.57	288.70	273.12	260.09	249.04
14000	387.86	356.28	331.22	310.90	294.13	280.09	268.19
15000	415.56	381.73	354.88	333.11	315.14	300.10	287.35
16000	443.27	407.18	378.54	355.32	336.15	320.11	306.51
17000	470.97	432.63	402.20	377.53	357.16	340.11	325.66
18000	498.68	458.08	425.86	399.73	378.17	360.12	344.82
19000	526.38	483.53	449.52	421.94	399.18	380.13	363.98
20000	554.08	508.98	473.18	444.15	420.19	400.13	383.14
21000	581.79	534.43	496.84	466.35	441.20	420.14	402.29
22000	609.49	559.87	520.50	488.56	462.21	440.14	421.45
23000	637.20	585.32	544.15	510.77	483.22	460.15	440.61
24000	664.90	610.77	567.81	532.98	504.23	480.16	459.76
25000	692.60	636.22	591.47	555.18	525.24	500.16	478.92
26000	720.31	661.67	615.13	577.39	546.25	520.17	498.08
27000	748.01	687.12	638.79	599.60	567.26	540.18	517.23
28000	775.72	712.57	662.45	621.81	588.27	560.18	536.39
29000	803.42	738.02	686.11	644.01	609.28	580.19	555.55
30000	831.13	763.46	709.77	666.22	630.28	600.20	574.70
31000	858.83	788.91	733.43	688.43	651.29	620.20	593.86
32000	886.53	814.36	757.08	710.64	672.30	640.21	613.02
33000	914.24	839.81	780.74	732.84	693.31	660.22	632.17
34000	941.94	865.26	804.40	755.05	714.32	680.22	651.33
35000	969.65	890.71	828.06	777.26	735.33	700.23	670.49
40000	1108.17	1017.95	946.36	888.29	840.38	800.26	766.27
45000	1246.69	1145.20	1064.65	999.33	945.43	900.30	862.05
50000	1385.21	1272.44	1182.95	1110.37	1050.47	1000.33	957.84
55000	1523.73	1399.69	1301.24	1221.41	1155.52	1100.36	1053.62
60000	1662.25	1526.93	1419.53	1332.44	1260.57	1200.40	1149.41
65000	1800.77	1654.17	1537.83	1443.48	1365.62	1300.43	1245.19
70000	1939.29	1781.42	1656.12	1554.52	1470.66	1400.46	1340.97

14¾% Monthly Loan Payments

LOAN AMOUNT	7½ YEARS	8 YEARS	8½ YEARS	9 YEARS	9½ YEARS	10 YEARS	10½ YEARS
100	1.84	1.78	1.73	1.68	1.64	1.60	1.56
200	3.69	3.56	3.45	3.36	3.27	3.20	3.13
300	5.53	5.34	5.18	5.03	4.91	4.79	4.69
400	7.37	7.12	6.90	6.71	6.54	6.39	6.26
500	9.21	8.90	8.63	8.39	8.18	7.99	7.82
600	11.06	10.68	10.35	10.07	9.81	9.59	9.39
700	12.90	12.46	12.08	11.74	11.45	11.19	10.95
800	14.74	14.24	13.80	13.42	13.08	12.78	12.52
900	16.59	16.02	15.53	15.10	14.72	14.38	14.08
1000	18.43	17.80	17.25	16.78	16.35	15.98	15.65
1500	27.64	26.70	25.88	25.16	24.53	23.97	23.47
2000	36.86	35.60	34.51	33.55	32.71	31.96	31.30
2500	46.07	44.50	43.14	41.94	40.89	39.95	39.12
3000	55.29	53.40	51.76	50.33	49.06	47.94	46.95
3500	64.50	62.30	60.39	58.71	57.24	55.93	54.77
4000	73.72	71.20	69.02	67.10	65.42	63.92	62.60
4500	82.93	80.10	77.64	75.49	73.59	71.91	70.42
5000	92.15	89.01	86.27	83.88	81.77	79.90	78.24
5500	101.36	97.91	94.90	92.27	89.95	87.89	86.07
6000	110.58	106.81	103.53	100.65	98.12	95.88	93.89
6500	119.79	115.71	112.15	109.04	106.30	103.87	101.72
7000	129.00	124.61	120.78	117.43	114.48	111.87	109.54
7500	138.22	133.51	129.41	125.82	122.66	119.86	117.37
8000	147.43	142.41	138.04	134.21	130.83	127.85	125.19
8500	156.65	151.31	146.66	142.59	139.01	135.84	133.01
9000	165.86	160.21	155.29	150.98	147.19	143.83	140.84
9500	175.08	169.11	163.92	159.37	155.36	151.82	148.66
10000	184.29	178.01	172.54	167.76	163.54	159.81	156.49
11000	202.72	195.81	189.80	184.53	179.89	175.79	172.14
12000	221.15	213.61	207.05	201.31	196.25	191.77	187.79
13000	239.58	231.41	224.31	218.08	212.60	207.75	203.43
14000	258.01	249.21	241.56	234.86	228.96	223.73	219.08
15000	276.44	267.02	258.82	251.64	245.31	239.71	234.73
16000	294.87	284.82	276.07	268.41	261.66	255.69	250.38
17000	313.30	302.62	293.33	285.19	278.02	271.67	266.03
18000	331.73	320.42	310.58	301.96	294.37	287.65	281.68
19000	350.16	338.22	327.83	318.74	310.73	303.63	297.33
20000	368.59	356.02	345.09	335.51	327.08	319.61	312.98
21000	387.01	373.82	362.34	352.29	343.43	335.60	328.62
22000	405.44	391.62	379.60	369.07	359.79	351.58	344.27
23000	423.87	409.42	396.85	385.84	376.14	367.56	359.92
24000	442.30	427.22	414.11	402.62	392.50	383.54	375.57
25000	460.73	445.03	431.36	419.39	408.85	399.52	391.22
26000	479.16	462.83	448.61	436.17	425.20	415.50	406.87
27000	497.59	480.63	465.87	452.94	441.56	431.48	422.52
28000	516.02	498.43	483.12	469.72	457.91	447.46	438.17
29000	534.45	516.23	500.38	486.50	474.27	463.44	453.81
30000	552.88	534.03	517.63	503.27	490.62	479.42	469.46
31000	571.31	551.83	534.89	520.05	506.98	495.40	485.11
32000	589.74	569.63	552.14	536.82	523.33	511.38	500.76
33000	608.17	587.43	569.40	553.60	539.68	527.36	516.41
34000	626.60	605.24	586.65	570.37	556.04	543.35	532.06
35000	645.02	623.04	603.90	587.15	572.39	559.33	547.71
40000	737.17	712.04	690.18	671.03	654.16	639.23	625.95
45000	829.32	801.05	776.45	754.91	735.93	719.13	704.20
50000	921.46	890.05	862.72	838.79	817.70	799.04	782.44
55000	1013.61	979.06	948.99	922.66	899.47	878.94	860.68
60000	1105.76	1068.06	1035.27	1006.54	981.24	958.84	938.93
65000	1197.90	1157.07	1121.54	1090.42	1063.01	1038.75	1017.17
70000	1290.05	1246.07	1207.81	1174.30	1144.78	1118.65	1095.42

Monthly Loan Payments 14¾%

LOAN AMOUNT	11 YEARS	11½ YEARS	12 YEARS	12½ YEARS	13 YEARS	14 YEARS	15 YEARS
100	1.54	1.51	1.48	1.46	1.44	1.41	1.38
200	3.07	3.02	2.97	2.93	2.89	2.82	2.77
300	4.61	4.53	4.45	4.39	4.33	4.23	4.15
400	6.14	6.03	5.94	5.85	5.78	5.64	5.53
500	7.68	7.54	7.42	7.32	7.22	7.05	6.91
600	9.21	9.05	8.91	8.78	8.66	8.46	8.30
700	10.75	10.56	10.39	10.24	10.11	9.87	9.68
800	12.28	12.07	11.88	11.71	11.55	11.28	11.06
900	13.82	13.58	13.36	13.17	12.99	12.69	12.44
1000	15.35	15.09	14.85	14.63	14.44	14.10	13.83
1500	23.03	22.63	22.27	21.95	21.66	21.15	20.74
2000	30.70	30.17	29.70	29.27	28.88	28.21	27.65
2500	38.38	37.72	37.12	36.58	36.10	35.26	34.56
3000	46.06	45.26	44.54	43.90	43.32	42.31	41.48
3500	53.73	52.80	51.97	51.22	50.54	49.36	48.39
4000	61.41	60.35	59.39	58.53	57.75	56.41	55.30
4500	69.09	67.89	66.82	65.85	64.97	63.46	62.21
5000	76.76	75.43	74.24	73.17	72.19	70.51	69.13
5500	84.44	82.98	81.67	80.48	79.41	77.57	76.04
6000	92.11	90.52	89.09	87.80	86.63	84.62	82.95
6500	99.79	98.06	96.51	95.12	93.85	91.67	89.86
7000	107.47	105.61	103.94	102.43	101.07	98.72	96.78
7500	115.14	113.15	111.36	109.75	108.29	105.77	103.69
8000	122.82	120.70	118.79	117.07	115.51	112.82	110.60
8500	130.50	128.24	126.21	124.38	122.73	119.87	117.51
9000	138.17	135.78	133.63	131.70	129.95	126.93	124.43
9500	145.85	143.33	141.06	139.01	137.17	133.98	131.34
10000	153.52	150.87	148.48	146.33	144.39	141.03	138.25
11000	168.88	165.96	163.33	160.96	158.83	155.13	152.08
12000	184.23	181.04	178.18	175.60	173.26	169.23	165.90
13000	199.58	196.13	193.03	190.23	187.70	183.34	179.73
14000	214.93	211.22	207.88	204.86	202.14	197.44	193.55
15000	230.29	226.30	222.72	219.50	216.58	211.54	207.38
16000	245.64	241.39	237.57	234.13	231.02	225.65	221.20
17000	260.99	256.48	252.42	248.76	245.46	239.75	235.03
18000	276.34	271.56	267.27	263.40	259.90	253.85	248.85
19000	291.70	286.65	282.12	278.03	274.34	267.95	262.68
20000	307.05	301.74	296.97	292.66	288.77	282.06	276.50
21000	322.40	316.83	311.81	307.30	303.21	296.16	290.33
22000	337.75	331.91	326.66	321.93	317.65	310.26	304.15
23000	353.11	347.00	341.51	336.56	332.09	324.36	317.98
24000	368.46	362.09	356.36	351.20	346.53	338.47	331.80
25000	383.81	377.17	371.21	365.83	360.97	352.57	345.63
26000	399.16	392.26	386.05	380.46	375.41	366.67	359.45
27000	414.52	407.35	400.90	395.09	389.85	380.78	373.28
28000	429.87	422.43	415.75	409.73	404.28	394.88	387.10
29000	445.22	437.52	430.60	424.36	418.72	408.98	400.93
30000	460.57	452.61	445.45	438.99	433.16	423.08	414.75
31000	475.93	467.69	460.30	453.63	447.60	437.19	428.58
32000	491.28	482.78	475.14	468.26	462.04	451.29	442.40
33000	506.63	497.87	489.99	482.89	476.48	465.39	456.23
34000	521.98	512.95	504.84	497.53	490.92	479.50	470.05
35000	537.34	528.04	519.69	512.16	505.36	493.60	483.88
40000	614.10	603.48	593.93	585.33	577.55	564.11	553.00
45000	690.86	678.91	668.17	658.49	649.74	634.63	622.13
50000	767.62	754.35	742.41	731.66	721.94	705.14	691.25
55000	844.38	829.78	816.65	804.82	794.13	775.65	760.38
60000	921.15	905.21	890.90	877.99	866.32	846.17	829.50
65000	997.91	980.65	965.14	951.15	938.52	916.68	898.63
70000	1074.67	1056.08	1039.38	1024.32	1010.71	987.20	967.75

15%   Monthly Loan Payments

LOAN AMOUNT	½ YEAR	1 YEAR	1½ YEARS	2 YEARS	2½ YEARS	3 YEARS	3½ YEARS
100	17.40	9.03	6.24	4.85	4.02	3.47	3.07
200	34.81	18.05	12.48	9.70	8.04	6.93	6.15
300	52.21	27.08	18.72	14.55	12.05	10.40	9.22
400	69.61	36.10	24.95	19.39	16.07	13.87	12.30
500	87.02	45.13	31.19	24.24	20.09	17.33	15.37
600	104.42	54.15	37.43	29.09	24.11	20.80	18.45
700	121.82	63.18	43.67	33.94	28.12	24.27	21.52
800	139.23	72.21	49.91	38.79	32.14	27.73	24.60
900	156.63	81.23	56.15	43.64	36.16	31.20	27.67
1000	174.03	90.26	62.38	48.49	40.18	34.67	30.75
1500	261.05	135.39	93.58	72.73	60.27	52.00	46.12
2000	348.07	180.52	124.77	96.97	80.36	69.33	61.50
2500	435.08	225.65	155.96	121.22	100.45	86.66	76.87
3000	522.10	270.77	187.15	145.46	120.54	104.00	92.25
3500	609.12	315.90	218.35	169.70	140.62	121.33	107.62
4000	696.14	361.03	249.54	193.95	160.71	138.66	123.00
4500	783.15	406.16	280.73	218.19	180.80	155.99	138.37
5000	870.17	451.29	311.92	242.43	200.89	173.33	153.75
5500	957.19	496.42	343.12	266.68	220.98	190.66	169.12
6000	1044.20	541.55	374.31	290.92	241.07	207.99	184.49
6500	1131.22	586.68	405.50	315.16	261.16	225.32	199.87
7000	1218.24	631.81	436.69	339.41	281.25	242.66	215.24
7500	1305.25	676.94	467.89	363.65	301.34	259.99	230.62
8000	1392.27	722.07	499.08	387.89	321.43	277.32	245.99
8500	1479.29	767.20	530.27	412.14	341.52	294.66	261.37
9000	1566.30	812.32	561.46	436.38	361.61	311.99	276.74
9500	1653.32	857.45	592.66	460.62	381.70	329.32	292.12
10000	1740.34	902.58	623.85	484.87	401.79	346.65	307.49
11000	1914.37	992.84	686.23	533.35	441.96	381.32	338.24
12000	2088.41	1083.10	748.62	581.84	482.14	415.98	368.99
13000	2262.44	1173.36	811.00	630.33	522.32	450.65	399.74
14000	2436.47	1263.62	873.39	678.81	562.50	485.31	430.49
15000	2610.51	1353.87	935.77	727.30	602.68	519.98	461.24
16000	2784.54	1444.13	998.16	775.79	642.86	554.65	491.98
17000	2958.57	1534.39	1060.54	824.27	683.04	589.31	522.73
18000	3132.61	1624.65	1122.93	872.76	723.21	623.98	553.48
19000	3306.64	1714.91	1185.31	921.25	763.39	658.64	584.23
20000	3480.68	1805.17	1247.70	969.73	803.57	693.31	614.98
21000	3654.71	1895.42	1310.08	1018.22	843.75	727.97	645.73
22000	3828.74	1985.68	1372.47	1066.71	883.93	762.64	676.48
23000	4002.78	2075.94	1434.85	1115.19	924.11	797.30	707.23
24000	4176.81	2166.20	1497.23	1163.68	964.29	831.97	737.98
25000	4350.85	2256.46	1559.62	1212.17	1004.46	866.63	768.73
26000	4524.88	2346.72	1622.00	1260.65	1044.64	901.30	799.48
27000	4698.91	2436.97	1684.39	1309.14	1084.82	935.96	830.22
28000	4872.95	2527.23	1746.77	1357.63	1125.00	970.62	860.97
29000	5046.98	2617.49	1809.16	1406.11	1165.18	1005.29	891.72
30000	5221.01	2707.75	1871.54	1454.60	1205.36	1039.96	922.47
31000	5395.05	2798.01	1933.93	1503.09	1245.53	1074.63	953.22
32000	5569.08	2888.27	1996.31	1551.57	1285.71	1109.29	983.97
33000	5743.12	2978.52	2058.70	1600.06	1325.89	1143.96	1014.72
34000	5917.15	3068.78	2121.08	1648.55	1366.07	1178.62	1045.47
35000	6091.18	3159.04	2183.47	1697.03	1406.25	1213.29	1076.22
40000	6961.35	3610.33	2495.39	1939.47	1607.14	1386.61	1229.96
45000	7831.52	4061.62	2807.32	2181.90	1808.03	1559.94	1383.71
50000	8701.69	4512.92	3119.24	2424.33	2008.93	1733.27	1537.45
55000	9571.86	4964.21	3431.16	2666.77	2209.82	1906.59	1691.20
60000	10442.03	5415.50	3743.09	2909.20	2410.71	2079.92	1844.94
65000	11312.20	5866.79	4055.01	3151.63	2611.61	2253.25	1998.69
70000	12182.37	6318.08	4366.94	3394.07	2812.50	2426.57	2152.43

Monthly Loan Payments   15%

LOAN AMOUNT	4 YEARS	4½ YEARS	5 YEARS	5½ YEARS	6 YEARS	6½ YEARS	7 YEARS
100	2.78	2.56	2.38	2.23	2.11	2.01	1.93
200	5.57	5.12	4.76	4.47	4.23	4.03	3.86
300	8.35	7.67	7.14	6.70	6.34	6.04	5.79
400	11.13	10.23	9.52	8.94	8.46	8.06	7.72
500	13.92	12.79	11.89	11.17	10.57	10.07	9.65
600	16.70	15.35	14.27	13.40	12.69	12.09	11.58
700	19.48	17.90	16.65	15.64	14.80	14.10	13.51
800	22.26	20.46	19.03	17.87	16.92	16.12	15.44
900	25.05	23.02	21.41	20.11	19.03	18.13	17.37
1000	27.83	25.58	23.79	22.34	21.15	20.14	19.30
1500	41.75	38.37	35.68	33.51	31.72	30.22	28.95
2000	55.66	51.16	47.58	44.68	42.29	40.29	38.59
2500	69.58	63.94	59.47	55.85	52.86	50.36	48.24
3000	83.49	76.73	71.37	67.02	63.44	60.43	57.89
3500	97.41	89.52	83.26	78.19	74.01	70.51	67.54
4000	111.32	102.31	95.16	89.36	84.58	80.58	77.19
4500	125.24	115.10	107.05	100.53	95.15	90.65	86.84
5000	139.15	127.89	118.95	111.70	105.73	100.72	96.48
5500	153.07	140.68	130.84	122.87	116.30	110.79	106.13
6000	166.98	153.47	142.74	134.04	126.87	120.87	115.78
6500	180.90	166.25	154.63	145.21	137.44	130.94	125.43
7000	194.82	179.04	166.53	156.38	148.02	141.01	135.08
7500	208.73	191.83	178.42	167.55	158.59	151.08	144.73
8000	222.65	204.62	190.32	178.73	169.16	161.15	154.37
8500	236.56	217.41	202.21	189.90	179.73	171.23	164.02
9000	250.48	230.20	214.11	201.07	190.31	181.30	173.67
9500	264.39	242.99	226.00	212.24	200.88	191.37	183.32
10000	278.31	255.78	237.90	223.41	211.45	201.44	192.97
11000	306.14	281.35	261.69	245.75	232.60	221.59	212.26
12000	333.97	306.93	285.48	268.08	253.74	241.73	231.56
13000	361.80	332.51	309.27	290.43	274.89	261.88	250.86
14000	389.63	358.09	333.06	312.77	296.03	282.02	270.15
15000	417.46	383.66	356.85	335.11	317.18	302.17	289.45
16000	445.29	409.24	380.64	357.45	338.32	322.31	308.75
17000	473.12	434.82	404.43	379.79	359.47	342.45	328.04
18000	500.95	460.40	428.22	402.13	380.61	362.60	347.34
19000	528.78	485.97	452.01	424.47	401.76	382.74	366.64
20000	556.61	511.55	475.80	446.81	422.90	402.89	385.94
21000	584.45	537.13	499.59	469.15	444.05	423.03	405.23
22000	612.28	562.71	523.38	491.49	465.19	443.18	424.53
23000	640.11	588.28	547.17	513.83	486.34	463.32	443.83
24000	667.94	613.86	570.96	536.18	507.48	483.46	463.12
25000	695.77	639.44	594.75	558.52	528.63	503.61	482.42
26000	723.60	665.02	618.54	580.86	549.77	523.75	501.72
27000	751.43	690.60	642.33	603.20	570.92	543.90	521.01
28000	779.26	716.17	666.12	625.54	592.06	564.04	540.31
29000	807.09	741.75	689.91	647.88	613.21	584.19	559.61
30000	834.92	767.33	713.70	670.22	634.35	604.33	578.90
31000	862.75	792.91	737.49	692.56	655.50	624.48	598.20
32000	890.58	818.48	761.28	714.90	676.64	644.62	617.50
33000	918.41	844.06	785.07	737.24	697.79	664.76	636.79
34000	946.25	869.64	808.86	759.58	718.93	684.91	656.09
35000	974.08	895.22	832.65	781.92	740.08	705.05	675.39
40000	1113.23	1023.10	951.60	893.63	845.80	805.77	771.87
45000	1252.38	1150.99	1070.55	1005.33	951.53	906.50	868.35
50000	1391.54	1278.88	1189.50	1117.03	1057.25	1007.22	964.84
55000	1530.69	1406.77	1308.45	1228.74	1162.98	1107.94	1061.32
60000	1669.84	1534.66	1427.40	1340.44	1268.70	1208.66	1157.81
65000	1809.00	1662.54	1546.35	1452.14	1374.43	1309.38	1254.29
70000	1948.15	1790.43	1665.30	1563.85	1480.15	1410.10	1350.77

15% Monthly Loan Payments

LOAN AMOUNT	7½ YEARS	8 YEARS	8½ YEARS	9 YEARS	9½ YEARS	10 YEARS	10½ YEARS
100	1.86	1.79	1.74	1.69	1.65	1.61	1.58
200	3.71	3.59	3.48	3.38	3.30	3.23	3.16
300	5.57	5.38	5.22	5.08	4.95	4.84	4.74
400	7.43	7.18	6.96	6.77	6.60	6.45	6.32
500	9.29	8.97	8.70	8.46	8.25	8.07	7.90
600	11.14	10.77	10.44	10.15	9.90	9.68	9.48
700	13.00	12.56	12.18	11.85	11.55	11.29	11.06
800	14.86	14.36	13.92	13.54	13.20	12.91	12.64
900	16.71	16.15	15.66	15.23	14.85	14.52	14.22
1000	18.57	17.95	17.40	16.92	16.50	16.13	15.80
1500	27.86	26.92	26.10	25.39	24.76	24.20	23.71
2000	37.14	35.89	34.80	33.85	33.01	32.27	31.61
2500	46.43	44.86	43.50	42.31	41.26	40.33	39.51
3000	55.71	53.84	52.20	50.77	49.51	48.40	47.41
3500	65.00	62.81	60.90	59.24	57.77	56.47	55.31
4000	74.29	71.78	69.60	67.70	66.02	64.53	63.21
4500	83.57	80.75	78.30	76.16	74.27	72.60	71.12
5000	92.86	89.73	87.00	84.62	82.52	80.67	79.02
5500	102.14	98.70	95.71	93.08	90.78	88.73	86.92
6000	111.43	107.67	104.41	101.55	99.03	96.80	94.82
6500	120.71	116.65	113.11	110.01	107.28	104.87	102.72
7000	130.00	125.62	121.81	118.47	115.53	112.93	110.62
7500	139.29	134.59	130.51	126.93	123.79	121.00	118.53
8000	148.57	143.56	139.21	135.39	132.04	129.07	126.43
8500	157.86	152.54	147.91	143.86	140.29	137.13	134.33
9000	167.14	161.51	156.61	152.32	148.54	145.20	142.23
9500	176.43	170.48	165.31	160.78	156.80	153.27	150.13
10000	185.71	179.45	174.01	169.24	165.05	161.33	158.04
11000	204.29	197.40	191.41	186.17	181.55	177.47	173.84
12000	222.86	215.34	208.81	203.09	198.06	193.60	189.64
13000	241.43	233.29	226.21	220.02	214.56	209.74	205.45
14000	260.00	251.24	243.61	236.94	231.07	225.87	221.25
15000	278.57	269.18	261.01	253.87	247.57	242.00	237.05
16000	297.14	287.13	278.42	270.79	264.08	258.14	252.86
17000	315.71	305.07	295.82	287.71	280.58	274.27	268.66
18000	334.29	323.02	313.22	304.64	297.09	290.40	284.46
19000	352.86	340.96	330.62	321.56	313.59	306.54	300.27
20000	371.43	358.91	348.02	338.49	330.09	322.67	316.07
21000	390.00	376.85	365.42	355.41	346.60	338.80	331.87
22000	408.57	394.80	382.82	372.34	363.10	354.94	347.68
23000	427.14	412.74	400.22	389.26	379.61	371.07	363.48
24000	445.72	430.69	417.62	406.18	396.11	387.20	379.29
25000	464.29	448.64	435.02	423.11	412.62	403.34	395.09
26000	482.86	466.58	452.42	440.03	429.12	419.47	410.89
27000	501.43	484.53	469.83	456.96	445.63	435.60	426.70
28000	520.00	502.47	487.23	473.88	462.13	451.74	442.50
29000	538.57	520.42	504.63	490.81	478.64	467.87	458.30
30000	557.14	538.36	522.03	507.73	495.14	484.00	474.11
31000	575.72	556.31	539.43	524.65	511.65	500.14	489.91
32000	594.29	574.25	556.83	541.58	528.15	516.27	505.71
33000	612.86	592.20	574.23	558.50	544.66	532.41	521.52
34000	631.43	610.14	591.63	575.43	561.16	548.54	537.32
35000	650.00	628.09	609.03	592.35	577.67	564.67	553.12
40000	742.86	717.82	696.04	676.97	660.19	645.34	632.14
45000	835.72	807.54	783.04	761.60	742.71	726.01	711.16
50000	928.57	897.27	870.05	846.22	825.24	806.67	790.18
55000	1021.43	987.00	957.05	930.84	907.76	887.34	869.20
60000	1114.29	1076.72	1044.06	1015.46	990.28	968.01	948.21
65000	1207.14	1166.45	1131.06	1100.08	1072.81	1048.68	1027.23
70000	1300.00	1256.18	1218.07	1184.70	1155.33	1129.34	1106.25

Monthly Loan Payments 15%

LOAN AMOUNT	11 YEARS	11½ YEARS	12 YEARS	12½ YEARS	13 YEARS	14 YEARS	15 YEARS
100	1.55	1.52	1.50	1.48	1.46	1.43	1.40
200	3.10	3.05	3.00	2.96	2.92	2.85	2.80
300	4.65	4.57	4.50	4.44	4.38	4.28	4.20
400	6.20	6.10	6.00	5.92	5.84	5.71	5.60
500	7.75	7.62	7.50	7.40	7.30	7.14	7.00
600	9.31	9.15	9.01	8.88	8.76	8.56	8.40
700	10.86	10.67	10.51	10.36	10.22	9.99	9.80
800	12.41	12.20	12.01	11.84	11.68	11.42	11.20
900	13.96	13.72	13.51	13.32	13.14	12.84	12.60
1000	15.51	15.25	15.01	14.80	14.60	14.27	14.00
1500	23.26	22.87	22.51	22.19	21.90	21.41	20.99
2000	31.02	30.49	30.02	29.59	29.21	28.54	27.99
2500	38.77	38.11	37.52	36.99	36.51	35.68	34.99
3000	46.53	45.74	45.03	44.39	43.81	42.81	41.99
3500	54.28	53.36	52.53	51.78	51.11	49.95	48.99
4000	62.04	60.98	60.04	59.18	58.41	57.08	55.98
4500	69.79	68.60	67.54	66.58	65.71	64.22	62.98
5000	77.55	76.23	75.04	73.98	73.01	71.35	69.98
5500	85.30	83.85	82.55	81.38	80.32	78.49	76.98
6000	93.05	91.47	90.05	88.77	87.62	85.62	83.98
6500	100.81	99.10	97.56	96.17	94.92	92.76	90.97
7000	108.56	106.72	105.06	103.57	102.22	99.89	97.97
7500	116.32	114.34	112.57	110.97	109.52	107.03	104.97
8000	124.07	121.96	120.07	118.36	116.82	114.16	111.97
8500	131.83	129.59	127.57	125.76	124.12	121.30	118.96
9000	139.58	137.21	135.08	133.16	131.43	128.43	125.96
9500	147.34	144.83	142.58	140.56	138.73	135.57	132.96
10000	155.09	152.46	150.09	147.95	146.03	142.70	139.96
11000	170.60	167.70	165.10	162.75	160.63	156.97	153.95
12000	186.11	182.95	180.11	177.55	175.23	171.24	167.95
13000	201.62	198.19	195.11	192.34	189.84	185.52	181.95
14000	217.13	213.44	210.12	207.14	204.44	199.79	195.94
15000	232.64	228.68	225.13	221.93	219.04	214.06	209.94
16000	248.15	243.93	240.14	236.73	233.65	228.33	223.93
17000	263.66	259.17	255.15	251.52	248.25	242.60	237.93
18000	279.16	274.42	270.16	266.32	262.85	256.87	251.93
19000	294.67	289.67	285.17	281.11	277.45	271.14	265.92
20000	310.18	304.91	300.18	295.91	292.06	285.41	279.92
21000	325.69	320.16	315.18	310.71	306.66	299.68	293.91
22000	341.20	335.40	330.19	325.50	321.26	313.95	307.91
23000	356.71	350.65	345.20	340.30	335.87	328.22	321.91
24000	372.22	365.89	360.21	355.09	350.47	342.49	335.90
25000	387.73	381.14	375.22	369.89	365.07	356.76	349.90
26000	403.24	396.38	390.23	384.68	379.67	371.03	363.89
27000	418.75	411.63	405.24	399.48	394.28	385.30	377.89
28000	434.26	426.88	420.25	414.27	408.88	399.57	391.88
29000	449.77	442.12	435.25	429.07	423.48	413.84	405.88
30000	465.27	457.37	450.26	443.86	438.09	428.11	419.88
31000	480.78	472.61	465.27	458.66	452.69	442.38	433.87
32000	496.29	487.86	480.28	473.46	467.29	456.65	447.87
33000	511.80	503.10	495.29	488.25	481.89	470.92	461.86
34000	527.31	518.35	510.30	503.05	496.50	485.19	475.86
35000	542.82	533.59	525.31	517.84	511.10	499.46	489.86
40000	620.37	609.82	600.35	591.82	584.11	570.82	559.83
45000	697.91	686.05	675.39	665.80	657.13	642.17	629.81
50000	775.46	762.28	750.44	739.77	730.14	713.52	699.79
55000	853.00	838.50	825.48	813.75	803.16	784.87	769.77
60000	930.55	914.73	900.53	887.73	876.17	856.22	839.75
65000	1008.09	990.96	975.57	961.71	949.19	927.58	909.73
70000	1085.64	1067.19	1050.61	1035.68	1022.20	998.93	979.71

15¼%   Monthly Loan Payments

LOAN AMOUNT	½ YEAR	1 YEAR	1½ YEARS	2 YEARS	2½ YEARS	3 YEARS	3½ YEAR
100	17.42	9.04	6.25	4.86	4.03	3.48	3.0
200	34.83	18.08	12.50	9.72	8.06	6.96	6.1
300	52.25	27.11	18.75	14.58	12.09	10.44	9.2
400	69.66	36.15	25.00	19.44	16.12	13.92	12.3
500	87.08	45.19	31.25	24.30	20.15	17.39	15.4
600	104.49	54.23	37.50	29.16	24.18	20.87	18.5
700	121.91	63.26	43.75	34.02	28.21	24.35	21.6
800	139.33	72.30	50.00	38.88	32.24	27.83	24.7
900	156.74	81.34	56.25	43.74	36.27	31.31	27.7
1000	174.16	90.38	62.50	48.61	40.30	34.79	30.8
1500	261.24	135.56	93.75	72.91	60.45	52.18	46.3
2000	348.32	180.75	125.01	97.21	80.60	69.58	61.
2500	435.39	225.94	156.26	121.51	100.75	86.97	77.
3000	522.47	271.13	187.51	145.82	120.90	104.36	92.
3500	609.55	316.32	218.76	170.12	141.05	121.76	108.0
4000	696.63	361.51	250.01	194.42	161.20	139.15	123.
4500	783.71	406.69	281.26	218.72	181.35	156.55	138.9
5000	870.79	451.88	312.51	243.03	201.50	173.94	154.
5500	957.87	497.07	343.76	267.33	221.65	191.33	169.
6000	1044.95	542.26	375.02	291.63	241.79	208.73	185.
6500	1132.03	587.45	406.27	315.94	261.94	226.12	200.
7000	1219.11	632.63	437.52	340.24	282.09	243.52	216.
7500	1306.18	677.82	468.77	364.54	302.24	260.91	231.
8000	1393.26	723.01	500.02	388.84	322.39	278.30	246.
8500	1480.34	768.20	531.27	413.15	342.54	295.70	262.
9000	1567.42	813.39	562.52	437.45	362.69	313.09	277.
9500	1654.50	858.58	593.77	461.75	382.84	330.48	293.
10000	1741.58	903.76	625.03	486.06	402.99	347.88	308.
11000	1915.74	994.14	687.53	534.66	443.29	382.67	339.
12000	2089.89	1084.52	750.03	583.27	483.59	417.45	370.
13000	2264.05	1174.89	812.53	631.87	523.89	452.24	401.
14000	2438.21	1265.27	875.04	680.48	564.19	487.03	432.
15000	2612.37	1355.64	937.54	729.08	604.49	521.82	463.
16000	2786.53	1446.02	1000.04	777.69	644.79	556.61	493.
17000	2960.68	1536.40	1062.54	826.29	685.08	591.39	524.
18000	3134.84	1626.77	1125.05	874.90	725.38	626.18	555.
19000	3309.00	1717.15	1187.55	923.50	765.68	660.97	586.
20000	3483.16	1807.53	1250.05	972.11	805.98	695.76	617.
21000	3657.32	1897.90	1312.55	1020.71	846.28	730.55	648.
22000	3831.47	1988.28	1375.06	1069.32	886.58	765.33	679.
23000	4005.63	2078.66	1437.56	1117.93	926.88	800.12	710.
24000	4179.79	2169.03	1500.06	1166.53	967.18	834.91	740.
25000	4353.95	2259.41	1562.56	1215.14	1007.48	869.70	771.
26000	4528.10	2349.78	1625.07	1263.74	1047.78	904.48	802.
27000	4702.26	2440.16	1687.57	1312.35	1088.07	939.27	833.
28000	4876.42	2530.54	1750.07	1360.95	1128.38	974.06	864.
29000	5050.58	2620.91	1812.57	1409.56	1168.67	1008.85	895.
30000	5224.74	2711.29	1875.08	1458.17	1208.97	1043.64	926.
31000	5398.89	2801.67	1937.58	1506.77	1249.27	1078.42	957.
32000	5573.05	2892.04	2000.08	1555.38	1289.57	1113.21	987.
33000	5747.21	2982.42	2062.58	1603.98	1329.87	1148.00	1018.
34000	5921.37	3072.79	2125.09	1652.59	1370.17	1182.79	1049.
35000	6095.53	3163.17	2187.59	1701.19	1410.47	1217.58	1080.
40000	6966.31	3615.05	2500.10	1944.22	1611.96	1391.52	1234.
45000	7837.10	4066.93	2812.61	2187.25	1813.46	1565.45	1389.
50000	8707.89	4518.82	3125.13	2430.28	2014.96	1739.39	1543.
55000	9578.68	4970.70	3437.64	2673.30	2216.45	1913.33	1698.
60000	10449.47	5422.58	3750.15	2916.33	2417.95	2087.27	1852.
65000	11320.26	5874.46	4062.66	3159.36	2619.44	2261.21	2006.
70000	12191.05	6326.34	4375.18	3402.39	2820.94	2435.15	2161.

Monthly Loan Payments   15¼%

LOAN AMOUNT	4 YEARS	4½ YEARS	5 YEARS	5½ YEARS	6 YEARS	6½ YEARS	7 YEARS
100	2.80	2.57	2.39	2.25	2.13	2.03	1.94
200	5.59	5.14	4.78	4.49	4.26	4.06	3.89
300	8.39	7.71	7.18	6.74	6.38	6.08	5.83
400	11.18	10.28	9.57	8.99	8.51	8.11	7.77
500	13.98	12.85	11.96	11.24	10.64	10.14	9.72
600	16.77	15.42	14.35	13.48	12.77	12.17	11.66
700	19.57	17.99	16.74	15.73	14.90	14.20	13.61
800	22.37	20.57	19.14	17.98	17.02	16.23	15.55
900	25.16	23.14	21.53	20.23	19.15	18.25	17.49
1000	27.96	25.71	23.92	22.47	21.28	20.28	19.44
1500	41.94	38.56	35.88	33.71	31.92	30.42	29.16
2000	55.92	51.41	47.84	44.95	42.56	40.57	38.87
2500	69.89	64.27	59.80	56.19	53.20	50.71	48.59
3000	83.87	77.12	71.76	67.42	63.84	60.85	58.31
3500	97.85	89.97	83.72	78.66	74.48	70.99	68.03
4000	111.83	102.83	95.69	89.90	85.12	81.13	77.75
4500	125.81	115.68	107.65	101.13	95.76	91.27	87.47
5000	139.79	128.53	119.61	112.37	106.41	101.41	97.19
5500	153.77	141.39	131.57	123.61	117.05	111.55	106.91
6000	167.75	154.24	143.53	134.85	127.69	121.70	116.62
6500	181.72	167.09	155.49	146.08	138.33	131.84	126.34
7000	195.70	179.95	167.45	157.32	148.97	141.98	136.06
7500	209.68	192.80	179.41	168.56	159.61	152.12	145.78
8000	223.66	205.65	191.37	179.79	170.25	162.26	155.50
8500	237.64	218.51	203.33	191.03	180.89	172.40	165.22
9000	251.62	231.36	215.29	202.27	191.53	182.54	174.94
9500	265.60	244.21	227.25	213.51	202.17	192.68	184.65
10000	279.58	257.07	239.21	224.74	212.81	202.83	194.37
11000	307.53	282.77	263.13	247.22	234.09	223.11	213.81
12000	335.49	308.48	287.06	269.69	255.37	243.39	233.25
13000	363.45	334.19	310.98	292.17	276.65	263.67	252.68
14000	391.41	359.89	334.90	314.64	297.93	283.96	272.12
15000	419.36	385.60	358.82	337.12	319.22	304.24	291.56
16000	447.32	411.31	382.74	359.59	340.50	324.52	311.00
17000	475.28	437.01	406.66	382.06	361.78	344.80	330.43
18000	503.24	462.72	430.58	404.54	383.06	365.09	349.87
19000	531.20	488.43	454.51	427.01	404.34	385.37	369.31
20000	559.15	514.14	478.43	449.49	425.62	405.65	388.75
21000	587.11	539.84	502.35	471.96	446.90	425.94	408.18
22000	615.07	565.55	526.27	494.44	468.18	446.22	427.62
23000	643.03	591.26	550.19	516.91	489.46	466.50	447.06
24000	670.98	616.96	574.11	539.38	510.74	486.78	466.49
25000	698.94	642.67	598.03	561.86	532.03	507.07	485.93
26000	726.90	668.38	621.96	584.33	553.31	527.35	505.37
27000	754.86	694.08	645.88	606.81	574.59	547.63	524.81
28000	782.81	719.79	669.80	629.28	595.87	567.91	544.24
29000	810.77	745.50	693.72	651.76	617.15	588.20	563.68
30000	838.73	771.20	717.64	674.23	638.43	608.48	583.12
31000	866.69	796.91	741.56	696.71	659.71	628.76	602.56
32000	894.64	822.62	765.48	719.18	680.99	649.04	621.99
33000	922.60	848.32	789.40	741.65	702.27	669.33	641.43
34000	950.56	874.03	813.33	764.13	723.55	689.61	660.87
35000	978.52	899.74	837.25	786.60	744.84	709.89	680.30
40000	1118.31	1028.27	956.85	898.97	851.24	811.31	777.49
45000	1258.09	1156.80	1076.46	1011.35	957.65	912.72	874.68
50000	1397.88	1285.34	1196.07	1123.72	1064.05	1014.13	971.86
55000	1537.67	1413.87	1315.67	1236.09	1170.46	1115.54	1069.05
60000	1677.46	1542.41	1435.28	1348.46	1276.86	1216.96	1166.24
65000	1817.25	1670.94	1554.89	1460.83	1383.27	1318.37	1263.42
70000	1957.03	1799.47	1674.50	1573.21	1489.67	1419.78	1360.61

15¼%   Monthly Loan Payments

LOAN AMOUNT	7½ YEARS	8 YEARS	8½ YEARS	9 YEARS	9½ YEARS	10 YEARS	10½ YEARS
100	1.87	1.81	1.75	1.71	1.67	1.63	1.60
200	3.74	3.62	3.51	3.41	3.33	3.26	3.19
300	5.61	5.43	5.26	5.12	5.00	4.89	4.79
400	7.49	7.24	7.02	6.83	6.66	6.51	6.38
500	9.36	9.05	8.77	8.54	8.33	8.14	7.98
600	11.23	10.85	10.53	10.24	9.99	9.77	9.58
700	13.10	12.66	12.28	11.95	11.66	11.40	11.17
800	14.97	14.47	14.04	13.66	13.32	13.03	12.77
900	16.84	16.28	15.79	15.37	14.99	14.66	14.36
1000	18.71	18.09	17.55	17.07	16.66	16.29	15.96
1500	28.07	27.14	26.32	25.61	24.98	24.43	23.94
2000	37.43	36.18	35.10	34.15	33.31	32.57	31.92
2500	46.79	45.23	43.87	42.68	41.64	40.72	39.90
3000	56.15	54.27	52.64	51.22	49.97	48.86	47.88
3500	65.50	63.32	61.42	59.76	58.30	57.00	55.86
4000	74.86	72.36	70.19	68.29	66.62	65.15	63.84
4500	84.21	81.41	78.97	76.83	74.95	73.29	71.82
5000	93.57	90.45	87.74	85.37	83.28	81.43	79.80
5500	102.93	99.50	96.51	93.90	91.61	89.58	87.77
6000	112.29	108.54	105.29	102.44	99.94	97.72	95.75
6500	121.64	117.59	114.06	110.98	108.26	105.87	103.73
7000	131.00	126.63	122.84	119.52	116.59	114.01	111.71
7500	140.36	135.68	131.61	128.05	124.92	122.15	119.69
8000	149.71	144.72	140.38	136.59	133.25	130.30	127.67
8500	159.07	153.77	149.16	145.13	141.58	138.44	135.65
9000	168.43	162.81	157.93	153.66	149.91	146.58	143.63
9500	177.79	171.86	166.71	162.20	158.23	154.73	151.61
10000	187.14	180.90	175.48	170.74	166.56	162.87	159.59
11000	205.86	198.99	193.03	187.81	183.22	179.16	175.55
12000	224.57	217.08	210.58	204.88	199.87	195.44	191.51
13000	243.28	235.17	228.13	221.96	216.53	211.73	207.47
14000	262.00	253.27	245.67	239.03	233.19	228.02	223.43
15000	280.71	271.36	263.22	256.10	249.84	244.30	239.39
16000	299.43	289.45	280.77	273.18	266.50	260.59	255.34
17000	318.14	307.54	298.32	290.25	283.15	276.88	271.30
18000	336.86	325.63	315.87	307.33	299.81	293.16	287.26
19000	355.57	343.72	333.41	324.40	316.47	309.45	303.22
20000	374.28	361.81	350.96	341.47	333.12	325.74	319.18
21000	393.00	379.90	368.51	358.55	349.78	342.03	335.14
22000	411.71	397.99	386.06	375.62	366.43	358.31	351.10
23000	430.43	416.08	403.61	392.69	383.09	374.60	367.06
24000	449.14	434.17	421.15	409.77	399.75	390.89	383.02
25000	467.86	452.26	438.70	426.84	416.40	407.17	398.98
26000	486.57	470.35	456.25	443.91	433.06	423.46	414.93
27000	505.28	488.44	473.80	460.99	449.72	439.75	430.89
28000	524.00	506.53	491.35	478.06	466.37	456.03	446.85
29000	542.71	524.62	508.89	495.13	483.03	472.32	462.81
30000	561.43	542.71	526.44	512.21	499.68	488.61	478.77
31000	580.14	560.80	543.99	529.28	516.34	504.89	494.73
32000	598.86	578.89	561.54	546.36	533.00	521.18	510.69
33000	617.57	596.98	579.09	563.43	549.65	537.47	526.65
34000	636.28	615.07	596.63	580.50	566.31	553.76	542.61
35000	655.00	633.16	614.18	597.58	582.96	570.04	558.57
40000	748.57	723.61	701.92	682.94	666.25	651.48	638.36
45000	842.14	814.07	789.66	768.31	749.53	732.91	718.16
50000	935.71	904.52	877.40	853.68	832.81	814.35	797.95
55000	1029.28	994.97	965.14	939.05	916.09	895.78	877.75
60000	1122.85	1085.42	1052.88	1024.42	999.37	977.22	957.54
65000	1216.42	1175.87	1140.63	1109.78	1082.65	1058.65	1037.34
70000	1310.00	1266.33	1228.37	1195.15	1165.93	1140.09	1117.13

122

Monthly Loan Payments 15¼%

LOAN AMOUNT	11 YEARS	11½ YEARS	12 YEARS	12½ YEARS	13 YEARS	14 YEARS	15 YEARS
100	1.57	1.54	1.52	1.50	1.48	1.44	1.42
200	3.13	3.08	3.03	2.99	2.95	2.89	2.83
300	4.70	4.62	4.55	4.49	4.43	4.33	4.25
400	6.27	6.16	6.07	5.98	5.91	5.78	5.67
500	7.83	7.70	7.59	7.48	7.38	7.22	7.08
600	9.40	9.24	9.10	8.98	8.86	8.66	8.50
700	10.97	10.78	10.62	10.47	10.34	10.11	9.92
800	12.53	12.32	12.14	11.97	11.81	11.55	11.33
900	14.10	13.86	13.65	13.46	13.29	12.99	12.75
1000	15.67	15.40	15.17	14.96	14.77	14.44	14.17
1500	23.50	23.11	22.76	22.44	22.15	21.66	21.25
2000	31.33	30.81	30.34	29.92	29.54	28.88	28.33
2500	39.17	38.51	37.93	37.40	36.92	36.10	35.42
3000	47.00	46.21	45.51	44.88	44.30	43.32	42.50
3500	54.83	53.92	53.10	52.36	51.69	50.54	49.59
4000	62.67	61.62	60.68	59.83	59.07	57.76	56.67
4500	70.50	69.32	68.27	67.31	66.46	64.97	63.75
5000	78.33	77.02	75.85	74.79	73.84	72.19	70.84
5500	86.17	84.73	83.44	82.27	81.22	79.41	77.92
6000	94.00	92.43	91.02	89.75	88.61	86.63	85.00
6500	101.83	100.13	98.61	97.23	95.99	93.85	92.09
7000	109.67	107.83	106.19	104.71	103.37	101.07	99.17
7500	117.50	115.54	113.78	112.19	110.76	108.29	106.26
8000	125.33	123.24	121.36	119.67	118.14	115.51	113.34
8500	133.17	130.94	128.95	127.15	125.53	122.73	120.42
9000	141.00	138.64	136.53	134.63	132.91	129.95	127.51
9500	148.83	146.35	144.12	142.11	140.29	137.17	134.59
10000	156.67	154.05	151.70	149.59	147.68	144.39	141.67
11000	172.33	169.45	166.87	164.54	162.45	158.83	155.84
12000	188.00	184.86	182.04	179.50	177.21	173.27	170.01
13000	203.67	200.26	197.21	194.46	191.98	187.70	184.18
14000	219.33	215.67	212.38	209.42	206.75	202.14	198.34
15000	235.00	231.07	227.55	224.38	221.52	216.58	212.51
16000	250.67	246.48	242.72	239.34	236.28	231.02	226.68
17000	266.33	261.88	257.89	254.30	251.05	245.46	240.85
18000	282.00	277.29	273.06	269.25	265.82	259.90	255.01
19000	297.67	292.69	288.23	284.21	280.59	274.34	269.18
20000	313.33	308.10	303.40	299.17	295.36	288.78	283.35
21000	329.00	323.50	318.57	314.13	310.12	303.21	297.52
22000	344.66	338.91	333.74	329.09	324.89	317.65	311.68
23000	360.33	354.31	348.91	344.05	339.66	332.09	325.85
24000	376.00	369.72	364.08	359.01	354.43	346.53	340.02
25000	391.66	385.12	379.25	373.96	369.19	360.97	354.19
26000	407.33	400.53	394.42	388.92	383.96	375.41	368.35
27000	423.00	415.93	409.59	403.88	398.73	389.85	382.52
28000	438.66	431.34	424.76	418.84	413.50	404.29	396.69
29000	454.33	446.74	439.93	433.80	428.27	418.72	410.86
30000	470.00	462.15	455.10	448.76	443.03	433.16	425.02
31000	485.66	477.55	470.27	463.72	457.80	447.60	439.19
32000	501.33	492.96	485.44	478.68	472.57	462.04	453.36
33000	517.00	508.36	500.61	493.63	487.34	476.48	467.53
34000	532.66	523.77	515.78	508.59	502.10	490.92	481.69
35000	548.33	539.17	530.95	523.55	516.87	505.36	495.86
40000	626.66	616.20	606.80	598.34	590.71	577.55	566.70
45000	705.00	693.22	682.65	673.14	664.55	649.74	637.54
50000	783.33	770.25	758.50	747.93	738.39	721.94	708.37
55000	861.66	847.27	834.35	822.72	812.23	794.13	779.21
60000	940.00	924.30	910.20	897.52	886.07	866.33	850.05
65000	1018.33	1001.32	986.05	972.31	959.91	938.52	920.89
70000	1096.66	1078.34	1061.90	1047.10	1033.74	1010.71	991.72

15½%   Monthly Loan Payments

LOAN AMOUNT	½ YEAR	1 YEAR	1½ YEARS	2 YEARS	2½ YEARS	3 YEARS	3½ YEAR
100	17.43	9.05	6.26	4.87	4.04	3.49	3.1
200	34.86	18.10	12.52	9.74	8.08	6.98	6.2
300	52.28	27.15	18.79	14.62	12.13	10.47	9.3
400	69.71	36.20	25.05	19.49	16.17	13.96	12.4
500	87.14	45.25	31.31	24.36	20.21	17.46	15.5
600	104.57	54.30	37.57	29.23	24.25	20.95	18.6
700	122.00	63.35	43.83	34.11	28.29	24.44	21.7
800	139.43	72.40	50.10	38.98	32.34	27.93	24.8
900	156.85	81.44	56.36	43.85	36.38	31.42	27.9
1000	174.28	90.49	62.62	48.72	40.42	34.91	31.0
1500	261.42	135.74	93.93	73.09	60.63	52.37	46.5
2000	348.56	180.99	125.24	97.45	80.84	69.82	62.0
2500	435.70	226.24	156.55	121.81	101.05	87.28	77.5
3000	522.85	271.48	187.86	146.17	121.26	104.73	93.0
3500	609.99	316.73	219.17	170.54	141.47	122.19	108.5
4000	697.13	361.98	250.48	194.90	161.68	139.64	123.9
4500	784.27	407.22	281.79	219.26	181.89	157.10	139.4
5000	871.41	452.47	313.10	243.62	202.10	174.55	154.9
5500	958.55	497.72	344.41	267.98	222.31	192.01	170.4
6000	1045.69	542.97	375.72	292.35	242.52	209.46	185.9
6500	1132.83	588.21	407.03	316.71	262.73	226.92	201.4
7000	1219.97	633.46	438.34	341.07	282.94	244.37	216.9
7500	1307.11	678.71	469.65	365.43	303.15	261.83	232.4
8000	1394.26	723.96	500.96	389.80	323.36	279.29	247.9
8500	1481.40	769.20	532.27	414.16	343.57	296.74	263.4
9000	1568.54	814.45	563.58	438.52	363.78	314.20	278.9
9500	1655.68	859.70	594.89	462.88	383.99	331.65	294.4
10000	1742.82	904.94	626.20	487.25	404.20	349.11	309.9
11000	1917.10	995.44	688.82	535.97	444.62	384.02	340.9
12000	2091.38	1085.93	751.44	584.69	485.04	418.93	371.9
13000	2265.67	1176.43	814.06	633.42	525.46	453.84	402.9
14000	2439.95	1266.92	876.68	682.14	565.88	488.75	433.9
15000	2614.23	1357.42	939.31	730.87	606.30	523.66	464.9
16000	2788.51	1447.91	1001.93	779.59	646.72	558.57	495.9
17000	2962.79	1538.41	1064.55	828.32	687.14	593.48	526.9
18000	3137.08	1628.90	1127.17	877.04	727.56	628.39	557.9
19000	3311.36	1719.39	1189.79	925.77	767.98	663.30	588.9
20000	3485.64	1809.89	1252.41	974.49	808.40	698.21	619.9
21000	3659.92	1900.38	1315.03	1023.22	848.82	733.12	650.9
22000	3834.20	1990.88	1377.65	1071.94	889.24	768.03	681.9
23000	4008.49	2081.37	1440.27	1120.66	929.66	802.95	712.9
24000	4182.77	2171.87	1502.89	1169.39	970.08	837.86	743.9
25000	4357.05	2262.36	1565.51	1218.11	1010.50	872.77	774.9
26000	4531.33	2352.85	1628.13	1266.84	1050.92	907.68	805.9
27000	4705.61	2443.35	1690.75	1315.56	1091.34	942.59	836.9
28000	4879.90	2533.84	1753.37	1364.29	1131.76	977.50	867.9
29000	5054.18	2624.34	1815.99	1413.01	1172.18	1012.41	898.9
30000	5228.46	2714.83	1878.61	1461.74	1212.60	1047.32	929.9
31000	5402.74	2805.33	1941.23	1510.46	1253.02	1082.23	960.9
32000	5577.02	2895.82	2003.85	1559.19	1293.44	1117.14	991.9
33000	5751.30	2986.32	2066.47	1607.91	1333.86	1152.05	1022.9
34000	5925.59	3076.81	2129.09	1656.63	1374.28	1186.96	1053.9
35000	6099.87	3167.30	2191.71	1705.36	1414.70	1221.87	1084.9
40000	6971.28	3619.78	2504.81	1948.98	1616.80	1396.43	1239.9
45000	7842.69	4072.25	2817.92	2192.60	1818.90	1570.98	1394.9
50000	8714.10	4524.72	3131.02	2436.23	2020.99	1745.53	1549.9
55000	9585.51	4977.19	3444.12	2679.85	2223.09	1920.09	1704.
60000	10456.92	5429.66	3757.22	2923.47	2425.19	2094.64	1859.
65000	11328.33	5882.14	4070.32	3167.10	2627.29	2269.19	2014.
70000	12199.74	6334.61	4383.44	3410.72	2829.39	2443.75	2169.

Monthly Loan Payments 15½%

LOAN AMOUNT	4 YEARS	4½ YEARS	5 YEARS	5½ YEARS	6 YEARS	6½ YEARS	7 YEARS
100	2.81	2.58	2.41	2.26	2.14	2.04	1.96
200	5.62	5.17	4.81	4.52	4.28	4.08	3.92
300	8.43	7.75	7.22	6.78	6.43	6.13	5.87
400	11.23	10.33	9.62	9.04	8.57	8.17	7.83
500	14.04	12.92	12.03	11.30	10.71	10.21	9.79
600	16.85	15.50	14.43	13.57	12.85	12.25	11.75
700	19.66	18.09	16.84	15.83	14.99	14.29	13.70
800	22.47	20.67	19.24	18.09	17.13	16.34	15.66
900	25.28	23.25	21.65	20.35	19.28	18.38	17.62
1000	28.08	25.84	24.05	22.61	21.42	20.42	19.58
1500	42.13	38.75	36.08	33.91	32.13	30.63	29.37
2000	56.17	51.67	48.11	45.22	42.83	40.84	39.16
2500	70.21	64.59	60.13	56.52	53.54	51.05	48.95
3000	84.25	77.51	72.16	67.83	64.25	61.26	58.74
3500	98.30	90.43	84.19	79.13	74.96	71.47	68.52
4000	112.34	103.35	96.21	90.43	85.67	81.69	78.31
4500	126.38	116.26	108.24	101.74	96.38	91.90	88.10
5000	140.42	129.18	120.27	113.04	107.09	102.11	97.89
5500	154.47	142.10	132.29	124.35	117.80	112.32	107.68
6000	168.51	155.02	144.32	135.65	128.50	122.53	117.47
6500	182.55	167.94	156.35	146.96	139.21	132.74	127.26
7000	196.59	180.85	168.37	158.26	149.92	142.95	137.05
7500	210.64	193.77	180.40	169.56	160.63	153.16	146.84
8000	224.68	206.69	192.43	180.87	171.34	163.37	156.63
8500	238.72	219.61	204.45	192.17	182.05	173.58	166.42
9000	252.76	232.53	216.48	203.48	192.76	183.79	176.21
9500	266.81	245.44	228.51	214.78	203.47	194.00	185.99
10000	280.85	258.36	240.53	226.09	214.17	204.21	195.78
11000	308.93	284.20	264.59	248.69	235.59	224.64	215.36
12000	337.02	310.04	288.64	271.30	257.01	245.06	234.94
13000	365.10	335.87	312.69	293.91	278.43	265.48	254.52
14000	393.19	361.71	336.74	316.52	299.84	285.90	274.10
15000	421.27	387.54	360.80	339.13	321.26	306.32	293.68
16000	449.36	413.38	384.85	361.74	342.68	326.74	313.25
17000	477.44	439.22	408.90	384.34	364.10	347.16	332.83
18000	505.53	465.05	432.96	406.95	385.51	367.59	352.41
19000	533.61	490.89	457.01	429.56	406.93	388.01	371.99
20000	561.70	516.73	481.06	452.17	428.35	408.43	391.57
21000	589.78	542.56	505.12	474.78	449.77	428.85	411.15
22000	617.87	568.40	529.17	497.39	471.18	449.27	430.72
23000	645.95	594.23	553.22	520.00	492.60	469.69	450.30
24000	674.04	620.07	577.28	542.60	514.02	490.11	469.88
25000	702.12	645.91	601.33	565.21	535.44	510.54	489.46
26000	730.21	671.74	625.38	587.82	556.85	530.96	509.04
27000	758.29	697.58	649.44	610.43	578.27	551.38	528.62
28000	786.38	723.42	673.49	633.04	599.69	571.80	548.19
29000	814.46	749.25	697.54	655.65	621.11	592.22	567.77
30000	842.55	775.09	721.60	678.26	642.52	612.64	587.35
31000	870.63	800.92	745.65	700.86	663.94	633.06	606.93
32000	898.72	826.76	769.70	723.47	685.36	653.49	626.51
33000	926.80	852.60	793.82	746.08	706.78	673.91	646.09
34000	954.89	878.43	817.81	768.69	728.19	694.33	665.66
35000	982.97	904.27	841.86	791.30	749.61	714.75	685.24
40000	1123.39	1033.45	962.13	904.34	856.70	816.86	783.13
45000	1263.82	1162.63	1082.39	1017.38	963.79	918.96	881.03
50000	1404.24	1291.81	1202.66	1130.43	1070.87	1021.07	978.92
55000	1544.67	1420.99	1322.93	1243.47	1177.96	1123.18	1076.81
60000	1685.09	1550.18	1443.19	1356.51	1285.05	1225.28	1174.70
65000	1825.52	1679.36	1563.46	1469.55	1392.14	1327.39	1272.59
70000	1965.94	1808.54	1683.72	1582.60	1499.22	1429.50	1370.48

125

15½%   Monthly Loan Payments

LOAN AMOUNT	7½ YEARS	8 YEARS	8½ YEARS	9 YEARS	9½ YEARS	10 YEARS	10½ YEARS
100	1.89	1.82	1.77	1.72	1.68	1.64	1.61
200	3.77	3.65	3.54	3.44	3.36	3.29	3.22
300	5.66	5.47	5.31	5.17	5.04	4.93	4.83
400	7.54	7.29	7.08	6.89	6.72	6.58	6.45
500	9.43	9.12	8.85	8.61	8.40	8.22	8.06
600	11.31	10.94	10.62	10.33	10.08	9.86	9.67
700	13.20	12.77	12.39	12.06	11.77	11.51	11.28
800	15.09	14.59	14.16	13.78	13.45	13.15	12.89
900	16.97	16.41	15.93	15.50	15.13	14.80	14.50
1000	18.86	18.24	17.70	17.22	16.81	16.44	16.12
1500	28.29	27.35	26.54	25.84	25.21	24.66	24.17
2000	37.72	36.47	35.39	34.45	33.62	32.88	32.23
2500	47.14	45.59	44.24	43.06	42.02	41.10	40.29
3000	56.57	54.71	53.09	51.67	50.42	49.32	48.35
3500	66.00	63.83	61.94	60.28	58.83	57.54	56.40
4000	75.43	72.94	70.78	68.89	67.23	65.76	64.46
4500	84.86	82.06	79.63	77.51	75.64	73.98	72.52
5000	94.29	91.18	88.48	86.12	84.04	82.21	80.58
5500	103.72	100.30	97.33	94.73	92.44	90.43	88.63
6000	113.15	109.42	106.17	103.34	100.85	98.65	96.69
6500	122.57	118.53	115.02	111.95	109.25	106.87	104.75
7000	132.00	127.65	123.87	120.56	117.66	115.09	112.81
7500	141.43	136.77	132.72	129.18	126.06	123.31	120.86
8000	150.86	145.89	141.57	137.79	134.47	131.53	128.92
8500	160.29	155.01	150.41	146.40	142.87	139.75	136.98
9000	169.72	164.12	159.26	155.01	151.27	147.97	145.04
9500	179.15	173.24	168.11	163.62	159.68	156.19	153.09
10000	188.58	182.36	176.96	172.24	168.08	164.41	161.15
11000	207.43	200.60	194.65	189.46	184.89	180.85	177.27
12000	226.29	218.83	212.35	206.68	201.70	197.29	193.38
13000	245.15	237.07	230.05	223.91	218.51	213.73	209.50
14000	264.01	255.30	247.74	241.13	235.31	230.17	225.61
15000	282.86	273.54	265.44	258.35	252.12	246.62	241.73
16000	301.72	291.77	283.13	275.58	268.93	263.06	257.84
17000	320.58	310.01	300.83	292.80	285.74	279.50	273.96
18000	339.44	328.25	318.52	310.02	302.55	295.94	290.07
19000	358.29	346.48	336.22	327.25	319.36	312.38	306.19
20000	377.15	364.72	353.92	344.47	336.16	328.82	322.30
21000	396.01	382.95	371.61	361.69	352.97	345.26	338.42
22000	414.87	401.19	389.31	378.92	369.78	361.70	354.53
23000	433.72	419.43	407.00	396.14	386.59	378.14	370.65
24000	452.58	437.66	424.70	413.36	403.40	394.59	386.76
25000	471.44	455.90	442.40	430.59	420.20	411.03	402.88
26000	490.30	474.13	460.09	447.81	437.01	427.47	418.99
27000	509.15	492.37	477.79	465.04	453.82	443.91	435.11
28000	528.01	510.61	495.48	482.26	470.63	460.35	451.22
29000	546.87	528.84	513.18	499.48	487.44	476.79	467.34
30000	565.73	547.08	530.87	516.71	504.24	493.23	483.46
31000	584.58	565.31	548.57	533.93	521.05	509.67	499.57
32000	603.44	583.55	566.27	551.15	537.86	526.11	515.69
33000	622.30	601.79	583.96	568.38	554.67	542.55	531.80
34000	641.16	620.02	601.66	585.60	571.48	559.00	547.92
35000	660.01	638.26	619.35	602.82	588.29	575.44	564.03
40000	754.30	729.44	707.83	688.94	672.33	657.64	644.61
45000	848.59	820.62	796.31	775.06	756.37	739.85	725.18
50000	942.88	911.80	884.79	861.18	840.41	822.05	805.76
55000	1037.16	1002.98	973.27	947.29	924.45	904.26	886.33
60000	1131.45	1094.16	1061.75	1033.41	1008.49	986.46	966.91
65000	1225.74	1185.33	1150.23	1119.53	1092.53	1068.67	1047.49
70000	1320.03	1276.51	1238.71	1205.65	1176.57	1150.87	1128.06

Monthly Loan Payments 15½%

LOAN AMOUNT	11 YEARS	11½ YEARS	12 YEARS	12½ YEARS	13 YEARS	14 YEARS	15 YEARS
100	1.58	1.56	1.53	1.51	1.49	1.46	1.43
200	3.16	3.11	3.07	3.02	2.99	2.92	2.87
300	4.75	4.67	4.60	4.54	4.48	4.38	4.30
400	6.33	6.23	6.13	6.05	5.97	5.84	5.74
500	7.91	7.78	7.67	7.56	7.47	7.30	7.17
600	9.49	9.34	9.20	9.07	8.96	8.76	8.60
700	11.08	10.90	10.73	10.59	10.45	10.23	10.04
800	12.66	12.45	12.27	12.10	11.95	11.69	11.47
900	14.24	14.01	13.80	13.61	13.44	13.15	12.91
1000	15.82	15.57	15.33	15.12	14.93	14.61	14.34
1500	23.74	23.35	23.00	22.68	22.40	21.91	21.51
2000	31.65	31.13	30.66	30.24	29.87	29.22	28.68
2500	39.56	38.91	38.33	37.81	37.33	36.52	35.85
3000	47.47	46.70	46.00	45.37	44.80	43.82	43.02
3500	55.39	54.48	53.66	52.93	52.27	51.13	50.19
4000	63.30	62.26	61.33	60.49	59.73	58.43	57.36
4500	71.21	70.04	68.99	68.05	67.20	65.74	64.53
5000	79.12	77.83	76.66	75.61	74.67	73.04	71.70
5500	87.04	85.61	84.33	83.17	82.13	80.34	78.87
6000	94.95	93.39	91.99	90.73	89.60	87.65	86.04
6500	102.86	101.17	99.66	98.30	97.07	94.95	93.21
7000	110.77	108.96	107.32	105.86	104.53	102.26	100.38
7500	118.69	116.74	114.99	113.42	112.00	109.56	107.55
8000	126.60	124.52	122.66	120.98	119.47	116.86	114.72
8500	134.51	132.30	130.32	128.54	126.93	124.17	121.89
9000	142.42	140.09	137.99	136.10	134.40	131.47	129.06
9500	150.34	147.87	145.65	143.66	141.87	138.78	136.23
10000	158.25	155.65	153.32	151.22	149.33	146.08	143.40
11000	174.07	171.22	168.65	166.35	164.27	160.69	157.74
12000	189.90	186.78	183.98	181.47	179.20	175.29	172.08
13000	205.72	202.35	199.32	196.59	194.13	189.90	186.42
14000	221.55	217.91	214.65	211.71	209.07	204.51	200.76
15000	237.37	233.48	229.98	226.84	224.00	219.12	215.10
16000	253.20	249.04	245.31	241.96	238.94	233.73	229.44
17000	269.02	264.61	260.64	257.08	253.87	248.33	243.78
18000	284.85	280.17	275.98	272.20	268.80	262.94	258.12
19000	300.67	295.74	291.31	287.33	283.74	277.55	272.46
20000	316.49	311.30	306.64	302.45	298.67	292.16	286.80
21000	332.32	326.87	321.97	317.57	313.60	306.77	301.14
22000	348.14	342.43	337.30	332.69	328.54	321.37	315.48
23000	363.97	358.00	352.64	347.82	343.47	335.98	329.82
24000	379.79	373.56	367.97	362.94	358.40	350.59	344.16
25000	395.62	389.13	383.30	378.06	373.34	365.20	358.50
26000	411.44	404.69	398.63	393.18	388.27	379.81	372.84
27000	427.27	420.26	413.97	408.31	403.20	394.41	387.18
28000	443.09	435.82	429.30	423.43	418.14	409.02	401.52
29000	458.92	451.39	444.63	438.55	433.07	423.63	415.86
30000	474.74	466.95	459.96	453.67	448.00	438.24	430.20
31000	490.57	482.52	475.29	468.80	462.94	452.84	444.54
32000	506.39	498.08	490.63	483.92	477.87	467.45	458.88
33000	522.22	513.65	505.96	499.04	492.80	482.06	473.22
34000	538.04	529.21	521.29	514.16	507.74	496.67	487.56
35000	553.87	544.78	536.62	529.29	522.67	511.28	501.90
40000	632.99	622.60	613.28	604.90	597.34	584.32	573.60
45000	712.11	700.43	689.94	680.51	672.01	657.36	645.30
50000	791.24	778.25	766.60	756.12	746.67	730.40	717.00
55000	870.36	856.08	843.26	831.74	821.34	803.43	788.69
60000	949.48	933.90	919.92	907.35	896.01	876.47	860.39
65000	1028.61	1011.73	996.58	982.96	970.67	949.51	932.09
70000	1107.73	1089.55	1073.24	1058.57	1045.34	1022.55	1003.79

15¾% Monthly Loan Payments

LOAN AMOUNT	½ YEAR	1 YEAR	1½ YEARS	2 YEARS	2½ YEARS	3 YEARS	3½ YEARS
100	17.44	9.06	6.27	4.88	4.05	3.50	3.11
200	34.88	18.12	12.55	9.77	8.11	7.01	6.22
300	52.32	27.18	18.82	14.65	12.16	10.51	9.34
400	69.76	36.25	25.10	19.54	16.22	14.01	12.45
500	87.20	45.31	31.37	24.42	20.27	17.52	15.56
600	104.64	54.37	37.64	29.31	24.32	21.02	18.67
700	122.08	63.43	43.92	34.19	28.38	24.52	21.79
800	139.52	72.49	50.19	39.07	32.43	28.03	24.90
900	156.97	81.55	56.46	43.96	36.49	31.53	28.01
1000	174.41	90.61	62.74	48.84	40.54	35.03	31.12
1500	261.61	135.92	94.11	73.27	60.81	52.55	46.69
2000	348.81	181.23	125.48	97.69	81.08	70.07	62.25
2500	436.02	226.53	156.85	122.11	101.35	87.58	77.8
3000	523.22	271.84	188.21	146.53	121.62	105.10	93.37
3500	610.42	317.14	219.58	170.95	141.89	122.62	108.9
4000	697.62	362.45	250.95	195.37	162.16	140.13	124.6
4500	784.83	407.76	282.32	219.80	182.43	157.65	140.0
5000	872.03	453.06	313.69	244.22	202.70	175.17	155.62
5500	959.23	498.37	345.06	268.64	222.97	192.69	171.1
6000	1046.44	543.68	376.43	293.06	243.25	210.20	186.7
6500	1133.64	588.98	407.80	317.48	263.52	227.72	202.3
7000	1220.84	634.29	439.17	341.91	283.79	245.24	217.8
7500	1308.05	679.59	470.54	366.33	304.06	262.75	233.4
8000	1395.25	724.90	501.91	390.75	324.33	280.27	248.9
8500	1482.45	770.21	533.28	415.17	344.60	297.79	264.5
9000	1569.65	815.51	564.64	439.59	364.87	315.30	280.1
9500	1656.86	860.82	596.01	464.02	385.14	332.82	295.6
10000	1744.06	906.13	627.38	488.44	405.41	350.34	311.2
11000	1918.47	996.74	690.12	537.28	445.95	385.37	342.3
12000	2092.87	1087.35	752.86	586.12	486.49	420.40	373.4
13000	2267.28	1177.96	815.60	634.97	527.03	455.44	404.6
14000	2441.69	1268.58	878.34	683.81	567.57	490.47	435.7
15000	2616.09	1359.19	941.07	732.66	608.11	525.51	466.8
16000	2790.50	1449.80	1003.81	781.50	648.65	560.54	497.9
17000	2964.90	1540.41	1066.55	830.34	689.20	595.57	529.1
18000	3139.31	1631.03	1129.29	879.19	729.74	630.61	560.2
19000	3313.72	1721.64	1192.03	928.03	770.28	665.64	591.3
20000	3488.12	1812.25	1254.77	976.87	810.82	700.67	622.4
21000	3662.53	1902.86	1317.50	1025.72	851.36	735.71	653.6
22000	3836.93	1993.48	1380.24	1074.56	891.90	770.74	684.7
23000	4011.34	2084.09	1442.98	1123.41	932.44	805.78	715.8
24000	4185.75	2174.70	1505.72	1172.25	972.98	840.81	746.9
25000	4360.15	2265.31	1568.46	1221.09	1013.52	875.84	778.1
26000	4534.56	2355.93	1631.20	1269.94	1054.06	910.88	809.2
27000	4708.96	2446.54	1693.93	1318.78	1094.60	945.91	840.3
28000	4883.37	2537.15	1756.67	1367.62	1135.14	980.94	871.4
29000	5057.78	2627.77	1819.41	1416.47	1175.69	1015.98	902.6
30000	5232.18	2718.38	1882.15	1465.31	1216.23	1051.01	933.7
31000	5406.59	2808.99	1944.89	1514.16	1256.77	1086.05	964.8
32000	5581.00	2899.60	2007.63	1563.00	1297.31	1121.08	995.9
33000	5755.40	2990.22	2070.36	1611.84	1337.85	1156.11	1027.0
34000	5929.81	3080.83	2133.10	1660.69	1378.39	1191.15	1058.2
35000	6104.21	3171.44	2195.84	1709.53	1418.93	1226.18	1089.3
40000	6976.24	3624.50	2509.53	1953.75	1621.64	1401.35	1244.9
45000	7848.27	4077.57	2823.22	2197.97	1824.34	1576.52	1400.5
50000	8720.31	4530.63	3136.92	2442.19	2027.04	1751.69	1556.2
55000	9592.34	4983.69	3450.61	2686.41	2229.75	1926.86	1711.8
60000	10464.37	5436.76	3764.30	2930.62	2432.45	2102.02	1867.4
65000	11336.40	5889.82	4077.99	3174.84	2635.16	2277.19	2023.0
70000	12208.43	6342.88	4391.68	3419.06	2837.86	2452.36	2178.6

Monthly Loan Payments 15¾%

LOAN AMOUNT	4 YEARS	4½ YEARS	5 YEARS	5½ YEARS	6 YEARS	6½ YEARS	7 YEARS
100	2.82	2.60	2.42	2.27	2.16	2.06	1.97
200	5.64	5.19	4.84	4.55	4.31	4.11	3.94
300	8.46	7.79	7.26	6.82	6.47	6.17	5.92
400	11.28	10.39	9.67	9.10	8.62	8.22	7.89
500	14.11	12.98	12.09	11.37	10.78	10.28	9.86
600	16.93	15.58	14.51	13.65	12.93	12.34	11.83
700	19.75	18.18	16.93	15.92	15.09	14.39	13.80
800	22.57	20.77	19.35	18.19	17.24	16.45	15.78
900	25.39	23.37	21.77	20.47	19.40	18.50	17.75
1000	28.21	25.97	24.19	22.74	21.55	20.56	19.72
1500	42.32	38.95	36.28	34.11	32.33	30.84	29.58
2000	56.42	51.93	48.37	45.49	43.11	41.12	39.44
2500	70.53	64.92	60.46	56.86	53.89	51.40	49.30
3000	84.64	77.90	72.56	68.23	64.66	61.68	59.16
3500	98.74	90.88	84.65	79.60	75.44	71.96	69.02
4000	112.85	103.86	96.74	90.97	86.22	82.24	78.88
4500	126.96	116.85	108.83	102.34	96.99	92.52	88.74
5000	141.06	129.83	120.93	113.72	107.77	102.80	98.60
5500	155.17	142.81	133.02	125.09	118.55	113.08	108.46
6000	169.27	155.80	145.11	136.46	129.33	123.36	118.32
6500	183.38	168.78	157.21	147.83	140.10	133.64	128.18
7000	197.49	181.76	169.30	159.20	150.88	143.92	138.04
7500	211.59	194.75	181.39	170.57	161.66	154.21	147.90
8000	225.70	207.73	193.48	181.94	172.44	164.49	157.76
8500	239.81	220.71	205.58	193.32	183.21	174.77	167.62
9000	253.91	233.70	217.67	204.69	193.99	185.05	177.48
9500	268.02	246.68	229.76	216.06	204.77	195.33	187.34
10000	282.12	259.66	241.85	227.43	215.54	205.61	197.20
11000	310.34	285.63	266.04	250.17	237.10	226.17	216.92
12000	338.55	311.59	290.23	272.92	258.65	246.73	236.64
13000	366.76	337.56	314.41	295.66	280.21	267.29	256.36
14000	394.97	363.53	338.60	318.40	301.76	287.85	276.08
15000	423.18	389.49	362.78	341.15	323.32	308.41	295.80
16000	451.40	415.46	386.97	363.89	344.87	328.97	315.52
17000	479.61	441.42	411.15	386.63	366.43	349.53	335.24
18000	507.82	467.39	435.34	409.38	387.98	370.09	354.96
19000	536.04	493.36	459.52	432.12	409.53	390.65	374.68
20000	564.25	519.32	483.71	454.86	431.09	411.21	394.40
21000	592.46	545.29	507.89	477.61	452.64	431.77	414.12
22000	620.67	571.26	532.08	500.35	474.20	452.34	433.84
23000	648.89	597.22	556.26	523.09	495.75	472.90	453.56
24000	677.10	623.19	580.45	545.83	517.31	493.46	473.28
25000	705.31	649.15	604.64	568.58	538.86	514.02	493.00
26000	733.52	675.12	628.82	591.32	560.42	534.58	512.72
27000	761.73	701.09	653.01	614.06	581.97	555.14	532.44
28000	789.95	727.05	677.19	636.81	603.52	575.70	552.16
29000	818.16	753.02	701.38	659.55	625.08	596.26	571.88
30000	846.37	778.98	725.56	682.29	646.63	616.82	591.60
31000	874.58	804.95	749.75	705.04	668.19	637.38	611.32
32000	902.80	830.92	773.93	727.78	689.74	657.94	631.04
33000	931.01	856.88	798.12	750.52	711.30	678.50	650.76
34000	959.22	882.85	822.30	773.27	732.85	699.06	670.48
35000	987.43	908.82	846.49	796.01	754.41	719.62	690.20
40000	1128.50	1038.65	967.42	909.72	862.18	822.43	788.80
45000	1269.56	1168.48	1088.34	1023.44	969.95	925.23	887.40
50000	1410.62	1298.31	1209.27	1137.16	1077.72	1028.03	986.00
55000	1551.68	1428.14	1330.20	1250.87	1185.49	1130.84	1084.60
60000	1692.74	1557.97	1451.13	1364.59	1293.27	1233.64	1183.20
65000	1833.81	1687.80	1572.05	1478.30	1401.04	1336.44	1281.80
70000	1974.87	1817.63	1692.98	1592.02	1508.81	1439.25	1380.40

15¾% Monthly Loan Payments

LOAN AMOUNT	7½ YEARS	8 YEARS	8½ YEARS	9 YEARS	9½ YEARS	10 YEARS	10½ YEARS
100	1.90	1.84	1.78	1.74	1.70	1.66	1.63
200	3.80	3.68	3.57	3.47	3.39	3.32	3.25
300	5.70	5.51	5.35	5.21	5.09	4.98	4.88
400	7.60	7.35	7.14	6.95	6.78	6.64	6.51
500	9.50	9.19	8.92	8.69	8.48	8.30	8.14
600	11.40	11.03	10.71	10.42	10.18	9.96	9.76
700	13.30	12.87	12.49	12.16	11.87	11.62	11.39
800	15.20	14.71	14.28	13.90	13.57	13.28	13.02
900	17.10	16.54	16.06	15.64	15.26	14.94	14.64
1000	19.00	18.38	17.84	17.37	16.96	16.60	16.27
1500	28.50	27.57	26.77	26.06	25.44	24.89	24.41
2000	38.00	36.76	35.69	34.75	33.92	33.19	32.54
2500	47.50	45.96	44.61	43.44	42.40	41.49	40.68
3000	57.00	55.15	53.53	52.12	50.88	49.79	48.82
3500	66.50	64.34	62.45	60.81	59.36	58.09	56.95
4000	76.01	73.53	71.38	69.50	67.84	66.38	65.09
4500	85.51	82.72	80.30	78.18	76.32	74.68	73.22
5000	95.01	91.91	89.22	86.87	84.80	82.98	81.36
5500	104.51	101.10	98.14	95.56	93.28	91.28	89.50
6000	114.01	110.29	107.07	104.24	101.77	99.58	97.63
6500	123.51	119.48	115.99	112.93	110.25	107.87	105.77
7000	133.01	128.67	124.91	121.62	118.73	116.17	113.90
7500	142.51	137.87	133.83	130.31	127.21	124.47	122.04
8000	152.01	147.06	142.75	138.99	135.69	132.77	130.18
8500	161.51	156.25	151.68	147.68	144.17	141.06	138.31
9000	171.01	165.44	160.60	156.37	152.65	149.36	146.45
9500	180.51	174.63	169.52	165.05	161.13	157.66	154.58
10000	190.01	183.82	178.44	173.74	169.61	165.96	162.72
11000	209.02	202.20	196.29	191.11	186.57	182.55	178.99
12000	228.02	220.58	214.13	208.49	203.53	199.15	195.26
13000	247.02	238.97	231.97	225.86	220.49	215.75	211.54
14000	266.02	257.35	249.82	243.24	237.45	232.34	227.81
15000	285.02	275.73	267.66	260.61	254.41	248.94	244.08
16000	304.02	294.11	285.51	277.99	271.37	265.53	260.35
17000	323.02	312.50	303.35	295.36	288.33	282.13	276.62
18000	342.02	330.88	321.20	312.73	305.30	298.73	292.90
19000	361.03	349.26	339.04	330.11	322.26	315.32	309.17
20000	380.03	367.64	356.88	347.48	339.22	331.92	325.44
21000	399.03	386.02	374.73	364.86	356.18	348.51	341.71
22000	418.03	404.41	392.57	382.23	373.14	365.11	357.98
23000	437.03	422.79	410.42	399.60	390.10	381.70	374.26
24000	456.03	441.17	428.26	416.98	407.06	398.30	390.53
25000	475.04	459.55	446.10	434.35	424.02	414.90	406.80
26000	494.04	477.93	463.95	451.73	440.98	431.49	423.07
27000	513.04	496.32	481.79	469.10	457.94	448.09	439.34
28000	532.04	514.70	499.64	486.47	474.90	464.68	455.62
29000	551.04	533.08	517.48	503.85	491.86	481.28	471.89
30000	570.04	551.46	535.33	521.22	508.83	497.88	488.16
31000	589.04	569.84	553.17	538.60	525.79	514.47	504.43
32000	608.05	588.23	571.01	555.97	542.75	531.07	520.70
33000	627.05	606.61	588.86	573.34	559.71	547.66	536.98
34000	646.05	624.99	606.70	590.72	576.67	564.26	553.25
35000	665.05	643.37	624.55	608.09	593.63	580.85	569.52
40000	760.06	735.28	713.77	694.96	678.43	663.83	650.88
45000	855.06	827.19	802.99	781.83	763.24	746.81	732.24
50000	950.07	919.10	892.21	868.70	848.04	829.79	813.60
55000	1045.08	1011.01	981.43	955.57	932.85	912.77	894.96
60000	1140.09	1102.92	1070.65	1042.44	1017.65	995.75	976.32
65000	1235.09	1194.83	1159.87	1129.31	1102.46	1078.73	1057.68
70000	1330.10	1286.74	1249.09	1216.19	1187.26	1161.71	1139.04

Monthly Loan Payments 15¾%

LOAN AMOUNT	11 YEARS	11½ YEARS	12 YEARS	12½ YEARS	13 YEARS	14 YEARS	15 YEARS
100	1.60	1.57	1.55	1.53	1.51	1.48	1.45
200	3.20	3.15	3.10	3.06	3.02	2.96	2.90
300	4.80	4.72	4.65	4.59	4.53	4.43	4.35
400	6.39	6.29	6.20	6.11	6.04	5.91	5.81
500	7.99	7.86	7.75	7.64	7.55	7.39	7.26
600	9.59	9.44	9.30	9.17	9.06	8.87	8.71
700	11.19	11.01	10.85	10.70	10.57	10.34	10.16
800	12.79	12.58	12.40	12.23	12.08	11.82	11.61
900	14.39	14.15	13.95	13.76	13.59	13.30	13.06
1000	15.98	15.73	15.49	15.29	15.10	14.78	14.51
1500	23.98	23.59	23.24	22.93	22.65	22.17	21.77
2000	31.97	31.45	30.99	30.57	30.20	29.56	29.03
2500	39.96	39.31	38.74	38.22	37.75	36.94	36.28
3000	47.95	47.18	46.48	45.86	45.30	44.33	43.54
3500	55.94	55.04	54.23	53.50	52.85	51.72	50.80
4000	63.93	62.90	61.98	61.15	60.40	59.11	58.05
4500	71.93	70.77	69.73	68.79	67.95	66.50	65.31
5000	79.92	78.63	77.47	76.44	75.50	73.89	72.57
5500	87.91	86.49	85.22	84.08	83.05	81.28	79.82
6000	95.90	94.36	92.97	91.72	90.60	88.67	87.08
6500	103.89	102.22	100.72	99.37	98.15	96.06	94.34
7000	111.89	110.08	108.46	107.01	105.70	103.44	101.59
7500	119.88	117.94	116.21	114.65	113.25	110.83	108.85
8000	127.87	125.81	123.96	122.30	120.80	118.22	116.10
8500	135.86	133.67	131.71	129.94	128.35	125.61	123.36
9000	143.85	141.53	139.45	137.58	135.90	133.00	130.62
9500	151.84	149.40	147.20	145.23	143.45	140.39	137.87
10000	159.84	157.26	154.95	152.87	151.00	147.78	145.13
11000	175.82	172.98	170.44	168.16	166.10	162.56	159.64
12000	191.80	188.71	185.94	183.44	181.20	177.33	174.16
13000	207.79	204.44	201.43	198.73	196.30	192.11	188.67
14000	223.77	220.16	216.93	214.02	211.40	206.89	203.18
15000	239.75	235.89	232.42	229.31	226.50	221.67	217.70
16000	255.74	251.61	247.92	244.59	241.60	236.44	232.21
17000	271.72	267.34	263.41	259.88	256.70	251.22	246.72
18000	287.70	283.07	278.91	275.17	271.80	266.00	261.24
19000	303.69	298.79	294.40	290.45	286.90	280.78	275.75
20000	319.67	314.52	309.90	305.74	302.00	295.56	290.26
21000	335.66	330.24	325.39	321.03	317.10	310.33	304.77
22000	351.64	345.97	340.89	336.32	332.20	325.11	319.29
23000	367.62	361.69	356.38	351.60	347.30	339.89	333.80
24000	383.61	377.42	371.87	366.89	362.40	354.67	348.31
25000	399.59	393.15	387.37	382.18	377.50	369.45	362.83
26000	415.57	408.87	402.86	397.46	392.60	384.22	377.34
27000	431.56	424.60	418.36	412.75	407.70	399.00	391.85
28000	447.54	440.32	433.85	428.04	422.80	413.78	406.37
29000	463.52	456.05	449.35	443.32	437.90	428.56	420.88
30000	479.51	471.78	464.84	458.61	453.00	443.33	435.39
31000	495.49	487.50	480.34	473.90	468.10	458.11	449.91
32000	511.48	503.23	495.83	489.19	483.20	472.89	464.42
33000	527.46	518.95	511.33	504.47	498.30	487.67	478.93
34000	543.44	534.68	526.82	519.76	513.40	502.45	493.44
35000	559.43	550.40	542.32	535.05	528.50	517.22	507.96
40000	639.34	629.03	619.79	611.48	604.00	591.11	580.52
45000	719.26	707.66	697.27	687.92	679.49	665.00	653.09
50000	799.18	786.29	774.74	764.35	754.99	738.89	725.65
55000	879.10	864.92	852.21	840.79	830.49	812.78	798.22
60000	959.02	943.55	929.69	917.22	905.99	886.67	870.78
65000	1038.93	1022.18	1007.16	993.66	981.49	960.56	943.35
70000	1118.85	1100.81	1084.63	1070.09	1056.99	1034.45	1015.92

16%   Monthly Loan Payments

LOAN AMOUNT	½ YEAR	1 YEAR	1½ YEARS	2 YEARS	2½ YEARS	3 YEARS	3½ YEARS
100	17.45	9.07	6.29	4.90	4.07	3.52	3.12
200	34.91	18.15	12.57	9.79	8.13	7.03	6.25
300	52.36	27.22	18.86	14.69	12.20	10.55	9.37
400	69.81	36.29	25.14	19.59	16.26	14.06	12.50
500	87.27	45.37	31.43	24.48	20.33	17.58	15.62
600	104.72	54.44	37.71	29.38	24.40	21.09	18.75
700	122.17	63.51	44.00	34.27	28.46	24.61	21.87
800	139.62	72.58	50.29	39.17	32.53	28.13	25.00
900	157.08	81.66	56.57	44.07	36.60	31.64	28.12
1000	174.53	90.73	62.86	48.96	40.66	35.16	31.25
1500	261.80	136.10	94.28	73.44	60.99	52.74	46.87
2000	349.06	181.46	125.71	97.93	81.32	70.31	62.50
2500	436.33	226.83	157.14	122.41	101.66	87.89	78.12
3000	523.59	272.19	188.57	146.89	121.99	105.47	93.75
3500	610.86	317.56	220.00	171.37	142.32	123.05	109.37
4000	698.12	362.92	251.43	195.85	162.65	140.63	125.00
4500	785.39	408.29	282.85	220.33	182.98	158.21	140.62
5000	872.65	453.65	314.28	244.82	203.31	175.79	156.25
5500	959.92	499.02	345.71	269.30	223.64	193.36	171.87
6000	1047.18	544.39	377.14	293.78	243.97	210.94	187.50
6500	1134.45	589.75	408.57	318.26	264.30	228.52	203.12
7000	1221.71	635.12	440.00	342.74	284.63	246.10	218.75
7500	1308.98	680.48	471.42	367.22	304.97	263.68	234.37
8000	1396.24	725.85	502.85	391.70	325.30	281.26	250.00
8500	1483.51	771.21	534.28	416.19	345.63	298.83	265.62
9000	1570.77	816.58	565.71	440.67	365.96	316.41	281.25
9500	1658.04	861.94	597.14	465.15	386.29	333.99	296.87
10000	1745.30	907.31	628.56	489.63	406.62	351.57	312.50
11000	1919.83	998.04	691.42	538.59	447.28	386.73	343.74
12000	2094.36	1088.77	754.28	587.56	487.94	421.88	374.99
13000	2268.89	1179.50	817.13	636.52	528.61	457.04	406.24
14000	2443.42	1270.23	879.99	685.48	569.27	492.20	437.49
15000	2617.95	1360.96	942.85	734.45	609.93	527.36	468.74
16000	2792.48	1451.69	1005.70	783.41	650.59	562.51	499.99
17000	2967.01	1542.42	1068.56	832.37	691.26	597.67	531.24
18000	3141.54	1633.16	1131.42	881.34	731.92	632.83	562.49
19000	3316.08	1723.89	1194.27	930.30	772.58	667.98	593.74
20000	3490.61	1814.62	1257.13	979.26	813.24	703.14	624.99
21000	3665.14	1905.35	1319.99	1028.23	853.90	738.30	656.24
22000	3839.67	1996.08	1382.84	1077.19	894.57	773.45	687.49
23000	4014.20	2086.81	1445.70	1126.15	935.23	808.61	718.74
24000	4188.73	2177.54	1508.55	1175.11	975.89	843.77	749.99
25000	4363.26	2268.27	1571.41	1224.08	1016.55	878.93	781.24
26000	4537.79	2359.00	1634.27	1273.04	1057.21	914.08	812.49
27000	4712.32	2449.73	1697.12	1322.00	1097.88	949.24	843.74
28000	4886.85	2540.46	1759.98	1370.97	1138.54	984.40	874.99
29000	5061.38	2631.19	1822.84	1419.93	1179.20	1019.55	906.24
30000	5235.91	2721.93	1885.69	1468.89	1219.86	1054.71	937.49
31000	5410.44	2812.66	1948.55	1517.86	1260.52	1089.87	968.73
32000	5584.97	2903.39	2011.41	1566.82	1301.19	1125.03	999.98
33000	5759.50	2994.12	2074.26	1615.78	1341.85	1160.18	1031.23
34000	5934.03	3084.85	2137.12	1664.75	1382.51	1195.34	1062.48
35000	6108.56	3175.58	2199.98	1713.71	1423.17	1230.50	1093.73
40000	6981.21	3629.23	2514.26	1958.52	1626.48	1406.28	1249.98
45000	7853.86	4082.89	2828.54	2203.34	1829.79	1582.07	1406.23
50000	8726.51	4536.54	3142.82	2448.16	2033.10	1757.85	1562.48
55000	9599.17	4990.20	3457.10	2692.97	2236.41	1933.64	1718.72
60000	10471.82	5443.85	3771.39	2937.79	2439.72	2109.42	1874.97
65000	11344.47	5897.51	4085.67	3182.60	2643.04	2285.21	2031.22
70000	12217.12	6351.16	4399.95	3427.42	2846.35	2460.99	2187.47

Monthly Loan Payments 16%

LOAN AMOUNT	4 YEARS	4½ YEARS	5 YEARS	5½ YEARS	6 YEARS	6½ YEARS	7 YEARS
100	2.83	2.61	2.43	2.29	2.17	2.07	1.99
200	5.67	5.22	4.86	4.58	4.34	4.14	3.97
300	8.50	7.83	7.30	6.86	6.51	6.21	5.96
400	11.34	10.44	9.73	9.15	8.68	8.28	7.94
500	14.17	13.05	12.16	11.44	10.85	10.35	9.93
600	17.00	15.66	14.59	13.73	13.02	12.42	11.92
700	19.84	18.27	17.02	16.01	15.18	14.49	13.90
800	22.67	20.88	19.45	18.30	17.35	16.56	15.89
900	25.51	23.49	21.89	20.59	19.52	18.63	17.88
1000	28.34	26.10	24.32	22.88	21.69	20.70	19.86
1500	42.51	39.14	36.48	34.32	32.54	31.05	29.79
2000	56.68	52.19	48.64	45.76	43.38	41.40	39.72
2500	70.85	65.24	60.80	57.20	54.23	51.75	49.66
3000	85.02	78.29	72.95	68.63	65.08	62.10	59.59
3500	99.19	91.34	85.11	80.07	75.92	72.45	69.52
4000	113.36	104.39	97.27	91.51	86.77	82.80	79.45
4500	127.53	117.43	109.43	102.95	97.61	93.15	89.38
5000	141.70	130.48	121.59	114.39	108.46	103.50	99.31
5500	155.87	143.53	133.75	125.83	119.31	113.85	109.24
6000	170.04	156.58	145.91	137.27	130.15	124.20	119.17
6500	184.21	169.63	158.07	148.71	141.00	134.55	129.10
7000	198.38	182.67	170.23	160.15	151.84	144.90	139.03
7500	212.55	195.72	182.39	171.59	162.69	155.25	148.97
8000	226.72	208.77	194.54	183.03	173.53	165.60	158.90
8500	240.89	221.82	206.70	194.46	184.38	175.95	168.83
9000	255.06	234.87	218.86	205.90	195.23	186.30	178.76
9500	269.23	247.92	231.02	217.34	206.07	196.65	188.69
10000	283.40	260.96	243.18	228.78	216.92	207.00	198.62
11000	311.74	287.06	267.50	251.66	238.61	227.71	218.48
12000	340.08	313.16	291.82	274.54	260.30	248.41	238.34
13000	368.42	339.25	316.13	297.42	281.99	269.11	258.21
14000	396.76	365.35	340.45	320.29	303.69	289.81	278.07
15000	425.10	391.45	364.77	343.17	325.38	310.51	297.93
16000	453.44	417.54	389.09	366.05	347.07	331.21	317.79
17000	481.78	443.64	413.41	388.93	368.76	351.91	337.66
18000	510.13	469.73	437.73	411.81	390.45	372.61	357.52
19000	538.47	495.83	462.04	434.68	412.14	393.31	377.38
20000	566.81	521.93	486.36	457.56	433.84	414.01	397.24
21000	595.15	548.02	510.68	480.44	455.53	434.71	417.10
22000	623.49	574.12	535.00	503.32	477.22	455.41	436.97
23000	651.83	600.22	559.32	526.20	498.91	476.11	456.83
24000	680.17	626.31	583.63	549.08	520.60	496.81	476.69
25000	708.51	652.41	607.95	571.95	542.30	517.51	496.55
26000	736.85	678.51	632.27	594.83	563.99	538.21	516.41
27000	765.19	704.60	656.59	617.71	585.68	558.91	536.28
28000	793.53	730.70	680.91	640.59	607.37	579.61	556.14
29000	821.87	756.80	705.22	663.47	629.06	600.31	576.00
30000	850.21	782.89	729.54	686.34	650.76	621.01	595.86
31000	878.55	808.99	753.86	709.22	672.45	641.71	615.72
32000	906.89	835.08	778.18	732.10	694.14	662.41	635.59
33000	935.23	861.18	802.50	754.98	715.83	683.12	655.45
34000	963.57	887.28	826.81	777.86	737.52	703.82	675.31
35000	991.91	913.37	851.13	800.73	759.21	724.52	695.17
40000	1133.61	1043.86	972.72	915.13	867.67	828.02	794.48
45000	1275.31	1174.34	1094.31	1029.52	976.13	931.52	893.79
50000	1417.01	1304.82	1215.90	1143.91	1084.59	1035.02	993.10
55000	1558.72	1435.30	1337.49	1258.30	1193.05	1138.53	1092.41
60000	1700.42	1565.78	1459.08	1372.69	1301.51	1242.03	1191.72
65000	1842.12	1696.27	1580.67	1487.08	1409.97	1345.53	1291.03
70000	1983.82	1826.75	1702.26	1601.47	1518.43	1449.03	1390.34

16% Monthly Loan Payments

LOAN AMOUNT	7½ YEARS	8 YEARS	8½ YEARS	9 YEARS	9½ YEARS	10 YEARS	10½ YEARS
100	1.91	1.85	1.80	1.75	1.71	1.68	1.64
200	3.83	3.71	3.60	3.51	3.42	3.35	3.29
300	5.74	5.56	5.40	5.26	5.13	5.03	4.93
400	7.66	7.41	7.20	7.01	6.85	6.70	6.57
500	9.57	9.26	9.00	8.76	8.56	8.38	8.21
600	11.49	11.12	10.80	10.52	10.27	10.05	9.86
700	13.40	12.97	12.60	12.27	11.98	11.73	11.50
800	15.32	14.82	14.39	14.02	13.69	13.40	13.14
900	17.23	16.68	16.19	15.77	15.40	15.08	14.79
1000	19.15	18.53	17.99	17.53	17.11	16.75	16.43
1500	28.72	27.79	26.99	26.29	25.67	25.13	24.64
2000	38.29	37.06	35.99	35.05	34.23	33.50	32.86
2500	47.86	46.32	44.98	43.81	42.79	41.88	41.07
3000	57.44	55.59	53.98	52.58	51.34	50.25	49.29
3500	67.01	64.85	62.98	61.34	59.90	58.63	57.50
4000	76.58	74.12	71.97	70.10	68.46	67.01	65.72
4500	86.16	83.38	80.97	78.86	77.01	75.38	73.93
5000	95.73	92.64	89.97	87.63	85.57	83.76	82.15
5500	105.30	101.91	98.96	96.39	94.13	92.13	90.36
6000	114.88	111.17	107.96	105.15	102.69	100.51	98.58
6500	124.45	120.44	116.96	113.91	111.24	108.88	106.79
7000	134.02	129.70	125.95	122.68	119.80	117.26	115.01
7500	143.59	138.97	134.95	131.44	128.36	125.63	123.22
8000	153.17	148.23	143.95	140.20	136.91	134.01	131.44
8500	162.74	157.49	152.94	148.96	145.47	142.39	139.65
9000	172.31	166.76	161.94	157.73	154.03	150.76	147.87
9500	181.89	176.02	170.94	166.49	162.58	159.14	156.08
10000	191.46	185.29	179.93	175.25	171.14	167.51	164.30
11000	210.60	203.82	197.92	192.78	188.26	184.26	180.73
12000	229.75	222.35	215.92	210.30	205.37	201.02	197.15
13000	248.90	240.87	233.91	227.83	222.48	217.77	213.58
14000	268.04	259.40	251.90	245.35	239.60	234.52	230.01
15000	287.19	277.93	269.90	262.88	256.71	251.27	246.44
16000	306.33	296.46	287.89	280.40	273.83	268.02	262.87
17000	325.48	314.99	305.88	297.93	290.94	284.77	279.30
18000	344.63	333.52	323.88	315.45	308.06	301.52	295.73
19000	363.77	352.05	341.87	332.98	325.17	318.27	312.16
20000	382.92	370.58	359.86	350.51	342.28	335.03	328.59
21000	402.06	389.10	377.86	368.03	359.40	351.78	345.02
22000	421.21	407.63	395.85	385.56	376.51	368.53	361.45
23000	440.35	426.16	413.84	403.08	393.63	385.28	377.88
24000	459.50	444.69	431.84	420.61	410.74	402.03	394.31
25000	478.65	463.22	449.83	438.13	427.85	418.78	410.74
26000	497.79	481.75	467.82	455.66	444.97	435.53	427.17
27000	516.94	500.28	485.82	473.18	462.08	452.29	443.60
28000	536.08	518.81	503.81	490.71	479.20	469.04	460.03
29000	555.23	537.33	521.80	508.23	496.31	485.79	476.46
30000	574.38	555.86	539.79	525.76	513.43	502.54	492.89
31000	593.52	574.39	557.79	543.28	530.54	519.29	509.32
32000	612.67	592.92	575.78	560.81	547.65	536.04	525.75
33000	631.81	611.45	593.77	578.33	564.77	552.79	542.18
34000	650.96	629.98	611.77	595.86	581.88	569.54	558.60
35000	670.11	648.51	629.76	613.38	599.00	586.30	575.03
40000	765.83	741.15	719.73	701.01	684.57	670.05	657.18
45000	861.56	833.80	809.69	788.64	770.14	753.81	739.33
50000	957.29	926.44	899.66	876.26	855.71	837.57	821.48
55000	1053.02	1019.08	989.62	963.89	941.28	921.32	903.63
60000	1148.75	1111.73	1079.59	1051.52	1026.85	1005.08	985.77
65000	1244.48	1204.37	1169.56	1139.14	1112.42	1088.84	1067.92
70000	1340.21	1297.02	1259.52	1226.77	1197.99	1172.59	1150.07

Monthly Loan Payments 16%

LOAN AMOUNT	11 YEARS	11½ YEARS	12 YEARS	12½ YEARS	13 YEARS	14 YEARS	15 YEARS
100	1.61	1.59	1.57	1.55	1.53	1.49	1.47
200	3.23	3.18	3.13	3.09	3.05	2.99	2.94
300	4.84	4.77	4.70	4.64	4.58	4.48	4.41
400	6.46	6.35	6.26	6.18	6.11	5.98	5.87
500	8.07	7.94	7.83	7.73	7.63	7.47	7.34
600	9.69	9.53	9.39	9.27	9.16	8.97	8.81
700	11.30	11.12	10.96	10.82	10.69	10.46	10.28
800	12.91	12.71	12.53	12.36	12.21	11.96	11.75
900	14.53	14.30	14.09	13.91	13.74	13.45	13.22
1000	16.14	15.89	15.66	15.45	15.27	14.95	14.69
1500	24.21	23.83	23.49	23.18	22.90	22.42	22.03
2000	32.29	31.77	31.32	30.90	30.53	29.90	29.37
2500	40.36	39.72	39.15	38.63	38.17	37.37	36.72
3000	48.43	47.66	46.97	46.36	45.80	44.85	44.06
3500	56.50	55.61	54.80	54.08	53.43	52.32	51.40
4000	64.57	63.55	62.63	61.81	61.07	59.79	58.75
4500	72.64	71.49	70.46	69.54	68.70	67.27	66.09
5000	80.72	79.44	78.29	77.26	76.34	74.74	73.44
5500	88.79	87.38	86.12	84.99	83.97	82.22	80.78
6000	96.86	95.32	93.95	92.71	91.60	89.69	88.12
6500	104.93	103.27	101.78	100.44	99.24	97.16	95.47
7000	113.00	111.21	109.61	108.17	106.87	104.64	102.81
7500	121.07	119.16	117.44	115.89	114.50	112.11	110.15
8000	129.15	127.10	125.27	123.62	122.14	119.59	117.50
8500	137.22	135.04	133.10	131.35	129.77	127.06	124.84
9000	145.29	142.99	140.92	139.07	137.40	134.54	132.18
9500	153.36	150.93	148.75	146.80	145.04	142.01	139.53
10000	161.43	158.87	156.58	154.52	152.67	149.48	146.87
11000	177.57	174.76	172.24	169.98	167.94	164.43	161.56
12000	193.72	190.65	187.90	185.43	183.20	179.38	176.24
13000	209.86	206.54	203.56	200.88	198.47	194.33	190.93
14000	226.00	222.42	219.22	216.33	213.74	209.28	205.62
15000	242.15	238.31	234.87	231.79	229.01	224.23	220.31
16000	258.29	254.20	250.53	247.24	244.27	239.18	234.99
17000	274.43	270.09	266.19	262.69	259.54	254.12	249.68
18000	290.58	285.97	281.85	278.14	274.81	269.07	264.37
19000	306.72	301.86	297.51	293.60	290.07	284.02	279.05
20000	322.86	317.75	313.17	309.05	305.34	298.97	293.74
21000	339.01	333.64	328.82	324.50	320.61	313.92	308.43
22000	355.15	349.52	344.48	339.95	335.87	328.87	323.11
23000	371.29	365.41	360.14	355.41	351.14	343.81	337.80
24000	387.44	381.30	375.80	370.86	366.41	358.76	352.49
25000	403.58	397.18	391.46	386.31	381.68	373.71	367.18
26000	419.72	413.07	407.11	401.76	396.94	388.66	381.86
27000	435.87	428.96	422.77	417.22	412.21	403.61	396.55
28000	452.01	444.85	438.43	432.67	427.48	418.56	411.24
29000	468.15	460.73	454.09	448.12	442.74	433.51	425.92
30000	484.30	476.62	469.75	463.57	458.01	448.45	440.61
31000	500.44	492.51	485.41	479.02	473.28	463.40	455.30
32000	516.58	508.40	501.06	494.48	488.55	478.35	469.98
33000	532.72	524.28	516.72	509.93	503.81	493.30	484.67
34000	548.87	540.17	532.38	525.38	519.08	508.25	499.36
35000	565.01	556.06	548.04	540.83	534.35	523.20	514.05
40000	645.73	635.50	626.33	618.10	610.68	597.94	587.48
45000	726.44	714.93	704.62	695.36	687.02	672.68	660.92
50000	807.16	794.37	782.91	772.62	763.35	747.42	734.35
55000	887.87	873.81	861.20	849.88	839.69	822.16	807.79
60000	968.59	953.24	939.50	927.14	916.02	896.91	881.22
65000	1049.31	1032.68	1017.79	1004.41	992.36	971.65	954.66
70000	1130.02	1112.12	1096.08	1081.67	1068.69	1046.39	1028.09

16¼% Monthly Loan Payments

LOAN AMOUNT	½ YEAR	1 YEAR	1½ YEARS	2 YEARS	2½ YEARS	3 YEARS	3½ YEARS
100	17.47	9.08	6.30	4.91	4.08	3.53	3.14
200	34.93	18.17	12.59	9.82	8.16	7.06	6.28
300	52.40	27.25	18.89	14.72	12.24	10.58	9.41
400	69.86	36.34	25.19	19.63	16.31	14.11	12.55
500	87.33	45.42	31.49	24.54	20.39	17.64	15.69
600	104.79	54.51	37.78	29.45	24.47	21.17	18.83
700	122.26	63.59	44.08	34.36	28.55	24.70	21.96
800	139.72	72.68	50.38	39.27	32.63	28.22	25.10
900	157.19	81.76	56.68	44.17	36.71	31.75	28.24
1000	174.65	90.85	62.97	49.08	40.78	35.28	31.38
1500	261.98	136.27	94.46	73.62	61.18	52.92	47.06
2000	349.31	181.70	125.95	98.17	81.57	70.56	62.75
2500	436.64	227.12	157.44	122.71	101.96	88.20	78.44
3000	523.96	272.55	188.92	147.25	122.35	105.84	94.13
3500	611.29	317.97	220.41	171.79	142.74	123.48	109.81
4000	698.62	363.40	251.90	196.33	163.13	141.12	125.50
4500	785.95	408.82	283.39	220.87	183.53	158.76	141.19
5000	873.27	454.25	314.87	245.41	203.92	176.40	156.88
5500	960.60	499.67	346.36	269.95	224.31	194.04	172.56
6000	1047.93	545.10	377.85	294.50	244.70	211.68	188.25
6500	1135.25	590.52	409.34	319.04	265.09	229.32	203.94
7000	1222.58	635.94	440.82	343.58	285.48	246.96	219.63
7500	1309.91	681.37	472.31	368.12	305.88	264.60	235.32
8000	1397.24	726.79	503.80	392.66	326.27	282.24	251.00
8500	1484.56	772.22	535.28	417.20	346.66	299.88	266.69
9000	1571.89	817.64	566.77	441.74	367.05	317.53	282.38
9500	1659.22	863.07	598.26	466.29	387.44	335.17	298.07
10000	1746.55	908.49	629.75	490.83	407.83	352.81	313.75
11000	1921.20	999.34	692.72	539.91	448.62	388.09	345.13
12000	2095.85	1090.19	755.70	588.99	489.40	423.37	376.50
13000	2270.51	1181.04	818.67	638.07	530.19	458.65	407.88
14000	2445.16	1271.89	881.65	687.16	570.97	493.93	439.25
15000	2619.82	1362.74	944.62	736.24	611.75	529.21	470.63
16000	2794.47	1453.59	1007.59	785.32	652.54	564.49	502.01
17000	2969.13	1544.44	1070.57	834.40	693.32	599.77	533.38
18000	3143.78	1635.29	1133.54	883.49	734.10	635.05	564.76
19000	3318.44	1726.13	1196.52	932.57	774.89	670.33	596.13
20000	3493.09	1816.98	1259.49	981.65	815.67	705.61	627.51
21000	3667.74	1907.83	1322.47	1030.74	856.45	740.89	658.88
22000	3842.40	1998.68	1385.44	1079.82	897.24	776.17	690.26
23000	4017.05	2089.53	1448.42	1128.90	938.02	811.45	721.63
24000	4191.71	2180.38	1511.39	1177.98	978.80	846.73	753.00
25000	4366.36	2271.23	1574.37	1227.07	1019.59	882.01	784.38
26000	4541.02	2362.08	1637.34	1276.15	1060.37	917.30	815.76
27000	4715.67	2452.93	1700.32	1325.23	1101.15	952.58	847.13
28000	4890.33	2543.78	1763.29	1374.31	1141.94	987.86	878.51
29000	5064.98	2634.63	1826.27	1423.40	1182.72	1023.14	909.89
30000	5239.64	2725.48	1889.24	1472.48	1223.50	1058.42	941.26
31000	5414.29	2816.33	1952.21	1521.56	1264.29	1093.70	972.64
32000	5588.94	2907.17	2015.19	1570.64	1305.07	1128.98	1004.01
33000	5763.60	2998.02	2078.16	1619.73	1345.86	1164.26	1035.39
34000	5938.25	3088.87	2141.14	1668.81	1386.64	1199.54	1066.76
35000	6112.91	3179.72	2204.11	1717.89	1427.42	1234.82	1098.14
40000	6986.18	3633.97	2518.99	1963.31	1631.34	1411.22	1255.01
45000	7859.45	4088.21	2833.86	2208.72	1835.26	1587.63	1411.89
50000	8732.73	4542.46	3148.73	2454.13	2039.17	1764.03	1568.77
55000	9606.00	4996.71	3463.61	2699.55	2243.09	1940.43	1725.64
60000	10479.27	5450.95	3778.48	2944.96	2447.01	2116.83	1882.52
65000	11352.54	5905.20	4093.35	3190.37	2650.93	2293.24	2039.40
70000	12225.82	6359.44	4408.23	3435.79	2854.84	2469.64	2196.27

Monthly Loan Payments 16¼%

LOAN AMOUNT	4 YEARS	4½ YEARS	5 YEARS	5½ YEARS	6 YEARS	6½ YEARS	7 YEARS
100	2.85	2.62	2.45	2.30	2.18	2.08	2.00
200	5.69	5.25	4.89	4.60	4.37	4.17	4.00
300	8.54	7.87	7.34	6.90	6.55	6.25	6.00
400	11.39	10.49	9.78	9.21	8.73	8.34	8.00
500	14.23	13.11	12.23	11.51	10.91	10.42	10.00
600	17.08	15.74	14.67	13.81	13.10	12.50	12.00
700	19.93	18.36	17.12	16.11	15.28	14.59	14.00
800	22.77	20.98	19.56	18.41	17.46	16.67	16.00
900	25.62	23.60	22.01	20.71	19.65	18.76	18.00
1000	28.47	26.23	24.45	23.01	21.83	20.84	20.00
1500	42.70	39.34	36.68	34.52	32.74	31.26	30.01
2000	56.94	52.45	48.90	46.03	43.66	41.68	40.01
2500	71.17	65.57	61.13	57.53	54.57	52.10	50.01
3000	85.41	78.68	73.35	69.04	65.49	62.52	60.01
3500	99.64	91.79	85.58	80.55	76.40	72.94	70.02
4000	113.87	104.91	97.80	92.05	87.32	83.36	80.02
4500	128.11	118.02	110.03	103.56	98.23	93.78	90.02
5000	142.34	131.13	122.26	115.07	109.15	104.20	100.02
5500	156.58	144.25	134.48	126.57	120.06	114.62	110.03
6000	170.81	157.36	146.71	138.08	130.98	125.04	120.03
6500	185.05	170.48	158.93	149.59	141.89	135.46	130.03
7000	199.28	183.59	171.16	161.10	152.81	145.89	140.03
7500	213.51	196.70	183.38	172.60	163.72	156.31	150.04
8000	227.75	209.82	195.61	184.11	174.64	166.73	160.04
8500	241.98	222.93	207.83	195.62	185.55	177.15	170.04
9000	256.22	236.04	220.06	207.12	196.47	187.57	180.04
9500	270.45	249.16	232.29	218.63	207.38	197.99	190.04
10000	284.68	262.27	244.51	230.14	218.30	208.41	200.05
11000	313.15	288.50	268.96	253.15	240.13	229.25	220.05
12000	341.62	314.72	293.41	276.16	261.96	250.09	240.06
13000	370.09	340.95	317.86	299.18	283.79	270.93	260.06
14000	398.56	367.18	342.32	322.19	305.62	291.77	280.07
15000	427.03	393.40	366.77	345.20	327.45	312.61	300.07
16000	455.50	419.63	391.22	368.22	349.28	333.45	320.08
17000	483.96	445.86	415.67	391.23	371.11	354.29	340.08
18000	512.43	472.09	440.12	414.24	392.93	375.13	360.08
19000	540.90	498.31	464.57	437.26	414.76	395.97	380.09
20000	569.37	524.54	489.02	460.27	436.59	416.81	400.09
21000	597.84	550.77	513.47	483.29	458.42	437.66	420.10
22000	626.31	576.99	537.92	506.30	480.25	458.50	440.10
23000	654.78	603.22	562.38	529.31	502.08	479.34	460.11
24000	683.24	629.45	586.83	552.33	523.91	500.18	480.11
25000	711.71	655.67	611.28	575.34	545.74	521.02	500.12
26000	740.18	681.90	635.73	598.35	567.57	541.86	520.12
27000	768.65	708.13	660.18	621.37	589.40	562.70	540.13
28000	797.12	734.36	684.63	644.38	611.23	583.54	560.13
29000	825.59	760.58	709.08	667.39	633.06	604.38	580.14
30000	854.05	786.81	733.53	690.41	654.89	625.22	600.14
31000	882.52	813.04	757.98	713.42	676.72	646.06	620.15
32000	910.99	839.26	782.43	736.44	698.55	666.90	640.15
33000	939.46	865.49	806.89	759.45	720.38	687.74	660.16
34000	967.93	891.72	831.34	782.46	742.21	708.59	680.16
35000	996.40	917.94	855.79	805.48	764.04	729.43	700.16
40000	1138.74	1049.08	978.04	920.54	873.19	833.63	800.19
45000	1281.08	1180.21	1100.30	1035.61	982.34	937.83	900.21
50000	1423.42	1311.35	1222.55	1150.68	1091.49	1042.04	1000.24
55000	1565.77	1442.48	1344.81	1265.75	1200.63	1146.24	1100.26
60000	1708.11	1573.62	1467.07	1380.82	1309.78	1250.44	1200.28
65000	1850.45	1704.75	1589.32	1495.88	1418.93	1354.65	1300.31
70000	1992.79	1835.89	1711.58	1610.95	1528.08	1458.85	1400.33

16¼%   Monthly Loan Payments

LOAN AMOUNT	7½ YEARS	8 YEARS	8½ YEARS	9 YEARS	9½ YEARS	10 YEARS	10½ YEARS
100	1.93	1.87	1.81	1.77	1.73	1.69	1.66
200	3.86	3.74	3.63	3.54	3.45	3.38	3.32
300	5.79	5.60	5.44	5.30	5.18	5.07	4.98
400	7.72	7.47	7.26	7.07	6.91	6.76	6.64
500	9.65	9.34	9.07	8.84	8.63	8.45	8.29
600	11.57	11.21	10.89	10.61	10.36	10.14	9.95
700	13.50	13.07	12.70	12.37	12.09	11.84	11.61
800	15.43	14.94	14.51	14.14	13.81	13.53	13.27
900	17.36	16.81	16.33	15.91	15.54	15.22	14.93
1000	19.29	18.68	18.14	17.68	17.27	16.91	16.59
1500	28.94	28.01	27.21	26.52	25.90	25.36	24.88
2000	38.58	37.35	36.29	35.35	34.54	33.81	33.18
2500	48.23	46.69	45.36	44.19	43.17	42.27	41.47
3000	57.87	56.03	54.43	53.03	51.80	50.72	49.76
3500	67.52	65.37	63.50	61.87	60.44	59.18	58.06
4000	77.16	74.70	72.57	70.71	69.07	67.63	66.35
4500	86.81	84.04	81.64	79.55	77.71	76.08	74.64
5000	96.45	93.38	90.71	88.39	86.34	84.54	82.94
5500	106.10	102.72	99.79	97.22	94.98	92.99	91.23
6000	115.75	112.06	108.86	106.06	103.61	101.44	99.53
6500	125.39	121.39	117.93	114.90	112.24	109.90	107.82
7000	135.04	130.73	127.00	123.74	120.88	118.35	116.11
7500	144.68	140.07	136.07	132.58	129.51	126.81	124.41
8000	154.33	149.41	145.14	141.42	138.15	135.26	132.70
8500	163.97	158.75	154.21	150.25	146.78	143.71	141.00
9000	173.62	168.08	163.28	159.09	155.41	152.17	149.29
9500	183.26	177.42	172.36	167.93	164.05	160.62	157.58
10000	192.91	186.76	181.43	176.77	172.68	169.07	165.88
11000	212.20	205.44	199.57	194.45	189.95	185.98	182.47
12000	231.49	224.11	217.71	212.12	207.22	202.89	199.05
13000	250.78	242.79	235.86	229.80	224.49	219.80	215.64
14000	270.07	261.47	254.00	247.48	241.75	236.70	232.23
15000	289.36	280.14	272.14	265.16	259.02	253.61	248.82
16000	308.65	298.82	290.28	282.83	276.29	270.52	265.40
17000	327.94	317.49	308.43	300.51	293.56	287.43	281.99
18000	347.24	336.17	326.57	318.19	310.83	304.33	298.58
19000	366.53	354.85	344.71	335.86	328.10	321.24	315.17
20000	385.82	373.52	362.85	353.54	345.36	338.15	331.76
21000	405.11	392.20	381.00	371.22	362.63	355.06	348.34
22000	424.40	410.87	399.14	388.90	379.90	371.96	364.93
23000	443.69	429.55	417.28	406.57	397.17	388.87	381.52
24000	462.98	448.23	435.43	424.25	414.44	405.78	398.11
25000	482.27	466.90	453.57	441.93	431.70	422.69	414.69
26000	501.56	485.58	471.71	459.60	448.97	439.59	431.28
27000	520.85	504.25	489.85	477.28	466.24	456.50	447.87
28000	540.14	522.93	508.00	494.96	483.51	473.41	464.46
29000	559.43	541.61	526.14	512.63	500.78	490.32	481.05
30000	578.73	560.28	544.28	530.31	518.05	507.22	497.63
31000	598.02	578.96	562.42	547.99	535.31	524.13	514.22
32000	617.31	597.63	580.57	565.67	552.58	541.04	530.81
33000	636.60	616.31	598.71	583.34	569.85	557.95	547.40
34000	655.89	634.99	616.85	601.02	587.12	574.85	563.98
35000	675.18	653.66	635.00	618.70	604.39	591.76	580.57
40000	771.63	747.04	725.71	707.08	690.73	676.30	663.51
45000	868.09	840.42	816.42	795.47	777.07	760.83	746.45
50000	964.54	933.80	907.14	883.85	863.41	845.37	829.39
55000	1061.00	1027.18	997.85	972.24	949.75	929.91	912.33
60000	1157.45	1120.57	1088.56	1060.62	1036.09	1014.45	995.27
65000	1253.91	1213.95	1179.28	1149.01	1122.43	1098.98	1078.21
70000	1350.36	1307.33	1269.99	1237.39	1208.77	1183.52	1161.14

Monthly Loan Payments 16¼%

LOAN AMOUNT	11 YEARS	11½ YEARS	12 YEARS	12½ YEARS	13 YEARS	14 YEARS	15 YEARS
100	1.63	1.60	1.58	1.56	1.54	1.51	1.49
200	3.26	3.21	3.16	3.12	3.09	3.02	2.97
300	4.89	4.81	4.75	4.69	4.63	4.54	4.46
400	6.52	6.42	6.33	6.25	6.17	6.05	5.94
500	8.15	8.02	7.91	7.81	7.72	7.56	7.43
600	9.78	9.63	9.49	9.37	9.26	9.07	8.92
700	11.41	11.23	11.08	10.93	10.80	10.58	10.40
800	13.04	12.84	12.66	12.49	12.35	12.10	11.89
900	14.67	14.44	14.24	14.06	13.89	13.61	13.38
1000	16.30	16.05	15.82	15.62	15.43	15.12	14.86
1500	24.46	24.07	23.73	23.43	23.15	22.68	22.29
2000	32.61	32.10	31.64	31.24	30.87	30.24	29.72
2500	40.76	40.12	39.56	39.05	38.59	37.80	37.15
3000	48.91	48.15	47.47	46.86	46.30	45.36	44.59
3500	57.06	56.17	55.38	54.66	54.02	52.92	52.02
4000	65.21	64.20	63.29	62.47	61.74	60.48	59.45
4500	73.37	72.22	71.20	70.28	69.46	68.04	66.88
5000	81.52	80.25	79.11	78.09	77.17	75.60	74.31
5500	89.67	88.27	87.02	85.90	84.89	83.16	81.74
6000	97.82	96.30	94.93	93.71	92.61	90.72	89.17
6500	105.97	104.32	102.85	101.52	100.33	98.28	96.60
7000	114.12	112.35	110.76	109.33	108.04	105.84	104.03
7500	122.28	120.37	118.67	117.14	115.76	113.40	111.46
8000	130.43	128.40	126.58	124.95	123.48	120.96	118.89
8500	138.58	136.42	134.49	132.76	131.20	128.52	126.32
9000	146.73	144.45	142.40	140.57	138.91	136.08	133.76
9500	154.88	152.47	150.31	148.38	146.63	143.64	141.19
10000	163.03	160.50	158.22	156.18	154.35	151.20	148.62
11000	179.34	176.55	174.05	171.80	169.78	166.32	163.48
12000	195.64	192.60	189.87	187.42	185.22	181.44	178.34
13000	211.94	208.65	205.69	203.04	200.65	196.56	193.20
14000	228.25	224.70	221.51	218.66	216.09	211.68	208.06
15000	244.55	240.74	237.34	234.28	231.52	226.80	222.93
16000	260.85	256.79	253.16	249.90	246.96	241.92	237.79
17000	277.16	272.84	268.98	265.51	262.39	257.04	252.65
18000	293.46	288.89	284.80	281.13	277.83	272.16	267.51
19000	309.77	304.94	300.63	296.75	293.26	287.28	282.37
20000	326.07	320.99	316.45	312.37	308.70	302.40	297.23
21000	342.37	337.04	332.27	327.99	324.13	317.52	312.10
22000	358.68	353.09	348.09	343.61	339.57	332.64	326.96
23000	374.98	369.14	363.92	359.23	355.00	347.76	341.82
24000	391.28	385.19	379.74	374.84	370.44	362.88	356.68
25000	407.59	401.24	395.56	390.46	385.87	378.00	371.54
26000	423.89	417.29	411.38	406.08	401.31	393.12	386.40
27000	440.19	433.34	427.21	421.70	416.74	408.24	401.27
28000	456.50	449.39	443.03	437.32	432.18	423.36	416.13
29000	472.80	465.44	458.85	452.94	447.61	438.48	430.99
30000	489.10	481.49	474.67	468.55	463.05	453.60	445.85
31000	505.41	497.54	490.50	484.17	478.48	468.72	460.71
32000	521.71	513.59	506.32	499.79	493.92	483.84	475.57
33000	538.01	529.64	522.14	515.41	509.35	498.96	490.44
34000	554.32	545.69	537.96	531.03	524.79	514.07	505.30
35000	570.62	561.74	553.79	546.65	540.22	529.19	520.16
40000	652.14	641.99	632.90	624.74	617.40	604.79	594.47
45000	733.65	722.23	712.01	702.83	694.57	680.39	668.78
50000	815.17	802.48	791.12	780.92	771.75	755.99	743.08
55000	896.69	882.73	870.23	859.02	848.92	831.59	817.39
60000	978.21	962.98	949.35	937.11	926.10	907.19	891.70
65000	1059.72	1043.23	1028.46	1015.20	1003.27	982.79	966.01
70000	1141.24	1123.48	1107.57	1093.29	1080.45	1058.39	1040.32

16½%　Monthly Loan Payments

LOAN AMOUNT	½ YEAR	1 YEAR	1½ YEARS	2 YEARS	2½ YEARS	3 YEARS	3½ YEARS
100	17.48	9.10	6.31	4.92	4.09	3.54	3.15
200	34.96	18.19	12.62	9.84	8.18	7.08	6.30
300	52.43	27.29	18.93	14.76	12.27	10.62	9.45
400	69.91	36.39	25.24	19.68	16.36	14.16	12.60
500	87.39	45.48	31.55	24.60	20.45	17.70	15.75
600	104.87	54.58	37.86	29.52	24.54	21.24	18.90
700	122.35	63.68	44.17	34.44	28.63	24.78	22.05
800	139.82	72.77	50.47	39.36	32.72	28.32	25.20
900	157.30	81.87	56.78	44.28	36.81	31.86	28.35
1000	174.78	90.97	63.09	49.20	40.91	35.40	31.50
1500	262.17	136.45	94.64	73.80	61.36	53.11	47.25
2000	349.56	181.94	126.19	98.40	81.81	70.81	63.00
2500	436.95	227.42	157.73	123.01	102.26	88.51	78.75
3000	524.34	272.90	189.28	147.61	122.72	106.21	94.50
3500	611.73	318.39	220.83	172.21	143.17	123.92	110.26
4000	699.12	363.87	252.37	196.81	163.62	141.62	126.01
4500	786.50	409.35	283.92	221.41	184.07	159.32	141.76
5000	873.89	454.84	315.47	246.01	204.53	177.02	157.51
5500	961.28	500.32	347.01	270.61	224.98	194.72	173.26
6000	1048.67	545.81	378.56	295.21	245.43	212.43	189.01
6500	1136.06	591.29	410.10	319.82	265.88	230.13	204.76
7000	1223.45	636.77	441.65	344.42	286.34	247.83	220.51
7500	1310.84	682.26	473.20	369.02	306.79	265.53	236.26
8000	1398.23	727.74	504.74	393.62	327.24	283.24	252.01
8500	1485.62	773.22	536.29	418.22	347.69	300.94	267.76
9000	1573.01	818.71	567.84	442.82	368.15	318.64	283.51
9500	1660.40	864.19	599.38	467.42	388.60	336.34	299.26
10000	1747.79	909.68	630.93	492.02	409.05	354.04	315.01
11000	1922.57	1000.64	694.02	541.23	449.96	389.45	346.52
12000	2097.35	1091.61	757.12	590.43	490.86	424.85	378.02
13000	2272.12	1182.57	820.21	639.63	531.77	460.26	409.52
14000	2446.90	1273.55	883.30	688.83	572.67	495.66	441.02
15000	2621.68	1364.51	946.40	738.04	613.58	531.07	472.52
16000	2796.46	1455.48	1009.49	787.24	654.48	566.47	504.02
17000	2971.24	1546.45	1072.58	836.44	695.39	601.87	535.52
18000	3146.02	1637.42	1135.67	885.64	736.29	637.28	567.02
19000	3320.80	1728.39	1198.77	934.84	777.20	672.68	598.52
20000	3495.58	1819.35	1261.86	984.05	818.10	708.09	630.03
21000	3670.35	1910.32	1324.95	1033.25	859.01	743.49	661.53
22000	3845.13	2001.29	1388.05	1082.45	899.91	778.90	693.03
23000	4019.91	2092.26	1451.14	1131.65	940.82	814.30	724.53
24000	4194.69	2183.22	1514.23	1180.86	981.72	849.71	756.04
25000	4369.47	2274.19	1577.33	1230.06	1022.63	885.11	787.54
26000	4544.25	2365.16	1640.42	1279.26	1063.53	920.51	819.04
27000	4719.03	2456.13	1703.51	1328.46	1104.44	955.92	850.54
28000	4893.81	2547.09	1766.60	1377.67	1145.34	991.32	882.04
29000	5068.58	2638.06	1829.70	1426.87	1186.25	1026.73	913.54
30000	5243.36	2729.03	1892.79	1476.07	1227.15	1062.13	945.04
31000	5418.14	2820.00	1955.88	1525.27	1268.06	1097.54	976.55
32000	5592.92	2910.96	2018.98	1574.48	1308.96	1132.94	1008.05
33000	5767.70	3001.93	2082.07	1623.68	1349.87	1168.34	1039.55
34000	5942.48	3092.90	2145.16	1672.88	1390.77	1203.75	1071.05
35000	6117.26	3183.87	2208.26	1722.08	1431.68	1239.15	1102.55
40000	6991.15	3638.71	2523.72	1968.09	1636.20	1416.18	1260.06
45000	7865.04	4093.54	2839.19	2214.11	1840.73	1593.20	1417.57
50000	8738.94	4548.38	3154.65	2460.12	2045.26	1770.22	1575.07
55000	9612.83	5003.22	3470.12	2706.13	2249.78	1947.24	1732.58
60000	10486.73	5458.06	3785.58	2952.14	2454.31	2124.26	1890.09
65000	11360.62	5912.90	4101.05	3198.15	2658.83	2301.28	2047.60
70000	12234.51	6367.73	4416.51	3444.16	2863.36	2478.31	2205.10

Monthly Loan Payments 16½%

LOAN AMOUNT	4 YEARS	4½ YEARS	5 YEARS	5½ YEARS	6 YEARS	6½ YEARS	7 YEARS
100	2.86	2.64	2.46	2.31	2.20	2.10	2.01
200	5.72	5.27	4.92	4.63	4.39	4.20	4.03
300	8.58	7.91	7.38	6.94	6.59	6.29	6.04
400	11.44	10.54	9.83	9.26	8.79	8.39	8.06
500	14.30	13.18	12.29	11.57	10.98	10.49	10.07
600	17.16	15.81	14.75	13.89	13.18	12.59	12.09
700	20.02	18.45	17.21	16.20	15.38	14.69	14.10
800	22.88	21.09	19.67	18.52	17.57	16.79	16.12
900	25.74	23.72	22.13	20.83	19.77	18.88	18.13
1000	28.60	26.36	24.58	23.15	21.97	20.98	20.15
1500	42.90	39.54	36.88	34.72	32.95	31.47	30.22
2000	57.19	52.72	49.17	46.30	43.94	41.96	40.30
2500	71.49	65.89	61.46	57.87	54.92	52.45	50.37
3000	85.79	79.07	73.75	69.45	65.90	62.94	60.44
3500	100.09	92.25	86.05	81.02	76.89	73.44	70.52
4000	114.39	105.43	98.34	92.60	87.87	83.93	80.59
4500	128.69	118.61	110.63	104.17	98.86	94.42	90.67
5000	142.99	131.79	122.92	115.75	109.84	104.91	100.74
5500	157.28	144.97	135.21	127.32	120.82	115.40	110.81
6000	171.58	158.15	147.51	138.90	131.81	125.89	120.89
6500	185.88	171.33	159.80	150.47	142.79	136.38	130.96
7000	200.18	184.51	172.09	162.05	153.78	146.87	141.04
7500	214.48	197.68	184.38	173.62	164.76	157.36	151.11
8000	228.78	210.86	196.68	185.20	175.74	167.85	161.18
8500	243.07	224.04	208.97	196.77	186.73	178.34	171.26
9000	257.37	237.22	221.26	208.35	197.71	188.83	181.33
9500	271.67	250.40	233.55	219.92	208.70	199.32	191.40
10000	285.97	263.58	245.85	231.49	219.68	209.82	201.48
11000	314.57	289.94	270.43	254.64	241.65	230.80	221.63
12000	343.16	316.30	295.01	277.79	263.62	251.78	241.77
13000	371.76	342.65	319.60	300.94	285.58	272.76	261.92
14000	400.36	369.01	344.18	324.09	307.55	293.74	282.07
15000	428.96	395.37	368.77	347.24	329.52	314.72	302.22
16000	457.55	421.73	393.35	370.39	351.49	335.70	322.37
17000	486.15	448.09	417.94	393.54	373.46	356.69	342.51
18000	514.75	474.44	442.52	416.69	395.43	377.67	362.66
19000	543.34	500.80	467.11	439.84	417.39	398.65	382.81
20000	571.94	527.16	491.69	462.99	439.36	419.63	402.96
21000	600.54	553.52	516.27	486.14	461.33	440.61	423.11
22000	629.13	579.88	540.86	509.29	483.30	461.59	443.25
23000	657.73	606.23	565.44	532.44	505.27	482.57	463.40
24000	686.33	632.59	590.03	555.59	527.23	503.56	483.55
25000	714.93	658.95	614.61	578.74	549.20	524.54	503.70
26000	743.52	685.31	639.20	601.89	571.17	545.52	523.85
27000	772.12	711.67	663.78	625.04	593.14	566.50	543.99
28000	800.72	738.02	688.37	648.19	615.11	587.48	564.14
29000	829.31	764.38	712.95	671.34	637.07	608.46	584.29
30000	857.91	790.74	737.54	694.48	659.04	629.45	604.44
31000	886.51	817.10	762.12	717.63	681.01	650.43	624.58
32000	915.10	843.45	786.70	740.78	702.98	671.41	644.73
33000	943.70	869.81	811.29	763.93	724.95	692.39	664.88
34000	972.30	896.17	835.87	787.08	746.91	713.37	685.03
35000	1000.90	922.53	860.46	810.23	768.88	734.35	705.18
40000	1143.88	1054.32	983.38	925.98	878.72	839.26	805.92
45000	1286.87	1186.11	1106.30	1041.73	988.56	944.17	906.66
50000	1429.85	1317.90	1229.23	1157.47	1098.40	1049.08	1007.39
55000	1572.84	1449.69	1352.15	1273.22	1208.24	1153.98	1108.13
60000	1715.82	1581.49	1475.07	1388.97	1318.08	1258.89	1208.87
65000	1858.81	1713.27	1597.99	1504.72	1427.92	1363.80	1309.61
70000	2001.79	1845.06	1720.92	1620.46	1537.76	1468.71	1410.35

16½% Monthly Loan Payments

LOAN AMOUNT	7½ YEARS	8 YEARS	8½ YEARS	9 YEARS	9½ YEARS	10 YEARS	10½ YEARS
100	1.94	1.88	1.83	1.78	1.74	1.71	1.67
200	3.89	3.76	3.66	3.57	3.48	3.41	3.35
300	5.83	5.65	5.49	5.35	5.23	5.12	5.02
400	7.77	7.53	7.32	7.13	6.97	6.83	6.70
500	9.72	9.41	9.15	8.91	8.71	8.53	8.37
600	11.66	11.29	10.98	10.70	10.45	10.24	10.05
700	13.61	13.18	12.81	12.48	12.20	11.94	11.72
800	15.55	15.06	14.63	14.26	13.94	13.65	13.40
900	17.49	16.94	16.46	16.05	15.68	15.36	15.07
1000	19.44	18.82	18.29	17.83	17.42	17.06	16.75
1500	29.15	28.24	27.44	26.74	26.13	25.60	25.12
2000	38.87	37.65	36.59	35.66	34.85	34.13	33.49
2500	48.59	47.06	45.73	44.57	43.56	42.66	41.87
3000	58.31	56.47	54.88	53.49	52.27	51.19	50.24
3500	68.03	65.88	64.03	62.40	60.98	59.72	58.61
4000	77.75	75.30	73.17	71.32	69.69	68.26	66.99
4500	87.46	84.71	82.32	80.23	78.40	76.79	75.36
5000	97.18	94.12	91.46	89.15	87.11	85.32	83.73
5500	106.90	103.53	100.61	98.06	95.83	93.85	92.11
6000	116.62	112.94	109.76	106.98	104.54	102.39	100.48
6500	126.34	122.36	118.90	115.89	113.25	110.92	108.85
7000	136.05	131.77	128.05	124.81	121.96	119.45	117.23
7500	145.77	141.18	137.20	133.72	130.67	127.98	125.60
8000	155.49	150.59	146.34	142.64	139.38	136.51	133.97
8500	165.21	160.00	155.49	151.55	148.09	145.05	142.35
9000	174.93	169.42	164.64	160.47	156.81	153.58	150.72
9500	184.65	178.83	173.78	169.38	165.52	162.11	159.09
10000	194.36	188.24	182.93	178.29	174.23	170.64	167.47
11000	213.80	207.06	201.22	196.12	191.65	187.71	184.21
12000	233.24	225.89	219.51	213.95	209.07	204.77	200.96
13000	252.67	244.71	237.81	231.78	226.50	221.83	217.71
14000	272.11	263.54	256.10	249.61	243.92	238.90	234.45
15000	291.55	282.36	274.39	267.44	261.34	255.96	251.20
16000	310.98	301.18	292.69	285.27	278.77	273.03	267.95
17000	330.42	320.01	310.98	303.10	296.19	290.09	284.69
18000	349.86	338.83	329.27	320.93	313.61	307.16	301.44
19000	369.29	357.66	347.57	338.76	331.03	324.22	318.19
20000	388.73	376.48	365.86	356.59	348.46	341.28	334.93
21000	408.16	395.30	384.15	374.42	365.88	358.35	351.68
22000	427.60	414.13	402.44	392.25	383.30	375.41	368.43
23000	447.04	432.95	420.74	410.08	400.72	392.48	385.17
24000	466.47	451.78	439.03	427.91	418.15	409.54	401.92
25000	485.91	470.60	457.32	445.74	435.57	426.61	418.67
26000	505.35	489.42	475.62	463.57	452.99	443.67	435.41
27000	524.78	508.25	493.91	481.40	470.42	460.73	452.16
28000	544.22	527.07	512.20	499.23	487.84	477.80	468.91
29000	563.66	545.90	530.49	517.05	505.26	494.86	485.65
30000	583.09	564.72	548.79	534.88	522.68	511.93	502.40
31000	602.53	583.54	567.08	552.71	540.11	528.99	519.15
32000	621.97	602.37	585.37	570.54	557.53	546.06	535.89
33000	641.40	621.19	603.67	588.37	574.95	563.12	552.64
34000	660.84	640.02	621.96	606.20	592.38	580.18	569.39
35000	680.27	658.84	640.25	624.03	609.80	597.25	586.13
40000	777.46	752.96	731.72	713.18	696.91	682.57	669.87
45000	874.64	847.08	823.18	802.33	784.03	767.89	753.60
50000	971.82	941.20	914.65	891.47	871.14	853.21	837.33
55000	1069.00	1035.32	1006.11	980.62	958.26	938.53	921.07
60000	1166.18	1129.44	1097.57	1069.77	1045.37	1023.85	1004.80
65000	1263.37	1223.56	1189.04	1158.92	1132.48	1109.17	1088.53
70000	1360.55	1317.68	1280.50	1248.06	1219.60	1194.50	1172.27

142

Monthly Loan Payments 16½%

LOAN AMOUNT	11 YEARS	11½ YEARS	12 YEARS	12½ YEARS	13 YEARS	14 YEARS	15 YEARS
100	1.65	1.62	1.60	1.58	1.56	1.53	1.50
200	3.29	3.24	3.20	3.16	3.12	3.06	3.01
300	4.94	4.86	4.80	4.74	4.68	4.59	4.51
400	6.59	6.49	6.39	6.31	6.24	6.12	6.01
500	8.23	8.11	7.99	7.89	7.80	7.65	7.52
600	9.88	9.73	9.59	9.47	9.36	9.18	9.02
700	11.53	11.35	11.19	11.05	10.92	10.70	10.53
800	13.17	12.97	12.79	12.63	12.48	12.23	12.03
900	14.82	14.59	14.39	14.21	14.04	13.76	13.53
1000	16.46	16.21	15.99	15.79	15.60	15.29	15.04
1500	24.70	24.32	23.98	23.68	23.41	22.94	22.56
2000	32.93	32.43	31.97	31.57	31.21	30.58	30.07
2500	41.16	40.53	39.97	39.46	39.01	38.23	37.59
3000	49.39	48.64	47.96	47.36	46.81	45.88	45.11
3500	57.63	56.74	55.96	55.25	54.61	53.52	52.63
4000	65.86	64.85	63.95	63.14	62.41	61.17	60.15
4500	74.09	72.96	71.94	71.03	70.22	68.81	67.67
5000	82.32	81.06	79.94	78.93	78.02	76.46	75.19
5500	90.55	89.17	87.93	86.82	85.82	84.11	82.70
6000	98.79	97.28	95.92	94.71	93.62	91.75	90.22
6500	107.02	105.38	103.92	102.60	101.42	99.40	97.74
7000	115.25	113.49	111.91	110.50	109.22	107.04	105.26
7500	123.48	121.59	119.91	118.39	117.03	114.69	112.78
8000	131.72	129.70	127.90	126.28	124.83	122.34	120.30
8500	139.95	137.81	135.89	134.17	132.63	129.98	127.82
9000	148.18	145.91	143.89	142.07	140.43	137.63	135.33
9500	156.41	154.02	151.88	149.96	148.23	145.27	142.85
10000	164.64	162.13	159.87	157.85	156.04	152.92	150.37
11000	181.11	178.34	175.86	173.64	171.64	168.21	165.41
12000	197.57	194.55	191.85	189.42	187.24	183.50	180.45
13000	214.04	210.76	207.84	205.21	202.85	198.80	195.48
14000	230.50	226.98	223.82	220.99	218.45	214.09	210.52
15000	246.97	243.19	239.81	236.78	234.05	229.38	225.56
16000	263.43	259.40	255.80	252.56	249.66	244.67	240.59
17000	279.89	275.61	271.78	268.35	265.26	259.96	255.63
18000	296.36	291.83	287.77	284.13	280.86	275.26	270.67
19000	312.82	308.04	303.76	299.92	296.47	290.55	285.70
20000	329.29	324.25	319.75	315.71	312.07	305.84	300.74
21000	345.75	340.46	335.73	331.49	327.67	321.13	315.78
22000	362.22	356.68	351.72	347.28	343.28	336.42	330.82
23000	378.68	372.89	367.71	363.06	358.88	351.72	345.85
24000	395.15	389.10	383.70	378.85	374.49	367.01	360.89
25000	411.61	405.31	399.68	394.63	390.09	382.30	375.93
26000	428.07	421.53	415.67	410.42	405.69	397.59	390.96
27000	444.54	437.74	431.66	426.20	421.30	412.88	406.00
28000	461.00	453.95	447.65	441.99	436.90	428.18	421.04
29000	477.47	470.17	463.63	457.77	452.50	443.47	436.08
30000	493.93	486.38	479.62	473.56	468.11	458.76	451.11
31000	510.40	502.59	495.61	489.34	483.71	474.05	466.15
32000	526.86	518.80	511.59	505.13	499.31	489.34	481.19
33000	543.32	535.02	527.58	520.91	514.92	504.64	496.22
34000	559.79	551.23	543.57	536.70	530.52	519.93	511.26
35000	576.25	567.44	559.56	552.48	546.12	535.22	526.30
40000	658.58	648.50	639.49	631.41	624.14	611.68	601.48
45000	740.90	729.57	719.43	710.34	702.16	688.14	676.67
50000	823.22	810.63	799.37	789.26	780.18	764.60	751.85
55000	905.54	891.69	879.30	868.19	858.20	841.06	827.04
60000	987.86	972.76	959.24	947.12	936.21	917.52	902.23
65000	1070.18	1053.82	1039.18	1026.04	1014.23	993.98	977.41
70000	1152.51	1134.88	1119.11	1104.97	1092.25	1070.44	1052.60

16¾%   Monthly Loan Payments

LOAN AMOUNT	½ YEAR	1 YEAR	1½ YEARS	2 YEARS	2½ YEARS	3 YEARS	3½ YEARS
100	17.49	9.11	6.32	4.93	4.10	3.55	3.16
200	34.98	18.22	12.64	9.86	8.21	7.11	6.33
300	52.47	27.33	18.96	14.80	12.31	10.66	9.49
400	69.96	36.43	25.28	19.73	16.41	14.21	12.65
500	87.45	45.54	31.61	24.66	20.51	17.76	15.81
600	104.94	54.65	37.93	29.59	24.62	21.32	18.98
700	122.43	63.76	44.25	34.53	28.72	24.87	22.14
800	139.92	72.87	50.57	39.46	32.82	28.42	25.30
900	157.41	81.98	56.89	44.39	36.92	31.98	28.47
1000	174.90	91.09	63.21	49.32	41.03	35.53	31.63
1500	262.35	136.63	94.82	73.98	61.54	53.29	47.44
2000	349.81	182.17	126.42	98.64	82.05	71.06	63.26
2500	437.26	227.72	158.03	123.31	102.57	88.82	79.07
3000	524.71	273.26	189.63	147.97	123.08	106.59	94.88
3500	612.16	318.80	221.24	172.63	143.59	124.35	110.70
4000	699.61	364.34	252.85	197.29	164.11	142.11	126.51
4500	787.06	409.89	284.45	221.95	184.62	159.88	142.33
5000	874.52	455.43	316.06	246.61	205.13	177.64	158.14
5500	961.97	500.97	347.66	271.27	225.65	195.41	173.95
6000	1049.42	546.52	379.27	295.93	246.16	213.17	189.77
6500	1136.87	592.06	410.87	320.59	266.68	230.93	205.58
7000	1224.32	637.60	442.48	345.26	287.19	248.70	221.40
7500	1311.77	683.15	474.09	369.92	307.70	266.46	237.21
8000	1399.22	728.69	505.69	394.58	328.22	284.23	253.02
8500	1486.68	774.23	537.30	419.24	348.73	301.99	268.84
9000	1574.13	819.78	568.90	443.90	369.24	319.76	284.65
9500	1661.58	865.32	600.51	468.56	389.76	337.52	300.46
10000	1749.03	910.86	632.11	493.22	410.27	355.28	316.28
11000	1923.93	1001.95	695.33	542.54	451.30	390.81	347.90
12000	2098.84	1093.03	758.54	591.87	492.32	426.34	379.53
13000	2273.74	1184.12	821.75	641.19	533.35	461.87	411.16
14000	2448.64	1275.21	884.96	690.51	574.38	497.40	442.79
15000	2623.55	1366.29	948.17	739.83	615.40	532.93	474.42
16000	2798.45	1457.38	1011.38	789.16	656.43	568.45	506.05
17000	2973.35	1548.46	1074.60	838.48	697.46	603.98	537.67
18000	3148.26	1639.55	1137.81	887.80	738.48	639.51	569.30
19000	3323.16	1730.64	1201.02	937.12	779.51	675.04	600.93
20000	3498.06	1821.72	1264.23	986.44	820.54	710.57	632.56
21000	3672.96	1912.81	1327.44	1035.77	861.57	746.10	664.19
22000	3847.87	2003.90	1390.65	1085.09	902.59	781.63	695.81
23000	4022.77	2094.98	1453.86	1134.41	943.62	817.15	727.44
24000	4197.67	2186.07	1517.08	1183.73	984.65	852.68	759.07
25000	4372.58	2277.15	1580.29	1233.06	1025.67	888.21	790.70
26000	4547.48	2368.24	1643.50	1282.38	1066.70	923.74	822.33
27000	4722.38	2459.33	1706.71	1331.70	1107.73	959.27	853.95
28000	4897.29	2550.41	1769.92	1381.02	1148.75	994.80	885.58
29000	5072.19	2641.50	1833.13	1430.34	1189.78	1030.32	917.21
30000	5247.09	2732.58	1896.34	1479.67	1230.81	1065.85	948.84
31000	5422.00	2823.67	1959.56	1528.99	1271.83	1101.38	980.47
32000	5596.90	2914.76	2022.77	1578.31	1312.86	1136.91	1012.09
33000	5771.80	3005.84	2085.98	1627.63	1353.89	1172.44	1043.72
34000	5946.70	3096.93	2149.19	1676.96	1394.92	1207.97	1075.35
35000	6121.61	3188.02	2212.40	1726.28	1435.94	1243.50	1106.98
40000	6996.12	3643.45	2528.46	1972.89	1641.08	1421.14	1265.12
45000	7870.64	4098.88	2844.52	2219.50	1846.21	1598.78	1423.26
50000	8745.15	4554.31	3160.57	2466.11	2051.35	1776.42	1581.39
55000	9619.67	5009.74	3476.63	2712.72	2256.48	1954.06	1739.53
60000	10494.18	5465.17	3792.69	2959.33	2461.62	2131.71	1897.67
65000	11368.70	5920.60	4108.75	3205.94	2666.75	2309.35	2055.81
70000	12243.22	6376.03	4424.80	3452.56	2871.89	2486.99	2213.95

Monthly Loan Payments 16¾%

LOAN AMOUNT	4 YEARS	4½ YEARS	5 YEARS	5½ YEARS	6 YEARS	6½ YEARS	7 YEARS
100	2.87	2.65	2.47	2.33	2.21	2.11	2.03
200	5.75	5.30	4.94	4.66	4.42	4.22	4.06
300	8.62	7.95	7.42	6.99	6.63	6.34	6.09
400	11.49	10.60	9.89	9.31	8.84	8.45	8.12
500	14.36	13.24	12.36	11.64	11.05	10.56	10.15
600	17.24	15.89	14.83	13.97	13.26	12.67	12.17
700	20.11	18.54	17.30	16.30	15.47	14.79	14.20
800	22.98	21.19	19.77	18.63	17.69	16.90	16.23
900	25.85	23.84	22.25	20.96	19.90	19.01	18.26
1000	28.73	26.49	24.72	23.29	22.11	21.12	20.29
1500	43.09	39.73	37.08	34.93	33.16	31.68	30.44
2000	57.45	52.98	49.44	46.57	44.21	42.25	40.58
2500	71.81	66.22	61.80	58.21	55.27	52.81	50.73
3000	86.18	79.47	74.16	69.86	66.32	63.37	60.87
3500	100.54	92.71	86.51	81.50	77.37	73.93	71.02
4000	114.90	105.96	98.87	93.14	88.43	84.49	81.17
4500	129.27	119.20	111.23	104.79	99.48	95.05	91.31
5000	143.63	132.45	123.59	116.43	110.53	105.61	101.46
5500	157.99	145.69	135.95	128.07	121.59	116.18	111.60
6000	172.36	158.94	148.31	139.71	132.64	126.74	121.75
6500	186.72	172.18	160.67	151.36	143.69	137.30	131.90
7000	201.08	185.43	173.03	163.00	154.75	147.86	142.04
7500	215.44	198.67	185.39	174.64	165.80	158.42	152.19
8000	229.81	211.91	197.75	186.29	176.85	168.98	162.33
8500	244.17	225.16	210.11	197.93	187.91	179.54	172.48
9000	258.53	238.40	222.47	209.57	198.96	190.11	182.62
9500	272.90	251.65	234.82	221.22	210.02	200.67	192.77
10000	287.26	264.89	247.18	232.86	221.07	211.23	202.92
11000	315.98	291.38	271.90	256.14	243.18	232.35	223.21
12000	344.71	317.87	296.62	279.43	265.28	253.47	243.50
13000	373.44	344.36	321.34	302.72	287.39	274.60	263.79
14000	402.16	370.85	346.06	326.00	309.50	295.72	284.08
15000	430.89	397.34	370.78	349.29	331.60	316.84	304.37
16000	459.61	423.83	395.49	372.57	353.71	337.96	324.67
17000	488.34	450.32	420.21	395.86	375.82	359.09	344.96
18000	517.07	476.81	444.93	419.14	397.92	380.21	365.25
19000	545.79	503.30	469.65	442.43	420.03	401.33	385.54
20000	574.52	529.79	494.37	465.72	442.14	422.46	405.83
21000	603.24	556.28	519.09	489.00	464.24	443.58	426.12
22000	631.97	582.76	543.80	512.29	486.35	464.70	446.41
23000	660.69	609.25	568.52	535.57	508.46	485.82	466.71
24000	689.42	635.74	593.24	558.86	530.56	506.95	487.00
25000	718.15	662.23	617.96	582.15	552.67	528.07	507.29
26000	746.87	688.72	642.68	605.43	574.78	549.19	527.58
27000	775.60	715.21	667.40	628.72	596.89	570.32	547.87
28000	804.32	741.70	692.11	652.00	618.99	591.44	568.16
29000	833.05	768.19	716.83	675.29	641.10	612.56	588.46
30000	861.78	794.68	741.55	698.57	663.21	633.68	608.75
31000	890.50	821.17	766.27	721.86	685.31	654.81	629.04
32000	919.23	847.66	790.99	745.15	707.42	675.93	649.33
33000	947.95	874.15	815.71	768.43	729.53	697.05	669.62
34000	976.68	900.64	840.42	791.72	751.63	718.17	689.91
35000	1005.41	927.13	865.14	815.00	773.74	739.30	710.21
40000	1149.03	1059.57	988.73	931.43	884.27	844.91	811.66
45000	1292.66	1192.02	1112.33	1047.86	994.81	950.53	913.12
50000	1436.29	1324.47	1235.92	1164.29	1105.34	1056.14	1014.58
55000	1579.92	1456.91	1359.51	1280.72	1215.88	1161.75	1116.04
60000	1723.55	1589.36	1483.10	1397.15	1326.41	1267.37	1217.50
65000	1867.18	1721.80	1606.69	1513.58	1436.95	1372.98	1318.95
70000	2010.81	1854.25	1730.28	1630.01	1547.48	1478.59	1420.41

16¾%   Monthly Loan Payments

LOAN AMOUNT	7½ YEARS	8 YEARS	8½ YEARS	9 YEARS	9½ YEARS	10 YEARS	10½ YEARS
100	1.96	1.90	1.84	1.80	1.76	1.72	1.69
200	3.92	3.79	3.69	3.60	3.52	3.44	3.38
300	5.87	5.69	5.53	5.39	5.27	5.17	5.07
400	7.83	7.59	7.38	7.19	7.03	6.89	6.76
500	9.79	9.49	9.22	8.99	8.79	8.61	8.45
600	11.75	11.38	11.07	10.79	10.55	10.33	10.14
700	13.71	13.28	12.91	12.59	12.30	12.06	11.83
800	15.67	15.18	14.75	14.39	14.06	13.78	13.52
900	17.62	17.08	16.60	16.18	15.82	15.50	15.22
1000	19.58	18.97	18.44	17.98	17.58	17.22	16.91
1500	29.37	28.46	27.67	26.97	26.37	25.83	25.36
2000	39.17	37.94	36.89	35.97	35.16	34.44	33.81
2500	48.96	47.43	46.11	44.96	43.95	43.05	42.27
3000	58.75	56.92	55.33	53.95	52.73	51.67	50.72
3500	68.54	66.40	64.55	62.94	61.52	60.28	59.17
4000	78.33	75.89	73.77	71.93	70.31	68.89	67.62
4500	88.12	85.38	83.00	80.92	79.10	77.50	76.08
5000	97.91	94.86	92.22	89.91	87.89	86.11	84.53
5500	107.70	104.35	101.44	98.90	96.68	94.72	92.98
6000	117.50	113.83	110.66	107.90	105.47	103.33	101.44
6500	127.29	123.32	119.88	116.89	114.26	111.94	109.89
7000	137.08	132.81	129.11	125.88	123.05	120.55	118.34
7500	146.87	142.29	138.33	134.87	131.84	129.16	126.80
8000	156.66	151.78	147.55	143.86	140.62	137.77	135.25
8500	166.45	161.27	156.77	152.85	149.41	146.38	143.70
9000	176.45	170.75	165.99	161.84	158.20	155.00	152.16
9500	186.03	180.24	175.22	170.83	166.99	163.61	160.61
10000	195.83	189.72	184.44	179.83	175.78	172.22	169.06
11000	215.41	208.70	202.88	197.81	193.36	189.44	185.97
12000	234.99	227.67	221.32	215.79	210.94	206.66	202.87
13000	254.57	246.64	239.77	233.77	228.52	223.88	219.78
14000	274.16	265.61	258.21	251.76	246.09	241.10	236.69
15000	293.74	284.59	276.66	269.74	263.67	258.33	253.59
16000	313.32	303.56	295.10	287.72	281.25	275.55	270.50
17000	332.90	322.53	313.54	305.70	298.83	292.77	287.41
18000	352.49	341.50	331.99	323.69	316.41	309.99	304.31
19000	372.07	360.48	350.43	341.67	333.98	327.21	321.22
20000	391.65	379.45	368.87	359.65	351.56	344.43	338.12
21000	411.23	398.42	387.32	377.63	369.14	361.66	355.03
22000	430.82	417.39	405.76	395.62	386.72	378.88	371.94
23000	450.40	436.37	424.20	413.60	404.30	396.10	388.84
24000	469.98	455.34	442.65	431.58	421.87	413.32	405.75
25000	489.56	474.31	461.09	449.56	439.45	430.54	422.66
26000	509.15	493.28	479.54	467.55	457.03	447.76	439.56
27000	528.73	512.26	497.98	485.53	474.61	464.99	456.47
28000	548.31	531.23	516.42	503.51	492.19	482.21	473.37
29000	567.89	550.20	534.87	521.49	509.76	499.43	490.28
30000	587.48	569.17	553.31	539.48	527.34	516.65	507.19
31000	607.06	588.15	571.75	557.46	544.92	533.87	524.09
32000	626.64	607.12	590.20	575.44	562.50	551.09	541.00
33000	646.22	626.09	608.64	593.42	580.08	568.32	557.91
34000	665.81	645.06	627.09	611.41	597.66	585.54	574.81
35000	685.39	664.03	645.53	629.39	615.23	602.76	591.72
40000	783.30	758.90	737.75	719.30	703.12	688.87	676.25
45000	881.21	853.76	829.97	809.21	791.01	774.98	760.78
50000	979.13	948.62	922.18	899.13	878.90	861.08	845.31
55000	1077.04	1043.48	1014.40	989.04	966.79	947.19	929.84
60000	1174.95	1138.35	1106.62	1078.95	1054.69	1033.30	1014.37
65000	1272.86	1233.21	1198.84	1168.86	1142.58	1119.41	1098.91
70000	1370.78	1328.07	1291.06	1258.78	1230.47	1205.52	1183.44

Monthly Loan Payments 16¾%

LOAN AMOUNT	11 YEARS	11½ YEARS	12 YEARS	12½ YEARS	13 YEARS	14 YEARS	15 YEARS
100	1.66	1.64	1.62	1.60	1.58	1.55	1.52
200	3.33	3.28	3.23	3.19	3.15	3.09	3.04
300	4.99	4.91	4.85	4.79	4.73	4.64	4.56
400	6.65	6.55	6.46	6.38	6.31	6.19	6.09
500	8.31	8.19	8.08	7.98	7.89	7.73	7.61
600	9.98	9.83	9.69	9.57	9.46	9.28	9.13
700	11.64	11.46	11.31	11.17	11.04	10.83	10.65
800	13.30	13.10	12.92	12.76	12.62	12.37	12.17
900	14.96	14.74	14.54	14.36	14.20	13.92	13.69
1000	16.63	16.38	16.15	15.95	15.77	15.46	15.21
1500	24.94	24.56	24.23	23.93	23.66	23.20	22.82
2000	33.25	32.75	32.31	31.91	31.55	30.93	30.43
2500	41.57	40.94	40.38	39.88	39.43	38.66	38.03
3000	49.88	49.13	48.46	47.86	47.32	46.39	45.64
3500	58.19	57.32	56.54	55.83	55.21	54.13	53.25
4000	66.50	65.50	64.61	63.81	63.09	61.86	60.85
4500	74.82	73.69	72.69	71.79	70.98	69.59	68.46
5000	83.13	81.88	80.76	79.76	78.86	77.32	76.07
5500	91.44	90.07	88.84	87.74	86.75	85.06	83.67
6000	99.76	98.26	96.92	95.72	94.64	92.79	91.28
6500	108.07	106.45	104.99	103.69	102.52	100.52	98.89
7000	116.38	114.63	113.07	111.67	110.41	108.25	106.49
7500	124.70	122.82	121.15	119.65	118.30	115.99	114.10
8000	133.01	131.01	129.22	127.62	126.18	123.72	121.71
8500	141.32	139.20	137.30	135.60	134.07	131.45	129.31
9000	149.63	147.39	145.38	143.57	141.96	139.18	136.92
9500	157.95	155.57	153.45	151.55	149.84	146.92	144.53
10000	166.26	163.76	161.53	159.53	157.73	154.65	152.13
11000	182.89	180.14	177.68	175.48	173.50	170.11	167.35
12000	199.51	196.51	193.84	191.43	189.27	185.58	182.56
13000	216.14	212.89	209.99	207.39	205.05	201.04	197.77
14000	232.76	229.27	226.14	223.34	220.82	216.51	212.98
15000	249.39	245.64	242.29	239.29	236.59	231.97	228.20
16000	266.02	262.02	258.45	255.24	252.37	247.44	243.41
17000	282.64	278.40	274.60	271.20	268.14	262.90	258.62
18000	299.27	294.77	290.75	287.15	283.91	278.37	273.84
19000	315.89	311.15	306.91	303.10	299.69	293.83	289.05
20000	332.52	327.52	323.06	319.06	315.46	309.30	304.26
21000	349.15	343.90	339.21	335.01	331.23	324.76	319.48
22000	365.77	360.28	355.36	350.96	347.00	340.23	334.69
23000	382.40	376.65	371.52	366.91	362.78	355.69	349.90
24000	399.02	393.03	387.67	382.87	378.55	371.16	365.12
25000	415.65	409.41	403.82	398.82	394.32	386.62	380.33
26000	432.28	425.78	419.98	414.77	410.10	402.09	395.54
27000	448.90	442.16	436.13	430.72	425.87	417.55	410.76
28000	465.53	458.53	452.28	446.68	441.64	433.02	425.97
29000	482.15	474.91	468.44	462.63	457.41	448.48	441.18
30000	498.78	491.29	484.59	478.58	473.19	463.94	456.40
31000	515.41	507.66	500.74	494.54	488.96	479.41	471.61
32000	532.03	524.04	516.89	510.49	504.73	494.87	486.82
33000	548.66	540.42	533.05	526.44	520.51	510.34	502.04
34000	565.28	556.79	549.20	542.39	536.28	525.80	517.25
35000	581.91	573.17	565.35	558.35	552.05	541.27	532.46
40000	665.04	655.05	646.12	638.11	630.92	618.59	608.53
45000	748.17	736.93	726.88	717.87	709.78	695.92	684.59
50000	831.30	818.81	807.65	797.64	788.65	773.24	760.66
55000	914.43	900.69	888.41	877.40	867.51	850.57	836.73
60000	997.56	982.57	969.18	957.17	946.37	927.89	912.79
65000	1080.69	1064.46	1049.94	1036.93	1025.24	1005.21	988.86
70000	1163.82	1146.34	1130.71	1116.69	1104.10	1082.54	1064.92

17%   Monthly Loan Payments

LOAN AMOUNT	½ YEAR	1 YEAR	1½ YEARS	2 YEARS	2½ YEARS	3 YEARS	3½ YEARS
100	17.50	9.12	6.33	4.94	4.11	3.57	3.18
200	35.01	18.24	12.67	9.89	8.23	7.13	6.35
300	52.51	27.36	19.00	14.83	12.34	10.70	9.53
400	70.01	36.48	25.33	19.78	16.46	14.26	12.70
500	87.51	45.60	31.67	24.72	20.57	17.83	15.88
600	105.02	54.72	38.00	29.67	24.69	21.39	19.05
700	122.52	63.84	44.33	34.61	28.80	24.96	22.23
800	140.02	72.96	50.66	39.55	32.92	28.52	25.40
900	157.52	82.08	57.00	44.50	37.03	32.09	28.58
1000	175.03	91.20	63.33	49.44	41.15	35.65	31.75
1500	262.54	136.81	95.00	74.16	61.72	53.48	47.63
2000	350.05	182.41	126.66	98.88	82.30	71.31	63.51
2500	437.57	228.01	158.33	123.61	102.87	89.13	79.39
3000	525.08	273.61	189.99	148.33	123.45	106.96	95.26
3500	612.60	319.22	221.66	173.05	144.02	124.78	111.14
4000	700.11	364.82	253.32	197.77	164.60	142.61	127.02
4500	787.62	410.42	284.99	222.49	185.17	160.44	142.90
5000	875.14	456.02	316.65	247.21	205.74	178.26	158.77
5500	962.65	501.63	348.32	271.93	226.32	196.09	174.65
6000	1050.16	547.23	379.98	296.65	246.89	213.92	190.53
6500	1137.68	592.83	411.65	321.37	267.47	231.74	206.40
7000	1225.19	638.43	443.31	346.10	288.04	249.57	222.28
7500	1312.71	684.04	474.98	370.82	308.62	267.40	238.16
8000	1400.22	729.64	506.64	395.54	329.19	285.22	254.04
8500	1487.73	775.24	538.31	420.26	349.77	303.05	269.91
9000	1575.25	820.84	569.97	444.98	370.34	320.87	285.79
9500	1662.76	866.45	601.64	469.70	390.92	338.70	301.67
10000	1750.27	912.05	633.30	494.42	411.49	356.53	317.55
11000	1925.30	1003.25	696.63	543.86	452.64	392.18	349.30
12000	2100.33	1094.46	759.96	593.31	493.79	427.83	381.06
13000	2275.36	1185.66	823.29	642.75	534.94	463.49	412.81
14000	2450.38	1276.87	886.62	692.19	576.09	499.14	444.56
15000	2625.41	1368.07	949.95	741.63	617.23	534.79	476.32
16000	2800.44	1459.28	1013.28	791.08	658.38	570.44	508.07
17000	2975.47	1550.48	1076.61	840.52	699.53	606.10	539.83
18000	3150.49	1641.69	1139.94	889.96	740.68	641.75	571.58
19000	3325.52	1732.89	1203.27	939.40	781.83	677.40	603.34
20000	3500.55	1824.10	1266.60	988.85	822.98	713.05	635.09
21000	3675.58	1915.30	1329.93	1038.29	864.13	748.71	666.85
22000	3850.60	2006.50	1393.26	1087.73	905.28	784.36	698.60
23000	4025.63	2097.71	1456.59	1137.17	946.43	820.01	730.36
24000	4200.66	2188.91	1519.92	1186.61	987.58	855.67	762.11
25000	4375.69	2280.12	1583.25	1236.06	1028.72	891.32	793.86
26000	4550.71	2371.32	1646.58	1285.50	1069.87	926.97	825.62
27000	4725.74	2462.53	1709.91	1334.94	1111.02	962.62	857.37
28000	4900.77	2553.73	1773.24	1384.38	1152.17	998.28	889.13
29000	5075.80	2644.94	1836.57	1433.83	1193.32	1033.93	920.88
30000	5250.82	2736.14	1899.90	1483.27	1234.47	1069.58	952.64
31000	5425.85	2827.35	1963.23	1532.71	1275.62	1105.23	984.39
32000	5600.88	2918.55	2026.56	1582.15	1316.77	1140.89	1016.15
33000	5775.90	3009.76	2089.89	1631.59	1357.92	1176.54	1047.90
34000	5950.93	3100.96	2153.22	1681.04	1399.06	1212.19	1079.66
35000	6125.96	3192.17	2216.55	1730.48	1440.21	1247.85	1111.41
40000	7001.10	3648.19	2533.20	1977.69	1645.96	1426.11	1270.18
45000	7876.23	4104.21	2849.85	2224.90	1851.70	1604.37	1428.96
50000	8751.37	4560.24	3166.50	2472.11	2057.45	1782.64	1587.73
55000	9626.51	5016.26	3483.16	2719.32	2263.19	1960.90	1746.51
60000	10501.65	5472.29	3799.81	2966.54	2468.94	2139.16	1905.28
65000	11376.78	5928.31	4116.46	3213.75	2674.68	2317.43	2064.06
70000	12251.92	6384.33	4433.11	3460.96	2880.43	2495.69	2222.83

Monthly Loan Payments 17%

LOAN AMOUNT	4 YEARS	4½ YEARS	5 YEARS	5½ YEARS	6 YEARS	6½ YEARS	7 YEARS
100	2.89	2.66	2.49	2.34	2.22	2.13	2.04
200	5.77	5.32	4.97	4.68	4.45	4.25	4.09
300	8.66	7.99	7.46	7.03	6.67	6.38	6.13
400	11.54	10.65	9.94	9.37	8.90	8.51	8.17
500	14.43	13.31	12.43	11.71	11.12	10.63	10.22
600	17.31	15.97	14.91	14.05	13.35	12.76	12.26
700	20.20	18.63	17.40	16.40	15.57	14.89	14.31
800	23.08	21.30	19.88	18.74	17.80	17.01	16.35
900	25.97	23.96	22.37	21.08	20.02	19.14	18.39
1000	28.86	26.62	24.85	23.42	22.25	21.26	20.44
1500	43.28	39.93	37.28	35.13	33.37	31.90	30.65
2000	57.71	53.24	49.71	46.85	44.49	42.53	40.87
2500	72.14	66.55	62.13	58.56	55.62	53.16	51.09
3000	86.57	79.86	74.56	70.27	66.74	63.79	61.31
3500	100.99	93.17	86.98	81.98	77.86	74.43	71.53
4000	115.42	106.48	99.41	93.69	88.98	85.06	81.74
4500	129.85	119.79	111.84	105.40	100.11	95.69	91.96
5000	144.28	133.10	124.26	117.11	111.23	106.32	102.18
5500	158.70	146.42	136.69	128.82	122.35	116.95	112.40
6000	173.13	159.73	149.12	140.54	133.48	127.59	122.61
6500	187.56	173.04	161.54	152.25	144.60	138.22	132.83
7000	201.99	186.35	173.97	163.96	155.72	148.85	143.05
7500	216.41	199.66	186.39	175.67	166.85	159.48	153.27
8000	230.84	212.97	198.82	187.38	177.97	170.12	163.49
8500	245.27	226.28	211.25	199.09	189.09	180.75	173.70
9000	259.70	239.59	223.67	210.80	200.22	191.38	183.92
9500	274.12	252.90	236.10	222.51	211.34	202.01	194.14
10000	288.55	266.21	248.53	234.23	222.46	212.65	204.36
11000	317.41	292.83	273.38	257.65	244.71	233.91	224.79
12000	346.26	319.45	298.23	281.07	266.95	255.17	245.23
13000	375.12	346.07	323.08	304.49	289.20	276.44	265.67
14000	403.97	372.69	347.94	327.92	311.45	297.70	286.10
15000	432.83	399.31	372.79	351.34	333.69	318.97	306.54
16000	461.68	425.94	397.64	374.76	355.94	340.23	326.97
17000	490.54	452.56	422.49	398.18	378.18	361.50	347.41
18000	519.39	479.18	447.35	421.61	400.43	382.76	367.84
19000	548.25	505.80	472.20	445.03	422.68	404.03	388.28
20000	577.10	532.42	497.05	468.45	444.92	425.29	408.72
21000	605.96	559.04	521.90	491.87	467.17	446.56	429.15
22000	634.81	585.66	546.76	515.30	489.41	467.82	449.59
23000	663.67	612.28	571.61	538.72	511.66	489.08	470.02
24000	692.52	638.90	596.46	562.14	533.91	510.35	490.46
25000	721.38	665.52	621.31	585.56	556.15	531.61	510.90
26000	750.23	692.15	646.17	608.99	578.40	552.88	531.33
27000	779.09	718.77	671.02	632.41	600.65	574.14	551.77
28000	807.94	745.39	695.87	655.83	622.89	595.41	572.20
29000	836.80	772.01	720.72	679.25	645.14	616.67	592.64
30000	865.65	798.63	745.58	702.68	667.38	637.94	613.07
31000	894.51	825.25	770.43	726.10	689.63	659.20	633.51
32000	923.36	851.87	795.28	749.52	711.88	680.47	653.95
33000	952.22	878.49	820.14	772.94	734.12	701.73	674.38
34000	981.07	905.11	844.99	796.37	756.37	722.99	694.82
35000	1009.93	931.73	869.84	819.79	778.61	744.26	715.25
40000	1154.20	1064.84	994.10	936.90	889.85	850.58	817.43
45000	1298.48	1197.94	1118.37	1054.02	1001.08	956.90	919.61
50000	1442.75	1331.05	1242.63	1171.13	1112.31	1063.23	1021.79
55000	1587.03	1464.15	1366.89	1288.24	1223.54	1169.55	1123.97
60000	1731.30	1597.26	1491.15	1405.35	1334.77	1275.87	1226.15
65000	1875.58	1730.36	1615.42	1522.47	1446.00	1382.19	1328.33
70000	2019.85	1863.47	1739.68	1639.58	1557.23	1488.52	1430.51

17% Monthly Loan Payments

LOAN AMOUNT	7½ YEARS	8 YEARS	8½ YEARS	9 YEARS	9½ YEARS	10 YEARS	10½ YEARS
100	1.97	1.91	1.86	1.81	1.77	1.74	1.71
200	3.95	3.82	3.72	3.63	3.55	3.48	3.41
300	5.92	5.74	5.58	5.44	5.32	5.21	5.12
400	7.89	7.65	7.44	7.25	7.09	6.95	6.83
500	9.86	9.56	9.30	9.07	8.87	8.69	8.53
600	11.84	11.47	11.16	10.88	10.64	10.43	10.24
700	13.81	13.39	13.02	12.70	12.41	12.17	11.95
800	15.78	15.30	14.88	14.51	14.19	13.90	13.65
900	17.76	17.21	16.74	16.32	15.96	15.64	15.36
1000	19.73	19.12	18.60	18.14	17.73	17.38	17.07
1500	29.59	28.68	27.89	27.20	26.60	26.07	25.60
2000	39.46	38.24	37.19	36.27	35.47	34.76	34.13
2500	49.32	47.80	46.49	45.34	44.33	43.45	42.67
3000	59.19	57.36	55.79	54.41	53.20	52.14	51.20
3500	69.05	66.93	65.08	63.48	62.07	60.83	59.73
4000	78.92	76.49	74.38	72.54	70.94	69.52	68.27
4500	88.78	86.05	83.68	81.61	79.80	78.21	76.80
5000	98.65	95.61	92.98	90.68	88.67	86.90	85.33
5500	108.51	105.17	102.27	99.75	97.54	95.59	93.87
6000	118.37	114.73	111.57	108.82	106.40	104.28	102.40
6500	128.24	124.29	120.87	117.89	115.27	112.97	110.93
7000	138.10	133.85	130.17	126.95	124.14	121.66	119.47
7500	147.97	143.41	139.46	136.02	133.00	130.35	128.00
8000	157.83	152.97	148.76	145.09	141.87	139.04	136.53
8500	167.70	162.53	158.06	154.16	150.74	147.73	145.06
9000	177.56	172.09	167.36	163.23	159.61	156.42	153.60
9500	187.43	181.65	176.65	172.29	168.47	165.11	162.13
10000	197.29	191.21	185.95	181.36	177.34	173.80	170.66
11000	217.02	210.34	204.55	199.50	195.07	191.18	187.73
12000	236.75	229.46	223.14	217.63	212.81	208.56	204.80
13000	256.48	248.58	241.74	235.77	230.54	225.94	221.86
14000	276.21	267.70	260.33	253.91	248.28	243.32	238.93
15000	295.94	286.82	278.93	272.04	266.01	260.70	256.00
16000	315.67	305.94	297.52	290.18	283.74	278.08	273.06
17000	335.40	325.06	316.12	308.32	301.48	295.46	290.13
18000	355.12	344.19	334.71	326.45	319.21	312.84	307.20
19000	374.85	363.31	353.31	344.59	336.95	330.22	324.26
20000	394.58	382.43	371.90	362.72	354.68	347.60	341.33
21000	414.31	401.55	390.50	380.86	372.41	364.98	358.40
22000	434.04	420.67	409.09	399.00	390.15	382.35	375.46
23000	453.77	439.79	427.69	417.13	407.88	399.73	392.53
24000	473.50	458.91	446.28	435.27	425.62	417.11	409.60
25000	493.23	478.04	464.88	453.40	443.35	434.49	426.66
26000	512.96	497.16	483.47	471.54	461.08	451.87	443.73
27000	532.69	516.28	502.07	489.68	478.82	469.25	460.79
28000	552.42	535.40	520.66	507.81	496.55	486.63	477.86
29000	572.15	554.52	539.26	525.95	514.29	504.01	494.93
30000	591.87	573.64	557.85	544.09	532.02	521.39	511.99
31000	611.60	592.77	576.45	562.22	549.75	538.77	529.06
32000	631.33	611.89	595.04	580.36	567.49	556.15	546.13
33000	651.06	631.01	613.64	598.49	585.22	573.53	563.19
34000	670.79	650.13	632.23	616.63	602.96	590.91	580.26
35000	690.52	669.25	650.83	634.77	620.69	608.29	597.33
40000	789.17	764.86	743.80	725.45	709.36	695.19	682.66
45000	887.81	860.47	836.78	816.13	798.03	782.09	767.99
50000	986.46	956.07	929.75	906.81	886.70	868.99	853.32
55000	1085.10	1051.68	1022.73	997.49	975.37	955.89	938.66
60000	1183.75	1147.29	1115.70	1088.17	1064.04	1042.79	1023.99
65000	1282.39	1242.89	1208.68	1178.85	1152.71	1129.68	1109.32
70000	1381.04	1338.50	1301.65	1269.53	1241.38	1216.58	1194.65

Monthly Loan Payments 17%

LOAN AMOUNT	11 YEARS	11½ YEARS	12 YEARS	12½ YEARS	13 YEARS	14 YEARS	15 YEARS
100	1.68	1.65	1.63	1.61	1.59	1.56	1.54
200	3.36	3.31	3.26	3.22	3.19	3.13	3.08
300	5.04	4.96	4.90	4.84	4.78	4.69	4.62
400	6.72	6.62	6.53	6.45	6.38	6.26	6.16
500	8.39	8.27	8.16	8.06	7.97	7.82	7.70
600	10.07	9.92	9.79	9.67	9.57	9.38	9.23
700	11.75	11.58	11.42	11.28	11.16	10.95	10.77
800	13.43	13.23	13.06	12.90	12.75	12.51	12.31
900	15.11	14.89	14.69	14.51	14.35	14.07	13.85
1000	16.79	16.54	16.32	16.12	15.94	15.64	15.39
1500	25.18	24.81	24.48	24.18	23.91	23.46	23.09
2000	33.58	33.08	32.64	32.24	31.89	31.28	30.78
2500	41.97	41.35	40.80	40.30	39.86	39.10	38.48
3000	50.36	49.62	48.96	48.36	47.83	46.92	46.17
3500	58.76	57.89	57.12	56.42	55.80	54.73	53.87
4000	67.15	66.16	65.28	64.48	63.77	62.55	61.56
4500	75.55	74.43	73.44	72.54	71.74	70.37	69.26
5000	83.94	82.70	81.60	80.60	79.71	78.19	76.95
5500	92.34	90.97	89.76	88.67	87.69	86.01	84.65
6000	100.73	99.24	97.92	96.73	95.66	93.83	92.34
6500	109.12	107.51	106.07	104.79	103.63	101.65	100.04
7000	117.52	115.78	114.23	112.85	111.60	109.47	107.73
7500	125.91	124.05	122.39	120.91	119.57	117.29	115.43
8000	134.31	132.32	130.55	128.97	127.54	125.11	123.12
8500	142.70	140.59	138.71	137.03	135.52	132.93	130.82
9000	151.09	148.87	146.87	145.09	143.49	140.75	138.51
9500	159.49	157.14	155.03	153.15	151.46	148.56	146.21
10000	167.88	165.41	163.19	161.21	159.43	156.38	153.90
11000	184.67	181.95	179.51	177.33	175.37	172.02	169.29
12000	201.46	198.49	195.83	193.45	191.32	187.66	184.68
13000	218.25	215.03	212.15	209.57	207.26	203.30	200.07
14000	235.04	231.57	228.47	225.69	223.20	218.94	215.46
15000	251.82	248.11	244.79	241.81	239.14	234.58	230.85
16000	268.61	264.65	261.11	257.94	255.09	250.21	246.24
17000	285.40	281.19	277.43	274.06	271.03	265.85	261.63
18000	302.19	297.73	293.75	290.18	286.97	281.49	277.02
19000	318.98	314.27	310.07	306.30	302.92	297.13	292.41
20000	335.77	330.81	326.38	322.42	318.86	312.77	307.80
21000	352.55	347.35	342.70	338.54	334.80	328.41	323.19
22000	369.34	363.89	359.02	354.66	350.74	344.04	338.58
23000	386.13	380.43	375.34	370.78	366.69	359.68	353.97
24000	402.92	396.97	391.66	386.90	382.63	375.32	369.36
25000	419.71	413.51	407.98	403.02	398.57	390.96	384.75
26000	436.50	430.05	424.30	419.15	414.52	406.60	400.14
27000	453.28	446.60	440.62	435.27	430.46	422.24	415.53
28000	470.07	463.14	456.94	451.39	446.40	437.87	430.92
29000	486.86	479.68	473.26	467.51	462.35	453.51	446.31
30000	503.65	496.22	489.58	483.63	478.29	469.15	461.70
31000	520.44	512.76	505.90	499.75	494.23	484.79	477.09
32000	537.23	529.30	522.22	515.87	510.17	500.43	492.48
33000	554.01	545.84	538.53	531.99	526.12	516.07	507.87
34000	570.80	562.38	554.85	548.11	542.06	531.71	523.26
35000	587.59	578.92	571.17	564.23	558.00	547.34	538.65
40000	671.53	661.62	652.77	644.84	637.72	625.54	615.60
45000	755.47	744.33	734.37	725.44	717.43	703.73	692.55
50000	839.42	827.03	815.96	806.05	797.15	781.92	769.50
55000	923.36	909.73	897.56	886.65	876.86	860.11	846.45
60000	1007.30	992.43	979.15	967.26	956.58	938.30	923.40
65000	1091.24	1075.14	1060.75	1047.86	1036.29	1016.49	1000.35
70000	1175.18	1157.84	1142.35	1128.47	1116.01	1094.69	1077.30

17¼%   Monthly Loan Payments

LOAN AMOUNT	½ YEAR	1 YEAR	1½ YEARS	2 YEARS	2½ YEARS	3 YEARS	3½ YEARS
100	17.52	9.13	6.34	4.96	4.13	3.58	3.19
200	35.03	18.26	12.69	9.91	8.25	7.16	6.38
300	52.55	27.40	19.03	14.87	12.38	10.73	9.56
400	70.06	36.53	25.38	19.82	16.51	14.31	12.75
500	87.58	45.66	31.72	24.78	20.64	17.89	15.94
600	105.09	54.79	38.07	29.74	24.76	21.47	19.13
700	122.61	63.93	44.41	34.69	28.89	25.04	22.32
800	140.12	73.06	50.76	39.65	33.02	28.62	25.51
900	157.64	82.19	57.10	44.61	37.14	32.20	28.69
1000	175.15	91.32	63.45	49.56	41.27	35.78	31.88
1500	262.73	136.99	95.17	74.34	61.91	53.67	47.82
2000	350.30	182.65	126.90	99.12	82.54	71.55	63.76
2500	437.88	228.31	158.62	123.91	103.18	89.44	79.70
3000	525.46	273.97	190.35	148.69	123.81	107.33	95.64
3500	613.03	319.63	222.07	173.47	144.45	125.22	111.59
4000	700.61	365.29	253.80	198.25	165.08	143.11	127.53
4500	788.18	410.96	285.52	223.03	185.72	161.00	143.47
5000	875.76	456.62	317.24	247.81	206.36	178.89	159.41
5500	963.33	502.28	348.97	272.59	226.99	196.77	175.35
6000	1050.91	547.94	380.69	297.37	247.63	214.66	191.29
6500	1138.49	593.60	412.42	322.16	268.26	232.55	207.23
7000	1226.06	639.26	444.14	346.94	288.90	250.44	223.17
7500	1313.64	684.93	475.87	371.72	309.53	268.33	239.11
8000	1401.21	730.59	507.59	396.50	330.17	286.22	255.05
8500	1488.79	776.25	539.32	421.28	350.81	304.11	270.99
9000	1576.37	821.91	571.04	446.06	371.44	322.00	286.93
9500	1663.94	867.57	602.76	470.84	392.08	339.88	302.87
10000	1751.52	913.23	634.49	495.62	412.71	357.77	318.82
11000	1926.67	1004.56	697.94	545.19	453.98	393.55	350.70
12000	2101.82	1095.88	761.39	594.75	495.25	429.33	382.58
13000	2276.97	1187.20	824.83	644.31	536.53	465.11	414.46
14000	2452.13	1278.53	888.28	693.87	577.80	500.88	446.34
15000	2627.28	1369.85	951.73	743.44	619.07	536.66	478.22
16000	2802.43	1461.17	1015.18	793.00	660.34	572.44	510.11
17000	2977.58	1552.50	1078.63	842.56	701.61	608.21	541.99
18000	3152.73	1643.82	1142.08	892.12	742.88	643.99	573.87
19000	3327.88	1735.15	1205.53	941.69	784.15	679.77	605.75
20000	3503.04	1826.47	1268.98	991.25	825.42	715.55	637.63
21000	3678.19	1917.79	1332.43	1040.81	866.70	751.32	669.51
22000	3853.34	2009.12	1395.87	1090.37	907.97	787.10	701.39
23000	4028.49	2100.44	1459.32	1139.94	949.24	822.88	733.28
24000	4203.64	2191.76	1522.77	1189.50	990.51	858.65	765.16
25000	4378.80	2283.09	1586.22	1239.06	1031.78	894.43	797.04
26000	4553.95	2374.41	1649.67	1288.62	1073.05	930.21	828.92
27000	4729.10	2465.73	1713.12	1338.19	1114.32	965.99	860.80
28000	4904.25	2557.06	1776.57	1387.75	1155.59	1001.76	892.68
29000	5079.40	2648.38	1840.02	1437.31	1196.87	1037.54	924.57
30000	5254.55	2739.70	1903.46	1486.87	1238.14	1073.32	956.45
31000	5429.71	2831.03	1966.91	1536.44	1279.41	1109.10	988.33
32000	5604.86	2922.35	2030.36	1586.00	1320.68	1144.87	1020.21
33000	5780.01	3013.67	2093.81	1635.56	1361.95	1180.65	1052.09
34000	5955.16	3105.00	2157.26	1685.12	1403.22	1216.43	1083.98
35000	6130.31	3196.32	2220.71	1734.69	1444.49	1252.20	1115.86
40000	7006.07	3652.94	2537.95	1982.50	1650.85	1431.09	1275.26
45000	7881.83	4109.55	2855.20	2230.31	1857.20	1609.98	1434.67
50000	8757.59	4566.17	3172.44	2478.12	2063.56	1788.86	1594.08
55000	9633.35	5022.79	3489.68	2725.94	2269.92	1967.75	1753.49
60000	10509.11	5479.41	3806.93	2973.75	2476.27	2146.64	1912.89
65000	11384.87	5936.02	4124.17	3221.56	2682.63	2325.52	2072.30
70000	12260.63	6392.64	4441.42	3469.37	2888.98	2504.41	2231.71

Monthly Loan Payments 17¼%

LOAN AMOUNT	4 YEARS	4½ YEARS	5 YEARS	5½ YEARS	6 YEARS	6½ YEARS	7 YEARS
100	2.90	2.68	2.50	2.36	2.24	2.14	2.06
200	5.80	5.35	5.00	4.71	4.48	4.28	4.12
300	8.70	8.03	7.50	7.07	6.72	6.42	6.17
400	11.59	10.70	9.99	9.42	8.95	8.56	8.23
500	14.49	13.38	12.49	11.78	11.19	10.70	10.29
600	17.39	16.05	14.99	14.14	13.43	12.84	12.35
700	20.29	18.73	17.49	16.49	15.67	14.98	14.41
800	23.19	21.40	19.99	18.85	17.91	17.13	16.46
900	26.09	24.08	22.49	21.20	20.15	19.27	18.52
1000	28.98	26.75	24.99	23.56	22.39	21.41	20.58
1500	43.48	40.13	37.48	35.34	33.58	32.11	30.87
2000	57.97	53.51	49.97	47.12	44.77	42.81	41.16
2500	72.46	66.88	62.47	58.90	55.96	53.52	51.45
3000	86.95	80.26	74.96	70.68	67.16	64.22	61.74
3500	101.45	93.64	87.46	82.46	78.35	74.92	72.03
4000	115.94	107.01	99.95	94.24	89.54	85.63	82.32
4500	130.43	120.39	112.44	106.02	100.74	96.33	92.61
5000	144.92	133.77	124.94	117.80	111.93	107.03	102.90
5500	159.42	147.14	137.43	129.58	123.12	117.74	113.19
6000	173.91	160.52	149.92	141.36	134.32	128.44	123.48
6500	188.40	173.89	162.42	153.14	145.51	139.14	133.77
7000	202.89	187.27	174.91	164.92	156.70	149.85	144.06
7500	217.38	200.65	187.40	176.70	167.89	160.55	154.35
8000	231.88	214.02	199.90	188.48	179.09	171.25	164.64
8500	246.37	227.40	212.39	200.26	190.28	181.96	174.93
9000	260.86	240.78	224.88	212.04	201.47	192.66	185.22
9500	275.35	254.15	237.38	223.82	212.67	203.36	195.52
10000	289.85	267.53	249.87	235.60	223.86	214.07	205.81
11000	318.83	294.28	274.86	259.16	246.24	235.47	226.39
12000	347.81	321.04	299.85	282.72	268.63	256.88	246.97
13000	376.80	347.79	324.83	306.28	291.01	278.29	267.55
14000	405.78	374.54	349.82	329.84	313.40	299.69	288.13
15000	434.77	401.30	374.81	353.40	335.79	321.10	308.71
16000	463.75	428.05	399.80	376.96	358.17	342.51	329.29
17000	492.74	454.80	424.78	400.52	380.56	363.92	349.87
18000	521.72	481.55	449.77	424.08	402.95	385.32	370.45
19000	550.71	508.31	474.76	447.64	425.33	406.73	391.03
20000	579.69	535.06	499.74	471.19	447.72	428.14	411.61
21000	608.68	561.81	524.73	494.75	470.10	449.54	432.19
22000	637.66	588.57	549.72	518.31	492.49	470.95	452.77
23000	666.64	615.32	574.71	541.87	514.87	492.36	473.35
24000	695.63	642.07	599.69	565.43	537.26	513.76	493.93
25000	724.61	668.83	624.68	588.99	559.65	535.17	514.51
26000	753.60	695.58	649.67	612.55	582.03	556.58	535.09
27000	782.58	722.33	674.65	636.11	604.42	577.98	555.67
28000	811.57	749.09	699.64	659.67	626.80	599.39	576.26
29000	840.55	775.84	724.63	683.23	649.19	620.80	596.84
30000	869.54	802.59	749.62	706.79	671.58	642.20	617.42
31000	898.52	829.34	774.60	730.35	693.96	663.61	638.00
32000	927.51	856.10	799.59	753.91	716.35	685.02	658.58
33000	956.49	882.85	824.58	777.47	738.73	706.42	679.16
34000	985.47	909.60	849.56	801.03	761.12	727.83	699.74
35000	1014.46	936.36	874.55	824.59	783.51	749.24	720.32
40000	1159.38	1070.12	999.49	942.39	895.43	856.27	823.22
45000	1304.30	1203.89	1124.42	1060.19	1007.36	963.31	926.12
50000	1449.23	1337.65	1249.36	1177.99	1119.29	1070.34	1029.03
55000	1594.15	1471.42	1374.30	1295.79	1231.22	1177.37	1131.93
60000	1739.07	1605.18	1499.23	1413.58	1343.15	1284.41	1234.83
65000	1884.00	1738.95	1624.17	1531.38	1455.08	1391.44	1337.74
70000	2028.92	1872.71	1749.10	1649.18	1567.01	1498.47	1440.64

17¼%   Monthly Loan Payments

LOAN AMOUNT	7½ YEARS	8 YEARS	8½ YEARS	9 YEARS	9½ YEARS	10 YEARS	10½ YEARS
100	1.99	1.93	1.87	1.83	1.79	1.75	1.72
200	3.98	3.85	3.75	3.66	3.58	3.51	3.45
300	5.96	5.78	5.62	5.49	5.37	5.26	5.17
400	7.95	7.71	7.50	7.32	7.16	7.02	6.89
500	9.94	9.64	9.37	9.15	8.95	8.77	8.61
600	11.93	11.56	11.25	10.97	10.73	10.52	10.34
700	13.91	13.49	13.12	12.80	12.52	12.28	12.06
800	15.90	15.42	15.00	14.63	14.31	14.03	13.78
900	17.89	17.34	16.87	16.46	16.10	15.78	15.50
1000	19.88	19.27	18.75	18.29	17.89	17.54	17.23
1500	29.81	28.91	28.12	27.44	26.84	26.31	25.84
2000	39.75	38.54	37.49	36.58	35.78	35.08	34.45
2500	49.69	48.18	46.87	45.73	44.73	43.85	43.07
3000	59.63	57.81	56.24	54.87	53.67	52.62	51.68
3500	69.57	67.45	65.61	64.02	62.62	61.38	60.30
4000	79.51	77.08	74.99	73.16	71.56	70.15	68.91
4500	89.44	86.72	84.36	82.31	80.51	78.92	77.52
5000	99.38	96.36	93.74	91.45	89.45	87.69	86.14
5500	109.32	105.99	103.11	100.60	98.40	96.46	94.75
6000	119.26	115.63	112.48	109.74	107.34	105.23	103.36
6500	129.20	125.26	121.86	118.89	116.29	114.00	111.98
7000	139.13	134.90	131.23	128.03	125.23	122.77	120.59
7500	149.07	144.53	140.60	137.18	134.18	131.54	129.21
8000	159.01	154.17	149.98	146.32	143.12	140.31	137.82
8500	168.95	163.80	159.35	155.47	152.07	149.08	146.43
9000	178.89	173.44	168.72	164.61	161.01	157.85	155.05
9500	188.83	183.07	178.10	173.76	169.96	166.62	163.66
10000	198.76	192.71	187.47	182.90	178.91	175.39	172.27
11000	218.64	211.98	206.22	201.20	196.80	192.92	189.50
12000	238.52	231.25	224.96	219.49	214.69	210.46	206.73
13000	258.39	250.52	243.71	237.78	232.58	228.00	223.96
14000	278.27	269.79	262.46	256.07	250.47	245.54	241.18
15000	298.14	289.07	281.21	274.36	268.36	263.08	258.41
16000	318.02	308.34	299.95	292.65	286.25	280.62	275.64
17000	337.90	327.61	318.70	310.94	304.14	298.15	292.86
18000	357.77	346.88	337.45	329.23	322.03	315.69	310.09
19000	377.65	366.15	356.19	347.52	339.92	333.23	327.32
20000	397.53	385.42	374.94	365.81	357.81	350.77	344.55
21000	417.40	404.69	393.69	384.10	375.70	368.31	361.77
22000	437.28	423.96	412.43	402.39	393.59	385.85	379.00
23000	457.16	443.23	431.18	420.68	411.48	403.39	396.23
24000	477.03	462.51	449.93	438.97	429.37	420.92	413.46
25000	496.91	481.78	468.68	457.26	447.26	438.46	430.68
26000	516.78	501.05	487.42	475.55	465.15	456.00	447.91
27000	536.66	520.32	506.17	493.84	483.04	473.54	465.14
28000	556.54	539.59	524.92	512.13	500.93	491.08	482.37
29000	576.41	558.86	543.66	530.42	518.83	508.62	499.59
30000	596.29	578.13	562.41	548.71	536.72	526.16	516.82
31000	616.17	597.40	581.16	567.00	554.61	543.69	534.05
32000	636.04	616.67	599.90	585.29	572.50	561.23	551.28
33000	655.92	635.94	618.65	603.59	590.39	578.77	568.50
34000	675.80	655.22	637.40	621.88	608.28	596.31	585.73
35000	695.67	674.49	656.15	640.17	626.17	613.85	602.96
40000	795.05	770.84	749.88	731.62	715.62	701.54	689.09
45000	894.43	867.20	843.62	823.07	805.07	789.23	775.23
50000	993.82	963.55	937.35	914.52	894.53	876.93	861.37
55000	1093.20	1059.91	1031.09	1005.98	983.98	964.62	947.50
60000	1192.58	1156.26	1124.82	1097.43	1073.43	1052.31	1033.64
65000	1291.96	1252.62	1218.56	1188.88	1162.88	1140.00	1119.78
70000	1391.34	1348.97	1312.29	1280.33	1252.34	1227.70	1205.91

Monthly Loan Payments 17¼%

LOAN AMOUNT	11 YEARS	11½ YEARS	12 YEARS	12½ YEARS	13 YEARS	14 YEARS	15 YEARS
100	1.70	1.67	1.65	1.63	1.61	1.58	1.56
200	3.39	3.34	3.30	3.26	3.22	3.16	3.11
300	5.09	5.01	4.95	4.89	4.83	4.74	4.67
400	6.78	6.68	6.59	6.52	6.45	6.33	6.23
500	8.48	8.35	8.24	8.14	8.06	7.91	7.78
600	10.17	10.02	9.89	9.77	9.67	9.49	9.34
700	11.87	11.69	11.54	11.40	11.28	11.07	10.90
800	13.56	13.36	13.19	13.03	12.89	12.65	12.45
900	15.26	15.04	14.84	14.66	14.50	14.23	14.01
1000	16.95	16.71	16.49	16.29	16.11	15.81	15.57
1500	25.43	25.06	24.73	24.43	24.17	23.72	23.35
2000	33.90	33.41	32.97	32.58	32.23	31.63	31.14
2500	42.38	41.76	41.22	40.72	40.28	39.53	38.92
3000	50.85	50.12	49.46	48.87	48.34	47.44	46.70
3500	59.33	58.47	57.70	57.01	56.40	55.34	54.49
4000	67.81	66.82	65.94	65.16	64.45	63.25	62.27
4500	76.28	75.18	74.19	73.30	72.51	71.16	70.05
5000	84.76	83.53	82.43	81.45	80.57	79.06	77.84
5500	93.23	91.88	90.67	89.59	88.63	86.97	85.62
6000	101.71	100.23	98.92	97.74	96.68	94.88	93.41
6500	110.18	108.59	107.16	105.88	104.74	102.78	101.19
7000	118.66	116.94	115.40	114.03	112.80	110.69	108.97
7500	127.13	125.29	123.65	122.17	120.85	118.59	116.76
8000	135.61	133.64	131.89	130.32	128.91	126.50	124.54
8500	144.09	142.00	140.13	138.46	136.97	134.41	132.32
9000	152.56	150.35	148.38	146.61	145.02	142.31	140.11
9500	161.04	158.70	156.62	154.75	153.08	150.22	147.89
10000	169.51	167.06	164.86	162.90	161.14	158.13	155.68
11000	186.46	183.76	181.35	179.19	177.25	173.94	171.24
12000	203.42	200.47	197.83	195.48	193.36	189.75	186.81
13000	220.37	217.17	214.32	211.77	209.48	205.56	202.38
14000	237.32	233.88	230.81	228.06	225.59	221.38	217.95
15000	254.27	250.58	247.29	244.35	241.71	237.19	233.51
16000	271.22	267.29	263.78	260.64	257.82	253.00	249.08
17000	288.17	283.99	280.27	276.93	273.93	268.81	264.65
18000	305.12	300.70	296.75	293.22	290.05	284.63	280.22
19000	322.07	317.41	313.24	309.51	306.16	300.44	295.78
20000	339.03	334.11	329.72	325.80	322.27	316.25	311.35
21000	355.98	350.82	346.21	342.09	338.39	332.07	326.92
22000	372.93	367.52	362.70	358.38	354.50	347.88	342.49
23000	389.88	384.23	379.18	374.67	370.61	363.69	358.05
24000	406.83	400.93	395.67	390.96	386.73	379.50	373.62
25000	423.78	417.64	412.16	407.25	402.84	395.32	389.19
26000	440.73	434.34	428.64	423.54	418.96	411.13	404.76
27000	457.69	451.05	445.13	439.83	435.07	426.94	420.32
28000	474.64	467.76	461.61	456.12	451.18	442.75	435.89
29000	491.59	484.46	478.10	472.41	467.30	458.57	451.46
30000	508.54	501.17	494.59	488.70	483.41	474.38	467.03
31000	525.49	517.87	511.07	504.99	499.52	490.19	482.59
32000	542.44	534.58	527.56	521.28	515.64	506.00	498.16
33000	559.39	551.28	544.04	537.57	531.75	521.82	513.73
34000	576.34	567.99	560.53	553.86	547.87	537.63	529.30
35000	593.30	584.70	577.02	570.15	563.98	553.44	544.86
40000	678.05	668.22	659.45	651.59	644.55	632.51	622.70
45000	762.81	751.75	741.88	733.04	725.12	711.57	700.54
50000	847.56	835.28	824.31	814.49	805.68	790.63	778.38
55000	932.32	918.81	906.74	895.94	886.25	869.70	856.22
60000	1017.08	1002.33	989.17	977.39	966.82	948.76	934.05
65000	1101.83	1085.86	1071.60	1058.84	1047.39	1027.82	1011.89
70000	1186.59	1169.39	1154.03	1140.29	1127.96	1106.88	1089.73

17½%   Monthly Loan Payments

LOAN AMOUNT	½ YEAR	1 YEAR	1½ YEARS	2 YEARS	2½ YEARS	3 YEARS	3½ YEARS
100	17.53	9.14	6.36	4.97	4.14	3.59	3.20
200	35.06	18.29	12.71	9.94	8.28	7.18	6.40
300	52.58	27.43	19.07	14.90	12.42	10.77	9.60
400	70.11	36.58	25.43	19.87	16.56	14.36	12.80
500	87.64	45.72	31.78	24.84	20.70	17.95	16.00
600	105.17	54.87	38.14	29.81	24.84	21.54	19.21
700	122.69	64.01	44.50	34.78	28.98	25.13	22.41
800	140.22	73.15	50.85	39.75	33.11	28.72	25.61
900	157.75	82.30	57.21	44.71	37.25	32.31	28.81
1000	175.28	91.44	63.57	49.68	41.39	35.90	32.01
1500	262.91	137.16	95.35	74.52	62.09	53.85	48.01
2000	350.55	182.88	127.14	99.37	82.79	71.80	64.02
2500	438.18	228.61	158.92	124.21	103.48	89.76	80.02
3000	525.83	274.33	190.70	149.05	124.18	107.71	96.03
3500	613.47	320.05	222.49	173.89	144.88	125.66	112.03
4000	701.10	365.77	254.27	198.73	165.57	143.61	128.04
4500	788.74	411.49	286.05	223.57	186.27	161.56	144.04
5000	876.38	457.21	317.84	248.41	206.97	179.51	160.04
5500	964.02	502.93	349.62	273.26	227.67	197.46	176.05
6000	1051.66	548.65	381.41	298.10	248.36	215.41	192.05
6500	1139.30	594.37	413.19	322.94	269.06	233.36	208.06
7000	1226.93	640.10	444.97	347.78	289.76	251.31	224.06
7500	1314.57	685.82	476.76	372.62	310.45	269.27	240.07
8000	1402.21	731.54	508.54	397.46	331.15	287.22	256.07
8500	1489.85	777.26	540.33	422.30	351.85	305.17	272.08
9000	1577.49	822.98	572.11	447.15	372.54	323.12	288.08
9500	1665.13	868.70	603.89	471.99	393.24	341.07	304.08
10000	1752.76	914.42	635.68	496.83	413.94	359.02	320.09
11000	1928.04	1005.86	699.24	546.51	455.33	394.92	352.10
12000	2103.31	1097.31	762.81	596.19	496.72	430.82	384.11
13000	2278.59	1188.75	826.38	645.88	538.12	466.73	416.12
14000	2453.87	1280.19	889.95	695.56	579.51	502.63	448.12
15000	2629.14	1371.63	953.52	745.24	620.90	538.53	480.13
16000	2804.42	1463.08	1017.09	794.93	662.30	574.43	512.14
17000	2979.70	1554.52	1080.65	844.61	703.69	610.34	544.15
18000	3154.97	1645.96	1144.22	894.29	745.09	646.24	576.16
19000	3330.25	1737.40	1207.79	943.97	786.48	682.14	608.17
20000	3505.52	1828.84	1271.35	993.66	827.87	718.04	640.18
21000	3680.80	1920.29	1334.92	1043.34	869.27	753.94	672.19
22000	3856.08	2011.73	1398.49	1093.02	910.66	789.85	704.19
23000	4031.35	2103.17	1462.06	1142.71	952.05	825.75	736.20
24000	4206.63	2194.61	1525.62	1192.39	993.45	861.65	768.21
25000	4381.91	2286.06	1589.19	1242.07	1034.84	897.55	800.22
26000	4557.18	2377.50	1652.76	1291.75	1076.24	933.45	832.23
27000	4732.46	2468.94	1716.33	1341.44	1117.63	969.36	864.24
28000	4907.73	2560.38	1779.90	1391.12	1159.02	1005.26	896.25
29000	5083.01	2651.82	1843.46	1440.80	1200.42	1041.16	928.26
30000	5258.29	2743.27	1907.03	1490.49	1241.81	1077.06	960.27
31000	5433.56	2834.71	1970.60	1540.17	1283.20	1112.96	992.27
32000	5608.84	2926.15	2034.17	1589.85	1324.60	1148.87	1024.28
33000	5784.12	3017.59	2097.73	1639.53	1365.99	1184.77	1056.29
34000	5959.39	3109.03	2161.30	1689.22	1407.38	1220.67	1088.30
35000	6134.67	3200.48	2224.87	1738.90	1448.78	1256.57	1120.31
40000	7011.05	3657.69	2542.71	1987.31	1655.75	1436.08	1280.35
45000	7887.43	4114.90	2860.55	2235.73	1862.71	1615.59	1440.40
50000	8763.81	4572.11	3178.38	2484.14	2069.68	1795.10	1600.44
55000	9640.19	5029.32	3496.22	2732.56	2276.65	1974.61	1760.49
60000	10516.57	5486.55	3814.06	2980.97	2483.62	2154.12	1920.53
65000	11392.96	5943.74	4131.90	3229.39	2690.59	2333.63	2080.58
70000	12269.34	6400.95	4449.74	3477.80	2897.56	2513.14	2240.62

Monthly Loan Payments 17½%

LOAN AMOUNT	4 YEARS	4½ YEARS	5 YEARS	5½ YEARS	6 YEARS	6½ YEARS	7 YEARS
100	2.91	2.69	2.51	2.37	2.25	2.15	2.07
200	5.82	5.38	5.02	4.74	4.51	4.31	4.15
300	8.73	8.07	7.54	7.11	6.76	6.46	6.22
400	11.65	10.75	10.05	9.48	9.01	8.62	8.29
500	14.56	13.44	12.56	11.85	11.26	10.77	10.36
600	17.47	16.13	15.07	14.22	13.52	12.93	12.44
700	20.38	18.82	17.59	16.59	15.77	15.08	14.51
800	23.29	21.51	20.10	18.96	18.02	17.24	16.58
900	26.20	24.20	22.61	21.33	20.27	19.39	18.65
1000	29.11	26.89	25.12	23.70	22.53	21.55	20.73
1500	43.67	40.33	37.68	35.55	33.79	32.32	31.09
2000	58.23	53.77	50.24	47.39	45.05	43.10	41.45
2500	72.79	67.21	62.81	59.24	56.32	53.87	51.81
3000	87.34	80.66	75.37	71.09	67.58	64.65	62.18
3500	101.90	94.10	87.93	82.94	78.84	75.42	72.54
4000	116.46	107.54	100.49	94.79	90.10	86.20	82.90
4500	131.01	120.98	113.05	106.64	101.37	96.97	93.27
5000	145.57	134.43	125.61	118.49	112.63	107.75	103.63
5500	160.13	147.87	138.17	130.34	123.89	118.52	113.99
6000	174.69	161.31	150.73	142.18	135.16	129.30	124.35
6500	189.24	174.76	163.29	154.03	146.42	140.07	134.72
7000	203.80	188.20	175.86	165.88	157.68	150.85	145.08
7500	218.36	201.64	188.42	177.73	168.95	161.62	155.44
8000	232.91	215.08	200.98	189.58	180.21	172.40	165.81
8500	247.47	228.53	213.54	201.43	191.47	183.17	176.17
9000	262.03	241.97	226.10	213.28	202.73	193.95	186.53
9500	276.59	255.41	238.66	225.12	214.00	204.72	196.90
10000	291.14	268.85	251.22	236.97	225.26	215.50	207.26
11000	320.26	295.74	276.34	260.67	247.79	237.04	227.98
12000	349.37	322.63	301.47	284.37	270.31	258.59	248.71
13000	378.49	349.51	326.59	308.07	292.84	280.14	269.44
14000	407.60	376.40	351.71	331.76	315.36	301.69	290.16
15000	436.72	403.28	376.83	355.46	337.89	323.24	310.89
16000	465.83	430.17	401.96	379.16	360.42	344.79	331.61
17000	494.94	457.05	427.08	402.86	382.94	366.34	352.34
18000	524.06	483.94	452.20	426.55	405.47	387.89	373.06
19000	553.17	510.82	477.32	450.25	427.99	409.44	393.79
20000	582.29	537.71	502.44	473.95	450.52	430.99	414.52
21000	611.40	564.59	527.57	497.64	473.05	452.54	435.24
22000	640.52	591.48	552.69	521.34	495.57	474.09	455.97
23000	669.63	618.37	577.81	545.04	518.10	495.64	476.69
24000	698.74	645.25	602.93	568.74	540.63	517.19	497.42
25000	727.86	672.14	628.06	592.43	563.15	538.74	518.14
26000	756.97	699.02	653.18	616.13	585.68	560.29	538.87
27000	786.09	725.91	678.30	639.83	608.20	581.84	559.60
28000	815.20	752.79	703.42	663.53	630.73	603.39	580.32
29000	844.32	779.68	728.54	687.22	653.26	624.94	601.05
30000	873.43	806.56	753.67	710.92	675.78	646.49	621.77
31000	902.55	833.45	778.79	734.62	698.31	668.04	642.50
32000	931.66	860.34	803.91	758.32	720.83	689.58	663.23
33000	960.77	887.22	829.03	782.01	743.36	711.13	683.95
34000	989.89	914.11	854.16	805.71	765.89	732.68	704.68
35000	1019.00	940.99	879.28	829.41	788.41	754.23	725.40
40000	1164.57	1075.42	1004.89	947.89	901.04	861.98	829.03
45000	1310.15	1209.85	1130.50	1066.38	1013.67	969.73	932.66
50000	1455.72	1344.27	1256.11	1184.87	1126.30	1077.48	1036.29
55000	1601.29	1478.70	1381.72	1303.35	1238.93	1185.23	1139.92
60000	1746.86	1613.13	1507.33	1421.84	1351.56	1292.97	1243.55
65000	1892.43	1747.56	1632.94	1540.33	1464.19	1400.72	1347.18
70000	2038.01	1881.98	1758.55	1658.81	1576.82	1508.47	1450.81

17½% Monthly Loan Payments

LOAN AMOUNT	7½ YEARS	8 YEARS	8½ YEARS	9 YEARS	9½ YEARS	10 YEARS	10½ YEARS
100	2.00	1.94	1.89	1.84	1.80	1.77	1.74
200	4.00	3.88	3.78	3.69	3.61	3.54	3.48
300	6.01	5.83	5.67	5.53	5.41	5.31	5.22
400	8.01	7.77	7.56	7.38	7.22	7.08	6.96
500	10.01	9.71	9.45	9.22	9.02	8.85	8.69
600	12.01	11.65	11.34	11.07	10.83	10.62	10.43
700	14.02	13.59	13.23	12.91	12.63	12.39	12.17
800	16.02	15.54	15.12	14.76	14.44	14.16	13.91
900	18.02	17.48	17.01	16.60	16.24	15.93	15.65
1000	20.02	19.42	18.90	18.45	18.05	17.70	17.39
1500	30.04	29.13	28.35	27.67	27.07	26.55	26.08
2000	40.05	38.84	37.80	36.89	36.10	35.40	34.78
2500	50.06	48.55	47.25	46.11	45.12	44.24	43.47
3000	60.07	58.26	56.70	55.34	54.14	53.09	52.17
3500	70.08	67.97	66.15	64.56	63.17	61.94	60.86
4000	80.10	77.68	75.60	73.78	72.19	70.79	69.56
4500	90.11	87.40	85.05	83.00	81.21	79.64	78.25
5000	100.12	97.11	94.50	92.23	90.24	88.49	86.94
5500	110.13	106.82	103.95	101.45	99.26	97.34	95.64
6000	120.14	116.53	113.40	110.67	108.29	106.19	104.33
6500	130.16	126.24	122.85	119.89	117.31	115.04	113.03
7000	140.17	135.95	132.30	129.12	126.33	123.89	121.72
7500	150.18	145.66	141.75	138.34	135.36	132.73	130.42
8000	160.19	155.37	151.20	147.56	144.38	141.58	139.11
8500	170.20	165.08	160.65	156.79	153.41	150.43	147.81
9000	180.22	174.79	170.10	166.01	162.43	159.28	156.50
9500	190.23	184.50	179.55	175.23	171.45	168.13	165.19
10000	200.24	194.21	189.00	184.45	180.48	176.98	173.89
11000	220.26	213.63	207.90	202.90	198.52	194.68	191.28
12000	240.29	233.05	226.79	221.34	216.57	212.37	208.67
13000	260.31	252.48	245.69	239.79	234.62	230.07	226.06
14000	280.34	271.90	264.59	258.23	252.67	247.77	243.44
15000	300.36	291.32	283.49	276.68	270.72	265.47	260.83
16000	320.38	310.74	302.39	295.13	288.76	283.17	278.22
17000	340.41	330.16	321.29	313.57	306.81	300.86	295.61
18000	360.43	349.58	340.19	332.02	324.86	318.56	313.00
19000	380.46	369.00	359.09	350.46	342.91	336.26	330.39
20000	400.48	388.42	377.99	368.91	360.95	353.96	347.78
21000	420.51	407.85	396.89	387.35	379.00	371.66	365.17
22000	440.53	427.27	415.79	405.80	397.05	389.35	382.56
23000	460.55	446.69	434.69	424.24	415.10	407.05	399.94
24000	480.58	466.11	453.59	442.69	433.14	424.75	417.33
25000	500.60	485.53	472.49	461.13	451.19	442.45	434.72
26000	520.63	504.95	491.39	479.58	469.24	460.14	452.11
27000	540.65	524.37	510.29	498.02	487.29	477.84	469.50
28000	560.67	543.79	529.19	516.47	505.33	495.54	486.89
29000	580.70	563.22	548.09	534.91	523.38	513.24	504.28
30000	600.72	582.64	566.99	553.36	541.43	530.94	521.67
31000	620.75	602.06	585.89	571.81	559.48	548.63	539.06
32000	640.77	621.48	604.79	590.25	577.53	566.33	556.44
33000	660.79	640.90	623.69	608.70	595.57	584.03	573.83
34000	680.82	660.32	642.58	627.14	613.62	601.73	591.22
35000	700.84	679.74	661.48	645.59	631.67	619.43	608.61
40000	800.96	776.85	755.98	737.81	721.91	707.92	695.56
45000	901.08	873.95	850.48	830.04	812.15	796.40	782.50
50000	1001.20	971.06	944.98	922.27	902.38	884.89	869.44
55000	1101.32	1068.17	1039.48	1014.49	992.62	973.38	956.39
60000	1201.44	1165.27	1133.97	1106.72	1082.86	1061.87	1043.33
65000	1301.56	1262.38	1228.47	1198.95	1173.10	1150.36	1130.28
70000	1401.68	1359.48	1322.97	1291.17	1263.34	1238.85	1217.22

Monthly Loan Payments 17½%

LOAN AMOUNT	11 YEARS	11½ YEARS	12 YEARS	12½ YEARS	13 YEARS	14 YEARS	15 YEARS
100	1.71	1.69	1.67	1.65	1.63	1.60	1.57
200	3.42	3.37	3.33	3.29	3.26	3.20	3.15
300	5.13	5.06	5.00	4.94	4.89	4.80	4.72
400	6.85	6.75	6.66	6.58	6.51	6.40	6.30
500	8.56	8.44	8.33	8.23	8.14	7.99	7.87
600	10.27	10.12	9.99	9.88	9.77	9.59	9.45
700	11.98	11.81	11.66	11.52	11.40	11.19	11.02
800	13.69	13.50	13.32	13.17	13.03	12.79	12.60
900	15.40	15.18	14.99	14.81	14.66	14.39	14.17
1000	17.11	16.87	16.65	16.46	16.29	15.99	15.75
1500	25.67	25.31	24.98	24.69	24.43	23.98	23.62
2000	34.23	33.74	33.31	32.92	32.57	31.98	31.49
2500	42.79	42.18	41.63	41.15	40.71	39.97	39.36
3000	51.34	50.61	49.96	49.38	48.86	47.96	47.24
3500	59.90	59.05	58.29	57.61	57.00	55.96	55.11
4000	68.46	67.49	66.62	65.84	65.14	63.95	62.98
4500	77.02	75.92	74.94	74.07	73.28	71.94	70.86
5000	85.57	84.36	83.27	82.30	81.43	79.94	78.73
5500	94.13	92.79	91.60	90.53	89.57	87.93	86.60
6000	102.69	101.23	99.92	98.76	97.71	95.93	94.47
6500	111.25	109.66	108.25	106.99	105.85	103.92	102.35
7000	119.80	118.10	116.58	115.22	114.00	111.91	110.22
7500	128.36	126.53	124.90	123.45	122.14	119.91	118.09
8000	136.92	134.97	133.23	131.68	130.28	127.90	125.97
8500	145.48	143.41	141.56	139.91	138.42	135.89	133.84
9000	154.03	151.84	149.88	148.13	146.57	143.89	141.71
9500	162.59	160.28	158.21	156.36	154.71	151.88	149.58
10000	171.15	168.71	166.54	164.59	162.85	159.88	157.46
11000	188.26	185.58	183.19	181.05	179.14	175.86	173.20
12000	205.38	202.46	199.85	197.51	195.42	191.85	188.95
13000	222.49	219.33	216.50	213.97	211.71	207.84	204.70
14000	239.61	236.20	233.15	230.43	227.99	223.83	220.44
15000	256.72	253.07	249.81	246.89	244.28	239.81	236.19
16000	273.84	269.94	266.46	263.35	260.56	255.80	251.93
17000	290.95	286.81	283.12	279.81	276.85	271.79	267.68
18000	308.07	303.68	299.77	296.27	293.13	287.78	283.42
19000	325.18	320.55	316.42	312.73	309.42	303.76	299.17
20000	342.30	337.43	333.08	329.19	325.70	319.75	314.92
21000	359.41	354.30	349.73	345.65	341.99	335.74	330.66
22000	376.53	371.17	366.39	362.11	358.27	351.73	346.41
23000	393.64	388.04	383.04	378.57	374.56	367.71	362.15
24000	410.76	404.91	399.69	395.03	390.84	383.70	377.90
25000	427.87	421.78	416.35	411.49	407.13	399.69	393.64
26000	444.99	438.65	433.00	427.95	423.41	415.68	409.39
27000	462.10	455.52	449.65	444.40	439.70	431.66	425.14
28000	479.22	472.40	466.31	460.86	455.98	447.65	440.88
29000	496.33	489.27	482.96	477.32	472.27	463.64	456.63
30000	513.45	506.14	499.62	493.78	488.55	479.63	472.37
31000	530.56	523.01	516.27	510.24	504.84	495.62	488.12
32000	547.68	539.88	532.92	526.70	521.12	511.60	503.87
33000	564.79	556.75	549.58	543.16	537.41	527.59	519.61
34000	581.91	573.62	566.23	559.62	553.69	543.58	535.36
35000	599.02	590.49	582.89	576.08	569.98	559.57	551.10
40000	684.60	674.85	666.15	658.38	651.40	639.50	629.83
45000	770.17	759.21	749.42	740.67	732.83	719.46	708.56
50000	855.75	843.56	832.69	822.97	814.26	799.38	787.29
55000	941.32	927.92	915.96	905.27	895.68	879.32	866.02
60000	1026.90	1012.28	999.23	987.57	977.11	959.26	944.75
65000	1112.47	1096.63	1082.50	1069.86	1058.53	1039.19	1023.48
70000	1198.05	1180.99	1165.77	1152.16	1139.96	1119.13	1102.20

17¾% Monthly Loan Payments

LOAN AMOUNT	½ YEAR	1 YEAR	1½ YEARS	2 YEARS	2½ YEARS	3 YEARS	3½ YEARS
100	17.54	9.16	6.37	4.98	4.15	3.60	3.21
200	35.08	18.31	12.74	9.96	8.30	7.21	6.43
300	52.62	27.47	19.11	14.94	12.45	10.81	9.64
400	70.16	36.62	25.47	19.92	16.61	14.41	12.85
500	87.70	45.78	31.84	24.90	20.76	18.01	16.07
600	105.24	54.94	38.21	29.88	24.91	21.62	19.28
700	122.78	64.09	44.58	34.86	29.06	25.22	22.50
800	140.32	73.25	50.95	39.84	33.21	28.82	25.71
900	157.86	82.40	57.32	44.82	37.36	32.42	28.92
1000	175.40	91.56	63.69	49.80	41.52	36.03	32.14
1500	263.10	137.34	95.53	74.71	62.27	54.04	48.20
2000	350.80	183.12	127.37	99.61	83.03	72.05	64.27
2500	438.50	228.90	159.22	124.51	103.79	90.07	80.34
3000	526.20	274.68	191.06	149.41	124.55	108.08	96.41
3500	613.90	320.46	222.90	174.31	145.31	126.09	112.48
4000	701.60	366.24	254.75	199.21	166.07	144.11	128.55
4500	789.30	412.02	286.59	224.12	186.82	162.12	144.61
5000	877.00	457.81	318.43	249.02	207.58	180.14	160.68
5500	964.70	503.59	350.28	273.92	228.34	198.15	176.75
6000	1052.40	549.37	382.12	298.82	249.10	216.16	192.82
6500	1140.10	595.15	413.96	323.72	269.86	234.18	208.89
7000	1227.80	640.93	445.81	348.62	290.61	252.19	224.95
7500	1315.51	686.71	477.65	373.53	311.37	270.20	241.02
8000	1403.21	732.49	509.49	398.43	332.13	288.22	257.09
8500	1490.91	778.27	541.34	423.33	352.89	306.23	273.16
9000	1578.61	824.05	573.18	448.23	373.65	324.24	289.23
9500	1666.31	869.83	605.02	473.13	394.41	342.26	305.30
10000	1754.01	915.61	636.87	498.03	415.16	360.27	321.36
11000	1929.41	1007.17	700.55	547.84	456.68	396.30	353.50
12000	2104.81	1098.73	764.24	597.64	498.20	432.33	385.64
13000	2280.21	1190.29	827.93	647.44	539.71	468.35	417.77
14000	2455.61	1281.85	891.61	697.25	581.23	504.38	449.91
15000	2631.01	1373.42	955.30	747.05	622.74	540.41	482.05
16000	2806.41	1464.98	1018.99	796.85	664.26	576.43	514.18
17000	2981.81	1556.54	1082.67	846.66	705.78	612.46	546.32
18000	3157.21	1648.10	1146.36	896.46	747.29	648.49	578.46
19000	3332.61	1739.66	1210.05	946.26	788.81	684.52	610.59
20000	3508.01	1831.22	1273.73	996.07	830.33	720.54	642.73
21000	3683.41	1922.79	1337.42	1045.87	871.84	756.57	674.86
22000	3858.82	2014.34	1401.11	1095.67	913.36	792.60	707.00
23000	4034.22	2105.90	1464.79	1145.48	954.88	828.62	739.14
24000	4209.62	2197.47	1528.48	1195.28	996.39	864.65	771.27
25000	4385.02	2289.03	1592.17	1245.08	1037.91	900.68	803.41
26000	4560.42	2380.59	1655.85	1294.89	1079.42	936.70	835.55
27000	4735.82	2472.15	1719.54	1344.69	1120.94	972.73	867.68
28000	4911.22	2563.71	1783.23	1394.49	1162.46	1008.76	899.82
29000	5086.62	2655.27	1846.91	1444.30	1203.97	1044.79	931.96
30000	5262.02	2746.83	1910.60	1494.10	1245.49	1080.81	964.09
31000	5437.42	2838.39	1974.29	1543.91	1287.01	1116.84	996.23
32000	5612.82	2929.95	2037.97	1593.71	1328.52	1152.87	1028.37
33000	5788.22	3021.51	2101.66	1643.51	1370.04	1188.89	1060.50
34000	5963.62	3113.08	2165.35	1693.32	1411.55	1224.92	1092.64
35000	6139.02	3204.64	2229.03	1743.12	1453.07	1260.95	1124.77
40000	7016.03	3662.44	2547.47	1992.14	1660.65	1441.08	1285.46
45000	7893.02	4120.25	2865.90	2241.15	1868.23	1621.22	1446.14
50000	8770.04	4578.05	3184.33	2490.17	2075.82	1801.36	1606.82
55000	9647.02	5035.86	3502.77	2739.19	2283.40	1981.49	1767.50
60000	10524.04	5493.66	3821.20	2988.20	2490.98	2161.63	1928.18
65000	11401.05	5951.47	4139.63	3237.22	2698.56	2341.76	2088.87
70000	12278.05	6409.27	4458.07	3486.24	2906.14	2521.90	2249.55

Monthly Loan Payments 17¾%

LOAN AMOUNT	4 YEARS	4½ YEARS	5 YEARS	5½ YEARS	6 YEARS	6½ YEARS	7 YEARS
100	2.92	2.70	2.53	2.38	2.27	2.17	2.09
200	5.85	5.40	5.05	4.77	4.53	4.34	4.17
300	8.77	8.11	7.58	7.15	6.80	6.51	6.26
400	11.70	10.81	10.10	9.53	9.07	8.68	8.35
500	14.62	13.51	12.63	11.92	11.33	10.85	10.44
600	17.55	16.21	15.15	14.30	13.60	13.02	12.52
700	20.47	18.91	17.68	16.68	15.87	15.18	14.61
800	23.40	21.61	20.21	19.07	18.13	17.35	16.70
900	26.32	24.32	22.73	21.45	20.40	19.52	18.78
1000	29.24	27.02	25.26	23.84	22.67	21.69	20.87
1500	43.87	40.53	37.89	35.75	34.00	32.54	31.31
2000	58.49	54.04	50.52	47.67	45.33	43.39	41.74
2500	73.11	67.55	63.14	59.59	56.67	54.23	52.18
3000	87.73	81.05	75.77	71.51	68.00	65.08	62.61
3500	102.36	94.56	88.40	83.42	79.33	75.92	73.05
4000	116.98	108.07	101.03	95.34	90.67	86.77	83.49
4500	131.60	121.58	113.66	107.26	102.00	97.62	93.92
5000	146.22	135.09	126.29	119.18	113.33	108.46	104.36
5500	160.84	148.60	138.92	131.09	124.67	119.31	114.79
6000	175.47	162.11	151.55	143.01	136.00	130.16	125.23
6500	190.09	175.62	164.17	154.93	147.33	141.00	135.67
7000	204.71	189.13	176.80	166.85	158.67	151.85	146.10
7500	219.33	202.64	189.43	178.77	170.00	162.70	156.54
8000	233.96	216.15	202.06	190.68	181.33	173.54	166.97
8500	248.58	229.66	214.69	202.60	192.67	184.39	177.41
9000	263.20	243.16	227.32	214.52	204.00	195.23	187.84
9500	277.82	256.67	239.95	226.44	215.33	206.08	198.28
10000	292.45	270.18	252.58	238.35	226.67	216.93	208.72
11000	321.69	297.20	277.83	262.19	249.33	238.62	229.59
12000	350.93	324.22	303.09	286.02	272.00	260.31	250.46
13000	380.18	351.24	328.35	309.86	294.67	282.01	271.33
14000	409.42	378.26	353.61	333.70	317.33	303.70	292.20
15000	438.67	405.27	378.86	357.53	340.00	325.39	313.07
16000	467.91	432.29	404.12	381.37	362.67	347.08	333.94
17000	497.16	459.31	429.38	405.20	385.33	368.78	354.82
18000	526.40	486.33	454.64	429.04	408.00	390.47	375.69
19000	555.65	513.35	479.89	452.87	430.67	412.16	396.56
20000	584.89	540.36	505.15	476.71	453.33	433.85	417.43
21000	614.14	567.38	530.41	500.54	476.00	455.55	438.30
22000	643.38	594.40	555.67	524.38	498.67	477.24	459.17
23000	672.62	621.42	580.93	548.21	521.33	498.93	480.05
24000	701.87	648.44	606.18	572.05	544.00	520.63	500.92
25000	731.11	675.46	631.44	595.88	566.67	542.32	521.79
26000	760.36	702.47	656.70	619.72	589.33	564.01	542.66
27000	789.60	729.49	681.96	643.56	612.00	585.70	563.53
28000	818.85	756.51	707.21	667.39	634.67	607.40	584.40
29000	848.09	783.53	732.47	691.23	657.33	629.09	605.28
30000	877.34	810.55	757.73	715.06	680.00	650.78	626.15
31000	906.58	837.57	782.99	738.90	702.67	672.48	647.02
32000	935.82	864.58	808.24	762.73	725.33	694.17	667.89
33000	965.07	891.60	833.50	786.57	748.00	715.86	688.76
34000	994.31	918.62	858.76	810.40	770.67	737.55	709.63
35000	1023.56	945.64	884.02	834.24	793.33	759.25	730.50
40000	1169.78	1080.73	1010.30	953.42	906.67	867.71	834.86
45000	1316.00	1215.82	1136.59	1072.59	1020.00	976.17	939.22
50000	1462.23	1350.91	1262.88	1191.77	1133.33	1084.64	1043.58
55000	1608.45	1486.00	1389.17	1310.95	1246.67	1193.10	1147.94
60000	1754.67	1621.09	1515.46	1430.12	1360.00	1301.56	1252.29
65000	1900.89	1756.19	1641.75	1549.30	1473.33	1410.03	1356.65
70000	2047.12	1891.28	1768.03	1668.48	1586.67	1518.49	1461.01

17¾% Monthly Loan Payments

LOAN AMOUNT	7½ YEARS	8 YEARS	8½ YEARS	9 YEARS	9½ YEARS	10 YEARS	10½ YEARS
100	2.02	1.96	1.91	1.86	1.82	1.79	1.76
200	4.03	3.91	3.81	3.72	3.64	3.57	3.51
300	6.05	5.87	5.72	5.58	5.46	5.36	5.27
400	8.07	7.83	7.62	7.44	7.28	7.14	7.02
500	10.09	9.79	9.53	9.30	9.10	8.93	8.78
600	12.10	11.74	11.43	11.16	10.92	10.71	10.53
700	14.12	13.70	13.34	13.02	12.74	12.50	12.29
800	16.14	15.66	15.24	14.88	14.56	14.29	14.04
900	18.16	17.61	17.15	16.74	16.38	16.07	15.80
1000	20.17	19.57	19.05	18.60	18.21	17.86	17.55
1500	30.26	29.36	28.58	27.90	27.31	26.79	26.33
2000	40.34	39.14	38.11	37.20	36.41	35.72	35.10
2500	50.43	48.93	47.63	46.50	45.51	44.64	43.88
3000	60.52	58.72	57.16	55.80	54.62	53.57	52.65
3500	70.60	68.50	66.68	65.10	63.72	62.50	61.43
4000	80.69	78.29	76.21	74.40	72.82	71.43	70.20
4500	90.78	88.07	85.74	83.70	81.92	80.36	78.98
5000	100.86	97.86	95.26	93.00	91.03	89.29	87.76
5500	110.95	107.65	104.79	102.30	100.13	98.22	96.53
6000	121.03	117.43	114.32	111.60	109.23	107.15	105.31
6500	131.12	127.22	123.84	120.91	118.34	116.08	114.08
7000	141.21	137.00	133.37	130.21	127.44	125.01	122.86
7500	151.29	146.79	142.90	139.51	136.54	133.93	131.63
8000	161.38	156.58	152.42	148.81	145.64	142.86	140.41
8500	171.46	166.36	161.95	158.11	154.75	151.79	149.18
9000	181.55	176.15	171.47	167.41	163.85	160.72	157.96
9500	191.64	185.93	181.00	176.71	172.95	169.65	166.74
10000	201.72	195.72	190.53	186.01	182.05	178.58	175.51
11000	221.90	215.29	209.58	204.61	200.26	196.44	193.06
12000	242.07	234.86	228.63	223.21	218.47	214.29	210.61
13000	262.24	254.44	247.68	241.81	236.67	232.15	228.16
14000	282.41	274.01	266.74	260.41	254.88	250.01	245.71
15000	302.58	293.58	285.79	279.01	273.08	267.87	263.27
16000	322.76	313.15	304.84	297.61	291.29	285.73	280.82
17000	342.93	332.72	323.90	316.21	309.49	303.58	298.37
18000	363.10	352.29	342.95	334.81	327.70	321.44	315.92
19000	383.27	371.87	362.00	353.42	345.90	339.30	333.47
20000	403.45	391.44	381.05	372.02	364.11	357.16	351.02
21000	423.62	411.01	400.11	390.62	382.31	375.02	368.57
22000	443.79	430.58	419.16	409.22	400.52	392.87	386.12
23000	463.96	450.15	438.21	427.82	418.73	410.73	403.67
24000	484.14	469.73	457.26	446.42	436.93	428.59	421.23
25000	504.31	489.30	476.32	465.02	455.14	446.45	438.78
26000	524.48	508.87	495.37	483.62	473.34	464.30	456.33
27000	544.65	528.44	514.42	502.22	491.55	482.16	473.88
28000	564.83	548.01	533.48	520.82	509.75	500.02	491.43
29000	585.00	567.59	552.53	539.42	527.96	517.88	508.98
30000	605.17	587.16	571.58	558.02	546.16	535.74	526.53
31000	625.34	606.73	590.63	576.63	564.37	553.59	544.08
32000	645.51	626.30	609.69	595.23	582.57	571.45	561.63
33000	665.69	645.87	628.74	613.83	600.78	589.31	579.19
34000	685.86	665.45	647.79	632.43	618.99	607.17	596.74
35000	706.03	685.02	666.84	651.03	637.19	625.03	614.29
40000	806.89	782.88	762.11	744.03	728.22	714.32	702.04
45000	907.75	880.74	857.37	837.04	819.25	803.60	789.80
50000	1008.62	978.60	952.63	930.04	910.27	892.89	877.55
55000	1109.48	1076.46	1047.90	1023.04	1001.30	982.18	965.31
60000	1210.34	1174.32	1143.16	1116.05	1092.33	1071.47	1053.06
65000	1311.20	1272.18	1238.42	1209.05	1183.35	1160.76	1140.82
70000	1412.06	1370.04	1333.69	1302.06	1274.38	1250.05	1228.57

Monthly Loan Payments 17¾%

LOAN AMOUNT	11 YEARS	11½ YEARS	12 YEARS	12½ YEARS	13 YEARS	14 YEARS	15 YEARS
100	1.73	1.70	1.68	1.66	1.65	1.62	1.59
200	3.46	3.41	3.36	3.33	3.29	3.23	3.18
300	5.18	5.11	5.05	4.99	4.94	4.85	4.78
400	6.91	6.82	6.73	6.65	6.58	6.47	6.37
500	8.64	8.52	8.41	8.31	8.23	8.08	7.96
600	10.37	10.22	10.09	9.98	9.87	9.70	9.55
700	12.10	11.93	11.78	11.64	11.52	11.31	11.15
800	13.82	13.63	13.46	13.30	13.17	12.93	12.74
900	15.55	15.33	15.14	14.97	14.81	14.55	14.33
1000	17.28	17.04	16.82	16.63	16.46	16.16	15.92
1500	25.92	25.56	25.23	24.94	24.69	24.24	23.89
2000	34.56	34.08	33.64	33.26	32.91	32.33	31.85
2500	43.20	42.59	42.06	41.57	41.14	40.41	39.81
3000	51.84	51.11	50.47	49.89	49.37	48.49	47.77
3500	60.48	59.63	58.88	58.20	57.60	56.57	55.74
4000	69.12	68.15	67.29	66.52	65.83	64.65	63.70
4500	77.76	76.67	75.70	74.83	74.06	72.73	71.66
5000	86.40	85.19	84.11	83.15	82.29	80.82	79.62
5500	95.04	93.71	92.52	91.46	90.51	88.90	87.59
6000	103.68	102.23	100.93	99.78	98.74	96.98	95.55
6500	112.32	110.74	109.34	108.09	106.97	105.06	103.51
7000	120.95	119.26	117.76	116.41	115.20	113.14	111.47
7500	129.59	127.78	126.17	124.72	123.43	121.22	119.43
8000	138.23	136.30	134.58	133.04	131.66	129.31	127.40
8500	146.87	144.82	142.99	141.35	139.89	137.39	135.36
9000	155.51	153.34	151.40	149.67	148.12	145.47	143.32
9500	164.15	161.86	159.81	157.98	156.34	153.55	151.28
10000	172.79	170.38	168.22	166.30	164.57	161.63	159.25
11000	190.07	187.41	185.04	182.93	181.03	177.80	175.17
12000	207.35	204.45	201.87	199.56	197.49	193.96	191.10
13000	224.63	221.49	218.69	216.19	213.94	210.12	207.02
14000	241.91	238.53	235.51	232.82	230.40	226.28	222.95
15000	259.19	255.56	252.33	249.45	246.86	242.45	238.87
16000	276.47	272.60	269.16	266.07	263.32	258.61	254.79
17000	293.75	289.64	285.98	282.70	279.77	274.77	270.72
18000	311.03	306.68	302.80	299.33	296.23	290.94	286.64
19000	328.31	323.71	319.62	315.96	312.69	307.10	302.57
20000	345.58	340.75	336.44	332.59	329.14	323.26	318.49
21000	362.86	357.79	353.27	349.22	345.60	339.43	334.42
22000	380.14	374.83	370.09	365.85	362.06	355.59	350.34
23000	397.42	391.86	386.91	382.48	378.52	371.75	366.27
24000	414.70	408.90	403.73	399.11	394.97	387.92	382.19
25000	431.98	425.94	420.56	415.74	411.43	404.08	398.11
26000	449.26	442.98	437.38	432.37	427.89	420.24	414.04
27000	466.54	460.02	454.20	449.00	444.35	436.41	429.97
28000	483.82	477.05	471.02	465.63	460.80	452.57	445.89
29000	501.10	494.09	487.84	482.26	477.26	468.73	461.82
30000	518.38	511.13	504.67	498.89	493.72	484.90	477.74
31000	535.66	528.17	521.49	515.52	510.17	501.06	493.66
32000	552.94	545.20	538.31	532.15	526.63	517.22	509.59
33000	570.21	562.24	555.13	548.78	543.09	533.39	525.51
34000	587.49	579.28	571.95	565.41	559.55	549.55	541.44
35000	604.77	596.32	588.78	582.04	576.00	565.71	557.36
40000	691.17	681.50	672.89	665.19	658.29	646.53	636.99
45000	777.57	766.69	757.00	748.34	740.58	727.34	716.61
50000	863.96	851.88	841.11	831.48	822.86	808.16	796.23
55000	950.36	937.07	925.22	914.63	905.15	888.98	875.86
60000	1036.75	1022.26	1009.33	997.78	987.43	969.79	955.48
65000	1123.15	1107.44	1093.44	1080.93	1069.72	1050.61	1035.10
70000	1209.55	1192.63	1177.55	1164.08	1152.01	1131.42	1114.73

18% Monthly Loan Payments

LOAN AMOUNT	½ YEAR	1 YEAR	1½ YEARS	2 YEARS	2½ YEARS	3 YEARS	3½ YEARS
100	17.55	9.17	6.38	4.99	4.16	3.62	3.23
200	35.11	18.34	12.76	9.98	8.33	7.23	6.45
300	52.66	27.50	19.14	14.98	12.49	10.85	9.68
400	70.21	36.67	25.52	19.97	16.66	14.46	12.91
500	87.76	45.84	31.90	24.96	20.82	18.08	16.13
600	105.32	55.01	38.28	29.95	24.98	21.69	19.36
700	122.87	64.18	44.66	34.95	29.15	25.31	22.58
800	140.42	73.34	51.04	39.94	33.31	28.92	25.81
900	157.97	82.51	57.43	44.93	37.48	32.54	29.04
1000	175.53	91.68	63.81	49.92	41.64	36.15	32.26
1500	263.29	137.52	95.71	74.89	62.46	54.23	48.40
2000	351.05	183.36	127.61	99.85	83.28	72.30	64.53
2500	438.81	229.20	159.51	124.81	104.10	90.38	80.66
3000	526.58	275.04	191.42	149.77	124.92	108.46	96.79
3500	614.34	320.88	223.32	174.73	145.74	126.53	112.92
4000	702.10	366.72	255.22	199.70	166.56	144.61	129.06
4500	789.86	412.56	287.13	224.66	187.38	162.69	145.19
5000	877.63	458.40	319.03	249.62	208.20	180.76	161.32
5500	965.39	504.24	350.93	274.58	229.02	198.84	177.45
6000	1053.15	550.08	382.83	299.54	249.84	216.91	193.59
6500	1140.91	595.92	414.74	324.51	270.65	234.99	209.72
7000	1228.68	641.76	446.64	349.47	291.47	253.07	225.85
7500	1316.44	687.60	478.54	374.43	312.29	271.14	241.98
8000	1404.20	733.44	510.45	399.39	333.11	289.22	258.11
8500	1491.96	779.28	542.35	424.35	353.93	307.30	274.25
9000	1579.73	825.12	574.25	449.32	374.75	325.37	290.38
9500	1667.49	870.96	606.15	474.28	395.57	343.45	306.51
10000	1755.25	916.80	638.06	499.24	416.39	361.52	322.64
11000	1930.78	1008.48	701.86	549.17	458.03	397.68	354.91
12000	2106.30	1100.16	765.67	599.09	499.67	433.83	387.17
13000	2281.83	1191.84	829.48	649.01	541.31	469.98	419.44
14000	2457.35	1283.52	893.28	698.94	582.95	506.13	451.70
15000	2632.88	1375.20	957.09	748.86	624.59	542.29	483.96
16000	2808.40	1466.88	1020.89	798.79	666.23	578.44	516.23
17000	2983.93	1558.56	1084.70	848.71	707.87	614.59	548.49
18000	3159.45	1650.24	1148.50	898.63	749.51	650.74	580.76
19000	3334.98	1741.92	1212.31	948.56	791.14	686.90	613.02
20000	3510.50	1833.60	1276.12	998.48	832.78	723.05	645.29
21000	3686.03	1925.28	1339.92	1048.41	874.42	759.20	677.55
22000	3861.55	2016.96	1403.73	1098.33	916.06	795.35	709.81
23000	4037.08	2108.64	1467.53	1148.25	957.70	831.51	742.08
24000	4212.61	2200.32	1531.34	1198.18	999.34	867.66	774.34
25000	4388.13	2292.00	1595.14	1248.10	1040.98	903.81	806.61
26000	4563.66	2383.68	1658.95	1298.03	1082.62	939.96	838.87
27000	4739.18	2475.36	1722.76	1347.95	1124.26	976.11	871.13
28000	4914.71	2567.04	1786.56	1397.87	1165.90	1012.27	903.40
29000	5090.23	2658.72	1850.37	1447.80	1207.54	1048.42	935.66
30000	5265.76	2750.40	1914.17	1497.72	1249.18	1084.57	967.93
31000	5441.28	2842.08	1977.98	1547.65	1290.81	1120.72	1000.19
32000	5616.81	2933.76	2041.79	1597.57	1332.45	1156.88	1032.46
33000	5792.33	3025.44	2105.59	1647.50	1374.09	1193.03	1064.72
34000	5967.86	3117.12	2169.40	1697.42	1415.73	1229.18	1096.98
35000	6143.38	3208.80	2233.20	1747.34	1457.37	1265.33	1129.25
40000	7021.01	3667.20	2552.23	1996.96	1665.57	1446.10	1290.57
45000	7898.63	4125.60	2871.26	2246.58	1873.76	1626.86	1451.89
50000	8776.26	4584.00	3190.29	2496.21	2081.96	1807.62	1613.21
55000	9653.89	5042.40	3509.32	2745.83	2290.16	1988.38	1774.53
60000	10531.51	5500.80	3828.35	2995.45	2498.35	2169.14	1935.86
65000	11409.14	5959.20	4147.38	3245.07	2706.55	2349.91	2097.18
70000	12286.77	6417.60	4466.40	3494.69	2914.74	2530.67	2258.50

Monthly Loan Payments 18%

LOAN AMOUNT	4 YEARS	4½ YEARS	5 YEARS	5½ YEARS	6 YEARS	6½ YEARS	7 YEARS
100	2.94	2.72	2.54	2.40	2.28	2.18	2.10
200	5.87	5.43	5.08	4.79	4.56	4.37	4.20
300	8.81	8.15	7.62	7.19	6.84	6.55	6.31
400	11.75	10.86	10.16	9.59	9.12	8.73	8.41
500	14.69	13.58	12.70	11.99	11.40	10.92	10.51
600	17.62	16.29	15.24	14.38	13.68	13.10	12.61
700	20.56	19.01	17.78	16.78	15.97	15.29	14.71
800	23.50	21.72	20.31	19.18	18.25	17.47	16.81
900	26.44	24.44	22.85	21.58	20.53	19.65	18.92
1000	29.37	27.15	25.39	23.97	22.81	21.84	21.02
1500	44.06	40.73	38.09	35.96	34.21	32.75	31.53
2000	58.75	54.30	50.79	47.95	45.62	43.67	42.04
2500	73.44	67.88	63.48	59.93	57.02	54.59	52.54
3000	88.12	81.45	76.18	71.92	68.42	65.51	63.05
3500	102.81	95.03	88.88	83.91	79.83	76.43	73.56
4000	117.50	108.61	101.57	95.90	91.23	87.35	84.07
4500	132.19	122.18	114.27	107.88	102.64	98.26	94.58
5000	146.87	135.76	126.97	119.87	114.04	109.18	105.09
5500	161.56	149.33	139.66	131.86	125.44	120.10	115.60
6000	176.25	162.91	152.36	143.84	136.85	131.02	126.11
6500	190.94	176.48	165.06	155.83	148.25	141.94	136.62
7000	205.62	190.06	177.75	167.82	159.65	152.86	147.12
7500	220.31	203.64	190.45	179.80	171.06	163.77	157.63
8000	235.00	217.21	203.15	191.79	182.46	174.69	168.14
8500	249.69	230.79	215.84	203.78	193.87	185.61	178.65
9000	264.37	244.36	228.54	215.76	205.27	196.53	189.16
9500	279.06	257.94	241.24	227.75	216.67	207.45	199.67
10000	293.75	271.51	253.93	239.74	228.08	218.36	210.18
11000	323.12	298.67	279.33	263.71	250.89	240.20	231.20
12000	352.50	325.82	304.72	287.69	273.69	262.04	252.21
13000	381.87	352.97	330.11	311.66	296.50	283.87	273.23
14000	411.25	380.12	355.51	335.63	319.31	305.71	294.25
15000	440.62	407.27	380.90	359.61	342.12	327.55	315.27
16000	470.00	434.42	406.29	383.58	364.92	349.38	336.29
17000	499.37	461.57	431.69	407.56	387.73	371.22	357.30
18000	528.75	488.72	457.08	431.53	410.54	393.06	378.32
19000	558.12	515.88	482.48	455.50	433.35	414.89	399.34
20000	587.50	543.03	507.87	479.48	456.16	436.73	420.36
21000	616.87	570.18	533.26	503.45	478.96	458.57	441.37
22000	646.25	597.33	558.66	527.42	501.77	480.40	462.39
23000	675.62	624.48	584.05	551.40	524.58	502.24	483.41
24000	705.00	651.63	609.44	575.37	547.39	524.07	504.43
25000	734.37	678.78	634.84	599.35	570.19	545.91	525.45
26000	763.75	705.94	660.23	623.32	593.00	567.75	546.46
27000	793.12	733.09	685.62	647.29	615.81	589.58	567.48
28000	822.50	760.24	711.02	671.27	638.62	611.42	588.50
29000	851.87	787.39	736.41	695.24	661.43	633.26	609.52
30000	881.25	814.54	761.80	719.22	684.23	655.09	630.54
31000	910.62	841.69	787.20	743.19	707.04	676.93	651.55
32000	940.00	868.84	812.59	767.16	729.85	698.77	672.57
33000	969.37	896.00	837.98	791.14	752.66	720.60	693.59
34000	998.75	923.15	863.38	815.11	775.46	742.44	714.61
35000	1028.12	950.30	888.77	839.08	798.27	764.28	735.62
40000	1175.00	1086.06	1015.74	958.95	912.31	873.46	840.71
45000	1321.87	1221.81	1142.70	1078.82	1026.35	982.64	945.80
50000	1468.75	1357.57	1269.67	1198.69	1140.39	1091.82	1050.89
55000	1615.62	1493.33	1396.64	1318.56	1254.43	1201.00	1155.98
60000	1762.50	1629.08	1523.61	1438.43	1368.47	1310.19	1261.07
65000	1909.37	1764.84	1650.57	1558.30	1482.51	1419.37	1366.16
70000	2056.25	1900.60	1777.54	1678.17	1596.55	1528.55	1471.25

18%   Monthly Loan Payments

LOAN AMOUNT	7½ YEARS	8 YEARS	8½ YEARS	9 YEARS	9½ YEARS	10 YEARS	10½ YEARS
100	2.03	1.97	1.92	1.88	1.84	1.80	1.77
200	4.06	3.94	3.84	3.75	3.67	3.60	3.54
300	6.10	5.92	5.76	5.63	5.51	5.41	5.31
400	8.13	7.89	7.68	7.50	7.35	7.21	7.09
500	10.16	9.86	9.60	9.38	9.18	9.01	8.86
600	12.19	11.83	11.52	11.25	11.02	10.81	10.63
700	14.22	13.81	13.44	13.13	12.85	12.61	12.40
800	16.26	15.78	15.37	15.01	14.69	14.41	14.17
900	18.29	17.75	17.29	16.88	16.53	16.22	15.94
1000	20.32	19.72	19.21	18.76	18.36	18.02	17.71
1500	30.48	29.58	28.81	28.14	27.55	27.03	26.57
2000	40.64	39.45	38.41	37.51	36.73	36.04	35.43
2500	50.80	49.31	48.02	46.89	45.91	45.05	44.28
3000	60.96	59.17	57.62	56.27	55.09	54.06	53.14
3500	71.12	69.03	67.22	65.65	64.27	63.07	62.00
4000	81.28	78.89	76.83	75.03	73.46	72.07	70.86
4500	91.45	88.75	86.43	84.41	82.64	81.08	79.71
5000	101.61	98.62	96.03	93.78	91.82	90.09	88.57
5500	111.77	108.48	105.64	103.16	101.00	99.10	97.43
6000	121.93	118.34	115.24	112.54	110.18	108.11	106.28
6500	132.09	128.20	124.84	121.92	119.36	117.12	115.14
7000	142.25	138.06	134.44	131.30	128.55	126.13	124.00
7500	152.41	147.92	144.05	140.68	137.73	135.14	132.85
8000	162.57	157.79	153.65	150.06	146.91	144.15	141.71
8500	172.73	167.65	163.25	159.43	156.09	153.16	150.57
9000	182.89	177.51	172.86	168.81	165.27	162.17	159.43
9500	193.05	187.37	182.46	178.19	174.46	171.18	168.28
10000	203.21	197.23	192.06	187.57	183.64	180.19	177.14
11000	223.53	216.96	211.27	206.33	202.00	198.20	194.85
12000	243.85	236.68	230.48	225.08	220.37	216.22	212.57
13000	264.17	256.40	249.68	243.84	238.73	234.24	230.28
14000	284.50	276.12	268.89	262.60	257.09	252.26	247.99
15000	304.82	295.85	288.10	281.35	275.46	270.28	265.71
16000	325.14	315.57	307.30	300.11	293.82	288.30	283.42
17000	345.46	335.29	326.51	318.87	312.19	306.31	301.14
18000	365.78	355.02	345.71	337.62	330.55	324.33	318.85
19000	386.10	374.74	364.92	356.38	348.91	342.35	336.56
20000	406.42	394.46	384.13	375.14	367.28	360.37	354.28
21000	426.74	414.19	403.33	393.89	385.64	378.39	371.99
22000	447.06	433.91	422.54	412.65	404.00	396.41	389.71
23000	467.39	453.63	441.75	431.41	422.37	414.43	407.42
24000	487.71	473.36	460.95	450.17	440.73	432.44	425.13
25000	508.03	493.08	480.16	468.92	459.10	450.46	442.85
26000	528.35	512.80	499.37	487.68	477.46	468.48	460.56
27000	548.67	532.53	518.57	506.44	495.82	486.50	478.28
28000	568.99	552.25	537.78	525.19	514.19	504.52	495.99
29000	589.31	571.97	556.99	543.95	532.55	522.54	513.70
30000	609.63	591.70	576.19	562.71	550.92	540.56	531.42
31000	629.96	611.42	595.40	581.46	569.28	558.57	549.13
32000	650.28	631.14	614.60	600.22	587.64	576.59	566.84
33000	670.60	650.87	633.81	618.98	606.01	594.61	584.56
34000	690.92	670.59	653.02	637.73	624.37	612.63	602.27
35000	711.24	690.31	672.22	656.49	642.73	630.65	619.99
40000	812.85	788.93	768.26	750.28	734.55	720.74	708.56
45000	914.45	887.54	864.29	844.06	826.37	810.83	797.13
50000	1016.06	986.16	960.32	937.84	918.19	900.93	885.69
55000	1117.66	1084.78	1056.35	1031.63	1010.01	991.02	974.26
60000	1219.27	1183.39	1152.38	1125.41	1101.83	1081.11	1062.83
65000	1320.87	1282.01	1248.42	1219.20	1193.65	1171.20	1151.40
70000	1422.48	1380.62	1344.45	1312.98	1285.47	1261.30	1239.97

Monthly Loan Payments 18%

LOAN AMOUNT	11 YEARS	11½ YEARS	12 YEARS	12½ YEARS	13 YEARS	14 YEARS	15 YEARS
100	1.74	1.72	1.70	1.68	1.66	1.63	1.61
200	3.49	3.44	3.40	3.36	3.33	3.27	3.22
300	5.23	5.16	5.10	5.04	4.99	4.90	4.83
400	6.98	6.88	6.80	6.72	6.65	6.54	6.44
500	8.72	8.60	8.50	8.40	8.32	8.17	8.05
600	10.47	10.32	10.19	10.08	9.98	9.80	9.66
700	12.21	12.04	11.89	11.76	11.64	11.44	11.27
800	13.96	13.76	13.59	13.44	13.30	13.07	12.88
900	15.70	15.48	15.29	15.12	14.97	14.71	14.49
1000	17.44	17.20	16.99	16.80	16.63	16.34	16.10
1500	26.17	25.81	25.49	25.20	24.95	24.51	24.16
2000	34.89	34.41	33.98	33.60	33.26	32.68	32.21
2500	43.61	43.01	42.48	42.00	41.58	40.85	40.26
3000	52.33	51.61	50.97	50.40	49.89	49.02	48.31
3500	61.05	60.22	59.47	58.80	58.21	57.19	56.36
4000	69.78	68.82	67.96	67.20	66.52	65.36	64.42
4500	78.50	77.42	76.46	75.60	74.84	73.53	72.47
5000	87.22	86.02	84.96	84.00	83.15	81.70	80.52
5500	95.94	94.63	93.45	92.40	91.47	89.87	88.57
6000	104.67	103.23	101.95	100.80	99.78	98.04	96.63
6500	113.39	111.83	110.44	109.20	108.10	106.21	104.68
7000	122.11	120.43	118.94	117.60	116.41	114.38	112.73
7500	130.83	129.03	127.43	126.00	124.73	122.55	120.78
8000	139.55	137.64	135.93	134.40	133.04	130.72	128.83
8500	148.28	146.24	144.43	142.81	141.36	138.89	136.89
9000	157.00	154.84	152.92	151.21	149.67	147.06	144.94
9500	165.72	163.44	161.42	159.61	157.99	155.23	152.99
10000	174.44	172.05	169.91	168.01	166.30	163.40	161.04
11000	191.89	189.25	186.90	184.81	182.93	179.73	177.15
12000	209.33	206.46	203.89	201.61	199.56	196.07	193.25
13000	226.77	223.66	220.89	218.41	216.19	212.41	209.35
14000	244.22	240.86	237.88	235.21	232.82	228.75	225.46
15000	261.66	258.07	254.87	252.01	249.45	245.09	241.56
16000	279.11	275.27	271.86	268.81	266.08	261.43	257.67
17000	296.55	292.48	288.85	285.61	282.71	277.77	273.77
18000	314.00	309.68	305.84	302.41	299.34	294.11	289.88
19000	331.44	326.89	322.83	319.21	315.97	310.45	305.98
20000	348.88	344.09	339.82	336.01	332.60	326.79	322.08
21000	366.33	361.30	356.82	352.81	349.23	343.13	338.19
22000	383.77	378.50	373.81	369.61	365.86	359.47	354.29
23000	401.22	395.71	390.80	386.41	382.49	375.81	370.40
24000	418.66	412.91	407.79	403.21	399.12	392.15	386.50
25000	436.10	430.12	424.78	420.02	415.75	408.49	402.61
26000	453.55	447.32	441.77	436.82	432.38	424.83	418.71
27000	470.99	464.52	458.76	453.62	449.01	441.17	434.81
28000	488.44	481.73	475.75	470.42	465.64	457.51	450.92
29000	505.88	498.93	492.74	487.22	482.27	473.85	467.02
30000	523.33	516.14	509.74	504.02	498.90	490.19	483.13
31000	540.77	533.34	526.73	520.82	515.53	506.52	499.23
32000	558.21	550.55	543.72	537.62	532.16	522.86	515.33
33000	575.66	567.75	560.71	554.42	548.79	539.20	531.44
34000	593.10	584.96	577.70	571.22	565.42	555.54	547.54
35000	610.55	602.16	594.69	588.02	582.05	571.88	563.65
40000	697.77	688.18	679.65	672.02	665.20	653.58	644.17
45000	784.99	774.21	764.60	756.03	748.35	735.28	724.69
50000	872.21	860.23	849.56	840.03	831.50	816.98	805.21
55000	959.43	946.25	934.52	924.03	914.65	898.67	885.73
60000	1046.65	1032.28	1019.47	1008.04	997.80	980.37	966.25
65000	1133.87	1118.30	1104.43	1092.04	1080.95	1062.07	1046.77
70000	1221.09	1204.32	1189.38	1176.04	1164.10	1143.77	1127.29

18¼%   Monthly Loan Payments

LOAN AMOUNT	½ YEAR	1 YEAR	1½ YEARS	2 YEARS	2½ YEARS	3 YEARS	3½ YEARS
100	17.56	9.18	6.39	5.00	4.18	3.63	3.2
200	35.13	18.36	12.79	10.01	8.35	7.26	6.4
300	52.69	27.54	19.18	15.01	12.53	10.88	9.7
400	70.26	36.72	25.57	20.02	16.70	14.51	12.9
500	87.82	45.90	31.96	25.02	20.88	18.14	16.2
600	105.39	55.08	38.36	30.03	25.06	21.77	19.4
700	122.95	64.26	44.75	35.03	29.23	25.39	22.6
800	140.52	73.44	51.14	40.04	33.41	29.02	25.9
900	158.08	82.62	57.53	45.04	37.59	32.65	29.1
1000	175.65	91.80	63.93	50.04	41.76	36.28	32.3
1500	263.47	137.70	95.89	75.07	62.64	54.42	48.5
2000	351.30	183.60	127.85	100.09	83.52	72.56	64.7
2500	439.12	229.50	159.81	125.11	104.41	90.69	80.9
3000	526.95	275.40	191.78	150.13	125.29	108.83	97.1
3500	614.77	321.30	223.74	175.16	146.17	126.97	113.3
4000	702.60	367.20	255.70	200.18	167.05	145.11	129.5
4500	790.42	413.10	287.66	225.20	187.93	163.25	145.7
5000	878.25	459.00	319.63	250.22	208.81	181.39	161.9
5500	966.07	504.89	351.59	275.25	229.69	199.53	178.1
6000	1053.90	550.79	383.55	300.27	250.57	217.67	194.3
6500	1141.72	596.69	415.51	325.29	271.45	235.81	210.5
7000	1229.55	642.59	447.48	350.31	292.34	253.95	226.7
7500	1317.37	688.49	479.44	375.34	313.22	272.08	242.9
8000	1405.20	734.39	511.40	400.36	334.10	290.22	259.1
8500	1493.02	780.29	543.36	425.38	354.98	308.36	275.3
9000	1580.85	826.19	575.33	450.40	375.86	326.50	291.5
9500	1668.67	872.09	607.29	475.43	396.74	344.64	307.7
10000	1756.50	917.99	639.25	500.45	417.62	362.78	323.9
11000	1932.15	1009.79	703.18	550.49	459.38	399.06	356.3
12000	2107.80	1101.59	767.10	600.54	501.15	435.34	388.7
13000	2283.45	1193.39	831.03	650.58	542.91	471.61	421.1
14000	2459.10	1285.19	894.95	700.63	584.67	507.89	453.4
15000	2634.75	1376.99	958.88	750.67	626.43	544.17	485.8
16000	2810.40	1468.78	1022.80	800.72	668.20	580.45	518.2
17000	2986.05	1560.58	1086.73	850.76	709.96	616.72	550.6
18000	3161.70	1652.38	1150.65	900.81	751.72	653.00	583.0
19000	3337.35	1744.18	1214.58	950.85	793.48	689.28	615.4
20000	3513.00	1835.98	1278.50	1000.90	835.25	725.56	647.8
21000	3688.65	1927.78	1342.43	1050.94	877.01	761.84	680.2
22000	3864.29	2019.58	1406.35	1100.99	918.77	798.11	712.6
23000	4039.94	2111.38	1470.28	1151.03	960.53	834.39	745.0
24000	4215.59	2203.18	1534.20	1201.08	1002.29	870.67	777.4
25000	4391.24	2294.98	1598.13	1251.12	1044.06	906.95	809.8
26000	4566.89	2386.77	1662.05	1301.17	1085.82	943.23	842.2
27000	4742.54	2478.57	1725.98	1351.21	1127.58	979.50	874.5
28000	4918.19	2570.37	1789.90	1401.26	1169.34	1015.78	906.9
29000	5093.84	2662.17	1853.83	1451.30	1211.11	1052.06	939.3
30000	5269.49	2753.97	1917.75	1501.35	1252.87	1088.34	971.7
31000	5445.14	2845.77	1981.68	1551.39	1294.63	1124.62	1004.1
32000	5620.79	2937.57	2045.60	1601.44	1336.39	1160.89	1036.5
33000	5796.44	3029.37	2109.53	1651.48	1378.15	1197.17	1068.9
34000	5972.09	3121.17	2173.45	1701.53	1419.92	1233.45	1101.3
35000	6147.74	3212.97	2237.38	1751.57	1461.68	1269.73	1133.7
40000	7025.99	3671.96	2557.00	2001.80	1670.49	1451.12	1295.7
45000	7904.24	4130.96	2876.63	2252.02	1879.30	1632.51	1457.6
50000	8782.49	4589.95	3196.25	2502.25	2088.11	1813.90	1619.6
55000	9660.74	5048.95	3515.88	2752.47	2296.92	1995.29	1781.5
60000	10538.99	5507.94	3835.50	3002.70	2505.74	2176.68	1943.5
65000	11417.23	5966.94	4155.13	3252.92	2714.55	2358.07	2105.5
70000	12295.48	6425.93	4474.75	3503.15	2923.36	2539.46	2267.4

Monthly Loan Payments 18¼%

LOAN AMOUNT	4 YEARS	4½ YEARS	5 YEARS	5½ YEARS	6 YEARS	6½ YEARS	7 YEARS
100	2.95	2.73	2.55	2.41	2.29	2.20	2.12
200	5.90	5.46	5.11	4.82	4.59	4.40	4.23
300	8.85	8.19	7.66	7.23	6.88	6.59	6.35
400	11.80	10.91	10.21	9.65	9.18	8.79	8.47
500	14.75	13.64	12.76	12.06	11.47	10.99	10.58
600	17.70	16.37	15.32	14.47	13.77	13.19	12.70
700	20.65	19.10	17.87	16.88	16.06	15.39	14.82
800	23.60	21.83	20.42	19.29	18.36	17.58	16.93
900	26.56	24.56	22.98	21.70	20.65	19.78	19.05
1000	29.51	27.28	25.53	24.11	22.95	21.98	21.16
1500	44.26	40.93	38.29	36.17	34.42	32.97	31.75
2000	59.01	54.57	51.06	48.23	45.90	43.96	42.33
2500	73.76	68.21	63.82	60.28	57.37	54.95	52.91
3000	88.52	81.85	76.59	72.34	68.85	65.94	63.49
3500	103.27	95.50	89.35	84.39	80.32	76.93	74.08
4000	118.02	109.14	102.12	96.45	91.80	87.92	84.66
4500	132.78	122.78	114.88	108.51	103.27	98.91	95.24
5000	147.53	136.42	127.65	120.56	114.75	109.90	105.82
5500	162.28	150.07	140.41	132.62	126.22	120.89	116.41
6000	177.03	163.71	153.18	144.68	137.70	131.88	126.99
6500	191.79	177.35	165.94	156.73	149.17	142.87	137.57
7000	206.54	190.99	178.71	168.79	160.65	153.86	148.15
7500	221.29	204.64	191.47	180.85	172.12	164.85	158.73
8000	236.05	218.28	204.24	192.90	183.59	175.85	169.32
8500	250.80	231.92	217.00	204.96	195.07	186.84	179.90
9000	265.55	245.56	229.77	217.01	206.54	197.83	190.48
9500	280.31	259.21	242.53	229.07	218.02	208.82	201.06
10000	295.06	272.85	255.30	241.13	229.49	219.81	211.65
11000	324.56	300.13	280.83	265.24	252.44	241.79	232.81
12000	354.07	327.42	306.36	289.35	275.39	263.77	253.98
13000	383.58	354.70	331.89	313.47	298.34	285.75	275.14
14000	413.08	381.99	357.41	337.58	321.29	307.73	296.30
15000	442.59	409.27	382.94	361.69	344.24	329.71	317.47
16000	472.09	436.56	408.47	385.80	367.19	351.69	338.63
17000	501.60	463.84	434.00	409.92	390.14	373.67	359.80
18000	531.10	491.13	459.53	434.03	413.09	395.65	380.96
19000	560.61	518.41	485.06	458.14	436.04	417.63	402.13
20000	590.12	545.70	510.59	482.25	458.99	439.61	423.29
21000	619.62	572.98	536.12	506.37	481.94	461.59	444.46
22000	649.13	600.27	561.65	530.48	504.89	483.57	465.62
23000	678.63	627.55	587.18	554.59	527.83	505.55	486.79
24000	708.14	654.84	612.71	578.71	550.78	527.54	507.95
25000	737.64	682.12	638.24	602.82	573.73	549.52	529.12
26000	767.15	709.41	663.77	626.93	596.68	571.50	550.28
27000	796.66	736.69	689.30	651.04	619.63	593.48	571.44
28000	826.16	763.98	714.83	675.16	642.58	615.46	592.61
29000	855.67	791.26	740.36	699.27	665.53	637.44	613.77
30000	885.17	818.55	765.89	723.38	688.48	659.42	634.94
31000	914.68	845.83	791.42	747.50	711.43	681.40	656.10
32000	944.19	873.12	816.95	771.61	734.38	703.38	677.27
33000	973.69	900.40	842.48	795.72	757.33	725.36	698.43
34000	1003.20	927.69	868.01	819.83	780.28	747.34	719.60
35000	1032.70	954.97	893.54	843.95	803.23	769.32	740.76
40000	1180.23	1091.39	1021.18	964.51	917.97	879.23	846.59
45000	1327.76	1227.82	1148.83	1085.07	1032.72	989.13	952.41
50000	1475.29	1364.24	1276.48	1205.64	1147.47	1099.03	1058.23
55000	1622.82	1500.67	1404.13	1326.20	1262.21	1208.94	1164.05
60000	1770.35	1637.09	1531.78	1446.76	1376.96	1318.84	1269.88
65000	1917.88	1773.52	1659.43	1567.33	1491.71	1428.74	1375.70
70000	2065.41	1909.94	1787.07	1687.89	1606.45	1538.65	1481.52

18¼%   Monthly Loan Payments

LOAN AMOUNT	7½ YEARS	8 YEARS	8½ YEARS	9 YEARS	9½ YEARS	10 YEARS	10½ YEARS
100	2.05	1.99	1.94	1.89	1.85	1.82	1.79
200	4.09	3.98	3.87	3.78	3.70	3.64	3.58
300	6.14	5.96	5.81	5.67	5.56	5.45	5.36
400	8.19	7.95	7.74	7.57	7.41	7.27	7.15
500	10.24	9.94	9.68	9.46	9.26	9.09	8.94
600	12.28	11.93	11.62	11.35	11.11	10.91	10.73
700	14.33	13.91	13.55	13.24	12.97	12.73	12.51
800	16.38	15.90	15.49	15.13	14.82	14.54	14.30
900	18.42	17.89	17.42	17.02	16.67	16.36	16.09
1000	20.47	19.88	19.36	18.91	18.52	18.18	17.88
1500	30.71	29.81	29.04	28.37	27.78	27.27	26.82
2000	40.94	39.75	38.72	37.83	37.05	36.36	35.75
2500	51.18	49.69	48.40	47.28	46.31	45.45	44.69
3000	61.41	59.63	58.08	56.74	55.57	54.54	53.63
3500	71.65	69.56	67.76	66.20	64.83	63.63	62.57
4000	81.88	79.50	77.44	75.65	74.09	72.72	71.51
4500	92.12	89.44	87.12	85.11	83.35	81.81	80.45
5000	102.35	99.38	96.80	94.57	92.61	90.90	89.39
5500	112.59	109.31	106.48	104.02	101.88	99.99	98.33
6000	122.82	119.25	116.16	113.48	111.14	109.08	107.26
6500	133.06	129.19	125.84	122.94	120.40	118.17	116.20
7000	143.29	139.13	135.52	132.39	129.66	127.26	125.14
7500	153.53	149.06	145.21	141.85	138.92	136.35	134.08
8000	163.76	159.00	154.89	151.31	148.18	145.44	143.02
8500	174.00	168.94	164.57	160.77	157.44	154.53	151.96
9000	184.23	178.88	174.25	170.22	166.71	163.62	160.90
9500	194.47	188.81	183.93	179.68	175.97	172.71	169.83
10000	204.70	198.75	193.61	189.14	185.23	181.80	178.77
11000	225.18	218.63	212.97	208.05	203.75	199.98	196.65
12000	245.65	238.50	232.33	226.96	222.27	218.16	214.53
13000	266.12	258.38	251.69	245.88	240.80	236.34	232.41
14000	286.59	278.25	271.05	264.79	259.32	254.52	250.28
15000	307.06	298.13	290.41	283.70	277.84	272.70	268.16
16000	327.53	318.00	309.77	302.62	296.37	290.88	286.04
17000	348.00	337.88	329.13	321.53	314.89	309.06	303.91
18000	368.47	357.75	348.49	340.44	333.41	327.24	321.79
19000	388.94	377.63	367.85	359.36	351.93	345.42	339.67
20000	409.41	397.50	387.21	378.27	370.46	363.60	357.55
21000	429.88	417.38	406.57	397.18	388.98	381.78	375.42
22000	450.35	437.25	425.93	416.10	407.50	399.96	393.30
23000	470.82	457.13	445.30	435.01	426.03	418.13	411.18
24000	491.29	477.00	464.66	453.93	444.55	436.31	429.06
25000	511.76	496.88	484.02	472.84	463.07	454.49	446.93
26000	532.23	516.75	503.38	491.75	481.59	472.67	464.81
27000	552.70	536.63	522.74	510.67	500.12	490.85	482.69
28000	573.17	556.50	542.10	529.58	518.64	509.03	500.57
29000	593.64	576.38	561.46	548.49	537.16	527.21	518.44
30000	614.11	596.25	580.82	567.41	555.68	545.39	536.32
31000	634.58	616.13	600.18	586.32	574.21	563.57	554.20
32000	655.06	636.00	619.54	605.23	592.73	581.75	572.08
33000	675.53	655.88	638.90	624.15	611.25	599.93	589.95
34000	696.00	675.75	658.26	643.06	629.78	618.11	607.83
35000	716.47	695.63	677.62	661.97	648.30	636.29	625.71
40000	818.82	795.00	774.43	756.54	740.91	727.19	715.09
45000	921.17	894.38	871.23	851.11	833.53	818.09	804.48
50000	1023.52	993.75	968.03	945.68	926.14	908.99	893.87
55000	1125.88	1093.13	1064.84	1040.25	1018.76	999.89	983.25
60000	1228.23	1192.50	1161.64	1134.81	1111.37	1090.79	1072.64
65000	1330.58	1291.88	1258.44	1229.38	1203.98	1181.69	1162.03
70000	1432.93	1391.25	1355.25	1323.95	1296.60	1272.58	1251.41

Monthly Loan Payments   18¼%

LOAN AMOUNT	11 YEARS	11½ YEARS	12 YEARS	12½ YEARS	13 YEARS	14 YEARS	15 YEARS
100	1.76	1.74	1.72	1.70	1.68	1.65	1.63
200	3.52	3.47	3.43	3.39	3.36	3.30	3.26
300	5.28	5.21	5.15	5.09	5.04	4.95	4.89
400	7.04	6.95	6.86	6.79	6.72	6.61	6.51
500	8.80	8.69	8.58	8.49	8.40	8.26	8.14
600	10.57	10.42	10.30	10.18	10.08	9.91	9.77
700	12.33	12.16	12.01	11.88	11.76	11.56	11.40
800	14.09	13.90	13.73	13.58	13.44	13.21	13.03
900	15.85	15.64	15.44	15.27	15.12	14.86	14.66
1000	17.61	17.37	17.16	16.97	16.80	16.52	16.28
1500	26.41	26.06	25.74	25.46	25.21	24.77	24.43
2000	35.22	34.74	34.32	33.94	33.61	33.03	32.57
2500	44.02	43.43	42.90	42.43	42.01	41.29	40.71
3000	52.83	52.12	51.48	50.92	50.41	49.55	48.85
3500	61.63	60.80	60.06	59.40	58.81	57.81	57.00
4000	70.44	69.49	68.64	67.89	67.21	66.07	65.14
4500	79.24	78.18	77.22	76.37	75.62	74.32	73.28
5000	88.05	86.86	85.80	84.86	84.02	82.58	81.42
5500	96.85	95.55	94.38	93.35	92.42	90.84	89.56
6000	105.66	104.23	102.97	101.83	100.82	99.10	97.71
6500	114.46	112.92	111.55	110.32	109.22	107.36	105.85
7000	123.27	121.61	120.13	118.81	117.62	115.62	113.99
7500	132.07	130.29	128.71	127.29	126.03	123.87	122.13
8000	140.88	138.98	137.29	135.78	134.43	132.13	130.28
8500	149.68	147.66	145.87	144.26	142.83	140.39	138.42
9000	158.49	156.35	154.45	152.75	151.23	148.65	146.56
9500	167.29	165.04	163.03	161.24	159.63	156.91	154.70
10000	176.10	173.72	171.61	169.72	168.03	165.16	162.84
11000	193.71	191.09	188.77	186.69	184.84	181.68	179.13
12000	211.32	208.47	205.93	203.67	201.64	198.20	195.41
13000	228.93	225.84	223.09	220.64	218.44	214.71	211.70
14000	246.54	243.21	240.25	237.61	235.25	231.23	227.98
15000	264.15	260.58	257.41	254.58	252.05	247.75	244.27
16000	281.76	277.96	274.57	271.55	268.86	264.26	260.55
17000	299.37	295.33	291.73	288.53	285.66	280.78	276.83
18000	316.98	312.70	308.90	305.50	302.46	297.30	293.12
19000	334.59	330.07	326.06	322.47	319.27	313.81	309.40
20000	352.20	347.45	343.22	339.44	336.07	330.33	325.69
21000	369.81	364.82	360.38	356.42	352.87	346.85	341.97
22000	387.41	382.19	377.54	373.39	369.68	363.36	358.26
23000	405.02	399.56	394.70	390.36	386.48	379.88	374.54
24000	422.63	416.93	411.86	407.33	403.28	396.39	390.83
25000	440.24	434.31	429.02	424.30	420.09	412.91	407.11
26000	457.85	451.68	446.18	441.28	436.89	429.43	423.39
27000	475.46	469.05	463.34	458.25	453.69	445.94	439.68
28000	493.07	486.42	480.50	475.22	470.50	462.46	455.96
29000	510.68	503.80	497.66	492.19	487.30	478.98	472.25
30000	528.29	521.17	514.83	509.17	504.10	495.49	488.53
31000	545.90	538.54	531.99	526.14	520.91	512.01	504.82
32000	563.51	555.91	549.15	543.11	537.71	528.53	521.10
33000	581.12	573.28	566.31	560.08	554.51	545.04	537.39
34000	598.73	590.66	583.47	577.05	571.32	561.56	553.67
35000	616.34	608.03	600.63	594.03	588.12	578.08	569.95
40000	704.39	694.89	686.43	678.89	672.14	660.66	651.38
45000	792.44	781.75	772.24	763.75	756.16	743.24	732.80
50000	880.49	868.61	858.04	848.61	840.17	825.82	814.22
55000	968.54	955.47	943.85	933.47	924.19	908.40	895.64
60000	1056.59	1042.34	1029.65	1018.33	1008.21	990.99	977.06
65000	1144.63	1129.20	1115.45	1103.19	1092.22	1073.57	1058.49
70000	1232.68	1216.06	1201.26	1188.05	1176.24	1156.15	1139.91

18½%   Monthly Loan Payments

LOAN AMOUNT	½ YEAR	1 YEAR	1½ YEARS	2 YEARS	2½ YEARS	3 YEARS	3½ YEARS
100	17.58	9.19	6.40	5.02	4.19	3.64	3.2
200	35.15	18.38	12.81	10.03	8.38	7.28	6.5
300	52.73	27.58	19.21	15.05	12.57	10.92	9.7
400	70.31	36.77	25.62	20.07	16.75	14.56	13.0
500	87.89	45.96	32.02	25.08	20.94	18.20	16.2
600	105.46	55.15	38.43	30.10	25.13	21.84	19.5
700	123.04	64.34	44.83	35.12	29.32	25.48	22.7
800	140.62	73.53	51.24	40.13	33.51	29.12	26.0
900	158.20	82.73	57.64	45.15	37.70	32.76	29.2
1000	175.77	91.92	64.04	50.17	41.89	36.40	32.5
1500	263.66	137.88	96.07	75.25	62.83	54.61	48.7
2000	351.55	183.84	128.09	100.33	83.77	72.81	65.0
2500	439.44	229.80	160.11	125.42	104.71	91.01	81.3
3000	527.32	275.75	192.13	150.50	125.66	109.21	97.5
3500	615.21	321.71	224.16	175.58	146.60	127.41	113.8
4000	703.10	367.67	256.18	200.66	167.54	145.61	130.0
4500	790.98	413.63	288.20	225.75	188.48	163.82	146.3
5000	878.87	459.59	320.22	250.83	209.43	182.02	162.6
5500	966.76	505.55	352.24	275.91	230.37	200.22	178.8
6000	1054.65	551.51	384.27	301.00	251.31	218.42	195.1
6500	1142.53	597.47	416.29	326.08	272.26	236.62	211.3
7000	1230.42	643.43	448.31	351.16	293.20	254.83	227.6
7500	1318.31	689.39	480.33	376.25	314.14	273.03	243.9
8000	1406.19	735.34	512.36	401.33	335.08	291.23	260.1
8500	1494.08	781.30	544.38	426.41	356.03	309.43	276.4
9000	1581.97	827.26	576.40	451.49	376.97	327.63	292.6
9500	1669.86	873.22	608.42	476.58	397.91	345.84	308.9
10000	1757.74	919.18	640.44	501.66	418.86	364.04	325.2
11000	1933.52	1011.10	704.49	551.83	460.74	400.44	357.7
12000	2109.29	1103.02	768.53	601.99	502.63	436.84	390.2
13000	2285.07	1194.94	832.58	652.16	544.51	473.25	422.7
14000	2460.84	1286.85	896.62	702.32	586.40	509.65	455.2
15000	2636.62	1378.77	960.67	752.49	628.28	546.06	487.8
16000	2812.39	1470.69	1024.71	802.66	670.17	582.46	520.3
17000	2988.16	1562.61	1088.75	852.82	712.05	618.86	552.8
18000	3163.94	1654.53	1152.80	902.99	753.94	655.27	585.1
19000	3339.71	1746.44	1216.84	953.15	795.83	691.67	617.1
20000	3515.49	1838.36	1280.89	1003.32	837.71	728.07	650.4
21000	3691.26	1930.28	1344.93	1053.49	879.60	764.48	682.1
22000	3867.04	2022.20	1408.98	1103.65	921.48	800.88	715.4
23000	4042.81	2114.12	1473.02	1153.82	963.37	837.29	747.1
24000	4218.58	2206.03	1537.07	1203.98	1005.25	873.69	780.1
25000	4394.36	2297.95	1601.11	1254.15	1047.14	910.09	813.0
26000	4570.13	2389.87	1665.15	1304.32	1089.02	946.50	845.1
27000	4745.91	2481.79	1729.20	1354.48	1130.91	982.90	878.1
28000	4921.68	2573.71	1793.24	1404.65	1172.80	1019.30	910.1
29000	5097.46	2665.63	1857.29	1454.81	1214.68	1055.71	943.1
30000	5273.23	2757.54	1921.33	1504.98	1256.57	1092.11	975.1
31000	5449.01	2849.46	1985.38	1555.15	1298.45	1128.52	1008.1
32000	5624.78	2941.38	2049.42	1605.31	1340.34	1164.92	1040.1
33000	5800.55	3033.30	2113.46	1655.48	1382.22	1201.32	1073.1
34000	5976.33	3125.22	2177.51	1705.64	1424.11	1237.73	1105.1
35000	6152.10	3217.13	2241.55	1755.81	1465.99	1274.13	1138.1
40000	7030.97	3676.72	2561.78	2006.64	1675.42	1456.15	1300.1
45000	7909.85	4136.32	2882.00	2257.47	1884.85	1638.17	1463.1
50000	8788.72	4595.91	3202.22	2508.30	2094.28	1820.19	1626.1
55000	9667.59	5055.50	3522.44	2759.13	2303.71	2002.20	1788.1
60000	10546.46	5515.09	3842.66	3009.96	2513.13	2184.22	1951.1
65000	11425.33	5974.68	4162.88	3260.79	2722.56	2366.24	2113.1
70000	12304.21	6434.27	4483.11	3511.62	2931.99	2548.26	2276.1

Monthly Loan Payments 18½%

LOAN AMOUNT	4 YEARS	4½ YEARS	5 YEARS	5½ YEARS	6 YEARS	6½ YEARS	7 YEARS
100	2.96	2.74	2.57	2.43	2.31	2.21	2.13
200	5.93	5.48	5.13	4.85	4.62	4.43	4.26
300	8.89	8.23	7.70	7.28	6.93	6.64	6.39
400	11.85	10.97	10.27	9.70	9.24	8.85	8.52
500	14.82	13.71	12.83	12.13	11.55	11.06	10.66
600	17.78	16.45	15.40	14.55	13.85	13.28	12.79
700	20.75	19.19	17.97	16.98	16.16	15.49	14.92
800	23.71	21.93	20.53	19.40	18.47	17.70	17.05
900	26.67	24.68	23.10	21.83	20.78	19.91	19.18
1000	29.64	27.42	25.67	24.25	23.09	22.13	21.31
1500	44.46	41.13	38.50	36.38	34.64	33.19	31.97
2000	59.27	54.84	51.33	48.50	46.18	44.25	42.62
2500	74.09	68.55	64.17	60.63	57.73	55.31	53.28
3000	88.91	82.26	77.00	72.76	69.27	66.38	63.94
3500	103.73	95.97	89.83	84.88	80.82	77.44	74.59
4000	118.55	109.67	102.66	97.01	92.37	88.50	85.25
4500	133.37	123.38	115.50	109.13	103.91	99.56	95.90
5000	148.18	137.09	128.33	121.26	115.46	110.63	106.56
5500	163.00	150.80	141.16	133.39	127.00	121.69	117.22
6000	177.82	164.51	154.00	145.51	138.55	132.75	127.87
6500	192.64	178.22	166.83	157.64	150.09	143.81	138.53
7000	207.46	191.93	179.66	169.76	161.64	154.88	149.18
7500	222.28	205.64	192.50	181.89	173.19	165.94	159.84
8000	237.10	219.35	205.33	194.02	184.73	177.00	170.50
8500	251.91	233.06	218.16	206.14	196.28	188.07	181.15
9000	266.73	246.77	231.00	218.27	207.82	199.13	191.81
9500	281.55	260.48	243.83	230.39	219.37	210.19	202.46
10000	296.37	274.19	256.66	242.52	230.91	221.25	213.12
11000	326.01	301.61	282.33	266.77	254.00	243.38	234.43
12000	355.64	329.02	307.99	291.02	277.10	265.50	255.74
13000	385.28	356.44	333.66	315.28	300.19	287.63	277.05
14000	414.92	383.86	359.33	339.53	323.28	309.75	298.37
15000	444.55	411.28	384.99	363.78	346.37	331.88	319.68
16000	474.19	438.70	410.66	388.03	369.46	354.01	340.99
17000	503.83	466.12	436.33	412.28	392.55	376.13	362.30
18000	533.46	493.54	461.99	436.54	415.64	398.26	383.61
19000	563.10	520.96	487.66	460.79	438.74	420.38	404.93
20000	592.74	548.37	513.32	485.04	461.83	442.51	426.24
21000	622.38	575.79	538.99	509.29	484.92	464.63	447.55
22000	652.01	603.21	564.66	533.55	508.01	486.76	468.86
23000	681.65	630.63	590.32	557.80	531.10	508.88	490.17
24000	711.29	658.05	615.99	582.05	554.19	531.01	511.49
25000	740.92	685.47	641.66	606.30	577.28	553.13	532.80
26000	770.56	712.89	667.32	630.55	600.38	575.26	554.11
27000	800.20	740.31	692.99	654.81	623.47	597.38	575.42
28000	829.83	767.72	718.65	679.06	646.56	619.51	596.73
29000	859.47	795.14	744.32	703.31	669.65	641.63	618.05
30000	889.11	822.56	769.99	727.56	692.74	663.76	639.36
31000	918.74	849.98	795.65	751.81	715.83	685.88	660.67
32000	948.38	877.40	821.32	776.07	738.92	708.01	681.98
33000	978.02	904.82	846.98	800.32	762.01	730.14	703.29
34000	1007.66	932.24	872.65	824.57	785.11	752.26	724.61
35000	1037.29	959.66	898.32	848.82	808.20	774.39	745.92
40000	1185.48	1096.75	1026.65	970.08	923.65	885.01	852.48
45000	1333.66	1233.84	1154.98	1091.34	1039.11	995.64	959.04
50000	1481.85	1370.94	1283.31	1212.60	1154.57	1106.27	1065.60
55000	1630.03	1508.03	1411.64	1333.86	1270.02	1216.89	1172.16
60000	1778.21	1645.12	1539.97	1455.12	1385.48	1327.52	1278.72
65000	1926.40	1782.22	1668.30	1576.38	1500.94	1438.15	1385.27
70000	2074.58	1919.31	1796.63	1697.64	1616.39	1548.77	1491.83

18½%   Monthly Loan Payments

LOAN AMOUNT	7½ YEARS	8 YEARS	8½ YEARS	9 YEARS	9½ YEARS	10 YEARS	10½ YEARS
100	2.06	2.00	1.95	1.91	1.87	1.83	1.80
200	4.12	4.01	3.90	3.81	3.74	3.67	3.61
300	6.19	6.01	5.85	5.72	5.60	5.50	5.41
400	8.25	8.01	7.81	7.63	7.47	7.34	7.22
500	10.31	10.01	9.76	9.54	9.34	9.17	9.02
600	12.37	12.02	11.71	11.44	11.21	11.00	10.82
700	14.43	14.02	13.66	13.35	13.08	12.84	12.63
800	16.50	16.02	15.61	15.26	14.95	14.67	14.43
900	18.56	18.02	17.56	17.16	16.81	16.51	16.24
1000	20.62	20.03	19.52	19.07	18.68	18.34	18.04
1500	30.93	30.04	29.27	28.61	28.02	27.51	27.06
2000	41.24	40.05	39.03	38.14	37.36	36.68	36.08
2500	51.55	50.07	48.79	47.68	46.71	45.85	45.10
3000	61.86	60.08	58.55	57.21	56.05	55.02	54.12
3500	72.17	70.10	68.30	66.75	65.39	64.19	63.15
4000	82.48	80.11	78.06	76.28	74.73	73.37	72.17
4500	92.79	90.12	87.82	85.82	84.07	82.54	81.19
5000	103.10	100.14	97.58	95.35	93.41	91.71	90.21
5500	113.41	110.15	107.34	104.89	102.75	100.88	99.23
6000	123.72	120.16	117.09	114.42	112.09	110.05	108.25
6500	134.03	130.18	126.85	123.96	121.44	119.22	117.27
7000	144.34	140.19	136.61	133.50	130.78	128.39	126.29
7500	154.65	150.21	146.37	143.03	140.12	137.56	135.31
8000	164.96	160.22	156.12	152.57	149.46	146.73	144.33
8500	175.27	170.23	165.88	162.10	158.80	155.90	153.35
9000	185.58	180.25	175.64	171.64	168.14	165.07	162.37
9500	195.89	190.26	185.40	181.17	177.48	174.25	171.39
10000	206.20	200.27	195.16	190.71	186.82	183.42	180.41
11000	226.82	220.30	214.67	209.78	205.51	201.76	198.46
12000	247.44	240.33	234.19	228.85	224.19	220.10	216.50
13000	268.06	260.36	253.70	247.92	242.87	238.44	234.54
14000	288.68	280.38	273.22	266.99	261.55	256.78	252.58
15000	309.31	300.41	292.73	286.06	280.24	275.12	270.62
16000	329.93	320.44	312.25	305.13	298.92	293.47	288.66
17000	350.55	340.47	331.76	324.20	317.60	311.81	306.70
18000	371.17	360.49	351.28	343.27	336.28	330.15	324.75
19000	391.79	380.52	370.79	362.35	354.97	348.49	342.79
20000	412.41	400.55	390.31	381.42	373.65	366.83	360.83
21000	433.03	420.58	409.83	400.49	392.33	385.17	378.87
22000	453.65	440.60	429.34	419.56	411.01	403.52	396.91
23000	474.27	460.63	448.86	438.63	429.70	421.86	414.95
24000	494.89	480.66	468.37	457.70	448.38	440.20	432.99
25000	515.51	500.69	487.89	476.77	467.06	458.54	451.04
26000	536.13	520.71	507.40	495.84	485.74	476.88	469.08
27000	556.75	540.74	526.92	514.91	504.43	495.22	487.12
28000	577.37	560.77	546.43	533.98	523.11	513.57	505.16
29000	597.99	580.80	565.95	553.05	541.79	531.91	523.20
30000	618.61	600.82	585.47	572.12	560.47	550.25	541.24
31000	639.23	620.85	604.98	591.20	579.16	568.59	559.28
32000	659.85	640.88	624.50	610.27	597.84	586.93	577.33
33000	680.47	660.91	644.01	629.34	616.52	605.27	595.37
34000	701.09	680.93	663.53	648.41	635.20	623.62	613.41
35000	721.71	700.96	683.04	667.48	653.89	641.96	631.45
40000	824.81	801.10	780.62	762.83	747.30	733.67	721.66
45000	927.92	901.23	878.20	858.19	840.71	825.37	811.86
50000	1031.02	1001.37	975.78	953.54	934.12	917.08	902.07
55000	1134.12	1101.51	1073.35	1048.89	1027.53	1008.79	992.28
60000	1237.22	1201.65	1170.93	1144.25	1120.95	1100.50	1082.49
65000	1340.32	1301.78	1268.51	1239.60	1214.36	1192.21	1172.69
70000	1443.42	1401.92	1366.09	1334.96	1307.77	1283.92	1262.90

Monthly Loan Payments 18½%

LOAN AMOUNT	11 YEARS	11½ YEARS	12 YEARS	12½ YEARS	13 YEARS	14 YEARS	15 YEARS
100	1.78	1.75	1.73	1.71	1.70	1.67	1.65
200	3.56	3.51	3.47	3.43	3.40	3.34	3.29
300	5.33	5.26	5.20	5.14	5.09	5.01	4.94
400	7.11	7.02	6.93	6.86	6.79	6.68	6.59
500	8.89	8.77	8.67	8.57	8.49	8.35	8.23
600	10.67	10.52	10.40	10.29	10.19	10.02	9.88
700	12.44	12.28	12.13	12.00	11.88	11.69	11.53
800	14.22	14.03	13.86	13.72	13.58	13.36	13.17
900	16.00	15.79	15.60	15.43	15.28	15.02	14.82
1000	17.78	17.54	17.33	17.14	16.98	16.69	16.47
1500	26.66	26.31	26.00	25.72	25.47	25.04	24.70
2000	35.55	35.08	34.66	34.29	33.96	33.39	32.93
2500	44.44	43.85	43.33	42.86	42.44	41.74	41.16
3000	53.33	52.62	51.99	51.43	50.93	50.08	49.40
3500	62.22	61.39	60.66	60.01	59.42	58.43	57.63
4000	71.10	70.16	69.32	68.58	67.91	66.78	65.86
4500	79.99	78.93	77.99	77.15	76.40	75.12	74.09
5000	88.88	87.70	86.66	85.72	84.89	83.47	82.33
5500	97.77	96.47	95.32	94.29	93.38	91.82	90.56
6000	106.66	105.24	103.99	102.87	101.87	100.16	98.79
6500	115.54	114.01	112.65	111.44	110.35	108.51	107.02
7000	124.43	122.78	121.32	120.01	118.84	116.86	115.26
7500	133.32	131.55	129.98	128.58	127.33	125.21	123.49
8000	142.21	140.32	138.65	137.16	135.82	133.55	131.72
8500	151.10	149.09	147.31	145.73	144.31	141.90	139.95
9000	159.98	157.86	155.98	154.30	152.80	150.25	148.19
9500	168.87	166.64	164.65	162.87	161.29	158.59	156.42
10000	177.76	175.41	173.31	171.44	169.78	166.94	164.65
11000	195.54	192.95	190.64	188.59	186.75	183.63	181.12
12000	213.31	210.49	207.97	205.73	203.73	200.33	197.58
13000	231.09	228.03	225.30	222.88	220.71	217.02	214.05
14000	248.86	245.57	242.64	240.02	237.69	233.72	230.51
15000	266.64	263.11	259.97	257.17	254.66	250.41	246.98
16000	284.42	280.65	277.30	274.31	271.64	267.10	263.44
17000	302.19	298.19	294.63	291.45	288.62	283.80	279.91
18000	319.97	315.73	311.96	308.60	305.60	300.49	296.37
19000	337.74	333.27	329.29	325.74	322.57	317.19	312.84
20000	355.52	350.81	346.62	342.89	339.55	333.88	329.30
21000	373.30	368.35	363.95	360.03	356.53	350.58	345.77
22000	391.07	385.89	381.29	377.18	373.51	367.27	362.24
23000	408.85	403.43	398.62	394.32	390.48	383.96	378.70
24000	426.62	420.97	415.95	411.47	407.46	400.66	395.17
25000	444.40	438.51	433.28	428.61	424.44	417.35	411.63
26000	462.18	456.05	450.61	445.75	441.42	434.05	428.10
27000	479.95	473.59	467.94	462.90	458.39	450.74	444.56
28000	497.73	491.14	485.27	480.04	475.37	467.43	461.03
29000	515.50	508.68	502.60	497.19	492.35	484.13	477.49
30000	533.28	526.22	519.93	514.33	509.33	500.82	493.96
31000	551.06	543.76	537.27	531.48	526.30	517.52	510.42
32000	568.83	561.30	554.60	548.62	543.28	534.21	526.89
33000	586.61	578.84	571.93	565.77	560.26	550.90	543.35
34000	604.38	596.38	589.26	582.91	577.24	567.60	559.82
35000	622.16	613.92	606.59	600.05	594.21	584.29	576.28
40000	711.04	701.62	693.25	685.78	679.10	667.76	658.61
45000	799.92	789.32	779.90	771.50	763.99	751.23	740.94
50000	888.85	877.03	866.56	857.22	848.88	834.70	823.26
55000	977.68	964.73	953.21	942.94	933.76	918.17	905.59
60000	1066.56	1052.43	1039.87	1028.66	1018.65	1001.64	987.91
65000	1155.44	1140.14	1126.52	1114.39	1103.54	1085.11	1070.24
70000	1244.32	1227.84	1213.18	1200.11	1188.43	1168.58	1152.57

18¾% Monthly Loan Payments

LOAN AMOUNT	½ YEAR	1 YEAR	1½ YEARS	2 YEARS	2½ YEARS	3 YEARS	3½ YEARS
100	17.59	9.20	6.42	5.03	4.20	3.65	3.2
200	35.18	18.41	12.83	10.06	8.40	7.31	6.5
300	52.77	27.61	19.25	15.09	12.60	10.96	9.7
400	70.36	36.81	25.67	20.11	16.80	14.61	13.0
500	87.95	46.02	32.08	25.14	21.00	18.26	16.3
600	105.54	55.22	38.50	30.17	25.21	21.92	19.5
700	123.13	64.43	44.91	35.20	29.41	25.57	22.8
800	140.72	73.63	51.33	40.23	33.61	29.22	26.1
900	158.31	82.83	57.75	45.26	37.81	32.88	29.3
1000	175.90	92.04	64.16	50.29	42.01	36.53	32.6
1500	263.85	138.06	96.25	75.43	63.01	54.79	48.9
2000	351.80	184.07	128.33	100.57	84.02	73.06	65.3
2500	439.75	230.09	160.41	125.72	105.02	91.32	81.6
3000	527.70	276.11	192.49	150.86	126.03	109.59	97.9
3500	615.65	322.13	224.57	176.01	147.03	127.85	114.2
4000	703.60	368.15	256.66	201.15	168.04	146.12	130.6
4500	791.55	414.17	288.74	226.29	189.04	164.38	146.9
5000	879.49	460.19	320.82	251.44	210.05	182.65	163.2
5500	967.44	506.21	352.90	276.58	231.05	200.91	179.5
6000	1055.39	552.22	384.98	301.72	252.05	219.18	195.9
6500	1143.34	598.24	417.07	326.87	273.06	237.44	212.2
7000	1231.29	644.26	449.15	352.01	294.06	255.71	228.5
7500	1319.24	690.28	481.23	377.15	315.07	273.97	244.8
8000	1407.19	736.30	513.31	402.30	336.07	292.24	261.2
8500	1495.14	782.32	545.39	427.44	357.07	310.50	277.5
9000	1583.09	828.34	577.47	452.59	378.08	328.77	293.8
9500	1671.04	874.35	609.56	477.73	399.09	347.03	310.1
10000	1758.99	920.37	641.64	502.87	420.09	365.30	326.5
11000	1934.88	1012.41	705.80	553.16	462.10	401.83	359.1
12000	2110.79	1104.45	769.97	603.45	504.11	438.36	391.7
13000	2286.69	1196.48	834.13	653.73	546.12	474.89	424.4
14000	2462.59	1288.52	898.29	704.02	588.13	511.42	457.0
15000	2638.48	1380.56	962.46	754.31	630.14	547.95	489.7
16000	2814.38	1472.60	1026.62	804.60	672.14	584.48	522.
17000	2990.28	1564.63	1090.79	854.88	714.15	621.01	555.
18000	3166.18	1656.67	1154.95	905.17	756.16	657.54	587.
19000	3342.08	1748.71	1219.11	955.46	798.17	694.07	620.
20000	3517.98	1840.75	1283.28	1005.74	840.18	730.59	652.
21000	3693.88	1932.78	1347.44	1056.03	882.19	767.12	685.
22000	3869.78	2024.82	1411.61	1106.32	924.20	803.65	718.
23000	4045.68	2116.86	1475.77	1156.61	966.21	840.18	750.
24000	4221.58	2208.90	1539.93	1206.89	1008.22	876.71	783.
25000	4397.47	2300.93	1604.10	1257.18	1050.23	913.24	816.
26000	4573.37	2392.97	1668.26	1307.47	1092.23	949.77	848.
27000	4749.27	2485.01	1732.42	1357.76	1134.24	986.30	881.
28000	4925.17	2577.04	1796.59	1408.04	1176.25	1022.83	914.
29000	5101.07	2669.08	1860.75	1458.33	1218.26	1059.36	946.
30000	5276.97	2761.12	1924.92	1508.62	1260.27	1095.89	979.
31000	5452.87	2853.16	1989.08	1558.90	1302.28	1132.42	1012.
32000	5628.77	2945.19	2053.24	1609.19	1344.29	1168.95	1044.
33000	5804.67	3037.23	2117.41	1659.48	1386.30	1205.48	1077.
34000	5980.57	3129.27	2181.57	1709.77	1428.31	1242.01	1110.
35000	6156.46	3221.31	2245.74	1760.05	1470.32	1278.54	1142.
40000	7035.96	3681.49	2566.55	2011.49	1680.36	1461.19	1305.
45000	7915.45	4141.68	2887.37	2262.93	1890.41	1643.84	1469
50000	8794.95	4601.87	3208.19	2514.36	2100.45	1826.49	1632.
55000	9674.44	5062.05	3529.01	2765.80	2310.50	2009.14	1795.
60000	10553.94	5522.24	3849.83	3017.23	2520.54	2191.78	1958.
65000	11433.43	5982.42	4170.65	3268.67	2730.59	2374.43	2122.
70000	12312.93	6442.61	4491.47	3520.11	2940.63	2557.08	2285.

Monthly Loan Payments 18¾%

LOAN AMOUNT	4 YEARS	4½ YEARS	5 YEARS	5½ YEARS	6 YEARS	6½ YEARS	7 YEARS
100	2.98	2.76	2.58	2.44	2.32	2.23	2.15
200	5.95	5.51	5.16	4.88	4.65	4.45	4.29
300	8.93	8.27	7.74	7.32	6.97	6.68	6.44
400	11.91	11.02	10.32	9.76	9.29	8.91	8.58
500	14.88	13.78	12.90	12.20	11.62	11.14	10.73
600	17.86	16.53	15.48	14.64	13.94	13.36	12.88
700	20.84	19.29	18.06	17.07	16.26	15.59	15.02
800	23.81	22.04	20.64	19.51	18.59	17.82	17.17
900	26.79	24.80	23.22	21.95	20.91	20.04	19.31
1000	29.77	27.55	25.80	24.39	23.23	22.27	21.46
1500	44.65	41.33	38.70	36.59	34.85	33.41	32.19
2000	59.54	55.11	51.61	48.78	46.47	44.54	42.92
2500	74.42	68.88	64.51	60.98	58.08	55.68	53.65
3000	89.31	82.66	77.41	73.18	69.70	66.81	64.38
3500	104.19	96.44	90.31	85.37	81.32	77.95	75.11
4000	119.07	110.21	103.21	97.57	92.94	89.08	85.84
4500	133.96	123.99	116.11	109.76	104.55	100.22	96.57
5000	148.84	137.76	129.02	121.96	116.17	111.35	107.30
5500	163.73	151.54	141.92	134.15	127.79	122.49	118.03
6000	178.61	165.32	154.82	146.35	139.40	133.62	128.76
6500	193.49	179.09	167.72	158.55	151.02	144.76	139.49
7000	208.38	192.87	180.62	170.74	162.64	155.89	150.22
7500	223.26	206.65	193.52	182.94	174.25	167.03	160.95
8000	238.15	220.42	206.43	195.13	185.87	178.16	171.68
8500	253.03	234.20	219.33	207.33	197.49	189.30	182.41
9000	267.92	247.98	232.23	219.53	209.10	200.43	193.14
9500	282.80	261.75	245.13	231.72	220.72	211.57	203.87
10000	297.68	275.53	258.03	243.92	232.34	222.70	214.60
11000	327.45	303.08	283.84	268.31	255.57	244.98	236.06
12000	357.22	330.64	309.64	292.70	278.81	267.25	257.52
13000	386.99	358.19	335.44	317.09	302.04	289.52	278.98
14000	416.76	385.74	361.24	341.48	325.27	311.79	300.44
15000	446.53	413.29	387.05	365.88	348.51	334.06	321.90
16000	476.29	440.85	412.85	390.27	371.74	356.33	343.36
17000	506.06	468.40	438.65	414.66	394.97	378.60	364.82
18000	535.83	495.95	464.46	439.05	418.21	400.87	386.27
19000	565.60	523.51	490.26	463.44	441.44	423.14	407.73
20000	595.37	551.06	516.06	487.84	464.68	445.41	429.19
21000	625.14	578.61	541.87	512.23	487.91	467.68	450.65
22000	654.90	606.16	567.67	536.62	511.14	489.95	472.11
23000	684.67	633.72	593.47	561.01	534.38	512.22	493.57
24000	714.44	661.27	619.28	585.40	557.61	534.49	515.03
25000	744.21	688.82	645.08	609.79	580.85	556.76	536.49
26000	773.98	716.38	670.88	634.19	604.08	579.03	557.95
27000	803.75	743.93	696.69	658.58	627.31	601.30	579.41
28000	833.51	771.48	722.49	682.97	650.55	623.57	600.87
29000	863.28	799.04	748.29	707.36	673.78	645.84	622.33
30000	893.05	826.59	774.10	731.75	697.01	668.11	643.79
31000	922.82	854.14	799.90	756.15	720.25	690.38	665.25
32000	952.59	881.69	825.70	780.54	743.48	712.65	686.71
33000	982.36	909.25	851.51	804.93	766.72	734.93	708.17
34000	1012.12	936.80	877.31	829.32	789.95	757.20	729.63
35000	1041.89	964.35	903.11	853.71	813.18	779.47	751.09
40000	1190.73	1102.12	1032.13	975.67	929.35	890.82	858.39
45000	1339.58	1239.88	1161.14	1097.63	1045.52	1002.17	965.69
50000	1488.42	1377.65	1290.16	1219.59	1161.69	1113.52	1072.99
55000	1637.26	1515.41	1419.18	1341.55	1277.86	1224.88	1180.28
60000	1786.10	1653.18	1548.19	1463.51	1394.03	1336.23	1287.58
65000	1934.94	1790.94	1677.21	1585.47	1510.20	1447.58	1394.88
70000	2083.78	1928.71	1806.22	1707.42	1626.37	1558.93	1502.18

18¾%　　Monthly Loan Payments

LOAN AMOUNT	7½ YEARS	8 YEARS	8½ YEARS	9 YEARS	9½ YEARS	10 YEARS	10½ YEARS
100	2.08	2.02	1.97	1.92	1.88	1.85	1.82
200	4.15	4.04	3.93	3.85	3.77	3.70	3.64
300	6.23	6.05	5.90	5.77	5.65	5.55	5.46
400	8.31	8.07	7.87	7.69	7.54	7.40	7.28
500	10.39	10.09	9.84	9.61	9.42	9.25	9.10
600	12.46	12.11	11.80	11.54	11.31	11.10	10.92
700	14.54	14.13	13.77	13.46	13.19	12.95	12.74
800	16.62	16.14	15.74	15.38	15.07	14.80	14.56
900	18.69	18.16	17.70	17.31	16.96	16.65	16.39
1000	20.77	20.18	19.67	19.23	18.84	18.50	18.21
1500	31.16	30.27	29.51	28.84	28.26	27.76	27.31
2000	41.54	40.36	39.34	38.46	37.69	37.01	36.41
2500	51.93	50.45	49.18	48.07	47.11	46.26	45.52
3000	62.31	60.54	59.01	57.69	56.53	55.51	54.62
3500	72.70	70.63	68.85	67.30	65.95	64.76	63.72
4000	83.08	80.72	78.68	76.91	75.37	74.02	72.82
4500	93.47	90.81	88.52	86.53	84.79	83.27	81.93
5000	103.85	100.90	98.35	96.14	94.21	92.52	91.03
5500	114.24	110.99	108.19	105.76	103.63	101.77	100.13
6000	124.62	121.08	118.03	115.37	113.06	111.02	109.24
6500	135.01	131.17	127.86	124.99	122.48	120.28	118.34
7000	145.40	141.26	137.70	134.60	131.90	129.53	127.44
7500	155.78	151.35	147.53	144.21	141.32	138.78	136.55
8000	166.17	161.44	157.37	153.83	150.74	148.03	145.65
8500	176.55	171.53	167.20	163.44	160.16	157.29	154.75
9000	186.94	181.62	177.04	173.06	169.58	166.54	163.86
9500	197.32	191.71	186.87	182.67	179.00	175.79	172.96
10000	207.71	201.80	196.71	192.29	188.43	185.04	182.06
11000	228.48	221.98	216.38	211.52	207.27	203.55	200.27
12000	249.25	242.16	236.05	230.74	226.11	222.05	218.47
13000	270.02	262.34	255.72	249.97	244.95	240.55	236.68
14000	290.79	282.53	275.39	269.20	263.80	259.06	254.89
15000	311.56	302.71	295.06	288.43	282.64	277.56	273.09
16000	332.33	322.89	314.74	307.66	301.48	296.07	291.30
17000	353.10	343.07	334.41	326.89	320.32	314.57	309.50
18000	373.87	363.25	354.08	346.12	339.17	333.07	327.71
19000	394.64	383.43	373.75	365.34	358.01	351.58	345.92
20000	415.41	403.61	393.42	384.57	376.85	370.08	364.12
21000	436.19	423.79	413.09	403.80	395.70	388.59	382.33
22000	456.96	443.97	432.76	423.03	414.54	407.09	400.54
23000	477.73	464.15	452.43	442.26	433.38	425.60	418.74
24000	498.50	484.33	472.10	461.49	452.22	444.10	436.95
25000	519.27	504.51	491.77	480.72	471.07	462.60	455.15
26000	540.04	524.69	511.44	499.95	489.91	481.11	473.36
27000	560.81	544.87	531.12	519.17	508.75	499.61	491.57
28000	581.58	565.05	550.79	538.40	527.59	518.12	509.77
29000	602.35	585.23	570.46	557.63	546.44	536.62	527.98
30000	623.12	605.41	590.13	576.86	565.28	555.12	546.18
31000	643.89	625.59	609.80	596.09	584.12	573.63	564.39
32000	664.66	645.77	629.47	615.32	602.96	592.13	582.60
33000	685.43	665.95	649.14	634.55	621.81	610.64	600.80
34000	706.20	686.13	668.81	653.77	640.65	629.14	619.01
35000	726.98	706.31	688.48	673.00	659.49	647.64	637.21
40000	830.83	807.22	786.84	769.15	753.71	740.17	728.25
45000	934.68	908.12	885.19	865.29	847.92	832.69	819.28
50000	1038.54	1009.02	983.55	961.43	942.13	925.21	910.31
55000	1142.39	1109.92	1081.90	1057.58	1036.34	1017.73	1001.34
60000	1246.24	1210.82	1180.26	1153.72	1130.56	1110.25	1092.37
65000	1350.10	1311.72	1278.61	1249.86	1224.77	1202.77	1183.40
70000	1453.95	1412.63	1376.97	1346.01	1318.98	1295.29	1274.43

Monthly Loan Payments 18¾%

LOAN AMOUNT	11 YEARS	11½ YEARS	12 YEARS	12½ YEARS	13 YEARS	14 YEARS	15 YEARS
100	1.79	1.77	1.75	1.73	1.72	1.69	1.66
200	3.59	3.54	3.50	3.46	3.43	3.37	3.33
300	5.38	5.31	5.25	5.20	5.15	5.06	4.99
400	7.18	7.08	7.00	6.93	6.86	6.75	6.66
500	8.97	8.85	8.75	8.66	8.58	8.44	8.32
600	10.77	10.63	10.50	10.39	10.29	10.12	9.99
700	12.56	12.40	12.25	12.12	12.01	11.81	11.65
800	14.35	14.17	14.00	13.85	13.72	13.50	13.32
900	16.15	15.94	15.75	15.59	15.44	15.19	14.98
1000	17.94	17.71	17.50	17.32	17.15	16.87	16.65
1500	26.91	26.56	26.25	25.98	25.73	25.31	24.97
2000	35.89	35.42	35.00	34.63	34.30	33.74	33.29
2500	44.86	44.27	43.76	43.29	42.88	42.18	41.62
3000	53.83	53.13	52.51	51.95	51.46	50.62	49.94
3500	62.80	61.98	61.26	60.61	60.03	59.05	58.26
4000	71.77	70.84	70.01	69.27	68.61	67.49	66.59
4500	80.74	79.69	78.76	77.93	77.19	75.93	74.91
5000	89.71	88.55	87.51	86.59	85.76	84.36	83.23
5500	98.69	97.40	96.26	95.24	94.34	92.80	91.56
6000	107.66	106.26	105.01	103.90	102.91	101.23	99.88
6500	116.63	115.11	113.76	112.56	111.49	109.67	108.20
7000	125.60	123.97	122.51	121.22	120.07	118.11	116.53
7500	134.57	132.82	131.27	129.88	128.64	126.54	124.85
8000	143.54	141.68	140.02	138.54	137.22	134.98	133.17
8500	152.51	150.53	148.77	147.20	145.79	143.41	141.50
9000	161.49	159.39	157.52	155.86	154.37	151.85	149.82
9500	170.46	168.24	166.27	164.51	162.95	160.29	158.14
10000	179.43	177.09	175.02	173.17	171.52	168.72	166.47
11000	197.37	194.80	192.52	190.49	188.67	185.60	183.11
12000	215.31	212.51	210.02	207.81	205.83	202.47	199.76
13000	233.26	230.22	227.53	225.12	222.98	219.34	216.41
14000	251.20	247.93	245.03	242.44	240.13	236.21	233.05
15000	269.14	265.64	262.53	259.76	257.28	253.08	249.70
16000	287.09	283.35	280.03	277.08	274.44	269.96	266.35
17000	305.03	301.06	297.54	294.39	291.59	286.83	282.99
18000	322.97	318.77	315.04	311.71	308.74	303.70	299.64
19000	340.91	336.48	332.54	329.03	325.89	320.57	316.29
20000	358.86	354.19	350.04	346.35	343.05	337.45	332.93
21000	376.80	371.90	367.54	363.66	360.20	354.32	349.58
22000	394.74	389.61	385.05	380.98	377.35	371.19	366.23
23000	412.69	407.32	402.55	398.30	394.50	388.06	382.87
24000	430.63	425.03	420.05	415.61	411.65	404.93	399.52
25000	448.57	442.74	437.55	432.93	428.81	421.81	416.17
26000	466.51	460.45	455.05	450.25	445.96	438.68	432.81
27000	484.46	478.16	472.56	467.57	463.11	455.55	449.46
28000	502.40	495.87	490.06	484.88	480.26	472.42	466.11
29000	520.34	513.58	507.56	502.20	497.42	489.30	482.75
30000	538.29	531.28	525.06	519.52	514.57	506.17	499.40
31000	556.23	548.99	542.56	536.84	531.72	523.04	516.05
32000	574.17	566.70	560.07	554.15	548.87	539.91	532.69
33000	592.11	584.41	577.57	571.47	566.02	556.79	549.34
34000	610.06	602.12	595.07	588.79	583.18	573.66	565.99
35000	628.00	619.83	612.57	606.10	600.33	590.53	582.63
40000	717.71	708.38	700.08	692.69	686.09	674.89	665.87
45000	807.43	796.93	787.59	779.28	771.85	759.25	749.10
50000	897.14	885.47	875.10	865.86	857.61	843.61	832.33
55000	986.86	974.02	962.61	952.45	943.37	927.98	915.57
60000	1076.57	1062.57	1050.12	1039.04	1029.14	1012.34	998.80
65000	1166.29	1151.12	1137.64	1125.62	1114.90	1096.70	1082.03
70000	1256.00	1239.66	1225.15	1212.21	1200.66	1181.06	1165.27

19%   Monthly Loan Payments

LOAN AMOUNT	½ YEAR	1 YEAR	1½ YEARS	2 YEARS	2½ YEARS	3 YEARS	3½ YEARS
100	17.60	9.22	6.43	5.04	4.21	3.67	3.28
200	35.20	18.43	12.86	10.08	8.43	7.33	6.56
300	52.81	27.65	19.29	15.12	12.64	11.00	9.83
400	70.41	36.86	25.71	20.16	16.85	14.66	13.11
500	88.01	46.08	32.14	25.20	21.07	18.33	16.39
600	105.61	55.29	38.57	30.25	25.28	21.99	19.67
700	123.22	64.51	45.00	35.29	29.49	25.66	22.94
800	140.82	73.73	51.43	40.33	33.71	29.32	26.22
900	158.42	82.94	57.86	45.37	37.92	32.99	29.50
1000	176.02	92.16	64.28	50.41	42.13	36.66	32.78
1500	264.04	138.23	96.43	75.61	63.20	54.98	49.17
2000	352.05	184.31	128.57	100.82	84.27	73.31	65.56
2500	440.06	230.39	160.71	126.02	105.33	91.64	81.95
3000	528.07	276.47	192.85	151.23	126.40	109.97	98.34
3500	616.08	322.55	224.99	176.43	147.46	128.30	114.72
4000	704.09	368.63	257.13	201.63	168.53	146.62	131.11
4500	792.11	414.70	289.28	226.84	189.60	164.95	147.50
5000	880.12	460.78	321.42	252.04	210.66	183.28	163.89
5500	968.13	506.86	353.56	277.25	231.73	201.61	180.28
6000	1056.14	552.94	385.70	302.45	252.80	219.94	196.67
6500	1144.15	599.02	417.84	327.66	273.86	238.26	213.06
7000	1232.17	645.10	449.98	352.86	294.93	256.59	229.45
7500	1320.18	691.17	482.13	378.06	316.00	274.92	245.84
8000	1408.19	737.25	514.27	403.27	337.06	293.25	262.23
8500	1496.20	783.33	546.41	428.47	358.13	311.58	278.62
9000	1584.21	829.41	578.55	453.68	379.19	329.90	295.01
9500	1672.22	875.49	610.69	478.88	400.26	348.23	311.40
10000	1760.24	921.57	642.83	504.09	421.33	366.56	327.78
11000	1936.26	1013.72	707.12	554.49	463.46	403.22	360.56
12000	2112.28	1105.88	771.40	604.90	505.59	439.87	393.34
13000	2288.31	1198.04	835.69	655.31	547.73	476.53	426.12
14000	2464.33	1290.19	899.97	705.72	589.86	513.18	458.90
15000	2640.36	1382.35	964.25	756.13	631.99	549.84	491.68
16000	2816.38	1474.51	1028.54	806.54	674.12	586.50	524.46
17000	2992.40	1566.66	1092.82	856.95	716.26	623.15	557.23
18000	3168.43	1658.82	1157.10	907.36	758.39	659.81	590.01
19000	3344.45	1750.97	1221.39	957.76	800.52	696.46	622.79
20000	3520.47	1843.13	1285.67	1008.17	842.65	733.12	655.57
21000	3696.50	1935.29	1349.95	1058.58	884.79	769.78	688.35
22000	3872.52	2027.44	1414.24	1108.99	926.92	806.43	721.13
23000	4048.54	2119.60	1478.52	1159.40	969.05	843.09	753.91
24000	4224.57	2211.76	1542.80	1209.81	1011.19	879.74	786.68
25000	4400.59	2303.91	1607.09	1260.22	1053.32	916.40	819.46
26000	4576.62	2396.07	1671.37	1310.62	1095.45	953.06	852.24
27000	4752.64	2488.23	1735.65	1361.03	1137.58	989.71	885.02
28000	4928.66	2580.38	1799.94	1411.44	1179.72	1026.37	917.80
29000	5104.69	2672.54	1864.22	1461.85	1221.85	1063.02	950.58
30000	5280.71	2764.70	1928.50	1512.26	1263.98	1099.68	983.35
31000	5456.73	2856.85	1992.79	1562.67	1306.11	1136.34	1016.13
32000	5632.76	2949.01	2057.07	1613.08	1348.25	1172.99	1048.91
33000	5808.78	3041.17	2121.36	1663.48	1390.38	1209.65	1081.69
34000	5984.80	3133.32	2185.64	1713.89	1432.51	1246.30	1114.47
35000	6160.83	3225.48	2249.92	1764.30	1474.65	1282.96	1147.25
40000	7040.95	3686.26	2571.34	2016.34	1685.31	1466.24	1311.14
45000	7921.07	4147.05	2892.76	2268.39	1895.97	1649.52	1475.03
50000	8801.18	4607.83	3214.17	2520.43	2106.64	1832.80	1638.92
55000	9681.30	5068.61	3535.59	2772.47	2317.30	2016.08	1802.82
60000	10561.42	5529.39	3857.01	3024.52	2527.96	2199.36	1966.71
65000	11441.54	5990.18	4178.43	3276.56	2738.63	2382.64	2130.60
70000	12321.66	6450.96	4499.84	3528.60	2949.29	2565.92	2294.49

Monthly Loan Payments 19%

LOAN AMOUNT	4 YEARS	4½ YEARS	5 YEARS	5½ YEARS	6 YEARS	6½ YEARS	7 YEARS
100	2.99	2.77	2.59	2.45	2.34	2.24	2.16
200	5.98	5.54	5.19	4.91	4.68	4.48	4.32
300	8.97	8.31	7.78	7.36	7.01	6.72	6.48
400	11.96	11.07	10.38	9.81	9.35	8.97	8.64
500	14.95	13.84	12.97	12.27	11.69	11.21	10.80
600	17.94	16.61	15.56	14.72	14.03	13.45	12.96
700	20.93	19.38	18.16	17.17	16.36	15.69	15.13
800	23.92	22.15	20.75	19.63	18.70	17.93	17.29
900	26.91	24.92	23.35	22.08	21.04	20.17	19.45
1000	29.90	27.69	25.94	24.53	23.38	22.42	21.61
1500	44.85	41.53	38.91	36.80	35.07	33.62	32.41
2000	59.80	55.37	51.88	49.06	46.75	44.83	43.22
2500	74.75	69.22	64.85	61.33	58.44	56.04	54.02
3000	89.70	83.06	77.82	73.60	70.13	67.25	64.82
3500	104.65	96.91	90.79	85.86	81.82	78.46	75.63
4000	119.60	110.75	103.76	98.13	93.51	89.66	86.43
4500	134.55	124.59	116.73	110.39	105.20	100.87	97.24
5000	149.50	138.44	129.70	122.66	116.88	112.08	108.04
5500	164.45	152.28	142.67	134.93	128.57	123.29	118.84
6000	179.40	166.12	155.64	147.19	140.26	134.50	129.65
6500	194.35	179.97	168.61	159.46	151.95	145.70	140.45
7000	209.30	193.81	181.58	171.72	163.64	156.91	151.26
7500	224.25	207.66	194.55	183.99	175.33	168.12	162.06
8000	239.20	221.50	207.52	196.26	187.01	179.33	172.86
8500	254.15	235.34	220.49	208.52	198.70	190.54	183.67
9000	269.10	249.19	233.46	220.79	210.39	201.74	194.47
9500	284.05	263.03	246.44	233.05	222.08	212.95	205.28
10000	299.00	276.87	259.41	245.32	233.77	224.16	216.08
11000	328.90	304.56	285.35	269.85	257.14	246.58	237.69
12000	358.80	332.25	311.29	294.38	280.52	268.99	259.30
13000	388.70	359.94	337.23	318.92	303.90	291.41	280.90
14000	418.60	387.62	363.17	343.45	327.27	313.83	302.51
15000	448.50	415.31	389.11	367.98	350.65	336.24	324.12
16000	478.40	443.00	415.05	392.51	374.03	358.66	345.73
17000	508.30	470.69	440.99	417.04	397.40	381.07	367.34
18000	538.20	498.37	466.93	441.57	420.78	403.49	388.94
19000	568.10	526.06	492.87	466.11	444.16	425.91	410.55
20000	598.00	553.75	518.81	490.64	467.53	448.32	432.16
21000	627.90	581.44	544.75	515.17	490.91	470.74	453.77
22000	657.80	609.12	570.69	539.70	514.29	493.15	475.38
23000	687.70	636.81	596.63	564.23	537.66	515.57	496.98
24000	717.60	664.50	622.57	588.77	561.04	537.99	518.59
25000	747.50	692.19	648.51	613.30	584.42	560.40	540.20
26000	777.40	719.87	674.45	637.83	607.79	582.82	561.81
27000	807.30	747.56	700.39	662.36	631.17	605.23	583.42
28000	837.20	775.25	726.34	686.89	654.55	627.65	605.02
29000	867.10	802.94	752.28	711.43	677.92	650.07	626.63
30000	897.00	830.62	778.22	735.96	701.30	672.48	648.24
31000	926.90	858.31	804.16	760.49	724.68	694.90	669.85
32000	956.80	886.00	830.10	785.02	748.06	717.32	691.46
33000	986.70	913.69	856.04	809.55	771.43	739.73	713.06
34000	1016.60	941.37	881.98	834.09	794.81	762.15	734.67
35000	1046.50	969.06	907.92	858.62	818.19	784.56	756.28
40000	1196.00	1107.50	1037.62	981.28	935.07	896.64	864.32
45000	1345.51	1245.94	1167.32	1103.94	1051.95	1008.72	972.36
50000	1495.01	1384.37	1297.03	1226.60	1168.84	1120.80	1080.40
55000	1644.51	1522.81	1426.73	1349.26	1285.72	1232.89	1188.44
60000	1794.01	1661.25	1556.43	1471.92	1402.60	1344.97	1296.48
65000	1943.51	1799.69	1686.14	1594.58	1519.49	1457.05	1404.52
70000	2093.01	1938.12	1815.84	1717.24	1636.37	1569.13	1512.56

19% Monthly Loan Payments

LOAN AMOUNT	7½ YEARS	8 YEARS	8½ YEARS	9 YEARS	9½ YEARS	10 YEARS	10½ YEARS
100	2.09	2.03	1.98	1.94	1.90	1.87	1.84
200	4.18	4.07	3.97	3.88	3.80	3.73	3.67
300	6.28	6.10	5.95	5.82	5.70	5.60	5.51
400	8.37	8.13	7.93	7.75	7.60	7.47	7.35
500	10.46	10.17	9.91	9.69	9.50	9.33	9.19
600	12.55	12.20	11.90	11.63	11.40	11.20	11.02
700	14.65	14.23	13.88	13.57	13.30	13.07	12.86
800	16.74	16.27	15.86	15.51	15.20	14.93	14.70
900	18.83	18.30	17.84	17.45	17.10	16.80	16.53
1000	20.92	20.33	19.83	19.39	19.00	18.67	18.37
1500	31.38	30.50	29.74	29.08	28.51	28.00	27.56
2000	41.84	40.67	39.65	38.77	38.01	37.33	36.74
2500	52.30	50.83	49.57	48.47	47.51	46.67	45.93
3000	62.76	61.00	59.48	58.16	57.01	56.00	55.11
3500	73.23	71.17	69.39	67.85	66.51	65.34	64.30
4000	83.69	81.34	79.31	77.55	76.01	74.67	73.49
4500	94.15	91.50	89.22	87.24	85.52	84.00	82.67
5000	104.61	101.67	99.13	96.94	95.02	93.34	91.86
5500	115.07	111.84	109.05	106.63	104.52	102.67	101.04
6000	125.53	122.00	118.96	116.32	114.02	112.00	110.23
6500	135.99	132.17	128.88	126.02	123.52	121.34	119.41
7000	146.45	142.34	138.79	135.71	133.02	130.67	128.60
7500	156.91	152.50	148.70	145.40	142.53	140.00	137.79
8000	167.37	162.67	158.62	155.10	152.03	149.34	146.97
8500	177.83	172.84	168.53	164.79	161.53	158.67	156.16
9000	188.29	183.00	178.44	174.48	171.03	168.01	165.34
9500	198.76	193.17	188.36	184.18	180.53	177.34	174.53
10000	209.22	203.34	198.27	193.87	190.03	186.67	183.71
11000	230.14	223.67	218.10	213.26	209.04	205.34	202.09
12000	251.06	244.01	237.92	232.64	228.04	224.01	220.46
13000	271.98	264.34	257.75	252.03	247.04	242.67	238.83
14000	292.90	284.67	277.58	271.42	266.05	261.34	257.20
15000	313.82	305.01	297.41	290.81	285.05	280.01	275.57
16000	334.75	325.34	317.23	310.19	304.05	298.68	293.94
17000	355.67	345.68	337.06	329.58	323.06	317.34	312.31
18000	376.59	366.01	356.88	348.97	342.06	336.01	330.69
19000	397.51	386.34	376.71	368.35	361.07	354.68	349.06
20000	418.43	406.68	396.54	387.74	380.07	373.34	367.43
21000	439.35	427.01	416.37	407.13	399.07	392.01	385.80
22000	460.28	447.35	436.19	426.52	418.08	410.68	404.17
23000	481.20	467.68	456.02	445.90	437.08	429.35	422.54
24000	502.12	488.01	475.85	465.29	456.08	448.01	440.92
25000	523.04	508.35	495.67	484.68	475.09	466.68	459.29
26000	543.96	528.68	515.50	504.06	494.09	485.35	477.66
27000	564.88	549.01	535.33	523.45	513.09	504.02	496.03
28000	585.81	569.35	555.15	542.84	532.10	522.68	514.40
29000	606.73	589.68	574.98	562.23	551.10	541.35	532.77
30000	627.65	610.02	594.81	581.61	570.10	560.02	551.14
31000	648.57	630.35	614.63	601.00	589.11	578.68	569.52
32000	669.49	650.68	634.46	620.39	608.11	597.35	587.89
33000	690.41	671.02	654.29	639.77	627.11	616.02	606.26
34000	711.34	691.35	674.12	659.16	646.12	634.69	624.63
35000	732.26	711.69	693.94	678.55	665.12	653.35	643.00
40000	836.87	813.35	793.08	775.48	760.14	746.69	734.86
45000	941.47	915.02	892.21	872.42	855.15	840.03	826.72
50000	1046.08	1016.69	991.35	969.35	950.17	933.36	918.57
55000	1150.69	1118.36	1090.48	1066.29	1045.19	1026.70	1010.43
60000	1255.30	1220.03	1189.62	1163.22	1140.21	1120.03	1102.29
65000	1359.91	1321.70	1288.75	1260.16	1235.22	1213.37	1194.15
70000	1464.52	1423.37	1387.89	1357.10	1330.24	1306.71	1286.00

Monthly Loan Payments 19%

LOAN AMOUNT	11 YEARS	11½ YEARS	12 YEARS	12½ YEARS	13 YEARS	14 YEARS	15 YEARS
100	1.81	1.79	1.77	1.75	1.73	1.71	1.68
200	3.62	3.58	3.53	3.50	3.47	3.41	3.37
300	5.43	5.36	5.30	5.25	5.20	5.12	5.05
400	7.24	7.15	7.07	7.00	6.93	6.82	6.73
500	9.06	8.94	8.84	8.75	8.66	8.53	8.41
600	10.87	10.73	10.60	10.49	10.40	10.23	10.10
700	12.68	12.52	12.37	12.24	12.13	11.94	11.78
800	14.49	14.30	14.14	13.99	13.86	13.64	13.46
900	16.30	16.09	15.91	15.74	15.59	15.35	15.15
1000	18.11	17.88	17.67	17.49	17.33	17.05	16.83
1500	27.17	26.82	26.51	26.24	25.99	25.58	25.24
2000	36.22	35.76	35.35	34.98	34.66	34.10	33.66
2500	45.28	44.70	44.18	43.73	43.32	42.63	42.07
3000	54.33	53.64	53.02	52.47	51.98	51.15	50.49
3500	63.39	62.58	61.86	61.22	60.65	59.68	58.90
4000	72.44	71.52	70.69	69.96	69.31	68.20	67.32
4500	81.50	80.46	79.53	78.71	77.97	76.73	75.73
5000	90.55	89.40	88.37	87.45	86.64	85.26	84.14
5500	99.61	98.33	97.21	96.20	95.30	93.78	92.56
6000	108.66	107.27	106.04	104.94	103.97	102.31	100.97
6500	117.72	116.21	114.88	113.69	112.63	110.83	109.39
7000	126.77	125.15	123.72	122.44	121.29	119.36	117.80
7500	135.83	134.09	132.55	131.18	129.96	127.88	126.22
8000	144.88	143.03	141.38	139.93	138.62	136.41	134.63
8500	153.94	151.97	150.23	148.67	147.28	144.93	143.04
9000	162.99	160.91	159.06	157.42	155.95	153.46	151.46
9500	172.05	169.85	167.90	166.16	164.61	161.99	159.87
10000	181.10	178.79	176.74	174.91	173.28	170.51	168.29
11000	199.21	196.67	194.41	192.40	190.60	187.56	185.12
12000	217.32	214.55	212.08	209.89	207.93	204.61	201.95
13000	235.43	232.43	229.76	227.38	225.26	221.66	218.77
14000	253.54	250.31	247.43	244.87	242.59	238.72	235.60
15000	271.65	268.19	265.10	262.36	259.91	255.77	252.43
16000	289.77	286.06	282.78	279.85	277.24	272.82	269.26
17000	307.88	303.94	300.45	297.34	294.57	289.87	286.09
18000	325.99	321.82	318.13	314.83	311.90	306.92	302.92
19000	344.10	339.70	335.80	332.32	329.22	323.97	319.75
20000	362.21	357.58	353.47	349.82	346.55	341.02	336.58
21000	380.32	375.46	371.15	367.31	363.88	358.07	353.40
22000	398.43	393.34	388.82	384.80	381.21	375.13	370.23
23000	416.54	411.22	406.49	402.29	398.54	392.18	387.06
24000	434.65	429.10	424.17	419.78	415.86	409.23	403.89
25000	452.76	446.98	441.84	437.27	433.19	426.28	420.72
26000	470.87	464.86	459.51	454.76	450.52	443.33	437.55
27000	488.98	482.73	477.19	472.25	467.85	460.38	454.38
28000	507.09	500.61	494.86	489.74	485.17	477.43	471.21
29000	525.20	518.49	512.54	507.23	502.50	494.48	488.03
30000	543.31	536.37	530.21	524.72	519.83	511.53	504.86
31000	561.42	554.25	547.88	542.21	537.16	528.59	521.69
32000	579.53	572.13	565.56	559.71	554.48	545.64	538.52
33000	597.64	590.01	583.23	577.20	571.81	562.69	555.35
34000	615.75	607.89	600.90	594.69	589.14	579.74	572.18
35000	633.86	625.77	618.58	612.18	606.47	596.79	589.01
40000	724.41	715.16	706.95	699.63	693.10	682.05	673.15
45000	814.96	804.56	795.31	787.09	779.74	767.30	757.29
50000	905.52	893.95	883.68	874.54	866.38	852.56	841.44
55000	996.07	983.35	972.05	961.99	953.02	937.81	925.58
60000	1086.62	1072.74	1060.42	1049.45	1039.66	1023.07	1009.73
65000	1177.17	1162.14	1148.79	1136.90	1126.30	1108.32	1093.87
70000	1267.72	1251.53	1237.16	1224.35	1212.93	1193.58	1178.01

183

19¼%   Monthly Loan Payments

LOAN AMOUNT	½ YEAR	1 YEAR	1½ YEARS	2 YEARS	2½ YEARS	3 YEARS	3½ YEARS
100	17.61	9.23	6.44	5.05	4.23	3.68	3.29
200	35.23	18.46	12.88	10.11	8.45	7.36	6.58
300	52.84	27.68	19.32	15.16	12.68	11.03	9.87
400	70.46	36.91	25.76	20.21	16.90	14.71	13.16
500	88.07	46.14	32.20	25.27	21.13	18.39	16.45
600	105.69	55.37	38.64	30.32	25.35	22.07	19.74
700	123.30	64.59	45.08	35.37	29.58	25.75	23.04
800	140.92	73.82	51.52	40.42	33.81	29.43	26.33
900	158.53	83.05	57.96	45.48	38.03	33.10	29.62
1000	176.15	92.28	64.40	50.53	42.26	36.78	32.91
1500	264.22	138.41	96.60	75.80	63.38	55.17	49.36
2000	352.30	184.55	128.81	101.06	84.51	73.57	65.82
2500	440.37	230.69	161.01	126.33	105.64	91.96	82.27
3000	528.45	276.83	193.21	151.59	126.77	110.35	98.72
3500	616.52	322.97	225.41	176.86	147.90	128.74	115.18
4000	704.59	369.10	257.61	202.12	169.03	147.13	131.63
4500	792.67	415.24	289.81	227.39	190.15	165.52	148.08
5000	880.74	461.38	322.02	252.65	211.28	183.91	164.54
5500	968.82	507.52	354.22	277.92	232.41	202.30	180.99
6000	1056.89	553.66	386.42	303.18	253.54	220.70	197.45
6500	1144.96	599.79	418.62	328.45	274.67	239.09	213.90
7000	1233.04	645.93	450.82	353.71	295.80	257.48	230.35
7500	1321.11	692.07	483.02	378.98	316.92	275.87	246.81
8000	1409.19	738.21	515.23	404.24	338.05	294.26	263.26
8500	1497.26	784.35	547.43	429.51	359.18	312.65	279.72
9000	1585.34	830.48	579.63	454.77	380.31	331.04	296.17
9500	1673.41	876.62	611.83	480.04	401.44	349.43	312.62
10000	1761.48	922.76	644.03	505.30	422.57	367.83	329.08
11000	1937.63	1015.04	708.44	555.83	464.82	404.61	361.99
12000	2113.78	1107.31	772.84	606.36	507.08	441.39	394.89
13000	2289.93	1199.59	837.24	656.89	549.34	478.17	427.80
14000	2466.08	1291.86	901.65	707.42	591.59	514.96	460.71
15000	2642.23	1384.14	966.05	757.95	633.85	551.74	493.62
16000	2818.37	1476.41	1030.45	808.48	676.11	588.52	526.52
17000	2994.52	1568.69	1094.85	859.01	718.36	625.30	559.43
18000	3170.67	1660.97	1159.26	909.54	760.62	662.09	592.34
19000	3346.82	1753.24	1223.66	960.07	802.88	698.87	625.25
20000	3522.97	1845.52	1288.06	1010.60	845.13	735.65	658.16
21000	3699.12	1937.79	1352.47	1061.13	887.39	772.43	691.06
22000	3875.26	2030.07	1416.87	1111.66	929.65	809.22	723.97
23000	4051.41	2122.35	1481.27	1162.19	971.90	846.00	756.88
24000	4227.56	2214.62	1545.68	1212.72	1014.16	882.78	789.79
25000	4403.71	2306.90	1610.08	1263.25	1056.42	919.56	822.69
26000	4579.86	2399.17	1674.48	1313.78	1098.67	956.35	855.60
27000	4756.01	2491.45	1738.89	1364.31	1140.93	993.13	888.51
28000	4932.15	2583.73	1803.29	1414.84	1183.19	1029.91	921.42
29000	5108.30	2676.00	1867.69	1465.37	1225.44	1066.69	954.33
30000	5284.45	2768.28	1932.10	1515.90	1267.70	1103.48	987.23
31000	5460.60	2860.55	1996.50	1566.44	1309.96	1140.26	1020.14
32000	5636.75	2952.83	2060.90	1616.97	1352.21	1177.04	1053.05
33000	5812.90	3045.11	2125.31	1667.50	1394.47	1213.82	1085.96
34000	5989.05	3137.38	2189.71	1718.03	1436.73	1250.61	1118.86
35000	6165.19	3229.66	2254.11	1768.56	1478.98	1287.39	1151.77
40000	7045.94	3691.04	2576.13	2021.21	1690.27	1471.30	1316.31
45000	7926.68	4152.42	2898.15	2273.86	1901.55	1655.21	1480.85
50000	8807.42	4613.80	3220.16	2526.51	2112.83	1839.13	1645.39
55000	9688.16	5075.18	3542.18	2779.16	2324.12	2023.04	1809.93
60000	10568.90	5536.56	3864.19	3031.81	2535.40	2206.95	1974.47
65000	11449.65	5997.94	4186.21	3284.46	2746.68	2390.87	2139.00
70000	12330.39	6459.32	4508.23	3537.11	2957.96	2574.78	2303.54

Monthly Loan Payments 19¼%

LOAN AMOUNT	4 YEARS	4½ YEARS	5 YEARS	5½ YEARS	6 YEARS	6½ YEARS	7 YEARS
100	3.00	2.78	2.61	2.47	2.35	2.26	2.18
200	6.01	5.56	5.22	4.93	4.70	4.51	4.35
300	9.01	8.35	7.82	7.40	7.06	6.77	6.53
400	12.01	11.13	10.43	9.87	9.41	9.02	8.70
500	15.02	13.91	13.04	12.34	11.76	11.28	10.88
600	18.02	16.69	15.65	14.80	14.11	13.54	13.05
700	21.02	19.48	18.25	17.27	16.46	15.79	15.23
800	24.03	22.26	20.86	19.74	18.82	18.05	17.41
900	27.03	25.04	23.47	22.21	21.17	20.31	19.58
1000	30.03	27.82	26.08	24.67	23.52	22.56	21.76
1500	45.05	41.73	39.12	37.01	35.28	33.84	32.64
2000	60.06	55.64	52.16	49.35	47.04	45.12	43.51
2500	75.08	69.56	65.20	61.68	58.80	56.41	54.39
3000	90.10	83.47	78.23	74.02	70.56	67.69	65.27
3500	105.11	97.38	91.27	86.35	82.32	78.97	76.15
4000	120.13	111.29	104.31	98.69	94.08	90.25	87.03
4500	135.14	125.20	117.35	111.03	105.84	101.53	97.91
5000	150.16	139.11	130.39	123.36	117.60	112.81	108.78
5500	165.18	153.02	143.43	135.70	129.36	124.09	119.66
6000	180.19	166.93	156.47	148.04	141.12	135.37	130.54
6500	195.21	180.85	169.51	160.37	152.88	146.65	141.42
7000	210.23	194.76	182.55	172.71	164.64	157.94	152.30
7500	225.24	208.67	195.59	185.04	176.40	169.22	163.18
8000	240.26	222.58	208.63	197.38	188.16	180.50	174.05
8500	255.27	236.49	221.67	209.72	199.92	191.78	184.93
9000	270.29	250.40	234.70	222.05	211.68	203.06	195.81
9500	285.31	264.31	247.74	234.39	223.44	214.34	206.69
10000	300.32	278.22	260.78	246.73	235.20	225.62	217.57
11000	330.35	306.05	286.86	271.40	258.72	248.18	239.33
12000	360.39	333.87	312.94	296.07	282.24	270.75	261.08
13000	390.42	361.69	339.02	320.74	305.76	293.31	282.84
14000	420.45	389.51	365.10	345.42	329.28	315.87	304.60
15000	450.48	417.34	391.17	370.09	352.80	338.43	326.35
16000	480.52	445.16	417.25	394.76	376.32	361.00	348.11
17000	510.55	472.98	443.33	419.43	399.84	383.56	369.87
18000	540.58	500.80	469.41	444.11	423.36	406.12	391.62
19000	570.61	528.63	495.49	468.78	446.88	428.68	413.38
20000	600.64	556.45	521.57	493.45	470.40	451.24	435.14
21000	630.68	584.27	547.64	518.12	493.92	473.81	456.89
22000	660.71	612.09	573.72	542.80	517.44	496.37	478.65
23000	690.74	639.92	599.80	567.47	540.96	518.93	500.41
24000	720.77	667.74	625.88	592.14	564.48	541.49	522.16
25000	750.81	695.56	651.96	616.81	588.00	564.05	543.92
26000	780.84	723.38	678.04	641.49	611.52	586.62	565.68
27000	810.87	751.21	704.11	666.16	635.04	609.18	587.43
28000	840.90	779.03	730.19	690.83	658.56	631.74	609.19
29000	870.93	806.85	756.27	715.50	682.08	654.30	630.95
30000	900.97	834.67	782.35	740.18	705.60	676.87	652.70
31000	931.00	862.49	808.43	764.85	729.12	699.43	674.46
32000	961.03	890.32	834.51	789.52	752.64	721.99	696.22
33000	991.06	918.14	860.58	814.19	776.16	744.55	717.98
34000	1021.09	945.96	886.66	838.87	799.68	767.11	739.73
35000	1051.13	973.78	912.74	863.54	823.20	789.68	761.49
40000	1201.29	1112.90	1043.13	986.90	940.80	902.49	870.27
45000	1351.45	1252.01	1173.52	1110.26	1058.40	1015.30	979.06
50000	1501.61	1391.12	1303.92	1233.63	1176.00	1128.11	1087.84
55000	1651.77	1530.23	1434.31	1356.99	1293.60	1240.92	1196.63
60000	1801.93	1669.34	1564.70	1480.35	1411.20	1353.73	1305.41
65000	1952.09	1808.46	1695.09	1603.71	1528.81	1466.54	1414.19
70000	2102.25	1947.57	1825.48	1727.08	1646.41	1579.35	1522.98

19¼% Monthly Loan Payments

LOAN AMOUNT	7½ YEARS	8 YEARS	8½ YEARS	9 YEARS	9½ YEARS	10 YEARS	10½ YEARS
100	2.11	2.05	2.00	1.95	1.92	1.88	1.85
200	4.21	4.10	4.00	3.91	3.83	3.77	3.71
300	6.32	6.15	6.00	5.86	5.75	5.65	5.56
400	8.43	8.20	7.99	7.82	7.67	7.53	7.41
500	10.54	10.24	9.99	9.77	9.58	9.42	9.27
600	12.64	12.29	11.99	11.73	11.50	11.30	11.12
700	14.75	14.34	13.99	13.68	13.42	13.18	12.98
800	16.86	16.39	15.99	15.64	15.33	15.06	14.83
900	18.97	18.44	17.99	17.59	17.25	16.95	16.68
1000	21.07	20.49	19.98	19.55	19.16	18.83	18.54
1500	31.61	30.73	29.98	29.32	28.75	28.25	27.81
2000	42.15	40.98	39.97	39.09	38.33	37.66	37.07
2500	52.68	51.22	49.96	48.87	47.91	47.08	46.34
3000	63.22	61.46	59.95	58.64	57.49	56.49	55.61
3500	73.76	71.71	69.94	68.41	67.08	65.91	64.88
4000	84.29	81.95	79.93	78.18	76.66	75.32	74.15
4500	94.83	92.20	89.93	87.96	86.24	84.74	83.42
5000	105.37	102.44	99.92	97.73	95.82	94.15	92.69
5500	115.90	112.68	109.91	107.50	105.41	103.57	101.96
6000	126.44	122.93	119.90	117.28	114.99	112.99	111.22
6500	136.98	133.17	129.89	127.05	124.57	122.40	120.49
7000	147.51	143.42	139.88	136.82	134.15	131.82	129.76
7500	158.05	153.66	149.88	146.60	143.74	141.23	139.03
8000	168.58	163.90	159.87	156.37	153.32	150.65	148.30
8500	179.12	174.15	169.86	166.14	162.90	160.06	157.57
9000	189.66	184.39	179.85	175.91	172.48	169.48	166.84
9500	200.19	194.63	189.84	185.69	182.07	178.89	176.11
10000	210.73	204.88	199.83	195.46	191.65	188.31	185.37
11000	231.80	225.37	219.82	215.01	210.81	207.14	203.91
12000	252.88	245.85	239.80	234.55	229.98	225.97	222.45
13000	273.95	266.34	259.79	254.10	249.14	244.80	240.99
14000	295.02	286.83	279.77	273.65	268.31	263.63	259.52
15000	316.10	307.32	299.75	293.19	287.47	282.46	278.06
16000	337.17	327.81	319.74	312.74	306.64	301.29	296.60
17000	358.24	348.29	339.72	332.28	325.80	320.13	315.14
18000	379.32	368.78	359.70	351.83	344.97	338.96	333.67
19000	400.39	389.27	379.69	371.38	364.13	357.79	352.21
20000	421.46	409.76	399.67	390.92	383.30	376.62	370.75
21000	442.54	430.25	419.65	410.47	402.46	395.45	389.29
22000	463.61	450.73	439.64	430.01	421.63	414.28	407.82
23000	484.68	471.22	459.62	449.56	440.79	433.11	426.36
24000	505.75	491.71	479.60	469.11	459.96	451.94	444.90
25000	526.83	512.20	499.59	488.65	479.12	470.77	463.43
26000	547.90	532.69	519.57	508.20	498.28	489.60	481.97
27000	568.97	553.17	539.55	527.74	517.45	508.44	500.51
28000	590.05	573.66	559.54	547.29	536.61	527.27	519.05
29000	611.12	594.15	579.52	566.84	555.78	546.10	537.58
30000	632.19	614.64	599.50	586.38	574.94	564.93	556.12
31000	653.27	635.12	619.49	605.93	594.11	583.76	574.66
32000	674.34	655.61	639.47	625.47	613.27	602.59	593.20
33000	695.41	676.10	659.45	645.02	632.44	621.42	611.73
34000	716.49	696.59	679.44	664.57	651.60	640.25	630.27
35000	737.56	717.08	699.42	684.11	670.77	659.08	648.81
40000	842.92	819.52	799.34	781.84	766.59	753.24	741.50
45000	948.29	921.96	899.26	879.57	862.42	847.39	834.18
50000	1053.66	1024.39	999.17	977.30	958.24	941.55	926.87
55000	1159.02	1126.83	1099.09	1075.03	1054.06	1035.70	1019.56
60000	1264.39	1229.27	1199.01	1172.77	1149.89	1129.86	1112.24
65000	1369.75	1331.71	1298.93	1270.50	1245.71	1224.01	1204.93
70000	1475.12	1434.15	1398.84	1368.23	1341.54	1318.17	1297.62

Monthly Loan Payments   19¼%

LOAN AMOUNT	11 YEARS	11½ YEARS	12 YEARS	12½ YEARS	13 YEARS	14 YEARS	15 YEARS
100	1.83	1.80	1.78	1.77	1.75	1.72	1.70
200	3.66	3.61	3.57	3.53	3.50	3.45	3.40
300	5.48	5.41	5.35	5.30	5.25	5.17	5.10
400	7.31	7.22	7.14	7.07	7.00	6.89	6.80
500	9.14	9.02	8.92	8.83	8.75	8.62	8.51
600	10.97	10.83	10.71	10.60	10.50	10.34	10.21
700	12.79	12.63	12.49	12.37	12.25	12.06	11.91
800	14.62	14.44	14.28	14.13	14.00	13.78	13.61
900	16.45	16.24	16.06	15.90	15.75	15.51	15.31
1000	18.28	18.05	17.85	17.66	17.50	17.23	17.01
1500	27.42	27.07	26.77	26.50	26.26	25.85	25.52
2000	36.56	36.10	35.69	35.33	35.01	34.46	34.02
2500	45.70	45.12	44.61	44.16	43.76	43.08	42.53
3000	54.84	54.15	53.54	52.99	52.51	51.69	51.03
3500	63.97	63.17	62.46	61.83	61.26	60.31	59.54
4000	73.11	72.20	71.38	70.66	70.01	68.92	68.05
4500	82.25	81.22	80.31	79.49	78.77	77.54	76.55
5000	91.39	90.25	89.23	88.32	87.52	86.15	85.06
5500	100.53	99.27	98.15	97.16	96.27	94.77	93.56
6000	109.67	108.30	107.08	105.99	105.02	103.38	102.07
6500	118.81	117.32	116.00	114.82	113.77	112.00	110.57
7000	127.95	126.34	124.92	123.65	122.53	120.61	119.08
7500	137.09	135.37	133.84	132.49	131.28	129.23	127.59
8000	146.23	144.39	142.77	141.32	140.03	137.84	136.09
8500	155.37	153.42	151.69	150.15	148.78	146.46	144.60
9000	164.51	162.44	160.61	158.98	157.53	155.08	153.10
9500	173.64	171.47	169.54	167.82	166.28	163.69	161.61
10000	182.78	180.49	178.46	176.65	175.04	172.31	170.11
11000	201.06	198.54	196.30	194.31	192.54	189.54	187.13
12000	219.34	216.59	214.15	211.98	210.04	206.77	204.14
13000	237.62	234.64	232.00	229.64	227.55	224.00	221.15
14000	255.90	252.69	249.84	247.31	245.05	241.23	238.16
15000	274.18	270.74	267.69	264.97	262.55	258.46	255.17
16000	292.45	288.79	285.53	282.64	280.06	275.69	272.18
17000	310.73	306.84	303.38	300.30	297.56	292.92	289.19
18000	329.01	324.89	321.23	317.97	315.06	310.15	306.21
19000	347.29	342.94	339.07	335.63	332.57	327.38	323.22
20000	365.57	360.98	356.92	353.30	350.07	344.61	340.23
21000	383.85	379.03	374.76	370.96	367.58	361.84	357.24
22000	402.13	397.08	392.61	388.63	385.08	379.07	374.25
23000	420.40	415.13	410.45	406.29	402.58	396.30	391.26
24000	438.68	433.18	428.30	423.96	420.09	413.53	408.27
25000	456.96	451.23	446.15	441.62	437.59	430.77	425.29
26000	475.24	469.28	463.99	459.29	455.09	448.00	442.30
27000	493.52	487.33	481.84	476.95	472.60	465.23	459.31
28000	511.80	505.38	499.68	494.62	490.10	482.46	476.32
29000	530.07	523.43	517.53	512.28	507.60	499.69	493.33
30000	548.35	541.48	535.38	529.95	525.11	516.92	510.34
31000	566.63	559.53	553.22	547.61	542.61	534.15	527.35
32000	584.91	577.58	571.07	565.28	560.12	551.38	544.37
33000	603.19	595.62	588.91	582.94	577.62	568.61	561.38
34000	621.47	613.67	606.76	600.61	595.12	585.84	578.39
35000	639.74	631.72	624.60	618.27	612.63	603.07	595.40
40000	731.14	721.97	713.83	706.60	700.14	689.22	680.46
45000	822.53	812.22	803.06	794.92	787.66	775.38	765.51
50000	913.92	902.46	892.29	883.25	875.18	861.53	850.57
55000	1005.31	992.71	981.52	971.57	962.70	947.68	935.63
60000	1096.71	1082.95	1070.75	1059.89	1050.22	1033.84	1020.69
65000	1188.10	1173.20	1159.98	1148.22	1137.73	1119.99	1105.74
70000	1279.49	1263.45	1249.21	1236.54	1225.25	1206.14	1190.80

19½%   Monthly Loan Payments

LOAN AMOUNT	½ YEAR	1 YEAR	1½ YEARS	2 YEARS	2½ YEARS	3 YEARS	3½ YEARS
100	17.63	9.24	6.45	5.07	4.24	3.69	3.30
200	35.25	18.48	12.90	10.13	8.48	7.38	6.61
300	52.88	27.72	19.36	15.20	12.71	11.07	9.91
400	70.51	36.96	25.81	20.26	16.95	14.76	13.21
500	88.14	46.20	32.26	25.33	21.19	18.45	16.52
600	105.76	55.44	38.71	30.39	25.43	22.15	19.82
700	123.39	64.68	45.17	35.46	29.67	25.84	23.13
800	141.02	73.92	51.62	40.52	33.90	29.53	26.43
900	158.65	83.16	58.07	45.59	38.14	33.22	29.73
1000	176.27	92.40	64.52	50.65	42.38	36.91	33.04
1500	264.41	138.59	96.78	75.98	63.57	55.36	49.56
2000	352.55	184.79	129.05	101.30	84.76	73.82	66.07
2500	440.68	230.99	161.31	126.63	105.95	92.27	82.59
3000	528.82	277.19	193.57	151.96	127.14	110.73	99.11
3500	616.96	323.38	225.83	177.28	148.33	129.18	115.63
4000	705.09	369.58	258.09	202.61	169.52	147.64	132.15
4500	793.23	415.78	290.35	227.93	190.71	166.09	148.67
5000	881.37	461.98	322.62	253.26	211.90	184.55	165.19
5500	969.50	508.17	354.88	278.59	233.09	203.00	181.71
6000	1057.64	554.37	387.14	303.91	254.28	221.46	198.22
6500	1145.78	600.57	419.40	329.24	275.47	239.91	214.74
7000	1233.91	646.77	451.66	354.56	296.67	258.37	231.26
7500	1322.05	692.97	483.92	379.89	317.86	276.82	247.78
8000	1410.19	739.16	516.18	405.22	339.05	295.27	264.30
8500	1498.32	785.36	548.45	430.54	360.24	313.73	280.82
9000	1586.46	831.56	580.71	455.87	381.43	332.18	297.34
9500	1674.59	877.76	612.97	481.19	402.62	350.64	313.85
10000	1762.73	923.95	645.23	506.52	423.81	369.09	330.37
11000	1939.00	1016.35	709.75	557.17	466.19	406.00	363.41
12000	2115.28	1108.74	774.28	607.82	508.57	442.91	396.45
13000	2291.55	1201.14	838.80	658.47	550.95	479.82	429.49
14000	2467.82	1293.54	903.32	709.13	593.33	516.73	462.52
15000	2644.10	1385.93	967.85	759.78	635.71	553.64	495.56
16000	2820.37	1478.33	1032.37	810.43	678.09	590.55	528.60
17000	2996.64	1570.72	1096.89	861.08	720.47	627.46	561.63
18000	3172.92	1663.12	1161.42	911.73	762.85	664.37	594.67
19000	3349.19	1755.51	1225.94	962.39	805.23	701.28	627.71
20000	3525.46	1847.91	1290.46	1013.04	847.62	738.19	660.75
21000	3701.74	1940.30	1354.98	1063.69	890.00	775.10	693.78
22000	3878.01	2032.70	1419.51	1114.34	932.38	812.00	726.82
23000	4054.28	2125.09	1484.03	1164.99	974.76	848.91	759.86
24000	4230.56	2217.49	1548.55	1215.65	1017.14	885.82	792.90
25000	4406.83	2309.88	1613.08	1266.30	1059.52	922.73	825.93
26000	4583.10	2402.28	1677.60	1316.95	1101.90	959.64	858.97
27000	4759.37	2494.68	1742.12	1367.60	1144.28	996.55	892.01
28000	4935.65	2587.07	1806.65	1418.25	1186.66	1033.46	925.04
29000	5111.92	2679.47	1871.17	1468.90	1229.04	1070.37	958.08
30000	5288.19	2771.86	1935.69	1519.56	1271.42	1107.28	991.12
31000	5464.47	2864.26	2000.22	1570.21	1313.80	1144.19	1024.16
32000	5640.74	2956.65	2064.74	1620.86	1356.18	1181.10	1057.19
33000	5817.01	3049.05	2129.26	1671.51	1398.56	1218.01	1090.23
34000	5993.29	3141.44	2193.79	1722.16	1440.95	1254.92	1123.27
35000	6169.56	3233.84	2258.31	1772.82	1483.33	1291.83	1156.31
40000	7050.93	3695.81	2580.92	2026.08	1695.23	1476.37	1321.49
45000	7932.29	4157.79	2903.54	2279.33	1907.13	1660.92	1486.68
50000	8813.66	4619.77	3226.15	2532.59	2119.04	1845.47	1651.87
55000	9695.02	5081.74	3548.77	2785.85	2330.94	2030.01	1817.05
60000	10576.39	5543.72	3871.39	3039.11	2542.85	2214.56	1982.24
65000	11457.75	6005.70	4194.00	3292.37	2754.75	2399.11	2147.43
70000	12339.12	6467.68	4516.62	3545.63	2966.65	2583.65	2312.61

Monthly Loan Payments 19½%

LOAN AMOUNT	4 YEARS	4½ YEARS	5 YEARS	5½ YEARS	6 YEARS	6½ YEARS	7 YEARS
100	3.02	2.80	2.62	2.48	2.37	2.27	2.19
200	6.03	5.59	5.24	4.96	4.73	4.54	4.38
300	9.05	8.39	7.86	7.44	7.10	6.81	6.57
400	12.07	11.18	10.49	9.93	9.47	9.08	8.76
500	15.08	13.98	13.11	12.41	11.83	11.35	10.95
600	18.10	16.77	15.73	14.89	14.20	13.63	13.14
700	21.12	19.57	18.35	17.37	16.56	15.90	15.33
800	24.13	22.37	20.97	19.85	18.93	18.17	17.52
900	27.15	25.16	23.59	22.33	21.30	20.44	19.72
1000	30.16	27.96	26.22	24.81	23.66	22.71	21.91
1500	45.25	41.94	39.32	37.22	35.50	34.06	32.86
2000	60.33	55.92	52.43	49.63	47.33	45.42	43.81
2500	75.41	69.89	65.54	62.03	59.16	56.77	54.77
3000	90.49	83.87	78.65	74.44	70.99	68.13	65.72
3500	105.58	97.85	91.76	86.85	82.82	79.48	76.67
4000	120.66	111.83	104.87	99.25	94.66	90.84	87.62
4500	135.74	125.81	117.97	111.66	106.49	102.19	98.58
5000	150.82	139.79	131.08	124.07	118.32	113.54	109.53
5500	165.91	153.77	144.19	136.47	130.15	124.90	120.48
6000	180.99	167.75	157.30	148.88	141.98	136.25	131.44
6500	196.07	181.72	170.41	161.29	153.82	147.61	142.39
7000	211.15	195.70	183.52	173.69	165.65	158.96	153.34
7500	226.23	209.68	196.62	186.10	177.48	170.32	164.30
8000	241.32	223.66	209.73	198.51	189.31	181.67	175.25
8500	256.40	237.64	222.84	210.91	201.14	193.02	186.20
9000	271.48	251.62	235.95	223.32	212.97	204.38	197.16
9500	286.56	265.60	249.06	235.73	224.81	215.73	208.11
10000	301.65	279.58	262.16	248.13	236.64	227.09	219.06
11000	331.81	307.53	288.38	272.95	260.30	249.80	240.97
12000	361.98	335.49	314.60	297.76	283.97	272.51	262.87
13000	392.14	363.45	340.81	322.58	307.63	295.21	284.78
14000	422.30	391.41	367.03	347.39	331.29	317.92	306.69
15000	452.47	419.37	393.25	372.20	354.96	340.63	328.59
16000	482.63	447.32	419.46	397.02	378.62	363.34	350.50
17000	512.80	475.28	445.68	421.83	402.29	386.05	372.40
18000	542.96	503.24	471.90	446.64	425.95	408.76	394.31
19000	573.13	531.20	498.11	471.46	449.61	431.47	416.22
20000	603.29	559.15	524.33	496.27	473.28	454.18	438.12
21000	633.46	587.11	550.55	521.08	496.94	476.88	460.03
22000	663.62	615.07	576.76	545.90	520.61	499.59	481.93
23000	693.79	643.03	602.98	570.71	544.27	522.30	503.84
24000	723.95	670.98	629.19	595.52	567.93	545.01	525.75
25000	754.12	698.94	655.41	620.34	591.60	567.72	547.65
26000	784.28	726.90	681.63	645.15	615.26	590.43	569.56
27000	814.44	754.86	707.84	669.96	638.92	613.14	591.47
28000	844.61	782.82	734.06	694.78	662.59	635.85	613.37
29000	874.77	810.77	760.28	719.59	686.25	658.55	635.28
30000	904.94	838.73	786.49	744.40	709.92	681.26	657.18
31000	935.10	866.69	812.71	769.22	733.58	703.97	679.09
32000	965.27	894.65	838.93	794.03	757.24	726.68	701.00
33000	995.43	922.60	865.14	818.85	780.91	749.39	722.90
34000	1025.60	950.56	891.36	843.66	804.57	772.10	744.81
35000	1055.76	978.52	917.58	868.47	828.24	794.81	766.71
40000	1206.58	1118.31	1048.66	992.54	946.56	908.35	876.24
45000	1357.41	1258.10	1179.74	1116.61	1064.87	1021.89	985.78
50000	1508.23	1397.88	1310.82	1240.67	1183.20	1135.44	1095.31
55000	1659.05	1537.67	1441.90	1364.74	1301.51	1248.98	1204.84
60000	1809.88	1677.46	1572.99	1488.81	1419.83	1362.53	1314.37
65000	1960.70	1817.25	1704.07	1612.88	1538.15	1476.07	1423.90
70000	2111.52	1957.04	1835.15	1736.94	1656.47	1589.61	1533.43

19½%   Monthly Loan Payments

LOAN AMOUNT	7½ YEARS	8 YEARS	8½ YEARS	9 YEARS	9½ YEARS	10 YEARS	10½ YEARS
100	2.12	2.06	2.01	1.97	1.93	1.90	1.87
200	4.25	4.13	4.03	3.94	3.87	3.80	3.74
300	6.37	6.19	6.04	5.91	5.80	5.70	5.61
400	8.49	8.26	8.06	7.88	7.73	7.60	7.48
500	10.61	10.32	10.07	9.85	9.66	9.50	9.35
600	12.74	12.39	12.08	11.82	11.60	11.40	11.22
700	14.86	14.45	14.10	13.79	13.53	13.30	13.09
800	16.98	16.51	16.11	15.76	15.46	15.20	14.96
900	19.10	18.58	18.13	17.74	17.39	17.10	16.83
1000	21.23	20.64	20.14	19.71	19.33	19.00	18.70
1500	31.84	30.96	30.21	29.56	28.99	28.49	28.06
2000	42.45	41.28	40.28	39.41	38.65	37.99	37.41
2500	53.06	51.61	50.35	49.26	48.32	47.49	46.76
3000	63.68	61.93	60.42	59.12	57.98	56.99	56.11
3500	74.29	72.25	70.49	68.97	67.64	66.48	65.46
4000	84.90	82.57	80.56	78.82	77.31	75.98	74.82
4500	95.51	92.89	90.63	88.68	86.97	85.48	84.17
5000	106.13	103.21	100.70	98.53	96.63	94.98	93.52
5500	116.74	113.53	110.77	108.38	106.30	104.47	102.87
6000	127.35	123.85	120.84	118.23	115.96	113.97	112.22
6500	137.96	134.18	130.91	128.09	125.62	123.47	121.58
7000	148.58	144.50	140.98	137.94	135.29	132.97	130.93
7500	159.19	154.82	151.05	147.79	144.95	142.46	140.28
8000	169.80	165.14	161.12	157.65	154.61	151.96	149.63
8500	180.41	175.46	171.19	167.50	164.28	161.46	158.98
9000	191.03	185.78	181.27	177.35	173.94	170.96	168.34
9500	201.64	196.10	191.34	187.20	183.60	180.45	177.69
10000	212.25	206.42	201.41	197.06	193.27	189.95	187.04
11000	233.48	227.07	221.55	216.76	212.59	208.95	205.74
12000	254.70	247.71	241.69	236.47	231.92	227.94	224.45
13000	275.93	268.35	261.83	256.17	251.25	246.94	243.15
14000	297.15	288.99	281.97	275.88	270.57	265.93	261.86
15000	318.38	309.64	302.11	295.58	289.90	284.93	280.56
16000	339.60	330.28	322.25	315.29	309.23	303.92	299.26
17000	360.83	350.92	342.39	334.99	328.56	322.92	317.97
18000	382.05	371.56	362.53	354.70	347.88	341.91	336.67
19000	403.28	392.21	382.67	374.41	367.21	360.91	355.37
20000	424.50	412.85	402.81	394.11	386.54	379.90	374.08
21000	445.73	433.49	422.95	413.82	405.86	398.90	392.78
22000	466.95	454.13	443.09	433.52	425.19	417.89	411.49
23000	488.18	474.78	463.23	453.23	444.52	436.89	430.19
24000	509.40	495.42	483.37	472.93	463.84	455.89	448.89
25000	530.63	516.06	503.51	492.64	483.17	474.88	467.60
26000	551.85	536.70	523.66	512.35	502.50	493.88	486.30
27000	573.08	557.35	543.80	532.05	521.82	512.87	505.01
28000	594.30	577.99	563.94	551.76	541.15	531.87	523.71
29000	615.53	598.63	584.08	571.46	560.48	550.86	542.41
30000	636.75	619.27	604.22	591.17	579.80	569.86	561.12
31000	657.98	639.92	624.36	610.88	599.13	588.85	579.82
32000	679.20	660.56	644.50	630.58	618.46	607.85	598.53
33000	700.43	681.20	664.64	650.29	637.78	626.84	617.23
34000	721.65	701.84	684.78	669.99	657.11	645.84	635.93
35000	742.88	722.49	704.92	689.70	676.44	664.83	654.64
40000	849.00	825.70	805.62	788.23	773.07	759.81	748.16
45000	955.13	928.91	906.33	886.75	869.70	854.78	841.68
50000	1061.25	1032.12	1007.03	985.28	966.34	949.76	935.20
55000	1167.38	1135.34	1107.73	1083.81	1062.97	1044.74	1028.72
60000	1273.50	1238.55	1208.44	1182.34	1159.61	1139.71	1122.24
65000	1379.63	1341.76	1309.14	1280.87	1256.24	1234.69	1215.76
70000	1485.75	1444.97	1409.84	1379.40	1352.87	1329.67	1309.28

Monthly Loan Payments 19½%

LOAN AMOUNT	11 YEARS	11½ YEARS	12 YEARS	12½ YEARS	13 YEARS	14 YEARS	15 YEARS
100	1.84	1.82	1.80	1.78	1.77	1.74	1.72
200	3.69	3.64	3.60	3.57	3.54	3.48	3.44
300	5.53	5.47	5.41	5.35	5.30	5.22	5.16
400	7.38	7.29	7.21	7.14	7.07	6.96	6.88
500	9.22	9.11	9.01	8.92	8.84	8.71	8.60
600	11.07	10.93	10.81	10.70	10.61	10.45	10.32
700	12.91	12.75	12.61	12.49	12.38	12.19	12.04
800	14.76	14.58	14.41	14.27	14.14	13.93	13.76
900	16.60	16.40	16.22	16.06	15.91	15.67	15.48
1000	18.45	18.22	18.02	17.84	17.68	17.41	17.19
1500	27.67	27.33	27.03	26.76	26.52	26.12	25.79
2000	36.89	36.44	36.04	35.68	35.36	34.82	34.39
2500	46.12	45.55	45.05	44.60	44.20	43.53	42.99
3000	55.34	54.66	54.06	53.52	53.04	52.23	51.58
3500	64.56	63.77	63.07	62.44	61.88	60.94	60.18
4000	73.79	72.88	72.07	71.36	70.72	69.64	68.78
4500	83.01	81.99	81.08	80.28	79.56	78.35	77.38
5000	92.24	91.10	90.09	89.20	88.40	87.05	85.97
5500	101.46	100.21	99.10	98.12	97.24	95.76	94.57
6000	110.68	109.32	108.11	107.04	106.08	104.46	103.17
6500	119.91	118.43	117.12	115.96	114.92	113.17	111.77
7000	129.13	127.54	126.13	124.88	123.76	121.87	120.36
7500	138.35	136.65	135.14	133.80	132.60	130.58	128.96
8000	147.58	145.76	144.15	142.72	141.44	139.29	137.56
8500	156.80	154.87	153.16	151.64	150.28	147.99	146.15
9000	166.02	163.98	162.17	160.56	159.12	156.70	154.75
9500	175.25	173.09	171.18	169.48	167.96	165.40	163.35
10000	184.47	182.20	180.19	178.40	176.80	174.11	171.95
11000	202.92	200.42	198.21	196.24	194.48	191.52	189.14
12000	221.37	218.64	216.22	214.08	212.16	208.93	206.34
13000	239.81	236.86	234.24	231.92	229.84	226.34	223.53
14000	258.26	255.08	252.26	249.76	247.52	243.75	240.73
15000	276.71	273.30	270.28	267.59	265.20	261.16	257.92
16000	295.15	291.52	288.30	285.43	282.88	278.57	275.12
17000	313.60	309.74	306.32	303.27	300.56	295.98	292.31
18000	332.05	327.96	324.34	321.11	318.24	313.39	309.50
19000	350.50	346.18	342.35	338.95	335.92	330.80	326.70
20000	368.94	364.40	360.37	356.79	353.60	348.21	343.89
21000	387.39	382.62	378.39	374.63	371.28	365.62	361.09
22000	405.84	400.84	396.41	392.47	388.96	383.04	378.28
23000	424.28	419.06	414.43	410.31	406.64	400.45	395.48
24000	442.73	437.28	432.45	428.15	424.33	417.86	412.67
25000	461.18	455.50	450.47	445.99	442.01	435.27	429.87
26000	479.62	473.72	468.48	463.83	459.69	452.68	447.06
27000	498.07	491.94	486.50	481.67	477.37	470.09	464.26
28000	516.52	510.16	504.52	499.51	495.05	487.50	481.45
29000	534.97	528.38	522.54	517.35	512.73	504.91	498.65
30000	553.41	546.60	540.56	535.19	530.41	522.32	515.84
31000	571.86	564.82	558.58	553.03	548.09	539.73	533.04
32000	590.31	583.04	576.60	570.87	565.77	557.14	550.23
33000	608.76	601.26	594.62	588.71	583.45	574.55	567.43
34000	627.20	619.48	612.63	606.55	601.13	591.96	584.62
35000	645.65	637.70	630.65	624.39	618.81	609.37	601.81
40000	737.89	728.80	720.75	713.59	707.21	696.43	687.79
45000	830.12	819.90	810.84	802.78	795.61	783.48	773.76
50000	922.36	911.00	900.93	891.98	884.01	870.54	859.74
55000	1014.59	1002.10	991.03	981.18	972.41	957.59	945.71
60000	1106.83	1093.20	1081.12	1070.38	1060.81	1044.64	1031.68
65000	1199.06	1184.30	1171.21	1159.58	1149.21	1131.70	1117.66
70000	1291.30	1275.40	1261.31	1248.78	1237.61	1218.75	1203.63

19¾% Monthly Loan Payments

LOAN AMOUNT	½ YEAR	1 YEAR	1½ YEARS	2 YEARS	2½ YEARS	3 YEARS	3½ YEAR
100	17.64	9.25	6.46	5.08	4.25	3.70	3.3
200	35.28	18.50	12.93	10.15	8.50	7.41	6.6
300	52.92	27.75	19.39	15.23	12.75	11.11	9.9
400	70.56	37.01	25.86	20.31	17.00	14.81	13.2
500	88.20	46.26	32.32	25.39	21.25	18.52	16.5
600	105.84	55.51	38.79	30.46	25.50	22.22	19.
700	123.48	64.76	45.25	35.54	29.75	25.93	23.
800	141.12	74.01	51.71	40.62	34.00	29.63	26.
900	158.76	83.26	58.18	45.70	38.25	33.33	29.
1000	176.40	92.51	64.64	50.77	42.51	37.04	33.
1500	264.60	138.77	96.96	76.16	63.76	55.55	49.
2000	352.80	185.03	129.29	101.55	85.01	74.07	66.
2500	440.99	231.29	161.61	126.93	106.26	92.59	82.
3000	529.19	277.54	193.93	152.32	127.52	111.11	99.
3500	617.39	323.80	226.25	177.71	148.77	129.63	116.
4000	705.59	370.06	258.57	203.10	170.02	148.15	132.
4500	793.79	416.32	290.89	228.48	191.27	166.66	149.
5000	881.99	462.57	323.22	253.87	212.53	185.18	165.
5500	970.19	508.83	355.54	279.26	233.78	203.70	182.
6000	1058.39	555.09	387.86	304.64	255.03	222.22	199.
6500	1146.59	601.35	420.18	330.03	276.28	240.74	215.
7000	1234.79	647.60	452.50	355.42	297.54	259.25	232.
7500	1322.98	693.86	484.82	380.80	318.79	277.77	248.
8000	1411.18	740.12	517.14	406.19	340.04	296.29	265.
8500	1499.38	786.38	549.47	431.58	361.29	314.81	281.
9000	1587.58	832.63	581.79	456.96	382.55	333.33	298.
9500	1675.78	878.89	614.11	482.35	403.80	351.85	315.
10000	1763.98	925.15	646.43	507.74	425.05	370.36	331.
11000	1940.38	1017.66	711.07	558.51	467.56	407.40	364.
12000	2116.78	1110.18	775.72	609.29	510.06	444.44	398.
13000	2293.17	1202.69	840.36	660.06	552.57	481.47	431.
14000	2469.57	1295.21	905.00	710.83	595.07	518.51	464.
15000	2645.97	1387.72	969.65	761.61	637.58	555.54	497.
16000	2822.37	1480.24	1034.29	812.38	680.08	592.58	530.
17000	2998.77	1572.75	1098.93	863.15	722.59	629.62	563.
18000	3175.16	1665.27	1163.58	913.93	765.09	666.65	597.
19000	3351.56	1757.78	1228.22	964.70	807.60	703.69	630.
20000	3527.96	1850.30	1292.86	1015.48	850.10	740.73	663.
21000	3704.36	1942.81	1357.50	1066.25	892.61	777.76	696.
22000	3880.75	2035.33	1422.15	1117.02	935.11	814.80	729
23000	4057.15	2127.84	1486.79	1167.80	977.62	851.84	762.
24000	4233.55	2220.36	1551.43	1218.57	1020.12	888.87	796.
25000	4409.95	2312.87	1616.08	1269.34	1062.63	925.91	829.
26000	4586.35	2405.39	1680.72	1320.12	1105.13	962.94	862.
27000	4762.74	2497.90	1745.36	1370.89	1147.64	999.98	895.
28000	4939.14	2590.42	1810.01	1421.67	1190.14	1037.02	928
29000	5115.54	2682.93	1874.65	1472.44	1232.65	1074.05	961
30000	5291.94	2775.45	1939.29	1523.21	1275.15	1111.09	995
31000	5468.34	2867.96	2003.94	1573.99	1317.66	1148.13	1028.
32000	5644.73	2960.48	2068.58	1624.76	1360.16	1185.16	1061
33000	5821.13	3052.99	2133.22	1675.53	1402.67	1222.20	1094
34000	5997.53	3145.51	2197.86	1726.31	1445.17	1259.24	1127
35000	6173.93	3238.02	2262.51	1777.08	1487.68	1296.27	1160
40000	7055.92	3700.60	2585.72	2030.95	1700.20	1481.45	1326
45000	7937.91	4163.17	2908.94	2284.82	1912.73	1666.63	1492
50000	8819.90	4625.74	3232.15	2538.69	2125.25	1851.82	1658
55000	9701.89	5088.32	3555.37	2792.56	2337.78	2037.00	1824
60000	10583.88	5550.89	3878.58	3046.43	2550.30	2222.18	1990
65000	11465.87	6013.47	4201.80	3300.29	2762.83	2407.36	2155
70000	12347.86	6476.04	4525.02	3554.16	2975.35	2592.54	2321

Monthly Loan Payments 19¾%

LOAN AMOUNT	4 YEARS	4½ YEARS	5 YEARS	5½ YEARS	6 YEARS	6½ YEARS	7 YEARS
100	3.03	2.81	2.64	2.50	2.38	2.29	2.21
200	6.06	5.62	5.27	4.99	4.76	4.57	4.41
300	9.09	8.43	7.91	7.49	7.14	6.86	6.62
400	12.12	11.24	10.54	9.98	9.52	9.14	8.82
500	15.15	14.05	13.18	12.48	11.90	11.43	11.03
600	18.18	16.86	15.81	14.97	14.28	13.71	13.23
700	21.21	19.67	18.45	17.47	16.67	16.00	15.44
800	24.24	22.47	21.08	19.96	19.05	18.28	17.64
900	27.27	25.28	23.72	22.46	21.43	20.57	19.85
1000	30.30	28.09	26.35	24.95	23.81	22.86	22.06
1500	45.45	42.14	39.53	37.43	35.71	34.28	33.08
2000	60.59	56.19	52.71	49.91	47.62	45.71	44.11
2500	75.74	70.23	65.89	62.39	59.52	57.14	55.14
3000	90.89	84.28	79.06	74.86	71.42	68.57	66.17
3500	106.04	98.33	92.24	87.34	83.33	80.00	77.20
4000	121.19	112.37	105.42	99.82	95.23	91.42	88.22
4500	136.34	126.42	118.60	112.30	107.14	102.85	99.25
5000	151.49	140.47	131.77	124.77	119.04	114.28	110.28
5500	166.64	154.51	144.95	137.25	130.94	125.71	121.31
6000	181.78	168.56	158.13	149.73	142.85	137.13	132.34
6500	196.93	182.61	171.31	162.21	154.75	148.56	143.36
7000	212.08	196.65	184.48	174.68	166.66	159.99	154.39
7500	227.23	210.70	197.66	187.16	178.56	171.42	165.42
8000	242.38	224.75	210.84	199.64	190.47	182.85	176.45
8500	257.53	238.79	224.02	212.12	202.37	194.27	187.48
9000	272.68	252.84	237.19	224.59	214.27	205.70	198.50
9500	287.82	266.89	250.37	237.07	226.18	217.13	209.53
10000	302.97	280.93	263.55	249.55	238.08	228.56	220.56
11000	333.27	309.03	289.90	274.50	261.89	251.41	242.62
12000	363.57	337.12	316.26	299.46	285.70	274.27	264.67
13000	393.87	365.21	342.61	324.41	309.51	297.13	286.73
14000	424.16	393.31	368.97	349.37	333.31	319.98	308.78
15000	454.46	421.40	395.32	374.32	357.12	342.84	330.84
16000	484.76	449.49	421.68	399.28	380.93	365.69	352.89
17000	515.05	477.59	448.03	424.23	404.74	388.55	374.95
18000	545.35	505.68	474.39	449.19	428.55	411.40	397.01
19000	575.65	533.77	500.74	474.14	452.35	434.26	419.06
20000	605.95	561.87	527.10	499.10	476.16	457.12	441.12
21000	636.24	589.96	553.45	524.05	499.97	479.97	463.17
22000	666.54	618.05	579.81	549.01	523.78	502.83	485.23
23000	696.84	646.15	606.16	573.96	547.59	525.68	507.29
24000	727.14	674.24	632.52	598.92	571.40	548.54	529.34
25000	757.43	702.33	658.87	623.87	595.20	571.40	551.40
26000	787.73	730.43	685.23	648.83	619.01	594.25	573.45
27000	818.03	758.52	711.58	673.78	642.82	617.11	595.51
28000	848.33	786.61	737.94	698.74	666.63	639.96	617.57
29000	878.62	814.71	764.29	723.69	690.44	662.82	639.62
30000	908.92	842.80	790.65	748.65	714.24	685.67	661.68
31000	939.22	870.89	817.00	773.60	738.05	708.53	683.73
32000	969.51	898.99	843.36	798.56	761.86	731.39	705.79
33000	999.81	927.08	869.71	823.51	785.67	754.24	727.85
34000	1030.11	955.17	896.07	848.47	809.48	777.10	749.90
35000	1060.41	983.27	922.42	873.42	833.28	799.95	771.96
40000	1211.89	1123.73	1054.20	998.20	952.33	914.23	882.24
45000	1363.38	1264.20	1185.97	1122.97	1071.37	1028.51	992.52
50000	1514.87	1404.67	1317.75	1247.75	1190.41	1142.79	1102.80
55000	1666.35	1545.13	1449.52	1372.52	1309.45	1257.07	1213.08
60000	1817.84	1685.60	1581.30	1497.29	1428.49	1371.35	1323.35
65000	1969.33	1826.07	1713.07	1622.07	1547.53	1485.63	1433.63
70000	2120.81	1966.53	1844.85	1746.84	1666.57	1599.91	1543.91

19¾% Monthly Loan Payments

LOAN AMOUNT	7½ YEARS	8 YEARS	8½ YEARS	9 YEARS	9½ YEARS	10 YEARS	10½ YEARS
100	2.14	2.08	2.03	1.99	1.95	1.92	1.89
200	4.28	4.16	4.06	3.97	3.90	3.83	3.77
300	6.41	6.24	6.09	5.96	5.85	5.75	5.66
400	8.55	8.32	8.12	7.95	7.80	7.66	7.55
500	10.69	10.40	10.15	9.93	9.74	9.58	9.44
600	12.83	12.48	12.18	11.92	11.69	11.50	11.32
700	14.96	14.56	14.21	13.91	13.64	13.41	13.21
800	17.10	16.64	16.24	15.89	15.59	15.33	15.10
900	19.24	18.72	18.27	17.88	17.54	17.24	16.98
1000	21.38	20.80	20.30	19.87	19.49	19.16	18.87
1500	32.07	31.20	30.45	29.80	29.23	28.74	28.31
2000	42.76	41.60	40.60	39.73	38.98	38.32	37.74
2500	53.44	51.99	50.75	49.66	48.72	47.90	47.18
3000	64.13	62.39	60.89	59.60	58.47	57.48	56.61
3500	74.82	72.79	71.04	69.53	68.21	67.06	66.05
4000	85.51	83.19	81.19	79.46	77.96	76.64	75.48
4500	96.20	93.59	91.34	89.40	87.70	86.22	84.92
5000	106.89	103.99	101.49	99.33	97.45	95.80	94.36
5500	117.58	114.39	111.64	109.26	107.19	105.38	103.79
6000	128.27	124.79	121.79	119.19	116.94	114.96	113.23
6500	138.95	135.18	131.94	129.13	126.68	124.54	122.66
7000	149.64	145.58	142.09	139.06	136.43	134.12	132.10
7500	160.33	155.98	152.24	148.99	146.17	143.70	141.53
8000	171.02	166.38	162.39	158.93	155.93	153.28	150.97
8500	181.71	176.78	172.54	168.86	165.66	162.86	160.40
9000	192.40	187.18	182.68	178.79	175.40	172.44	169.84
9500	203.09	197.58	192.83	188.73	185.15	182.02	179.28
10000	213.78	207.98	202.98	198.66	194.89	191.60	188.71
11000	235.15	228.77	223.28	218.52	214.38	210.76	207.58
12000	256.53	249.57	243.58	238.39	233.87	229.92	226.45
13000	277.91	270.37	263.88	258.26	253.36	249.08	245.32
14000	299.29	291.17	284.18	278.12	272.85	268.24	264.19
15000	320.66	311.96	304.47	297.99	292.34	287.40	283.07
16000	342.04	332.76	324.77	317.85	311.83	306.56	301.94
17000	363.42	353.56	345.07	337.72	331.32	325.72	320.81
18000	384.80	374.36	365.37	357.58	350.81	344.88	339.68
19000	406.17	395.15	385.67	377.45	370.30	364.04	358.55
20000	427.55	415.95	405.96	397.32	389.79	383.20	377.42
21000	448.93	436.75	426.26	417.18	409.28	402.36	396.29
22000	470.31	457.55	446.56	437.05	428.77	421.52	415.16
23000	491.68	478.34	466.86	456.91	448.25	440.68	434.03
24000	513.06	499.14	487.16	476.78	467.74	459.84	452.91
25000	534.44	519.94	507.46	496.64	487.23	479.00	471.78
26000	555.82	540.74	527.75	516.51	506.72	498.16	490.65
27000	577.19	561.53	548.05	536.38	526.21	517.32	509.52
28000	598.57	582.33	568.35	556.24	545.70	536.48	528.39
29000	619.95	603.13	588.65	576.11	565.19	555.64	547.26
30000	641.33	623.93	608.95	595.97	584.68	574.80	566.13
31000	662.70	644.72	629.25	615.84	604.17	593.96	585.00
32000	684.08	665.52	649.54	635.71	623.66	613.12	603.87
33000	705.46	686.32	669.84	655.57	643.15	632.28	622.75
34000	726.84	707.12	690.14	675.44	662.64	651.44	641.62
35000	748.21	727.91	710.44	695.30	682.13	670.60	660.49
40000	855.10	831.90	811.93	794.63	779.57	766.40	754.84
45000	961.99	935.89	913.42	893.96	877.02	862.20	849.20
50000	1068.88	1039.88	1014.91	993.29	974.47	958.01	943.55
55000	1175.77	1143.87	1116.40	1092.62	1071.91	1053.81	1037.91
60000	1282.65	1247.85	1217.89	1191.95	1169.36	1149.61	1132.26
65000	1389.54	1351.84	1319.39	1291.28	1266.81	1245.41	1226.62
70000	1496.43	1455.83	1420.88	1390.61	1364.25	1341.21	1320.97

Monthly Loan Payments 19¾%

LOAN AMOUNT	11 YEARS	11½ YEARS	12 YEARS	12½ YEARS	13 YEARS	14 YEARS	15 YEARS
100	1.86	1.84	1.82	1.80	1.79	1.76	1.74
200	3.72	3.68	3.64	3.60	3.57	3.52	3.48
300	5.58	5.52	5.46	5.40	5.36	5.28	5.21
400	7.45	7.36	7.28	7.21	7.14	7.04	6.95
500	9.31	9.20	9.10	9.01	8.93	8.80	8.69
600	11.17	11.03	10.92	10.81	10.71	10.55	10.43
700	13.03	12.87	12.73	12.61	12.50	12.31	12.16
800	14.89	14.71	14.55	14.41	14.29	14.07	13.90
900	16.75	16.55	16.37	16.21	16.07	15.83	15.64
1000	18.62	18.39	18.19	18.02	17.86	17.59	17.38
1500	27.92	27.59	27.29	27.02	26.79	26.39	26.07
2000	37.23	36.78	36.38	36.03	35.71	35.18	34.76
2500	46.54	45.98	45.48	45.04	44.64	43.98	43.45
3000	55.85	55.17	54.58	54.05	53.57	52.77	52.14
3500	65.16	64.37	63.67	63.05	62.50	61.57	60.82
4000	74.47	73.57	72.77	72.06	71.43	70.37	69.51
4500	83.77	82.76	81.86	81.07	80.36	79.16	78.20
5000	93.08	91.96	90.96	90.08	89.29	87.96	86.89
5500	102.39	101.15	100.06	99.08	98.22	96.75	95.58
6000	111.70	110.35	109.15	108.09	107.14	105.55	104.27
6500	121.01	119.54	118.25	117.10	116.07	114.34	112.96
7000	130.32	128.74	127.34	126.11	125.00	123.14	121.65
7500	139.62	137.94	136.44	135.11	133.93	131.94	130.34
8000	148.93	147.13	145.54	144.12	142.86	140.73	139.03
8500	158.24	156.33	154.63	153.13	151.79	149.53	147.72
9000	167.55	165.52	163.73	162.14	160.72	158.32	156.41
9500	176.86	174.72	172.82	171.14	169.65	167.12	165.10
10000	186.16	183.91	181.92	180.15	178.57	175.91	173.79
11000	204.78	202.31	200.11	198.17	196.43	193.51	191.16
12000	223.40	220.70	218.30	216.18	214.29	211.10	208.54
13000	242.01	239.09	236.50	234.20	232.15	228.69	225.92
14000	260.63	257.48	254.69	252.21	250.00	246.28	243.30
15000	279.25	275.87	272.88	270.23	267.86	263.87	260.68
16000	297.86	294.26	291.07	288.24	285.72	281.46	278.06
17000	316.48	312.65	309.27	306.26	303.58	299.05	295.44
18000	335.10	331.05	327.46	324.27	321.43	316.64	312.81
19000	353.71	349.44	345.65	342.29	339.29	334.24	330.19
20000	372.33	367.83	363.84	360.30	357.15	351.83	347.57
21000	390.95	386.22	382.03	378.32	375.01	369.42	364.95
22000	409.56	404.61	400.23	396.33	392.86	387.01	382.33
23000	428.18	423.00	418.42	414.35	410.72	404.60	399.71
24000	446.79	441.39	436.61	432.36	428.58	422.19	417.09
25000	465.41	459.79	454.80	450.38	446.44	439.78	434.46
26000	484.03	478.18	472.99	468.39	464.29	457.38	451.84
27000	502.64	496.57	491.19	486.41	482.15	474.97	469.22
28000	521.26	514.96	509.38	504.42	500.01	492.56	486.60
29000	539.88	533.35	527.57	522.44	517.87	510.15	503.98
30000	558.49	551.74	545.76	540.45	535.72	527.74	521.36
31000	577.11	570.13	563.95	558.47	553.58	545.33	538.73
32000	595.73	588.53	582.15	576.48	571.44	562.92	556.11
33000	614.34	606.92	600.34	594.50	589.29	580.52	573.49
34000	632.96	625.31	618.53	612.51	607.15	598.11	590.87
35000	651.58	643.70	636.72	630.53	625.01	615.70	608.25
40000	744.66	735.66	727.68	720.60	714.30	703.66	695.14
45000	837.74	827.61	818.64	810.68	803.58	791.61	782.03
50000	930.82	919.57	909.60	900.75	892.87	879.57	868.93
55000	1023.90	1011.53	1000.56	990.83	982.16	967.53	955.82
60000	1116.99	1103.49	1091.52	1080.90	1071.45	1055.48	1042.71
65000	1210.07	1195.44	1182.48	1170.98	1160.73	1143.44	1129.61
70000	1303.15	1287.40	1273.44	1261.05	1250.02	1231.40	1216.50

20% Monthly Loan Payments

LOAN AMOUNT	½ YEAR	1 YEAR	1½ YEARS	2 YEARS	2½ YEARS	3 YEARS	3½ YEARS
100	17.65	9.26	6.48	5.09	4.26	3.72	3.3
200	35.30	18.53	12.95	10.18	8.53	7.43	6.6
300	52.96	27.79	19.43	15.27	12.79	11.15	9.9
400	70.61	37.05	25.91	20.36	17.05	14.87	13.3
500	88.26	46.32	32.38	25.45	21.31	18.58	16.6
600	105.91	55.58	38.86	30.54	25.58	22.30	19.9
700	123.57	64.84	45.33	35.63	29.84	26.01	23.3
800	141.22	74.11	51.81	40.72	34.10	29.73	26.6
900	158.87	83.37	58.29	45.81	38.37	33.45	29.9
1000	176.52	92.63	64.76	50.90	42.63	37.16	33.3
1500	264.78	138.95	97.14	76.34	63.94	55.75	49.9
2000	353.05	185.27	129.53	101.79	85.26	74.33	66.5
2500	441.31	231.59	161.91	127.24	106.57	92.91	83.2
3000	529.57	277.90	194.29	152.69	127.89	111.49	99.8
3500	617.83	324.22	226.67	178.14	149.20	130.07	116.5
4000	706.09	370.54	259.05	203.58	170.52	148.65	133.1
4500	794.35	416.86	291.43	229.03	191.83	167.24	149.8
5000	882.61	463.17	323.82	254.48	213.15	185.82	166.4
5500	970.88	509.49	356.20	279.93	234.46	204.40	183.1
6000	1059.14	555.81	388.58	305.37	255.78	222.98	199.7
6500	1147.40	602.12	420.96	330.82	277.09	241.56	216.4
7000	1235.66	648.44	453.34	356.27	298.41	260.15	233.0
7500	1323.92	694.76	485.72	381.72	319.72	278.73	249.7
8000	1412.18	741.08	518.11	407.17	341.04	297.31	266.3
8500	1500.44	787.39	550.49	432.61	362.35	315.89	283.0
9000	1588.71	833.71	582.87	458.06	383.67	334.47	299.6
9500	1676.97	880.03	615.25	483.51	404.98	353.05	316.3
10000	1765.23	926.35	647.63	508.96	426.30	371.64	332.9
11000	1941.75	1018.98	712.40	559.85	468.93	408.80	366.2
12000	2118.27	1111.61	777.16	610.75	511.56	445.96	399.5
13000	2294.80	1204.25	841.92	661.65	554.18	483.13	432.8
14000	2471.32	1296.88	906.68	712.54	596.81	520.29	466.1
15000	2647.84	1389.52	971.45	763.44	639.44	557.45	499.4
16000	2824.36	1482.15	1036.21	814.33	682.07	594.62	532.7
17000	3000.89	1574.79	1100.97	865.23	724.70	631.78	566.0
18000	3177.41	1667.42	1165.74	916.12	767.33	668.94	599.3
19000	3353.93	1760.06	1230.50	967.02	809.96	706.11	632.6
20000	3530.46	1852.69	1295.26	1017.92	852.59	743.27	665.9
21000	3706.98	1945.32	1360.03	1068.81	895.22	780.44	699.2
22000	3883.50	2037.96	1424.79	1119.71	937.85	817.60	732.5
23000	4060.02	2130.59	1489.55	1170.60	980.48	854.76	765.8
24000	4236.55	2223.23	1554.32	1221.50	1023.11	891.93	799.1
25000	4413.07	2315.86	1619.08	1272.40	1065.74	929.09	832.4
26000	4589.59	2408.50	1683.84	1323.29	1108.37	966.25	865.7
27000	4766.12	2501.13	1748.61	1374.19	1151.00	1003.42	899.
28000	4942.64	2593.77	1813.37	1425.08	1193.63	1040.58	932.
29000	5119.16	2686.40	1878.13	1475.98	1236.26	1077.74	965.
30000	5295.68	2779.04	1942.90	1526.87	1278.89	1114.91	998.
31000	5472.21	2871.67	2007.66	1577.77	1321.52	1152.07	1032.
32000	5648.73	2964.30	2072.42	1628.67	1364.15	1189.23	1065.
33000	5825.25	3056.94	2137.19	1679.56	1406.78	1226.40	1098.8
34000	6001.77	3149.57	2201.95	1730.46	1449.41	1263.56	1132.
35000	6178.30	3242.21	2266.71	1781.35	1492.04	1300.73	1165.
40000	7060.91	3705.38	2590.53	2035.83	1705.18	1486.54	1331.
45000	7943.53	4168.55	2914.34	2290.31	1918.33	1672.36	1498.
50000	8826.14	4631.73	3238.16	2544.79	2131.48	1858.18	1664.
55000	9708.75	5094.90	3561.98	2799.27	2344.63	2044.00	1831.
60000	10591.37	5558.07	3885.79	3053.75	2557.78	2229.82	1997.
65000	11473.98	6021.24	4209.61	3308.23	2770.92	2415.63	2164.
70000	12356.59	6484.42	4533.42	3562.71	2984.07	2601.45	2330.

Monthly Loan Payments 20%

LOAN AMOUNT	4 YEARS	4½ YEARS	5 YEARS	5½ YEARS	6 YEARS	6½ YEARS	7 YEARS
100	3.04	2.82	2.65	2.51	2.40	2.30	2.22
200	6.09	5.65	5.30	5.02	4.79	4.60	4.44
300	9.13	8.47	7.95	7.53	7.19	6.90	6.66
400	12.17	11.29	10.60	10.04	9.58	9.20	8.88
500	15.22	14.11	13.25	12.55	11.98	11.50	11.10
600	18.26	16.94	15.90	15.06	14.37	13.80	13.32
700	21.30	19.76	18.55	17.57	16.77	16.10	15.54
800	24.34	22.58	21.20	20.08	19.16	18.40	17.76
900	27.39	25.41	23.84	22.59	21.56	20.70	19.99
1000	30.43	28.23	26.49	25.10	23.95	23.00	22.21
1500	45.65	42.34	39.74	37.65	35.93	34.51	33.31
2000	60.86	56.46	52.99	50.19	47.91	46.01	44.41
2500	76.08	70.57	66.23	62.74	59.88	57.51	55.52
3000	91.29	84.69	79.48	75.29	71.86	69.01	66.62
3500	106.51	98.80	92.73	87.84	83.83	80.51	77.72
4000	121.72	112.92	105.98	100.39	95.81	92.01	88.82
4500	136.94	127.03	119.22	112.94	107.79	103.52	99.93
5000	152.15	141.15	132.47	125.48	119.76	115.02	111.03
5500	167.37	155.26	145.72	138.03	131.74	126.52	122.13
6000	182.58	169.38	158.96	150.58	143.72	138.02	133.24
6500	197.80	183.49	172.21	163.13	155.69	149.52	144.34
7000	213.01	197.61	185.46	175.68	167.67	161.02	155.44
7500	228.23	211.72	198.70	188.23	179.65	172.53	166.55
8000	243.44	225.83	211.95	200.77	191.62	184.03	177.65
8500	258.66	239.95	225.20	213.32	203.60	195.53	188.75
9000	273.87	254.06	238.44	225.87	215.58	207.03	199.86
9500	289.09	268.18	251.69	238.42	227.55	218.53	210.96
10000	304.30	282.29	264.94	250.97	239.53	230.03	222.06
11000	334.73	310.52	291.43	276.06	263.48	253.04	244.27
12000	365.16	338.75	317.93	301.16	287.43	276.04	266.47
13000	395.59	366.98	344.42	326.26	311.39	299.04	288.68
14000	426.03	395.21	370.91	351.35	335.34	322.05	310.89
15000	456.46	423.44	397.41	376.45	359.29	345.05	333.09
16000	486.89	451.67	423.90	401.55	383.25	368.05	355.30
17000	517.32	479.90	450.40	426.64	407.20	391.06	377.51
18000	547.75	508.13	476.89	451.74	431.15	414.06	399.71
19000	578.18	536.36	503.38	476.84	455.10	437.06	421.92
20000	608.61	564.59	529.88	501.93	479.06	460.07	444.12
21000	639.04	592.82	556.37	527.03	503.01	483.07	466.33
22000	669.47	621.04	582.87	552.13	526.96	506.07	488.54
23000	699.90	649.27	609.36	577.22	550.91	529.08	510.74
24000	730.33	677.50	635.85	602.32	574.87	552.08	532.95
25000	760.76	705.73	662.35	627.42	598.82	575.08	555.15
26000	791.19	733.96	688.84	652.51	622.77	598.09	577.36
27000	821.62	762.19	715.33	677.61	646.73	621.09	599.57
28000	852.05	790.42	741.83	702.71	670.68	644.09	621.77
29000	882.48	818.65	768.32	727.80	694.63	667.10	643.98
30000	912.91	846.88	794.82	752.90	718.58	690.10	666.19
31000	943.34	875.11	821.31	778.00	742.54	713.10	688.39
32000	973.77	903.34	847.80	803.10	766.49	736.11	710.60
33000	1004.20	931.57	874.30	828.19	790.44	759.11	732.80
34000	1034.63	959.80	900.79	853.29	814.40	782.11	755.01
35000	1065.06	988.03	927.29	878.39	838.35	805.12	777.22
40000	1217.21	1129.17	1059.76	1003.87	958.11	920.13	888.25
45000	1369.37	1270.32	1192.22	1129.35	1077.88	1035.15	999.28
50000	1521.52	1411.46	1324.69	1254.84	1197.64	1150.17	1110.31
55000	1673.67	1552.61	1457.16	1380.32	1317.41	1265.18	1221.34
60000	1825.82	1693.76	1589.63	1505.80	1437.17	1380.20	1332.37
65000	1977.97	1834.90	1722.10	1631.29	1556.93	1495.22	1443.40
70000	2130.13	1976.05	1854.57	1756.77	1676.70	1610.23	1554.43

20% Monthly Loan Payments

LOAN AMOUNT	7½ YEARS	8 YEARS	8½ YEARS	9 YEARS	9½ YEARS	10 YEARS	10½ YEARS
100	2.15	2.10	2.05	2.00	1.97	1.93	1.90
200	4.31	4.19	4.09	4.01	3.93	3.87	3.81
300	6.46	6.29	6.14	6.01	5.90	5.80	5.71
400	8.61	8.38	8.18	8.01	7.86	7.73	7.62
500	10.77	10.48	10.23	10.01	9.83	9.66	9.52
600	12.92	12.57	12.27	12.02	11.79	11.60	11.42
700	15.07	14.67	14.32	14.02	13.76	13.53	13.33
800	17.22	16.76	16.37	16.02	15.72	15.46	15.23
900	19.38	18.86	18.41	18.02	17.69	17.39	17.13
1000	21.53	20.95	20.46	20.03	19.65	19.33	19.04
1500	32.30	31.43	30.68	30.04	29.48	28.99	28.56
2000	43.06	41.91	40.91	40.05	39.30	38.65	38.08
2500	53.83	52.38	51.14	50.07	49.13	48.31	47.60
3000	64.59	62.86	61.37	60.08	58.96	57.98	57.12
3500	75.36	73.34	71.60	70.09	68.78	67.64	66.64
4000	86.12	83.81	81.83	80.11	78.61	77.30	76.16
4500	96.89	94.29	92.05	90.12	88.44	86.97	85.67
5000	107.65	104.77	102.28	100.13	98.26	96.63	95.19
5500	118.42	115.24	112.51	110.15	108.09	106.29	104.71
6000	129.18	125.72	122.74	120.16	117.91	115.95	114.23
6500	139.95	136.20	132.97	130.17	127.74	125.62	123.75
7000	150.71	146.67	143.20	140.18	137.57	135.28	133.27
7500	161.48	157.15	153.42	150.20	147.39	144.94	142.79
8000	172.24	167.63	163.65	160.21	157.22	154.60	152.31
8500	183.01	178.10	173.88	170.23	167.05	164.27	161.83
9000	193.77	188.58	184.11	180.24	176.87	173.93	171.35
9500	204.54	199.06	194.34	190.26	186.70	183.59	180.87
10000	215.31	209.53	204.56	200.27	196.52	193.26	190.39
11000	236.84	230.49	225.02	220.29	216.18	212.58	209.43
12000	258.37	251.44	245.48	240.32	235.83	231.91	228.47
13000	279.90	272.39	265.93	260.34	255.48	251.23	247.50
14000	301.43	293.34	286.39	280.37	275.13	270.56	266.54
15000	322.96	314.30	306.85	300.40	294.79	289.88	285.58
16000	344.49	335.25	327.30	320.42	314.44	309.21	304.62
17000	366.02	356.20	347.76	340.45	334.09	328.53	323.66
18000	387.55	377.16	368.22	360.48	353.74	347.86	342.70
19000	409.08	398.11	388.67	380.50	373.40	367.19	361.74
20000	430.61	419.06	409.13	400.53	393.05	386.51	380.78
21000	452.14	440.02	429.59	420.56	412.70	405.84	399.81
22000	473.67	460.97	450.04	440.58	432.35	425.16	418.85
23000	495.20	481.92	470.50	460.61	452.01	444.49	437.89
24000	516.73	502.88	490.95	480.64	471.66	463.81	456.93
25000	538.26	523.83	511.41	500.66	491.31	483.14	475.97
26000	559.79	544.78	531.87	520.69	510.96	502.46	495.01
27000	581.32	565.74	552.32	540.72	530.62	521.79	514.05
28000	602.86	586.69	572.78	560.74	550.27	541.12	533.09
29000	624.39	607.64	593.24	580.77	569.92	560.44	552.12
30000	645.92	628.60	613.69	600.80	589.57	579.77	571.16
31000	667.45	649.55	634.15	620.82	609.23	599.09	590.20
32000	688.98	670.50	654.61	640.85	628.88	618.42	609.24
33000	710.51	691.46	675.06	660.87	648.53	637.74	628.28
34000	732.04	712.41	695.52	680.90	668.18	657.07	647.32
35000	753.57	733.36	715.98	700.93	687.84	676.39	666.36
40000	861.22	838.13	818.26	801.06	786.10	773.02	761.55
45000	968.87	942.89	920.54	901.19	884.36	869.65	856.75
50000	1076.53	1047.66	1022.82	1001.33	982.62	966.28	951.94
55000	1184.18	1152.43	1125.10	1101.46	1080.88	1062.91	1047.13
60000	1291.83	1257.19	1227.39	1201.59	1179.15	1159.53	1142.33
65000	1399.49	1361.96	1329.67	1301.72	1277.41	1256.16	1237.52
70000	1507.14	1466.72	1431.95	1401.86	1375.67	1352.79	1332.72

Monthly Loan Payments 20%

LOAN AMOUNT	11 YEARS	11½ YEARS	12 YEARS	12½ YEARS	13 YEARS	14 YEARS	15 YEARS
100	1.88	1.86	1.84	1.82	1.80	1.78	1.76
200	3.76	3.71	3.67	3.64	3.61	3.55	3.51
300	5.64	5.57	5.51	5.46	5.41	5.33	5.27
400	7.51	7.43	7.35	7.28	7.21	7.11	7.03
500	9.39	9.28	9.18	9.10	9.02	8.89	8.78
600	11.27	11.14	11.02	10.91	10.82	10.66	10.54
700	13.15	12.99	12.86	12.73	12.62	12.44	12.29
800	15.03	14.85	14.69	14.55	14.43	14.22	14.05
900	16.91	16.71	16.53	16.37	16.23	16.00	15.81
1000	18.79	18.56	18.37	18.19	18.04	17.77	17.56
1500	28.18	27.85	27.55	27.29	27.05	26.66	26.34
2000	37.57	37.13	36.73	36.38	36.07	35.55	35.13
2500	46.97	46.41	45.92	45.48	45.09	44.43	43.91
3000	56.36	55.69	55.10	54.57	54.11	53.32	52.69
3500	65.75	64.97	64.28	63.67	63.12	62.20	61.47
4000	75.15	74.25	73.46	72.76	72.14	71.09	70.25
4500	84.54	83.54	82.65	81.86	81.16	79.98	79.03
5000	93.93	92.82	91.83	90.95	90.18	88.86	87.81
5500	103.32	102.10	101.01	100.05	99.19	97.75	96.60
6000	112.72	111.38	110.20	109.15	108.21	106.64	105.38
6500	122.11	120.66	119.38	118.24	117.23	115.52	114.16
7000	131.50	129.94	128.56	127.34	126.25	124.41	122.94
7500	140.90	139.23	137.75	136.43	135.26	133.29	131.72
8000	150.29	148.51	146.93	145.53	144.28	142.18	140.50
8500	159.68	157.79	156.11	154.62	153.30	151.07	149.29
9000	169.08	167.07	165.29	163.72	162.32	159.95	158.07
9500	178.47	176.35	174.48	172.81	171.33	168.84	166.85
10000	187.86	185.63	183.66	181.91	180.35	177.73	175.63
11000	206.65	204.20	202.03	200.10	198.39	195.50	193.19
12000	225.44	222.76	220.39	218.29	216.42	213.27	210.76
13000	244.22	241.32	238.76	236.48	234.46	231.04	228.32
14000	263.01	259.89	257.13	254.67	252.49	248.82	245.88
15000	281.80	278.45	275.49	272.86	270.53	266.59	263.44
16000	300.58	297.01	293.86	291.06	288.56	284.36	281.01
17000	319.37	315.58	312.22	309.25	306.60	302.14	298.57
18000	338.15	334.14	330.59	327.44	324.63	319.91	316.13
19000	356.94	352.71	348.96	345.63	342.67	337.68	333.70
20000	375.73	371.27	367.32	363.82	360.70	355.45	351.26
21000	394.51	389.83	385.69	382.01	378.74	373.23	368.82
22000	413.30	408.40	404.05	400.20	396.77	391.00	386.39
23000	432.09	426.96	422.42	418.39	414.81	408.77	403.95
24000	450.87	445.52	440.79	436.58	432.85	426.54	421.51
25000	469.66	464.09	459.15	454.77	450.88	444.32	439.07
26000	488.44	482.65	477.52	472.96	468.92	462.09	456.64
27000	507.23	501.21	495.88	491.16	486.95	479.86	474.20
28000	526.02	519.78	514.25	509.35	504.99	497.63	491.76
29000	544.80	538.34	532.62	527.54	523.02	515.41	509.33
30000	563.59	556.90	550.98	545.73	541.06	533.18	526.89
31000	582.38	575.47	569.35	563.92	559.09	550.95	544.45
32000	601.16	594.03	587.71	582.11	577.13	568.72	562.01
33000	619.95	612.59	606.08	600.30	595.16	586.50	579.58
34000	638.74	631.16	624.45	618.49	613.20	604.27	597.14
35000	657.52	649.72	642.81	636.68	631.23	622.04	614.70
40000	751.45	742.54	734.64	727.64	721.41	710.91	702.52
45000	845.39	835.35	826.47	818.59	811.58	799.77	790.33
50000	939.32	928.17	918.30	909.55	901.76	888.63	878.15
55000	1033.25	1020.99	1010.12	1000.50	991.94	977.50	965.96
60000	1127.18	1113.81	1101.97	1091.46	1082.11	1066.36	1053.78
65000	1221.11	1206.62	1193.80	1182.41	1172.29	1155.22	1141.59
70000	1315.04	1299.44	1285.63	1273.37	1262.47	1244.09	1229.41

20½% Monthly Loan Payments

LOAN AMOUNT	½ YEAR	1 YEAR	1½ YEARS	2 YEARS	2½ YEARS	3 YEARS	3½ YEARS
100	17.68	9.29	6.50	5.11	4.29	3.74	3.36
200	35.35	18.57	13.00	10.23	8.58	7.48	6.71
300	53.03	27.86	19.50	15.34	12.86	11.23	10.07
400	70.71	37.15	26.00	20.46	17.15	14.97	13.42
500	88.39	46.44	32.50	25.57	21.44	18.71	16.78
600	106.06	55.72	39.00	30.68	25.73	22.45	20.14
700	123.74	65.01	45.50	35.80	30.02	26.19	23.49
800	141.42	74.30	52.00	40.91	34.30	29.94	26.85
900	159.10	83.59	58.50	46.03	38.59	33.68	30.20
1000	176.77	92.87	65.00	51.14	42.88	37.42	33.56
1500	265.16	139.31	97.51	76.71	64.32	56.13	50.34
2000	353.55	185.75	130.01	102.28	85.76	74.84	67.12
2500	441.93	232.18	162.51	127.85	107.20	93.55	83.90
3000	530.32	278.62	195.01	153.42	128.64	112.26	100.68
3500	618.70	325.06	227.51	178.99	150.08	130.97	117.45
4000	707.09	371.50	260.01	204.56	171.52	149.68	134.23
4500	795.48	417.93	292.52	230.13	192.96	168.38	151.01
5000	883.86	464.37	325.02	255.70	214.40	187.09	167.79
5500	972.25	510.81	357.52	281.27	235.84	205.80	184.57
6000	1060.64	557.24	390.02	306.84	257.28	224.51	201.35
6500	1149.02	603.68	422.52	332.41	278.72	243.22	218.13
7000	1237.41	650.12	455.03	357.98	300.15	261.93	234.91
7500	1325.79	696.55	487.53	383.55	321.59	280.64	251.69
8000	1414.18	742.99	520.03	409.12	343.03	299.35	268.47
8500	1502.57	789.43	552.53	434.69	364.47	318.06	285.25
9000	1590.95	835.87	585.03	460.26	385.91	336.77	302.03
9500	1679.34	882.30	617.54	485.83	407.35	355.48	318.80
10000	1767.73	928.74	650.04	511.40	428.79	374.19	335.58
11000	1944.50	1021.61	715.04	562.54	471.67	411.61	369.14
12000	2121.27	1114.49	780.05	613.68	514.55	449.03	402.70
13000	2298.04	1207.36	845.05	664.83	557.43	486.44	436.26
14000	2474.82	1300.24	910.05	715.97	600.31	523.86	469.82
15000	2651.59	1393.11	975.06	767.11	643.19	561.28	503.38
16000	2828.36	1485.98	1040.06	818.25	686.07	598.70	536.94
17000	3005.13	1578.86	1105.06	869.39	728.95	636.12	570.49
18000	3181.91	1671.73	1170.07	920.53	771.83	673.54	604.05
19000	3358.68	1764.61	1235.07	971.67	814.71	710.96	637.61
20000	3535.45	1857.48	1300.08	1022.81	857.59	748.38	671.17
21000	3712.22	1950.35	1365.08	1073.95	900.46	785.80	704.73
22000	3889.00	2043.23	1430.08	1125.09	943.34	823.21	738.29
23000	4065.77	2136.10	1495.09	1176.23	986.22	860.63	771.8
24000	4242.54	2228.98	1560.09	1227.37	1029.10	898.05	805.4
25000	4419.31	2321.85	1625.10	1278.51	1071.98	935.47	838.9
26000	4596.09	2414.72	1690.10	1329.65	1114.86	972.89	872.5
27000	4772.86	2507.60	1755.10	1380.79	1157.74	1010.31	906.0
28000	4949.63	2600.47	1820.11	1431.93	1200.62	1047.73	939.6
29000	5126.41	2693.35	1885.11	1483.07	1243.50	1085.15	973.1
30000	5303.18	2786.22	1950.11	1534.21	1286.38	1122.57	1006.7
31000	5479.95	2879.09	2015.12	1585.35	1329.26	1159.98	1040.3
32000	5656.72	2971.97	2080.12	1636.49	1372.14	1197.40	1073.8
33000	5833.50	3064.84	2145.13	1687.63	1415.02	1234.82	1107.4
34000	6010.27	3157.72	2210.13	1738.77	1457.89	1272.24	1140.9
35000	6187.04	3250.59	2275.13	1789.91	1500.77	1309.66	1174.5
40000	7070.90	3714.96	2600.15	2045.62	1715.17	1496.75	1342.3
45000	7954.77	4179.33	2925.17	2301.32	1929.57	1683.85	1510.1
50000	8838.63	4643.70	3250.19	2557.02	2143.96	1870.94	1677.9
55000	9722.49	5108.07	3575.21	2812.72	2358.36	2058.04	1845.7
60000	10606.36	5572.44	3900.23	3068.42	2572.76	2245.13	2013.5
65000	11490.22	6036.81	4225.25	3324.13	2787.15	2432.22	2181.2
70000	12374.08	6501.18	4550.27	3579.83	3001.55	2619.32	2349.0

Monthly Loan Payments 20½%

LOAN AMOUNT	4 YEARS	4½ YEARS	5 YEARS	5½ YEARS	6 YEARS	6½ YEARS	7 YEARS
100	3.07	2.85	2.68	2.54	2.42	2.33	2.25
200	6.14	5.70	5.35	5.08	4.85	4.66	4.50
300	9.21	8.55	8.03	7.61	7.27	6.99	6.75
400	12.28	11.40	10.71	10.15	9.70	9.32	9.00
500	15.35	14.25	13.39	12.69	12.12	11.65	11.25
600	18.42	17.10	16.06	15.23	14.55	13.98	13.50
700	21.49	19.95	18.74	17.77	16.97	16.31	15.76
800	24.56	22.80	21.42	20.31	19.39	18.64	18.01
900	27.63	25.65	24.10	22.84	21.82	20.97	20.26
1000	30.70	28.50	26.77	25.38	24.24	23.30	22.51
1500	46.05	42.75	40.16	38.07	36.37	34.95	33.76
2000	61.39	57.00	53.55	50.76	48.49	46.60	45.02
2500	76.74	71.26	66.93	63.45	60.61	58.25	56.27
3000	92.09	85.51	80.32	76.14	72.73	69.90	67.52
3500	107.44	99.76	93.71	88.84	84.85	81.55	78.78
4000	122.79	114.01	107.09	101.53	96.97	93.20	90.03
4500	138.14	128.26	120.48	114.22	109.10	104.85	101.29
5000	153.49	142.51	133.86	126.91	121.22	116.50	112.54
5500	168.84	156.76	147.25	139.60	133.34	128.15	123.80
6000	184.18	171.01	160.64	152.29	145.46	139.80	135.05
6500	199.53	185.26	174.02	164.98	157.58	151.45	146.30
7000	214.88	199.52	187.41	177.67	169.70	163.10	157.56
7500	230.23	213.77	200.80	190.36	181.83	174.75	168.81
8000	245.58	228.02	214.18	203.05	193.95	186.40	180.07
8500	260.93	242.27	227.57	215.74	206.07	198.05	191.32
9000	276.28	256.52	240.96	228.43	218.19	209.70	202.57
9500	291.63	270.77	254.34	241.13	230.31	221.35	213.83
10000	306.97	285.02	267.73	253.82	242.44	233.00	225.08
11000	337.67	313.53	294.50	279.20	266.68	256.30	247.59
12000	368.37	342.03	321.27	304.58	290.92	279.60	270.10
13000	399.07	370.53	348.05	329.96	315.17	302.90	292.61
14000	429.76	399.03	374.82	355.34	339.41	326.20	315.12
15000	460.46	427.53	401.59	380.72	363.65	349.50	337.62
16000	491.16	456.04	428.37	406.11	387.90	372.80	360.13
17000	521.86	484.54	455.14	431.49	412.14	396.10	382.64
18000	552.55	513.04	481.91	456.87	436.38	419.40	405.15
19000	583.25	541.54	508.68	482.25	460.63	442.70	427.66
20000	613.95	570.05	535.46	507.63	484.87	466.00	450.16
21000	644.65	598.55	562.23	533.01	509.11	489.30	472.67
22000	675.34	627.05	589.00	558.40	533.36	512.60	495.18
23000	706.04	655.55	615.78	583.78	557.60	535.89	517.69
24000	736.74	684.06	642.55	609.16	581.84	559.19	540.20
25000	767.43	712.56	669.32	634.54	606.09	582.49	562.71
26000	798.13	741.06	696.09	659.92	630.33	605.79	585.21
27000	828.83	769.56	722.87	685.30	654.58	629.09	607.72
28000	859.53	798.06	749.64	710.68	678.82	652.39	630.23
29000	890.22	826.57	776.41	736.07	703.06	675.69	652.74
30000	920.92	855.07	803.19	761.45	727.31	698.99	675.25
31000	951.62	883.57	829.96	786.83	751.55	722.29	697.76
32000	982.32	912.07	856.73	812.21	775.79	745.59	720.26
33000	1013.01	940.58	883.50	837.59	800.04	768.89	742.77
34000	1043.71	969.08	910.28	862.97	824.28	792.19	765.28
35000	1074.41	997.58	937.05	888.36	848.52	815.49	787.79
40000	1227.90	1140.09	1070.91	1015.26	969.74	931.99	900.33
45000	1381.38	1282.60	1204.78	1142.17	1090.96	1048.49	1012.87
50000	1534.87	1425.12	1338.64	1269.08	1212.18	1164.99	1125.41
55000	1688.36	1567.63	1472.51	1395.99	1333.39	1281.49	1237.95
60000	1841.84	1710.14	1606.37	1522.90	1454.61	1397.99	1350.49
65000	1995.33	1852.65	1740.24	1649.80	1575.83	1514.49	1463.04
70000	2148.82	1995.16	1874.10	1776.71	1697.05	1630.98	1575.58

20½%   Monthly Loan Payments

LOAN AMOUNT	7½ YEARS	8 YEARS	8½ YEARS	9 YEARS	9½ YEARS	10 YEARS	10½ YEARS
100	2.18	2.13	2.08	2.03	2.00	1.97	1.94
200	4.37	4.25	4.15	4.07	4.00	3.93	3.88
300	6.55	6.38	6.23	6.10	5.99	5.90	5.81
400	8.74	8.51	8.31	8.14	7.99	7.86	7.75
500	10.92	10.63	10.39	10.17	9.99	9.83	9.69
600	13.10	12.76	12.46	12.21	11.99	11.79	11.63
700	15.29	14.89	14.54	14.24	13.99	13.76	13.56
800	17.47	17.01	16.62	16.28	15.98	15.73	15.50
900	19.65	19.14	18.70	18.31	17.98	17.69	17.44
1000	21.84	21.27	20.77	20.35	19.98	19.66	19.38
1500	32.76	31.90	31.16	30.52	29.97	29.49	29.06
2000	43.68	42.53	41.55	40.70	39.96	39.32	38.75
2500	54.60	53.17	51.94	50.87	49.95	49.15	48.44
3000	65.51	63.80	62.32	61.05	59.94	58.97	58.13
3500	76.43	74.43	72.71	71.22	69.93	68.80	67.82
4000	87.35	85.06	83.10	81.40	79.92	78.63	77.50
4500	98.27	95.70	93.49	91.57	89.91	88.46	87.19
5000	109.19	106.33	103.87	101.75	99.90	98.29	96.88
5500	120.11	116.96	114.26	111.92	109.89	108.12	106.57
6000	131.03	127.60	124.65	122.10	119.88	117.95	116.26
6500	141.95	138.23	135.03	132.27	129.87	127.78	125.94
7000	152.87	148.86	145.42	142.45	139.86	137.61	135.63
7500	163.79	159.50	155.81	152.62	149.85	147.44	145.32
8000	174.70	170.13	166.20	162.80	159.84	157.27	155.01
8500	185.62	180.76	176.58	172.97	169.83	167.09	164.70
9000	196.54	191.39	186.97	183.15	179.82	176.92	174.38
9500	207.46	202.03	197.36	193.32	189.81	186.75	184.07
10000	218.38	212.66	207.75	203.50	199.80	196.58	193.76
11000	240.22	233.93	228.52	223.85	219.78	216.24	213.14
12000	262.06	255.19	249.29	244.20	239.76	235.90	232.51
13000	283.89	276.46	270.07	264.54	259.75	255.56	251.89
14000	305.73	297.72	290.84	284.89	279.73	275.22	271.26
15000	327.57	318.99	311.62	305.24	299.71	294.87	290.64
16000	349.41	340.26	332.39	325.59	319.69	314.53	310.02
17000	371.25	361.52	353.17	345.94	339.67	334.19	329.39
18000	393.09	382.79	373.94	366.29	359.65	353.85	348.77
19000	414.92	404.06	394.72	386.64	379.63	373.51	368.14
20000	436.76	425.32	415.49	406.99	399.61	393.16	387.52
21000	458.60	446.59	436.26	427.34	419.59	412.82	406.90
22000	480.44	467.85	457.04	447.69	439.57	432.48	426.27
23000	502.28	489.12	477.81	468.04	459.55	452.14	445.65
24000	524.11	510.39	498.59	488.39	479.53	471.80	465.02
25000	545.95	531.65	519.36	508.74	499.51	491.46	484.40
26000	567.79	552.92	540.14	529.09	519.49	511.11	503.78
27000	589.63	574.18	560.91	549.44	539.47	530.77	523.15
28000	611.47	595.45	581.69	569.79	559.45	550.43	542.53
29000	633.30	616.72	602.46	590.14	579.43	570.09	561.90
30000	655.14	637.98	623.24	610.49	599.41	589.75	581.28
31000	676.98	659.25	644.01	630.84	619.39	609.41	600.66
32000	698.82	680.51	664.78	651.19	639.37	629.06	620.03
33000	720.66	701.78	685.56	671.54	659.35	648.72	639.41
34000	742.49	723.05	706.33	691.89	679.33	668.38	658.78
35000	764.33	744.31	727.11	712.24	699.31	688.04	678.16
40000	873.52	850.64	830.98	813.98	799.22	786.35	775.04
45000	982.71	956.97	934.85	915.73	899.12	884.62	871.92
50000	1091.90	1063.30	1038.73	1017.48	999.02	982.91	968.80
55000	1201.09	1169.63	1142.60	1119.23	1098.92	1081.20	1065.68
60000	1310.28	1275.96	1246.47	1220.98	1198.82	1179.49	1162.56
65000	1419.47	1382.29	1350.34	1322.72	1298.73	1277.78	1259.44
70000	1528.66	1488.62	1454.22	1424.47	1398.63	1376.08	1356.32

Monthly Loan Payments 20½%

LOAN AMOUNT	11 YEARS	11½ YEARS	12 YEARS	12½ YEARS	13 YEARS	14 YEARS	15 YEARS
100	1.91	1.89	1.87	1.85	1.84	1.81	1.79
200	3.83	3.78	3.74	3.71	3.68	3.63	3.59
300	5.74	5.67	5.61	5.56	5.52	5.44	5.38
400	7.65	7.56	7.49	7.42	7.36	7.25	7.17
500	9.56	9.45	9.36	9.27	9.20	9.07	8.97
600	11.48	11.35	11.23	11.13	11.04	10.88	10.76
700	13.39	13.24	13.10	12.98	12.87	12.70	12.55
800	15.30	15.13	14.97	14.84	14.71	14.51	14.35
900	17.22	17.02	16.84	16.69	16.55	16.32	16.14
1000	19.13	18.91	18.72	18.54	18.39	18.14	17.93
1500	28.69	28.36	28.07	27.82	27.59	27.21	26.90
2000	38.26	37.82	37.43	37.09	36.79	36.27	35.87
2500	47.82	47.27	46.79	46.36	45.98	45.34	44.83
3000	57.38	56.73	56.15	55.63	55.18	54.41	53.80
3500	66.95	66.18	65.51	64.91	64.37	63.48	62.77
4000	76.51	75.64	74.86	74.18	73.57	72.55	71.73
4500	86.08	85.09	84.22	83.45	82.77	81.62	80.70
5000	95.64	94.55	93.58	92.72	91.96	90.68	89.67
5500	105.20	104.00	102.94	102.00	101.16	99.75	98.63
6000	114.77	113.46	112.30	111.27	110.36	108.82	107.60
6500	124.33	122.91	121.65	120.54	119.55	117.89	116.57
7000	133.90	132.36	131.01	129.81	128.75	126.96	125.53
7500	143.46	141.82	140.37	139.08	137.94	136.03	134.50
8000	153.02	151.27	149.73	148.36	147.14	145.10	143.47
8500	162.59	160.73	159.09	157.63	156.34	154.16	152.43
9000	172.15	170.18	168.44	166.90	165.53	163.23	161.40
9500	181.72	179.64	177.80	176.17	174.73	172.30	170.37
10000	191.28	189.09	187.16	185.45	183.93	181.37	179.33
11000	210.41	208.00	205.87	203.99	202.32	199.51	197.27
12000	229.53	226.91	224.59	222.54	220.71	217.64	215.20
13000	248.66	245.82	243.31	241.08	239.10	235.78	233.14
14000	267.79	264.73	262.02	259.62	257.50	253.92	251.07
15000	286.92	283.64	280.74	278.17	275.89	272.05	269.00
16000	306.05	302.55	299.45	296.71	294.28	290.19	286.94
17000	325.17	321.46	318.17	315.26	312.67	308.33	304.87
18000	344.30	340.37	336.89	333.80	331.07	326.46	322.80
19000	363.43	359.27	355.60	352.35	349.46	344.60	340.74
20000	382.56	378.18	374.32	370.89	367.85	362.74	358.67
21000	401.69	397.09	393.03	389.44	386.24	380.88	376.60
22000	420.81	416.00	411.75	407.98	404.64	399.01	394.54
23000	439.94	434.91	430.47	426.53	423.03	417.15	412.47
24000	459.07	453.82	449.18	445.07	441.42	435.29	430.40
25000	478.20	472.73	467.90	463.62	459.81	453.42	448.34
26000	497.33	491.64	486.61	482.16	478.21	471.56	466.27
27000	516.45	510.55	505.33	500.70	496.60	489.70	484.20
28000	535.58	529.46	524.05	519.25	514.99	507.83	502.14
29000	554.71	548.37	542.76	537.79	533.38	525.97	520.07
30000	573.84	567.28	561.48	556.34	551.78	544.11	538.00
31000	592.97	586.19	580.19	574.88	570.17	562.24	555.94
32000	612.09	605.09	598.91	593.43	588.56	580.38	573.87
33000	631.22	624.00	617.62	611.97	606.96	598.52	591.80
34000	650.35	642.91	636.34	630.52	625.35	616.65	609.74
35000	669.48	661.82	655.06	649.06	643.74	634.79	627.67
40000	765.12	756.37	748.64	741.79	735.70	725.48	717.34
45000	860.76	850.91	842.22	834.51	827.67	816.16	807.01
50000	956.40	945.46	935.79	927.23	919.63	906.85	896.67
55000	1052.04	1040.01	1029.37	1019.95	1011.59	997.53	986.34
60000	1147.67	1134.55	1122.95	1112.68	1103.56	1088.21	1076.01
65000	1243.31	1229.10	1216.53	1205.40	1195.52	1178.90	1165.68
70000	1338.95	1323.64	1310.11	1298.12	1287.48	1269.58	1255.34

203

21% Monthly Loan Payments

LOAN AMOUNT	½ YEAR	1 YEAR	1½ YEARS	2 YEARS	2½ YEARS	3 YEARS	3½ YEARS
100	17.70	9.31	6.52	5.14	4.31	3.77	3.3
200	35.40	18.62	13.05	10.28	8.63	7.54	6.7
300	53.11	27.93	19.57	15.42	12.94	11.30	10.1
400	70.81	37.25	26.10	20.55	17.25	15.07	13.5
500	88.51	46.56	32.62	25.69	21.56	18.84	16.9
600	106.21	55.87	39.15	30.83	25.88	22.61	20.2
700	123.92	65.18	45.67	35.97	30.19	26.37	23.6
800	141.62	74.49	52.20	41.11	34.50	30.14	27.0
900	159.32	83.80	58.72	46.25	38.82	33.91	30.4
1000	177.02	93.11	65.24	51.39	43.13	37.68	33.8
1500	265.53	139.67	97.87	77.08	64.69	56.51	50.7
2000	354.05	186.23	130.49	102.77	86.26	75.35	67.6
2500	442.56	232.78	163.11	128.46	107.82	94.19	84.5
3000	531.07	279.34	195.73	154.15	129.39	113.03	101.4
3500	619.58	325.90	228.36	179.85	150.95	131.86	118.3
4000	708.09	372.46	260.98	205.54	172.52	150.70	135.2
4500	796.60	419.01	293.60	231.24	194.08	169.54	152.1
5000	885.11	465.57	326.22	256.93	215.65	188.38	169.1
5500	973.62	512.13	358.85	282.62	237.21	207.21	186.0
6000	1062.14	558.68	391.47	308.31	258.78	226.05	202.9
6500	1150.65	605.24	424.09	334.01	280.34	244.89	219.8
7000	1239.16	651.80	456.71	359.70	301.91	263.73	236.7
7500	1327.67	698.35	489.34	385.39	323.47	282.56	253.6
8000	1416.18	744.91	521.96	411.09	345.04	301.40	270.5
8500	1504.69	791.47	554.58	436.78	366.60	320.24	287.4
9000	1593.20	838.02	587.20	462.47	388.17	339.08	304.3
9500	1681.71	884.58	619.83	488.16	409.73	357.91	321.3
10000	1770.23	931.14	652.45	513.86	431.30	376.75	338.2
11000	1947.25	1024.25	717.69	565.24	474.43	414.43	372.0
12000	2124.27	1117.37	782.94	616.63	517.56	452.10	405.8
13000	2301.29	1210.48	848.18	668.01	560.69	489.78	439.6
14000	2478.32	1303.59	913.43	719.40	603.82	527.45	473.4
15000	2655.34	1396.71	978.67	770.78	646.95	565.13	507.3
16000	2832.36	1489.82	1043.92	822.17	690.08	602.80	541.1
17000	3009.38	1582.93	1109.16	873.56	733.21	640.48	574.9
18000	3186.41	1676.05	1174.41	924.94	776.34	678.15	608.7
19000	3363.43	1769.16	1239.65	976.33	819.47	715.83	642.5
20000	3540.45	1862.28	1304.90	1027.71	862.60	753.50	676.4
21000	3717.47	1955.39	1370.14	1079.10	905.72	791.18	710.2
22000	3894.50	2048.50	1435.39	1130.48	948.85	828.85	744.0
23000	4071.52	2141.62	1500.63	1181.87	991.98	866.53	777.
24000	4248.54	2234.73	1565.88	1233.26	1035.11	904.20	811.
25000	4425.56	2327.84	1631.12	1284.64	1078.24	941.88	845.
26000	4602.59	2420.96	1696.37	1336.03	1121.37	979.55	879.
27000	4779.61	2514.07	1761.61	1387.41	1164.50	1017.23	913.
28000	4956.63	2607.19	1826.86	1438.80	1207.63	1054.90	946.
29000	5133.65	2700.30	1892.10	1490.18	1250.76	1092.58	980.
30000	5310.68	2793.41	1957.35	1541.57	1293.89	1130.25	1014.
31000	5487.70	2886.53	2022.59	1592.96	1337.02	1167.93	1048.
32000	5664.72	2979.64	2087.84	1644.34	1380.15	1205.60	1082.
33000	5841.74	3072.75	2153.08	1695.73	1423.28	1243.28	1116.
34000	6018.77	3165.87	2218.33	1747.11	1466.41	1280.95	1149.
35000	6195.79	3258.98	2283.57	1798.50	1509.54	1318.63	1183.
40000	7080.90	3724.55	2609.80	2055.43	1725.19	1507.00	1352.
45000	7966.02	4190.12	2936.02	2312.35	1940.84	1695.38	1521.
50000	8851.13	4655.69	3262.25	2569.28	2156.49	1883.75	1691
55000	9736.24	5121.26	3588.47	2826.21	2372.14	2072.13	1860.
60000	10621.35	5586.83	3914.70	3083.14	2587.79	2260.50	2029
65000	11506.47	6052.40	4240.92	3340.07	2803.43	2448.88	2198
70000	12391.58	6517.96	4567.14	3597.00	3019.08	2637.25	2367

Monthly Loan Payments 21%

LOAN AMOUNT	4 YEARS	4½ YEARS	5 YEARS	5½ YEARS	6 YEARS	6½ YEARS	7 YEARS
100	3.10	2.88	2.71	2.57	2.45	2.36	2.28
200	6.19	5.76	5.41	5.13	4.91	4.72	4.56
300	9.29	8.63	8.12	7.70	7.36	7.08	6.84
400	12.39	11.51	10.82	10.27	9.81	9.44	9.12
500	15.48	14.39	13.53	12.83	12.27	11.80	11.41
600	18.58	17.27	16.23	15.40	14.72	14.16	13.69
700	21.68	20.14	18.94	17.97	17.18	16.52	15.97
800	24.77	23.02	21.64	20.53	19.63	18.88	18.25
900	27.87	25.90	24.35	23.10	22.08	21.24	20.53
1000	30.97	28.78	27.05	25.67	24.54	23.60	22.81
1500	46.45	43.17	40.58	38.50	36.80	35.40	34.22
2000	61.93	57.55	54.11	51.34	49.07	47.20	45.62
2500	77.41	71.94	67.63	64.17	61.34	59.00	57.03
3000	92.90	86.33	81.16	77.00	73.61	70.79	68.44
3500	108.38	100.72	94.69	89.84	85.88	82.59	79.84
4000	123.86	115.11	108.21	102.67	98.14	94.39	91.25
4500	139.35	129.50	121.74	115.51	110.41	106.19	102.66
5000	154.83	143.88	135.27	128.34	122.68	117.99	114.06
5500	170.31	158.27	148.79	141.17	134.95	129.79	125.47
6000	185.79	172.66	162.32	154.01	147.22	141.59	136.87
6500	201.28	187.05	175.85	166.84	159.48	153.39	148.28
7000	216.76	201.44	189.37	179.68	171.75	165.19	159.69
7500	232.73	215.83	202.90	192.51	184.02	176.99	171.09
8000	247.73	230.21	216.43	205.35	196.29	188.78	182.50
8500	263.21	244.60	229.95	218.18	208.56	200.58	193.90
9000	278.69	258.99	243.48	231.01	220.82	212.38	205.31
9500	294.17	273.38	257.01	243.85	233.09	224.18	216.72
10000	309.66	287.77	270.53	256.68	245.36	235.98	228.12
11000	340.62	316.54	297.59	282.35	269.90	259.58	250.93
12000	371.59	345.32	324.64	308.02	294.43	283.18	273.75
13000	402.55	374.10	351.69	333.69	318.97	306.77	296.56
14000	433.52	402.87	378.75	359.35	343.50	330.37	319.37
15000	464.49	431.65	405.80	385.02	368.04	353.97	342.18
16000	495.45	460.43	432.85	410.69	392.58	377.57	365.00
17000	526.42	489.20	459.91	436.36	417.11	401.17	387.81
18000	557.38	517.98	486.96	462.03	441.65	424.77	410.62
19000	588.35	546.76	514.01	487.69	466.18	448.36	433.43
20000	619.31	575.53	541.07	513.36	490.72	471.96	456.24
21000	650.28	604.31	568.12	539.03	515.26	495.56	479.06
22000	681.25	633.09	595.17	564.70	539.79	519.16	501.87
23000	712.21	661.86	622.23	590.37	564.33	542.76	524.68
24000	743.18	690.64	649.28	616.04	588.86	566.35	547.49
25000	774.14	719.42	676.33	641.70	613.40	589.95	570.31
26000	805.11	748.19	703.39	667.37	637.94	613.55	593.12
27000	836.07	776.97	730.44	693.04	662.47	637.15	615.93
28000	867.04	805.75	757.49	718.71	687.01	660.75	638.74
29000	898.01	834.52	784.55	744.38	711.54	684.34	661.55
30000	928.97	863.30	811.60	770.04	736.08	707.94	684.37
31000	959.94	892.08	838.65	795.71	760.62	731.54	707.18
32000	990.90	920.85	865.71	821.38	785.15	755.14	729.99
33000	1021.87	949.63	892.76	847.05	809.69	778.74	752.80
34000	1052.83	978.41	919.81	872.72	834.22	802.33	775.62
35000	1083.80	1007.19	946.87	898.38	858.76	825.93	798.43
40000	1238.63	1151.07	1082.13	1026.73	981.44	943.92	912.49
45000	1393.46	1294.95	1217.40	1155.07	1104.12	1061.91	1026.55
50000	1548.28	1438.84	1352.67	1283.41	1226.80	1179.90	1140.61
55000	1703.11	1582.72	1487.93	1411.75	1349.48	1297.89	1254.67
60000	1857.94	1726.60	1623.20	1540.09	1472.16	1415.88	1368.73
65000	2012.77	1870.49	1758.47	1668.43	1594.84	1533.87	1482.79
70000	2167.60	2014.37	1893.74	1796.77	1717.52	1651.86	1596.86

21% Monthly Loan Payments

LOAN AMOUNT	7½ YEARS	8 YEARS	8½ YEARS	9 YEARS	9½ YEARS	10 YEARS	10½ YEARS
100	2.21	2.16	2.11	2.07	2.03	2.00	1.97
200	4.43	4.32	4.22	4.13	4.06	4.00	3.94
300	6.64	6.47	6.33	6.20	6.09	6.00	5.91
400	8.86	8.63	8.44	8.27	8.12	8.00	7.89
500	11.07	10.79	10.55	10.34	10.16	10.00	9.86
600	13.29	12.95	12.66	12.40	12.19	12.00	11.83
700	15.50	15.11	14.77	14.47	14.22	14.00	13.80
800	17.72	17.26	16.88	16.54	16.25	15.99	15.77
900	19.93	19.42	18.99	18.61	18.28	17.99	17.74
1000	22.15	21.58	21.09	20.67	20.31	19.99	19.72
1500	33.22	32.37	31.64	31.01	30.47	29.99	29.57
2000	44.30	43.16	42.19	41.35	40.62	39.99	39.43
2500	55.37	53.95	52.74	51.69	50.78	49.98	49.29
3000	66.44	64.74	63.28	62.02	60.93	59.98	59.15
3500	77.52	75.53	73.83	72.36	71.09	69.98	69.00
4000	88.59	86.32	84.38	82.70	81.24	79.97	78.86
4500	99.66	97.11	94.93	93.04	91.40	89.97	88.72
5000	110.74	107.91	105.47	103.37	101.55	99.97	98.58
5500	121.81	118.70	116.02	113.71	111.71	109.96	108.44
6000	132.89	129.49	126.57	124.05	121.86	119.96	118.29
6500	143.96	140.28	137.12	134.39	132.02	129.96	128.15
7000	155.03	151.07	147.66	144.72	142.17	139.95	138.01
7500	166.11	161.86	158.21	155.06	152.33	149.95	147.87
8000	177.18	172.65	168.76	165.40	162.48	159.95	157.72
8500	188.25	183.44	179.30	175.74	172.64	169.94	167.58
9000	199.33	194.23	189.85	186.07	182.80	179.94	177.44
9500	210.40	205.02	200.40	196.41	192.95	189.94	187.30
10000	221.48	215.81	210.95	206.75	203.11	199.93	197.15
11000	243.62	237.39	232.04	227.42	223.42	219.92	216.87
12000	265.77	258.97	253.14	248.10	243.73	239.92	236.59
13000	287.92	280.55	274.23	268.77	264.04	259.91	256.30
14000	310.07	302.13	295.33	289.45	284.35	279.90	276.02
15000	332.21	323.72	316.42	310.12	304.66	299.90	295.73
16000	354.36	345.30	337.52	330.80	324.97	319.89	315.45
17000	376.51	366.88	358.61	351.47	345.28	339.88	335.16
18000	398.66	388.46	379.70	372.15	365.59	359.88	354.88
19000	420.80	410.04	400.80	392.82	385.90	379.87	374.59
20000	442.95	431.62	421.89	413.50	406.21	399.86	394.31
21000	465.10	453.20	442.99	434.17	426.52	419.86	414.03
22000	487.25	474.78	464.08	454.85	446.83	439.85	433.74
23000	509.39	496.36	485.18	475.52	467.14	459.84	453.46
24000	531.54	517.94	506.27	496.20	487.45	479.84	473.17
25000	553.69	539.53	527.37	516.87	507.77	499.83	492.89
26000	575.84	561.11	548.46	537.55	528.08	519.82	512.60
27000	597.99	582.69	569.56	558.22	548.39	539.82	532.32
28000	620.13	604.27	590.65	578.90	568.70	559.81	552.03
29000	642.28	625.85	611.75	599.57	589.01	579.80	571.75
30000	664.43	647.43	632.84	620.25	609.32	599.80	591.46
31000	686.58	669.01	653.94	640.92	629.63	619.79	611.18
32000	708.72	690.59	675.03	661.60	649.94	639.78	630.90
33000	730.87	712.17	696.13	682.27	670.25	659.77	650.61
34000	753.02	733.75	717.22	702.95	690.56	679.77	670.33
35000	775.17	755.34	738.31	723.62	710.87	699.76	690.04
40000	885.90	863.24	843.79	826.99	812.42	799.73	788.62
45000	996.64	971.15	949.26	930.37	913.98	899.69	887.20
50000	1107.38	1079.05	1054.74	1033.74	1015.53	999.66	985.77
55000	1218.12	1186.96	1160.21	1137.12	1117.08	1099.62	1084.35
60000	1328.86	1294.86	1265.68	1240.49	1218.64	1199.59	1182.93
65000	1439.59	1402.77	1371.16	1343.87	1320.19	1299.56	1281.51
70000	1550.33	1510.67	1476.63	1447.24	1421.74	1399.52	1380.08

Monthly Loan Payments 21%

LOAN AMOUNT	11 YEARS	11½ YEARS	12 YEARS	12½ YEARS	13 YEARS	14 YEARS	15 YEARS
100	1.95	1.93	1.91	1.89	1.88	1.85	1.83
200	3.89	3.85	3.81	3.78	3.75	3.70	3.66
300	5.84	5.78	5.72	5.67	5.63	5.55	5.49
400	7.79	7.70	7.63	7.56	7.50	7.40	7.32
500	9.74	9.63	9.53	9.45	9.38	9.25	9.15
600	11.68	11.55	11.44	11.34	11.25	11.10	10.98
700	13.63	13.48	13.35	13.23	13.13	12.95	12.81
800	15.58	15.41	15.25	15.12	15.00	14.80	14.64
900	17.52	17.33	17.16	17.01	16.88	16.65	16.48
1000	19.47	19.26	19.07	18.90	18.75	18.50	18.31
1500	29.21	28.89	28.60	28.35	28.13	27.76	27.46
2000	38.94	38.51	38.14	37.80	37.50	37.01	36.61
2500	48.68	48.14	47.67	47.25	46.88	46.26	45.77
3000	58.42	57.77	57.20	56.70	56.26	55.51	54.92
3500	68.15	67.40	66.74	66.15	65.63	64.76	64.07
4000	77.89	77.03	76.27	75.60	75.01	74.01	73.22
4500	87.62	86.66	85.81	85.05	84.39	83.27	82.38
5000	97.36	96.29	95.34	94.50	93.76	92.52	91.53
5500	107.09	105.92	104.87	103.95	103.14	101.77	100.68
6000	116.83	115.54	114.41	113.40	112.51	111.02	109.84
6500	126.57	125.17	123.94	122.85	121.89	120.27	118.99
7000	136.30	134.80	133.48	132.30	131.27	129.52	128.14
7500	146.04	144.43	143.01	141.75	140.64	138.78	137.30
8000	155.77	154.06	152.54	151.20	150.02	148.03	146.45
8500	165.51	163.69	162.08	160.66	159.39	157.28	155.60
9000	175.25	173.32	171.61	170.11	168.77	166.53	164.76
9500	184.98	182.94	181.15	179.56	178.15	175.78	173.91
10000	194.72	192.57	190.68	189.01	187.52	185.03	183.06
11000	214.19	211.83	209.75	207.91	206.27	203.54	201.37
12000	233.66	231.09	228.82	226.81	225.03	222.04	219.67
13000	253.13	250.34	247.88	245.71	243.78	240.54	237.98
14000	272.61	269.60	266.95	264.61	262.53	259.05	256.29
15000	292.08	288.86	286.02	283.51	281.28	277.55	274.59
16000	311.55	308.12	305.09	302.41	300.04	296.05	292.90
17000	331.02	327.37	324.16	321.31	318.79	314.56	311.20
18000	350.49	346.63	343.22	340.21	337.54	333.06	329.51
19000	369.96	365.89	362.29	359.11	356.29	351.56	347.82
20000	389.44	385.15	381.36	378.01	375.04	370.07	366.12
21000	408.91	404.40	400.43	396.91	393.80	388.57	384.43
22000	428.38	423.66	419.50	415.81	412.55	407.07	402.73
23000	447.85	442.92	438.56	434.71	431.30	425.58	421.04
24000	467.32	462.18	457.63	453.61	450.05	444.08	439.35
25000	486.80	481.43	476.70	472.51	468.81	462.58	457.65
26000	506.27	500.69	495.77	491.42	487.56	481.09	475.96
27000	525.74	519.95	514.84	510.32	506.31	499.59	494.27
28000	545.21	539.20	533.90	529.22	525.06	518.09	512.57
29000	564.68	558.46	552.97	548.12	543.81	536.60	530.88
30000	584.15	577.72	572.04	567.02	562.57	555.10	549.18
31000	603.63	596.98	591.11	585.92	581.32	573.61	567.49
32000	623.10	616.23	610.18	604.82	600.07	592.11	585.80
33000	642.57	635.49	629.24	623.72	618.82	610.61	604.10
34000	662.04	654.75	648.31	642.62	637.58	629.12	622.41
35000	681.51	674.01	667.38	661.52	656.33	647.62	640.71
40000	778.87	770.29	762.72	756.02	750.09	740.14	732.24
45000	876.23	866.58	858.06	850.53	843.85	832.65	823.78
50000	973.59	962.86	953.40	945.03	937.61	925.17	915.31
55000	1070.95	1059.15	1048.74	1039.53	1031.37	1017.69	1006.84
60000	1168.31	1155.44	1144.08	1134.04	1125.13	1110.20	1098.37
65000	1265.67	1251.72	1239.42	1228.54	1218.89	1202.72	1189.90
70000	1363.03	1348.01	1334.76	1323.04	1312.66	1295.24	1281.43

21½% Monthly Loan Payments

LOAN AMOUNT	½ YEAR	1 YEAR	1½ YEARS	2 YEARS	2½ YEARS	3 YEARS	3½ YEARS
100	17.73	9.34	6.55	5.16	4.34	3.79	3.41
200	35.45	18.67	13.10	10.33	8.68	7.59	6.82
300	53.18	28.01	19.65	15.49	13.01	11.38	10.23
400	70.91	37.34	26.19	20.65	17.35	15.17	13.63
500	88.64	46.68	32.74	25.82	21.69	18.97	17.04
600	106.36	56.01	39.29	30.98	26.03	22.76	20.45
700	124.09	65.35	45.84	36.14	30.37	26.55	23.86
800	141.82	74.68	52.39	41.31	34.70	30.35	27.27
900	159.55	84.02	58.94	46.47	39.04	34.14	30.68
1000	177.27	93.35	65.49	51.63	43.38	37.93	34.08
1500	265.91	140.03	98.23	77.45	65.07	56.90	51.13
2000	354.55	186.71	130.97	103.26	86.76	75.86	68.17
2500	443.18	233.38	163.72	129.08	108.45	94.83	85.21
3000	531.82	280.06	196.46	154.89	130.14	113.80	102.25
3500	620.45	326.74	229.20	180.71	151.83	132.76	119.29
4000	709.09	373.42	261.95	206.53	173.52	151.73	136.34
4500	797.73	420.09	294.69	232.34	195.21	170.70	153.38
5000	886.36	466.77	327.43	258.16	216.91	189.66	170.42
5500	975.00	513.45	360.18	283.97	238.60	208.63	187.46
6000	1063.64	560.12	392.92	309.79	260.29	227.59	204.50
6500	1152.27	606.80	425.66	335.61	281.98	246.56	221.55
7000	1240.91	653.48	458.41	361.42	303.67	265.53	238.59
7500	1329.55	700.15	491.15	387.24	325.36	284.49	255.63
8000	1418.18	746.83	523.89	413.05	347.05	303.46	272.67
8500	1506.82	793.51	556.64	438.87	368.74	322.42	289.71
9000	1595.45	840.19	589.38	464.68	390.43	341.39	306.76
9500	1684.09	886.86	622.12	490.50	412.12	360.36	323.80
10000	1772.73	933.54	654.87	516.32	433.81	379.32	340.84
11000	1950.00	1026.89	720.35	567.95	477.19	417.26	374.92
12000	2127.27	1120.25	785.84	619.58	520.57	455.19	409.01
13000	2304.54	1213.60	851.32	671.21	563.95	493.12	443.09
14000	2481.82	1306.95	916.81	722.84	607.33	531.05	477.17
15000	2659.09	1400.31	982.30	774.47	650.72	568.98	511.26
16000	2836.36	1493.66	1047.78	826.11	694.10	606.92	545.34
17000	3013.64	1587.02	1113.27	877.74	737.48	644.85	579.43
18000	3190.91	1680.37	1178.76	929.37	780.86	682.78	613.51
19000	3368.18	1773.72	1244.24	981.00	824.24	720.71	647.59
20000	3545.45	1867.08	1309.73	1032.63	867.62	758.65	681.68
21000	3722.73	1960.43	1375.22	1084.26	911.00	796.58	715.76
22000	3900.00	2053.79	1440.70	1135.89	954.38	834.51	749.85
23000	4077.27	2147.14	1506.19	1187.53	997.76	872.44	783.93
24000	4254.54	2240.49	1571.68	1239.16	1041.15	910.37	818.01
25000	4431.82	2333.85	1637.16	1290.79	1084.53	948.31	852.10
26000	4609.09	2427.20	1702.65	1342.42	1127.91	986.24	886.18
27000	4786.36	2520.56	1768.14	1394.05	1171.29	1024.17	920.27
28000	4963.64	2613.91	1833.62	1445.68	1214.67	1062.10	954.35
29000	5140.91	2707.26	1899.11	1497.32	1258.05	1100.04	988.43
30000	5318.18	2800.62	1964.60	1548.95	1301.43	1137.97	1022.52
31000	5495.45	2893.97	2030.08	1600.58	1344.81	1175.90	1056.60
32000	5672.73	2987.33	2095.57	1652.21	1388.19	1213.83	1090.69
33000	5850.00	3080.68	2161.06	1703.84	1431.58	1251.77	1124.77
34000	6027.27	3174.03	2226.54	1755.47	1474.96	1289.70	1158.85
35000	6204.54	3267.39	2292.03	1807.10	1518.34	1327.63	1192.94
40000	7090.91	3734.16	2619.46	2065.26	1735.24	1517.29	1363.36
45000	7977.27	4200.93	2946.89	2323.42	1952.15	1706.95	1533.78
50000	8863.63	4667.70	3274.33	2581.58	2169.05	1896.61	1704.20
55000	9750.00	5134.47	3601.76	2839.74	2385.96	2086.28	1874.61
60000	10636.36	5601.23	3929.19	3097.89	2602.86	2275.94	2045.03
65000	11522.72	6068.00	4256.62	3356.05	2819.77	2465.60	2215.45
70000	12409.09	6534.77	4584.06	3614.21	3036.67	2655.26	2385.87

208

Monthly Loan Payments 21½%

LOAN AMOUNT	4 YEARS	4½ YEARS	5 YEARS	5½ YEARS	6 YEARS	6½ YEARS	7 YEARS
100	3.12	2.91	2.73	2.60	2.48	2.39	2.31
200	6.25	5.81	5.47	5.19	4.97	4.78	4.62
300	9.37	8.72	8.20	7.79	7.45	7.17	6.94
400	12.49	11.62	10.93	10.38	9.93	9.56	9.25
500	15.62	14.53	13.67	12.98	12.42	11.95	11.56
600	18.74	17.43	16.40	15.57	14.90	14.34	13.87
700	21.86	20.34	19.13	18.17	17.38	16.73	16.18
800	24.99	23.24	21.87	20.77	19.86	19.12	18.49
900	28.11	26.15	24.60	23.36	22.35	21.51	20.81
1000	31.24	29.05	27.34	25.96	24.83	23.90	23.12
1500	46.85	43.58	41.00	38.93	37.25	35.85	34.68
2000	62.47	58.11	54.67	51.91	49.66	47.80	46.24
2500	78.09	72.63	68.34	64.89	62.08	59.75	57.80
3000	93.71	87.16	82.01	77.87	74.49	71.69	69.35
3500	109.32	101.68	95.67	90.85	86.91	83.64	80.91
4000	124.94	116.21	109.34	103.83	99.32	95.59	92.47
4500	140.56	130.74	123.01	116.80	111.74	107.54	104.03
5000	156.18	145.26	136.68	129.78	124.15	119.49	115.59
5500	171.79	159.79	150.34	142.76	136.57	131.44	127.15
6000	187.41	174.32	164.01	155.74	148.98	143.39	138.71
6500	203.03	188.84	177.68	168.72	161.40	155.34	150.27
7000	218.65	203.37	191.35	181.69	173.81	167.29	161.83
7500	234.26	217.89	205.02	194.67	186.23	179.24	173.39
8000	249.88	232.42	218.68	207.65	198.64	191.19	184.95
8500	265.50	246.95	232.35	220.63	211.06	203.13	196.50
9000	281.12	261.47	246.02	233.61	223.47	215.08	208.06
9500	296.73	276.00	259.69	246.58	235.89	227.03	219.62
10000	312.35	290.53	273.35	259.56	248.30	238.98	231.18
11000	343.59	319.58	300.69	285.52	273.13	262.88	254.30
12000	374.82	348.63	328.02	311.48	297.96	286.78	277.42
13000	406.06	377.68	355.36	337.43	322.79	310.68	300.54
14000	437.29	406.74	382.70	363.39	347.62	334.57	323.65
15000	468.53	435.79	410.03	389.34	372.45	358.47	346.77
16000	499.76	464.84	437.37	415.30	397.28	382.37	369.89
17000	531.00	493.89	464.70	441.26	422.11	406.27	393.01
18000	562.23	522.95	492.04	467.21	446.94	430.17	416.13
19000	593.47	552.00	519.37	493.17	471.77	454.07	439.24
20000	624.71	581.05	546.71	519.13	496.60	477.96	462.36
21000	655.94	610.10	574.04	545.08	521.43	501.86	485.48
22000	687.18	639.16	601.38	571.04	546.26	525.76	508.60
23000	718.41	668.21	628.71	596.99	571.09	549.66	531.72
24000	749.65	697.26	656.05	622.95	595.92	573.56	554.84
25000	780.88	726.31	683.38	648.91	620.75	597.45	577.95
26000	812.12	755.37	710.72	674.86	645.59	621.35	601.07
27000	843.35	784.42	738.06	700.82	670.42	645.25	624.19
28000	874.59	813.47	765.39	726.78	695.25	669.15	647.31
29000	905.82	842.52	792.73	752.73	720.08	693.05	670.43
30000	937.06	871.58	820.06	778.69	744.91	716.95	693.54
31000	968.29	900.63	847.40	804.65	769.74	740.84	716.66
32000	999.53	929.68	874.73	830.60	794.57	764.74	739.78
33000	1030.76	958.73	902.07	856.56	819.40	788.64	762.90
34000	1062.00	987.79	929.40	882.51	844.23	812.54	786.02
35000	1093.23	1016.84	956.74	908.47	869.06	836.44	809.13
40000	1249.41	1162.10	1093.42	1038.25	993.21	955.93	924.73
45000	1405.59	1307.36	1230.09	1168.03	1117.36	1075.42	1040.32
50000	1561.76	1452.63	1366.77	1297.81	1241.51	1194.91	1155.91
55000	1717.94	1597.89	1503.45	1427.60	1365.66	1314.40	1271.50
60000	1874.12	1743.15	1640.12	1557.38	1489.81	1433.89	1387.09
65000	2030.29	1888.41	1776.80	1687.16	1613.96	1553.38	1502.68
70000	2186.47	2033.68	1913.48	1816.94	1738.11	1672.87	1618.27

21½%   Monthly Loan Payments

LOAN AMOUNT	7½ YEARS	8 YEARS	8½ YEARS	9 YEARS	9½ YEARS	10 YEARS	10½ YEARS
100	2.25	2.19	2.14	2.10	2.06	2.03	2.01
200	4.49	4.38	4.28	4.20	4.13	4.07	4.01
300	6.74	6.57	6.43	6.30	6.19	6.10	6.02
400	8.98	8.76	8.57	8.40	8.26	8.13	8.02
500	11.23	10.95	10.71	10.50	10.32	10.17	10.03
600	13.48	13.14	12.85	12.60	12.39	12.20	12.03
700	15.72	15.33	14.99	14.70	14.45	14.23	14.04
800	17.97	17.52	17.13	16.80	16.51	16.26	16.05
900	20.21	19.71	19.28	18.90	18.58	18.30	18.05
1000	22.46	21.90	21.42	21.00	20.64	20.33	20.06
1500	33.69	32.85	32.13	31.50	30.96	30.50	30.09
2000	44.92	43.80	42.83	42.00	41.29	40.66	40.11
2500	56.15	54.75	53.54	52.51	51.61	50.83	50.14
3000	67.38	65.69	64.25	63.01	61.93	60.99	60.17
3500	78.61	76.64	74.96	73.51	72.25	71.16	70.20
4000	89.84	87.59	85.67	84.01	82.57	81.32	80.23
4500	101.07	98.54	96.38	94.51	92.89	91.49	90.26
5000	112.30	109.49	107.09	105.01	103.22	101.65	100.29
5500	123.53	120.44	117.79	115.51	113.54	111.82	110.31
6000	134.75	131.39	128.50	126.01	123.86	121.98	120.34
6500	145.98	142.34	139.21	136.52	134.18	132.15	130.37
7000	157.21	153.29	149.92	147.02	144.50	142.31	140.40
7500	168.44	164.24	160.63	157.52	154.82	152.48	150.43
8000	179.67	175.18	171.34	168.02	165.14	162.64	160.46
8500	190.90	186.13	182.04	178.52	175.47	172.81	170.49
9000	202.13	197.08	192.75	189.02	185.79	182.97	180.52
9500	213.36	208.03	203.46	199.52	196.11	193.14	190.54
10000	224.59	218.98	214.17	210.02	206.43	203.30	200.57
11000	247.05	240.88	235.59	231.03	227.07	223.63	220.63
12000	269.51	262.78	257.00	252.03	247.72	243.96	240.69
13000	291.97	284.67	278.42	273.03	268.36	264.29	260.74
14000	314.43	306.57	299.84	294.03	289.00	284.62	280.80
15000	336.89	328.47	321.26	315.03	309.65	304.96	300.86
16000	359.35	350.37	342.67	336.04	330.29	325.29	320.92
17000	381.81	372.27	364.09	357.04	350.93	345.62	340.97
18000	404.26	394.16	385.51	378.04	371.57	365.95	361.03
19000	426.72	416.06	406.92	399.04	392.22	386.28	381.09
20000	449.18	437.96	428.34	420.05	412.86	406.61	401.14
21000	471.64	459.86	449.76	441.05	433.50	426.94	421.20
22000	494.10	481.76	471.17	462.05	454.15	447.27	441.26
23000	516.56	503.65	492.59	483.05	474.79	467.60	461.32
24000	539.02	525.55	514.01	504.06	495.43	487.93	481.37
25000	561.48	547.45	535.43	525.06	516.08	508.26	501.43
26000	583.94	569.35	556.84	546.06	536.72	528.59	521.49
27000	606.40	591.25	578.26	567.06	557.36	548.92	541.55
28000	628.86	613.14	599.68	588.06	578.00	569.25	561.60
29000	651.32	635.04	621.09	609.07	598.65	589.58	581.66
30000	673.77	656.94	642.51	630.07	619.29	609.91	601.72
31000	696.23	678.84	663.93	651.07	639.93	630.24	621.77
32000	718.69	700.74	685.34	672.07	660.58	650.57	641.83
33000	741.15	722.63	706.76	693.08	681.22	670.90	661.89
34000	763.61	744.53	728.18	714.08	701.86	691.23	681.95
35000	786.07	766.43	749.60	735.08	722.51	711.56	702.00
40000	898.37	875.92	856.68	840.09	825.72	813.21	802.29
45000	1010.66	985.41	963.77	945.10	928.94	914.87	902.58
50000	1122.96	1094.90	1070.85	1050.12	1032.15	1016.52	1002.86
55000	1235.25	1204.39	1177.94	1155.13	1135.37	1118.17	1103.15
60000	1347.55	1313.88	1285.02	1260.14	1238.58	1219.82	1203.43
65000	1459.84	1423.37	1392.11	1365.15	1341.80	1321.47	1303.72
70000	1572.14	1532.86	1499.19	1470.16	1445.01	1423.12	1404.01

Monthly Loan Payments   21½%

LOAN AMOUNT	11 YEARS	11½ YEARS	12 YEARS	12½ YEARS	13 YEARS	14 YEARS	15 YEARS
100	1.98	1.96	1.94	1.93	1.91	1.89	1.87
200	3.96	3.92	3.88	3.85	3.82	3.77	3.74
300	5.95	5.88	5.83	5.78	5.73	5.66	5.60
400	7.93	7.84	7.77	7.70	7.65	7.55	7.47
500	9.91	9.80	9.71	9.63	9.56	9.44	9.34
600	11.89	11.76	11.65	11.56	11.47	11.32	11.21
700	13.87	13.73	13.60	13.48	13.38	13.21	13.08
800	15.85	15.69	15.54	15.41	15.29	15.10	14.94
900	17.84	17.65	17.48	17.33	17.20	16.98	16.81
1000	19.82	19.61	19.42	19.26	19.11	18.87	18.68
1500	29.73	29.41	29.13	28.89	28.67	28.31	28.02
2000	39.64	39.22	38.84	38.52	38.23	37.74	37.36
2500	49.54	49.02	48.56	48.15	47.79	47.18	46.70
3000	59.45	58.82	58.27	57.78	57.34	56.62	56.04
3500	69.36	68.63	67.98	67.41	66.90	66.05	65.38
4000	79.27	78.43	77.69	77.04	76.46	75.49	74.72
4500	89.18	88.23	87.40	86.66	86.01	84.92	84.06
5000	99.09	98.04	97.11	96.29	95.57	94.36	93.40
5500	109.00	107.84	106.82	105.92	105.13	103.80	102.74
6000	118.91	117.65	116.53	115.55	114.68	113.23	112.09
6500	128.82	127.45	126.25	125.18	124.24	122.67	121.43
7000	138.73	137.25	135.96	134.81	133.80	132.10	130.77
7500	148.63	147.06	145.67	144.44	143.36	141.54	140.11
8000	158.54	156.86	155.38	154.07	152.91	150.98	149.45
8500	168.45	166.66	165.09	163.70	162.47	160.41	158.79
9000	178.36	176.47	174.80	173.33	172.03	169.85	168.13
9500	188.27	186.27	184.51	182.96	181.58	179.28	177.47
10000	198.18	196.08	194.22	192.59	191.14	188.72	186.81
11000	218.00	215.68	213.65	211.85	210.25	207.59	205.49
12000	237.82	235.29	233.07	231.11	229.37	226.46	224.17
13000	257.63	254.90	252.49	250.36	248.48	245.34	242.85
14000	277.45	274.51	271.91	269.62	267.60	264.21	261.53
15000	297.27	294.11	291.34	288.88	286.71	283.08	280.21
16000	317.09	313.72	310.76	308.14	305.83	301.95	298.89
17000	336.90	333.33	330.18	327.40	324.94	320.82	317.57
18000	356.72	352.94	349.60	346.66	344.05	339.70	336.26
19000	376.54	372.55	369.03	365.92	363.17	358.57	354.94
20000	396.36	392.15	388.45	385.18	382.28	377.44	373.62
21000	416.18	411.76	407.87	404.43	401.40	396.31	392.30
22000	435.99	431.37	427.29	423.69	420.51	415.18	410.98
23000	455.81	450.98	446.71	442.95	439.62	434.06	429.66
24000	475.63	470.58	466.14	462.21	458.74	452.93	448.34
25000	495.45	490.19	485.56	481.47	477.85	471.80	467.02
26000	515.27	509.80	504.98	500.73	496.97	490.67	485.70
27000	535.08	529.41	524.40	519.99	516.08	509.54	504.38
28000	554.90	549.01	543.83	539.25	535.19	528.42	523.06
29000	574.72	568.62	563.25	558.51	554.31	547.29	541.74
30000	594.54	588.23	582.67	577.76	573.42	566.16	560.43
31000	614.36	607.84	602.09	597.02	592.54	585.03	579.11
32000	634.17	627.44	621.52	616.28	611.65	603.90	597.79
33000	653.99	647.05	640.94	635.54	630.76	622.78	616.47
34000	673.81	666.66	660.36	654.80	649.88	641.65	635.15
35000	693.63	686.27	679.78	674.06	668.99	660.52	653.83
40000	792.72	784.31	776.90	770.35	764.56	754.88	747.23
45000	891.81	882.34	874.01	866.65	860.13	849.24	840.64
50000	990.90	980.38	971.12	962.94	955.70	943.60	934.04
55000	1089.99	1078.42	1068.23	1059.23	1051.27	1037.96	1027.45
60000	1189.08	1176.46	1165.34	1155.53	1146.85	1132.32	1120.85
65000	1288.17	1274.50	1262.45	1251.82	1242.42	1226.68	1214.26
70000	1387.26	1372.54	1359.57	1348.12	1337.99	1321.04	1307.66

22%   Monthly Loan Payments

LOAN AMOUNT	½ YEAR	1 YEAR	1½ YEARS	2 YEARS	2½ YEARS	3 YEARS	3½ YEARS
100	17.75	9.36	6.57	5.19	4.36	3.82	3.4
200	35.50	18.72	13.15	10.38	8.73	7.64	6.8
300	53.26	28.08	19.72	15.56	13.09	11.46	10.3
400	71.01	37.44	26.29	20.75	17.45	15.28	13.7
500	88.76	46.80	32.86	25.94	21.82	19.10	17.1
600	106.51	56.16	39.44	31.13	26.18	22.91	20.6
700	124.27	65.52	46.01	36.31	30.54	26.73	24.0
800	142.02	74.88	52.58	41.50	34.91	30.55	27.4
900	159.77	84.23	59.16	46.69	39.27	34.37	30.9
1000	177.52	93.59	65.73	51.88	43.63	38.19	34.3
1500	266.28	140.39	98.59	77.82	65.45	57.29	51.5
2000	355.05	187.19	131.46	103.76	87.27	76.38	68.7
2500	443.81	233.99	164.32	129.70	109.08	95.48	85.8
3000	532.57	280.78	197.19	155.63	130.90	114.57	103.0
3500	621.33	327.58	230.05	181.57	152.72	133.67	120.2
4000	710.09	374.38	262.91	207.51	174.53	152.76	137.3
4500	798.85	421.17	295.78	233.45	196.35	171.86	154.5
5000	887.61	467.97	328.64	259.39	218.17	190.95	171.7
5500	976.38	514.77	361.51	285.33	239.98	210.05	188.9
6000	1065.14	561.57	394.37	311.27	261.80	229.14	206.0
6500	1153.90	608.36	427.24	337.21	283.62	248.24	223.2
7000	1242.66	655.16	460.10	363.15	305.43	267.33	240.4
7500	1331.42	701.96	492.96	389.09	327.25	286.43	257.6
8000	1420.18	748.76	525.83	415.03	349.07	305.52	274.7
8500	1508.95	795.55	558.69	440.96	370.88	324.62	291.9
9000	1597.71	842.35	591.56	466.90	392.70	343.71	309.1
9500	1686.47	889.15	624.42	492.84	414.52	362.81	326.3
10000	1775.23	935.94	657.29	518.78	436.33	381.90	343.4
11000	1952.75	1029.54	723.02	570.66	479.97	420.09	377.8
12000	2130.28	1123.13	788.74	622.54	523.60	458.29	412.1
13000	2307.80	1216.73	854.47	674.42	567.23	496.48	446.5
14000	2485.32	1310.32	920.20	726.29	610.86	534.67	480.8
15000	2662.84	1403.92	985.93	778.17	654.50	572.86	515.2
16000	2840.37	1497.51	1051.66	830.05	698.13	611.05	549.5
17000	3017.89	1591.10	1117.39	881.93	741.76	649.24	583.9
18000	3195.41	1684.70	1183.12	933.81	785.40	687.43	618.2
19000	3372.94	1778.29	1248.84	985.68	829.03	725.62	652.6
20000	3550.46	1871.89	1314.57	1037.56	872.66	763.81	686.9
21000	3727.98	1965.48	1380.30	1089.44	916.30	802.00	721.3
22000	3905.51	2059.08	1446.03	1141.32	959.93	840.19	755.6
23000	4083.03	2152.67	1511.76	1193.20	1003.56	878.38	790.0
24000	4260.55	2246.27	1577.49	1245.08	1047.20	916.57	824.3
25000	4438.07	2339.86	1643.22	1296.95	1090.83	954.76	858.7
26000	4615.60	2433.45	1708.94	1348.83	1134.46	992.95	893.0
27000	4793.12	2527.05	1774.67	1400.71	1178.10	1031.14	927.4
28000	4970.64	2620.64	1840.40	1452.59	1221.73	1069.33	961.7
29000	5148.17	2714.24	1906.13	1504.47	1265.36	1107.52	996.1
30000	5325.69	2807.83	1971.86	1556.34	1309.00	1145.71	1030.4
31000	5503.21	2901.43	2037.59	1608.22	1352.63	1183.90	1064.8
32000	5680.74	2995.02	2103.32	1660.10	1396.26	1222.09	1099.1
33000	5858.26	3088.61	2169.05	1711.98	1439.90	1260.28	1133.5
34000	6035.78	3182.21	2234.77	1763.86	1483.53	1298.48	1167.8
35000	6213.30	3275.80	2300.50	1815.74	1527.16	1336.67	1202.1
40000	7100.92	3743.78	2629.15	2075.13	1745.33	1527.62	1373.9
45000	7988.53	4211.75	2957.79	2334.52	1963.49	1718.57	1545.6
50000	8876.15	4679.72	3286.43	2593.91	2181.66	1909.52	1717.4
55000	9763.76	5147.69	3615.08	2853.30	2399.83	2100.47	1889.1
60000	10651.38	5615.66	3943.72	3112.69	2617.99	2291.43	2060.9
65000	11538.99	6083.63	4272.36	3372.08	2836.16	2482.38	2232.6
70000	12426.61	6551.61	4601.01	3631.47	3054.32	2673.33	2404.3

Monthly Loan Payments 22%

LOAN AMOUNT	4 YEARS	4½ YEARS	5 YEARS	5½ YEARS	6 YEARS	6½ YEARS	7 YEARS
100	3.15	2.93	2.76	2.62	2.51	2.42	2.34
200	6.30	5.87	5.52	5.25	5.03	4.84	4.69
300	9.45	8.80	8.29	7.87	7.54	7.26	7.03
400	12.60	11.73	11.05	10.50	10.05	9.68	9.37
500	15.75	14.66	13.81	13.12	12.56	12.10	11.71
600	18.90	17.60	16.57	15.75	15.08	14.52	14.06
700	22.05	20.53	19.33	18.37	17.59	16.94	16.40
800	25.20	23.46	22.10	21.00	20.10	19.36	18.74
900	28.36	26.40	24.86	23.62	22.61	21.78	21.08
1000	31.51	29.33	27.62	26.25	25.13	24.20	23.43
1500	47.26	43.99	41.43	39.37	37.69	36.30	35.14
2000	63.01	58.66	55.24	52.49	50.25	48.40	46.85
2500	78.77	73.32	69.05	65.62	62.82	60.50	58.56
3000	94.52	87.99	82.86	78.74	75.38	72.60	70.28
3500	110.27	102.65	96.67	91.86	87.94	84.70	81.99
4000	126.02	117.32	110.48	104.98	100.50	96.80	93.70
4500	141.78	131.98	124.29	118.11	113.07	108.90	105.42
5000	157.53	146.65	138.09	131.23	125.63	121.00	117.13
5500	173.28	161.31	151.90	144.35	138.19	133.10	128.84
6000	189.04	175.98	165.71	157.48	150.76	145.20	140.56
6500	204.79	190.64	179.52	170.60	163.32	157.30	152.27
7000	220.54	205.31	193.33	183.72	175.88	169.40	163.98
7500	236.30	219.97	207.14	196.85	188.45	181.50	175.69
8000	252.05	234.64	220.95	209.97	201.01	193.60	187.41
8500	267.80	249.30	234.76	223.09	213.57	205.70	199.12
9000	283.55	263.97	248.57	236.21	226.14	217.80	210.83
9500	299.31	278.63	262.38	249.34	238.70	229.90	222.55
10000	315.06	293.30	276.19	262.46	251.26	242.00	234.26
11000	346.57	322.63	303.81	288.71	276.39	266.20	257.69
12000	378.07	351.96	331.43	314.95	301.51	290.40	281.11
13000	409.58	381.29	359.05	341.20	326.64	314.60	304.54
14000	441.09	410.62	386.66	367.45	351.77	338.80	327.96
15000	472.59	439.95	414.28	393.69	376.89	363.00	351.39
16000	504.10	469.28	441.90	419.94	402.02	387.20	374.82
17000	535.60	498.61	469.52	446.18	427.14	411.40	398.24
18000	567.11	527.94	497.14	472.43	452.27	435.60	421.67
19000	598.62	557.26	524.76	498.68	477.40	459.80	445.09
20000	630.12	586.59	552.38	524.92	502.52	484.00	468.52
21000	661.63	615.92	580.00	551.17	527.65	508.20	491.94
22000	693.13	645.25	607.62	577.41	552.77	532.40	515.37
23000	724.64	674.58	635.23	603.66	577.90	556.60	538.80
24000	756.15	703.91	662.85	629.91	603.03	580.80	562.22
25000	787.65	733.24	690.47	656.15	628.15	605.00	585.65
26000	819.16	762.57	718.09	682.40	653.28	629.20	609.07
27000	850.66	791.90	745.71	708.64	678.41	653.40	632.50
28000	882.17	821.23	773.33	734.89	703.53	677.60	655.93
29000	913.68	850.56	800.95	761.14	728.66	701.80	679.35
30000	945.18	879.89	828.57	787.38	753.78	726.00	702.78
31000	976.69	909.22	856.19	813.63	778.91	750.20	726.20
32000	1008.19	938.55	883.81	839.87	804.04	774.40	749.63
33000	1039.70	967.88	911.42	866.12	829.16	798.60	773.06
34000	1071.21	997.21	939.04	892.37	854.29	822.80	796.48
35000	1102.71	1026.54	966.66	918.61	879.41	847.00	819.91
40000	1260.24	1173.19	1104.76	1049.84	1005.05	968.01	937.04
45000	1417.77	1319.84	1242.85	1181.07	1130.68	1089.01	1054.17
50000	1575.30	1466.49	1380.95	1312.30	1256.31	1210.01	1171.30
55000	1732.83	1613.13	1519.04	1443.53	1381.94	1331.01	1288.43
60000	1890.36	1759.78	1657.13	1574.76	1507.57	1452.00	1405.56
65000	2047.90	1906.43	1795.23	1705.99	1633.20	1573.01	1522.69
70000	2205.43	2053.08	1933.32	1837.23	1758.83	1694.01	1639.82

22% Monthly Loan Payments

LOAN AMOUNT	7½ YEARS	8 YEARS	8½ YEARS	9 YEARS	9½ YEARS	10 YEARS	10½ YEARS
100	2.28	2.22	2.17	2.13	2.10	2.07	2.04
200	4.55	4.44	4.35	4.27	4.20	4.13	4.08
300	6.83	6.67	6.52	6.40	6.29	6.20	6.12
400	9.11	8.89	8.70	8.53	8.39	8.27	8.16
500	11.39	11.11	10.87	10.67	10.49	10.33	10.20
600	13.66	13.33	13.04	12.80	12.59	12.40	12.24
700	15.94	15.55	15.22	14.93	14.68	14.47	14.28
800	18.22	17.77	17.39	17.07	16.78	16.54	16.32
900	20.50	20.00	19.57	19.20	18.88	18.60	18.36
1000	22.77	22.22	21.74	21.33	20.98	20.67	20.40
1500	34.16	33.33	32.61	32.00	31.47	31.00	30.60
2000	45.55	44.43	43.48	42.66	41.96	41.34	40.80
2500	56.93	55.54	54.35	53.33	52.44	51.67	51.00
3000	68.32	66.65	65.22	64.00	62.93	62.01	61.20
3500	79.70	77.76	76.10	74.66	73.42	72.34	71.40
4000	91.09	88.87	86.97	85.33	83.91	82.68	81.60
4500	102.48	99.98	97.84	95.99	94.40	93.01	91.81
5000	113.86	111.09	108.71	106.66	104.89	103.35	102.01
5500	125.25	122.19	119.58	117.33	115.38	113.68	112.21
6000	136.64	133.30	130.45	127.99	125.87	124.02	122.41
6500	148.02	144.41	141.32	138.66	136.35	134.35	132.61
7000	159.41	155.52	152.19	149.32	146.84	144.69	142.81
7500	170.79	166.63	163.06	159.99	157.33	155.02	153.01
8000	182.18	177.74	173.93	170.66	167.82	165.36	163.21
8500	193.57	188.85	184.80	181.32	178.31	175.69	173.41
9000	204.95	199.95	195.67	191.99	188.80	186.03	183.61
9500	216.34	211.06	206.54	202.65	199.29	196.36	193.81
10000	227.73	222.17	217.41	213.32	209.78	206.70	204.01
11000	250.50	244.39	239.16	234.65	230.75	227.37	224.41
12000	273.27	266.60	260.90	255.98	251.73	248.04	244.81
13000	296.04	288.82	282.64	277.31	272.71	268.71	265.22
14000	318.82	311.04	304.38	298.65	293.69	289.38	285.62
15000	341.59	333.26	326.12	319.98	314.66	310.05	306.02
16000	364.36	355.47	347.86	341.31	335.64	330.72	326.42
17000	387.14	377.69	369.60	362.64	356.62	351.38	346.82
18000	409.91	399.91	391.35	383.97	377.60	372.05	367.22
19000	432.68	422.12	413.09	405.31	398.57	392.72	387.62
20000	455.45	444.34	434.83	426.64	419.55	413.39	408.02
21000	478.23	466.56	456.57	447.97	440.53	434.06	428.43
22000	501.00	488.78	478.31	469.30	461.51	454.73	448.83
23000	523.77	510.99	500.05	490.63	482.48	475.40	469.23
24000	546.54	533.21	521.79	511.97	503.46	496.07	489.63
25000	569.32	555.43	543.54	533.30	524.44	516.74	510.03
26000	592.09	577.64	565.28	554.63	545.42	537.41	530.43
27000	614.86	599.86	587.02	575.96	566.39	558.08	550.83
28000	637.63	622.08	608.76	597.29	587.37	578.75	571.23
29000	660.41	644.30	630.50	618.63	608.35	599.42	591.63
30000	683.18	666.51	652.24	639.96	629.33	620.09	612.04
31000	705.95	688.73	673.98	661.29	650.30	640.76	632.44
32000	728.73	710.95	695.73	682.62	671.28	661.43	652.84
33000	751.50	733.16	717.47	703.95	692.26	682.10	673.24
34000	774.27	755.38	739.21	725.28	713.24	702.77	693.64
35000	797.04	777.60	760.95	746.62	734.21	723.44	714.04
40000	910.91	888.68	869.66	853.28	839.10	826.79	816.05
45000	1024.77	999.77	978.36	959.94	943.99	930.14	918.05
50000	1138.63	1110.85	1087.07	1066.60	1048.88	1033.48	1020.06
55000	1252.50	1221.94	1195.78	1173.25	1153.77	1136.83	1122.07
60000	1366.36	1333.02	1304.49	1279.91	1258.65	1240.18	1224.07
65000	1480.22	1444.11	1413.19	1386.57	1363.54	1343.53	1326.08
70000	1594.09	1555.20	1521.90	1493.23	1468.43	1446.88	1428.08

214

Monthly Loan Payments 22%

LOAN AMOUNT	11 YEARS	11½ YEARS	12 YEARS	12½ YEARS	13 YEARS	14 YEARS	15 YEARS
100	2.02	2.00	1.98	1.96	1.95	1.92	1.91
200	4.03	3.99	3.96	3.92	3.90	3.85	3.81
300	6.05	5.99	5.93	5.89	5.84	5.77	5.72
400	8.07	7.98	7.91	7.85	7.79	7.70	7.62
500	10.08	9.98	9.89	9.81	9.74	9.62	9.53
600	12.10	11.98	11.87	11.77	11.69	11.55	11.43
700	14.12	13.97	13.85	13.73	13.63	13.47	13.34
800	16.13	15.97	15.82	15.70	15.58	15.39	15.25
900	18.15	17.96	17.80	17.66	17.53	17.32	17.15
1000	20.17	19.96	19.78	19.62	19.48	19.24	19.06
1500	30.25	29.94	29.67	29.43	29.22	28.86	28.59
2000	40.33	39.92	39.56	39.24	38.96	38.49	38.12
2500	50.42	49.90	49.45	49.05	48.70	48.11	47.64
3000	60.50	59.88	59.34	58.86	58.43	57.73	57.17
3500	70.58	69.86	69.23	68.67	68.17	67.35	66.70
4000	80.67	79.84	79.12	78.48	77.91	76.97	76.23
4500	90.75	89.82	89.01	88.29	87.65	86.59	85.76
5000	100.83	99.80	98.89	98.10	97.39	96.21	95.29
5500	110.91	109.78	108.78	107.91	107.13	105.84	104.82
6000	121.00	119.76	118.67	117.72	116.87	115.46	114.35
6500	131.08	129.74	128.56	127.52	126.61	125.08	123.87
7000	141.16	139.72	138.45	137.33	136.35	134.70	133.40
7500	151.25	149.70	148.34	147.14	146.09	144.32	142.93
8000	161.33	159.68	158.23	156.95	155.82	153.95	152.46
8500	171.41	169.66	168.12	166.76	165.56	163.56	161.99
9000	181.50	179.64	178.01	176.57	175.30	173.18	171.52
9500	191.58	189.62	187.90	186.38	185.04	182.81	181.05
10000	201.66	199.60	197.79	196.19	194.78	192.43	190.58
11000	221.83	219.56	217.57	215.81	214.26	211.67	209.63
12000	242.00	239.52	237.35	235.43	233.74	230.91	228.69
13000	262.16	259.48	257.13	255.05	253.22	250.16	247.75
14000	282.33	279.44	276.91	274.67	272.69	269.40	266.81
15000	302.49	299.40	296.68	294.29	292.17	288.64	285.86
16000	322.66	319.36	316.46	313.91	311.65	307.88	304.92
17000	342.83	339.32	336.24	333.53	331.13	327.13	323.98
18000	362.99	359.28	356.02	353.15	350.61	346.37	343.04
19000	383.16	379.24	375.80	372.76	370.08	365.61	362.09
20000	403.33	399.20	395.58	392.38	389.56	384.85	381.15
21000	423.49	419.16	415.36	412.00	409.04	404.10	400.21
22000	443.66	439.12	435.14	431.62	428.52	423.34	419.27
23000	463.82	459.08	454.92	451.24	448.00	442.58	438.32
24000	483.99	479.04	474.69	470.86	467.47	461.83	457.38
25000	504.16	499.00	494.47	490.48	486.95	481.07	476.44
26000	524.32	518.97	514.25	510.10	506.43	500.31	495.50
27000	544.49	538.93	534.03	529.72	525.91	519.55	514.55
28000	564.66	558.89	553.81	549.34	545.39	538.80	533.61
29000	584.82	578.85	573.59	568.96	564.86	558.04	552.67
30000	604.99	598.81	593.37	588.58	584.34	577.28	571.73
31000	625.15	618.77	613.15	608.19	603.82	596.52	590.78
32000	645.32	638.73	632.93	627.81	623.30	615.77	609.84
33000	665.49	658.69	652.70	647.43	642.78	635.01	628.90
34000	685.65	678.65	672.48	667.05	662.26	654.25	647.96
35000	705.82	698.61	692.26	686.67	681.73	673.50	667.01
40000	806.65	798.41	791.16	784.77	779.12	769.71	762.30
45000	907.48	898.21	890.05	882.86	876.51	865.92	857.59
50000	1008.31	998.01	988.95	980.96	973.90	962.14	952.88
55000	1109.15	1097.81	1087.84	1079.05	1071.29	1058.35	1048.17
60000	1209.98	1197.61	1186.74	1177.15	1168.69	1154.56	1143.45
65000	1310.81	1297.41	1285.63	1275.25	1266.08	1250.78	1238.74
70000	1411.64	1397.21	1384.53	1373.34	1363.47	1346.99	1334.03

22½%   Monthly Loan Payments

LOAN AMOUNT	½ YEAR	1 YEAR	1½ YEARS	2 YEARS	2½ YEARS	3 YEARS	3½ YEAR
100	17.78	9.38	6.60	5.21	4.39	3.84	3.
200	35.55	18.77	13.19	10.43	8.78	7.69	6.
300	53.33	28.15	19.79	15.64	13.17	11.53	10.
400	71.11	37.53	26.39	20.85	17.55	15.38	13.
500	88.89	46.92	32.99	26.06	21.94	19.22	17.
600	106.66	56.30	39.58	31.28	26.33	23.07	20.
700	124.44	65.68	46.18	36.49	30.72	26.91	24.
800	142.22	75.07	52.78	41.70	35.11	30.76	27.
900	160.00	84.45	59.37	46.91	39.50	34.60	31.
1000	177.77	93.84	65.97	52.13	43.89	38.45	34.
1500	266.66	140.75	98.96	78.19	65.83	57.67	51.
2000	355.55	187.67	131.94	104.25	87.77	76.90	69.
2500	444.43	234.59	164.93	130.31	109.72	96.12	86.
3000	533.32	281.51	197.91	156.38	131.66	115.35	103.
3500	622.21	328.42	230.90	182.44	153.60	134.57	121.
4000	711.09	375.34	263.89	208.50	175.54	153.80	138.
4500	799.98	422.26	296.87	234.56	197.49	173.02	155.
5000	888.87	469.18	329.86	260.63	219.43	192.25	173.
5500	977.75	516.09	362.84	286.69	241.37	211.47	190.
6000	1066.64	563.01	395.83	312.75	263.32	230.70	207.
6500	1155.53	609.93	428.81	338.82	285.26	249.92	224.
7000	1244.41	656.85	461.80	364.88	307.20	269.15	242.
7500	1333.30	703.76	494.78	390.94	329.15	288.37	259.
8000	1422.19	750.68	527.77	417.00	351.09	307.60	276.
8500	1511.07	797.60	560.76	443.07	373.03	326.82	294.
9000	1599.96	844.52	593.74	469.13	394.98	346.05	311.
9500	1688.85	891.43	626.73	495.19	416.92	365.27	328.
10000	1777.73	938.35	659.71	521.25	438.86	384.50	346.
11000	1955.51	1032.19	725.68	573.38	482.75	422.95	380.
12000	2133.28	1126.02	791.66	625.50	526.63	461.40	415.
13000	2311.05	1219.86	857.63	677.63	570.52	499.84	449.
14000	2488.83	1313.69	923.60	729.76	614.41	538.29	484.
15000	2666.60	1407.53	989.57	781.88	658.29	576.74	519.
16000	2844.38	1501.36	1055.54	834.01	702.18	615.19	553.
17000	3022.15	1595.20	1121.51	886.13	746.06	653.64	588.
18000	3199.92	1689.03	1187.48	938.26	789.95	692.09	623.
19000	3377.70	1782.87	1253.45	990.38	833.84	730.54	657.
20000	3555.47	1876.70	1319.43	1042.51	877.72	768.99	692.
21000	3733.24	1970.54	1385.40	1094.63	921.61	807.44	726.
22000	3911.02	2064.37	1451.37	1146.76	965.50	845.89	761.
23000	4088.79	2158.21	1517.34	1198.88	1009.38	884.34	796.
24000	4266.56	2252.04	1583.31	1251.01	1053.27	922.79	830.
25000	4444.34	2345.88	1649.28	1303.13	1097.15	961.24	865.
26000	4622.11	2439.71	1715.25	1355.26	1141.04	999.69	899.
27000	4799.88	2533.55	1781.22	1407.39	1184.93	1038.14	934.
28000	4977.66	2627.39	1847.20	1459.51	1228.81	1076.59	969.
29000	5155.43	2721.22	1913.17	1511.64	1272.70	1115.04	1003.
30000	5333.20	2815.06	1979.14	1563.76	1316.58	1153.49	1038.
31000	5510.98	2908.89	2045.11	1615.89	1360.47	1191.94	1073.
32000	5688.75	3002.73	2111.08	1668.01	1404.36	1230.39	1107.
33000	5866.52	3096.56	2177.05	1720.14	1448.24	1268.84	1142.
34000	6044.30	3190.40	2243.02	1772.26	1492.13	1307.29	1176.
35000	6222.07	3284.23	2308.99	1824.39	1536.02	1345.74	1211.
40000	7110.94	3753.41	2638.85	2085.02	1755.45	1537.98	1384.
45000	7999.81	4222.58	2968.71	2345.64	1974.88	1730.23	1557.
50000	8888.67	4691.76	3298.56	2606.27	2194.31	1922.48	1730.
55000	9777.54	5160.94	3628.42	2866.90	2413.74	2114.73	1903.
60000	10666.41	5630.11	3958.28	3127.52	2633.17	2306.98	2076.
65000	11555.27	6099.29	4288.13	3388.15	2852.60	2499.22	2249.
70000	12444.14	6568.46	4617.99	3648.78	3072.03	2691.47	2422.

Monthly Loan Payments 22½%

LOAN AMOUNT	4 YEARS	4½ YEARS	5 YEARS	5½ YEARS	6 YEARS	6½ YEARS	7 YEARS
100	3.18	2.96	2.79	2.65	2.54	2.45	2.37
200	6.36	5.92	5.58	5.31	5.08	4.90	4.75
300	9.53	8.88	8.37	7.96	7.63	7.35	7.12
400	12.71	11.84	11.16	10.61	10.17	9.80	9.49
500	15.89	14.80	13.95	13.27	12.71	12.25	11.87
600	19.07	17.76	16.74	15.92	15.25	14.70	14.24
700	22.24	20.73	19.53	18.58	17.80	17.15	16.61
800	25.42	23.69	22.32	21.23	20.34	19.60	18.99
900	28.60	26.65	25.11	23.88	22.88	22.05	21.36
1000	31.78	29.61	27.90	26.54	25.42	24.50	23.74
1500	47.67	44.41	41.86	39.81	38.14	36.76	35.60
2000	63.56	59.22	55.81	53.07	50.85	49.01	47.47
2500	79.45	74.02	69.76	66.34	63.56	61.26	59.34
3000	95.33	88.82	83.71	79.61	76.27	73.51	71.21
3500	111.22	103.63	97.66	92.88	88.98	85.76	83.07
4000	127.11	118.43	111.62	106.15	101.70	98.02	94.94
4500	143.00	133.24	125.57	119.42	114.41	110.27	106.81
5000	158.89	148.04	139.52	132.69	127.12	122.52	118.68
5500	174.78	162.85	153.47	145.96	139.83	134.77	130.55
6000	190.67	177.65	167.42	159.22	152.54	147.02	142.41
6500	206.56	192.45	181.38	172.49	165.25	159.28	154.28
7000	222.24	207.26	195.33	185.76	177.97	171.53	166.15
7500	238.34	222.06	209.28	199.03	190.68	183.78	178.02
8000	254.23	236.87	223.23	212.30	203.39	196.03	189.89
8500	270.11	251.67	237.18	225.57	216.10	208.28	201.75
9000	286.00	266.47	251.14	238.84	228.81	220.53	213.62
9500	301.89	281.28	265.09	252.11	241.53	232.79	225.49
10000	317.78	296.08	279.04	265.37	254.24	245.04	237.36
11000	349.56	325.69	306.94	291.91	279.66	269.54	261.09
12000	381.34	355.30	334.85	318.45	305.09	294.05	284.83
13000	413.12	384.91	362.75	344.99	330.51	318.55	308.56
14000	444.89	414.52	390.66	371.52	355.93	343.05	332.30
15000	476.67	444.12	418.56	398.06	381.36	367.56	356.03
16000	508.45	473.73	446.46	424.60	406.78	392.06	379.77
17000	540.23	503.34	474.37	451.14	432.20	416.57	403.51
18000	572.01	532.95	502.27	477.67	457.63	441.07	427.24
19000	603.78	562.56	530.17	504.21	483.05	465.57	450.98
20000	635.56	592.17	558.08	530.75	508.48	490.08	474.71
21000	667.34	621.77	585.98	557.29	533.90	514.58	498.45
22000	699.12	651.38	613.89	583.82	559.32	539.09	522.18
23000	730.90	680.99	641.79	610.36	584.75	563.59	545.92
24000	762.68	710.60	669.69	636.90	610.17	588.09	569.66
25000	794.45	740.21	697.60	663.44	635.59	612.60	593.39
26000	826.23	769.82	725.50	689.97	661.02	637.10	617.13
27000	858.01	799.42	753.41	716.51	686.44	661.60	640.86
28000	889.79	829.03	781.31	743.05	711.87	686.11	664.60
29000	921.57	858.64	809.21	769.59	737.29	710.61	688.33
30000	953.34	888.25	837.12	796.12	762.71	735.12	712.07
31000	985.12	917.86	865.02	822.66	788.14	759.62	735.80
32000	1016.90	947.47	892.93	849.20	813.56	784.12	759.54 •
33000	1048.68	977.07	920.83	875.74	838.98	808.63	783.28
34000	1080.46	1006.68	948.73	902.27	864.41	833.13	807.01
35000	1112.24	1036.29	976.64	928.81	889.83	857.64	830.75
40000	1271.13	1184.33	1116.16	1061.50	1016.95	980.15	949.43
45000	1430.01	1332.37	1255.68	1194.19	1144.07	1102.67	1068.10
50000	1588.91	1480.42	1395.20	1326.87	1271.19	1225.19	1186.78
55000	1747.80	1628.46	1534.72	1459.56	1398.31	1347.71	1305.46
60000	1906.69	1776.50	1674.24	1592.25	1525.43	1470.23	1424.14
65000	2065.58	1924.54	1813.76	1724.94	1652.54	1592.75	1542.82
70000	2224.47	2072.58	1953.28	1857.62	1779.66	1715.27	1661.49

22½% Monthly Loan Payments

LOAN AMOUNT	7½ YEARS	8 YEARS	8½ YEARS	9 YEARS	9½ YEARS	10 YEARS	10½ YEARS
100	2.31	2.25	2.21	2.17	2.13	2.10	2.07
200	4.62	4.51	4.41	4.33	4.26	4.20	4.15
300	6.93	6.76	6.62	6.50	6.39	6.30	6.22
400	9.24	9.02	8.83	8.67	8.53	8.40	8.30
500	11.54	11.27	11.03	10.83	10.66	10.51	10.37
600	13.85	13.52	13.24	13.00	12.79	12.61	12.45
700	16.16	15.78	15.45	15.16	14.92	14.71	14.52
800	18.47	18.03	17.65	17.33	17.05	16.81	16.60
900	20.78	20.28	19.86	19.50	19.18	18.91	18.67
1000	23.09	22.54	22.07	21.66	21.31	21.01	20.75
1500	34.63	33.81	33.10	32.50	31.97	31.52	31.12
2000	46.18	45.08	44.14	43.33	42.63	42.02	41.49
2500	57.72	56.35	55.17	54.16	53.29	52.53	51.87
3000	69.26	67.61	66.20	64.99	63.94	63.03	62.24
3500	80.81	78.88	77.24	75.82	74.60	73.54	72.62
4000	92.35	90.15	88.27	86.65	85.26	84.04	82.99
4500	103.90	101.42	99.31	97.49	95.91	94.55	93.36
5000	115.44	112.69	110.34	108.32	106.57	105.06	103.74
5500	126.98	123.96	121.37	119.15	117.23	115.56	114.11
6000	138.53	135.23	132.41	129.98	127.89	126.07	124.48
6500	150.07	146.50	143.44	140.81	138.54	136.57	134.86
7000	161.62	157.77	154.48	151.65	149.20	147.08	145.23
7500	173.16	169.04	165.51	162.48	159.86	157.58	155.60
8000	184.71	180.31	176.54	173.31	170.51	168.09	165.98
8500	196.25	191.57	187.58	184.14	181.17	178.60	176.35
9000	207.79	202.84	198.61	194.97	191.83	189.10	186.73
9500	219.34	214.11	209.65	205.80	202.49	199.61	197.10
10000	230.88	225.38	220.68	216.64	213.14	210.11	207.47
11000	253.97	247.92	242.75	238.30	234.46	231.12	228.22
12000	277.06	270.46	264.81	259.96	255.77	252.13	248.97
13000	300.15	293.00	286.88	281.63	277.09	273.15	269.71
14000	323.23	315.53	308.95	303.29	298.40	294.16	290.46
15000	346.32	338.07	331.02	324.95	319.71	315.17	311.21
16000	369.41	360.61	353.09	346.62	341.03	336.18	331.96
17000	392.50	383.15	375.15	368.28	362.34	357.19	352.70
18000	415.59	405.69	397.22	389.94	383.66	378.20	373.45
19000	438.67	428.22	419.29	411.61	404.97	399.21	394.20
20000	461.76	450.76	441.36	433.27	426.29	420.22	414.95
21000	484.85	473.30	463.43	454.94	447.60	441.23	435.69
22000	507.94	495.84	485.49	476.60	468.91	462.25	456.44
23000	531.03	518.38	507.56	498.26	490.23	483.26	477.19
24000	554.12	540.92	529.63	519.93	511.54	504.27	497.93
25000	577.20	563.45	551.70	541.59	532.86	525.28	518.68
26000	600.29	585.99	573.77	563.25	554.17	546.29	539.43
27000	623.38	608.53	595.83	584.92	575.48	567.30	560.18
28000	646.47	631.07	617.90	606.58	596.80	588.31	580.92
29000	669.56	653.61	639.97	628.24	618.11	609.32	601.67
30000	692.64	676.14	662.04	649.91	639.43	630.34	622.42
31000	715.73	698.68	684.10	671.57	660.74	651.35	643.17
32000	738.82	721.22	706.17	693.23	682.06	672.36	663.91
33000	761.91	743.76	728.24	714.90	703.37	693.37	684.66
34000	785.00	766.30	750.31	736.56	724.68	714.38	705.41
35000	808.08	788.84	772.38	758.23	746.00	735.39	726.16
40000	923.53	901.53	882.72	866.50	852.57	840.45	829.89
45000	1038.97	1014.22	993.06	974.86	959.14	945.50	933.63
50000	1154.41	1126.91	1103.40	1083.18	1065.71	1050.56	1037.36
55000	1269.85	1239.60	1213.73	1191.50	1172.28	1155.62	1141.10
60000	1385.29	1352.29	1324.07	1299.81	1278.86	1260.67	1244.84
65000	1500.73	1464.98	1434.41	1408.13	1385.43	1365.73	1348.57
70000	1616.17	1577.67	1544.75	1516.45	1492.00	1470.78	1452.31

Monthly Loan Payments 22½%

LOAN AMOUNT	11 YEARS	11½ YEARS	12 YEARS	12½ YEARS	13 YEARS	14 YEARS	15 YEARS
100	2.05	2.03	2.01	2.00	1.98	1.96	1.94
200	4.10	4.06	4.03	4.00	3.97	3.92	3.89
300	6.16	6.09	6.04	5.99	5.95	5.88	5.83
400	8.21	8.13	8.06	7.99	7.94	7.85	7.77
500	10.26	10.16	10.07	9.99	9.92	9.81	9.72
600	12.31	12.19	12.08	11.99	11.91	11.77	11.66
700	14.36	14.22	14.10	13.99	13.89	13.73	13.61
800	16.41	16.25	16.11	15.99	15.88	15.69	15.55
900	18.47	18.28	18.12	17.98	17.86	17.65	17.49
1000	20.52	20.31	20.14	19.98	19.84	19.62	19.44
1500	30.78	30.47	30.21	29.97	29.77	29.42	29.15
2000	41.03	40.63	40.28	39.96	39.69	39.23	38.87
2500	51.29	50.79	50.34	49.95	49.61	49.04	48.59
3000	61.55	60.94	60.41	59.94	59.53	58.85	58.31
3500	71.81	71.10	70.48	69.94	69.45	68.65	68.03
4000	82.07	81.26	80.55	79.93	79.38	78.46	77.74
4500	92.33	91.42	90.62	89.92	89.30	88.27	87.46
5000	102.58	101.57	100.69	99.91	99.22	98.08	97.18
5500	112.84	111.73	110.76	109.90	109.14	107.88	106.90
6000	123.10	121.89	120.83	119.89	119.07	117.69	116.62
6500	133.36	132.05	130.89	129.88	128.99	127.50	126.34
7000	143.62	142.20	140.96	139.87	138.91	137.31	136.05
7500	153.88	152.36	151.03	149.86	148.83	147.12	145.77
8000	164.13	162.52	161.10	159.85	158.75	156.92	155.49
8500	174.39	172.68	171.17	169.84	168.68	166.73	165.21
9000	184.65	182.83	181.24	179.83	178.60	176.54	174.93
9500	194.91	192.99	191.31	189.83	188.52	186.35	184.64
10000	205.17	203.15	201.38	199.82	198.44	196.15	194.36
11000	225.68	223.46	221.51	219.80	218.29	215.77	213.80
12000	246.20	243.78	241.65	239.78	238.13	235.39	233.23
13000	266.72	264.09	261.79	259.76	257.97	255.00	252.67
14000	287.23	284.41	281.93	279.74	277.82	274.62	272.11
15000	307.75	304.72	302.06	299.72	297.66	294.23	291.54
16000	328.27	325.04	322.20	319.71	317.51	313.85	310.98
17000	348.79	345.35	342.34	339.69	337.35	333.46	330.42
18000	369.30	365.67	362.48	359.67	357.20	353.08	349.85
19000	389.82	385.98	382.61	379.65	377.04	372.69	369.29
20000	410.34	406.30	402.75	399.63	396.88	392.31	388.72
21000	430.85	426.61	422.89	419.61	416.73	411.92	408.16
22000	451.37	446.93	443.03	439.60	436.57	431.54	427.60
23000	471.89	467.24	463.17	459.58	456.42	451.16	447.03
24000	492.40	487.56	483.30	479.56	476.26	470.77	466.47
25000	512.92	507.87	503.44	499.54	496.10	490.39	485.90
26000	533.44	528.19	523.58	519.52	515.95	510.00	505.34
27000	553.95	548.50	543.72	539.50	535.79	529.62	524.78
28000	574.47	568.82	563.85	559.49	555.64	549.23	544.21
29000	594.99	589.13	583.99	579.47	575.48	568.85	563.65
30000	615.50	609.45	604.13	599.45	595.33	588.46	583.09
31000	636.02	629.76	624.27	619.43	615.17	608.08	602.52
32000	656.54	650.08	644.40	639.41	635.01	627.69	621.96
33000	677.05	670.39	664.54	659.39	654.86	647.31	641.39
34000	697.57	690.71	684.68	679.38	674.70	666.93	660.83
35000	718.09	711.02	704.82	699.36	694.55	686.54	680.27
40000	820.67	812.60	805.50	799.27	793.77	784.62	777.45
45000	923.26	914.17	906.19	899.17	892.99	882.69	874.63
50000	1025.84	1015.74	1006.88	999.08	992.21	980.77	971.81
55000	1128.42	1117.32	1107.57	1098.99	1091.43	1078.85	1068.99
60000	1231.01	1218.89	1208.26	1198.90	1190.65	1176.93	1166.17
65000	1333.59	1320.47	1308.95	1298.81	1289.87	1275.00	1263.35
70000	1436.17	1422.04	1409.63	1398.72	1389.09	1373.08	1360.53

23%   Monthly Loan Payments

LOAN AMOUNT	½ YEAR	1 YEAR	1½ YEARS	2 YEARS	2½ YEARS	3 YEARS	3½ YEAR
100	17.80	9.41	6.62	5.24	4.41	3.87	3.
200	35.60	18.82	13.24	10.47	8.83	7.74	6.
300	53.41	28.22	19.86	15.71	13.24	11.61	10.
400	71.21	37.63	26.49	20.95	17.66	15.48	13.
500	89.01	47.04	33.11	26.19	22.07	19.35	17.
600	106.81	56.45	39.73	31.42	26.48	23.23	20.
700	124.62	65.85	46.35	36.66	30.90	27.10	24.
800	142.42	75.26	52.97	41.90	35.31	30.97	27.
900	160.22	84.67	59.59	47.14	39.73	34.84	31.
1000	178.02	94.08	66.21	52.37	44.14	38.71	34.
1500	267.04	141.11	99.32	78.56	66.21	58.06	52.
2000	356.05	188.15	132.43	104.75	88.28	77.42	69.
2500	445.06	235.19	165.54	130.93	110.35	96.77	87.
3000	534.07	282.23	198.64	157.12	132.42	116.13	104.
3500	623.08	329.27	231.75	183.31	154.49	135.48	122.
4000	712.10	376.31	264.86	209.49	176.56	154.84	139.
4500	801.11	423.34	297.96	235.68	198.63	174.19	156.
5000	890.12	470.38	331.07	261.87	220.70	193.55	174.
5500	979.13	517.42	364.18	288.05	242.77	212.90	191.
6000	1068.14	564.46	397.29	314.24	264.84	232.26	209.
6500	1157.16	611.50	430.39	340.43	286.91	251.61	226.
7000	1246.17	658.53	463.50	366.61	308.98	270.97	244.
7500	1335.18	705.57	496.61	392.80	331.05	290.32	261.
8000	1424.19	752.61	529.72	418.99	353.12	309.68	279.
8500	1513.20	799.65	562.82	445.17	375.19	329.03	296.
9000	1602.22	846.69	595.93	471.36	397.26	348.39	313.
9500	1691.23	893.73	629.04	497.55	419.33	367.74	331.
10000	1780.24	940.76	662.14	523.73	441.40	387.10	348.
11000	1958.26	1034.84	728.36	576.11	485.54	425.81	383.
12000	2136.29	1128.92	794.57	628.48	529.68	464.52	418.
13000	2314.31	1222.99	860.79	680.85	573.82	503.23	453.
14000	2492.34	1317.07	927.00	733.23	617.96	541.94	488.
15000	2670.36	1411.14	993.22	785.60	662.10	580.65	523.
16000	2848.39	1505.22	1059.43	837.97	706.24	619.36	558.
17000	3026.41	1599.30	1125.64	890.35	750.38	658.07	592.
18000	3204.43	1693.37	1191.86	942.72	794.52	696.77	627.
19000	3382.46	1787.45	1258.07	995.09	838.66	735.48	662.
20000	3560.48	1881.53	1324.29	1047.47	882.80	774.19	697.
21000	3738.51	1975.60	1390.50	1099.84	926.94	812.90	732.
22000	3916.53	2069.68	1456.72	1152.21	971.08	851.61	767.
23000	4094.55	2163.76	1522.93	1204.59	1015.22	890.32	802.
24000	4272.58	2257.83	1589.15	1256.96	1059.36	929.03	837.
25000	4450.60	2351.91	1655.36	1309.33	1103.50	967.74	872.
26000	4628.63	2445.98	1721.57	1361.71	1147.64	1006.45	906.
27000	4806.65	2540.06	1787.79	1414.08	1191.78	1045.16	941.
28000	4984.67	2634.14	1854.00	1466.45	1235.92	1083.87	976.
29000	5162.70	2728.21	1920.22	1518.83	1280.06	1122.58	1011.
30000	5340.72	2822.29	1986.43	1571.20	1324.20	1161.29	1046.
31000	5518.75	2916.37	2052.65	1623.57	1368.34	1200.00	1081.
32000	5696.77	3010.44	2118.86	1675.95	1412.48	1238.71	1116.
33000	5874.79	3104.52	2185.07	1728.32	1456.62	1277.42	1151.
34000	6052.82	3198.59	2251.29	1780.69	1500.76	1316.13	1185.
35000	6230.84	3292.67	2317.50	1833.07	1544.90	1354.84	1220.
40000	7120.96	3763.05	2648.58	2094.94	1765.60	1548.39	1395.
45000	8011.08	4233.43	2979.65	2356.80	1986.30	1741.94	1569.
50000	8901.20	4703.82	3310.72	2618.67	2207.00	1935.49	1744.
55000	9791.32	5174.20	3641.79	2880.53	2427.70	2129.03	1918.
60000	10681.44	5644.58	3972.86	3142.40	2648.40	2322.58	2092.
65000	11571.56	6114.96	4303.93	3404.26	2869.10	2516.13	2267.
70000	12461.68	6585.34	4635.01	3666.13	3089.80	2709.68	2441.

Monthly Loan Payments 23%

LOAN AMOUNT	4 YEARS	4½ YEARS	5 YEARS	5½ YEARS	6 YEARS	6½ YEARS	7 YEARS
100	3.21	2.99	2.82	2.68	2.57	2.48	2.40
200	6.41	5.98	5.64	5.37	5.14	4.96	4.81
300	9.62	8.97	8.46	8.05	7.72	7.44	7.21
400	12.82	11.96	11.28	10.73	10.29	9.92	9.62
500	16.03	14.94	14.10	13.42	12.86	12.40	12.02
600	19.23	17.93	16.91	16.10	15.43	14.89	14.43
700	22.44	20.92	19.73	18.78	18.01	17.37	16.83
800	25.64	23.91	22.55	21.46	20.58	19.85	19.24
900	28.85	26.90	25.37	24.15	23.15	22.33	21.64
1000	32.05	29.89	28.19	26.83	25.72	24.81	24.05
1500	48.08	44.83	42.29	40.25	38.58	37.21	36.07
2000	64.10	59.78	56.38	53.66	51.45	49.62	48.09
2500	80.13	74.72	70.48	67.08	64.31	62.02	60.12
3000	96.15	89.66	84.57	80.49	77.17	74.43	72.14
3500	112.18	104.61	98.67	93.91	90.03	86.83	84.17
4000	128.21	119.55	112.76	107.32	102.89	99.24	96.19
4500	144.23	134.50	126.86	120.74	115.75	111.64	108.21
5000	160.26	149.44	140.95	134.15	128.62	124.05	120.24
5500	176.28	164.39	155.05	147.57	141.48	136.45	132.26
6000	192.31	179.33	169.14	160.98	154.34	148.86	144.28
6500	208.33	194.27	183.24	174.40	167.20	161.26	156.31
7000	224.36	209.22	197.33	187.81	180.06	173.67	168.33
7500	240.39	224.16	211.43	201.23	192.92	186.07	180.35
8000	256.41	239.11	225.52	214.64	205.78	198.48	192.38
8500	272.44	254.05	239.62	228.06	218.65	210.88	204.40
9000	288.46	268.99	253.71	241.47	231.51	223.28	216.42
9500	304.49	283.94	267.81	254.89	244.37	235.69	228.45
10000	320.51	298.88	281.90	268.30	257.23	248.09	240.47
11000	352.57	328.77	310.10	295.14	282.95	272.90	264.52
12000	384.62	358.66	338.29	321.97	308.68	297.71	288.57
13000	416.67	388.55	366.48	348.80	334.40	322.52	312.61
14000	448.72	418.44	394.67	375.63	360.12	347.33	336.66
15000	480.77	448.32	422.86	402.46	385.85	372.14	360.71
16000	512.82	478.21	451.05	429.29	411.57	396.95	384.76
17000	544.88	508.10	479.24	456.12	437.29	421.76	408.80
18000	576.93	537.99	507.43	482.95	463.02	446.57	432.85
19000	608.98	567.88	535.62	509.78	488.74	471.38	456.90
20000	641.03	597.77	563.81	536.61	514.46	496.19	480.94
21000	673.08	627.65	592.00	563.44	540.19	521.00	504.99
22000	705.13	657.54	620.19	590.27	565.91	545.81	529.04
23000	737.19	687.43	648.38	617.10	591.63	570.62	553.09
24000	769.24	717.32	676.57	643.93	617.35	595.43	577.13
25000	801.29	747.21	704.76	670.76	643.08	620.24	601.18
26000	833.34	777.09	732.95	697.59	668.80	645.04	625.23
27000	865.39	806.98	761.14	724.42	694.52	669.85	649.27
28000	897.44	836.87	789.33	751.25	720.25	694.66	673.32
29000	929.49	866.76	817.52	778.08	745.97	719.47	697.37
30000	961.52	896.65	845.71	804.91	771.69	744.28	721.42
31000	993.60	926.54	873.90	831.74	797.42	769.09	745.46
32000	1025.65	956.42	902.10	858.58	823.14	793.90	769.51
33000	1057.70	986.31	930.29	885.41	848.86	818.71	793.56
34000	1089.75	1016.20	958.48	912.24	874.59	843.52	817.60
35000	1121.80	1046.09	986.67	939.07	900.31	868.33	841.65
40000	1282.06	1195.53	1127.62	1073.22	1028.92	992.38	961.89
45000	1442.32	1344.97	1268.57	1207.37	1157.54	1116.42	1082.12
50000	1602.57	1494.41	1409.52	1341.52	1286.16	1240.47	1202.36
55000	1762.83	1643.85	1550.48	1475.68	1414.77	1364.52	1322.60
60000	1923.09	1793.30	1691.43	1609.83	1543.39	1488.56	1442.83
65000	2083.35	1942.74	1832.38	1743.98	1672.00	1612.61	1563.07
70000	2243.60	2092.18	1973.33	1878.13	1800.62	1736.66	1683.30

23% Monthly Loan Payments

LOAN AMOUNT	7½ YEARS	8 YEARS	8½ YEARS	9 YEARS	9½ YEARS	10 YEARS	10½ YEARS
100	2.34	2.29	2.24	2.20	2.17	2.14	2.11
200	4.68	4.57	4.48	4.40	4.33	4.27	4.22
300	7.02	6.86	6.72	6.60	6.50	6.41	6.33
400	9.36	9.14	8.96	8.80	8.66	8.54	8.44
500	11.70	11.43	11.20	11.00	10.83	10.68	10.55
600	14.04	13.72	13.44	13.20	12.99	12.81	12.66
700	16.38	16.00	15.68	15.40	15.16	14.95	14.77
800	18.72	18.29	17.92	17.60	17.32	17.08	16.88
900	21.06	20.58	20.16	19.80	19.49	19.22	18.99
1000	23.41	22.86	22.40	22.00	21.65	21.35	21.10
1500	35.11	34.29	33.59	33.00	32.48	32.03	31.64
2000	46.81	45.72	44.79	43.99	43.31	42.71	42.19
2500	58.51	57.15	55.99	54.99	54.13	53.39	52.74
3000	70.22	68.58	67.19	65.99	64.96	64.06	63.29
3500	81.92	80.01	78.38	76.99	75.79	74.74	73.83
4000	93.62	91.44	89.59	87.99	86.61	85.42	84.38
4500	105.32	102.88	100.78	98.99	97.44	96.10	94.93
5000	117.03	114.31	111.98	109.99	108.27	106.77	105.48
5500	128.73	125.74	123.18	120.99	119.09	117.45	116.03
6000	140.43	137.17	134.38	131.98	129.92	128.13	126.57
6500	152.14	148.60	145.58	142.98	140.74	138.81	137.12
7000	163.84	160.03	156.77	153.98	151.57	149.48	147.67
7500	175.54	171.46	167.97	164.98	162.40	160.16	158.22
8000	187.24	182.89	179.17	175.98	173.22	170.84	168.76
8500	198.95	194.32	190.37	186.98	184.05	181.52	179.31
9000	210.65	205.75	201.57	197.98	194.88	192.19	189.86
9500	222.35	217.18	212.77	208.97	205.70	202.87	200.41
10000	234.06	228.61	223.96	219.97	216.53	213.55	210.95
11000	257.46	251.47	246.36	241.97	238.18	234.90	232.05
12000	280.87	274.33	268.76	263.97	259.84	256.26	253.15
13000	304.27	297.20	291.15	285.97	281.49	277.61	274.24
14000	327.68	320.06	313.55	307.96	303.14	298.97	295.34
15000	351.08	342.92	335.95	329.96	324.80	320.32	316.43
16000	374.49	365.78	358.34	351.96	346.45	341.68	337.53
17000	397.89	388.64	380.74	373.95	368.10	363.03	358.62
18000	421.30	411.50	403.14	395.95	389.75	384.39	379.72
19000	444.71	434.36	425.53	417.95	411.41	405.74	400.81
20000	468.11	457.22	447.93	439.95	433.06	427.10	421.91
21000	491.52	480.09	470.32	461.94	454.71	448.45	443.01
22000	514.92	502.95	492.72	483.94	476.37	469.81	464.10
23000	538.33	525.81	515.12	505.94	498.02	491.16	485.20
24000	561.73	548.67	537.51	527.94	519.67	512.51	506.29
25000	585.14	571.53	559.91	549.93	541.33	533.87	527.39
26000	608.54	594.39	582.31	571.93	562.98	555.22	548.48
27000	631.95	617.25	604.70	593.93	584.63	576.58	569.58
28000	655.35	640.11	627.10	615.93	606.28	597.93	590.67
29000	678.76	662.97	649.50	637.92	627.94	619.29	611.77
30000	702.17	685.84	671.89	659.92	649.59	640.64	632.86
31000	725.57	708.70	694.29	681.92	671.24	662.00	653.96
32000	748.98	731.56	716.68	703.91	692.90	683.35	675.05
33000	772.38	754.42	739.08	725.91	714.55	704.71	696.15
34000	795.79	777.28	761.48	747.91	736.20	726.06	717.25
35000	819.19	800.14	783.87	769.91	757.86	747.42	738.34
40000	936.22	914.45	895.86	879.89	866.12	854.19	843.82
45000	1053.25	1028.75	1007.84	989.88	974.39	960.97	949.30
50000	1170.28	1143.06	1119.82	1099.87	1082.65	1067.74	1054.77
55000	1287.30	1257.37	1231.80	1209.85	1190.92	1174.51	1160.25
60000	1404.33	1371.67	1343.78	1319.84	1299.18	1281.29	1265.73
65000	1521.36	1485.98	1455.77	1429.83	1407.45	1388.06	1371.21
70000	1638.39	1600.28	1567.75	1539.81	1515.71	1494.83	1476.68

Monthly Loan Payments 23%

LOAN AMOUNT	11 YEARS	11½ YEARS	12 YEARS	12½ YEARS	13 YEARS	14 YEARS	15 YEARS
100	2.09	2.07	2.05	2.03	2.02	2.00	1.98
200	4.17	4.13	4.10	4.07	4.04	4.00	3.96
300	6.26	6.20	6.15	6.10	6.06	6.00	5.94
400	8.35	8.27	8.20	8.14	8.08	8.00	7.93
500	10.43	10.34	10.25	10.17	10.11	10.00	9.91
600	12.52	12.40	12.30	12.21	12.13	11.99	11.89
700	14.61	14.47	14.35	14.24	14.15	13.99	13.87
800	16.70	16.54	16.40	16.28	16.17	15.99	15.85
900	18.78	18.60	18.45	18.31	18.19	17.99	17.83
1000	20.87	20.67	20.50	20.35	20.21	19.99	19.82
1500	31.30	31.01	30.75	30.52	30.32	29.99	29.72
2000	41.74	41.34	41.00	40.69	40.42	39.98	39.63
2500	52.17	51.68	51.25	50.87	50.53	49.98	49.54
3000	62.61	62.01	61.50	61.04	60.64	59.97	59.45
3500	73.04	72.35	71.74	71.21	70.74	69.97	69.36
4000	83.48	82.69	81.99	81.38	80.85	79.96	79.27
4500	93.91	93.02	92.24	91.56	90.96	89.96	89.17
5000	104.35	103.36	102.49	101.73	101.06	99.95	99.08
5500	114.78	113.69	112.74	111.90	111.17	109.95	108.99
6000	125.22	124.03	122.99	122.08	121.27	119.94	118.90
6500	135.65	134.37	133.24	132.25	131.38	129.94	128.81
7000	146.09	144.70	143.49	142.42	141.49	139.93	138.72
7500	156.52	155.04	153.74	152.60	151.59	149.93	148.62
8000	166.96	165.37	163.99	162.77	161.70	159.92	158.53
8500	177.39	175.71	174.24	172.94	171.80	169.92	168.44
9000	187.82	186.04	184.49	183.12	181.91	179.91	178.35
9500	198.26	196.38	194.73	193.29	192.02	189.91	188.26
10000	208.69	206.72	204.98	203.46	202.12	199.90	198.17
11000	229.56	227.39	225.48	223.81	222.33	219.89	217.98
12000	250.43	248.06	245.98	244.15	242.55	239.88	237.80
13000	271.30	268.73	266.48	264.50	262.76	259.87	257.62
14000	292.17	289.40	286.98	284.85	282.97	279.86	277.43
15000	313.04	310.07	307.48	305.19	303.18	299.85	297.25
16000	333.91	330.75	327.97	325.54	323.40	319.84	317.07
17000	354.78	351.42	348.47	345.88	343.61	339.83	336.88
18000	375.65	372.09	368.97	366.23	363.82	359.82	356.70
19000	396.52	392.76	389.47	386.58	384.03	379.81	376.52
20000	417.39	413.43	409.97	406.92	404.25	399.80	396.33
21000	438.26	434.10	430.47	427.27	424.46	419.80	416.15
22000	459.13	454.78	450.96	447.62	444.67	439.78	435.97
23000	480.00	475.45	471.46	467.96	464.88	459.77	455.78
24000	500.87	496.12	491.96	488.31	485.09	479.77	475.60
25000	521.73	516.79	512.46	508.65	505.31	499.75	495.42
26000	542.60	537.46	532.96	529.00	525.52	519.74	515.23
27000	563.47	558.13	553.46	549.35	545.73	539.73	535.05
28000	584.34	578.81	573.95	569.69	565.94	559.72	554.87
29000	605.21	599.48	594.45	590.04	586.16	579.71	574.68
30000	626.08	620.15	614.95	610.39	606.37	599.70	594.50
31000	646.95	640.82	635.45	630.73	626.58	619.69	614.32
32000	667.82	661.49	655.95	651.08	646.79	639.68	634.13
33000	688.69	682.16	676.45	671.42	667.00	659.67	653.95
34000	709.56	702.84	696.94	691.77	687.22	679.66	673.77
35000	730.43	723.51	717.44	712.12	707.43	699.65	693.58
40000	834.78	826.87	819.93	813.85	808.49	799.60	792.67
45000	939.12	930.22	922.43	915.58	909.55	899.55	891.75
50000	1043.47	1033.58	1024.92	1017.31	1010.61	999.50	990.83
55000	1147.82	1136.94	1127.41	1119.04	1111.67	1099.45	1089.91
60000	1252.16	1240.30	1229.90	1220.77	1212.74	1199.40	1189.00
65000	1356.51	1343.66	1332.39	1322.50	1313.80	1299.36	1288.08
70000	1460.86	1447.02	1434.89	1424.23	1414.86	1399.31	1387.16

23½%   Monthly Loan Payments

LOAN AMOUNT	½ YEAR	1 YEAR	1½ YEARS	2 YEARS	2½ YEARS	3 YEARS	3½ YEARS
100	17.83	9.43	6.65	5.26	4.44	3.90	3.5
200	35.65	18.86	13.29	10.52	8.88	7.79	7.0
300	53.48	28.30	19.94	15.79	13.32	11.69	10.5
400	71.31	37.73	26.58	21.05	17.76	15.59	14.0
500	89.14	47.16	33.23	26.31	22.20	19.49	17.5
600	106.96	56.59	39.87	31.57	26.64	23.38	21.0
700	124.79	66.02	46.52	36.84	31.08	27.28	24.6
800	142.62	75.45	53.17	42.10	35.52	31.18	28.1
900	160.45	84.89	59.81	47.36	39.96	35.07	31.6
1000	178.27	94.32	66.46	52.62	44.39	38.97	35.1
1500	267.41	141.48	99.69	78.93	66.59	58.46	52.7
2000	356.55	188.64	132.92	105.24	88.79	77.94	70.3
2500	445.69	235.79	166.14	131.55	110.99	97.43	87.8
3000	534.82	282.95	199.37	157.87	133.18	116.91	105.4
3500	623.96	330.11	232.60	184.18	155.38	136.40	123.0
4000	713.10	377.27	265.83	210.49	177.58	155.88	140.5
4500	802.24	424.43	299.06	236.80	199.78	175.37	158.1
5000	891.37	471.59	332.29	263.11	221.97	194.85	175.7
5500	980.51	518.75	365.52	289.42	244.17	214.34	193.3
6000	1069.65	565.91	398.75	315.73	266.37	233.82	210.8
6500	1158.79	613.07	431.98	342.04	288.56	253.31	228.4
7000	1247.92	660.22	465.21	368.35	310.76	272.80	246.0
7500	1337.06	707.38	498.43	394.66	332.96	292.28	263.6
8000	1426.20	754.54	531.66	420.97	355.16	311.77	281.1
8500	1515.34	801.70	564.89	447.29	377.35	331.25	298.7
9000	1604.47	848.86	598.12	473.60	399.55	350.74	316.3
9500	1693.61	896.02	631.35	499.91	421.75	370.22	333.9
10000	1782.50	943.18	664.58	526.22	443.95	389.71	351.4
11000	1961.02	1037.50	731.04	578.84	488.34	428.68	386.6
12000	2139.30	1131.81	797.50	631.46	532.73	467.65	421.7
13000	2317.57	1226.13	863.95	684.08	577.13	506.62	456.9
14000	2495.85	1320.45	930.41	736.71	621.52	545.59	492.0
15000	2674.12	1414.77	996.87	789.33	665.92	584.56	527.2
16000	2852.40	1509.08	1063.33	841.95	710.31	623.53	562.3
17000	3030.67	1603.40	1129.79	894.57	754.71	662.50	597.5
18000	3208.95	1697.72	1196.24	947.19	799.10	701.47	632.6
19000	3387.22	1792.04	1262.70	999.82	843.50	740.45	667.8
20000	3565.50	1886.36	1329.16	1052.44	887.89	779.42	702.9
21000	3743.77	1980.67	1395.62	1105.06	932.28	818.39	738.1
22000	3922.05	2074.99	1462.08	1157.68	976.68	857.36	773.2
23000	4100.32	2169.31	1528.53	1210.30	1021.07	896.33	808.4
24000	4278.60	2263.63	1594.99	1262.92	1065.47	935.30	843.5
25000	4456.87	2357.94	1661.45	1315.55	1109.86	974.27	878.7
26000	4635.15	2452.26	1727.91	1368.17	1154.26	1013.24	913.8
27000	4813.42	2546.58	1794.37	1420.79	1198.65	1052.21	949.0
28000	4991.70	2640.90	1860.82	1473.41	1243.05	1091.18	984.1
29000	5169.97	2735.22	1927.28	1526.03	1287.44	1130.15	1019.3
30000	5348.25	2829.53	1993.74	1578.66	1331.84	1169.12	1054.4
31000	5526.52	2923.85	2060.20	1631.28	1376.23	1208.09	1089.6
32000	5704.80	3018.17	2126.66	1683.90	1420.62	1247.07	1124.7
33000	5883.07	3112.49	2193.11	1736.52	1465.02	1286.04	1159.9
34000	6061.35	3206.80	2259.57	1789.14	1509.41	1325.01	1195.0
35000	6239.62	3301.12	2326.03	1841.77	1553.81	1363.98	1230.1
40000	7130.99	3772.71	2658.32	2104.87	1775.78	1558.83	1405.9
45000	8022.37	4244.30	2990.61	2367.98	1997.75	1753.69	1581.6
50000	8913.74	4715.89	3322.90	2631.09	2219.73	1948.54	1757.4
55000	9805.12	5187.48	3655.19	2894.20	2441.70	2143.39	1933.1
60000	10696.49	5659.07	3987.48	3157.31	2663.67	2338.25	2108.9
65000	11587.87	6130.66	4319.77	3420.42	2885.64	2533.10	2284.6
70000	12479.24	6602.25	4652.06	3683.53	3107.62	2727.96	2460.3

Monthly Loan Payments 23½%

LOAN AMOUNT	4 YEARS	4½ YEARS	5 YEARS	5½ YEARS	6 YEARS	6½ YEARS	7 YEARS
100	3.23	3.02	2.85	2.71	2.60	2.51	2.44
200	6.47	6.03	5.70	5.43	5.20	5.02	4.87
300	9.70	9.05	8.54	8.14	7.81	7.54	7.31
400	12.93	12.07	11.39	10.85	10.41	10.05	9.74
500	16.16	15.08	14.24	13.56	13.01	12.56	12.18
600	19.40	18.10	17.09	16.28	15.61	15.07	14.62
700	22.63	21.12	19.93	18.99	18.22	17.58	17.05
800	25.86	24.14	22.78	21.70	20.82	20.09	19.49
900	29.09	27.15	25.63	24.41	23.42	22.61	21.92
1000	32.33	30.17	28.48	27.13	26.02	25.12	24.36
1500	48.49	45.25	42.72	40.69	39.04	37.68	36.54
2000	64.65	60.34	56.96	54.25	52.05	50.23	48.72
2500	80.82	75.42	71.20	67.81	65.06	62.79	60.90
3000	96.98	90.51	85.44	81.38	78.07	75.35	73.08
3500	113.14	105.59	99.67	94.94	91.08	87.91	85.26
4000	129.30	120.68	113.91	108.50	104.10	100.47	97.44
4500	145.47	135.76	128.15	122.06	117.11	113.03	109.62
5000	161.63	150.85	142.39	135.63	130.12	125.58	121.80
5500	177.79	165.93	156.63	149.19	143.13	138.14	133.98
6000	193.96	181.02	170.87	162.75	156.14	150.70	146.16
6500	210.12	196.10	185.11	176.31	169.16	163.26	158.34
7000	226.28	211.19	199.35	189.88	182.17	175.82	170.52
7500	242.45	226.27	213.59	203.44	195.18	188.38	182.70
8000	258.61	241.36	227.83	217.00	208.19	200.93	194.88
8500	274.77	256.44	242.07	230.56	221.21	213.49	207.07
9000	290.93	271.53	256.31	244.13	234.22	226.05	219.25
9500	307.10	286.61	270.55	257.69	247.23	238.61	231.43
10000	323.26	301.70	284.78	271.25	260.24	251.17	243.61
11000	355.59	331.87	313.26	298.38	286.27	276.28	267.97
12000	387.91	362.03	341.74	325.50	312.29	301.40	292.33
13000	420.24	392.20	370.22	352.63	338.31	326.52	316.69
14000	452.56	422.37	398.70	379.75	364.34	351.63	341.05
15000	484.89	452.54	427.18	406.88	390.36	376.75	365.41
16000	517.22	482.71	455.66	434.00	416.39	401.87	389.77
17000	549.54	512.88	484.13	461.13	442.41	426.98	414.13
18000	581.87	543.05	512.61	488.25	468.43	452.10	438.49
19000	614.19	573.22	541.09	515.38	494.46	477.22	462.85
20000	646.52	603.39	569.57	542.50	520.48	502.33	487.21
21000	678.85	633.56	598.05	569.63	546.51	527.45	511.57
22000	711.17	663.73	626.53	596.75	572.53	552.57	535.93
23000	743.50	693.90	655.01	623.88	598.56	577.68	560.29
24000	775.82	724.07	683.48	651.00	624.58	602.80	584.65
25000	808.15	754.24	711.96	678.13	650.60	627.92	609.01
26000	840.48	784.41	740.44	705.25	676.63	653.03	633.38
27000	872.80	814.58	768.92	732.38	702.65	678.15	657.74
28000	905.13	844.75	797.40	759.50	728.68	703.27	682.10
29000	937.46	874.92	825.88	786.63	754.70	728.38	706.46
30000	969.78	905.09	854.35	813.75	780.72	753.50	730.82
31000	1002.11	935.26	882.83	840.88	806.75	778.62	755.18
32000	1034.43	965.43	911.31	868.00	832.77	803.73	779.54
33000	1066.76	995.60	939.79	895.13	858.80	828.85	803.90
34000	1099.09	1025.77	968.27	922.25	884.82	853.97	828.26
35000	1131.41	1055.94	996.75	949.38	910.84	879.08	852.62
40000	1293.04	1206.78	1139.14	1085.00	1040.97	1004.67	974.42
45000	1454.67	1357.63	1281.53	1220.63	1171.09	1130.25	1096.23
50000	1616.30	1508.48	1423.92	1356.25	1301.21	1255.84	1218.03
55000	1777.93	1659.33	1566.32	1491.88	1431.33	1381.42	1339.83
60000	1939.56	1810.17	1708.71	1627.50	1561.45	1507.00	1461.64
65000	2101.19	1961.02	1851.10	1763.13	1691.57	1632.59	1583.44
70000	2262.82	2111.87	1993.49	1898.75	1821.69	1758.17	1705.24

23½%   Monthly Loan Payments

LOAN AMOUNT	7½ YEARS	8 YEARS	8½ YEARS	9 YEARS	9½ YEARS	10 YEARS	10½ YEARS
100	2.37	2.32	2.27	2.23	2.20	2.17	2.14
200	4.74	4.64	4.55	4.47	4.40	4.34	4.29
300	7.12	6.96	6.82	6.70	6.60	6.51	6.43
400	9.49	9.27	9.09	8.93	8.80	8.68	8.58
500	11.86	11.59	11.36	11.17	11.00	10.85	10.72
600	14.23	13.91	13.64	13.40	13.20	13.02	12.87
700	16.61	16.23	15.91	15.63	15.40	15.19	15.01
800	18.98	18.55	18.18	17.87	17.60	17.36	17.16
900	21.35	20.87	20.45	20.10	19.79	19.53	19.30
1000	23.72	23.19	22.73	22.33	21.99	21.70	21.45
1500	35.59	34.78	34.09	33.50	32.99	32.55	32.17
2000	47.45	46.37	45.45	44.67	43.99	43.40	42.89
2500	59.31	57.97	56.82	55.83	54.98	54.25	53.61
3000	71.17	69.56	68.18	67.00	65.98	65.10	64.34
3500	83.04	81.15	79.54	78.17	76.98	75.95	75.06
4000	94.90	92.74	90.91	89.33	87.98	86.80	85.78
4500	106.76	104.34	102.27	100.50	98.97	97.65	96.51
5000	118.62	115.93	113.63	111.67	109.97	108.50	107.23
5500	130.49	127.52	125.00	122.83	120.97	119.35	117.95
6000	142.35	139.12	136.36	134.00	131.96	130.20	128.67
6500	154.21	150.71	147.72	145.17	142.96	141.05	139.40
7000	166.07	162.30	159.09	156.33	153.96	151.90	150.12
7500	177.94	173.90	170.45	167.50	164.95	162.75	160.84
8000	189.80	185.49	181.82	178.66	175.95	173.60	171.57
8500	201.66	197.08	193.18	189.83	186.95	184.45	182.29
9000	213.52	208.68	204.54	201.00	197.94	195.30	193.01
9500	225.39	220.27	215.91	212.16	208.94	206.15	203.73
10000	237.25	231.86	227.27	223.33	219.94	217.00	214.46
11000	260.97	255.05	250.00	245.66	241.93	238.70	235.90
12000	284.70	278.23	272.72	268.00	263.93	260.41	257.35
13000	308.42	301.42	295.45	290.33	285.92	282.11	278.79
14000	332.15	324.61	318.18	312.66	307.91	303.81	300.24
15000	355.87	347.79	340.90	335.00	329.91	325.51	321.69
16000	379.60	370.98	363.63	357.33	351.90	347.21	343.13
17000	403.32	394.17	386.36	379.66	373.90	368.91	364.58
18000	427.05	417.35	409.08	402.00	395.89	390.61	386.02
19000	450.77	440.54	431.81	424.33	417.88	412.31	407.47
20000	474.50	463.72	454.54	446.66	439.88	434.01	428.92
21000	498.22	486.91	477.26	468.99	461.87	455.71	450.36
22000	521.95	510.10	499.99	491.33	483.86	477.41	471.81
23000	545.67	533.28	522.72	513.66	505.86	499.11	493.25
24000	569.40	556.47	545.45	535.99	527.85	520.81	514.70
25000	593.12	579.65	568.17	558.33	549.85	542.51	536.14
26000	616.85	602.84	590.90	580.66	571.84	564.21	557.59
27000	640.57	626.03	613.63	602.99	593.83	585.91	579.04
28000	664.30	649.21	636.35	625.33	615.83	607.61	600.48
29000	688.02	672.40	659.08	647.66	637.82	629.31	621.93
30000	711.75	695.59	681.81	669.99	659.82	651.01	643.37
31000	735.47	718.77	704.53	692.33	681.81	672.71	664.82
32000	759.19	741.96	727.26	714.66	703.80	694.41	686.26
33000	782.92	765.14	749.99	736.99	725.80	716.11	707.71
34000	806.64	788.33	772.71	759.33	747.79	737.81	729.16
35000	830.37	811.52	795.44	781.66	769.78	759.52	750.60
40000	948.99	927.45	909.08	893.32	879.75	868.02	857.83
45000	1067.62	1043.38	1022.71	1004.99	989.72	976.52	965.06
50000	1186.24	1159.31	1136.34	1116.65	1099.69	1085.02	1072.29
55000	1304.87	1275.24	1249.98	1228.32	1209.66	1193.52	1179.52
60000	1423.49	1391.17	1363.61	1339.99	1319.63	1302.03	1286.75
65000	1542.11	1507.10	1477.25	1451.65	1429.60	1410.53	1393.97
70000	1660.74	1623.03	1590.88	1563.32	1539.57	1519.03	1501.20

Monthly Loan Payments 23½%

LOAN AMOUNT	11 YEARS	11½ YEARS	12 YEARS	12½ YEARS	13 YEARS	14 YEARS	15 YEARS
100	2.12	2.10	2.09	2.07	2.06	2.04	2.02
200	4.24	4.21	4.17	4.14	4.12	4.07	4.04
300	6.37	6.31	6.26	6.21	6.17	6.11	6.06
400	8.49	8.41	8.34	8.29	8.23	8.15	8.08
500	10.61	10.52	10.43	10.36	10.29	10.18	10.10
600	12.73	12.62	12.52	12.43	12.35	12.22	12.12
700	14.86	14.72	14.60	14.50	14.41	14.26	14.14
800	16.98	16.82	16.69	16.57	16.47	16.29	16.16
900	19.10	18.93	18.78	18.64	18.52	18.33	18.18
1000	21.22	21.03	20.86	20.71	20.58	20.37	20.20
1500	31.84	31.55	31.29	31.07	30.87	30.55	30.30
2000	42.45	42.06	41.72	41.43	41.16	40.73	40.40
2500	53.06	52.58	52.15	51.78	51.46	50.92	50.50
3000	63.67	63.09	62.58	62.14	61.75	61.10	60.60
3500	74.28	73.61	73.01	72.49	72.04	71.28	70.70
4000	84.90	84.12	83.44	82.85	82.33	81.47	80.80
4500	95.51	94.64	93.88	93.21	92.62	91.65	90.89
5000	106.12	105.15	104.31	103.56	102.91	101.83	100.99
5500	116.73	115.67	114.74	113.92	113.20	112.02	111.09
6000	127.34	126.18	125.17	124.28	123.49	122.20	121.19
6500	137.96	136.70	135.60	134.63	133.78	132.38	131.29
7000	148.57	147.21	146.03	144.99	144.08	142.57	141.39
7500	159.18	157.73	156.46	155.35	154.37	152.75	151.49
8000	169.79	168.24	166.89	165.70	164.66	162.93	161.59
8500	180.40	178.76	177.32	176.06	174.95	173.12	171.69
9000	191.02	189.27	187.75	186.41	185.24	183.30	181.79
9500	201.63	199.79	198.18	196.77	195.53	193.48	191.89
10000	212.24	210.30	208.61	207.13	205.82	203.67	201.99
11000	233.46	231.34	229.47	227.84	226.41	224.03	222.19
12000	254.69	252.37	250.33	248.55	246.99	244.40	242.39
13000	275.91	273.40	271.19	269.26	267.57	264.77	262.58
14000	297.14	294.43	292.06	289.98	288.15	285.13	282.78
15000	318.36	315.46	312.92	310.69	308.73	305.50	302.98
16000	339.58	336.49	333.78	331.40	329.32	325.87	323.18
17000	360.81	357.52	354.64	352.12	349.90	346.23	343.38
18000	382.03	378.55	375.50	372.83	370.48	366.60	363.58
19000	403.26	399.58	396.36	393.54	391.06	386.97	383.78
20000	424.48	420.61	417.22	414.25	411.65	407.33	403.98
21000	445.70	441.64	438.08	434.97	432.23	427.70	424.18
22000	466.93	462.67	458.95	455.68	452.81	448.06	444.37
23000	488.15	483.70	479.81	476.39	473.39	468.43	464.57
24000	509.38	504.73	500.67	497.10	493.98	488.80	484.77
25000	530.60	525.76	521.53	517.82	514.56	509.16	504.97
26000	551.82	546.79	542.39	538.53	535.14	529.53	525.17
27000	573.05	567.82	563.25	559.24	555.72	549.90	545.37
28000	594.27	588.85	584.11	579.96	576.30	570.26	565.57
29000	615.50	609.88	604.97	600.67	596.89	590.63	585.77
30000	636.72	630.91	625.83	621.38	617.47	611.00	605.97
31000	657.94	651.94	646.70	642.09	638.05	631.36	626.16
32000	679.17	672.98	667.56	662.81	658.63	651.73	646.36
33000	700.39	694.01	688.42	683.52	679.22	672.10	666.56
34000	721.62	715.04	709.28	704.23	699.80	692.46	686.76
35000	742.84	736.07	730.14	724.94	720.38	712.83	706.96
40000	848.96	841.22	834.45	828.51	823.29	814.66	807.95
45000	955.08	946.37	938.75	932.07	926.20	916.50	908.95
50000	1061.20	1051.52	1043.06	1035.63	1029.11	1018.33	1009.94
55000	1167.32	1156.68	1147.36	1139.20	1132.03	1120.16	1110.94
60000	1273.44	1261.83	1251.67	1242.76	1234.94	1221.99	1211.93
65000	1379.56	1366.98	1355.97	1346.32	1337.85	1323.83	1312.92
70000	1485.68	1472.13	1460.28	1449.89	1440.76	1425.66	1413.92

24% Monthly Loan Payments

LOAN AMOUNT	½ YEAR	1 YEAR	1½ YEARS	2 YEARS	2½ YEARS	3 YEARS	3½ YEAR
100	17.85	9.46	6.67	5.29	4.46	3.92	3.5
200	35.71	18.91	13.34	10.57	8.93	7.85	7.
300	53.56	28.37	20.01	15.86	13.39	11.77	10.
400	71.41	37.82	26.68	21.15	17.86	15.69	14.1
500	89.26	47.28	33.35	26.44	22.32	19.62	17.7
600	107.12	56.74	40.02	31.72	26.79	23.54	21.2
700	124.97	66.19	46.69	37.01	31.25	27.46	24.7
800	142.82	75.65	53.36	42.30	35.72	31.39	28.3
900	160.67	85.10	60.03	47.58	40.18	35.31	31.8
1000	178.53	94.56	66.70	52.87	44.65	39.23	35.4
1500	267.79	141.84	100.05	79.31	66.97	58.85	53.1
2000	357.05	189.12	133.40	105.74	89.30	78.47	70.8
2500	446.31	236.40	166.76	132.18	111.62	98.08	88.5
3000	535.58	283.68	200.11	158.61	133.95	117.70	106.3
3500	624.84	330.96	233.46	185.05	156.27	137.31	123.9
4000	714.10	378.24	266.81	211.48	178.60	156.93	141.6
4500	803.37	425.52	300.16	237.92	200.92	176.55	159.3
5000	892.63	472.80	333.51	264.36	223.25	196.16	177.0
5500	981.89	520.08	366.86	290.79	245.57	215.78	194.8
6000	1071.15	567.36	400.21	317.23	267.90	235.40	212.5
6500	1160.42	614.64	433.56	343.66	290.22	255.01	230.2
7000	1249.68	661.92	466.91	370.10	312.55	274.63	247.9
7500	1338.94	709.20	500.27	396.53	334.87	294.25	265.6
8000	1428.21	756.48	533.62	422.97	357.20	313.86	283.3
8500	1517.47	803.76	566.97	449.40	379.52	333.48	301.0
9000	1606.73	851.04	600.32	475.84	401.85	353.10	318.7
9500	1696.00	898.32	633.67	502.28	424.17	372.71	336.4
10000	1785.26	945.60	667.02	528.71	446.50	392.33	354.1
11000	1963.78	1040.16	733.72	581.58	491.15	431.56	389.5
12000	2142.31	1134.72	800.43	634.45	535.80	470.79	425.0
13000	2320.84	1229.27	867.13	687.32	580.45	510.03	460.4
14000	2499.36	1323.83	933.83	740.20	625.10	549.26	495.8
15000	2677.89	1418.39	1000.53	793.07	669.75	588.49	531.2
16000	2856.41	1512.95	1067.23	845.94	714.40	627.73	566.6
17000	3034.94	1607.51	1133.94	898.81	759.05	666.96	602.0
18000	3213.46	1702.07	1200.64	951.68	803.70	706.19	637.5
19000	3391.99	1796.63	1267.34	1004.55	848.35	745.42	672.9
20000	3570.52	1891.19	1334.04	1057.42	893.00	784.66	708.3
21000	3749.04	1985.75	1400.74	1110.29	937.65	823.89	743.7
22000	3927.57	2080.31	1467.45	1163.16	982.30	863.12	779.1
23000	4106.09	2174.87	1534.15	1216.04	1026.95	902.36	814.6
24000	4284.62	2269.43	1600.85	1268.91	1071.60	941.59	850.0
25000	4463.15	2363.99	1667.55	1321.78	1116.25	980.82	885.4
26000	4641.67	2458.55	1734.25	1374.65	1160.90	1020.05	920.8
27000	4820.20	2553.11	1800.96	1427.52	1205.55	1059.29	956.2
28000	4998.72	2647.67	1867.66	1480.39	1250.20	1098.52	991.6
29000	5177.25	2742.23	1934.36	1533.26	1294.85	1137.75	1027.1
30000	5355.77	2836.79	2001.06	1586.13	1339.50	1176.99	1062.5
31000	5534.30	2931.35	2067.77	1639.00	1384.15	1216.22	1097.9
32000	5712.83	3025.91	2134.47	1691.88	1428.80	1255.45	1133.3
33000	5891.35	3120.47	2201.17	1744.75	1473.45	1294.68	1168.7
34000	6069.88	3215.03	2267.87	1797.62	1518.10	1333.92	1204.1
35000	6248.40	3309.59	2334.57	1850.49	1562.75	1373.15	1239.6
40000	7141.03	3782.38	2668.08	2114.84	1786.00	1569.31	1416.6
45000	8033.66	4255.18	3001.59	2379.20	2009.25	1765.48	1593.7
50000	8926.29	4727.98	3335.11	2643.55	2232.50	1961.64	1770.8
55000	9818.92	5200.78	3668.62	2907.91	2455.75	2157.81	1947.9
60000	10711.55	5673.58	4002.13	3172.27	2679.00	2353.97	2125.0
65000	11604.18	6146.37	4335.64	3436.62	2902.24	2550.14	2302.1
70000	12496.81	6619.17	4669.15	3700.98	3125.49	2746.30	2479.2

Monthly Loan Payments 24%

LOAN AMOUNT	4 YEARS	4½ YEARS	5 YEARS	5½ YEARS	6 YEARS	6½ YEARS	7 YEARS
100	3.26	3.05	2.88	2.74	2.63	2.54	2.47
200	6.52	6.09	5.75	5.48	5.27	5.09	4.94
300	9.78	9.14	8.63	8.23	7.90	7.63	7.40
400	13.04	12.18	11.51	10.97	10.53	10.17	9.87
500	16.30	15.23	14.38	13.71	13.16	12.71	12.34
600	19.56	18.27	17.26	16.45	15.80	15.26	14.81
700	22.82	21.32	20.14	19.19	18.43	17.80	17.27
800	26.08	24.36	23.01	21.94	21.06	20.34	19.74
900	29.34	27.41	25.89	24.68	23.69	22.88	22.21
1000	32.60	30.45	28.77	27.42	26.33	25.43	24.68
1500	48.90	45.68	43.15	41.13	39.49	38.14	37.01
2000	65.20	60.90	57.54	54.84	52.65	50.85	49.35
2500	81.50	76.13	71.92	68.55	65.82	63.56	61.69
3000	97.81	91.36	86.30	82.26	78.98	76.28	74.03
3500	114.11	106.58	100.69	95.97	92.14	88.99	86.37
4000	130.41	121.81	115.07	109.68	105.31	101.70	98.70
4500	146.71	137.04	129.46	123.40	118.47	114.42	111.04
5000	163.01	152.26	143.84	137.11	131.63	127.13	123.38
5500	179.31	167.49	158.22	150.82	144.80	139.84	135.72
6000	195.61	182.71	172.61	164.53	157.96	152.55	148.05
6500	211.91	197.94	186.99	178.24	171.12	165.27	160.39
7000	228.21	213.17	201.38	191.95	184.29	177.98	172.73
7500	244.51	228.39	215.76	205.66	197.45	190.69	185.07
8000	260.81	243.62	230.14	219.37	210.61	203.41	197.41
8500	277.12	258.84	244.53	233.08	223.78	216.12	209.74
9000	293.42	274.07	258.91	246.79	236.94	228.83	222.08
9500	309.72	289.30	273.30	260.50	250.10	241.54	234.42
10000	326.02	304.52	287.68	274.21	263.27	254.26	246.76
11000	358.62	334.97	316.45	301.63	289.60	279.68	271.43
12000	391.22	365.43	345.22	329.05	315.92	305.11	296.11
13000	423.82	395.88	373.98	356.48	342.25	330.53	320.79
14000	456.43	426.33	402.75	383.90	368.58	355.96	345.46
15000	489.03	456.78	431.52	411.32	394.90	381.39	370.14
16000	521.63	487.24	460.29	438.74	421.23	406.81	394.81
17000	554.23	517.69	489.06	466.16	447.56	432.24	419.49
18000	586.83	548.14	517.82	493.58	473.88	457.66	444.16
19000	619.43	578.59	546.59	521.00	500.21	483.09	468.84
20000	652.04	609.05	575.36	548.42	526.54	508.52	493.52
21000	684.64	639.50	604.13	575.85	552.86	533.94	518.19
22000	717.24	669.95	632.90	603.27	579.19	559.37	542.87
23000	749.84	700.40	661.66	630.69	605.52	584.79	567.54
24000	782.44	730.85	690.43	658.11	631.84	610.22	592.22
25000	815.05	761.31	719.20	685.53	658.17	635.64	616.90
26000	847.65	791.76	747.97	712.95	684.50	661.07	641.57
27000	880.25	822.21	776.74	740.37	710.82	686.50	666.25
28000	912.85	852.66	805.50	767.79	737.15	711.92	690.92
29000	945.45	883.12	834.27	795.22	763.48	737.35	715.60
30000	978.06	913.57	863.04	822.64	789.80	762.77	740.27
31000	1010.66	944.02	891.81	850.06	816.13	788.20	764.95
32000	1043.26	974.47	920.57	877.48	842.46	813.62	789.63
33000	1075.86	1004.92	949.34	904.90	868.79	839.05	814.30
34000	1108.46	1035.38	978.11	932.32	895.11	864.48	838.98
35000	1141.06	1065.83	1006.88	959.74	921.44	889.90	863.65
40000	1304.07	1218.09	1150.72	1096.85	1053.07	1017.03	987.03
45000	1467.08	1370.35	1294.56	1233.96	1184.71	1144.16	1110.41
50000	1630.09	1522.61	1438.40	1371.06	1316.34	1271.29	1233.79
55000	1793.10	1674.87	1582.24	1508.17	1447.98	1398.42	1357.17
60000	1956.11	1827.14	1726.08	1645.27	1579.61	1525.55	1480.55
65000	2119.12	1979.40	1869.92	1782.38	1711.24	1652.67	1603.93
70000	2282.13	2131.66	2013.76	1919.49	1842.88	1779.80	1727.31

24%   Monthly Loan Payments

LOAN AMOUNT	7½ YEARS	8 YEARS	8½ YEARS	9 YEARS	9½ YEARS	10 YEARS	10½ YEARS
100	2.40	2.35	2.31	2.27	2.23	2.20	2.18
200	4.81	4.70	4.61	4.53	4.47	4.41	4.36
300	7.21	7.05	6.92	6.80	6.70	6.61	6.54
400	9.62	9.41	9.22	9.07	8.93	8.82	8.72
500	12.02	11.76	11.53	11.34	11.17	11.02	10.90
600	14.43	14.11	13.84	13.60	13.40	13.23	13.08
700	16.83	16.46	16.14	15.87	15.64	15.43	15.26
800	19.24	18.81	18.45	18.14	17.87	17.64	17.44
900	21.64	21.16	20.75	20.40	20.10	19.84	19.62
1000	24.05	23.51	23.06	22.67	22.34	22.05	21.80
1500	36.07	35.27	34.59	34.01	33.51	33.07	32.70
2000	48.09	47.03	46.12	45.34	44.67	44.10	43.60
2500	60.12	58.78	57.65	56.68	55.84	55.12	54.50
3000	72.14	70.54	69.18	68.01	67.01	66.14	65.39
3500	84.16	82.30	80.71	79.35	78.18 ·	77.17	76.29
4000	96.18	94.05	92.24	90.68	89.35	88.19	87.19
4500	108.21	105.81	103.77	102.02	100.52	99.22	98.09
5000	120.23	117.57	115.30	113.35	111.68	110.24	108.99
5500	132.25	129.32	126.83	124.69	122.85	121.26	119.89
6000	144.28	141.08	138.36	136.03	134.02	132.29	130.79
6500	156.30	152.84	149.89	147.36	145.19	143.31	141.69
7000	168.32	164.59	161.42	158.70	156.36	154.34	152.59
7500	180.35	176.35	172.95	170.03	167.53	165.36	163.49
8000	192.37	188.11	184.47	181.37	178.69	176.38	174.38
8500	204.39	199.86	196.00	192.70	189.86	187.41	185.28
9000	216.41	211.62	207.53	204.04	201.03	198.43	196.18
9500	228.44	223.37	219.06	215.37	212.20	209.46	207.08
10000	240.46	235.13	230.59	226.71	223.37	220.48	217.98
11000	264.51	258.64	253.65	249.38	245.70	242.53	239.78
12000	288.55	282.16	276.71	272.05	268.04	264.58	261.58
13000	312.60	305.67	299.77	294.72	290.38	286.63	283.37
14000	336.64	329.18	322.83	317.39	312.71	308.67	305.17
15000	360.69	352.70	345.89	340.06	335.05	330.72	326.97
16000	384.74	376.21	368.95	362.73	357.39	352.77	348.77
17000	408.78	399.72	392.01	385.40	379.72	374.82	370.57
18000	432.83	423.24	415.07	408.08	402.06	396.87	392.36
19000	456.87	446.75	438.13	430.75	424.40	418.91	414.16
20000	480.92	470.26	461.19	453.42	446.73	440.96	435.96
21000	504.97	493.78	484.25	476.09	469.07	463.01	457.76
22000	529.01	517.29	507.31	498.76	491.41	485.06	479.56
23000	553.06	540.80	530.37	521.43	513.74	507.11	501.35
24000	577.10	564.32	553.42	544.10	536.08	529.15	523.15
25000	601.15	587.83	576.48	566.77	558.42	551.20	544.95
26000	625.20	611.34	599.54	589.44	580.75	573.25	566.75
27000	649.24	634.85	622.60	612.11	603.09	595.30	588.55
28000	673.29	658.37	645.66	634.78	625.43	617.35	610.34
29000	697.33	681.88	668.72	657.45	647.76	639.39	632.14
30000	721.38	705.39	691.78	680.13	670.10	661.44	653.94
31000	745.43	728.91	714.84	702.80	692.44	683.49	675.74
32000	769.47	752.42	737.90	725.47	714.77	705.54	697.54
33000	793.52	775.93	760.96	748.14	737.11	727.59	719.33
34000	817.56	799.45	784.02	770.81	759.45	749.64	741.13
35000	841.61	822.96	807.08	793.48	781.78	771.68	762.93
40000	961.84	940.53	922.37	906.83	893.47	881.92	871.92
45000	1082.07	1058.09	1037.67	1020.19	1005.15	992.16	980.91
50000	1202.30	1175.66	1152.97	1133.54	1116.83	1102.40	1089.90
55000	1322.53	1293.22	1268.26	1246.90	1228.52	1212.65	1198.89
60000	1442.76	1410.79	1383.56	1360.25	1340.20	1322.89	1307.88
65000	1562.99	1528.35	1498.86	1473.61	1451.88	1433.13	1416.87
70000	1683.22	1645.92	1614.15	1586.96	1563.57	1543.37	1525.86

Monthly Loan Payments 24%

LOAN AMOUNT	11 YEARS	11½ YEARS	12 YEARS	12½ YEARS	13 YEARS	14 YEARS	15 YEARS
100	2.16	2.14	2.12	2.11	2.10	2.07	2.06
200	4.32	4.28	4.25	4.22	4.19	4.15	4.12
300	6.47	6.42	6.37	6.32	6.29	6.22	6.17
400	8.63	8.56	8.49	8.43	8.38	8.30	8.23
500	10.79	10.70	10.61	10.54	10.48	10.37	10.29
600	12.95	12.83	12.74	12.65	12.57	12.45	12.35
700	15.11	14.97	14.86	14.76	14.67	14.52	14.41
800	17.26	17.11	16.98	16.86	16.76	16.60	16.47
900	19.42	19.25	19.10	18.97	18.86	18.67	18.52
1000	21.58	21.39	21.23	21.08	20.95	20.74	20.58
1500	32.37	32.09	31.84	31.62	31.43	31.12	30.87
2000	43.16	42.78	42.45	42.16	41.91	41.49	41.17
2500	53.95	53.48	53.06	52.70	52.39	51.86	51.46
3000	64.74	64.17	63.68	63.24	62.86	62.23	61.75
3500	75.53	74.87	74.29	73.78	73.34	72.61	72.04
4000	86.32	85.57	84.90	84.32	83.82	82.98	82.33
4500	97.11	96.26	95.52	94.86	94.29	93.35	92.62
5000	107.90	106.96	106.13	105.41	104.77	103.72	102.91
5500	118.69	117.65	116.74	115.95	115.25	114.10	113.21
6000	129.48	128.35	127.36	126.49	125.73	124.47	123.50
6500	140.27	139.04	137.97	137.03	136.20	134.84	133.79
7000	151.06	149.74	148.58	147.57	146.68	145.21	144.08
7500	161.86	160.43	159.19	158.11	157.16	155.59	154.37
8000	172.65	171.13	169.81	168.65	167.63	165.96	164.66
8500	183.44	181.83	180.42	179.19	178.11	176.33	174.95
9000	194.23	192.52	191.03	189.73	188.59	186.70	185.24
9500	205.02	203.22	201.65	200.27	199.07	197.08	195.54
10000	215.81	213.91	212.26	210.81	209.54	207.45	205.83
11000	237.39	235.30	233.48	231.89	230.50	228.19	226.41
12000	258.97	256.70	254.71	252.97	251.45	248.94	246.99
13000	280.55	278.09	275.94	274.05	272.40	269.68	267.58
14000	302.13	299.48	297.16	295.14	293.36	290.43	288.16
15000	323.71	320.87	318.39	316.22	314.31	311.17	308.74
16000	345.29	342.26	339.61	337.30	335.27	331.92	329.32
17000	366.87	363.65	360.84	358.38	356.22	352.66	349.91
18000	388.45	385.04	382.07	379.46	377.18	373.41	370.49
19000	410.03	406.43	403.29	400.54	398.13	394.15	391.07
20000	431.61	427.83	424.52	421.62	419.08	414.90	411.65
21000	453.19	449.22	445.74	442.70	440.04	435.64	432.24
22000	474.77	470.61	466.97	463.78	460.99	456.39	452.82
23000	496.36	492.00	488.19	484.87	481.95	477.13	473.40
24000	517.94	513.39	509.42	505.95	502.90	497.88	493.99
25000	539.52	534.78	530.65	527.03	523.86	518.62	514.57
26000	561.10	556.17	551.87	548.11	544.81	539.37	535.15
27000	582.68	577.56	573.10	569.19	565.76	560.11	555.73
28000	604.26	598.96	594.32	590.27	586.72	580.86	576.32
29000	625.84	620.35	615.55	611.35	607.67	601.60	596.90
30000	647.42	641.74	636.78	632.43	628.63	622.35	617.48
31000	669.00	663.13	658.00	653.51	649.58	643.09	638.06
32000	690.58	684.52	679.23	674.60	670.53	663.84	658.65
33000	712.16	705.91	700.45	695.68	691.49	684.58	679.23
34000	733.74	727.30	721.68	716.76	712.44	705.33	699.81
35000	755.32	748.69	742.91	737.84	733.40	726.07	720.40
40000	863.23	855.65	849.03	843.24	838.17	829.79	823.31
45000	971.13	962.61	955.16	948.65	942.94	933.52	926.22
50000	1079.03	1069.56	1061.29	1054.06	1047.71	1037.24	1029.14
55000	1186.94	1176.52	1167.42	1159.46	1152.48	1140.97	1132.05
60000	1294.84	1283.48	1273.55	1264.87	1257.25	1244.69	1234.96
65000	1402.74	1390.43	1379.68	1370.27	1362.02	1348.42	1337.88
70000	1510.65	1497.39	1485.81	1475.68	1466.79	1452.14	1440.79

Capital Accumulation Projections

In planning for the future it may b
desirable to know how much a series of monthl
deposits or investments will accumulate to ove
time. This table shows the total amount that wi
accumulate when monthly deposits or inves
ments are made over a specified period of time a
a specified interest rate. The table is based o
monthly compounding. It covers interest rate
ranging from 5% to 18% and shows accumulate
values for monthly deposits or investments rang
ing from $10 to $1,000 for a term of 5 to 25 years
Here are some illustrative situations to help yo
understand and use the table:

Situation 1

Mr. Johnson wants to know how much a $50.00-per-month investment is expected to grow to if it is invested for 10 years in an account that will earn 9% for the 10-year term. He can determine the amount by (1) locating the 9% page, (2) locating the 10-year column, (3) looking down the left side of the page to the $50.00 line, and (4) scanning across to the 10-year column. The table shows that if Mr. Johnson puts away $50.00 per month for 10 years at an interest rate of 9% compounded monthly, he will accumulate $9,748.28.

Situation 2

Mrs. Reed plans to invest $100.00 per month for 20 years and expects that the investment will earn 10% interest. She wants to know how much money she will have after the 20 years. She must (1) locate the 10% page, (2) find the 20-year column, (3) look down the left side of the page to the $100.00 line, and (4) scan across to the 20-year column. The number shown is 76,569.69; therefore, Mrs. Reed will have accumulated $76,569.69.

5% Capital Accumulation Projections

MONTHLY AMOUNT	5 YEARS	10 YEARS	15 YEARS	20 YEARS	25 YEARS
10	682.89	1559.29	2684.03	4127.46	5979.91
20	1365.79	3118.59	5368.05	8254.93	11959.82
30	2048.68	4677.88	8052.08	12382.39	17939.73
40	2731.58	6237.17	10736.11	16509.85	23919.64
50	3414.47	7796.46	13420.13	20637.32	29899.55
60	4097.37	9355.76	16104.16	24764.78	35879.46
70	4780.26	10915.05	18788.19	28892.24	41859.37
80	5463.16	12474.34	21472.21	33019.70	47839.28
90	6146.05	14033.64	24156.24	37147.17	53819.19
100	6828.94	15592.93	26840.26	41274.63	59799.10
110	7511.84	17152.22	29524.29	45402.09	65779.01
120	8194.73	18711.51	32208.32	49529.56	71758.92
130	8877.63	20270.81	34892.34	53657.02	77738.83
140	9560.52	21830.10	37576.37	57784.48	83718.74
150	10243.42	23389.39	40260.40	61911.95	89698.65
160	10926.31	24948.69	42944.42	66039.41	95678.56
170	11609.20	26507.98	45628.45	70166.87	101658.47
180	12292.10	28067.27	48312.48	74294.34	107638.38
190	12974.99	29626.56	50996.50	78421.80	113618.29
200	13657.89	31185.86	53680.53	82549.26	119598.20
210	14340.78	32745.15	56364.56	86676.72	125578.11
220	15023.68	34304.44	59048.58	90804.19	131558.02
230	15706.57	35863.74	61732.61	94931.65	137537.93
240	16389.47	37423.03	64416.64	99059.11	143517.84
250	17072.36	38982.32	67100.66	103186.58	149497.75
260	17755.25	40541.62	69784.69	107314.04	155477.66
270	18438.15	42100.91	72468.71	111441.50	161457.57
280	19121.04	43660.20	75152.74	115568.97	167437.48
290	19803.94	45219.49	77836.77	119696.43	173417.39
300	20486.83	46778.79	80520.79	123823.89	179397.30
310	21169.73	48338.08	83204.82	127951.36	185377.21
320	21852.62	49897.37	85888.85	132078.82	191357.12
330	22535.52	51456.67	88572.87	136206.28	197337.03
340	23218.41	53015.96	91256.90	140333.74	203316.94
350	23901.30	54575.25	93940.93	144461.21	209296.85
360	24584.20	56134.54	96624.95	148588.67	215276.76
370	25267.09	57693.84	99308.98	152716.13	221256.67
380	25949.99	59253.13	101993.01	156843.60	227236.58
390	26632.88	60812.42	104677.03	160971.06	233216.49
400	27315.78	62371.72	107361.06	165098.52	239196.40
410	27998.67	63931.01	110045.09	169225.99	245176.31
420	28681.57	65490.30	112729.11	173353.45	251156.22
430	29364.46	67049.59	115413.14	177480.91	257136.13
440	30047.35	68608.89	118097.16	181608.38	263116.04
450	30730.25	70168.18	120781.19	185735.84	269095.95
460	31413.14	71727.47	123465.22	189863.30	275075.86
470	32096.04	73286.77	126149.24	193990.77	281055.77
480	32778.93	74846.06	128833.27	198118.23	287035.68
490	33461.83	76405.35	131517.30	202245.69	293015.59
500	34144.72	77964.64	134201.32	206373.15	298995.50
550	37559.19	85761.11	147621.46	227010.47	328895.05
600	40973.66	93557.57	161041.59	247647.79	358794.60
650	44388.14	101354.04	174461.72	268285.10	388694.15
700	47802.61	109150.50	187881.85	288922.42	418593.70
750	51217.08	116946.97	201301.99	309559.73	448493.25
800	54631.55	124743.43	214722.12	330197.05	478392.80
850	58046.03	132539.90	228142.25	350834.36	508292.35
900	61460.50	140336.36	241562.38	371471.68	538191.90
950	64874.97	148132.82	254982.52	392108.99	568091.45
1000	68289.44	155929.29	268402.65	412746.31	597991.00

Capital Accumulation Projections 6%

MONTHLY AMOUNT	5 YEARS	10 YEARS	15 YEARS	20 YEARS	25 YEARS
10	701.19	1646.99	2922.73	4643.51	6964.59
20	1402.38	3293.97	5845.46	9287.02	13929.18
30	2103.57	4940.96	8768.18	13930.53	20893.77
40	2804.76	6587.95	11690.91	18574.04	27858.36
50	3505.94	8234.94	14613.64	23217.55	34822.95
60	4207.13	9881.92	17536.37	27861.07	41787.54
70	4908.32	11528.91	20459.10	32504.58	48752.13
80	5609.51	13175.90	23381.82	37148.09	55716.71
90	6310.70	14822.89	26304.55	41791.60	62681.30
100	7011.89	16469.87	29227.28	46435.11	69645.89
110	7713.08	18116.86	32150.01	51078.62	76610.48
120	8414.27	19763.85	35072.74	55722.13	83575.07
130	9115.45	21410.84	37995.46	60365.64	90539.66
140	9816.64	23057.82	40918.19	65009.15	97504.25
150	10517.83	24704.81	43840.92	69652.66	104468.84
160	11219.02	26351.80	46763.65	74296.18	111433.43
170	11920.21	27998.79	49686.38	78939.69	118398.02
180	12621.40	29645.77	52609.11	83583.20	125362.61
190	13322.59	31292.76	55531.83	88226.71	132327.20
200	14023.78	32939.75	58454.56	92870.22	139291.79
210	14724.96	34586.74	61377.29	97513.73	146256.38
220	15426.15	36233.72	64300.02	102157.24	153220.97
230	16127.34	37880.71	67222.75	106800.75	160185.55
240	16828.53	39527.70	70145.47	111444.26	167150.14
250	17529.72	41174.69	73068.20	116087.77	174114.73
260	18230.91	42821.67	75990.93	120731.29	181079.32
270	18932.10	44468.66	78913.66	125374.80	188043.91
280	19633.29	46115.65	81836.39	130018.31	195008.50
290	20334.48	47762.64	84759.11	134661.82	201973.09
300	21035.66	49409.62	87681.84	139305.33	208937.68
310	21736.85	51056.61	90604.57	143948.84	215902.27
320	22438.04	52703.60	93527.30	148592.35	222866.86
330	23139.23	54350.59	96450.03	153235.86	229831.45
340	23840.42	55997.57	99372.75	157879.37	236796.04
350	24541.61	57644.56	102295.48	162522.88	243760.63
360	25242.80	59291.55	105218.21	167166.40	250725.22
370	25943.99	60938.54	108140.94	171809.91	257689.80
380	26645.17	62585.52	111063.67	176453.42	264654.39
390	27346.36	64232.51	113986.39	181096.93	271618.98
400	28047.55	65879.50	116909.12	185740.44	278583.57
410	28748.74	67526.48	119831.85	190383.95	285548.16
420	29449.93	69173.47	122754.58	195027.46	292512.75
430	30151.12	70820.46	125677.31	199670.97	299477.34
440	30852.31	72467.45	128600.03	204314.48	306441.93
450	31553.50	74114.43	131522.76	208957.99	313406.52
460	32254.69	75761.42	134445.49	213601.51	320371.11
470	32955.87	77408.41	137368.22	218245.02	327335.70
480	33657.06	79055.40	140290.95	222888.53	334300.29
490	34358.25	80702.38	143213.67	227532.04	341264.88
500	35059.44	82349.37	146136.40	232175.55	348229.47
550	38565.38	90584.31	160750.04	255393.10	383052.41
600	42071.33	98819.25	175363.68	278610.66	417875.36
650	45577.27	107054.18	189977.32	301828.21	452698.31
700	49083.22	115289.12	204590.96	325045.77	487521.25
750	52589.16	123524.06	219204.60	348263.32	522344.20
800	56095.10	131758.99	233818.24	371480.88	557167.15
850	59601.05	139993.93	248431.89	394698.43	591990.09
900	63106.99	148228.87	263045.53	417915.99	626813.04
950	66612.94	156463.81	277659.17	441133.54	661635.99
1000	70118.88	164698.74	292272.81	464351.10	696458.93

7% Capital Accumulation Projections

MONTHLY AMOUNT	5 YEARS	10 YEARS	15 YEARS	20 YEARS	25 YEARS
10	720.11	1740.94	3188.11	5239.65	8147.
20	1440.21	3481.89	6376.22	10479.31	16295.
30	2160.32	5222.83	9564.34	15718.96	24443.
40	2880.42	6963.78	12752.45	20958.62	32591.
50	3600.53	8704.72	15940.56	26198.27	40739.
60	4320.63	10445.67	19128.67	31437.92	48887.
70	5040.74	12186.61	22316.79	36677.58	57035.
80	5760.84	13927.56	25504.90	41917.23	65183.
90	6480.95	15668.50	28693.01	47156.89	73331.
100	7201.05	17409.45	31881.12	52396.54	81479.
110	7921.16	19150.39	35069.24	57636.19	89627.
120	8641.26	20891.34	38257.35	62875.85	97775.
130	9361.37	22632.28	41445.46	68115.50	105923.
140	10081.47	24373.23	44633.57	73355.16	114071.
150	10801.58	26114.17	47821.69	78594.81	122219.
160	11521.68	27855.12	51009.80	83834.46	130367.
170	12241.79	29596.06	54197.91	89074.12	138515.
180	12961.89	31337.00	57386.02	94313.77	146663.
190	13682.00	33077.95	60574.14	99553.43	154811.
200	14402.11	34818.89	63762.25	104793.08	162959.
210	15122.21	36559.84	66950.36	110032.73	171107.
220	15842.32	38300.78	70138.47	115272.39	179255.
230	16562.42	40041.73	73326.59	120512.04	187403.
240	17282.53	41782.67	76514.70	125751.70	195551.
250	18002.63	43523.62	79702.81	130991.35	203699.
260	18722.74	45264.56	82890.92	136231.00	211847.
270	19442.84	47005.51	86079.04	141470.66	219995.
280	20162.95	48746.45	89267.15	146710.31	228143.
290	20883.05	50487.40	92455.26	151949.97	236291.
300	21603.16	52228.34	95643.37	157189.62	244439.
310	22323.26	53969.29	98831.49	162429.27	252587.
320	23043.37	55710.23	102019.60	167668.93	260735.
330	23763.47	57451.17	105207.71	172908.58	268883.
340	24483.58	59192.12	108395.82	178148.24	277031.
350	25203.68	60933.06	111583.94	183387.89	285178.
360	25923.79	62674.01	114772.05	188627.54	293326.
370	26643.89	64414.95	117960.16	193867.20	301474.
380	27364.00	66155.90	121148.27	199106.85	309622.
390	28084.11	67896.84	124336.38	204346.51	317770.
400	28804.21	69637.79	127524.50	209586.16	325918.
410	29524.32	71378.73	130712.61	214825.81	334066.
420	30244.42	73119.68	133900.72	220065.47	342214.
430	30964.53	74860.62	137088.83	225305.12	350362.
440	31684.63	76601.57	140276.95	230544.78	358510.
450	32404.74	78342.51	143465.06	235784.43	366658.
460	33124.85	80083.46	146653.17	241024.08	374806.
470	33844.95	81824.40	149841.28	246263.74	382954.
480	34565.05	83565.35	153029.40	251503.39	391102.
490	35285.16	85306.29	156217.51	256743.05	399250.
500	36005.26	87047.23	159405.62	261982.70	407398.
550	39605.79	95751.96	175346.18	288180.97	448138.
600	43206.32	104456.68	191286.75	314379.24	488878.
650	46806.84	113161.40	207227.31	340577.51	529618.
700	50407.37	121866.13	223167.87	366775.78	570357.
750	54007.90	130570.85	239108.43	392974.05	611097.
800	57608.42	139275.58	255048.99	419172.32	651837.
850	61208.95	147980.30	270989.56	445370.59	692577.
900	64809.47	156685.02	286930.12	471568.86	733317.
950	68410.00	165389.75	302870.68	497767.13	774057.
1000	72010.53	174094.47	318811.24	523965.40	814797.

Capital Accumulation Projections 8%

MONTHLY AMOUNT	5 YEARS	10 YEARS	15 YEARS	20 YEARS	25 YEARS
10	739.67	1841.66	3483.45	5929.47	9573.67
20	1479.33	3683.31	6966.90	11858.94	19147.33
30	2219.00	5524.97	10450.35	17788.42	28721.00
40	2958.67	7366.63	13933.81	23717.89	38294.66
50	3698.34	9208.28	17417.26	29647.36	47868.33
60	4438.00	11049.94	20900.71	35576.83	57441.99
70	5177.67	12891.60	24384.16	41506.31	67015.66
80	5917.34	14733.25	27867.61	47435.78	76589.33
90	6657.00	16574.91	31351.06	53365.25	86162.99
100	7396.67	18416.57	34834.51	59294.72	95736.66
110	8136.34	20258.22	38317.97	65224.19	105310.32
120	8876.00	22099.88	41801.42	71153.67	114883.99
130	9615.67	23941.54	45284.87	77083.14	124457.65
140	10355.34	25783.19	48768.32	83012.61	134031.32
150	11095.01	27624.85	52251.77	88942.08	143604.99
160	11834.67	29466.51	55735.22	94871.55	153178.65
170	12574.34	31308.16	59218.67	100801.03	162752.32
180	13314.01	33149.82	62702.13	106730.50	172325.98
190	14053.67	34991.48	66185.58	112659.97	181899.65
200	14793.34	36833.14	69669.03	118589.44	191473.31
210	15533.01	38674.79	73152.48	124518.92	201046.98
220	16272.67	40516.45	76635.93	130448.39	210620.65
230	17012.34	42358.11	80119.38	136377.86	220194.31
240	17752.01	44199.76	83602.83	142307.33	229767.98
250	18491.68	46041.42	87086.29	148236.80	239341.64
260	19231.34	47883.08	90569.74	154166.28	248915.31
270	19971.01	49724.73	94053.19	160095.75	258488.97
280	20710.68	51566.39	97536.64	166025.22	268062.64
290	21450.34	53408.05	101020.09	171954.69	277636.31
300	22190.01	55249.70	104503.54	177884.17	287209.97
310	22929.68	57091.36	107986.99	183813.64	296783.64
320	23669.34	58933.02	111470.45	189743.11	306357.30
330	24409.01	60774.67	114953.90	195672.58	315930.97
340	25148.68	62616.33	118437.35	201602.05	325504.63
350	25888.35	64457.99	121920.80	207531.53	335078.30
360	26628.01	66299.64	125404.25	213461.00	344651.97
370	27367.68	68141.30	128887.70	219390.47	354225.63
380	28107.35	69982.96	132371.15	225319.94	363799.30
390	28847.01	71824.61	135854.61	231249.42	373372.96
400	29586.68	73666.27	139338.06	237178.89	382946.63
410	30326.35	75507.93	142821.51	243108.36	392520.29
420	31066.01	77349.58	146304.96	249037.83	402093.96
430	31805.68	79191.24	149788.41	254967.30	411667.63
440	32545.35	81032.90	153271.86	260896.78	421241.29
450	33285.02	82874.55	156755.31	266826.25	430814.96
460	34024.68	84716.21	160238.77	272755.72	440388.62
470	34764.35	86557.87	163722.22	278685.19	449962.29
480	35504.02	88399.52	167205.67	284614.66	459535.95
490	36243.68	90241.18	170689.12	290544.14	469109.62
500	36983.35	92082.84	174172.57	296473.61	478683.29
550	40681.69	101291.12	191589.83	326120.97	526551.61
600	44380.02	110499.41	209007.09	355768.33	574419.94
650	48078.36	119707.69	226424.34	385415.69	622288.27
700	51776.69	128915.97	243841.60	415063.05	670156.60
750	55475.03	138124.26	261258.86	444710.41	718024.93
800	59173.36	147332.54	278676.11	474357.77	765893.26
850	62871.70	156540.82	296093.37	504005.14	813761.58
900	66570.03	165749.11	313510.63	533652.50	861629.91
950	70268.37	174957.39	330927.89	563299.86	909498.24
1000	73966.70	184165.68	348345.14	592947.22	957366.57

9% Capital Accumulation Projections

MONTHLY AMOUNT	5 YEARS	10 YEARS	15 YEARS	20 YEARS	25 YEARS
10	759.90	1949.66	3812.44	6728.96	11295.30
20	1519.80	3899.31	7624.88	13457.92	22590.61
30	2279.69	5848.97	11437.31	20186.88	33885.91
40	3039.59	7798.63	15249.75	26915.84	45181.21
50	3799.49	9748.28	19062.19	33644.80	56476.52
60	4559.39	11697.94	22874.63	40373.76	67771.82
70	5319.29	13647.59	26687.07	47102.72	79067.12
80	6079.19	15597.25	30499.50	53831.68	90362.43
90	6839.08	17546.91	34311.94	60560.64	101657.73
100	7598.98	19496.56	38124.38	67289.60	112953.04
110	8358.88	21446.22	41936.82	74018.56	124248.34
120	9118.78	23395.88	45749.26	80747.52	135543.64
130	9878.68	25345.53	49561.70	87476.48	146838.95
140	10638.57	27295.19	53374.13	94205.44	158134.25
150	11398.47	29244.85	57186.57	100934.40	169429.55
160	12158.37	31194.50	60999.01	107663.36	180724.86
170	12918.27	33144.16	64811.45	114392.32	192020.16
180	13678.17	35093.81	68623.89	121121.28	203315.46
190	14438.07	37043.47	72436.32	127850.24	214610.77
200	15197.96	38993.13	76248.76	134579.20	225906.07
210	15957.86	40942.78	80061.20	141308.16	237201.37
220	16717.76	42892.44	83873.64	148037.12	248496.68
230	17477.66	44842.10	87686.08	154766.08	259791.98
240	18237.56	46791.75	91498.51	161495.05	271087.28
250	18997.45	48741.41	95310.95	168224.01	282382.59
260	19757.35	50691.06	99123.39	174952.97	293677.89
270	20517.25	52640.72	102935.83	181681.93	304973.19
280	21277.15	54590.38	106748.27	188410.89	316268.50
290	22037.05	56540.03	110560.71	195139.85	327563.80
300	22796.95	58489.69	114373.14	201868.81	338859.11
310	23556.84	60439.35	118185.58	208597.77	350154.41
320	24316.74	62389.00	121998.02	215326.73	361449.71
330	25076.64	64338.66	125810.46	222055.69	372745.02
340	25836.54	66288.32	129622.90	228784.65	384040.32
350	26596.44	68237.97	133435.33	235513.61	395335.62
360	27356.33	70187.63	137247.77	242242.57	406630.93
370	28116.23	72137.28	141060.21	248971.53	417926.23
380	28876.13	74086.94	144872.65	255700.49	429221.53
390	29636.03	76036.60	148685.09	262429.45	440516.84
400	30395.93	77986.25	152497.52	269158.41	451812.14
410	31155.83	79935.91	156309.96	275887.37	463107.44
420	31915.72	81885.57	160122.40	282616.33	474402.75
430	32675.62	83835.22	163934.84	289345.29	485698.05
440	33435.52	85784.88	167747.28	296074.25	496993.35
450	34195.42	87734.54	171559.72	302803.21	508288.66
460	34955.32	89684.19	175372.15	309532.17	519583.96
470	35715.21	91633.85	179184.59	316261.13	530879.27
480	36475.11	93583.50	182997.03	322990.09	542174.57
490	37235.01	95533.16	186809.47	329719.05	553469.87
500	37994.91	97482.82	190621.91	336448.01	564765.18
550	41794.40	107231.10	209684.10	370092.81	621241.69
600	45593.89	116979.38	228746.29	403737.61	677718.21
650	49393.38	126727.66	247808.48	437382.41	734194.73
700	53192.87	136475.94	266870.67	471027.22	790671.25
750	56992.36	146224.23	285932.86	504672.02	847147.76
800	60791.85	155972.51	304995.05	538316.82	903624.28
850	64591.35	165720.79	324057.24	571961.62	960100.80
900	68390.84	175469.07	343119.43	605606.42	1016577.32
950	72190.33	185217.35	362181.62	639251.22	1073053.83
1000	75989.82	194965.63	381243.81	672896.02	1129530.35

Capital Accumulation Projections 10%

MONTHLY AMOUNT	5 YEARS	10 YEARS	15 YEARS	20 YEARS	25 YEARS
10	780.82	2065.52	4179.24	7656.97	13378.90
20	1561.65	4131.04	8358.49	15313.94	26757.81
30	2342.47	6196.56	12537.73	22970.91	40136.71
40	3123.30	8262.08	16716.97	30627.88	53515.61
50	3904.12	10327.60	20896.21	38284.85	66894.52
60	4684.94	12393.12	25075.46	45941.81	80273.42
70	5465.77	14458.64	29254.70	53598.78	93652.32
80	6246.59	16524.16	33433.94	61255.75	107031.23
90	7027.41	18589.68	37613.18	68912.72	120410.13
100	7808.24	20655.20	41792.43	76569.69	133789.03
110	8589.06	22720.72	45971.67	84226.66	147167.94
120	9369.89	24786.24	50150.91	91883.63	160546.84
130	10150.71	26851.76	54330.15	99540.60	173925.75
140	10931.53	28917.28	58509.40	107197.57	187304.65
150	11712.36	30982.80	62688.64	114854.54	200683.55
160	12493.18	33048.32	66867.88	122511.51	214062.46
170	13274.00	35113.84	71047.13	130168.47	227441.36
180	14054.83	37179.36	75226.37	137825.44	240820.26
190	14835.65	39244.88	79405.61	145482.41	254199.17
200	15616.48	41310.40	83584.85	153139.38	267578.07
210	16397.30	43375.92	87764.10	160796.35	280956.97
220	17178.12	45441.44	91943.34	168453.32	294335.88
230	17958.95	47506.96	96122.58	176110.29	307714.78
240	18739.77	49572.48	100301.82	183767.26	321093.68
250	19520.60	51638.01	104481.07	191424.23	334472.59
260	20301.42	53703.53	108660.31	199081.20	347851.49
270	21082.24	55769.05	112839.55	206738.17	361230.39
280	21863.07	57834.57	117018.79	214395.13	374609.30
290	22643.89	59900.09	121198.04	222052.10	387988.20
300	23424.71	61965.61	125377.28	229709.07	401367.10
310	24205.54	64031.13	129556.52	237366.04	414746.01
320	24986.36	66096.65	133735.77	245023.01	428124.91
330	25767.19	68162.17	137915.01	252679.98	441503.81
340	26548.01	70227.69	142094.25	260336.95	454882.72
350	27328.83	72293.21	146273.49	267993.92	468261.62
360	28109.66	74358.73	150452.74	275650.89	481640.53
370	28890.48	76424.26	154631.98	283307.86	495019.43
380	29671.30	78489.77	158811.22	290964.83	508398.33
390	30452.13	80555.29	162990.46	298621.79	521777.24
400	31232.95	82620.81	167169.71	306278.76	535156.14
410	32013.78	84686.33	171348.95	313935.73	548535.04
420	32794.60	86751.85	175528.19	321592.70	561913.95
430	33575.42	88817.37	179707.43	329249.67	575292.85
440	34356.25	90882.89	183886.68	336906.64	588671.75
450	35137.07	92948.41	188065.92	344563.61	602050.66
460	35917.90	95013.93	192245.16	352220.58	615429.56
470	36698.72	97079.45	196424.40	359877.55	628808.46
480	37479.54	99144.97	200603.65	367534.52	642187.37
490	38260.37	101210.49	204782.89	375191.49	655566.27
500	39041.19	103276.01	208962.13	382848.45	668945.17
550	42945.31	113603.61	229858.35	421133.30	735839.69
600	46849.43	123931.21	250754.56	459418.15	802734.21
650	50753.55	134258.81	271650.77	497702.99	869628.73
700	54657.67	144586.41	292546.99	535987.84	936523.24
750	58561.79	154914.02	313443.20	574272.68	1003417.76
800	62465.90	165241.62	334339.41	612557.53	1070312.28
850	66370.02	175569.22	355235.63	650842.37	1137206.80
900	70274.14	185896.82	376131.84	689127.22	1204101.31
950	74178.26	196224.42	397028.05	727412.06	1270995.83
1000	78082.38	206552.02	417924.27	765696.91	1337890.35

11% Capital Accumulation Projections

MONTHLY AMOUNT	5 YEARS	10 YEARS	15 YEARS	20 YEARS	25 YEARS
10	802.47	2189.87	4588.58	8735.73	15905.81
20	1604.94	4379.75	9177.15	17471.46	31811.62
30	2407.41	6569.62	13765.73	26207.19	47717.44
40	3209.88	8759.49	18354.30	34942.92	63623.25
50	4012.35	10949.36	22942.88	43678.65	79529.06
60	4814.82	13139.24	27531.45	52414.38	95434.87
70	5617.29	15329.11	32120.03	61150.11	111340.68
80	6419.76	17518.98	36708.61	69885.84	127246.50
90	7222.23	19708.86	41297.18	78621.57	143152.31
100	8024.70	21898.73	45885.76	87357.31	159058.12
110	8827.17	24088.60	50474.33	96093.04	174963.93
120	9629.64	26278.47	55062.91	104828.77	190869.74
130	10432.11	28468.35	59651.48	113564.50	206775.55
140	11234.58	30658.22	64240.06	122300.23	222681.37
150	12037.05	32848.09	68828.63	131035.96	238587.18
160	12839.52	35037.97	73417.21	139771.69	254492.99
170	13641.99	37227.84	78005.79	148507.42	270398.80
180	14444.46	39417.71	82594.36	157243.15	286304.61
190	15246.93	41607.58	87182.94	165978.88	302210.43
200	16049.40	43797.46	91771.51	174714.61	318116.24
210	16851.87	45987.33	96360.09	183450.34	334022.05
220	17654.34	48177.20	100948.66	192186.07	349927.86
230	18456.81	50367.08	105537.24	200921.80	365833.67
240	19259.28	52556.95	110125.82	209657.53	381739.49
250	20061.75	54746.82	114714.39	218393.26	397645.30
260	20864.22	56936.69	119302.97	227128.99	413551.11
270	21666.69	59126.57	123891.54	235864.72	429456.92
280	22469.16	61316.44	128480.12	244600.45	445362.73
290	23271.63	63506.31	133068.69	253336.19	461268.54
300	24074.10	65696.19	137657.27	262071.92	477174.36
310	24876.57	67886.06	142245.84	270807.65	493080.17
320	25679.04	70075.93	146834.42	279543.38	508985.98
330	26481.51	72265.81	151423.00	288279.11	524891.79
340	27283.98	74455.68	156011.57	297014.84	540797.60
350	28086.45	76645.55	160600.15	305750.57	556703.42
360	28888.92	78835.42	165188.72	314486.30	572609.23
370	29691.39	81025.30	169777.30	323222.03	588515.04
380	30493.86	83215.17	174365.87	331957.76	604420.85
390	31296.33	85405.04	178954.45	340693.49	620326.66
400	32098.80	87594.92	183543.03	349429.22	636232.48
410	32901.27	89784.79	188131.60	358164.95	652138.29
420	33703.74	91974.66	192720.18	366900.68	668044.10
430	34506.21	94164.53	197308.75	375636.41	683949.91
440	35308.68	96354.41	201897.33	384372.14	699855.72
450	36111.15	98544.28	206485.90	393107.87	715761.54
460	36913.62	100734.15	211074.48	401843.60	731667.35
470	37716.09	102924.03	215663.05	410579.34	747573.16
480	38518.56	105113.90	220251.63	419315.07	763478.97
490	39321.03	107303.77	224840.21	428050.80	779384.78
500	40123.50	109493.64	229428.78	436786.53	795290.59
550	44135.85	120443.01	252371.66	480465.18	874819.68
600	48148.20	131392.37	275314.54	524143.83	954348.71
650	52160.55	142341.74	298257.42	567822.48	1033877.77
700	56172.90	153291.10	321200.29	611501.14	1113406.83
750	60185.25	164240.47	344143.17	655179.79	1192935.89
800	64197.60	175189.83	367086.05	698858.44	1272464.95
850	68209.95	186139.19	390028.93	742537.10	1351994.01
900	72222.30	197088.56	412971.81	786215.75	1431523.07
950	76234.65	208037.92	435914.68	829894.40	1511052.13
1000	80247.00	218987.29	458857.56	873573.05	1590581.19

Capital Accumulation Projections 12%

MONTHLY AMOUNT	5 YEARS	10 YEARS	15 YEARS	20 YEARS	25 YEARS
10	824.86	2323.39	5045.76	9991.48	18976.35
20	1649.73	4646.78	10091.52	19982.96	37952.70
30	2474.59	6970.17	15137.28	29974.44	56929.05
40	3299.45	9293.56	20183.04	39965.92	75905.40
50	4124.32	11616.95	25228.80	49957.40	94881.75
60	4949.18	13940.34	30274.56	59948.88	113858.11
70	5774.05	16263.74	35320.32	69940.35	132834.46
80	6598.91	18587.13	40366.08	79931.83	151810.81
90	7423.77	20910.52	45411.84	89923.31	170787.16
100	8248.64	23233.91	50457.60	99914.79	189763.51
110	9073.50	25557.30	55503.36	109906.27	208739.86
120	9898.36	27880.69	60549.12	119897.75	227716.21
130	10723.23	30204.08	65594.88	129889.23	246692.56
140	11548.09	32527.47	70640.64	139880.71	265668.91
150	12372.95	34850.86	75686.40	149872.19	284645.26
160	13197.82	37174.25	80732.16	159863.67	303621.61
170	14022.68	39497.64	85777.92	169855.15	322597.97
180	14847.55	41821.03	90823.68	179846.63	341574.32
190	15672.41	44144.42	95869.44	189838.10	360550.67
200	16497.27	46467.82	100915.20	199829.58	379527.02
210	17322.14	48791.21	105960.96	209821.06	398503.37
220	18147.00	51114.60	111006.72	219812.54	417479.72
230	18971.86	53437.99	116052.48	229804.02	436456.07
240	19796.73	55761.38	121098.24	239795.50	455432.42
250	20621.59	58084.77	126144.00	249786.98	474408.77
260	21446.46	60408.16	131189.76	259778.46	493385.12
270	22271.32	62731.55	136235.52	269769.94	512361.47
280	23096.18	65054.94	141281.28	279761.42	531337.83
290	23921.05	67378.33	146327.04	289752.90	550314.18
300	24745.91	69701.72	151372.80	299744.38	569290.53
310	25570.77	72025.11	156418.56	309735.85	588266.88
320	26395.64	74348.50	161464.32	319727.33	607243.23
330	27220.50	76671.90	166510.08	329718.81	626219.58
340	28045.36	78995.29	171555.84	339710.29	645195.93
350	28870.23	81318.68	176601.60	349701.77	664172.28
360	29695.09	83642.07	181647.36	359693.25	683148.63
370	30519.96	85965.46	186693.12	369684.73	702124.98
380	31344.82	88288.85	191738.88	379676.21	721101.34
390	32169.68	90612.24	196784.64	389667.69	740077.69
400	32994.55	92935.63	201830.40	399659.17	759054.04
410	33819.41	95259.02	206876.16	409650.65	778030.39
420	34644.27	97582.41	211921.92	419642.13	797006.74
430	35469.14	99905.80	216967.68	429633.61	815983.09
440	36294.00	102229.19	222013.44	439625.08	834959.44
450	37118.86	104552.58	227059.20	449616.56	853935.79
460	37943.73	106875.98	232104.96	459608.04	872912.14
470	38768.59	109199.37	237150.72	469599.52	891888.49
480	39593.46	111522.76	242196.48	479591.00	910864.84
490	40418.32	113846.15	247242.24	489582.48	929841.20
500	41243.18	116169.54	252288.00	499573.96	948817.55
550	45367.50	127786.49	277516.80	549531.36	1043699.30
600	49491.82	139403.45	302745.60	599488.75	1138581.06
650	53616.14	151020.40	327974.40	649446.15	1233462.81
700	57740.46	162637.35	353203.20	699403.54	1328344.56
750	61864.77	174254.31	378432.00	749360.94	1423226.32
800	65989.09	185871.26	403660.80	799318.34	1518108.07
850	70113.41	197488.21	428889.60	849275.73	1612989.83
900	74237.73	209105.17	454118.40	899233.13	1707871.58
950	78362.05	220722.12	479347.20	949190.52	1802753.34
1000	82486.37	232339.08	504576.00	999147.92	1897635.09

13% Capital Accumulation Projections

MONTHLY AMOUNT	5 YEARS	10 YEARS	15 YEARS	20 YEARS	25 YEARS
10	848.03	2466.81	5556.81	11455.19	22714.35
20	1696.07	4933.61	11113.63	22910.38	45428.70
30	2544.10	7400.42	16670.44	34365.57	68143.05
40	3392.13	9867.23	22227.25	45820.77	90857.40
50	4240.17	12334.03	27784.06	57275.96	113571.75
60	5088.20	14800.84	33340.88	68731.15	136286.10
70	5936.23	17267.65	38897.69	80186.34	159000.45
80	6784.26	19734.45	44454.50	91641.53	181714.80
90	7632.30	22201.26	50011.32	103096.72	204429.15
100	8480.33	24668.07	55568.13	114551.91	227143.50
110	9328.36	27134.87	61124.94	126007.11	249857.85
120	10176.40	29601.68	66681.75	137462.30	272572.20
130	11024.43	32068.48	72238.57	148917.49	295286.55
140	11872.46	34535.29	77795.38	160372.68	318000.90
150	12720.50	37002.10	83352.19	171827.87	340715.25
160	13568.53	39468.90	88909.00	183283.06	363429.60
170	14416.56	41935.71	94465.82	194738.25	386143.95
180	15264.60	44402.52	100022.63	206193.45	408858.30
190	16112.63	46869.32	105579.44	217648.64	431572.65
200	16960.66	49336.13	111136.26	229103.83	454287.00
210	17808.69	51802.94	116693.07	240559.02	477001.35
220	18656.73	54269.74	122249.88	252014.21	499715.70
230	19504.76	56736.55	127806.69	263469.40	522430.05
240	20352.79	59203.36	133363.51	274924.59	545144.40
250	21200.83	61670.16	138920.32	286379.79	567858.75
260	22048.86	64136.97	144477.13	297834.98	590573.10
270	22896.89	66603.78	150033.95	309290.17	613287.45
280	23744.93	69070.58	155590.76	320745.36	636001.80
290	24592.96	71537.39	161147.57	332200.55	658716.15
300	25440.99	74004.20	166704.38	343655.74	681430.50
310	26289.02	76471.00	172261.20	355110.93	704144.85
320	27137.06	78937.81	177818.01	366566.13	726859.20
330	27985.09	81404.61	183374.82	378021.32	749573.55
340	28833.12	83871.42	188931.63	389476.51	772287.90
350	29681.16	86338.23	194488.45	400931.70	795002.25
360	30529.19	88805.03	200045.26	412386.89	817716.60
370	31377.22	91271.84	205602.07	423842.08	840430.95
380	32225.26	93738.65	211158.89	435297.28	863145.30
390	33073.29	96205.45	216715.70	446752.47	885859.65
400	33921.32	98672.26	222272.51	458207.66	908574.00
410	34769.36	101139.07	227829.32	469662.85	931288.35
420	35617.39	103605.87	233386.14	481118.04	954002.71
430	36465.42	106072.68	238942.95	492573.23	976717.06
440	37313.45	108539.49	244499.76	504028.42	999431.41
450	38161.49	111006.29	250056.58	515483.62	1022145.76
460	39009.52	113473.10	255613.39	526938.81	1044860.11
470	39857.55	115939.91	261170.20	538394.00	1067574.46
480	40705.59	118406.71	266727.01	549849.19	1090288.81
490	41553.62	120873.52	272283.83	561304.38	1113003.16
500	42401.65	123340.33	277840.64	572759.57	1135717.51
550	46641.82	135674.36	305624.70	630035.53	1249289.26
600	50881.98	148008.39	333408.77	687311.49	1362861.01
650	55122.15	160342.42	361192.83	744587.44	1476432.76
700	59362.31	172676.46	388976.89	801863.40	1590004.51
750	63602.48	185010.49	416760.96	859139.36	1703576.26
800	67842.64	197344.52	444545.02	916415.32	1817148.01
850	72082.81	209678.55	472329.09	973691.27	1930719.76
900	76322.98	222012.59	500113.15	1030967.23	2044291.51
950	80563.14	234346.62	527897.21	1088243.19	2157863.26
1000	84803.31	246680.65	555681.28	1145519.14	2271435.01

Capital Accumulation Projections 14%

MONTHLY AMOUNT	5 YEARS	10 YEARS	15 YEARS	20 YEARS	25 YEARS
10	872.01	2620.91	6128.54	13163.46	27272.78
20	1744.01	5241.83	12257.08	26326.93	54545.55
30	2616.02	7862.74	18385.61	39490.39	81818.33
40	3488.03	10483.66	24514.15	52653.85	109091.11
50	4360.04	13104.57	30642.69	65817.31	136363.89
60	5232.04	15725.48	36771.23	78980.78	163636.66
70	6104.05	18346.40	42899.76	92144.24	190909.44
80	6976.06	20967.31	49028.30	105307.70	218182.22
90	7848.07	23588.22	55156.84	118471.16	245454.99
100	8720.07	26209.14	61285.38	131634.63	272727.77
110	9592.08	28830.05	67413.92	144798.09	300000.55
120	10464.09	31450.97	73542.45	157961.55	327273.33
130	11336.10	34071.88	79670.99	171125.02	354546.10
140	12208.10	36692.79	85799.53	184288.48	381818.88
150	13080.11	39313.71	91928.07	197451.94	409091.66
160	13952.12	41934.62	98056.60	210615.40	436364.43
170	14824.12	44555.54	104185.14	223778.87	463637.21
180	15696.13	47176.45	110313.68	236942.33	490909.99
190	16568.14	49797.36	116442.22	250105.79	518182.77
200	17440.15	52418.28	122570.76	263269.26	545455.54
210	18312.15	55039.19	128699.29	276432.72	572728.32
220	19184.16	57660.10	134827.83	289596.18	600001.10
230	20056.17	60281.02	140956.37	302759.64	627273.87
240	20928.18	62901.93	147084.91	315923.11	654546.65
250	21800.18	65522.85	153213.44	329086.57	681819.43
260	22672.19	68143.76	159341.98	342250.03	709092.21
270	23544.20	70764.67	165470.52	355413.49	736364.98
280	24416.21	73385.59	171599.06	368576.96	763637.76
290	25288.21	76006.50	177727.60	381740.42	790910.54
300	26160.22	78627.41	183856.13	394903.88	818183.31
310	27032.23	81248.33	189984.67	408067.35	845456.09
320	27904.24	83869.24	196113.21	421230.81	872728.87
330	28776.24	86490.16	202241.75	434394.27	900001.65
340	29648.25	89111.07	208370.28	447557.73	927274.42
350	30520.26	91731.98	214498.82	460721.20	954547.20
360	31392.26	94352.90	220627.36	473884.66	981819.98
370	32264.27	96973.81	226755.90	487048.12	1009092.75
380	33136.28	99594.73	232884.44	500211.58	1036365.53
390	34008.29	102215.64	239012.97	513375.05	1063638.31
400	34880.29	104836.55	245141.51	526538.51	1090911.09
410	35752.30	107457.47	251270.05	539701.97	1118183.86
420	36624.31	110078.38	257398.59	552865.44	1145456.64
430	37496.32	112699.29	263527.12	566028.90	1172729.42
440	38368.32	115320.21	269655.66	579192.36	1200002.19
450	39240.33	117941.12	275784.20	592355.82	1227274.97
460	40112.34	120562.04	281912.74	605519.29	1254547.75
470	40984.35	123182.95	288041.28	618682.75	1281820.53
480	41856.35	125803.86	294169.81	631846.21	1309093.30
490	42728.36	128424.78	300298.35	645009.67	1336366.08
500	43600.37	131045.69	306426.89	658173.14	1363638.86
550	47960.40	144150.26	337069.58	723990.45	1500002.74
600	52320.44	157254.83	367712.27	789807.77	1636366.63
650	56680.48	170359.40	398354.96	855625.08	1772730.51
700	61040.51	183463.97	428997.65	921442.39	1909094.40
750	65400.55	196568.54	459640.33	987259.71	2045458.29
800	69760.59	209673.11	490283.02	1053077.02	2181822.17
850	74120.62	222777.68	520925.71	1118894.33	2318186.06
900	78480.66	235882.24	551568.40	1184711.65	2454549.94
950	82840.70	248986.81	582211.09	1250528.96	2590913.83
1000	87200.73	262091.38	612853.78	1316346.28	2727277.72

15% Capital Accumulation Projections

MONTHLY AMOUNT	5 YEARS	10 YEARS	15 YEARS	20 YEARS	25 YEARS
10	896.82	2786.57	6768.63	15159.55	32840.7
20	1793.63	5573.15	13537.26	30319.10	65681.4
30	2690.45	8359.72	20305.89	45478.65	98522.2
40	3587.27	11146.29	27074.52	60638.20	131362.9
50	4484.08	13932.86	33843.15	75797.75	164203.6
60	5380.90	16719.44	40611.79	90957.30	197044.4
70	6277.72	19506.01	47380.42	106116.85	229885.1
80	7174.54	22292.58	54149.05	121276.40	262725.9
90	8071.35	25079.15	60917.68	136435.95	295566.6
100	8968.17	27865.73	67686.31	151595.50	328407.3
110	9864.99	30652.30	74454.94	166755.05	361248.1
120	10761.80	33438.87	81223.57	181914.60	394088.8
130	11658.62	36225.45	87992.20	197074.15	426929.5
140	12555.44	39012.02	94760.83	212233.70	459770.3
150	13452.25	41798.59	101529.46	227393.25	492611.0
160	14349.07	44585.16	108298.10	242552.80	525451.8
170	15245.89	47371.74	115066.73	257712.35	558292.5
180	16142.70	50158.31	121835.36	272871.90	591133.2
190	17039.52	52944.88	128603.99	288031.45	623974.0
200	17936.34	55731.45	135372.62	303190.99	656814.7
210	18833.15	58518.03	142141.25	318350.54	689655.4
220	19729.97	61304.60	148909.88	333510.09	722496.2
230	20626.79	64091.17	155678.51	348669.64	755336.9
240	21523.61	66877.75	162447.14	363829.19	788177.7
250	22420.42	69664.32	169215.77	378988.74	821018.4
260	23317.24	72450.89	175984.40	394148.29	853859.1
270	24214.06	75237.46	182753.04	409307.84	886699.9
280	25110.87	78024.04	189521.67	424467.39	919540.6
290	26007.69	80810.61	196290.30	439626.94	952381.3
300	26904.51	83597.18	203058.93	454786.49	985222.1
310	27801.32	86383.75	209827.56	469946.04	1018062.8
320	28698.14	89170.33	216596.19	485105.59	1050903.6
330	29594.96	91956.90	223364.82	500265.14	1083744.3
340	30491.77	94743.47	230133.45	515424.69	1116585.0
350	31388.59	97530.05	236902.08	530584.24	1149425.8
360	32285.41	100316.62	243670.71	545743.79	1182266.5
370	33182.22	103103.19	250439.34	560903.34	1215107.2
380	34079.04	105889.76	257207.98	576062.89	1247948.0
390	34975.86	108676.34	263976.61	591222.44	1280788.7
400	35872.68	111462.91	270745.24	606381.99	1313629.4
410	36769.49	114249.48	277513.87	621541.54	1346470.2
420	37666.31	117036.05	284282.50	636701.09	1379310.9
430	38563.13	119822.63	291051.13	651860.64	1412151.7
440	39459.94	122609.20	297819.76	667020.19	1444992.4
450	40356.76	125395.77	304588.39	682179.74	1477833.1
460	41253.58	128182.34	311357.02	697339.29	1510673.9
470	42150.39	130968.92	318125.65	712498.84	1543514.6
480	43047.21	133755.49	324894.29	727658.39	1576355.3
490	43944.03	136542.06	331662.92	742817.94	1609196.1
500	44840.84	139328.64	338431.55	757977.49	1642036.8
550	49324.93	153261.50	372274.70	833775.24	1806240.5
600	53809.01	167194.36	406117.86	909572.98	1970444.2
650	58293.10	181127.23	439961.01	985370.73	2134647.9
700	62777.18	195060.09	473804.17	1061168.48	2298851.6
750	67261.27	208992.95	507647.32	1136966.23	2463055.3
800	71745.35	222925.82	541490.48	1212763.98	2627258.9
850	76229.44	236858.68	575333.63	1288561.73	2791462.6
900	80713.52	250791.54	609176.78	1364359.48	2955666.3
950	85197.60	264724.41	643019.94	1440157.23	3119870.0
1000	89681.69	278657.27	676863.09	1515954.97	3284073.7

Capital Accumulation Projections 16%

MONTHLY AMOUNT	5 YEARS	10 YEARS	15 YEARS	20 YEARS	25 YEARS
10	922.49	2964.72	7485.80	17494.61	39652.18
20	1844.99	5929.43	14971.60	34989.22	79304.36
30	2767.48	8894.15	22457.40	52483.83	118956.53
40	3689.97	11858.86	29943.20	69978.43	158608.71
50	4612.47	14823.58	37429.00	87473.04	198260.89
60	5534.96	17788.29	44914.80	104967.65	237913.07
70	6457.45	20753.01	52400.60	122462.26	277565.25
80	7379.95	23717.72	59886.40	139956.87	317217.43
90	8302.44	26682.44	67372.20	157451.48	356869.60
100	9224.93	29647.15	74858.00	174946.09	396521.78
110	10147.43	32611.87	82343.80	192440.69	436173.96
120	11069.92	35576.58	89829.60	209935.30	475826.14
130	11992.41	38541.30	97315.40	227429.91	515478.32
140	12914.91	41506.01	104801.20	244924.52	555130.49
150	13837.40	44470.73	112287.00	262419.13	594782.67
160	14759.89	47435.44	119772.80	279913.74	634434.85
170	15682.38	50400.16	127258.60	297408.35	674087.03
180	16604.88	53364.87	134744.40	314902.95	713739.21
190	17527.37	56329.59	142230.20	332397.56	753391.39
200	18449.86	59294.30	149716.00	349892.17	793043.56
210	19372.36	62259.01	157201.80	367386.78	832695.74
220	20294.85	65223.73	164687.60	384881.39	872347.92
230	21217.34	68188.45	172173.40	402376.00	912000.10
240	22139.84	71153.16	179659.20	419870.61	951652.28
250	23062.33	74117.88	187145.00	437365.22	991304.45
260	23984.82	77082.59	194630.80	454859.82	1030956.63
270	24907.32	80047.31	202116.60	472354.43	1070608.81
280	25829.81	83012.02	209602.40	489849.04	1110260.99
290	26752.30	85976.74	217088.20	507343.65	1149913.17
300	27674.80	88941.45	224574.00	524838.26	1189565.34
310	28597.29	91906.17	232059.80	542332.87	1229217.52
320	29519.78	94870.88	239545.60	559827.48	1268869.70
330	30442.28	97835.60	247031.40	577322.08	1308521.88
340	31364.77	100800.31	254517.20	594816.69	1348174.06
350	32287.26	103765.03	262003.00	612311.30	1387826.24
360	33209.76	106729.74	269488.80	629805.91	1427478.41
370	34132.25	109694.46	276974.60	647300.52	1467130.59
380	35054.74	112659.17	284460.40	664795.13	1506782.77
390	35977.24	115623.89	291946.20	682289.74	1546434.95
400	36899.73	118588.60	299432.00	699784.34	1586087.13
410	37822.22	121553.32	306917.80	717278.95	1625739.30
420	38744.72	124518.03	314403.60	734773.56	1665391.48
430	39667.21	127482.75	321889.40	752268.17	1705043.66
440	40589.70	130447.46	329375.20	769762.78	1744695.84
450	41512.20	133412.18	336861.00	787257.39	1784348.02
460	42434.69	136376.89	344346.80	804752.00	1824000.20
470	43357.18	139341.61	351832.60	822246.60	1863652.37
480	44279.68	142306.32	359318.40	839741.21	1903304.55
490	45202.17	145271.04	366804.20	857235.82	1942956.73
500	46124.66	148235.75	374290.00	874730.43	1982608.91
550	50737.13	163059.33	411719.00	962203.47	2180869.80
600	55349.59	177882.91	449147.99	1049676.52	2379130.69
650	59962.06	192706.48	486576.99	1137149.56	2577391.58
700	64574.53	207530.06	524005.99	1224622.60	2775652.47
750	69186.99	222353.63	561434.99	1312095.65	2973913.36
800	73799.46	237177.21	598863.99	1399568.69	3172174.25
850	78411.92	252000.78	636292.99	1487041.73	3370435.14
900	83024.39	266824.36	673721.99	1574514.77	3568696.03
950	87636.86	281647.93	711150.99	1661987.82	3766956.93
1000	92249.32	296471.51	748579.99	1749460.86	3965217.82

17% Capital Accumulation Projections

MONTHLY AMOUNT	5 YEARS	10 YEARS	15 YEARS	20 YEARS	25 YEARS
10	949.07	3156.35	8289.90	20229.17	47996.72
20	1898.14	6312.70	16579.80	40458.33	95993.44
30	2847.21	9469.05	24869.70	60687.50	143990.15
40	3796.28	12625.40	33159.60	80916.67	191986.87
50	4745.35	15781.75	41449.50	101145.83	239983.59
60	5694.41	18938.11	49739.40	121375.00	287980.31
70	6643.48	22094.46	58029.30	141604.17	335977.02
80	7592.55	25250.81	66319.20	161833.33	383973.74
90	8541.62	28407.16	74609.10	182062.50	431970.46
100	9490.69	31563.51	82899.00	202291.67	479967.18
110	10439.76	34719.86	91188.90	222520.83	527963.90
120	11388.83	37876.21	99478.80	242750.00	575960.61
130	12337.90	41032.56	107768.70	262979.17	623957.33
140	13286.97	44188.91	116058.60	283208.33	671954.05
150	14236.04	47345.26	124348.50	303437.50	719950.77
160	15185.11	50501.62	132638.40	323666.67	767947.48
170	16134.18	53657.97	140928.30	343895.83	815944.20
180	17083.24	56814.32	149218.20	364125.00	863940.92
190	18032.31	59970.67	157508.10	384354.17	911937.64
200	18981.38	63127.02	165798.00	404583.33	959934.36
210	19930.45	66283.37	174087.90	424812.50	1007931.07
220	20879.52	69439.72	182377.80	445041.67	1055927.79
230	21828.59	72596.07	190667.70	465270.83	1103924.51
240	22777.66	75752.42	198957.60	485500.00	1151921.23
250	23726.73	78908.77	207247.50	505729.17	1199917.94
260	24675.80	82065.13	215537.40	525958.33	1247914.66
270	25624.87	85221.48	223827.30	546187.50	1295911.38
280	26573.94	88377.83	232117.20	566416.67	1343908.10
290	27523.01	91534.18	240407.10	586645.83	1391904.82
300	28472.07	94690.53	248697.00	606875.00	1439901.53
310	29421.14	97846.88	256986.90	627104.17	1487898.25
320	30370.21	101003.23	265276.80	647333.33	1535894.97
330	31319.28	104159.58	273566.70	667562.50	1583891.69
340	32268.35	107315.93	281856.60	687791.67	1631888.40
350	33217.42	110472.28	290146.50	708020.83	1679885.12
360	34166.49	113628.64	298436.40	728250.00	1727881.84
370	35115.56	116784.99	306726.30	748479.17	1775878.56
380	36064.63	119941.34	315016.20	768708.33	1823875.27
390	37013.70	123097.69	323306.10	788937.50	1871871.99
400	37962.77	126254.04	331596.00	809166.67	1919868.71
410	38911.84	129410.39	339885.90	829395.83	1967865.42
420	39860.90	132566.74	348175.80	849625.00	2015862.14
430	40809.97	135723.09	356465.70	869854.17	2063858.86
440	41759.04	138879.44	364755.60	890083.33	2111855.57
450	42708.11	142035.79	373045.50	910312.50	2159852.29
460	43657.18	145192.14	381335.40	930541.67	2207849.01
470	44606.25	148348.50	389625.30	950770.83	2255845.72
480	45555.32	151504.85	397915.20	971000.00	2303842.44
490	46504.39	154661.20	406205.10	991229.17	2351839.16
500	47453.46	157817.55	414495.00	1011458.33	2399835.88
550	52198.80	173599.30	455944.50	1112604.17	2639819.46
600	56944.15	189381.06	497394.00	1213750.00	2879803.05
650	61689.49	205162.81	538843.50	1314895.83	3119786.63
700	66434.84	220944.57	580293.00	1416041.67	3359770.21
750	71180.19	236726.32	621742.50	1517187.50	3599753.80
800	75925.53	252508.08	663192.00	1618333.33	3839737.48
850	80670.88	268289.83	704641.50	1719479.16	4079721.06
900	85416.22	284071.59	746091.01	1820625.00	4319704.66
950	90161.57	299853.34	787540.51	1921770.83	4559688.19
1000	94906.91	315635.10	828990.01	2022916.66	4799671.79

Capital Accumulation Projections 18%

MONTHLY AMOUNT	5 YEARS	10 YEARS	15 YEARS	20 YEARS	25 YEARS
10	976.58	3362.58	9192.09	23434.87	58233.12
20	1953.16	6725.15	18384.18	46869.74	116466.24
30	2929.74	10087.73	27576.27	70304.62	174699.36
40	3906.31	13450.30	36768.36	93739.49	232932.48
50	4882.89	16812.88	45960.44	117174.36	291165.61
60	5859.47	20175.45	55152.53	140609.23	349398.73
70	6836.05	23538.03	64344.62	164044.10	407631.85
80	7812.63	26900.60	73536.71	187478.97	465864.97
90	8789.21	30263.18	82728.80	210913.85	524098.09
100	9765.79	33625.75	91920.89	234348.72	582331.21
110	10742.37	36988.33	101112.98	257783.59	640564.33
120	11718.94	40350.90	110305.07	281218.46	698797.45
130	12695.52	43713.48	119497.15	304653.33	757030.57
140	13672.10	47076.05	128689.24	328088.21	815263.70
150	14648.68	50438.63	137881.33	351523.08	873496.82
160	15625.26	53801.20	147073.42	374957.95	931729.94
170	16601.84	57163.78	156265.51	398392.82	989963.06
180	17578.42	60526.35	165457.60	421827.69	1048196.18
190	18555.00	63888.93	174649.69	445262.57	1106429.30
200	19531.57	67251.50	183841.78	468697.44	1164662.42
210	20508.15	70614.08	193033.86	492132.31	1222895.54
220	21484.73	73976.65	202225.95	515567.18	1281128.66
230	22461.31	77339.23	211418.04	539002.05	1339361.78
240	23437.89	80701.80	220610.13	562436.92	1397594.91
250	24414.47	84064.38	229802.22	585871.80	1455828.03
260	25391.05	87426.95	238994.31	609306.67	1514061.15
270	26367.63	90789.53	248186.40	632741.54	1572294.27
280	27344.20	94152.10	257378.49	656176.41	1630527.39
290	28320.78	97514.68	266570.58	679611.28	1688760.51
300	29297.36	100877.25	275762.66	703046.16	1746993.63
310	30273.94	104239.83	284954.75	726481.03	1805226.75
320	31250.52	107602.40	294146.84	749915.90	1863459.87
330	32227.10	110964.98	303338.93	773350.77	1921693.00
340	33203.68	114327.55	312531.02	796785.64	1979926.12
350	34180.26	117690.13	321723.11	820220.52	2038159.24
360	35156.83	121052.71	330915.20	843655.39	2096392.36
370	36133.41	124415.28	340107.29	867090.26	2154625.48
380	37109.99	127777.86	349299.37	890525.13	2212858.60
390	38086.57	131140.43	358491.46	913960.00	2271091.72
400	39063.15	134503.01	367683.55	937394.87	2329324.84
410	40039.73	137865.58	376875.64	960829.75	2387557.96
420	41016.31	141228.16	386067.73	984264.62	2445791.09
430	41992.88	144590.73	395259.82	1007699.49	2504024.21
440	42969.46	147953.31	404451.91	1031134.36	2562257.33
450	43946.04	151315.88	413644.00	1054569.23	2620490.45
460	44922.62	154678.46	422836.08	1078004.11	2678723.57
470	45899.20	158041.03	432028.17	1101438.98	2736956.69
480	46875.78	161403.61	441220.26	1124873.85	2795189.81
490	47852.36	164766.18	450412.35	1148308.72	2853422.93
500	48828.94	168128.76	459604.44	1171743.59	2911656.05
550	53711.83	184941.63	505564.88	1288917.95	3202821.66
600	58594.72	201754.51	551525.33	1406092.31	3493987.26
650	63477.62	218567.38	597485.77	1523266.67	3785152.87
700	68360.51	235380.26	643446.22	1640441.03	4076318.48
750	73243.40	252193.14	689406.66	1757615.39	4367484.08
800	78126.30	269006.01	735367.10	1874789.75	4658649.69
850	83009.19	285818.89	781327.55	1991964.11	4949815.29
900	87892.08	302631.76	827287.99	2109138.47	5240980.90
950	92774.98	319444.64	873248.44	2226312.83	5532146.50
1000	97657.87	336257.51	919208.88	2343487.19	5823312.11

Life Expectancy of Accumulated Savings

In planning for the future it may b
desirable to know how long a specific sum o
money will last if monthly withdrawals are made
If someone wishes to withdraw a fixed amoun
each month from accumulated savings, he or sh
may use this table to estimate how many equa
monthly payments will be possible before th
accumulated savings is depleted. For this purpos
it is assumed that the same specified rate of in
terest will be earned throughout the period o
withdrawal and that compounding will be on
monthly basis.

The table that follows covers interest rate
from 5% to 18% and is based on monthly with
drawals. The starting sum of money ranges fron
$10,000 to $100,000. Note that the number o
months it would take to deplete the savings i
shown in whole numbers, and therefore, there ma
be an additional sum left over that is smaller tha
the regular monthly withdrawal. Here are some il
lustrative situations to help you understand an
use the table:

Situation 1

Mr. Thompson wants to know how many months his $10,000.00 of savings is expected to last if it earns 12% interest and he withdraws $200.00 per month. He can find the answer by (1) locating the pages based on savings of $10,000.00, (2) finding the 12%-interest column, (3) looking down the left side of the page to the $200.00 line, and (4) scanning across to the 12%-interest column. The number of months is 69.

Situation 2

Mrs. Walsh has $20,000.00 earning 15% interest in a savings fund. She would like to know the maximum amount of money she can withdraw monthly over the next 4 years. To find the answer she must (1) locate the pages based on $20,000.00 savings, (2) find the 15%-interest column, (3) scan down the column to the number closest to, but not less than, 48 (12 months per year x 4 years = 48 months), and (4) scan across the 48 line to the left to determine the monthly withdrawal. The amount shown is $550.00.

Life Expectancy of Accumulated Savings
Based on Monthly Withdrawals from Savings of $10,000

MONTHLY WITHDRAWAL	INTEREST RATES						
	5%	6%	7%	8%	9%	10%	11%
100	129	138	150	165	185	215	272
110	114	121	129	140	153	170	196
120	102	108	114	122	131	142	158
130	92	97	102	108	115	123	133
140	84	88	92	97	102	108	116
150	78	81	84	88	92	97	103
160	72	75	77	81	84	88	93
170	67	69	72	74	77	81	84
180	63	65	67	69	72	74	78
190	59	61	63	65	67	69	72
200	56	57	59	61	62	64	67
210	53	54	55	57	59	60	62
220	50	51	52	54	55	57	59
230	48	49	50	51	52	54	55
240	45	46	47	48	50	51	52
250	43	44	45	46	47	48	50
260	42	42	43	44	45	46	47
270	40	41	41	42	43	44	45
280	38	39	39	40	40	42	43
290	37	37	38	39	40	40	41
300	35	36	37	37	38	39	39
310	34	35	35	36	37	37	38
320	33	34	34	35	35	36	36
330	32	32	33	33	34	35	35
340	31	31	32	32	33	33	34
350	30	30	31	31	32	32	33
360	29	29	30	30	31	31	32
370	28	29	29	29	30	30	31
380	27	28	28	28	29	29	30
390	27	27	27	28	28	28	29
400	26	26	27	27	27	28	28
410	25	26	26	26	27	27	27
420	25	25	25	26	26	26	26
430	24	24	25	25	25	25	26
440	23	24	24	24	25	25	25
450	23	23	23	23	24	24	24
460	22	23	23	23	23	24	24
470	22	22	22	22	23	23	23
480	21	22	22	22	22	22	23
490	21	21	21	22	22	22	22
500	20	21	21	21	21	21	22
510	20	20	20	21	21	21	21
520	20	20	20	20	20	21	21
530	19	19	20	20	20	20	20
540	19	19	19	19	20	20	20
550	18	19	19	19	19	19	19
560	18	18	18	19	19	19	19
570	18	18	18	18	18	19	19
580	17	18	18	18	18	18	18
590	17	17	17	18	18	18	18
600	17	17	17	17	17	17	18
625	16	16	16	16	17	17	17
650	15	16	16	16	16	16	16
675	15	15	15	15	15	15	15
700	14	14	14	15	15	15	15
725	14	14	14	14	14	14	14
750	13	13	13	14	14	14	14
775	13	13	13	13	13	13	13
800	12	12	13	13	13	13	13
825	12	12	12	12	12	12	12

*Monthly withdrawal is less than the interest earned, thus the accumulated savings will never be depleted.

Life Expectancy of Accumulated Savings
Based on Monthly Withdrawals from Savings of $10,000

MONTHLY WITHDRAWAL	INTEREST RATES						
	12%	13%	14%	15%	16%	17%	18%
100	*	*	*	*	*	*	*
110	240	388	*	*	*	*	*
120	180	216	308	*	*	*	*
130	147	166	196	262	*	*	*
140	125	137	154	179	229	*	*
150	110	118	129	144	165	205	*
160	98	104	112	122	135	154	186
170	89	94	99	106	115	127	143
180	81	85	90	95	101	109	120
190	75	78	82	86	91	97	104
200	69	72	75	78	82	87	93
210	64	67	69	72	76	79	84
220	60	62	65	67	70	73	76
230	57	59	61	63	65	68	70
240	54	55	57	59	61	63	65
250	51	52	54	55	57	59	61
260	48	50	51	52	54	55	57
270	46	47	48	50	51	52	54
280	44	45	46	47	48	50	51
290	42	43	44	45	46	47	48
300	40	41	42	43	44	45	46
310	39	39	40	41	42	43	44
320	37	38	39	39	40	41	42
330	36	36	37	38	39	39	40
340	35	35	36	36	37	38	39
350	33	34	34	35	36	36	37
360	32	33	33	34	34	35	36
370	31	32	32	33	33	34	34
380	30	31	31	32	32	33	33
390	29	30	30	31	31	32	32
400	28	29	29	30	30	31	31
410	28	28	28	29	29	30	30
420	27	27	28	28	28	29	29
430	26	26	27	27	28	28	28
440	25	26	26	26	27	27	28
450	25	25	25	26	26	26	27
460	24	24	25	25	25	26	26
470	24	24	24	24	25	25	25
480	23	23	24	24	24	24	25
490	22	23	23	23	23	24	24
500	22	22	22	23	23	23	23
510	21	22	22	22	22	23	23
520	21	21	21	22	22	22	22
530	21	21	21	21	21	22	22
540	20	20	20	21	21	21	21
550	20	20	20	20	20	21	21
560	19	19	20	20	20	20	20
570	19	19	19	19	20	20	20
580	19	19	19	19	19	19	20
590	18	18	18	19	19	19	19
600	18	18	18	18	18	19	19
625	17	17	17	17	18	18	18
650	16	16	17	17	17	17	17
675	16	16	16	16	16	16	16
700	15	15	15	15	15	16	16
725	14	15	15	15	15	15	15
750	14	14	14	14	14	14	14
775	13	13	14	14	14	14	14
800	13	13	13	13	13	13	13
825	12	13	13	13	13	13	13

*Monthly withdrawal is less than the interest earned, thus the accumulated savings will never be depleted.

Life Expectancy of Accumulated Savings
Based on Monthly Withdrawals from Savings of $20,000

MONTHLY WITHDRAWAL	INTEREST RATES						
	5%	6%	7%	8%	9%	10%	11%
100	430	*	*	*	*	*	*
110	340	480	*	*	*	*	*
120	285	359	616	*	*	*	*
130	246	293	391	*	*	*	*
140	217	251	308	458	*	*	*
150	195	220	258	330	*	*	*
160	176	196	224	269	371	*	*
170	162	177	199	230	286	473	*
180	149	162	179	203	239	313	*
190	138	149	163	182	208	252	367
200	129	138	150	165	185	215	272
210	121	129	139	151	167	190	226
220	114	121	129	140	153	170	196
230	108	114	121	130	141	155	174
240	102	108	114	122	131	142	158
250	97	102	108	114	122	132	144
260	92	97	102	108	115	123	133
270	88	92	97	102	108	115	124
280	84	88	92	97	102	108	116
290	81	84	88	92	97	103	109
300	78	81	84	88	92	97	103
310	75	78	81	84	88	92	98
320	72	75	77	81	84	88	93
330	69	72	75	77	81	84	88
340	67	69	72	74	77	81	84
350	65	67	69	72	74	77	81
360	63	65	67	69	72	74	78
370	61	63	65	67	69	72	74
380	59	61	63	65	67	69	72
390	57	59	61	62	64	67	69
400	56	57	59	61	62	64	67
410	54	56	57	59	60	62	64
420	53	54	55	57	59	60	62
430	51	53	54	55	57	59	60
440	50	51	52	54	55	57	59
450	49	50	51	52	54	55	57
460	48	49	50	51	52	54	55
470	46	47	49	50	51	52	54
480	45	46	47	48	50	51	52
490	44	45	46	47	48	50	51
500	43	44	45	46	47	48	50
510	42	43	44	45	46	47	48
520	42	42	43	44	45	46	47
530	41	41	42	43	44	45	46
540	40	41	41	42	43	44	45
550	39	40	40	41	42	43	44
560	38	39	39	40	41	42	43
570	38	38	39	40	40	41	42
580	37	37	38	39	39	40	41
590	36	37	37	38	39	39	40
600	35	36	37	37	38	39	39
625	34	34	35	36	36	37	38
650	32	33	34	34	35	35	36
675	31	32	32	33	33	34	36
700	30	30	31	31	32	32	33
725	29	29	30	30	31	31	31
750	28	28	29	29	29	30	30
775	27	27	28	28	28	29	29
800	26	26	27	27	27	28	28
825	25	25	26	26	26	27	27

*Monthly withdrawal is less than the interest earned, thus the accumulated savings will never be depleted.

Life Expectancy of Accumulated Savings
Based on Monthly Withdrawals from Savings of $20,000

MONTHLY WITHDRAWAL	12%	13%	14%	15%	16%	17%	18%
			INTEREST RATES				
200	*	*	*	*	*	*	*
210	305	*	*	*	*	*	*
220	240	388	*	*	*	*	*
230	204	264	*	*	*	*	*
240	180	216	308	*	*	*	*
250	161	186	233	*	*	*	*
260	147	166	196	262	*	*	*
270	135	150	172	209	331	*	*
280	125	137	154	179	229	*	*
290	117	127	140	159	190	268	*
300	110	118	129	144	165	205	*
310	104	111	120	132	148	174	230
320	98	104	112	122	135	154	186
330	93	99	105	114	124	139	161
340	89	94	99	106	115	127	143
350	85	89	94	100	108	117	130
360	81	85	90	95	101	109	120
370	78	81	85	90	96	103	111
380	75	78	82	86	91	97	104
390	72	75	78	82	86	92	98
400	69	72	75	78	82	87	93
410	67	69	72	75	79	83	88
420	64	67	69	72	76	79	84
430	62	65	67	70	73	76	80
440	60	62	65	67	70	73	76
450	59	60	63	65	67	70	73
460	57	59	61	63	65	68	70
470	55	57	59	61	63	65	68
480	54	55	57	59	61	63	65
490	52	54	55	57	59	61	63
500	51	52	54	55	57	59	61
510	50	51	52	54	55	57	59
520	48	50	51	52	54	55	57
530	47	48	50	51	52	54	56
540	46	47	48	50	51	52	54
550	45	46	47	48	50	51	52
560	44	45	46	47	48	50	51
570	43	44	45	46	47	48	50
580	42	43	44	45	46	47	48
590	41	42	43	44	45	46	47
600	40	41	42	43	44	45	46
625	38	39	40	41	41	42	43
650	36	37	38	39	39	40	41
675	35	35	36	37	37	38	39
700	33	34	34	35	36	36	37
725	32	32	33	34	34	35	35
750	31	31	32	32	33	33	34
775	29	30	30	31	31	32	32
800	28	29	30	30	31	31	32
825	27	28	28	29	29	29	30
850	26	27	27	28	28	28	29
875	26	26	26	27	27	27	28
900	25	25	25	26	26	27	27
925	24	24	25	25	26	26	27
950	23	24	24	24	24	25	25
975	23	23	23	23	24	24	24
1000	22	22	22	23	23	23	23
1025	21	22	22	22	22	23	23
1050	21	21	21	21	22	22	23
1075	20	20	21	21	21	21	21

*Monthly withdrawal is less than the interest earned, thus the accumulated savings will never be depleted.

Life Expectancy of Accumulated Savings
Based on Monthly Withdrawals from Savings of $30,000

MONTHLY WITHDRAWAL	INTEREST RATES						
	5%	6%	7%	8%	9%	10%	11%
100	*	*	*	*	*	*	*
110	*	*	*	*	*	*	*
120	*	*	*	*	*	*	*
130	783	*	*	*	*	*	*
140	537	*	*	*	*	*	*
150	430	*	*	*	*	*	*
160	365	555	*	*	*	*	*
170	319	429	*	*	*	*	*
180	285	359	616	*	*	*	*
190	257	312	436	*	*	*	*
200	235	277	357	*	*	*	*
210	217	251	308	458	*	*	*
220	201	229	272	360	*	*	*
230	188	211	245	306	512	*	*
240	176	196	224	269	371	*	*
250	166	183	206	242	308	*	*
260	157	172	192	220	268	392	*
270	149	162	179	203	239	313	*
280	142	153	168	188	217	269	441
290	135	146	159	176	200	238	324
300	129	138	150	165	185	215	272
310	124	132	142	155	173	197	239
320	119	126	136	147	162	183	214
330	114	121	129	140	153	170	196
340	110	116	124	133	145	160	181
350	106	112	119	127	137	150	168
360	102	108	114	122	131	142	158
370	99	104	110	117	125	135	149
380	95	100	106	112	120	129	140
390	92	97	102	108	115	123	133
400	90	94	98	104	110	118	127
410	87	91	95	100	106	113	121
420	84	88	92	97	102	108	116
430	82	86	89	94	99	104	111
440	80	83	87	91	95	101	107
450	78	81	84	88	92	97	103
460	76	79	82	85	89	94	99
470	74	77	80	83	87	91	96
480	72	75	77	81	84	88	93
490	70	73	75	78	82	86	90
500	69	71	74	76	80	83	87
510	67	69	72	74	77	81	84
520	66	68	70	73	75	78	82
530	64	66	68	71	73	76	80
540	63	65	67	69	72	74	78
550	62	63	65	68	70	73	75
560	60	62	64	66	68	71	74
570	59	61	63	65	67	69	72
580	58	59	61	63	65	67	70
590	57	58	60	62	64	66	68
600	56	57	59	61	62	64	67
625	53	55	56	58	59	61	63
650	51	52	53	55	56	58	60
675	49	50	51	52	54	55	57
700	47	48	49	50	51	53	54
725	45	46	47	48	49	50	52
750	43	44	45	46	47	48	50
775	42	43	44	44	45	46	48
800	40	41	42	43	44	45	46
825	39	40	40	41	42	43	44

*Monthly withdrawal is less than the interest earned, thus the accumulated savings will never be depleted.

Life Expectancy of Accumulated Savings
Based on Monthly Withdrawals from Savings of $30,000

MONTHLY WITHDRAWAL	INTEREST RATES						
	12%	13%	14%	15%	16%	17%	18%
300	*	*	*	*	*	*	*
310	345	*	*	*	*	*	*
320	278	*	*	*	*	*	*
330	240	388	*	*	*	*	*
340	215	289	*	*	*	*	*
350	195	244	*	*	*	*	*
360	180	216	308	*	*	*	*
370	167	195	251	*	*	*	*
380	156	179	218	348	*	*	*
390	147	166	196	262	*	*	*
400	139	155	179	223	*	*	*
410	132	146	165	198	280	*	*
420	125	137	154	179	229	*	*
430	120	130	144	165	201	316	*
440	115	124	136	153	181	240	*
450	110	118	129	144	165	205	*
460	106	113	123	135	153	183	257
470	102	109	117	128	143	166	212
480	98	104	112	122	135	154	186
490	95	101	108	116	127	143	168
500	92	97	103	111	121	134	154
510	89	94	99	106	115	127	143
520	86	91	96	102	110	120	134
530	83	88	93	98	106	115	127
540	81	85	90	95	101	109	120
550	79	82	87	92	98	105	114
560	77	80	84	89	94	101	109
570	75	78	82	86	91	97	104
580	73	76	79	83	88	93	100
590	71	74	77	81	85	90	96
600	69	72	75	78	82	87	93
625	65	68	70	73	77	80	85
650	62	64	66	69	72	75	79
675	59	60	63	65	67	70	73
700	56	57	59	61	63	66	69
725	53	55	56	58	60	62	65
750	51	52	54	55	57	59	61
775	49	50	51	53	54	56	58
800	47	48	49	50	52	53	55
825	45	46	47	48	50	51	52
850	43	44	45	46	48	49	50
875	42	43	44	45	46	47	48
900	40	41	42	43	44	45	46
925	39	40	40	41	42	43	44
950	38	38	39	40	41	42	43
975	36	37	38	39	39	40	41
1000	35	36	37	37	38	39	40
1025	34	35	36	36	37	38	38
1050	33	34	34	35	36	36	37
1075	32	33	33	34	35	35	36
1100	32	32	33	33	34	34	35
1125	31	31	32	32	33	33	34
1150	30	30	31	31	32	32	33
1175	29	30	30	30	31	31	32
1200	28	29	29	30	30	31	31
1225	28	28	29	29	29	30	30
1250	27	27	28	28	29	29	29
1275	26	27	27	28	28	28	29
1300	26	26	27	27	27	28	28
1325	25	26	26	26	27	27	27

Monthly withdrawal is less than the interest earned, thus the accumulated savings will ever be depleted.

Life Expectancy of Accumulated Savings
Based on Monthly Withdrawals from Savings of $40,000

MONTHLY WITHDRAWAL	5%	6%	7%	8%	9%	10%	11%
				INTEREST RATES			
150	*	*	*	*	*	*	*
160	*	*	*	*	*	*	*
170	945	*	*	*	*	*	*
180	625	*	*	*	*	*	*
190	504	*	*	*	*	*	*
200	430	*	*	*	*	*	*
210	379	610	*	*	*	*	*
220	340	480	*	*	*	*	*
230	310	408	*	*	*	*	*
240	285	359	616	*	*	*	*
250	264	322	465	*	*	*	*
260	246	293	391	*	*	*	*
270	230	270	343	661	*	*	*
280	217	251	308	458	*	*	*
290	205	234	280	379	*	*	*
300	195	220	258	330	459	*	*
310	185	207	240	296	371	*	*
320	176	196	224	269	320	*	*
330	169	186	211	248	320	*	*
340	162	177	199	230	286	473	*
350	155	169	188	215	260	366	*
360	149	162	179	203	239	313	516
370	143	155	171	191	222	278	367
380	138	149	163	182	208	252	308
390	134	144	156	173	196	232	308
400	129	138	150	165	185	215	272
410	125	134	144	158	176	202	246
420	121	129	139	151	167	190	226
430	117	125	134	145	160	179	209
440	114	121	129	140	153	170	196
450	111	117	125	135	147	162	184
460	108	114	121	130	141	155	174
470	105	111	117	126	136	148	166
480	102	108	114	122	131	142	158
490	99	105	111	118	126	137	151
500	97	102	108	114	122	132	144
510	95	99	105	111	118	127	139
520	92	97	102	108	115	123	133
530	90	94	99	105	111	119	128
540	88	92	97	102	108	115	124
550	86	90	94	99	105	112	120
560	84	88	92	97	102	108	116
570	83	86	90	94	100	105	112
580	81	84	88	92	97	103	109
590	79	83	86	90	95	100	106
600	78	81	84	88	92	97	103
625	74	77	80	83	87	91	96
650	71	73	76	79	82	86	90
675	68	70	72	75	78	82	85
700	65	67	69	72	74	77	81
725	62	64	66	69	71	74	77
750	60	62	64	66	68	70	73
775	58	59	61	63	65	67	70
800	56	57	59	61	62	64	67
825	54	55	57	58	60	62	64
850	52	53	55	56	58	59	61
875	50	52	53	54	56	57	59
900	49	50	51	52	54	55	57
925	47	48	49	51	52	53	55
950	46	47	48	49	50	52	53

*Monthly withdrawal is less than the interest earned, thus the accumulated savings will never be depleted.

Life Expectancy of Accumulated Savings
Based on Monthly Withdrawals from Savings of $40,000

MONTHLY WITHDRAWAL	INTEREST RATES						
	12%	13%	14%	15%	16%	17%	18%
400	•	•	•	•	•	•	•
410	373	•	•	•	•	•	•
420	305	•	•	•	•	•	•
430	267	•	•	•	•	•	•
440	240	388	•	•	•	•	•
450	220	305	•	•	•	•	•
460	204	264	•	•	•	•	•
470	191	236	426	•	•	•	•
480	180	216	308	•	•	•	•
490	170	200	262	•	•	•	•
500	161	186	233	•	•	•	•
510	154	175	212	316	•	•	•
520	147	166	196	262	•	•	•
530	141	157	183	231	•	•	•
540	135	150	172	209	331	•	•
550	130	143	162	193	263	•	•
560	125	137	154	179	229	•	•
570	121	132	147	168	207	365	•
580	117	127	140	159	190	268	•
590	113	123	134	151	176	229	•
600	110	118	129	144	165	205	•
625	102	109	118	129	144	168	216
650	96	101	109	118	129	146	172
675	90	95	101	108	117	130	147
700	85	89	94	100	108	117	130
725	80	84	88	94	100	108	118
750	76	80	83	88	93	100	108
775	72	76	79	83	87	93	99
800	69	72	75	78	82	87	93
825	66	69	71	74	78	82	87
850	63	66	68	71	74	78	82
875	61	63	65	68	70	74	77
900	59	60	63	65	67	70	73
925	56	58	60	62	64	67	70
950	54	56	58	60	62	64	67
975	53	54	56	57	59	61	64
1000	51	52	54	55	57	59	61
1025	49	50	52	53	55	57	59
1050	48	49	50	52	53	55	56
1075	46	47	49	50	51	53	54
1100	45	46	47	48	50	51	52
1125	44	45	46	47	48	49	51
1150	42	43	44	45	47	48	49
1175	41	42	43	44	45	46	48
1200	40	41	42	43	44	45	46
1225	39	40	41	42	43	44	45
1250	38	39	40	41	41	42	43
1275	37	38	39	40	40	41	42
1300	36	37	38	39	39	40	41
1325	36	36	37	38	38	39	40
1350	35	35	36	37	37	38	39
1375	34	35	35	36	37	37	38
1400	33	34	35	35	36	36	37
1425	33	33	34	34	35	36	36
1450	32	32	33	34	34	35	35
1475	31	32	32	33	33	34	35
1500	31	31	32	32	33	33	34
1525	30	31	31	31	32	33	33
1550	29	30	30	31	31	32	32
1575	29	29	30	30	31	31	32

•Monthly withdrawal is less than the interest earned, thus the accumulated savings will never be depleted.

Life Expectancy of Accumulated Savings
Based on Monthly Withdrawals from Savings of $50,000

MONTHLY WITHDRAWAL	5%	6%	7%	8%	9%	10%	11%
200	*	*	*	*	*	*	*
210	1163	*	*	*	*	*	*
220	706	*	*	*	*	*	*
230	568	*	*	*	*	*	*
240	487	*	*	*	*	*	*
250	430	*	*	*	*	*	*
260	388	653	*	*	*	*	*
270	355	521	*	*	*	*	*
280	327	447	*	*	*	*	*
290	304	397	*	*	*	*	*
300	285	359	616	*	*	*	*
310	268	329	486	*	*	*	*
320	253	304	416	*	*	*	*
330	239	284	370	*	*	*	*
340	228	266	335	591	*	*	*
350	217	251	308	458	*	*	*
360	207	237	285	391	*	*	*
370	199	225	266	347	*	*	*
380	191	215	250	315	579	*	*
390	183	205	236	290	436	*	*
400	176	196	224	269	371	*	*
410	170	188	213	252	329	*	*
420	164	181	203	237	298	582	*
430	159	174	194	224	275	418	*
440	154	168	186	213	255	353	*
450	149	162	179	203	239	313	*
460	145	157	172	194	225	284	615
470	140	152	166	185	213	262	405
480	136	147	160	178	203	244	339
490	133	143	155	171	193	228	300
500	129	138	150	165	185	215	272
510	126	135	145	159	177	204	250
520	123	131	141	154	170	194	233
530	120	127	137	149	164	185	219
540	117	124	133	144	158	177	207
550	114	121	129	140	153	170	196
560	111	118	126	136	148	164	186
570	109	115	123	132	143	158	178
580	107	113	120	128	139	152	171
590	104	110	117	125	135	147	164
600	102	108	114	122	131	142	158
625	97	102	108	114	122	132	144
650	92	97	102	108	115	123	133
675	88	92	97	102	108	115	124
700	84	88	92	97	102	108	116
725	81	84	88	92	97	103	109
750	78	81	84	88	92	97	103
775	75	78	81	84	88	92	98
800	72	75	77	81	84	88	93
825	69	72	75	77	81	84	88
850	67	69	72	74	77	81	84
875	65	67	69	72	74	77	81
900	63	65	67	69	72	74	78
925	61	63	65	67	69	72	74
950	59	61	63	65	67	69	72
975	57	59	61	62	64	67	69
1000	56	57	59	61	62	64	67
1025	54	56	57	59	60	62	64
1050	53	54	55	57	59	60	6
1075	51	53	53	54	55	57	6

*Monthly withdrawal is less than the interest earned, thus the accumulated savings will never be depleted.

Life Expectancy of Accumulated Savings
Based on Monthly Withdrawals from Savings of $50,000

MONTHLY WITHDRAWAL	INTEREST RATES						
	12%	13%	14%	15%	16%	17%	18%
500	*	*	*	*	*	*	*
510	395	*	*	*	*	*	*
520	327	*	*	*	*	*	*
530	288	*	*	*	*	*	*
540	261	*	*	*	*	*	*
550	240	388	*	*	*	*	*
560	224	317	*	*	*	*	*
570	210	278	*	*	*	*	*
580	199	252	*	*	*	*	*
590	188	232	386	*	*	*	*
600	180	216	308	*	*	*	*
625	161	186	233	*	*	*	*
650	147	166	196	262	*	*	*
675	135	150	172	209	331	*	*
700	125	137	154	179	229	*	*
725	117	127	140	159	190	268	*
750	110	118	129	144	165	205	*
775	104	111	120	132	148	174	230
800	98	104	112	122	135	154	186
825	93	99	105	114	124	139	161
850	89	94	99	106	115	127	143
875	85	89	94	100	108	117	130
900	81	85	90	95	101	109	120
925	78	81	85	90	96	103	111
950	75	78	82	86	91	97	104
975	72	75	78	82	86	92	98
1000	69	72	75	78	82	87	93
1025	67	69	72	75	79	83	88
1050	64	67	69	72	76	79	84
1075	62	65	67	70	73	76	80
1100	60	62	65	67	70	73	76
1125	59	60	63	65	67	70	73
1150	57	59	61	63	65	68	70
1175	55	57	59	61	63	65	68
1200	54	55	57	59	61	63	65
1225	52	54	55	57	59	61	63
1250	51	52	54	55	57	59	61
1275	50	51	52	54	55	57	59
1300	48	50	51	52	54	55	59
1325	47	48	50	51	52	54	56
1350	46	47	48	50	51	52	54
1375	45	46	47	48	50	51	52
1400	44	45	46	47	48	50	51
1425	43	44	45	46	47	48	50
1450	42	43	44	45	46	47	48
1475	41	42	43	44	45	46	47
1500	40	41	42	43	44	45	46
1525	39	40	41	42	43	44	45
1550	39	39	40	41	42	43	44
1575	38	39	39	40	41	42	43
1600	37	38	39	39	40	41	42
1625	36	37	38	39	39	40	41
1650	36	36	37	38	39	39	40
1675	35	36	36	37	38	39	39
1700	35	35	36	36	37	38	39
1725	34	34	35	36	36	37	38
1750	33	34	34	35	36	36	37
1775	33	33	34	34	35	36	36
1800	32	33	33	34	34	35	36
1825	32	32	33	33	34	34	35

*onthly withdrawal is less than the interest earned, thus the accumulated savings will ꞏer be depleted.

Life Expectancy of Accumulated Savings
Based on Monthly Withdrawals from Savings of $60,000

MONTHLY WITHDRAWAL	5%	6%	7%	8%	9%	10%	11
				INTEREST RATES			
250	*	*	*	*	*	*	*
260	783	*	*	*	*	*	*
270	625	*	*	*	*	*	*
280	537	*	*	*	*	*	*
290	476	*	*	*	*	*	*
300	430	*	*	*	*	*	*
310	394	688	*	*	*	*	*
320	365	555	*	*	*	*	*
330	340	480	*	*	*	*	*
340	319	429	*	*	*	*	*
350	301	390	*	*	*	*	*
360	285	359	616	*	*	*	*
370	270	333	501	*	*	*	*
380	257	312	436	*	*	*	*
390	246	293	391	*	*	*	*
400	235	277	357	*	*	*	*
410	226	263	330	558	*	*	*
420	217	251	308	458	*	*	*
430	209	239	289	400	*	*	*
440	201	229	272	360	*	*	*
450	195	220	258	330	*	*	*
460	188	211	245	306	512	*	*
470	182	203	234	286	422	*	*
480	176	196	224	269	371	*	*
490	171	189	215	255	335	*	*
500	166	183	206	242	308	*	*
510	162	177	199	230	286	473	*
520	157	172	192	220	268	392	*
530	153	167	185	211	253	346	*
540	149	162	179	203	239	313	*
550	145	158	173	195	228	288	*
560	142	153	168	188	217	269	4
570	138	149	163	182	208	252	3
580	135	146	159	176	200	238	3
590	132	142	154	170	192	226	2
600	129	138	150	165	185	215	2
625	122	131	141	153	170	193	2
650	116	124	132	143	157	176	2
675	111	117	125	135	147	162	1
700	106	112	119	127	137	150	1
725	101	107	113	120	129	140	1
750	97	102	108	114	122	132	1
775	93	98	103	109	116	124	1
800	90	94	98	104	110	118	1
825	86	90	94	99	105	112	1
850	83	87	91	95	100	106	1
875	80	84	87	91	96	102	1
900	78	81	84	88	92	97	
925	75	78	81	85	89	93	
950	73	76	79	82	85	90	
975	71	73	76	79	82	86	
1000	69	71	74	76	80	83	
1025	67	69	71	74	77	80	
1050	65	67	69	72	74	77	
1075	63	65	67	70	72	75	
1100	62	63	65	68	70	73	
1125	60	62	64	66	68	70	
1150	58	60	62	64	66	68	
1175	57	59	60	62	64	66	
1200	56	57	59	61	62	64	

*Monthly withdrawal is less than the interest earned, thus the accumulated savings will never be depleted.

Life Expectancy of Accumulated Savings
Based on Monthly Withdrawals from Savings of $60,000

MONTHLY WITHDRAWAL	INTEREST RATES						
	12%	13%	14%	15%	16%	17%	18%
600	•	•	•	•	•	•	•
625	323	•	•	•	•	•	•
650	257	•	•	•	•	•	•
675	220	305	•	•	•	•	•
700	195	244	•	•	•	•	•
725	176	210	290	•	•	•	•
750	161	186	233	•	•	•	•
775	149	169	201	276	•	•	•
800	139	155	179	223	•	•	•
825	130	143	162	193	263	•	•
850	122	134	149	172	213	•	•
875	116	126	138	156	185	252	•
900	110	118	129	144	165	205	•
925	105	112	121	134	151	178	242
950	100	106	115	125	139	160	197
975	96	101	109	118	129	146	172
1000	92	97	103	111	121	134	154
1025	88	93	99	105	114	125	141
1050	85	89	94	100	108	117	130
1075	82	86	90	96	102	111	121
1100	79	82	87	92	98	105	114
1125	76	80	83	88	93	100	108
1150	74	77	80	85	89	95	102
1175	71	74	78	81	86	91	97
1200	69	72	75	78	82	87	93
1225	67	70	73	76	79	84	89
1250	65	68	70	73	77	80	85
1275	63	66	68	71	74	78	82
1300	62	64	66	69	72	75	79
1325	60	62	64	67	69	72	76
1350	59	60	63	65	67	70	73
1375	57	59	61	63	65	68	71
1400	56	57	59	61	63	66	69
1425	54	56	58	60	62	64	67
1450	53	55	56	58	60	62	65
1475	52	53	55	57	59	61	63
1500	51	52	54	55	57	59	61
1525	50	51	52	54	56	57	59
1550	49	50	51	53	54	56	58
1575	48	49	50	52	53	55	56
1600	47	48	49	50	52	53	55
1625	46	47	48	49	51	52	54
1650	45	46	47	48	50	51	52
1675	44	45	46	47	49	50	52
1700	43	44	45	46	48	49	50
1725	42	43	44	45	47	48	49
1750	42	43	44	45	46	47	48
1775	41	42	43	44	45	46	47
1800	40	41	42	43	44	45	46
1825	40	40	41	42	43	44	45
1850	39	40	40	41	42	43	44
1875	38	39	40	41	41	42	43
1900	38	38	39	40	41	42	43
1925	37	38	38	39	40	41	42
1950	36	37	38	39	39	40	41
1975	36	37	37	38	39	40	40
2000	35	36	37	37	38	39	40
2050	34	35	36	36	37	38	38
2100	33	34	34	35	36	37	37
2150	32	33	33	34	35	35	36

*Monthly withdrawal is less than the interest earned, thus the accumulated savings will never be depleted.

Life Expectancy of Accumulated Savings
Based on Monthly Withdrawals from Savings of $70,000

MONTHLY WITHDRAWAL	INTEREST RATES						
	5%	6%	7%	8%	9%	10%	11%
300	861	*	*	*	*	*	*
310	680	*	*	*	*	*	*
320	583	*	*	*	*	*	*
330	517	*	*	*	*	*	*
340	469	*	*	*	*	*	*
350	430	*	*	*	*	*	*
360	399	718	*	*	*	*	*
370	373	585	*	*	*	*	*
380	350	509	*	*	*	*	*
390	331	456	*	*	*	*	*
400	314	416	*	*	*	*	*
410	298	385	*	*	*	*	*
420	285	359	946	*	*	*	*
430	272	337	616	*	*	*	*
440	261	318	513	*	*	*	*
450	251	301	409	*	*	*	*
460	241	286	375	*	*	*	*
470	233	273	349	744	*	*	*
480	225	261	326	539	*	*	*
490	217	251	308	458	*	*	*
500	210	241	291	407	*	*	*
510	204	232	277	371	*	*	*
520	197	224	264	342	*	*	*
530	192	216	253	319	624	*	*
540	186	209	242	300	479	*	*
550	181	202	233	284	413	*	*
560	176	196	224	269	371	*	*
570	172	190	216	257	339	*	*
580	168	185	209	245	315	*	*
590	164	180	202	235	295	540	*
600	160	175	196	226	278	431	*
625	151	164	182	206	245	326	*
650	143	155	170	190	220	274	477
675	136	146	159	176	201	240	329
700	129	138	150	165	185	215	272
725	123	132	142	155	172	196	237
750	118	126	135	146	161	181	212
775	113	120	128	138	151	168	192
800	109	115	122	131	142	157	177
825	104	110	117	125	135	147	164
850	101	106	112	119	128	139	154
875	97	102	108	114	122	132	144
900	94	98	103	109	117	125	136
925	91	95	100	105	112	120	129
950	88	92	96	101	107	114	123
975	85	89	93	98	103	109	112
1000	82	86	90	94	99	105	107
1025	80	83	87	91	96	101	103
1050	78	81	84	88	92	97	99
1075	76	78	82	85	89	94	97
1100	74	76	79	83	86	91	95
1125	72	74	77	80	84	88	92
1150	70	72	75	78	81	85	89
1175	68	70	73	76	79	82	86
1200	66	69	71	74	77	80	83
1225	65	67	69	72	74	77	81
1250	63	65	67	70	72	75	78
1275	62	64	66	68	71	73	76
1300	61	62	64	66	69	71	74
1325	59	61	63	65	67	69	72

*Monthly withdrawal is less than the interest earned, thus the accumulated savings will never be depleted.

Life Expectancy of Accumulated Savings
Based on Monthly Withdrawals from Savings of $70,000

MONTHLY WITHDRAWAL	INTEREST RATES						
	12%	13%	14%	15%	16%	17%	18%
725	338	*	*	*	*	*	*
750	272	*	*	*	*	*	*
775	234	356	*	*	*	*	*
800	208	274	*	*	*	*	*
825	189	233	396	*	*	*	*
850	174	206	279	*	*	*	*
875	161	186	233	*	*	*	*
900	151	171	205	288	*	*	*
925	142	159	184	234	*	*	*
950	134	148	169	204	305	*	*
975	127	139	156	183	238	*	*
1000	120	131	146	167	204	340	*
1025	115	124	137	154	182	243	*
1050	110	118	129	144	165	205	*
1075	105	113	122	135	153	181	252
1100	101	108	116	127	142	164	207
1125	97	104	111	121	133	151	181
1150	94	99	106	115	126	140	164
1175	91	96	102	109	119	132	150
1200	87	92	98	105	113	124	139
1225	85	89	94	100	108	117	130
1250	82	86	91	96	103	112	123
1275	80	83	88	93	99	106	116
1300	77	81	85	89	95	102	110
1325	75	78	82	86	92	98	105
1350	73	76	80	84	88	94	101
1375	71	74	77	81	85	90	96
1400	69	72	75	78	82	87	93
1425	67	70	73	76	80	84	89
1450	66	68	71	74	77	81	86
1475	64	66	69	72	75	79	83
1500	63	65	67	70	73	76	80
1525	61	63	66	68	71	74	78
1550	60	62	64	66	69	72	75
1575	59	60	63	65	67	70	73
1600	57	59	61	63	66	68	71
1625	56	58	60	62	64	66	69
1650	55	57	58	60	62	65	67
1675	54	55	57	59	61	63	66
1700	53	54	56	58	60	62	64
1725	52	53	55	56	58	60	63
1750	51	52	54	55	57	59	61
1775	50	51	53	54	56	58	60
1800	49	50	52	53	55	56	58
1825	48	49	51	52	54	55	57
1850	47	48	50	51	53	54	56
1875	46	48	49	50	51	53	55
1900	46	47	48	49	51	52	54
1925	45	46	47	48	50	51	52
1950	44	45	46	47	49	50	51
1975	43	44	46	47	48	49	50
2000	43	44	45	46	47	48	50
2050	41	42	43	44	45	46	48
2100	40	41	42	43	44	45	46
2150	39	40	41	42	42	43	45
2200	38	39	39	40	41	42	43
2250	37	38	38	39	40	41	42
2300	36	37	37	38	39	40	40
2400	34	35	35	36	37	37	38
2500	33	33	34	34	35	35	36

Monthly withdrawal is less than the interest earned, thus the accumulated savings will ever be depleted.

Life Expectancy of Accumulated Savings
Based on Monthly Withdrawals from Savings of $80,000

MONTHLY WITHDRAWAL	INTEREST RATES						
	5%	6%	7%	8%	9%	10%	11
300	*	*	*	*	*	*	*
310	*	*	*	*	*	*	*
320	*	*	*	*	*	*	*
330	*	*	*	*	*	*	*
340	945	*	*	*	*	*	*
350	732	*	*	*	*	*	*
360	625	*	*	*	*	*	*
370	555	*	*	*	*	*	*
380	504	*	*	*	*	*	*
390	463	*	*	*	*	*	*
400	430	*	*	*	*	*	*
410	403	744	*	*	*	*	*
420	379	610	*	*	*	*	*
430	358	533	*	*	*	*	*
440	340	480	*	*	*	*	*
450	324	440	*	*	*	*	*
460	310	408	*	*	*	*	*
470	297	381	850	*	*	*	*
480	285	359	616	*	*	*	*
490	274	339	523	*	*	*	*
500	264	322	465	*	*	*	*
510	254	307	423	*	*	*	*
520	246	293	391	*	*	*	*
530	238	281	365	*	*	*	*
540	230	270	343	661	*	*	*
550	224	260	324	526	*	*	*
560	217	251	308	458	*	*	*
570	211	242	293	412	*	*	*
580	205	234	280	379	*	*	*
590	200	227	269	352	*	*	*
600	195	220	258	330	*	*	*
625	183	204	236	288	430	*	*
650	172	191	217	258	343	*	*
675	163	180	202	234	294	529	*
700	155	169	188	215	260	366	*
725	148	160	177	200	235	303	4
750	141	152	167	186	215	264	41
775	135	145	158	175	199	237	32
800	129	138	150	165	185	215	27
825	124	132	143	156	173	198	24
850	119	127	136	148	163	184	21
875	115	122	131	141	154	172	19
900	111	117	125	135	147	162	18
925	107	113	120	129	139	153	17
950	103	109	116	124	133	145	16
975	100	105	111	119	127	138	15
1000	97	102	108	114	122	132	14
1025	94	99	104	110	117	126	13
1050	91	96	101	106	113	121	13
1075	89	93	97	103	109	116	12
1100	86	90	94	99	105	112	12
1125	84	88	92	96	101	108	11
1150	82	85	89	93	98	104	11
1175	80	83	87	91	95	100	10
1200	78	81	84	88	92	97	10
1225	76	79	82	86	90	94	10
1250	74	77	80	83	87	91	9
1275	72	75	78	81	85	89	9
1300	71	73	76	79	82	86	9
1325	69	72	74	77	80	84	8

*Monthly withdrawal is less than the interest earned, thus the accumulated savings will never be depleted.

Life Expectancy of Accumulated Savings
Based on Monthly Withdrawals from Savings of $80,000

MONTHLY WITHDRAWAL	INTEREST RATES						
	12%	13%	14%	15%	16%	17%	18%
850	284	*	*	*	*	*	*
875	246	431	*	*	*	*	*
900	220	305	*	*	*	*	*
925	201	256	*	*	*	*	*
950	185	225	348	*	*	*	*
975	172	203	271	*	*	*	*
1000	161	186	233	*	*	*	*
1025	152	173	208	298	*	*	*
1050	144	161	189	245	*	*	*
1075	137	152	174	214	366	*	*
1100	130	143	162	193	263	*	*
1125	124	136	152	176	223	*	*
1150	119	130	143	163	198	300	*
1175	114	124	136	153	179	237	*
1200	110	118	129	144	165	205	*
1225	106	114	123	136	154	184	261
1250	102	109	118	129	144	168	216
1275	99	105	113	123	136	156	190
1300	96	101	109	118	129	146	172
1325	93	98	105	113	123	137	158
1350	90	95	101	108	117	130	147
1375	87	92	97	104	112	123	138
1400	85	89	94	100	108	117	130
1425	82	86	91	97	104	112	123
1450	80	84	88	94	100	108	118
1475	78	82	86	91	96	103	112
1500	76	80	83	88	93	100	108
1525	74	77	81	85	90	96	103
1550	72	76	79	83	87	93	99
1575	71	74	77	81	85	90	96
1600	69	72	75	78	82	87	93
1625	68	70	73	76	80	84	90
1650	66	69	71	74	78	82	87
1675	65	67	70	73	76	80	84
1700	63	66	68	71	74	78	82
1725	62	64	67	69	72	76	79
1750	61	63	65	68	70	74	77
1775	60	62	64	66	69	72	75
1800	59	60	63	65	67	70	73
1825	57	59	61	63	66	68	71
1850	56	58	60	62	64	67	70
1875	55	57	59	61	63	65	68
1900	54	56	58	60	62	64	67
1925	53	55	57	58	60	63	65
1950	53	54	56	57	59	61	64
1975	52	53	55	56	58	60	62
2000	51	52	54	55	57	59	61
2050	49	50	52	53	55	57	59
2100	48	49	50	52	53	55	56
2150	46	47	49	50	51	53	54
2200	45	46	47	48	50	51	52
2250	44	45	46	47	48	49	51
2300	42	43	44	45	47	48	49
2400	40	41	42	43	44	45	46
2500	38	39	40	41	41	42	43
2600	36	37	38	39	39	40	41
2700	35	35	36	37	37	38	39
2800	33	34	34	35	36	36	37
2900	32	32	33	34	34	35	35
3000	31	31	32	32	33	33	34

*Monthly withdrawal is less than the interest earned, thus the accumulated savings will never be depleted.

265

Life Expectancy of Accumulated Savings
Based on Monthly Withdrawals from Savings of $90,000

MONTHLY WITHDRAWAL	INTEREST RATES						
	5%	6%	7%	8%	9%	10%	11%
350	*	*	*	*	*	*	*
360	*	*	*	*	*	*	*
370	*	*	*	*	*	*	*
380	1041	*	*	*	*	*	*
390	783	*	*	*	*	*	*
400	666	*	*	*	*	*	*
410	591	*	*	*	*	*	*
420	537	*	*	*	*	*	*
430	494	*	*	*	*	*	*
440	459	*	*	*	*	*	*
450	430	*	*	*	*	*	*
460	406	767	*	*	*	*	*
470	384	632	*	*	*	*	*
480	365	555	*	*	*	*	*
490	348	502	*	*	*	*	*
500	333	461	*	*	*	*	*
510	319	429	*	*	*	*	*
520	307	402	*	*	*	*	*
530	295	379	801	*	*	*	*
540	285	359	616	*	*	*	*
550	275	341	531	*	*	*	*
560	266	326	476	*	*	*	*
570	257	312	436	*	*	*	*
580	250	299	405	*	*	*	*
590	242	288	379	*	*	*	*
600	235	277	357	*	*	*	*
625	220	255	315	484	*	*	*
650	206	236	283	386	*	*	*
675	195	220	258	330	*	*	*
700	184	206	238	292	445	*	*
725	175	194	221	264	357	*	*
750	166	183	206	242	308	*	*
775	159	174	194	223	274	413	*
800	152	165	183	208	248	334	*
825	145	158	173	195	228	288	*
850	139	151	165	184	211	257	386
875	134	144	157	174	197	234	313
900	129	138	150	165	185	215	272
925	125	133	144	157	175	200	243
950	120	128	138	150	165	187	222
975	116	124	132	143	157	176	205
1000	113	119	127	137	150	167	191
1025	109	115	123	132	143	158	179
1050	106	112	119	127	137	150	168
1075	103	108	115	122	132	144	159
1100	100	105	111	118	127	137	151
1125	97	102	108	114	122	132	144
1150	94	99	104	111	118	127	138
1175	92	96	101	107	114	122	132
1200	90	94	98	104	110	118	127
1225	87	91	96	101	107	114	122
1250	85	89	93	98	103	110	118
1275	83	87	91	95	100	106	114
1300	81	85	88	93	98	103	110
1325	80	83	86	90	95	100	106
1350	78	81	84	88	92	97	103
1375	76	79	82	86	90	95	100
1400	74	77	80	84	88	92	97
1425	73	76	79	82	85	90	94
1450	71	74	77	80	83	87	92

*Monthly withdrawal is less than the interest earned, thus the accumulated savings will never be depleted.

Life Expectancy of Accumulated Savings
Based on Monthly Withdrawals from Savings of $90,000

MONTHLY WITHDRAWAL	INTEREST RATES						
	12%	13%	14%	15%	16%	17%	18%
850	*	*	*	*	*	*	*
875	*	*	*	*	*	*	*
900	*	*	*	*	*	*	*
925	362	*	*	*	*	*	*
950	295	*	*	*	*	*	*
975	257	*	*	*	*	*	*
1000	231	342	*	*	*	*	*
1025	211	280	*	*	*	*	*
1050	195	244	*	*	*	*	*
1075	182	220	324	*	*	*	*
1100	171	201	266	*	*	*	*
1125	161	186	233	*	*	*	*
1150	153	174	210	308	*	*	*
1175	145	164	193	254	*	*	*
1200	139	155	179	223	*	*	*
1225	133	147	167	201	293	*	*
1250	127	140	157	185	243	*	*
1275	122	134	149	172	213	*	*
1300	118	128	142	161	193	280	*
1325	114	123	135	152	178	232	*
1350	110	118	129	144	165	205	*
1375	106	114	124	137	155	186	269
1400	103	110	119	131	146	171	223
1425	100	106	115	125	139	160	197
1450	97	103	111	120	132	150	179
1475	94	100	107	115	126	142	165
1500	92	97	103	111	121	134	154
1525	89	94	100	107	116	128	145
1550	87	92	97	104	112	122	137
1575	85	89	94	100	108	117	130
1600	83	87	92	97	104	113	124
1625	81	85	89	94	101	109	119
1650	79	82	87	92	98	105	114
1675	77	80	84	89	95	101	110
1700	75	79	82	87	92	98	106
1725	74	77	80	85	89	95	102
1750	72	75	78	82	87	92	99
1775	71	73	77	80	85	90	96
1800	69	72	75	78	82	87	93
1825	68	70	73	77	80	85	90
1850	66	69	72	75	78	83	87
1875	65	68	70	73	77	80	85
1900	64	66	69	72	75	79	83
1925	63	65	67	70	73	77	81
1950	62	64	66	69	72	75	79
1975	61	63	65	67	70	73	77
2000	60	62	64	66	69	72	75
2050	58	59	61	64	66	69	72
2100	56	57	59	61	63	66	69
2150	54	56	57	59	61	63	66
2200	52	54	55	57	59	61	63
2250	51	52	54	55	57	59	61
2300	49	51	52	54	55	57	59
2400	47	48	49	50	52	53	55
2500	44	45	46	48	49	50	52
2600	42	43	44	45	46	47	49
2700	40	41	42	43	44	45	46
2800	38	39	40	41	42	43	44
2900	37	38	38	39	40	41	42
3000	35	36	37	37	38	39	40

Monthly withdrawal is less than the interest earned, thus the accumulated savings will never be depleted.

Life Expectancy of Accumulated Savings
Based on Monthly Withdrawals from Savings of $100,000

MONTHLY WITHDRAWAL	INTEREST RATES						
	5%	6%	7%	8%	9%	10%	11%
350	*	*	*	*	*	*	*
360	*	*	*	*	*	*	*
370	*	*	*	*	*	*	*
380	*	*	*	*	*	*	*
390	*	*	*	*	*	*	*
400	*	*	*	*	*	*	*
410	*	*	*	*	*	*	*
420	1163	*	*	*	*	*	*
430	835	*	*	*	*	*	*
440	706	*	*	*	*	*	*
450	625	*	*	*	*	*	*
460	568	*	*	*	*	*	*
470	523	*	*	*	*	*	*
480	487	*	*	*	*	*	*
490	456	*	*	*	*	*	*
500	430	*	*	*	*	*	*
510	408	788	*	*	*	*	*
520	388	653	*	*	*	*	*
530	370	575	*	*	*	*	*
540	355	521	*	*	*	*	*
550	340	480	*	*	*	*	*
560	327	447	*	*	*	*	*
570	315	420	*	*	*	*	*
580	304	397	*	*	*	*	*
590	294	377	770	*	*	*	*
600	285	359	616	*	*	*	*
625	264	322	465	*	*	*	*
650	246	293	391	*	*	*	*
675	230	270	343	661	*	*	*
700	217	251	308	458	*	*	*
725	205	234	280	379	*	*	*
750	195	220	258	330	*	*	*
775	185	207	240	296	459	*	*
800	176	196	224	269	371	*	*
825	169	186	211	248	320	*	*
850	162	177	199	230	286	473	*
875	155	169	188	215	260	366	*
900	149	162	179	203	239	313	*
925	143	155	171	191	222	278	51
950	138	149	163	182	208	252	36
975	134	144	156	173	196	232	30
1000	129	138	150	165	185	215	27
1025	125	134	144	158	176	202	24
1050	121	129	139	151	167	190	22
1075	117	125	134	145	160	179	20
1100	114	121	129	140	153	170	19
1125	111	117	125	135	147	162	18
1150	108	114	121	130	141	155	17
1175	105	111	117	126	136	148	16
1200	102	108	114	122	131	142	15
1225	99	105	111	118	126	137	15
1250	97	102	108	114	122	132	14
1275	95	99	105	111	118	127	13
1300	92	97	102	108	115	123	13
1325	90	94	99	105	111	119	12
1350	88	92	97	102	108	115	12
1375	86	90	94	99	105	112	12
1400	84	88	92	97	102	108	1
1425	83	86	90	94	100	105	1
1450	81	84	88	92	97	103	10

*Monthly withdrawal is less than the interest earned, thus the accumulated savings will never be depleted.

Life Expectancy of Accumulated Savings
Based on Monthly Withdrawals from Savings of $100,000

MONTHLY WITHDRAWAL	INTEREST RATES						
	12%	13%	14%	15%	16%	17%	18%
850	*	*	*	*	*	*	*
875	*	*	*	*	*	*	*
900	*	*	*	*	*	*	*
925	*	*	*	*	*	*	*
950	*	*	*	*	*	*	*
975	*	*	*	*	*	*	*
1000	*	*	*	*	*	*	*
1025	373	*	*	*	*	*	*
1050	305	*	*	*	*	*	*
1075	267	*	*	*	*	*	*
1100	240	388	*	*	*	*	*
1125	220	305	*	*	*	*	*
1150	204	264	*	*	*	*	*
1175	191	236	426	*	*	*	*
1200	180	216	308	*	*	*	*
1225	170	200	262	*	*	*	*
1250	161	186	233	*	*	*	*
1275	1E4	175	212	316	*	*	*
1300	147	166	196	262	*	*	*
1325	141	157	183	231	*	*	*
1350	135	150	172	209	331	*	*
1375	130	143	162	193	263	*	*
1400	125	137	154	179	229	*	*
1425	121	132	147	168	207	365	*
1450	117	127	140	159	190	268	*
1475	113	123	134	151	176	229	*
1500	110	118	129	144	165	205	*
1525	107	115	124	137	156	187	276
1550	104	111	120	132	148	174	230
1575	101	108	116	127	141	163	204
1600	98	104	112	122	135	154	186
1625	96	101	109	118	129	146	172
1650	93	99	105	114	124	139	161
1675	91	96	102	110	120	132	151
1700	89	94	99	106	115	127	143
1725	87	91	97	103	111	122	136
1750	85	89	94	100	108	117	130
1775	83	87	92	98	105	113	125
1800	81	85	90	95	101	109	120
1825	79	83	87	92	99	106	115
1850	78	81	85	90	96	103	111
1875	76	80	83	88	93	100	108
1900	75	78	82	86	91	97	104
1925	73	76	80	84	89	94	101
1950	72	75	78	82	86	92	98
1975	70	73	77	80	84	89	95
2000	69	72	75	78	82	87	93
2050	67	69	72	75	79	83	88
2100	64	67	69	72	76	79	84
2150	62	65	67	70	73	76	80
2200	60	62	65	67	70	73	76
2250	59	60	63	65	67	70	73
2300	57	59	61	63	65	68	70
2400	54	55	57	59	61	63	65
2500	51	52	54	55	57	59	61
2600	48	50	51	52	54	55	57
2700	46	47	48	50	51	52	54
2800	44	45	46	47	48	50	51
2900	42	43	44	45	46	47	48
3000	40	41	42	43	44	45	46

Monthly withdrawal is less than the interest earned, thus the accumulated savings will ever be depleted.

Glossary

amortization The process of repaying a loan through a series of installment payments at periodic intervals.

annual interest rate A percentage that, when multiplied by the principal, gives the amount of money that the principal will earn over the period of a year.

annuity A series of payments over a specified period of time.

assets Anything owned that has exchange value.

capital The assets of a person or a company. Capital may be cash or other valuables.

CD *See* certificate of deposit.

certificate of deposit (CD) A document issued to a person to indicate how much money, in long-term savings, he or she has on deposit with a bank.

compounding The process of reinvesting interest to earn more interest.

credit Money borrowed now with the promise to pay later.

current account A bank account from which money can be withdrawn at will.

demand deposit A bank account that has no penalty for withdrawals.

deposit account A bank account from which withdrawals are restricted.

discounted loan A loan that is reduced by the interest charges at the time the loan is given.

Federal Deposit Insurance Corporation (FDIC) An agency of the government that insures savings up to a maximum amount.

installment loan A loan in which a series of regular payments pays off the principal and the interest.

interest The amount of money that the principal earns during a specified period of time.

principal The initial amount of money invested or borrowed.

time deposit An investment for a specified period of time at a higher interest rate than is available with a passbook account. This usually requires a minimum amount of money, and the time period may vary from one month to several years.

yield The return on an investment.

More selected BARRON'S titles:

DICTIONARY OF ACCOUNTING TERMS
Joel Siegel and Jae Shim
Approximately 2500 terms are defined for accountants, business managers, students, and small business persons.
Paperback, $8.95, Canada $12.95/ISBN 3766-9

DICTIONARY OF ADVERTISING AND DIRECT MAIL TERM
Jane Imber and Betsy-Ann Toffler
Approximately 3000 terms are defined as reference for ad industr professionals, students, and consumers.
Paperback, $8.95, Canada $12.95/ISBN 3765-0

DICTIONARY OF BUSINESS TERMS
Jack P. Friedman, general editor
Over 6000 entries define a wide range of terms used throughout business, real estate, taxes, banking, investment, more.
Paperback, $8.95, Canada $12.95/ISBN 3775-8

DICTIONARY OF COMPUTER TERMS
Douglas Downing and Michael Covington
Over 600 key computer terms are clearly explained, and sample programs included. Paperback, $8.95, Canada $12.95/ISBN 2905

DICTIONARY OF INSURANCE TERMS, by Harvey W. Rubin
Approximately 2500 insurance terms are defined as they relate to property, casualty, life, health, and other types of insurance.
Paperback, $8.95, Canada $12.95/ISBN 3722-3, 448 pages

BARRON'S BUSINESS REVIEW SERIES
Self-instruction guides cover topics taught in a college-level busin course, presenting essential concepts in an easy-to-follow format.
Each book paperback $9.95, Canada $13.95, approx. 228 pages
ACCOUNTING, by Peter J. Eisen/ISBN 3574-7
BUSINESS LAW, by Hardwicke and Emerson/ISBN 3495-3
BUSINESS STATISTICS, by Downing and Clark/ISBN 3576-3
ECONOMICS, by Walter J. Wessels/ISBN 3560-7
FINANCE, by A. A. Groppelli and Ehsan Nikhbakht/ISBN 3561
MANAGEMENT, by Montana and Charnov/ISBN 3559-3
MARKETING, by Richard L. Sandhusen/ISBN 3494-5
QUANTITATIVE METHODS, by Downing and Clark. $10.95,
Canada $15.95/ISBN 3947-5

BARRON'S TALKING BUSINESS SERIES:
BILINGUAL DICTIONARIES
Five bilingual dictionaries translate about 3000 terms not found most foreign phrasebooks. Includes words related to accounting, sales, banking, computers, export/import and finance.
Each book paperback, $6.95, Canada $9.95, approx. 256 pages
TALKING BUSINESS IN FRENCH, by Beppie LeGal/ISBN 374
TALKING BUSINESS IN GERMAN, by Henry Strutz/ISBN 374
TALKING BUSINESS IN ITALIAN, by Frank Rakus/ISBN 3754
TALKING BUSINESS IN JAPANESE, by C. & N. Akiyama/
ISBN 3848-7
TALKING BUSINESS IN SPANISH, by Fryer and Faria/ISBN 37

All prices are in U.S. and Canadian dollars and subject to change without notic At your bookseller, or order direct adding 10% postage (minimum charge $1.50), N.Y. residents add sales tax.

Barron's Educational Series, Inc.
250 Wireless Boulevard, Hauppauge, NY 11788
Call toll-free: 1-800-645-3476, in NY 1-800-257-5729
In Canada: 195 Allstate Parkway, Markham, Ontario L3R4T8

More selected BARRON'S titles:

DICTIONARY OF FINANCE AND INVESTMENT TERMS
John Downes and Jordan Goodman
Defines and explains over 2500 Wall Street terms for professionals, business students, and average investors.
Paperback $8.95, Canada $12.95/ISBN 2522-9, 495 pages
"This is an invaluable fog-cutter for investors."
—William S. Rukeyser, Managing Editor, FORTUNE Magazine

DICTIONARY OF REAL ESTATE TERMS
Jack P. Friedman, Jack C. Harris, and Bruce Lindeman
Defines over 1200 terms, with examples and illustrations. A key reference for everyone in real estate. Comprehensive and current.
Paperback $8.95, Canada $12.95/ISBN 2521-0, 224 pages

REAL ESTATE HANDBOOK
Jack P. Friedman, Jack C. Harris, and Bruce Lindeman
A dictionary/reference for everyone in real estate. Defines over 1500 legal, financial, and architectural terms.
Cloth $19.95, Canada $28.95/ISBN 5758-9, 700 pages

HOW TO PREPARE FOR REAL ESTATE LICENSING EXAMINATIONS-SALESPERSON AND BROKER, 3rd EDITION
Jack P. Friedman and Bruce Lindeman
Reviews current exam topics and features updated model exams and supplemental exams, all with explained answers.
Paperback, $9.95, Canada $13.95/ISBN 2996-8, 340 pages

BARRON'S FINANCE AND INVESTMENT HANDBOOK
John Downes and Jordan Goodman
This hard-working handbook of essential information defines more than 2500 key terms, and explores 30 basic investment opportunities with a description and discussion of the pros and cons of each. The investment information reflects new Federal Tax Act provisions effective in 1987.
Cloth $21.95, Canada $31.95/ISBN 5729-5, 864 pages
"...an excellent investment guide...almost any serious investor will want this book."—Christian Science Monitor

BARRON'S FINANCIAL TABLES FOR BETTER MONEY MANAGEMENT
Stephen S. Solomon, Dr. Clifford Marshall, and Martin Pepper
Pocket-sized handbooks of interest and investment rates tables that can be used easily by average investors and mortgage holders.
Volume 1: Savings and Loans
Paperback $5.50, Canada $7.95/ISBN 2745-0, 272 pages
Volume 2: Real Estate Loans
Paperback $5.50, Canada $7.95/ISBN 2744-2, 336 pages
Volume 3: Mortgage Payments
Paperback $5.50, Canada $7.95/ISBN 2728-0, 304 pages
Volume 4: Stocks and Bonds
Paperback $5.50, Canada $7.95/ISBN 2727-2, 256 pages
Volume 5: Comprehensive Annuities
Paperback $5.50, Canada $7.95/ISBN 2726-4, 160 pages
Volume 6: Canadian Mortgage Payments
Paperback $5.50, Canada $7.95/ISBN 3939-4, 336 pages

All prices are in U.S. and Canadian dollars and subject to change without notice. At your bookseller, or order direct adding 10% postage (minimum charge $1.50), N.Y. residents add sales tax.

Barron's Educational Series, Inc.
250 Wireless Boulevard, Hauppauge, NY 11788
Call toll-free: 1-800-645-3476, in NY 1-800-257-5729
In Canada: 195 Allstate Parkway, Markham, Ontario L3R4T8

NOTES

NOTES

NOTES

NOTES

NOTES

NOTES

NOTES

NOTES

NOTES

NOTES

NOTES